ALVIN W. GOULDNER is Max Weber Research
Professor of Social Theory at Washington University, St. Louis. He is the author of several
major sociological works, including *Enter Plato*
(1965) and *Patterns of Industrial Bureaucracy*
(1954). He has also lectured abroad at the
London School of Economics, Stockholm School
of Economics, the Hebrew University, and the
University of Warsaw.

THE
COMING CRISIS
OF
WESTERN
SOCIOLOGY

BOOKS BY ALVIN W. GOULDNER

Studies in Leadership (editor)
Patterns of Industrial Bureaucracy
Wildcat Strike
Emile Durkheim's *Socialism and Saint-Simon* (editor)
Notes on Technology and the Moral Order (with R. A. Peterson)
Modern Sociology (with H. P. Gouldner)
Applied Sociology (editor, with S. M. Miller)
Enter Plato

STUDIES IN THE SERIES ON
THE SOCIAL ORIGINS OF SOCIAL THEORY
Enter Plato
The Coming Crisis of Western Sociology

THE
COMING CRISIS
OF
WESTERN
SOCIOLOGY

ALVIN W. GOULDNER

Max Weber Research Professor of Social Theory
Washington University, St. Louis

BASIC BOOKS, INC.

PUBLISHERS

New York   *London*

THIRD PRINTING
© 1970 by Alvin W. Gouldner
Library of Congress Catalog Card Number: 77–110771
SBN 465–01278–7
Manufactured in the United States of America
DESIGNED BY VINCENT TORRE

Dedicated with Love to

JANET WALKER GOULDNER

"Here are the priests; and although they are my enemies . . . my blood is related to theirs."

FRIEDRICH NIETZSCHE
Thus Spake Zarathustra

Preface

Social theorists today work within a crumbling social matrix of
paralyzed urban centers and battered campuses. Some may put
cotton in their ears, but their bodies still feel the shock waves. It is
no exaggeration to say that we theorize today within the sound of
guns. The old order has the picks of a hundred rebellions thrust into
its hide.

While I was working on this study, one of the popular songs of
the time was "Come on Baby, Light My Fire." It is characteristic of
our time that this song, which is an ode to urban conflagration, was
made into a singing commercial by an auto manufacturer in
Detroit, the very city whose burning and looting it celebrated. One
wonders: Is this "repressive tolerance," or is it, more simply, that
they just do not understand? It is this context of social contradictions and conflicts that is the historical matrix of what I have called
"The Coming Crisis of Western Sociology." What I shall be examining here is the reflection of these conflicts in the idiom of social
theory.

The present study is part of a larger work plan, whose first
product was *Enter Plato,* and whose objective is to contribute to an
historically informed sociology of social theory. The plan envisages
a series of studies called "The Social Origins of Western Social
Theory," and I am now at work on two other volumes in it. One of
these is on the relation of the nineteenth century Romantic movement to social theory, and another is a study in which I hope to
connect the various analytic threads, presenting a more systematic
and generalized sociological theory about social theories.

Like others, I owe much to many. I am particularly grateful to Dennis Wrong for a massive critique, at once sensitive and sensible, of the entire study. I am also indebted to Robin Blackburn, Wolf Heydebrand, Robert Merton, and S. Michael Miller for their trenchant suggestions concerning the chapter "What Happened in Sociology." I am deeply indebted to my graduate students at Washington University, perhaps most especially to Barry Thompson and Robert Wicke, for their criticism and encouragement of my work, in and out of our seminars together. My ideas on "methodological dualism" were developed in the course of working with William Yancey while I was his dissertation advisor. Admirers of England's Raymond Williams will also recognize that I have been much influenced by his emphasis on the "structure of sentiments."

I am also grateful to Orville Brim and the Russell Sage Foundation of New York for assistance that helped to make possible extensive European travel during 1965–1966 and without which this study would be a much different and, indeed, poorer one. While in Europe I was fortunate in having the assistance of a multilingual secretary, Manuela Wingate, and in the United States I had the great help of Adeline Sneider in preparing the manuscript. My thanks to both of them for their unflagging good humor, their technical skill, and their great capacity for work.

As I mentioned, this study is a part of a larger series on which I have been working and for which I have been preparing for the last twenty years. I have therefore felt free to draw upon certain of my previous publications and to use them here where they seemed appropriate. Conceiving of the present study as a work of synthesis, I have not felt compelled to inundate its pages with a sea of footnotes. If the substance and logic of what I say here does not convince, neither will the conventional rituals of scholarship. I shall not impose upon the reader's intelligence by making the usual perfunctory statement about where the final responsibility for the defects of this work resides.

ALVIN W. GOULDNER

January 1970
Washington University
St. Louis, Missouri

Contents

PART I

Sociology: Contradictions and Infrastructure

PART II
The World of Talcott Parsons

PART III
The Coming Crisis of Western Sociology

PART IV

Epilogue: The Theorist Pulls Himself Together, Partially

PART I

Sociology: Contradictions and Infrastructure

1

Introduction: Toward a Critique of Sociology

The criticism and transformation of society can be divorced only at our peril from the criticism and transformation of theories about society. Yet the gap between theory and practice, so common in the history of American radical movements, is in some quarters growing wider. Some of the most militant of American radicals, in the New Left or in the movement for Black liberation, have at least temporarily avoided any serious concern with social theory.

This neglect of theory doubtless has various origins. In some part it is due to the fact that these social movements are still new and their political activism consumes their necessarily limited energies and resources; the new radicalisms will, in short, need time to produce their new theories. Although the neglect of theory is scarcely peculiar to Americans, it is in part also due to the fact that American radicals are often more American than they know and may prefer the tangible outcomes of pragmatic politics to the intangible outputs of theory. Again, part of their neglect of theoretical problems is probably due to the close links that some young radicals have with the "hippie" contingent of their generation, whose more expressive and aesthetic styles of rejecting American culture dispose them to avoid what they take to be the sterile "hassles" of intellectual confrontation. There is also a vocal minority who, as has been said, feel personally excluded when they hear an appeal to reason.

SOCIOLOGY AS POPULAR CULTURE

There are, however, other important sources of theoretical apathy among young American radicals today, and these, among other things, distinguish them from the radicals of the 1930's. One of these may well be the emergence of sociology, between the 1940's and the 1960's, as part of popular culture. Sociology then came of age, institutionally if not intellectually. It became a viable part of the academic scene: hundreds of thousands of American college students took courses in sociology; literally thousands of sociology books were written. At the same time, the newly emerging paperback book industry made these available as mass literature. They were sold in drugstores, railway stations, air terminals, hotels, and grocery stores, while, at the same time, increasing middle-class affluence made it easier for students to purchase them, even when not required as textbooks.

This mass availability of sociology (and the other social sciences) as part of everyday culture has had a paradoxical effect on the attitudes that some young people developed toward social theory and social problems. On the one side, the bookstore mingling of social science with other expressions of popular literature identified social science, by association, as part and parcel of the larger culture that the radicals rejected. Some young radicals thus came to distrust social theory because they experienced it as part of the prevailing culture. On the other side, however, sheer familiarity with the social sciences led some to accept it uncritically. For some young people the paperback sociology of the bookstore began to take the place of the earlier literature of radical criticism and protest.

Assimilating the social sciences as part of everyday culture, reading books about the nature of prejudice or poverty, the facts of life in America often seemed quite clear to them. Efforts to discuss theory might then seem to be an unnecessary obfuscation, a substitution of talking about problems for doing something about them. Viewing these researches against the background of their own values, they often experienced a simple moral revulsion rather than an intellectual stimulation. Theorizing, some came to believe, was a form of escapism, if not of moral cowardice.

Yet the neglect of self-conscious theory by radicals is both dangerous and ironic, for such a posture implies that—although they lay claim to being radical—they have in effect surrendered to one of the most vulgar currents of American culture: to its small-town,

Babbitt-like anti-intellectualism and know-nothingism. Moreover, if radicals wish to change their world, they must surely expect to do so only against the resistance of some and with the help of others. Yet those whom they oppose, as well as those with whom they may wish to ally themselves, will in fact often be guided by certain theories. Without self-conscious theory, radicals will be unable to understand, let alone change, either their enemies or their friends. Radicals who believe that they can separate the task of developing theory from that of changing society are not in fact acting without a theory, but *with* one that is tacit and therefore unexaminable and uncorrectable. If they do not learn to use their theory self-consciously, they will be used by it. Unable either to control or to understand their theories, radicals will thus in effect submit to one form of the very alienation that they commonly reject.

The profound transformation of society that many radicals seek cannot be accomplished by political means alone; it cannot be confined to a purely political embodiment. For the old society is not held together merely by force and violence, or expedience and prudence. The old society maintains itself also through theories and ideologies that establish its hegemony over the minds of men, who therefore do not merely bite their tongues but submit to it willingly. It will be impossible either to emancipate men from the old society or to build a humane new one, without beginning, here and now, the construction of a total counter-culture, including new social theories; and it is impossible to do this without a critique of the social theories dominant today.

The ambivalence toward theory among some sectors of the New Left, the simultaneous sense of its irrelevance and of its necessity, was clearly expressed by Daniel Cohn-Bendit, one of the leading activists in the French student rebellion that began at Nanterre in the spring of 1968: the anarchists, he remarked, "have influenced me more by certain activities than by their theories . . . theoreticians are laughable." At the same time, however, Cohn-Bendit also observed "the existence of a gap between theory and practice . . . we are trying to effectively develop a theory."[1]

That theory has had an effect upon the emerging New Left, whatever the attitude toward it, is evidenced, among other things, by the role of the "Frankfurt school of critical sociology"—including Jurgen Habermas, Theodor Adorno, and Max Horkheimer—which has been said to be "as important as any single event"[2] in the political revitalization of the *Sozialisticher Deutscher Studentbund* from 1961–1965. Also, there is the international responsiveness of the new radicals to the work of another member of that school, Herbert Marcuse, whose practical importance was backhandedly acknowledged by recent Soviet critiques of his theory. Yet even here, within the critical school of sociology, the continuing tension between theory and practice was evidenced by the polemical exchange between Habermas and the young militants during the fall of 1968, after their demonstrations at Frankfurt.

Lacking the time or the impulse to reformulate old theories or to develop their own new theories, the radicals' need of a theory is today sometimes satisfied by a hastily gulped, vulgar Marxism. Yet even this seems better than another alternative often taken today, namely, merely to label one's own views as "Marxist." This self-characterization may express solidarity with a powerful intellectual tradition but, lacking any true assimilation of it, provides no real help. Indeed, this "magic naming" may do harm, since it can distract critical attention from the rather different theory that the individual may, in point of fact, actually be using. Thus, on one occasion I heard a young radical deliver an extended critique of modern sociology, particularly of Talcott Parsons' version of Functionalism, from what he claimed to be a Marxist standpoint, when he was actually viewing it only from the standpoint of another, somewhat different version of Functional theory.

At its best, such uses of Marxism by American radicals, even when they are more than merely invocatory, are fundamentally regressive and primitivistic. This is particularly true in the United States, where, apart from a very few economists and a slightly larger number of capable historians, Marxism itself has developed hardly at all; where its intellectual caliber remains fixated on the stunted level of the 1930's, when it was blighted by Stalinism; and where it has hardly begun to assimilate even the older contributions of a Georg Lukacs or an Antonio Gramsei, let alone those of the brilliant German, Italian, and French contemporaries. American Marxists have been among the less original and creative contingents of world Marxism; they have usually only applied, but practically never deepened, Marxist theory. Unless one is willing to believe that the academic social sciences have contributed nothing of value to an understanding of modern society during the last thirty years, the flight back to an unreconstructed Marxism is an act, at best, of desperation, and at worst, of irresponsibility or bad faith. Many young radicals today, however, have no impulse to retreat to a rote Marxism. Indeed, many are deeply critical of what they take to be its ingrained disposition toward a totalitarian *Realpolitik;* for some, this becomes still one further reason to suspect and avoid theory.

NEW SENTIMENTS, OLD THEORIES

My reading of the contemporary radical condition is that we are now living in a fluid transitional era when a younger generation has emerged with a sharply different structure of sentiments, with collective feelings that are not resonated by the very different kinds of sentiments that have been historically deposited in older theories, and this makes some among the younger generation either coldly indifferent or hotly antagonistic to the older theories. There is, in short, a gap between the newly emerging structure of sentiments among young radicals and the older "languages" or theories, a gap that has not yet been bridged by the development of a new theoretical language in which young radicals might more fully express themselves and their own conception of reality.

From this standpoint, the crux of the issue is the lack of "fit" between new sentiments and old theories. It is precisely because of this that certain young radicals do not simply feel the old theories are "wrong" and should be criticized in detail; their more characteristic response to the older theories is a feeling of their sheer *irrelevance*. Their inclination is not to disprove or argue with the old theories, but to ridicule or avoid them.

At this juncture, academic social theorists might reply that in this respect the New Left is simply being wrong-headed, for what have theories and personal sentiments to do with one another? One should not assume, the academic sociologist might say, that theories need to be consonant with men's sentiments before they are accepted or rejected. However, my own contrary assumption —to be elaborated later—is that the fit between theories and sentiments has a good deal to do with the career of a theory. Much of the theoretical apathy of some young radicals, their ritual Marxism, their efforts to restore the young Marx of alienation, or their clutching at new theories such as ethnomethodology, all are, I believe, various expressions of the existence of an unfilled theoretical need that derives from the gap between their own new structure of sentiments or their own sense of what is real, on the one hand, and, on the other hand, the older theories now available in the academic and social surround.

As some young American radicals now experience it, their important need at this moment in history is to activate and to assert their emerging radical sentiments, and to consolidate and to preserve their new radical identity. It may be that in the beginning this can be done by a militant politics of activistic demonstration.

R. D. Laing, whose views have often articulated the feelings of young radicals, has expressed this well in his *Politics of Experience,* where he remarks: "No one can begin to think, feel or act now except from the starting point of his own alienation . . . we do not need theory so much as the experience that is the source of the theory."[3]

The feeling that one's sentiments are valid, that one has a right to have and to hold them, is rooted partially in the sense of reality that derives from personal experience and in the solidarity with others who share these experiences and sentiments. The felt validity of sentiments is thus fundamentally a matter of consensual validation, not of analytic power, or refined conceptualization, or even of "evidence." The young radical thus draws lines in terms of generational solidarities and cleavages, of emotional rather than ideological affinities: "trust no one over thirty." Whether or not it "should be," social theory is always rooted in the theorist's experiences. Whether or not it should be, the sensed validity of a theory depends therefore upon the sharing of experience and of the sentiments to which such experience gives rise, among those who offer and those who listen to the theory.

Apart from the sheer cultural obsolescence of traditional social theories because of their rooting in older personal realities, and apart from the inability of old theories to resonate new sentiments, theory is sometimes suspect today because it is something received from the past. Theory is commonly transmitted by older men to younger men who are in some way dependent upon them. The theoretical apathy of a young radical is thus sometimes an expression of his vigorous striving toward individuality and autonomy, and of his need to become and live as a man, and, if possible, as a better man than his elders have been. Somewhere in the young radical's thoughts is the suspicion that not only are received, traditional theories wrong or irrelevant, but that they are also *unmanly;* he sees them as the timidity-generating creations of timid men.

Still not "professionalized," the young radical does not view a theory as pure, isolated, and alone, but sees through the theory to the theorist. He sees theory as a communication by a whole man. His judgment about a theory and theorizing will be influenced by his feeling about the whole man who produces it. And he often sees this man as someone who has "copped out," retreated from life's struggles, compromised his own highest ideals, accommodated himself to injustice and suffering, and made a comfortable career out of studying the misery of others. The young radical observes that, for all his sympathetic writing about the "culture of poverty," the social scientist, nevertheless, does not share his book royalties even with the poor whom he has studied and who have made them possible. The young radical observes that, for all his sympathetic commentary about the suffering of Blacks, hardly any sociologist of repute can be recruited to teach in Black colleges in the south. The young radical's grievance is often, then, that the sociologist and social theorist is not a whole man, and that his life does not give consistent expression to his own values. In short, he is prone to see the sociologist as he sees other elders, as something of an exploiter and hypocrite. He observes that there are no martyrs among sociologists.

Interpreting social theory in terms of what he sees in the theorist, and viewing it as a falsification of what he himself has seen in the social world, the young radical often defines *all* of Academic Sociology and social theory as an undifferentiated obfuscation of life, as an ideology discolored by a pervasive conservative bias in the service of the status quo.

SOCIOLOGY AND THE NEW LEFT: A PARADOX

Yet there is a deepgoing paradox here, and the young radical himself has already begun to confront it. Some, for example, have noticed that in the past decade or so an Academic Sociology akin to that in the United States has also emerged in the Soviet Union, alongside of traditional Marxism-Leninism. This development has been intellectually troublesome to those radicals who, out of a rote Marxism, have concluded that American Academic Sociology is an instrument of American corporate capitalism. For clearly the conservative character of American sociology cannot be attributed to its subservience to corporate capitalism if an essentially similar sociology has emerged where, as in the Soviet Union, there is no corporate capitalism.

But this is only one of the paradoxes generated by a blanket critique that views all of sociology as the conservative instrument of a repressive society. For example, many of the most visible leaders of student rebellions throughout the world, from Nanterre to Columbia Universities, have been students of sociology. France's Cohn-Bendit is just one of the most obvious cases in point. Leslie Fiedler has more generally observed that "at the root of any [student] demonstration there is a character who is . . . a student of sociology . . . [and] a Jew . . . [and] an outsider," or who possesses at least two of these characteristics.[4] Without endorsing the validity

of all of Mr. Fiedler's designations, I do believe that there is considerable merit in his observation of the prominent role of young
sociologists in current student rebellions. Yet, if this is so, how
can sociology be an unmitigated expression of political conservatism?

Another version of this paradox was evidenced at the Boston
meetings of the American Sociological Association in August 1968.
There were, in a way, actually two concurrent meetings at Boston:
the official one, routinely managed by the American Sociological
Association; and, alongside of it, a series of unscheduled "shadow"
meetings, organized by the young men and women of the "radical
caucus," the Sociology Liberation Movement, with a noticeable
leavening of Columbia University militants. These two tracks
paralleled one another without touching until the climactic plenary
session of the ASA meetings, when more than a thousand gathered
to hear the Secretary of Health, Education, and Welfare. Scheduled
to have been a dull, honorific occasion, it became what may in
a modest way be an historic event when ASA President Philip M.
Hauser, having heard that the radical caucus planned to demonstrate at the secretary's talk, invited the caucus to express its
dissenting views from the platform.

The key dissenting talk was made by a young sociologist, Martin
Nicolaus, then from Canada's Simon Fraser University and one of
the contributing editors of the New Left journal, *Viet Report.* In
icy, measured tones, Mr. Nicolaus declared:

> The Secretary of HEW is a military officer in the domestic front of the
> war against the people . . . the Department of which the man is head is
> more accurately described as the agency which watches over the in-
> equitable distribution of preventable diseases, over the funding of do-
> mestic propaganda and indoctrination, over the preservation of a cheap
> and docile labor force. . . . This assembly [of sociologists] here tonight
> . . . is a conclave of high and low priests, scribes, intellectual valets, and
> their innocent victims, engaged in the mutual affirmation of a falsehood
> . . . the profession is an outgrowth of nineteenth-century European tra-
> ditionalism and conservatism, wedded to twentieth-century American
> corporation liberalism . . . the professional eyes of the sociologist are
> on the down people, and the professional palm of the sociologist is
> stretched toward the up people . . . he is an Uncle Tom not only for
> this government and ruling class but for any.

These harsh words were applauded vigorously by the caucus and
its sympathizers, hissed by a few of the older ex-radicals, and met
by a larger group with shocked, stony forbearance. Now, even those
who concur, as I do, in many of Mr. Nicolaus' acerbic judgments,
must also acknowledge that their sheer utterance implies a
dilemma. It is not so much that he was allowed to speak by

officials of the ASA that expresses this dilemma, but, rather, that he wanted to speak. It was not so much that he was allowed to say what he saw, but that he saw as much as he did, that expresses the dilemma. For Nicolaus' very utterances, as well as the vigor and activity of the radical caucus at this same convention, themselves demonstrate that not all sociologists are "intellectual valets" and that not all are "Uncle Toms" of the ruling class.

There is a problem here: How can one account for the very radicalism of those sociologists who accuse sociology of being conservative? Much of what I say in subsequent chapters will, indeed, stress the conservative character of certain dominant trends in American sociology. At the same time, however, the fact that it is often sociologists themselves who criticize sociology for being conservative implies that sociology may produce radicals as well as conservatives. My point then is that sociology may produce, not merely recruit, radicals; that it may generate, not merely tolerate, radicalization.

It is undoubtedly correct that sociology often attracts young men and women of reformist inclination and prior radical outlook, and that some of their subsequent criticism of sociology may indeed derive from their frustrated expectations. Yet I doubt that this is the whole story. For there are other questions that need to be considered: If sociology often attracts radicals, what is there about sociology itself that attracts them? Can we believe that the young reformer's initial attraction to sociology was simply a case of mistaken identity?

Moreover, it is certain that many, but not all, of the radicals attracted become conservative. Not all the young socialists of the 1930's who became sociologists also became pillars of the status quo, and neither will all those of the New Left of today. While it cannot be central to the volume that follows and will not be examined here in any detail, I believe that there are aspects of the character of and outlook intrinsic to Academic Sociology itself that sustain rather than tame the radical impulse. I believe that, in the normal course of working as a sociologist, there are things that happen that may radicalize a man and have a liberating rather than repressive effect upon him. In brief, and in the language of a non-Academic Sociology, I believe that sociology has its own "internal contradictions," which, despite its powerful link to the status quo and its deepgoing conservative bent, have the unwitting but inherent consequence of fostering anti-Establishment and radicalizing tendencies, particularly among young people.

The relationship between sociology and the New Left is a complex one. Certainly I do not intend to imply that it was the emergence of sociology and its penetration into popular culture that energized the New Left. Nonetheless, the sheer visibility of sociologists in the student revolts at various universities, the importance of the German school of critical sociology for the New Left in Germany and elsewhere, as well as the early role of C. Wright Mills in articulating the emerging sentiments of the new American radicalism, all suggest that sociology has not simply served as a foil for the New Left. They suggest the possibility that some styles and aspects of sociology have also, wittingly and unwittingly, contributed productively to it. This in turn implies that sociology is by no means totally repressive or uniformly conservative in character, but possesses also a liberating or radicalizing potential, susceptible to further growth.

Sociology has a dialectical character and contains both repressive and liberative dimensions. The extrication and further development of its liberative potential will depend, in important part, on the penetration of an historically informed critique of sociology as a theory and as a social institution.

Sociology today is akin to early nineteenth-century Hegelianism, especially in the ambivalence of its political implications. Despite Hegelianism's predominantly conservative and authoritarian cast, it contained powerful radical implications that Marx was able to extricate and to incorporate into a transcending system of thought. The extrication of the liberative potential of modern Academic Sociology from its encompassing conservative structure is a major task of contemporary cultural criticism. It is a task that parallels the similar effort of some of the new radicals today, to extricate Marxism itself from its own conservative and repressive components, and in particular from the bureaucratic and totalitarian proclivities to which it is vulnerable. In neither case, however, will this be possible apart from the sharpest and most probing of criticism. In neither case will it be possible simply to assume that the only important question is the empirical validity or factuality of the intellectual systems involved, and that the viable parts of each theoretical system can be sifted out by "research" alone. The question here is not simply which parts of an intellectual system are empirically true or false, but also which are liberative and which repressive in their consequences. In short, the problem is: What are the social and political consequences of the intellectual system under examination? Do they liberate or repress men? Do they bind men into the social world that now exists, or do they enable men to transcend it?

Any and every statement about the social world, as well as the methodologies by which it is reached, has consequences that may be viewed quite apart from its intellectual validity. When it is said that a social science should be appraised solely in terms of its own autonomous standards, this is a value choice that cannot be justified by "purely scientific" considerations alone; it depends upon anterior, nonscientific assumptions about what a social science is for. That the ideological implications and social consequences of an intellectual system do not determine its validity, for theory does indeed have a measure of autonomy, is not in the least denied here. Certainly the *cognitive* validity of an intellectual system cannot and should not be judged by its ideological implications or its social consequences. But it does not follow from this that an intellectual system should be (or, for that matter, ever is) judged only in terms of its cognitive validity, its truth or falsity. In short, it is never simply a question of whether an intellectual system, or a statement that it implies, is true or false. Those who affirm that it is are simply choosing to ignore or to devalue other meanings and consequences of theories, and are in effect refusing to take responsibility for them even though they do exist.

There is no reason why one should be required to evaluate the formula for a new poison gas solely in terms of its mathematical elegance or of other purely technical criteria. And there is little point in pretending that such a formula is a purely neutral bit of information, useful for the furtherance of any and all social values: the thing is meant to kill and, precisely because it is technically adequate, it does so. To limit judgment solely to "autonomous" technical criteria is in effect not only to allow but to require men to be moral cretins in their technical roles. It is to make psychopathic behavior culturally required in the conduct of scientific roles. Insofar as our culture conventionally construes technical, scientific, and professional roles as those that obligate men to ignore all but the technical implications of their work, the very social structure itself is inherently pathogenic. The social function of such a segmented role structure is akin to that of the reflexive obedience induced by military training. The function of such a technical role structure, as of military discipline, is to sever the normal moral sensibilities and responsibilities of civilians and soldiers, and to enable them to be used as deployables, willing to pursue practically any objective. In the last analysis, such arrangements produce an unthinking readiness to kill or to hurt others—or to produce things that do so—on order.

The extrication of the liberative potential of Academic Sociology, no less than that of historical Marxism, is not to be accomplished by research alone. It will also require action and criticism, efforts to change the social world and efforts to change social science, both of which are profoundly interconnected, if for no other reason than that social science is a *part* of the social world as well as a *conception* of it.

In a later study I hope to be able to contribute to a sociologically informed critique of Marxism. In this volume, however, I shall seek to contribute to a critique of modern sociology in some of its dominant institutional and intellectual characteristics, as a part of a larger critique of modern society and culture. The critique of contemporary society cannot be deepened except insofar as the intellectual instruments of this critique, including sociology and the other social sciences, are themselves critically sharpened. Correspondingly, a critique of sociology will be superficial unless the discipline is seen as the flawed product of a flawed society and unless we begin to specify the details of this interconnection. What is required therefore is an analysis on different levels, in which sociology is seen in its relation to larger historical trends, to the macro-institutional level, and especially to the state; it also means seeing sociology in the setting of its most immediate locale, the university; it means seeing it as a way in which men work as teachers and researchers, and operate within an intellectual community with a received occupational culture, where they pursue careers, livelihoods, material ambitions, as well as intellectual aspirations.

Finally, and centrally, a critique of sociology also requires detailed and specific analysis of the dominant theoretical and intellectual products that sociology has created. It is these intellectual products that distinguish sociology from other activities, that justify its existence, and that produce its distinctive impact on the larger surrounding society. There can be no serious critique of sociology without a fine-grained, close analysis of its theories and its theorists.

The intellectual scope and output of modern sociology, let alone the sheer size of its operating establishments and the number of its personnel, are vast and complex; there can be no question, therefore, of exhaustive coverage of all its varying expressions and tendencies, here in this volume. Rather than a superficial effort at pseudo-systematic and exhaustive coverage, what I have therefore essayed is a close critique of a few important standpoints and issues: in particular, of what is by far the dominant system of American social theory, namely, that created by Talcott Parsons. Laborious though this effort will doubtless seem at times, let me repeat that I view it only as a very partial contribution to a critique of American sociology.

I am convinced that the extrication of the liberative potential of sociology today cannot be effected by sweeping generalizations that ignore detail; it must proceed by confronting the theories, point by point, and the theorists, man by man. This process, of working through the details of these theories and our own reactions to them, is necessary if we are to transcend them, liberate ourselves from their penetrating conservative influence, and incorporate their viable dimensions in new standpoints. Without this painful process, a radical criticism of society or sociology runs the continual risk of falling into a sterile polemicism that yields no enduring guidance and will be dangerously lacking in self-awareness.

Just as the sharpest critics of Marxism have usually been Marxists, the keenest critics of sociology today have usually been sociologists and students of sociology. They have commonly been men who regard themselves as sociologists and who have critically evaluated sociology from a sociological perspective. Their prototype, of course, is C. Wright Mills. Thus even the most polemical of their criticisms have an ambiguous implication. At one and the same time, they testify both to the profound flaws and to the continuing value, to the painful predicaments and to the perduring potentialities, of the sociological perspective.

Often enough the men whose rejection of such criticism is most vehement are those who live *off* sociology, while the most vehement critics are those who live *for* it. Often, but not always. For it is well to notice that there are critics and critics. They too may be divided among those who live for and those who live off sociology. Criticism is sometimes a way in which men can draw a quick notice to themselves without making solid contributions of their own. In short, men sometimes play the critic because they expect that the door to repute can be opened with a key of brass. The serious critics, however, are those marked by an ability to resist conventional success or by an ability to transcend failure as conventionally defined. C. Wright Mills never became a full professor; his "failure" may remind us that the serious players are always those who have an ability to pay costs.

CRITICISM AND THE HISTORICAL PERSPECTIVE

We might suggest that those who live off sociology in the most opportunistic ways, in brief, the careerists who accept sociology very largely as it is, are not, strangely enough, the most ambitious. In a way, their very careerism tokens a low level of ambition, or at least a type of ambition relatively easily satisfied within the framework of a routine career. The most unswerving critics of an intellectual establishment, those who cannot be satisfied by and within it, are usually those who do not treasure the coin of its realm, but value other, rather different kinds of fulfillments. Often these are attainable only by men with a vivid historical sense, who view themselves as historical actors and as part of a longer social and intellectual tradition. In effect, the gratifications they seek cannot be given them by their contemporaries, and the responsibilities they feel are not to contemporaries alone. They are therefore less vulnerable to the temptations and seductions of the present. From the standpoint of their more conventional contemporaries, such men are often seen as flawed. Yet they are frequently flawed in a productive manner; for being less subject to the influence of the dominant surround, they are often critically sensitive to the limitations of established intellectual paradigms and can work in a manner that is creatively at variance with them.

One of the most important functions of the "classics" in sociology is to root the sociologist in history and to enable him to live among and to take the role of truly great men. The classics implant standards of great, though often unfulfillable, achievement; they make it difficult for a man to be impressed or intimidated by those around him. An historical approach to theory puts one in the company of greatness, and it inevitably raises the standard by which one measures accomplishment. History thus insulates us from the vulgarities, no less than the gratifications, of the present.

Yet to be in love with history is dangerous, for in delivering us from the present, it may also place us in bondage to the past. It may induce an insensitivity to the new problems or needs of the present as well as to the novelty and genuine creativity of new responses to these new needs. It may produce an interminable, pedantic exegesis of the past and encourage a petulant refusal to acknowledge contemporary achievement as valuably new. The historically sensitive critic who lives too much in the shadow of the great may suffer a failure of nerve that paralyzes his creative originality; he may therefore devalue the achievements of his peers and contemporaries. In short, his criticism of contemporaries may be animated not only by *their* failure to measure up to the standards of greatness but also by his *own*. The life of criticism is therefore a precarious one not only because those criticized take a dim view of the critic, but also because it produces inner vulnerabilities that easily sour the critic. Yet the continuing development of the social sciences and its liberative potential cannot be accomplished without risking the sharpest criticism.

During an earlier period, prior to the present full-scale effort to professionalize sociology, career-seeking young men often manifested their mettle by assaulting the ideas of their seniors and, what some thought to be safer, those of classical sociologists now safely deceased. With the growth of professionalization, however, young sociologists were increasingly encouraged to seek out what was "right" in the work of others, not what was wrong. In effect they were enjoined to adopt a constructive attitude, a positive rather than a critical or negative attitude. Rather than a call for criticism, the watchwords of professionalized sociology became: continuity, codification, convergence, and cumulation. Talcott Parsons' *Structure of Social Action* was the paradigm of such a posture, and its ideology of "continuity" was taken up and amplified by his students.

This ideology is essentially an extension of the perspective that nineteenth-century sociological Positivism developed in the course of its opposition to what it regarded as the "negative" criticism of the French Revolution and the *philosophes*. The modern ideology of continuity is an extension of this earlier Positivist view of *society* into a view of *sociology* itself, into the methodology of scholarly practice, and into the training of the young scholar. The search for convergences with and in the past, for which it calls, seeks to reveal a tacit consensus of great minds and, by showing this, to lend credence to the conclusions that they are held to have converged upon unwittingly. Convergence thus becomes a rhetoric, a way of persuading men to accept certain views. The implication is that if these great men, tacitly or explicitly, agreed on a given view, it must have a *prima facie* cogency. Convergence, then, is one way in which views come, in practice, to be "tested," even though this is at variance with the canons of scientific method formally espoused by these same men.

The ideology of convergence implies that if great theorists can be shown to have come to a consensus unbeknownst to themselves, then it is these tacit *agreements* that are theoretically productive, rather than the polemics to which the men themselves often gave focal attention. Underneath the manifest disagreements of theory, the cunning of history—it is implied—has contrived to produce a truly valuable residue of intellectual consensus. This is an Americanized version of Hegelianism, in which historical development presumably occurs not through polemic, struggle, and conflict, but through consensus.

The theorist proceeding in this manner has found an ingenious way of linking his own position to the past, while at the same time manifesting his own superiority to it. Seemingly subordinating his own claims to personal priority, in apparent conformity to a higher, selfless principle, the theorist puts himself forward modestly, as a discoverer of consensus rather than as an originator of ideas. Yet in the very act of "discovering" theoretical convergences and continuities in the work of earlier men, and in particular by holding that these were unwitting, the modern theorist tacitly presents himself as now revealing things hitherto hidden from the founding fathers, and as saying them more precisely and clearly. For all his decorous regard for the past, the contemporary exponent of continuity thus manages to communicate his own originality and creativity.

The call to intellectual convergence and cumulation began to crystallize in the United States under certain distinctive social conditions. It began to emerge with—and it congenially resonated —sentiments appropriate to the "united front" solidarity of the political and military struggle against Nazism. It was in effect the academic counterpart of wartime domestic unity and of international unity between the Western powers and the Soviet Union. In short, the American call to convergence and continuity in social theory had its social foundation in collective sentiments that favored all kinds of social unity, and which had developed in response to the military and political exigencies of World War II. Correspondingly, however, with the breakdown of national unity after the war as well as with the later growth of widespread racial conflict and student rebellion, the ideology of convergence and continuity no longer resonated collective sentiment. A more critical standpoint could re-emerge.

The ideology of convergence and continuity, however, did not only reflect general national and international conditions, but was also congenial to the drive to professionalize sociology that was mounted about the same time. For such an ideology is less congenial to men who see themselves as intellectuals than to those who aspire to be professionals and technicians. The call to continuity and convergence is a methodological slogan more congenial to the guild-like sentiments of professionals, who commonly affirm their solidarity and who deplore the indecorous public display of their internal disputes. If this slogan of "continuity-convergence" serves to strengthen the mutual solidarity of professionals, it most often does so, however, at the cost of a blanketing mood of consensus that smothers intellectual criticism and innovation. If it opens some bridges to the past, it does so at the cost of barricading bridges to the future. There is no possible way of transcending the present and the past from which it derives, without a thoroughgoing criticism of it. And there is no way of moving beyond contemporary sociology without a criticism of its theory and its practice, its establishments and its ideas.

NOTES

1. "Interview with Daniel Cohn-Bendit," *Our Generation*, VI, Nos. 1–2 (May, June, July 1968), 98–99.

2. John and Barbara Ehrenreich, "The European Student Movements," *Monthly Review*, XX (September 1968), 17.

3. R. D. Laing, *The Politics of Experience* (New York: Ballantine Books, 1968), pp. 12, 17.

4. *Village Voice*, September 19, 1968, p. 59.

2

Sociology and Sub-Sociology

Seeded in Western Europe in the first half of the nineteenth century, sociology lay in a territory that did not know what to do with the new discipline. Sociology did not find its first supporting environment or first achieve successful institutionalization in Western Europe. Its most fertile ground was in time found elsewhere in the East and West. Sociology achieved successful embodiment in supporting establishments only after it underwent a kind of "binary fission," only after the two parts into which it became differentiated found different strata and different nations to sponsor it. One part of sociology, "Marxism," moved eastward and became at length, after World War I, the official social science of the then new Soviet Union. The other part, which I will call "Academic Sociology," moved westward and came to a different kind of fruition within American culture. Both are different sides of Western sociology.

The diffusion of sociology in each direction was carried by a different social stratum. Marxism was borne by unattached intelligentsia, by political groups and parties oriented to lower strata groups who were in rebellion against an emerging bourgeois society that excluded them. Academic Sociology was developed in the United States by university academicians who were oriented to the established middle class, and who sought pragmatically to reform rather than systematically to rebel against the status quo. Both, however, were early linked with social movements, in particular to what Anthony Wallace has called movements of "cultural revitalization." Each embodied a different conception of how the established order around it was failing and needed revision, and each had its own vision of a *new* social order.

After World War I, American sociology found itself becoming entrenched at the University of Chicago, in a metropolitan environment in which industrialism had burgeoned and was proliferating problems. It conceived of these as the problems of "urban communities." That is, they were viewed as due to the vast size and anonymity of urban communities, which were taken to be essentially alike, rather than as varying with the economy, the class system, or the property institutions of the particular city.

Marxism, on the other hand, took root in parts of Europe where industrialization had been slow and relatively retarded. When the Leninist version of Marxism seized power in Russia, its task was to accelerate and to consolidate industrialization. Marxism had defined European problems as essentially due to "capitalism," that is, to the perpetuation of an archaic class system and of property institutions that were seen as, at some point, impeding industrial development.

Early Marxism and Academic Sociology both agreed that modern society was experiencing problems that could be solved only by building or borrowing *new* patterns. Certainly neither thought that its culture's problems were due to the intrusion of "alien" elements that would now have to be expelled, or to the neglect or disuse of old traditional elements that could be restored. While Academic Sociology sometimes looked nostalgically to the past to find models for the future and sometimes judged the fragmented city in terms of the more cohesive rural countryside, it knew it could not go back. Both Academic Sociology and Marxism understood that something new was needed; and each thought its sociology could help surmount the defects of the society in which it found itself. They differed, however, in that Academic Sociology tended to think that the problems would in time be remedied by a society that it regarded as slowly maturing and fundamentally sound, while Marxism viewed these problems as rooted in conflicts inherent in the new society and therefore insoluble within its master framework.

The two sociologies were fostered by, and their fortunes varied with, the two nations by which they came to be sponsored. Following the Soviet Revolution, there were some efforts to continue the intellectual development of Marxism there, but these, closely connected with violent political struggles in that society, were soon brought to a halt. With the growth of Stalinism, Marxism in the Soviet Union ceased to develop *intellectually*, and because of its international dominance over Marxism elsewhere, even the theoretical creativity of a Georg Lukàcs or an Antonio Gramsei re-

mained largely unassimilated until the crackup of Stalinism following World War II.

In the United States, sociology took hold as an academic discipline during the 1920's largely under the aegis of the University of
Chicago. It began to move eastward during the 1930's, and its
continued development, during the 1940's and 1950's, was dominated by Harvard and Columbia Universities. By the mid-1960's,
with the financing of the Welfare State, American sociology became more institutionally polycentric; the hegemony of these three
leading sociological centers became less pronounced with the
growth of competing centers elsewhere in the country. In the view
of many American sociologists, during the 1960's the dominant
American center had moved once more, this time to the University
of California at Berkeley.

Although conceived in Western Europe, then, one form of
sociology achieved its most powerful social impact and influence
in Eastern Europe, while another found a supportive environment
in the United States, where it became institutionalized within the
university system.

The tremendous growth of sociology in the United States is one
manifestation of the continuing efforts of American culture to
explore, to cope with, and to control its changing environment.
Sociology has grown as rapidly as perhaps any other aspect of
American intellectual culture. To much of the world today, sociology is practically synonymous with American sociology. The
preeminence of American sociology in its professional sphere
throughout the world may be even greater than the corresponding
world influence of most other American cultural efforts, even of
American mathematics, physics, or the other physical sciences. Its
techniques are everywhere emulated, and its theories shape the
terms in which world discussion of sociology is cast and the issues
around which intellectual debate centers.

In two generations, American sociologists devised a number of
research techniques and invented another handful of complex
theoretical perspectives; they completed and published thousands
of researches; they trained a cadre of full-time specialists at least
two or three times larger than that of all European countries combined; they established many new periodicals, research institutes,
departments; they developed academic influence and won wide
public attention, if not uniform respect; and they committed every
form of gaucherie and vulgarity that can be expected of an *arriviste*
discipline. Yet, for all its vulnerabilities, it did establish itself firmly
as a part of American culture, and each year sees it even more
deeply institutionalized in the United States. The modern era, as

C. Wright Mills said, is indeed the era of sociology. And this is largely because it is the era of the Welfare State.

After World War II and under the stimulus of the Welfare State, American sociology grew at a more rapid rate than ever before. As it grew, sociology increasingly lost its academic isolation, and sociologists were exposed to new pressures, temptations, and opportunities. Sociologists began to peer increasingly into the cracks and crannies of their own culture, often unrecognized by other middle-class professionals. At the same time they began traveling abroad more than ever before and began experiencing a reverberating "culture shock." Sociologists, then, grew more numerous, more worldly, more experienced, more affluent, more powerful, and more academically secure. They have, especially since World War II, gone up in the world. Often, all too often, this has meant a smug complacency; but occasionally it has also meant that some sociologists developed a greater need to reformulate their own deeply held intellectual perspectives.

These recent developments within the sociological establishment in America have merged with others external to it, with new and mounting social problems both domestic and foreign. It is thus almost certain that American sociology will soon undergo profound and radical changes. At the same time that these factors bring American sociology to the threshold of a basic reorientation, other developments at the eastern perimeter of European culture, in the Soviet world, also testify to changes in their sociology that promise to be no less profound and critical. Although painfully slow and far from fully underway, the process of unthawing Soviet Marxism is clearly visible. It appears, then, that the two major poles around which world sociology developed during the last half century, Academic Sociology in the United States and Marxism in the Soviet Union, are more or less simultaneously being exposed to powerful social forces that will move each toward major change. As with the prongs of a tuning fork, the movements of each will resonate the other, accelerating the crisis in sociology throughout the world.

I have said that American sociology today is, for all practical purposes, the model of Academic Sociology throughout the world. One of the problems to which the discussion that follows will address itself is an effort to sketch out a preliminary answer to the question: What *is* an Academic Sociology? The question cannot be answered, even in a preliminary way, however, by restricting attention to American sociology. We cannot begin to understand Academic Sociology except historically, as having come from somewhere and as going somewhere, and I shall therefore have to roam broadly in search of an answer. I shall suggest that recent Soviet developments offer some interesting clues about the social origins of Academic Sociology. Like other sociologists of my time, I have witnessed some of the events to be discussed. I shall therefore refer occasionally to things that I have seen and heard at first hand, either through casual encounter or deliberate study. In doing so, however, it is not my intention to insinuate a place for myself among the men whose work I shall call into evidence. Yet, like any other man, I must place reliance as much on my own personal experience as on the books I have read.

What, then, is Academic Sociology, and who is the Academic sociologist? It is a curious question, because today most sociologists think it hardly worth raising except in the most elementary textbooks, where the answer commonly given is correspondingly simplistic.

At the beginnings of French sociology, after Henri Saint-Simon had died, his students began a series of lectures. On one street there were lectures given by Auguste Comte, and on another there were competitive lectures given by Enfantin and Bazard. Each kept circling around this question: Who and what is the sociologist? In the end, all of them made it clear that they were bent on establishing a new religion, a religion of humanity, and that they believed its priesthood would be sociologists. In short, the sociologist was first conceived as a kind of priest.

It might be thought that this linkage between priest and sociologist existed only at the beginnings of sociology, but is now archaic and no longer exists for the modern, professionally-oriented sociology. Such a conclusion, however, may well be premature. In a study of the American Sociological Association, Timothy Sprehe and I polled its 6,762 members by mail on a variety of questions. Among the 3,441 who replied, it was found that, as late as 1964, more than one-quarter (27.6 per cent) of the sociologists who responded had thought, at one time or another, of becoming clergymen. Moreover, as I shall discuss at a later point, those who were friendly to the dominant school of sociological thought, Functionalism, were more likely to have thought of becoming clergymen and to attend church more frequently than those who were unfriendly toward it.

TOWARD A SOCIOLOGY OF SOCIOLOGY

Outlandish as this early priestly conception of the sociologist may now seem, it gave an answer to the question of who the sociologist is that is probably far more serious, and certainly more interesting, than the one sociologists now conventionally give. Our usual answer today is that the sociologist is someone who studies group life, examines man-in-society, and does researches into human relationships. Now this is not a very serious answer. It is as if a policeman were to describe his role by saying that he catches criminals; as if a businessman were to say, he makes soap; as if a priest were to say, he celebrates mass; as if a congressman were to say, he passes laws. While none of these answers is in itself untrue, they all betray a narrowness of vision. The answer is restricted to some part of what each is *supposed* to do, in effect reassuring us that he is doing what he should be; but it gives us little inkling of his full role in the larger scheme of things. Such an answer is for-givable when made by a policeman or a businessman; but it is difficult to avoid the feeling that, when made by a sociologist, it is peculiarly inappropriate and, in a way, self-contradictory. For if, as the sociologist says, it is his special job to see man-in-society, then shouldn't he also see and talk about *himself* in society?

Unfortunately, no more than other men do sociologists tell us what they are really doing in the world, as distinct from what they think they should be doing. Here in this study, however, I am very much concerned with what sociologists, and particularly social theorists, are really up to. I greatly doubt that all they are doing in the world can be described by saying that they study it. I greatly doubt that all they want from the world is just to be adequately supported but otherwise left alone, so that they can continue to study it.

The sociologists' task today is not only to see people as they see themselves, nor to see themselves as others see them; it is also to see *themselves* as they see other people. What is needed is a new and heightened self-awareness among sociologists, which would lead them to ask the same kinds of questions about themselves as they do about taxicab drivers or doctors, and to answer them in the same ways. Above all, this means that we must acquire the in-grained habit of viewing our own beliefs as we would those held by others. It means, for example, that when we are asked why it is that some sociologists believe sociology must be a "value-free discipline," we do not simply reply with the logical arguments on its behalf. Sociologists must surrender the human but elitist assumption that *others* believe out of need whereas *they* believe because of the dictates of logic and reason.

It will be relatively easy for sociologists to adopt such a stand-point with respect to their *professional* beliefs; it will be far harder, however, for them to do so with respect to their *scientific* beliefs and behavior. It will be difficult for them to feel in their bones, for example, that "scientific method" is not simply a logic but also a morality; that it is, moreover, the ideology of a small-scale social movement whose object is the reform—a very singular and dis-tinctive kind of reform—of sociology itself, and whose social character is not much different from that of any other social movement. It will be extremely difficult for many sociologists to recognize that we presently lack any serious understanding of how it happens that one piece of social research is regarded as good and another as poor, or why it is that sociologists move from one theory to another. For, like other men, sociologists still commonly confuse the moral answer with the empirical, thinking that what should be, is. That is, we too readily suppose that a change, particularly if it is to a theory that we ourselves happen to accept, has been made primarily because it was required by the findings of studies done in conformity with scientific method; we thus hasten to affirm our moral convictions rather than allow the question to remain un-answered until the studies, by which alone it could be answered, have been done.

Sociologists must cease assuming that there are two distinct breeds of men, subjects and objects, sociologists and laymen, whose behavior needs to be viewed in different ways. There is only one race of men; it is time we sociologists acknowledged all the im-plications of our membership in it. Like other sociologists, I will undoubtedly have difficulty in viewing sociologists as just another tribe in the race of men, but I mean to go as far as I can in this direction.

My aim, then, is to search out some critical understanding of the social mission of Academic Sociology, and to formulate some tentative ideas about the social mandate with which it operates, the ideologies it expresses, and the link it has to the larger society. An effort will be made to define the character of Academic Sociology by focusing on its dominant school of thought, Function-alism, and its dominant theorist, Talcott Parsons. While his stand-point is by no means the only one in American sociology today, it is without doubt the leading one. Any effort to understand the changes impending in American sociology today must confront its central intellectual tendencies. And since intellectual tendencies do not develop in a social vacuum, any effort to understand American sociology today must relate it to the nature and problems of the society in which it developed. In a later section, I shall briefly explore certain emerging characteristics of the new sociology in Eastern Europe, which I had opportunity to witness during 1965 and 1966. One of the most important reasons for focusing on the new sociology of Eastern Europe is that it provides a case of the emergence of an academic type of sociology in *statu nascendi:* it can thus refine our understanding of the social conditions under which an Academic Sociology emerges and help provide a basis for answering the question, What is Academic Sociology?

THE CHARACTER OF SOCIOLOGY

How and where one seeks this answer will depend, of course, on how sociology is conceived, on what it is taken to be. In their image of sociology, many practitioners stress that it is a social *science* and regard its scientific side as its most distinguishing and important feature. They wish to become, and to be thought of as, scientists; they wish to make their work more rigorous, more mathematical, more formal, and more powerfully instrumented. To them it is the scientific method of study itself, not the object studied or the way the object is conceived, that is the emotionally central if not the logically defining characteristic of sociology. In contrast to such a view, held by many but by no means all sociologists, the approach I take to the question of the character of sociology may seem curious. I do not intend to focus on sociology as a science, or on its "method."

Whatever their different emphases on the place of methodological rigor in sociology, most sociologists agree that a knowledge of social life requires that, at some point, researches be undertaken, that suppositions be subjected to some empirical test, that logical inferences be submitted to sensory observations. Most agree that there must be a looking at and a listening to people. Should it not suffice, therefore, to define the character of sociology simply in terms of its interest in knowing the social world empirically? Should not our question about the character of sociology be confined to the question: Under what conditions do men begin to study the social world empirically? Important as this question is, I do not think so.

One reason for not formulating the problem in this manner is that there are many different ways in which the social world can be studied, all of which may be equally scientific or empirical. There seems no reason to believe that the work of economists, political scientists, anthropologists, or social psychologists is less scientific than that of sociologists, though it is often manifestly different. Moreover, the empirical study of the social world premises that men already have certain conceptions of it. They have, at the very least, assumed that it is knowable by an empirical science, much as other parts of the world are by other sciences, and that, like them, it is possessed of lawful regularities. In short, whether or not an empirical study of social life develops, and the kind of study it is, depends upon certain prior assumptions about society and men, and, indeed, certain feelings about and relations to society and men.

Yet, if the formal purpose of sociology is to discover the character of the social world, how can it be based upon prior assumptions concerning this character? Doesn't this smuggle the rabbit into the hat and require that the things sociology discovers about the social world be limited by, or depend upon, what it already assumes about it? In some part this must be true; sociology can do no other. Sociology necessarily operates within the limits of its assumptions. But when it is acting self-consciously, it can at least put these assumptions to the test; it can appraise which are warranted and which are unfounded. Nonetheless, to a very large extent, these assumptions still must provide the axis of decision and discovery; they establish the limiting terms by which imputed attributes of the social world are affirmed or denied.

Like it or not, and know it or not, sociologists will organize their researches in terms of their prior assumptions; the character of sociology will depend upon them and will change when they change. To explore the character of a sociology, to know what a sociology is, therefore requires us to identify its deepest assumptions about man and society. For these reasons it will not be to its *methods* of study to which I will look for an understanding of its character, but rather to its assumptions about man and society. The use of particular methods of study implies the existence of particular assumptions about man and society.

When I speak of the "assumptions" that define the character of a sociology, however, I do not limit myself to those that sociologists make explicit in their "theories." One reason for this is that, in the last analysis, I am seeking to understand these theories as a human and social product. I want to be able to step back from the deliberately wrought theories, and I therefore need something to step back onto, so that I may begin to develop ideas that can account for the theories themselves. Ultimately, I want to be able to explain, not only logically but sociologically, why sociologists adopt certain theories and reject others, and why they change from one set of theories to another. The study here is a step in that direction.

BACKGROUND AND DOMAIN ASSUMPTIONS

Deliberately formulated social theories, we might say with deliberate oversimplification, contain at least two distinguishable elements. One element is the explicitly formulated assumptions, which may be called "postulations." But they contain a good deal more. They also contain a second set of assumptions that are unpostulated and unlabeled, and these I will term "background assumptions." I call them background assumptions because, on the one hand, they provide the background out of which the postulations in part emerge and, on the other hand, not being expressly formulated, they remain in the background of the theorist's attention. Postulations are brought into focalized attention, while background assumptions are part of what Michael Polanyi calls the theorist's "subsidiary attention."[1] Background assumptions are embedded in a theory's postulations. Operating within and alongside of them, they are, as it were, "silent partners" in the theoretical enterprise. Background assumptions provide some of the bases of choice and the invisible cement for linking together postulations. From beginning to end, they influence a theory's formulation and the researchers to which it leads.

Background assumptions also influence the *social* career of a theory, influencing the responses of those to whom it is communicated. For, in some part, theories are accepted or rejected because of the background assumptions embedded in them. In particular, a social theory is more likely to be accepted by those who share the theory's background assumptions and find them agreeable. Over and above their stipulated connotations, social theories and their component concepts contain a charge of surplus meanings derived in part from their background assumptions, and these may congenially resonate the compatible background assumptions of their hearers or may generate a painful dissonance.

Commitment to a social theory, in this view, occurs through a process rather different, and certainly more complex, than is supposedly the case in the canons of scientific method. The latter conceives of the process of commitment to a theory, or withdrawal from it, very largely in cerebral and rational terms; it emphasizes that the rejecting or accepting process is governed by a deliberate inspection and rational appraisal of the theory's formal logic and supporting evidence. That sociologists content themselves with such a limited view testifies to their readiness to explain their own behavior in a manner radically different from that by which they explain the behavior of others. It testifies to our readiness to account for our own behavior as if it were shaped solely by a willing conformity to the morality of scientific method.

That sociologists content themselves with such a view testifies to the fact that we have failed to become *aware* of ourselves and to take our own *experience* seriously. For as anyone who has ever dealt with theories knows, some are in fact accepted as convincing and others are rejected as unconvincing, long before the supporting evidence is in hand. Students do this frequently. Some theories are simply experienced, even by experienced sociologists, as *intuitively* convincing; others are not. How does this happen? What makes a theory intuitively convincing?

One reason is that its background assumptions coincide or are compatible with, consensually validate or bring to psychic closure, the background assumptions held by the viewer. The theory felt to be intuitively convincing is commonly experienced as *déjà vu*, as something previously known or already suspected. It is congenial because it confirms or complements an assumption already held by the respondent, but an assumption that was seen only dimly by him precisely because it was a "background" assumption. The intuitively convincing theory or concept is one that "sensitizes" the viewer, as Herbert Blumer suggests; but it sensitizes him not merely to some hidden part of the world outside, but also to some hitherto obscured part of the world *inside* himself. We do not know how much of what we now regard as "good" social theory is favored for these reasons. We can be sure, however, that it is a great deal more than those with scientific pretensions assume.

Background assumptions come in different sizes, they govern domains of different scope. They are arranged, one might say, like an inverted cone, standing on its point. At the top are background assumptions with the largest circumference, those that have no limited domain to which alone they apply. These are beliefs about the world that are so general that they may, in principle, be applied to any subject matter without restriction. They are, as Stephan Pepper calls them, "world hypotheses."[2] Being primitive presuppositions about the world and everything in it, they serve to provide the most general of orientations, which enable unfamiliar experiences to be made meaningful. They provide the terms of reference by which the less general assumptions, further down the cone, are themselves limited and influenced. World hypotheses are the most pervasive and primitive beliefs about what is real. They may involve, for example, an inclination to believe that the world and the things in it are "really" *one* or are "truly" *many*. Or, again, they may involve a disposition to believe that the world is "really" highly integrated and cohesive (regardless of whether it is one or many), or only loosely stranded together and dispersive. World hypotheses—the cat may as well be let out of the bag—are what are sometimes called "metaphysics."

Background assumptions of more limited application, for example, about man and society, are what I shall call "domain assumptions." Domain assumptions are the background assumptions applied only to members of a single domain; they are, in effect, the metaphysics of a domain. Domain assumptions about man and society might include, for example, dispositions to believe that men are rational or irrational; that society is precarious or fundamentally stable; that social problems will correct themselves without planned intervention; that human behavior is unpredictable; that man's true humanity resides in his feelings and sentiments. I say that these "might" be examples of domain assumptions made about man and society, because whether they are or not is a matter that can be decided finally only be determining what people, including sociologists, believe about a given domain.

Domain assumptions are of less general application than world hypotheses, although both are background assumptions. We might say that world hypotheses are a special or limiting case of domain assumptions, the case in which no restrictions are applied to the subject matter to which its assumptions refer. Domain assumptions are the things attributed to all members of a domain; in part they are shaped by the thinker's world hypotheses and, in turn, they shape his deliberately wrought theories. They are an aspect of the larger culture that is most intimately related to the postulations of theory. They are also one of the important links between the theorist's work and the larger society.

There are at least two different questions that may be raised about the role of background assumptions, whether world hypotheses or domain assumptions, in social science. One is whether social science must, for logical reasons, rest inescapably on some such assumptions. Whether social theories *unavoidably* require and must rest *logically* on some background assumptions is a question that simply does not concern me here. It is, I think, an important problem, but one primarily for logicians and philosophers of science. Another question does, however, interest me. This is whether social scientists do, in point of fact, tend to commit themselves to domain assumptions about man and society, with significant consequences for their theory. I think it probable and prudent to assume that they do.

What I am saying, then, is that the work of sociologists, as of others, is influenced by a sub-theoretical set of *beliefs,* for that is what background assumptions are: beliefs about all members of symbolically constituted domains. I am not saying that the work of sociologists should be influenced by background assumptions; this is a problem for methodological moralists. Nor am I saying that sociology logically requires and necessarily rests upon background assumptions; this is a problem for philosophers of science. What I am saying is that sociologists *do* use and are influenced by background assumptions; this is an empirical matter that sociologists themselves can study and confirm.

I think it is in the essential nature of background assumptions that they are not originally adopted for instrumental reasons, the way, for example, one might select a statistical test of significance or pick a screwdriver out of a tool kit. In short, they are not selected with a calculated view to their utility. This is so because they are often internalized in us long before the intellectual age of consent. They are affectively-laden cognitive tools that are developed early in the course of our socialization into a particular culture and are built deeply into our character structure. They are therefore likely to change with changes in modal or "social character," to vary with changes in socialization experiences and practices, and therefore to differ with different age or peer groups.

We begin the lifelong process of learning background assumptions while learning our first language, for the language gives us categories that constitute the domains to which the domain assumptions refer. As we learn the categories and the domains that they demarcate, we also acquire a variety of assumptions or beliefs about all members of the domain. In simple truth, all of these domain-constituting categories derive from and function in much the same manner as "stereotypes." Thus, as children are taught the category of Negro, they also learn certain background assumptions—and "prejudices"—about Negroes. Certain *existential* background assumptions are learned about what Negroes presumably *are,* for example, "lazy and shiftless." We also learn *normative* background assumptions, that is, beliefs about their moral value, their goodness or badness. Indeed, normative and existential assumptions are so closely intertwined as to be inseparable, except analytically. In a similar way, we learn linguistic categories such as man, society, group, friend, parent, poor, woman; accompanying each of these are background assumptions, dispositions to attribute certain things to all members of the constituted domain. For example, friends are helpful, or will betray you; man is a weak, or a strong, animal; society is powerful, or precarious; the poor are deserving, or undeserving.

The domains that come to be constituted vary with the languages learned and used, and the background assumptions accompanying them vary with the cultures or subcultures in which they are learned and used. To suggest that they operate in much the same manner as racial stereotypes and prejudices entails a set of strong and specifiable assumptions: (1) there is a disposition to believe that there are certain attributes that will be manifested by *all* members of the domain, which (2) is acquired well before the believer has had a personal experience with anything like a true sample of the members of the domain, and perhaps even before he has had any, but which (3) may, nonetheless, entail the strongest feelings about them, (4) shape his subsequent encounters with them, and that (5) are not at all easily shaken or changed, even when these encounters produce experiences discrepant with the assumptions. In short, they are often resistant to "evidence." To say, then, that sociology is shaped by the background assumptions of its practitioners is only to say that they have a human vulnerability to prejudice. These prejudices, however, may be even more difficult to escape than racial prejudice, insofar as they do not manifestly impair the interests of special groups whose struggle against the prejudice may heighten public awareness of it.

It would seem to be one implication of Charles Osgood's work on the "semantic differential" that certain kinds of background assumptions will be made *universally*, about all linguistically constituted domains.[3] For example, they may always be judged in terms of their weakness or strength, their activity or passivity; most importantly, they will always be defined in terms of their "goodness" or "badness." In short, if linguistic categories constitute domains and thus define reality, they inescapably entail an imputation about moral worth and value. As in the realm of physics, where there is no quality without some quantity, so in the social realm, there is no reality without value; the real and the ideal are different dimensions, but they are simultaneously constituted by and inseparably fused in the linguistic categories that constitute social domains.

In brief, to understand the character of Academic Sociology we have to understand the background assumptions, the world hypotheses and domain assumptions, with which it works. These may be inferred from the stipulated social theories with which it operates. The theories thus constitute part but not all of the data by which we can glean a theorist's background assumptions. I say "part but not all" of the data, because theorists leave other trace-marks than their formal publications; they write letters, have conversations, give informal lectures, and take political positions. In short, they do not merely write technical articles; they live in all the revealing ways that other men do. Indeed, they may even submit to interviews.

Background assumptions provide the inherited intellectual "capital" with which a theorist is endowed long before he becomes a theorist, and which he later invests in his intellectual and scientific roles, fusing it to his technical training. Sub-theoretical in character, background assumptions endow the stipulated theory with its appeal, its power, its reach; they establish its maneuver ground for technical development. At some point in this development, however, old background assumptions may come to operate in new conditions, scientifically or socially unsuitable, and thus create an uncomfortable dissonance for the theorist. They then become boundaries which confine and inhibit the theory's further development. When this occurs, it is no small technical rectification that is required; rather, a basic intellectual shift impends. Again, a new generation may arise with new background assumptions, ones that are not resonated congenially by theories based on older assumptions which the young generation feels to be wrong or absurd. It is then we can say that a theory, or the discipline based on it, verges on crisis.

The most basic changes in any science commonly derive not so much from the invention of new research techniques but rather from new ways of looking at data that may have long existed. Indeed, they may neither refer to nor be occasioned by "data," old or new. The most basic changes are in theory and in conceptual schemes, especially those that embody new background assumptions. They are thus changes in the way the world is seen, in what is believed to be real and valuable. To understand the impending crisis in sociology, therefore, it is necessary to understand its dominant intellectual schemes and theories; it is necessary to see the ways in which their background assumptions, by no means new, are being brought to a painful dissonance by new developments in the larger society.

It is an essential element in my theory about sociology that its articulated theories in part derive from, rest on, and are sustained by the usually tacit assumptions that theorists make about the domains with which they concern themselves. Articulate social theory, I shall hold, is in part an extrusion from, and develops in interaction with, the theorist's tacit domain assumptions. Believing this to be the case for other theorists, I shall be obliged at various points in the discussion to present my own domain assumptions, for reasons of candor as well as of consistency.

It is of the essence of domain assumptions that they are intellectually consequential, which is to say, they are theory-shaping, not because they rest on evidence nor even because they are provable; a social domain defined as real is real in its consequences for theory-making. In setting out one's domain assumptions, however, there is considerable danger that one will dissemble precisely because one wants to be "reasonable." One does not want to acknowledge as one's own an assumption for which one can give no "good" reason, and there is a great disposition to adorn or disguise a domain assumption in a reasonable argument, even if that is not the reason one holds it. And it is an almost overpowering temptation, particularly for those sociologists who need to think of themselves as scientists, to present their domain assumptions as if they were empirically substantiated "facts."

Yet the presentation of one's domain assumptions may provide an occasion when the theorist may glimpse whether or not he has a right to believe in them. The point, then, at which the theorist sees the importance of and attempts to present his domain assumptions is an ambiguous moment. It has the contradictory potential of increasing his self-awareness or his self-deception, of disclosing or dissembling, of activating growth-inducing forces or foreclosing the possibilities of basic intellectual development. It may be a fruitful but always is a dangerous moment in the lives of theorists.

Two things are needed to grasp it productively. First, the theorist must recognize that what is at issue here is not only what is in the world but also what is in himself; he must have a capacity to hear his own voice, not simply those of others. Second, he must have the courage of his convictions, or at least courage enough to acknowledge his beliefs as his, whether or not legitimated by reason and evidence. Unless he delivers his domain assumptions from the dim realm of subsidiary awareness into the clearer realm of focal awareness, where they can be held firmly in view, they can never be brought before the bar of reason or submitted to the test of evidence. The theorist lacking in such insight and courage is in the wrong business.

The important thing in setting forth one's domain assumptions is to have the insight to see what one believes and the courage to say what one sees. And since insight and courage are scarce moral resources, the important thing in reading someone else's account of his domain assumptions is to be continually aware that at some point you are going to be deceived.

THE IMPORTANCE OF DOMAIN ASSUMPTIONS:
A RESEARCH NOTE

That domain assumptions are in fact consequential for, or at least very importantly related to, a great variety of other professional and theoretical beliefs held by sociologists, despite there being no sense in which they rest on "evidence," may be gleaned from the national opinion survey of American sociologists conducted by Timothy Sprehe and me in 1964.[4] A very large number of questions concerning a great variety of areas were answered by the more than 3,400 sociologists who replied. Among the areas explored were the sociologists' conceptions of their role in society, their attitudes toward sociology as a "value-free" discipline, their attitudes toward specific theories, research techniques and methodologies, and their attitudes toward professionalization and professionalism. We also asked a variety of questions designed to explore sociologists' domain assumptions. For example, we asked them whether they believe men are rational, whether social problems are self-correcting or require planned intervention, whether human behavior is unpredictable, whether the ultimate reality of group life was located in unity or diversity, whether changing people is more important than understanding them, whether human behavior is more or less complex than it seems. Most of these questions were unqualified, and aimed to discern what sociologists attributed to such entire domains as "human behavior," "modern society," "the world," or "groups." Some methodological purists might object that such questions cannot be answered, or are "meaningless," or are lacking in specificity. Basically, however, such an objection either rests on the assumption that sociologists are fundamentally different from other human beings and do not hold the same kind of vague and "unproven" beliefs that others do, or else it wishes to blur the issue, which is an empirical one, with the irrelevant notion that sociologists *should* not have such beliefs. But, if our approach needs any defense, it was one of the elemental findings of our research that sociologists seem to have no more difficulty than anyone else in answering such broad questions, and, like other men, they do indeed hold the kind of beliefs that I have characterized as domain assumptions.

More than that, however, our research also indicated that domain assumptions are a rather important type of belief when compared to the other types of belief by a factor analysis of the questionnaire data. This factor analysis (an orthogonal, "Varimax" rotation) isolated seven factors as the most important dimensions underlying the large number of specific questions that were asked. One of these was the dimension bearing on domain assumptions, which was composed of the items about rationality, predictability, etcetera, mentioned above. When the seven factors were correlated with one another and listed in order of their average correlations with all other factors, the "domain assumption" factor was discovered to be the most important of them; that is, it had a substantially larger mean correlation with all the other factors than did any of the other six. A second method used for appraising the relative importance of domain assumptions was to make a multiple regression analysis, in which each factor was treated as a dependent variable and the degree to which it was accounted for by the other six was measured by its partial regression coefficient (or *beta* weight). It was thereby possible to determine the contribution of each factor to any other, by holding all the others constant and then, summing the beta scores, to measure the contribution of any one factor to *all* the others. With this method, the domain assumptions factor showed the second highest score, and not much less than the first. Finally, using an oblique (or "Oblimax") rotation to extract the factors, when the resulting factors were all correlated with one another, domain assumptions had the most consistently high correlation with all the other factors.

SENTIMENTS AND THEORY

One of the reasons that domain assumptions have importance as part of the entire sub-theoretical matrix on which theory rests is that they provide foci for feelings, affective states, and sentiments, although they are by no means the only structures around which sentiments come to be organized. To say, for example, that someone "believes" Negroes are lazy and also "believes" this is bad, is not entirely correct. For, those viewing this as "bad" do more than *believe* it; they *feel* it and may indeed feel it strongly. They may have sentiments of disgust and avoidance, or a wish to punish, associated with their assumptions about what the Negro is and with their devaluation of him. Sentiments entail a hormone-eliciting, muscle-tensing, tissue-embedded, fight-or-flight disposition of the total organism. While sentiments often may be organized around or elicited by domain assumptions, they are not the same thing. And they may, of course, be organized around or elicited by a great many things other than domain assumptions, for instance, individual persons or concrete situations.

Furthermore, people may have sentiments that are not conventionally called for by the domain assumptions that they have learned, but they are not for that reason any the less powerful and body-gripping. There may, in brief, be various forms of dissonance between the existential and normative beliefs that people learn in connection with domain-constituting categories, and the sentiments that they feel toward members of that category. Thus, for instance, a White woman may *feel* sexually aroused and attracted to a Black man, even though she also believes that Blacks are "dirty" and "disgusting." A man may *feel* pessimistic and despairing, resigned and quiescent, even though he also believes that men are good and that society progresses, simply because he himself is ill or aging. Correspondingly, a man may, when young, feel optimistic and energetically activistic, even though he may believe that the world is on a collision course with disaster and that there is little that can be done about it.

I am, of course, not suggesting that young men are invariably more optimistic than old ones, but what I am intimating, using age only as an example, is that people may feel things at variance with their domain assumptions, with their existential beliefs or normative values; feelings emerge from people's experience with the world, during which they often come to need and learn things that are somewhat different from what they are supposed to need or were deliberately taught to learn. If Freud and other psychologists are right about the Oedipal Complex, many men in Western societies feel hostility toward their fathers even though they have never been taught to do so, and in fact have been taught to love and honor them. In short, men may have feelings at variance with those of their culturally prescribed "languages" that is, with the domain assumptions conventional to their group of society. Such sentiments may be idiosyncratic to an individual and derive from his unique experience, or they may be shared by large numbers and derive from an experience common to them, even if not culturally prescribed for them. Thus, at least since about the early nineteenth century, many young people in Western countries seem to be subjected to a common experience that induces them to be somewhat more anti-authoritarian, rebellious, or critical of the political and cultural status quo than were their elders.

The prescribed domain assumptions, then, are one thing; the sentiments men have may be quite another. When they diverge, when the things men feel are at variance with their domain assumptions, there is a dissonance or tension between the two levels. Sometimes this is dealt with simply by giving ritualistic "lip service" to the domain assumptions required and taught in the culture; sometimes men may openly rebel against them, adopting or seeking new domain assumptions more consonant with the feelings they actually have. But there is likely to be an intrinsic difficulty in such an open and active rebellion: first, unless there are already alternatives formulated, men may find it easier to live with the old uncomfortable assumptions than with none at all; second, men often experience their own deviant feelings as "wrong" and as perilous to their own security, and consequently may conceal their unprescribed feelings even from themselves; third, as a consequence of this, they may not openly communicate their deviant feelings to others who might share and therefore encourage and support them.

In consequence then, when a gap opens between the sentiments men feel and the domain assumptions they have been taught, their most immediate response may be to suppress or privatize the experienced dissonance. They may allow the tension to fester; or they may begin a kind of sporadic, cultural, guerrilla warfare against the prevailing domain assumptions, in which their dissatisfaction is intermittently expressed in squeaks of black humor or by an inertial apathy. This situation, very much like the attitude of some young radicals today toward academic sociology, begins to change importantly when domain categories and assumptions emerge that are more consonant with what people feel. When resistance to established assumptions lacks alternatives, it may at first be manifested socially among those who, while lacking a new language, do nonetheless recognize their common possession of deviant sentiments, and therefore may enter into informal solidarities with one another against those who they commonly feel share other sentiments. The current "generation gap" seems a case in point. When, however, the new sentiments begin to find or create their own appropriate language, the possibilities of larger solidarities and of rational public discussion are extended.

It is in part because social theories are shaped by and express domain assumptions that they are also sentiment-relevant: reactions to social theories involve the sentiments of the men who read and write them. Whether a theory is accepted or rejected, whether it undergoes change or remains essentially unchanged, is not simply a cerebral decision; it is in some part contingent upon the gratifications or tensions that it generates by dint of its relation to the sentiments of those involved. Social theories may be sentiment-relevant in various ways and to varying degrees may inhibit or arouse the expression of certain sentiments. As a limiting case, the degree to which they impinge upon sentiments may be so small that, for all practical purposes, they may be said to be "neutral" in their sentiment-relevance. Yet even this last case is consequential for reactions to the theory, for the sentiment-neutral theory may simply be eliciting apathetic or disinterested responses, the feeling that the theory is somehow "irrelevant," and thus induce avoidance of, if not active opposition to, it. Moreover, reactions to a social theory may also depend upon the *kinds* of sentiments that are aroused directly or by association. The activation of particular sentiments may at some times and for some people be enjoyable, or it may be discomfiting and painful.

Max Weber's theory of bureaucracy, for example, stressing, as it does, the inevitable proliferation of bureaucratic forms in the increasingly large and complex modern social organizations, tends to elicit and resonate sentiments of pessimism concerning the possibilities of large-scale social change that could successfully remedy human alienation. Those committed to efforts at such change will experience such sentiments as dissonant and may therefore react critically to the theory, attempting to change it in ways that strip it of such consequences, or they may reject it altogether. Conversely, those who never had—or who once had but then relinquished—aspirations for social change, or whose inclination is to seek limited intra-system reforms, may for their part not experience the Weberian theory as inducing an unpleasant pessimism.

In one case, then, a theory may have a coherence-inducing or integrating effect, while in another it may have a tension- or conflict-inducing effect; each has different consequences for the individual's ability to pursue certain courses of *action* in the world and has different implications for different lines of political conduct. It is thus through its sentiment-relevance as well as through its domain assumptions that a social theory takes on political meanings and implications quite apart from whether these were knowingly intended or recognized either by those who formulated or those who accepted it. In the example mentioned above, concerning Weber's theory of bureaucracy, it is commonly understood that the theory has strongly antisocialist implications, for it implies that change toward socialism will not prevent bureaucratization and alienation.

PERSONAL REALITY AND SOCIAL THEORY

If every social theory is thus a tacit theory of politics, every theory is also a personal theory, inevitably expressing, coping, and infused with the personal experience of the individuals who author it.

Every social theory has both political and personal relevance, which, according to the technical canons of social theory, it is not supposed to have. Consequently, both the man and his politics are commonly screened out in what is deemed the proper presentation of presumably "autonomous" social theory.

Yet, however disguised, an appreciable part of any sociological enterprise devolves from the sociologist's effort to explore, to objectify, and to universalize some of his own most deeply personal experiences. Much of any man's effort to know the social world around him is prompted by an effort, more or less disguised or deliberate, to know things that are personally important to him; which is to say, he aims at knowing himself and the experiences he has had in his social world (his relationship to it), and at *changing* this relationship in some manner. Like it or not, and know it or not, in confronting the social world the theorist is also confronting himself. While this has no bearing on the validity of the resultant theory, it does bear on another legitimate interest: the sources, the motives, and the aims of the sociological quest.

Whatever their other differences, all sociologists seek to study something in the social world that they take to be real; and, whatever their philosophy of science, they seek to explain it in terms of something that they *feel* to be real. Like other men, sociologists impute reality to certain things in their social world. This is to say, they believe, sometimes with focal and sometimes only with subsidiary awareness, that certain things are truly attributable to the social world. In important part, their conception of what is "real" derives from the domain assumptions they have learned in their culture. These culturally standardized assumptions are, however, differentiated by personal experience in different parts of the social structure. Individually accented by particular sentiment-generating experiences, the common domain assumptions in time assume personal arrangements; they become part of a man's personal reality.

For simplicity's sake, I suggest that there are two kinds of "reality" with which sociologists must come to terms. One consists of "role realities," the things they learn as sociologists; these include what they believe to be the "facts" yielded by previous researches, whether conducted by themselves or others. The "facts," of course, entail imputations made by men about the world. To assign factuality to some imputation about the world is also to express a personal conviction about its truth, as well as about the propriety of the process by which it was made. To believe an imputation to be "factual" is to assign a high value to it, setting it above such things as "opinions" or "prejudices."

Inevitably, to assign factuality to an imputation is to make it an anchor point in the self's relation to the world, to make it or claim

it should be central to the self. To assign factuality to an imputa-
ion is to invoke an obligation and duty upon the self: one must
"take the facts into account" under certain conditions. There is the
further obligation to inspect severely and to examine critically (in
short to defend against) attacks on one's "factual" beliefs; a denial
of beliefs previously thought to be factual is thus a self-mobilizing
"challenge." Within scientific communities, therefore, men engage
in committed personal efforts—through contest, conflict, struggle,
and negotiation—to establish and maintain the facts. The facts are
not automatically produced by the impersonal machinery of research. To assign factuality to a belief is a self-involving commitment; the person makes a claim upon the credence of another, or
himself lends credence to the claim of another. In these and other
ways, the factual becomes part of the sociologist's personal reality.

In particular those imputations that a sociologist makes about
the factuality of beliefs based on research tend to become aspects
of his reality, part of his *focal awareness* as a *sociologist*. Deemed
relevant to his work as a sociologist and derived in accordance with
methodological decorum, the sociologist commonly feels that he
may with propriety publicly endorse such beliefs. Indeed, these
must explicitly be attended to by him under certain conditions. In
short, he must not ignore them, and he need not conceal his belief
in them.

A second order of conceptions about reality held by sociologists
consists of the "personally real." These are imputations about "realities" in the social world that sociologists make, not because of
"evidence" or "research," but simply because of what they have seen,
heard, been told, or read. While these beliefs differ from "facts"
systematically gathered and scientifically evaluated, the sociologist
nonetheless *experiences* them as no less real—and it is well for
his sanity that he does. Still, while these are every bit as real to
him as facts garnered through research, if not more so, the sociologist *qua* sociologist is not supposed to credit or attend to them in
the same way that he treats "facts"; indeed, he may feel obliged as
a sociologist to subject them to systematic doubt. Imputations
about the world that are part of the sociologist's *personal* reality
may therefore sink into his subsidiary awareness rather than remaining consciously available to him, when he acts as a conforming sociologist. But this, of course, is very far from saying that they
thereby cease to have consequences for his work as a sociologist
or social theorist. In practice, the sociologist's role realities and his
personal realities interpenetrate and mutually influence one another.

During the 1940's and 1950's, largely under the influence of
Talcott Parsons, many sociologists stressed the importance of

theory in structuring research. Starting from the commonplace that sociologists did not view all parts of the social world as equally important, but rather focused their attention upon it selectively, they concluded that this perceptual organization was largely the result of the "theories," tacit or explicit, which were held. "Facts" were thus seen as the product of an effort to pursue the inferences of theories and, indeed, as being constituted by the conceptual schemes embedded in the theories. Facts were seen, at least primarily, as interacting with theories, confirming or disproving them, and thus as cumulatively shaping theoretical development; perceptual selectivity, and hence the focus of research, was largely accounted for in terms of the sociologist's theoretical commitment.

This emphasis tended to deprecate the earlier tradition of methodological empiricism, which had stressed the primary value of data and research. If the empiricists had stressed that sociologists are or should be guided by the facts yielded by properly conducted research, theory-stressing sociologists tended to reply that sociologists are or should be guided by articulate, explicit, and hence testable theory. From the standpoint presented here, however, both seem to have been at least partially mistaken.

Those who emphasized theory tended unduly to deprecate the self-implicating, perception-anchoring, and stabilizing role of "facts" (as distinct from their validity-testing function); the empiricists tended to miss the importance of previously held theoretical assumptions. Both, in addition, made a common error in limiting themselves to only one order of the imputably real, namely, the "factual." What both missed is that scientific factuality is only a special case of a larger set of beliefs, those imputing reality; both failed to see that whether an aspect of "role reality" or "personal reality," the imputably real has a special force in structuring the perception of the sociologist and shaping his subsequent theorizing and research. The theorists in particular failed to see the importance of the sub-theoretical level, including the "personally real," as consequential for theory and research. A situation defined as real is real in its consequences, for sociologists as for other men.

Whether part of his role reality or his personal reality, things to which the sociologist imputes reality play a role in his work in several ways. They may be elements that he is concerned to explain, in short, as "dependent variables" or effects; they may be part of his explanatory effort, serving as "independent variables" or possible "causes"; or, again, they may be used as explicit models or tacit paradigms that he employs to clarify the nature of what he wants to explain or the factors that explain it.

To amplify the latter point: the imputably real enters importantly into theory construction by being regarded as possessed of *generalizable* significance, by being treated as an example or case of, or a model or paradigm of, a larger set of things. Sociologists assume that things they have researched, or with which they have otherwise become personally acquainted and hence "know," are like (and may be used to understand) other things with which they are unacquainted at first hand or have not yet researched. Thus, while aiming to account for a set of events that extend beyond the sociologist's facts or personal realities, social theories are at the same time also influenced by his prior imputations about what is real in the world, whether these are his facts or personal realities. For example, Max Weber's general theory of bureaucracy was influenced both by his historical, scholarly researches and by his first-hand acquaintance with German bureaucracy and, in particular, with governmental rather than private bureaucracy. The German governmental bureaucracy, both as experienced social structure and as cultural ideal, constituted for Weber a personal reality that served as his central paradigm for all bureaucracies; it provided a framework for organizing and assimilating the facts yielded by his scholarly researches.

If personal reality shapes scholarly research, scholarly research is also a source of personal reality, not only of role reality. A man's research or work is commonly more than just a way he spends time; it is often a vital part of his life and a central part of the experience that shapes his personal reality. If this were not so, then all relevant research would be equally significant to a sociologist. But the truth is that researches and discoveries made by the scholar himself have a special importance for him; a man's own researches become a part of his personal reality in ways that the work of his colleagues usually does not. If nothing else, they become personal commitments that he wishes to defend.

The limited parts of the social world with which a sociologist's research bring him into contact are endowed with a compelling reality precisely because they are part of his personal experience. Limited though they are, they often come to be used as paradigms for other, unknown parts, and serve as the basis for generalizing about larger wholes. Thus, for example, *one* reason Malinowski's theory of magic differed from that of A. R. Radcliffe-Brown was because the different kinds of magic each had first closely studied came to stand for all other kinds of magic. Although Malinowski had focused on work- and subsistence-getting magic, and Radcliffe-Brown on childbirth magic, each treated his limited experience as a paradigm, exemplary of and essentially akin to other kinds of magic. Evidence incorporated into personal experience became part of a permeating personal reality to which the larger world was assimilated and by which it was shaped.

Sociologists, of course, are familiar with these dangers, at least *en principe*, and they seek to use systematic sampling as a way of obviating them. Nonetheless, systematic sampling cannot fully avoid the problem, for it provides a basis for testing a theory only subsequent to its formulation. Disciplined research entails the use of a systematic sample in order to test inferences from a theory, but, in the nature of the case, the theory must be formulated prior to the sample. Indeed, the more the sociologist stresses the importance of articulate theory, the more this is likely to be the case. The theory will therefore tend to devolve around, and consequently be shaped by, the limited facts and personal realities available to the theorist, and *in particular by those imputed realities that he treats as paradigms.*

Systematic sampling serves primarily as a restraint on unjustified generalization from "facts"; but it does not similarly restrain the influence of "personal realities." Since the latter commonly remains only at the fringes of subsidiary awareness, being deemed scientifically irrelevant, it is often (and mistakenly) assumed that it is scientifically inconsequential. In point of fact, the personally real and problematic often enough becomes the starting point for systematic inquiry—and, indeed, there is no scientific reason this should not be so.

What is personally real to men is real, frequently though not always, primarily because it is not unique to them—in the sense of idiosyncratic to, or uniquely different for, them—but rather is socially and collectively true. Since the sense of the reality of things often depends on mutual agreement or consensual validation, collectively held notions of reality are among the most firmly constituted components of an individual's personal reality. Yet the personally real does not entirely consist of or derive from collective definitions of social reality. It may also emerge from recurrent personal experience, whether unique to the person or shared with a few others. What becomes personally real to one individual, then, need not be personally real to others. But whether derived from collective definitions or from recurrent personal experiences, a man believes that some things are real; and these imputed realities are of special importance to the kinds of theories that he formulates, even if he happens to be a sociologist.

THE INFRASTRUCTURE OF SOCIAL THEORY

From this perspective all social theory is immersed in a sub-theoretical level of domain assumptions and sentiments which both liberate and constrain it. This sub-theoretical level is shaped by and shared with the larger culture and society, at least to some extent, as well as being individually organized, accented, differentiated, and changed by personal experience in the world. I call this sub-theoretical level the "infrastructure" of theory.

This infrastructure is important not because it is the ultimate determinant of the character of social theory, but because it is part of the most immediate, local surround from which the theory-work eventuates in theory-performances and theory-products. Theory-work is surely linked to, even if not solely determined by, the character of the theorist doing it. This infrastructure can never really be left behind, even in the most isolated and lonely moments of theory-work, when a man finally puts pen to paper in a room where there is no one but himself. The world is, of course, there in the room with him, in him; he has not escaped it. But it is not *the* world, not *the* society and *the* culture that is there with him, but *his* limited version and partial experience of it.

However individual a work of theory is, nonetheless, some (and perhaps much) of its individuality is conventional in character. The individuality of theory-work is, in part, a socially sanctioned illusion. For there are the assistants who have helped the theorist do his research and writing; there are the colleagues and the students, the friends and the lovers, on whom he has informally "tested" his ideas; there are those from whom he has learned and taken and those whom he opposes. All theory is not merely influenced but actually produced by a group. Behind each theory-product is not only the author whose name appears upon the work, but an entire shadow group for whom, we might say, the "author" is the emblem; in a way, the author's name serves as the name of an intellectual team.

Yet the "author" is not merely the puppet of these group forces, because to some extent he selects his team, recruits members to and eliminates them from his theory-working group, responds selectively to the things they suggest and the criticisms they make, accepting some and ignoring others, attending to some more closely than others. Thus, while authorship is always in some measure conventional, it is also in some measure the expression of the real activities and initiatives of an individual theorist whose "infrastructure" helps shape both the ideas and the shadow group whose tacit collaboration eventuates in theoretical performances.

A concern with sub-theory or the infrastructure of theory is not the expression of an inclination to psychologize theory and is certainly not a form of psychological reductionism. It is, rather, the outcome of a concern for empirical realism, an effort to come close to the human systems to which any theoretical work is most visibly and intimately linked. It is an effort that is peculiarly necessary for those working within a sociological tradition that tends to obscure and to cast doubt upon the importance and reality of persons, and to view them as the creatures of grander social structures. For those, such as myself, who have lived within a sociological tradition, the importance of the larger social structures and historical processes is not in doubt. What is intellectually in question, when the significance of theoretical infrastructure is raised, is the analytic means by which we may move between persons and social structures, between society and the local, more narrowly bounded environments from which social theory discernibly derives. My own view is that any sociological explanation or generalization implies (at least tacitly) certain psychological assumptions; correspondingly, any psychological generalization tacitly implies certain sociological conditions. In directing attention to the importance of the theoretical infrastructure, I have sought not to psychologize social theory and remove it from the larger social system, but rather to specify the analytic means by which I hope to *link it more firmly* with the larger social world.

THEORETICAL INFRASTRUCTURE AND IDEOLOGY

Rooted in a limited personal reality, resonating some sentiments but not others, and embedded in certain domain assumptions, every social theory facilitates the pursuit of some but not of all courses of *action*, and thus encourages us to change or to accept the world as it is, to say yea or nay to it. In a way, every theory is a discreet obituary or celebration for some social system.

The sentiments resonated by a social theory provide an immediate but privatized mood, an experience that inhibits or fosters anticipated courses of public and political conduct, and thus may exacerbate or resolve internal uncertainties or conflicts about the possibilities of successful outcomes. Similarly, domain assumptions

entail beliefs about what is real in the world and thus have implications about what it is possible to *do,* to *change* in the world;
the values they entail indicate what courses of action are desirable
and thus shape conduct. In this sense, every theory and every
theorist ideologizes social reality.

The ideologizing of sociology is not an archaism manifested only
by long-dead "founding fathers" but absent from more truly
modern sociologists. Indeed, it is fully manifest in the school of
thought that has been most insistent on the importance of profes-
sionalizing sociology and of maintaining its intellectual autonomy,
namely, that developed by Talcott Parsons. This may be noted even
in a recent collection of essays on *American Sociology,* edited by
Parsons in 1968.[5] The dominant mood of this volume, published in
the midst of the ongoing war in Vietnam and written during a
period when hostilities between the Black and White communities
in American cities had reached the point of recurrent summer
violence and rioting, was, despite this, one of self-congratulatory
celebration.

One convenience of this volume is that, being intended for popular consumption—indeed, originally prepared for the Voice of
America broadcasts—its essays are swathed in fewer layers of
gauzy jargon. One can more readily see the domain assumptions on
which they rest, the sentiments that they resonate, the politics they
imply. S. M. Lipset, in his essay, for example, remarks that "basic
structural changes while maintaining traditional legitimacy in
political institutions would appear to be the best way to avoid
political tensions."[6] But is the avoidance of political tensions always
best, for whom? If I can fathom Mr. Lipset's meaning here, he is
saying that political stability would be achieved if efforts at social
change prudently stopped short of changing established ways of
allocating and justifying power. I doubt this, for it seems to me that
the clinging to established legitimations of political power is one
of the ways in which elites seek to block all other "basic structural
changes." Moreover, what of countries where political legitimacy
itself is based on revolution? One also wonders whether Lipset
would apply his assumptions about continuity to Soviet Russia and
tell Soviet liberals that they too should adapt their reform impulses
to their nation's traditional mode of legitimating political power,
thus maintaining its autocratic political traditions. Politically, Lipset's argument is the classical conservative brief against abrupt
tensionful change which might disrupt legitimacy, continuity, and
gradualism.

The self-congratulatory tone of this volume is raised to patriotic
pitch when Mr. Lipset argues that exceptional grace was bestowed
on American society when George Washington, for reasons unex-

plained, refused the crown. This triumphal theme is carried forward by Albert Cohen, who implicitly answers those who call America a sick society by maintaining that, to the contrary, "the United States is a dynamic, growing, prosperous, more or less democratic society."[7] The celebration continues: Thomas Pettigrew recounts the story of Black progress in the United States, where, he holds, "one out of every three Negro Americans today can be sociologically classified . . . as middle class."[8] He reassures us that racial violence today, far from being a symptom of societal malaise, is, to the contrary, proof of the "rapid social progress taking place."[9] "Rapid" from whose standpoint?

Reinhard Bendix also assures us that, in modern society, the words "ruler" and "ruled" no longer have "clear meaning."[10] Presumably this is so, because the people now exercise "control through periodic elections . . . [and] the fact that every adult has the vote is a token of the regard in which he is held as an individual and a citizen."[11] The franchise, Bendix tells us, has been "extended." One wonders if that is how the matter would be put by those who were arrested, beaten, and killed in the struggle during the 1960's to enfranchise Blacks in the American South: would *they* see what had happened as an "extension" of the franchise?

In all this, a very selective, one-sided picture of American society is made persuasive by a number of techniques. One is to call the partly-filled glass of water half-filled, rather than half-empty; for example, American Blacks are described as one-third middle class, rather than as two-thirds miserable. There is also the strategy of the Great Omission. In this volume there is scarcely anything about war, not an echo of the new revisionist historiography; indeed, the word "imperialism" does not appear in the book's index, and there is nothing about the relation between democracy, affluence, and war. Furthermore, we may note how myths are woven into the total view of social reality, deeply but invisibly, by the entire structure of language and conceptualization. When, for instance, the bloody struggle to register Blacks in the South is rendered as the mechanical "extension" of the franchise, a much larger view of social change and of men is implicitly communicated.

METHODOLOGY AS IDEOLOGY

Domain assumptions concerning man and society are built not only into substantive social theory but into methodology itself. Charles Tilly's essay on urbanization, in Parsons' volume, presents an interesting case of the latter, revealing the manner in which research methods predicate domain assumptions and how, at the same time, these methods generate dispositions of political relevance. "No country," complains Tilly, "has a social accounting system allowing the quick, reliable detection of changes in organizational membership, kinship organization, religious adherence, or even occupational mobility."[12] From Tilly's standpoint as a research-oriented sociologist, this is a bad thing. Yet what kind of country would it be that would have such a relentless, "quick, reliable" all-embracing system of information about its population? Surely it would be a nation in which the potentialities (at least) for the most complete totalitarianism were at hand. Undoubtedly Tilly would reject such a society as quickly as I. Yet he and many other sociologists fail to see that the conventional methodologies of social research often premise and foster a deep-going authoritarianism, a readiness to lie to and manipulate people: they betray a bureaucratic numbness.

As Chris Argyris has put it (but not in Parsons' *American Sociology*), conformity to "rigorous research criteria would create a world for the subject in which his behavior is defined, controlled, evaluated, manipulated, and reported to a degree that is comparable to the behavior of workers in the most mechanized assembly-line conditions." Stated otherwise, information-gathering systems or research methods always premise the existence and use of some system of social control. It is not only that the information they yield may be used *by* systems of social control, but that they themselves *are* systems of control.

Every research method makes some assumptions about how information may be secured from people and what may be done with people, or to them, in order to secure it; this, in turn, rests on certain domain assumptions concerning *who and what people are*. To the degree that the social sciences are modelled on the physical sciences, they entail the domain assumption that people are "things" which may be treated and controlled in much the same manner that other sciences control their non-human materials: people are "subjects" which may be subjected to the control of the experimenter for purposes they need not understand or even consent to. Such social science will thoughtlessly drift into buying increments of information at the cost of human autonomy and dignity.

When viewed from one standpoint, "methodology" seems a purely technical concern devoid of ideology; presumably it deals only with methods of extracting reliable information from the world, collecting data, constructing questionnaires, sampling, and analyzing returns. Yet it is always a good deal more than that, for it is commonly infused with ideologically resonant assumptions about what the social world is, who the sociologist is, and what the nature of the relation between them is.

THE AUTONOMY OF SOCIAL STRUCTURE
AS DOMAIN ASSUMPTION

It is not only in its basic methodological conceptions, however, that sociology is embedded in domain assumptions having ideological resonance, but also in its most fundamental conceptions of what its subject matter is and what the characteristics are of the distinctive domains it studies. For example, in Peter Blau's contribution to Parsons' *American Sociology*, there is the conventional but unexamined assumption that, "once firmly organized," an organization tends to assume an identity of its own which makes it independent of the people who have founded it or of those who constitute its membership."[13] Although flatly asserted as fact, Blau's statement is, being a characterization of *all* formal organizations, clearly a domain assumption. The evidence that would allow *all* formal organizations to be thus characterized is trivial in comparison to the scope of the generalization. But there is nothing novel in this; it is the common way of men with domain assumptions.

Whether Blau's statement is actually a fact or only a domain assumption parading as one, there is still a consequential choice of how to view it. It makes a substantial difference whether one views the autonomy or alienation of social structures from people as a normal condition to be accepted or as an endemic and recurrent disease to be opposed. It is inherent in the very occupational ideology of many modern sociologists, faced as they are with the professional task of distinguishing their own from competing academic disciplines, not only to stress the potency and autonomy of social structures—and therefore the dependence of persons—but also to accept this as normal, rather than asking: Under what conditions does it occur? Are there not differences in the degree to which social structures get out of hand and live independently of their members? What accounts for these differences?

In short, then, from the substantive domain assumption that human beings are the raw materials of independent social structures, to the methodological domain assumption that men may be treated and studied like other "things," there is a repressive technocratic current in sociology and the other social sciences, as well as in the general society. It is a current that has great social importance because it congenially resonates the sentiments of any modern elite in bureaucratized societies who view social problems in terms of technological paradigms, as a kind of engineering task.

The domain assumptions of sociological analysis are embedded in—both expressed and concealed by—its most central programmatic concepts, its most elemental vision of "society" and "culture." The *focal* implications of these concepts stress the manner in which men are shaped and influenced by their groups and group heritage. Yet since the social sciences emerged in the secularized world of the "self-made" bourgeoisie that surfaced after the French Revolution in nineteenth-century Europe, these concepts also tacitly imply that man *makes* his own societies and cultures. They imply the potency of man. But this vision of the potency of man, in contrast to that of society and culture, tends to be confined to the merely subsidiary attention of Academic Sociology rather than to its focal concerns.

Academic Sociology's emphasis on the potency of society and the subordination of men to it is itself an historical product that contains an historical truth. The modern concepts of society and of culture arose in a social world that, following the French Revolution, men could believe they themselves had made. They could see that it was through their struggles that kings had been overthrown and an ancient religion disestablished. Yet, at the same time men could also see that this was a world out of control, not amenable to men's designs. It was therefore a grotesque, contradictory world: a world made by men but, despite this, not *their* world.

No thinker better grasped this paradoxical character of the new social world than Rousseau. It was central to his conception that man was corrupted by the very advance of the arts and sciences, that he had lost something vital in the very midst of his highest achievements. This paradoxical vision also underlies his conception of man as born free but now living everywhere in chains: man creates society through a willing contract but must then subject himself to his own creation.

Culture and society thus emerged as ambiguous conceptions, as being man's own creations but also having lives and histories of their own. It is precisely this ambiguity to which the central conceptions of sociological analysis, "culture" and "society," give continued expression. Both culture and society are seen, in sociological analysis, as having a life apart from the men who create, embody, and enact them. The concepts of culture and society tacitly predicate that men have created a social world from which they have been alienated. The germinal concepts of the social sciences, then, are imprinted with the birth trauma of a social world from which men saw themselves alienated from their own creations; in which men felt themselves to be at once newly potent and tragically impotent. The emerging academic social sciences thus commonly came to conceive of society and culture as *autonomous* things: things that are independent and exist for themselves. Society and culture were then amenable to being viewed like any other "natural" phenomena, as having laws of their own that operated quite apart from the intentions and plans of men, while the disciplines that studied them could be viewed as natural sciences like any other. Method, then, follows domain assumption. In other words, sociology emerged as a "natural" science when certain domain assumptions and sentiments became prevalent: when men felt alienated from a society that they thought they had made but could not control. Whereas European men had once expressed their estrangement from themselves in terms of traditional religion and metaphysics, they now began to do so through academic social science, and scientism became, in this way, a modern substitute for a decaying traditional religion.

The concepts of society and culture, which are at the very foundation of the academic social sciences, are in part based upon a reaction to an historical defeat: man's failure to possess the social world that he created. To that extent, the academic social sciences are the social sciences of an alienated age and alienated man. From this standpoint the possibility of "objectivity" in, and the call to "objectivity" by, the academic social sciences has a rather different meaning than that conventionally assigned. The "objectivity" of the social sciences is not the expression of a dispassionate and detached view of the social world; it is, rather, an ambivalent effort to accommodate to alienation *and* to express a muted resentment of it.

In one part, then, the dominant expressions of the academic social sciences embody an accommodation to the alienation of men in contemporary society, rather than a determined effort to transcend it. The core concepts of society and culture, as held by the social sciences, entail the view that their autonomy and uncontrollability are a normal and natural condition, rather than intrinsically a kind of pathology. It is this assumption that is at the heart of the *repressive* component of sociology.

At the same time, however, the social sciences' accommodation to alienation is an ambivalent and resentful one. It is in this muted resentment that there is the suppressed *liberative* potential of sociology. And it is this total conception of man—the dominant focal view of him as the controlled product of society and culture, combined with the subsidiary conception of man as the maker of society and culture—that shapes the unique contradiction distinctive of sociology.

It is not simply that one or another "school" of sociology embodies these contradictory domain assumptions about men and society, but that these dwell in the basic charter of Academic Sociology as a discipline. These assumptions resonate certain sentiments about the grotesqueness of the social world that began to emerge during the nineteenth century, and they are rooted in a contradictory personal reality widely shared by men who, then as now, felt that they were somehow living in a world that they made but did not control.

THE CONTRADICTION OF AUTONOMY

When sociologists stress the autonomy of sociology—that it should (and, therefore, that it can) be pursued entirely in terms of its own standards, free of the influences of the surrounding society—they are giving testimony of their loyalty to the rational credo of their profession. At the same time, however, they are also contradicting themselves as sociologists, for surely the strongest general assumption of sociology is that men are shaped in countless ways by the press of their social surround. Looked at with bland innocence, then, the sociologists' claim to autonomy entails a contradiction between the claims of sociology and the claims of reason and "profession."

In large measure, this contradiction is hidden, in daily practice, by sociologists who premise a dualistic reality in which their own behavior is tacitly held to be different from the behavior of those they study. It is hidden by employing the focal sociological assumption, that men are shaped by culture and social structure, when sociologists study *others,* yet tacitly employing the assumption that men make their own cultures, when sociologists think about *themselves.* The *operating* premise of the sociologist claiming autonomy for his discipline is that he is free from the very social pressures whose importance he affirms when thinking about other men. In effect, the sociologist conjugates his basic domain assumptions by saying: *they* are bound by society; *I* am free of it.

The sociologist thus resolves his contradictory assumptions by splitting them and applying each to different persons or groups: one for himself and his peers, another for his "subjects." Implicit in such a split is an image of self and other, in which the two are assumed to be deeply different and thus to be differentially evaluated, the "self" tacitly viewed as a kind of elite, the "other" as a kind of mass.

One reason for this split is that the focal sociological assumption about the governing influence of the social surround violates the sociologist's own sense of personal reality. He, after all, *knows* with direct inner certainty that his own behavior is *not* socially determined; but the freedom of the others whom he studies is an aspect only of their personal reality, not of his own. When he premises that their behavior is socially determined, the sociologist is not violating *his* sense of personal reality, but only *theirs*.

The methodological dualism by which the sociologist keeps two sets of books, one for the study of "laymen" and another when he thinks about himself, evidences one of the most profound ways in which the sociologist's personal reality shapes his methodological and theoretical practice. It cannot be stressed too strongly that in everyday practice the sociologist believes himself capable of making hundreds of purely rational decisions—the choice of research problems, sites, question formulations, statistical tests, or sampling methods. He thinks of these as free technical decisions and of himself as acting in autonomous conformity with technical standards, rather than as a creature molded by social structure and culture. If he finds he has gone wrong, he thinks of himself as having made a "mistake." A "mistake" is an outcome produced not by any social necessity, but by a corrigible ignorance, a lack of careful thought or rigorous training, a hasty assessment.

When this inconsistency is called to the sociologist's attention, he will acknowledge that his behavior, too, is influenced by social forces. He will acknowledge, for example, that there is or can be such a thing as a sociology of knowledge or a sociology of sociology, in which even the sociologist's own behavior may be shown to be socially influenced. But such acknowledgments are usually made *en principe;* they are begrudging concessions; they are formally acknowledged for reasons of consistency; but, not being consistent with his own feelings of freedom and personal reality, they are not deeply convincing to the sociologist. In short, they are not really an operating part of his normal way of thinking about his own everyday work.

Another way in which this inconsistency is maintained is through the use of "self-obscuring" methodologies. That is, they obscure the sociologist from himself. The more prestigious and "high science" these methodologies are, the less likely it is that the sociologist will recognize himself as implicated in his research or will see his findings as having implications about himself. Not being constrained to see his research as having a bearing upon his own life, he can more readily maintain a different set of assumptions concerning it.

More specifically, a high science methodology tends to distil the complexity of social situations into a search for the effects of a few highly formalized and specially defined "variables," whose presence often cannot be gauged by direct inspection but requires special instruments employed under special conditions. Thus the "variables" sociologists study often do not exist for laymen; they are not what laymen see when they look about themselves. High science methodologies, in effect, create a gap between what the sociologist as sociologist deals with and what he (like others) confronts as an ordinary person, experiencing his *own* existence. Thus even when he undertakes studies in the sociology of knowledge, exploring, say, the effects of "class position," "reference groups," or "income levels" on intellectual activities, it is easy for him to feel that he is talking about someone else, perhaps some other sociologist, not about himself and his own life.

It is a function of high science methodologies to widen the gap between what the sociologist is studying and his own personal reality. Even if one were to assume that this serves to fortify objectivity and reduce bias, it seems likely that it has been bought at the price of the dimming of the sociologist's self-awareness. In other words, it seems that, at some point, the formula is: the more rigorous the methodology, the more dimwitted the sociologist; the more reliable his information about the social world, the less insightful his knowledge about himself.

A concern with the problem of the sociologist's autonomy clearly must confront the manifold ways in which the sociologist's own social surround affects his work. But if we do not talk about this in ways enabling the sociologist to recognize this surround as his own, he will never recognize himself in it. When, however, an exploration of this problem is informed by a sensitivity to the importance of the sociologist's personal reality, it can then lead him to a view of "society," not as exotic and external to him, but as his familiar practice and mundane experience. A concern with his personal reality leads to an insistence on the unusual importance of the most mundane experience for the sociologist. It can lead to a concern with the recognizable *texture* of his experienced situation rather than with only a few sifted-out, technically defined "variables." Awareness of textured reality enables "variables" to be seen as *self*-experience and allows them to be mobilized for self-understanding. The sociologist is not what he eats; but the sociologist is what he sees, does, and wants every day, in all his activities, morning, noon, and night, whether as sociologist or not. To understand him and his personal reality we must see how he lives as well as how he works.

To take a few singular examples: some sociologists I know conceive of themselves as gentlemen-professors. They invest considerable energies not merely in their work but in their total style of life. One I know starts his day by breakfasting in his luxury apartment, and then, donning his smoking jacket, returns to bed where he reads or writes in presumably unruffled serenity until noon, when, as is his unvarying habit, he goes to the university. To indicate that matters cannot be simplified, I should also add that he holds relatively radical views about the value of peasant revolutions. Still other sociologists I know are gentlemen-farmers and gentlemen-ranchers. Most live suburban existences; not a few have summer homes; many do extensive traveling. Most of the sociologists I know seem to have little interest in "culture" and are rarely in evidence at galleries, concerts, or plays.

Like other men, sociologists also have sexual lives, and "even this" may be intellectually consequential. In loyalty tinged with bitterness, most stick it out to the end with the wives who saw them through graduate school, while others practice serial polygamy. And a few are hidden homosexuals, often tensely preoccupied by the dangers of self-disclosure in a "straight" world. My point is not that this is especially important, but that even this remote sexual dimension of existence reaches into and is linked with the sociologist's world of work. For example, it is my strong but undocumented impression that when some sociologists change their work interests, problems, or styles, they also change mistresses or wives. Again, and while I do not know why it is so, I also believe that some well-known "schools" of American sociology— both the people whom they produce and the teachers who produce them—seem to be dominantly "masculine" and even "studsy" in group tone; others, however, seem to be more "feminine" in their personal behavior and in the more aesthetically refined sensibility that their work manifests.

Some sociologists I know are deeply involved in the stock market, and have been for quite a while. When they gather together they will often proudly inform one another of their recent triumphs or bemoan their losses and pass on current gossip about promising stocks. Sometimes they are making money from the very wars that, as liberals, they denounce. They are also much interested in who is making how much money as a sociologist, or how much money it took to lure someone from his old to a new university.

Many sociologists are also much interested in political power and in being close to men of power. It is not simply the academicians who were stockpiled at the Kennedy Center of Urban Affairs, and

not simply Harvard men, who tied their careers to political outcomes in the years preceding the American election of 1968. Some
had pinned their hopes on the election of Robert Kennedy, and,
when the latter was assassinated, it was for them not only a
national tragedy but also a career calamity. Being close to power
also involves being close to funds, funds for research, of course;
and despite protestations to the contrary, this is also linked to
appreciable increments in professional prestige and personal
income.

Nor is it simply the pull of larger, distant things and great public
events but the press of smaller, nearer things that punctuates the
rhythm of academic days: the Byzantine conniving about the chair-
manship of departments; the upward and onward press toward
promotion and keeping up with those with whom one had been at
graduate school; the daily exposure to young, still unshaped minds,
and the wallowing in their admiration, or the bitterness at their
ingratitude when it is not forthcoming; the comparing of the size
of class enrollments at the beginning of each semester, while
pretending not to care about something as vulgar as that; the
careful noting of who has been invited to whose home and the
pain of being excluded.

These and countless other things comprise the texture of the
sociologist's world, which is probably not altogether different from
other worlds. It is really quite impossible to imagine that men who
care as much about the world as sociologists do, will be untouched
by it. It is fantasy to believe that a man's work will be autonomous
from his life or that his life will not be profoundly consequential
for his work. The daily texture of the sociologist's life integrates
him into the world as it is; more than that, it makes this world,
and indeed its very problems, a source of gratification. It is a
world in which the sociologist has moved onward and upward,
with increasing access to the corridors of power, with growing
public acknowledgment and respect, and with an income and a
style of life increasingly like that of comfortably privileged strata
(or, if a younger man, with considerable prospects). Sociologists
have, in short, become men with a very substantial stake in
society.

Their own personal experience of success suffuses with congenial
sentiment their conception of the society within which this happened. It colors their personal reality with a tacit conviction of the
opportunity in and viability of the status quo. At the same time,
however, the sociologist's work often brings him to a first-hand
acquaintance with suffering. The complacency and yea-saying born
of the sociologist's personal success thus often conflicts with what
he sees as a sociologist.

This tension is neither casual nor accidental, but is the inevitable outcome of his contradictory role in the world. The sociologist's value to his social world depends in substantial measure upon its failures and its consequent need for ideas and information that will enable it to cope with them. The sociologist's personal opportunities thus grow as the crisis of his society deepens. His very efforts to fulfill his social mandate, the studies for which he is rewarded and the rewards that link him to the status quo thus also bring him closer to society's failures. His awareness of these failures, however, is largely seen from his perspective of realized personal ambitions. The failures of society, that is, do not resonate the sociologist's *own* sense of personal failure; they are seen through the softening lens of a personal reality that *knows* success to be possible within this society.

The tension between the sociologist's personal reality of success and his occupationally-induced awareness of societal failure often finds its resolution in political liberalism, for this is an ideology that allows him to seek remedies for the failures of society without challenging its essential premises. It is an ideology that allows him to seek change in his society while still working within and, indeed, for it. The ideology of liberalism is the political counterpart of the contemporary sociologist's claim to autonomy. Liberalism is the politics toward which the conventional professional ideology of autonomy is disposed to drift.

In the end, however, a critique of the ideology of autonomy, as of liberalism, must recognize that it does serve as a brake upon the sociologist's full assimilation into his society. The ideology of autonomy involves partial acquiescence, but it is better by far than an ideology sanctioning total submission to society. "Autonomy" is the timid form of the verb "to resist." Like liberalism, it means: accept the system, work within it, but also try to maintain some distance from it. A critique of the ideology of autonomy must show what autonomy means in practice, that it entails a measure of contradiction with the very claims of sociology itself. Yet such a critique does not make the most fair case if it merely affirms that autonomy is a myth. For autonomy is still a regulative ideal, even if it (like others) can never be perfectly fulfilled. Rather, the problem is that autonomy is too often given only ritualistic lip service by successful men comfortable within the status quo, and frequently is not pursued even to its achievable potentialities.

From one perspective, to affirm the value of autonomy is to insist that the story the sociologist tells be his own story, that it be an account in which *he* truly believes and to which *he* commits himself. Autonomy is, in one form, an insistence upon authenticity. It says that if a man can never tell the "whole truth," then at least he should strive to tell his own truth. It may be that this is the closest we can get to "objectivity" within the framework of liberal assumption. At any rate, the claim to autonomy may provide leverage for those who believe that there can, even now, be a great deal more of it than one presently finds. The claim to autonomy at least legitimates efforts to know more about the textured reality that is part of the sociologist's daily surround, for it says to him: you must find out what it is that actually limits your autonomy and makes you and your work less than you want it to be. Such analysis can lead us to begin to know the larger implications of what the sociologist is doing in the world and to extend his self-awareness.

The object of a critique of the ideology of autonomy, then, is not to unmask the sociologist but, by confronting him with the frailty and ambiguity of his own professions, to stir his self-awareness. Its object is not to discredit his efforts at autonomy but to enable these to be realized more fully by heightening awareness of the social forces that, surrounding and penetrating the sociologist, subvert his own ideals.

NOTES

1. M. Polanyi, *Personal Knowledge* (New York: Harper & Row, 1964).

2. Stephan C. Pepper, *World Hypotheses: A Study in Evidence* (Berkeley: University of California Press, 1942).

3. Charles E. Osgood, George Suci, and Percy Tannenbaum, *The Measurement of Meaning* (Urbana: University of Illinois Press, 1957).

4. See J. T. Sprehe, "The Climate of Opinion in Sociology: A Study of the Professional Value and Belief Systems of Sociologists" (Ph.D. Dissertation, Washington, January 1967).

5. *American Sociology*, T. Parsons, ed. (New York: Basic Books, 1968).

6. S. M. Lipset, "Political Sociology," in Parsons, *American Sociology*, p. 159.

7. *American Sociology*, p. 237.

8. *Ibid.*, p. 263.

9. *Ibid.*, p. 270.

10. *Ibid.*, p. 278.

11. *Ibid.*, p. 279.

12. Charles Tilly, "The Forms of Urbanization," in Parsons, *American Sociology*, p. 77.

13. Peter Blau, "The Study of Formal Organization," in Parsons, *American Sociology*, p. 54.

3

Utilitarian Culture and Sociology

The modern period of sociology that was launched by Talcott Parsons in the United States during the late 1930's began, significantly enough, with a pointed critique of the theory of utilitarianism. Utilitarianism, however, was not only a theory of academicians and philosophers; it was also a central component of the everyday culture of middle-class society. The more encompassing problem, then, is a critique not of utilitarian theory but of the diffuse utilitarian *culture* that was its mundane matrix. This is crucial to an understanding of Parsons and of Western sociology through all its stages of development, from the early nineteenth century to the present, in its Marxist no less than its Academic expressions. In many ways, Western sociology was and remains a response to a utilitarian culture. Before this sociology is explored, therefore, I will briefly examine what it was responding to, namely, utilitarian culture and the middle class that was its historical bearer.

THE MIDDLE CLASS AND UTILITARIAN CULTURE

With the growing influence of the middle class in the eighteenth century, utility emerged as a dominant social standard. What is relevant here is utilitarianism not as a technical philosophy but as a part of the popular, everyday culture of the middle class; for with its advent a major revolution was wrought in the value system by which men and social roles were now to be judged.

This development is historically traceable to the nature of the feudal regimes in which the middle class was incubated and to the "old regimes" against which it rebelled in the course of its birth. In the feudal context the middle class was submerged among the "commoners" and had only a negative or residual identity, legally and socially; it was an identity assigned to all who were *not* clergy, *not* noble, and *not* serfs. As the middle class proliferated this single status came to encompass an enormous variety of life styles and circumstances, including both the master and his servant, the banker and the bootmaker.

This residual and negative identity reflected the historical emergence of the middle class as a stratum only casually articulated to a feudal structure, which centered its legal system and its strategic identities—peasant or serf and lord—around relationships to the land. Moreover, middle-class activities were also irrelevant to the medieval Church's central religious interest in the salvation of souls, and indeed were often directly at variance with religious values calling for worldly renunciation. The middle class was, in most ways, distant from the center of feudal culture and thus slowly developed an institutional life and culture of its own, which was *parallel* to the feudal one and protected by being a relatively insulated extrusion into the emerging towns.

Living to the side, as it were, of the prized concerns of Christian culture and of the feudal order, and without a firm and honored place in them, middle-class life was not esteemed but was tolerated by the elites because of its sheer usefulness. From the standpoint of the feudal order's system of social identities, the middle class did not exist; it was nothing, socially speaking. It is in this vein that the Abbé Sièyes, asking *What Is the Third Estate?*, replies that it is "nothing," but wants to be "something." From the feudal standpoint it was not what the middle class *was* that counted, but what it *did:* the services and functions it performed. In time, however, the middle class came to pride itself upon its very utility and came to measure all other social strata by their utility or imputed lack of it. The wheel came full circle when the middle-class standard of utility was adopted and prized by other groups. Sheer utility then became a claim to respect rather than merely a basis for begrudging tolerance.

The middle-class standard of utility developed in the course of its polemic against the feudal norms and aristocratic claims of the "old regimes," in which the rights of men were held to be derived from and limited by their estate, class, birth, or lineage: in short, by what they "were" rather than by what they *did*. In contrast, the new middle class held in highest esteem those talents, skills, and energies of individuals that contributed to their own individual accomplishments and achievements. The middle-class standard of utility implied that rewards should be proportioned to men's personal work and contribution. The usefulness of men, it was now held, should control the station to which they might rise or the work and authority they might have, rather than that their station should govern and admit them to employment and privileges.

In the eighteenth century, then, adults and adult roles came increasingly to be judged by the middle class in terms of the usefulness imputed to them. Thus, on the eve of the French Revolution the Abbé Sièyes proclaimed: "Take away the privileged orders, and the nation is not smaller but greater . . . [the] privileged class is assuredly foreign to the nation by its do-nothing uselessness." Here, of course, Sièyes was thinking largely of the aristocracy, which, despite its growing commercial interests, still commonly rejected the full-time pursuit of business or of civic professions other than the clergy, and which, unless impoverished, usually did not even manage its own estates. During the Revolution the rich middle class was itself denounced by the most militant or Jacobin wing of revolutionaries, partly for taking venal advantage of the national peril but, also and emphatically, as useless "idlers." By the nineteenth century few intellectuals would have argued with Flaubert when he held that the creed of the bourgeoisie was that "one must establish oneself . . . one must be useful . . . one must work."

Looked at in terms of how it appeared to those involved, the rising middle class's demand for usefulness was above all an attempt to revise the bases *on* which, and hence the groups *to* which, public rewards and opportunities would be open. "Utility" took on meaning in a specific context involving a particular set of social relations, where it was used initially to dislodge the aristocracy from preeminence and to legitimate the claims and social identity of the rising middle class. In this regard the standard of utility entailed a claim that rewards should be allocated not on the basis of birth or of inherited social identity, but on the basis of talent and energy manifested in individual achievement. This was antitraditionalistic and antiascriptive, proachievement and proindividualistic. It entailed an emphasis on what the individual did, rather than on who he was or on what he was born. From the new middle-class standpoint, all feudal social identities were obsolete and no longer a basis for valid claims. There were now only individuals; all were "citizens" fundamentally alike in that all were endowed with the same "natural rights"; all were to be judged from the same standpoint, in terms of the same single set of values.

Utilitarianism was naturally linked to the extension of *universalism*. In other words, the middle-class value of utility, as well as its other values, was held to apply to *all* men—all were expected to be useful. In this respect the structure of middle-class values differed importantly from feudal or aristocratic values, which had held that different groups or estates were obliged to manifest the different values appropriate to themselves. The privileges and obligations of the aristocracy were not expected to be those of the commoners. As Cesar Graña remarks, "The bourgeoisie was the first ruling class in history whose values could be acquired by all classes, and bourgeois culture was, in this sense, the first true democratic culture."[1]

At the same time that utilitarianism extended universalism, it also depersonalized the individual. In focusing public interest on the usefulness of the individual, it focused on a side of his life that had significance not in its personal uniqueness but only in its comparability, its inferior or superior usefulness, to others. Bourgeois utilitarianism was thus both individualistic and *impersonal*. Despite all its talk about the universal "rights of man," bourgeois utilitarianism saw men as having a kinship with other objects; all were now commonly judged by their usefulness and in terms of the consequences of their employment.

Developed in the course of its struggle against the nobility, the ideology of usefulness was in part a residual concept: the useful was that which the nobility was *not*. Identified as the opposite of the nobility, the useful were those whose lives manifestly did not turn on a round of leisure and entertainment, but who worked at routine economic roles in which they produced marketable goods and services. The middle class *experienced* itself as "useful" because, on the one hand, it conceived itself primarily as a producer rather than as a consumer like the nobility, and, on the other, because what it produced, it held, was what *others* wanted. The middle class thus maintained that their own interests could not be served apart from satisfying the interests of others: one was useful because one served.

It is clear that this concept of utility predicated the existence of a *market* on which men could buy what they wanted and for which others could produce what was wanted. Utilitarian culture was rooted in experience with and access to markets for goods and services. To appraise a man or an act from the standpoint of usefulness is to appraise their "consequences," which is a far more crucial concern in a market than in a manorial economy. A manorial economy is a self-sufficient one, where production and consumption are by the same people and under a single management; in a market economy, however, there is a gap between production and consumption. In a manorial economy the people and wants to be satisfied by production are relatively well known and stabilized by traditional standards; the problem, therefore, is the mobilization of resources sufficient for the maintenance of traditional styles of life. In a market economy the central problem is possible "overproduction," for production is for a changing, often fluctuating group of relatively unknown and uncontrollable consumers; the producer does not know which people, if any, will want or be able to buy what he has produced. His problem is not simply the mobilization of resources, but the *calculation* of the possible consequences of his own decisions. In a market economy the usefulness of production has to be calculated carefully in advance, yet one must then wait to see whether the production of certain things is wanted, and thereby rewarding to the producer. In a market economy "good intentions" are not enough to validate action; intention and action can be validated only by their consequences in an uncontrollable market. Since these consequences are uncertain, it is "results that count." The rise and spread of utilitarian culture thus predicated the transition from a manorial to a market economy, and the rise of a social class whose fortunes were linked with a market and whose disposition, therefore, was toward the calculation of consequences.

ANOMIE: THE NORMAL PATHOLOGY
OF UTILITARIANISM

A utilitarian culture, then, inevitably places a great stress upon winning or losing, upon success or failure as such, rather than upon the character of the intention that shapes a person's course of action or upon the conformity of his intention with a preestablished rule or model of propriety. No matter how well-intended— i.e., designed to conform—a given action is, it may still fail to have a benign outcome in a market economy. Moreover, if conformity with established rules were to be the basis for judging actions or roles, then this would have given precedence to the claims of the nobility, which, unlike those of the middle class, were sanctioned by tradition.

To a considerable extent, furthermore, utilitarian culture clashes with Christianity, which is an "intention morality," judging men and actions by the conformity of their intentions with established morality. The emerging utilitarianism of the middle class was dissonant with the Christian conception of morality as supernaturally sanctioned. The Baron d'Holbach argued during the Enlightenment that duties do not derive from God, but from man's own nature; and most of the *philosophes* accepted Touissant's definition of virtue as "fidelity in fulfilling obligations imposed by *reason.*" One should not hurt others, not because this is forbidden by the Mosaic code or the Golden Rule, but because it is not *prudent* to do so. Christianity thus contracted a terminal (or interminable) illness, and, in the last quarter of the nineteenth century, it was no surprise to many when Nietzsche pronounced the death of God.

Since the useful is judged in terms of the consequences of actions, the useful is a contingent thing that might vary with, or be relative to, time and place. Again, that which is useful is so only relative to that *for* which it is useful. Things are useful only in relation to something else, to an "end." There was a drift toward relativism in utilitarianism. Thus, while John Locke sought a single and universal standard of morality in "happiness," he also stressed that "there is scarcely a principle of morality to be named, or rule of virtue to be thought . . . which is not somewhere or other slighted and condemned by the fashion of whole societies of men, governed by practical opinions and rules of living quite opposite to others."

From the standpoint of utilitarian culture, it is not some transcendental standard above men, but men themselves and their own nature that become the measure. Things assume utility in relation to men, to their interests and happiness. To evaluate men or things in terms of their consequences is to evaluate them in terms of how they may be used to pursue an interest, rather than of what they are in themselves or because they may be deemed good in their own right. Things are good or evil not in themselves, but in whether they produce agreeable outcomes. Benjamin Franklin could therefore argue that even sexuality is not bad as such, for its meaning depends on its compatibility with health and repute. And Bernard de Mandeville, in his *Fable of the Bees* (1714), similarly maintained that even behavior flatly at variance with certain traditional moralities, for example, greed and luxury, might be the very basis of prosperity. "What we call evil in this world," he held, "is the grand principle that makes us social creatures." The transvaluation of values thus begins in utilitarianism.

Since utilitarian culture stresses the evaluation of consequences, whether anticipated or already existent, its center of attention begins to shift from moral to cognitive judgment. The question of whether an action is intrinsically "right" is increasingly superseded by efforts to appraise its consequences and therefore by efforts to determine what these *will be* or *are*. Questions about human behavior increasingly become factual rather than moral issues. In this vein, David Hume held that morality could not be deduced *a priori* from reason, but only inductively, by *inspecting and seeing* the consequences of behavior. The groundwork was thus being laid for the separation of facts and values, of empirical and moral questions, as, for example, in Kant's contention that "from the critical standpoint . . . the doctrine of morality and the doctrine of nature may each be true in its own sphere."

For all this variety of reasons, utilitarianism has a built-in tendency to restrict the sphere of morality; to enlarge the importance attributed to purely cognitive judgment; to diminish the credibility of an intention-oriented morality such as Christianity; to select courses of action on grounds independent of moral propriety or impropriety; and, in its future-orienting dependence on consequences not yet realized, to defer moral judgment by making it auxiliary to cognitive judgment. In brief, utilitarian culture has a tendency to ignore or deviate from established moral values, however hallowed by tradition or religion. This is in large part what Karl Marx was suggesting when he maintained that "the bourgeoisie, historically, has played a most revolutionary part . . . [it] has put an end to all feudal, patriarchical, idyllic relations. . . . It has drowned the most heavenly ecstasies of religious fervor, of chivalrous enthusiasm, of philistine sentimentalism, in the icy waters of egotistical calculation. It has resolved personal worth into exchange value . . . stripped of its halo every occupation hitherto honored and looked up to with reverent awe."

To put the matter in another, a Durkheimian manner, a bourgeois utilitarian culture has a "natural" or built-in disposition toward moral normlessness or "anomie," and this disposition derives from, among other things, the very character of its own commitments and emphases. It is not only that men abandon their moral code in a bourgeois society because its competitiveness induces them to disregard morally appropriate methods and to use any efficient means of achieving success, but more fundamentally that in all spheres of life their concern with the "useful" leads them to a prior and focal concern with the consequences of their actions, and thereby makes moral judgment auxiliary to factual questions concerning consequences. When men in a utilitarian culture focus on the useful, they are not abandoning but rather are giving conscientious conformity to the central requirements of their "moral" code.

The point here may be clarified by reference to Robert Merton's analysis of the sources of anomie in society. Merton remarks that when

the cultural emphasis shifts from the satisfactions deriving from competition itself to an almost exclusive concern with the outcome, the resultant stress makes for the breakdown of the regulatory structure. With this attenuation of institutional controls, there occurs an approximation to the situation erroneously held by the utilitarian philosophers to be typical of society, a situation in which calculations of personal advantage and fear of punishment are the only regulating agencies.[2]

The "almost exclusive concern with outcomes" to which Merton refers is a distinctive characteristic of utilitarian culture; it is not an aberration of utilitarian society but its normal cultural emphasis. Thus, if the utilitarian philosophers erroneously regarded this as "typical of society" in general, as Merton says, their theoretical statements were accurate reflections of the conditions growingly characteristic of their own bourgeois society.

To say that an action should be judged by its consequences does not *per se* indicate *how* these consequences should be evaluated. Utilitarian culture might be characterized, therefore, as having a standpoint which, while insistently focusing on the consequences of actions, does so without an equally insistent concern with the standards in terms of which these consequences will themselves be judged. The ultimate ends frequently reside only in subsidiary awareness. This implies that, even though things are "useful" only in relation to some goal, the goal itself is not dubious or problematic. Under what conditions is this likely to occur? For one, when the selection and pursuit of goals are felt to be "private matters," more or less protected from public criticism and debate because the individual is held to be the best judge of his own interests and of what is worth pursuing: *laissez faire, laissez seule*. To allow each to pursue goals of his own choosing premises that no common standards of value are more important than the right of each to pursue his own interests, and it implies, furthermore, a belief in the fundamental harmony of interests among men.

The ends of action may also be taken as "givens," because utilitarianism assumes they are more or less obvious to "anyone in his right mind." This occurs when there are certain ways in which a variety of different concrete ends are felt to be essentially alike; being alike, they need not be appraised and differentiated. No problem then resides in ordering or selecting among them, and there may therefore be little concern with clearly delineating moral standards in terms of which this could be done. The ends of action may also be taken as given when there are one or several things that can facilitate the achievement of a wide variety of different ends—that is, when there are some things that are, in effect, "all-purpose" utilities. These two conditions are precisely those that obtain in a market economy.

A large variety of concrete ends may be viewed as essentially alike when they are all for sale on the market and thus all have a *price*. And in a market economy there is a thing that permits the routine acquistion of a wide variety of different concrete ends, namely, *money*. Money is an all-purpose utility in middle-class society; possess it, and a great many desired things are no longer problematic but can be routinely bought. Under this condition, what is problematic is not what one wants or should want, but whether one has the money to buy it. Here, what is "useful" is what makes money.

There is one other all-purpose utility in middle-class society, and that is knowledge. In order to appraise consequences one must know them; in order to control consequences one must employ technology and science. Therefore, in a utilitarian culture knowledge and science are shaped by strongly instrumental conceptions. It is chiefly out of a desire for wealth, said de Tocqueville, "that a democratic people addicts itself to scientific pursuits." There is, however, something of a difference in emphasis among different sections of the middle class concerning these two all-purpose utilities. Propertied sections of the middle class tend to emphasize the importance of money, while educated and professional sections are somewhat more likely to stress knowledge and the education that will produce it.[3]

In emphasizing that bourgeois utilitarianism focuses upon the importance of appraising the consequences of actions, I do not of course mean to suggest that bourgeois culture is devoid of absolute moral commitments in which the concern is to do what is "right" for its own sake, but rather to focus on the pressures generated against such moral commitments by the bourgeois concern for utility. The rising bourgeoisie was, indeed, sometimes concerned with morality apart from utility even to the point of piety. Often the common image of the bourgeoisie quite correctly stressed the frequent conjunction of morality and utility. Thus Baudelaire's Leporello, symbol of the new bourgeois, was said to be "cold, reasonable and vulgar, [and] speaks of nothing but virtue and economy, two ideas that he naturally associates." The middle-class moral code often professed many of the same obligations demanded by traditional morality. What was new about it was not only that there were new individual items of belief in the code but that their priorities and emphases—especially the preeminence attached to the norm of utility—gave the moral code as a whole a new structuring. It was as if the Church's once subsidiary admonition of Prudence had been elevated to parity with, if not precedence over, the Golden Rule, Justice, Goodness, and Mercy.

In one of its first great public acts the French middle class had made a "Declaration of the Rights of Man and Citizen," in which it had formally outlined its moral code. It affirmed, among other things: that men were free and equal in their rights; that they had natural and imprescriptible rights to property, security, and resistance to oppression; that they had a natural right to do whatever did not harm another, and that this could be abridged only by law; that any man could do what was not forbidden by law; that men were presumed innocent until found guilty; that men had a right to the free communication of thoughts and opinions, to speak, write, and print freely; and that men could not be deprived of their property, since it is inviolable and sacred, except by certification of law and compensation in advance. In its affirmation that all social distinctions should be based upon a common utility, the Declaration of Rights indicated that "utility" was a *moral* value of the middle class and not just a pragmatic yardstick.

Middle-class thought, in fine, postulated a "natural" morality, one of whose central precepts was the morality of utility itself. It began, therefore, with an inherent tension. For, in affirming the centrality of utility it emphasized that men should concern themselves with the *consequences* of their actions, but in conceiving of men as having natural imprescriptible rights, it assumed that men also had *intrinsic* rights, the validity of which did *not* depend upon consequences. Since men often reveal their most salient concerns at the very beginning and end of their communications, it is notable that among the first words of the Declaration of Rights is an emphasis on utility and among the last is an emphasis on property rights. The very structure of the Declaration of Rights reveals the contradictory structure of bourgeois morality, boundaried by utility on the one side and by property on the other.

I have already suggested that there was an inherent tendency for the middle class's utilitarian concern with consequences to subvert any morality that demanded conformity with rules for their own sake; in short, there was in utilitarianism a continual tendency for bourgeois morality to drift toward an *anomic* normlessness. In some part, "utility" was always a thinly disguised rationalization for avarice and venality and the uninhibited pursuit of self-interest. Yet, in some part, utility was also a genuinely held and strongly felt precept of bourgeois morality itself. The bourgeois often felt a moral *obligation* to be useful. That the emerging bourgeoisie was indeed capable of a genuine moral passion was made perfectly plain by the austerities and moral zeal of the Jacobins. Thus, if utility tended to undermine a conformity with morality for its own sake, the resultant anomic normlessness was in part the paradoxical outcome of a commitment to utility that was itself moral.

The very precariousness of bourgeois morality was visible in that central document in which the middle classes most clearly affirmed their moral code, the Declaration of the Rights of Man. Here the point was expressly made that "no hindrance should be put in the way of anything not prohibited by law, nor may any man be forced to do what the law does not require." In effect, then, morality was divorced from law, and its claim upon men was limited. Law registered the public interest, and morality was now a private matter. In this context a man might still be a good citizen even if a moral leper. A man might now claim the protection of the law in his very refusal to conform with the moral code. In its net effect the Declaration of the Rights of Man circumscribed the claims of traditional morality even as it enlarged the new claims of utility.

I have suggested that at the core of bourgeois utilitarianism was the premise that a man's rewards should be proportioned to his abilities and contributions. More precisely, it might be said that, from the bourgeois standpoint, abilities, talent, and contribution were tacitly regarded only as a sufficient condition for reward, but not as a necessary condition of it. That is, it was held that talent should be rewarded, but not talent alone, for the bourgeois believed that his property and investments also were entitled to a return, quite apart from his own abilities and talents. In short, the bourgeoisie did not regard itself as entitled to managerial income alone. Indeed, this is precisely the meaning of the last clause in the Declaration of the Rights of Man, which held that property was a natural and sacred right of men and could not be expropriated without due process and compensation. The middle class never believed that its property-derived incomes—its right to rents, profits, interest—were justified only in terms of the utility of the property. The middle class insisted that property and men of property were useful to society and deserving of honor and other rewards because of this; but men of property also held that property was sacred in itself, and, in doing so, made a tacit claim that its rewards should not depend only upon its usefulness. The property interests of the middle class have thus always exerted a strain against its own utilitarian values, particularly when these were formulated in general and universal forms. When it was first developed as a polemic against "aristocratic uselessness," utilitarianism had asserted that the useless should *not* be rewarded. But the middle class was very reluctant to confine its claims to this one standard and was absolutely unwilling to do so with respect to property. In short, middle-class property has been one of the basic sources for the subversion of middle-class utilitarianism.

Middle-class property, indeed, has not only undermined its own norm of utility but has also subverted other aspects of its moral code. For example, the middle class's revolutionary slogan of Liberty and Equality was, at first, almost universally hedged with demands that there be property qualifications for the franchise. Thus Guizot spoke in the Chamber of Deputies in 1847 on the question of whether the franchise should be extended to men of intellectual attainments without regard to their income or property: though he boasted of his "infinite respect for intelligence," nonetheless he opposed this extension of the franchise. For all the use they saw in technology, and however much they vaunted reason, men of property were loath to allow scientists, if poor, to participate in governance. Middle-class culture thus embodied tensions between property and morality, between property and utility, as well as between morality and utility.

The utilitarian focus on consequences also began to influence social relationships; utility, as distinct from traditional rights and obligations, increasingly became the basis on which social relationships were maintained and justified. From a utilitarian standpoint, the rights of individuals came increasingly to be viewed as contingent on the useful contributions that they made to others. Correspondingly, the obligations of individuals were also increasingly viewed as contingent on the benefits that they received from others. Those not receiving benefits from others were not deemed to be obligated to provide benefits in return. Charity and *noblesse oblige* no longer applied; all was now increasingly contingent on reciprocity. One gave because others had given to one in the past and in order to encourage or obligate others to provide what one wanted in the future.

This affected not only the relationships between persons but also the relationships between citizens and the state. Political loyalty became increasingly contingent upon the state's contribution to the individual's well-being, not simply as a matter of fact but even as a matter of right and principle. As the Baron D'Holbach had remarked: "the pact that binds man to society . . . is conditional and reciprocal, and a society which cannot bring well-being to us loses all rights upon us." It is the state's duty to concern itself with and to protect the individual's well-being, and if it fails in this the individual is under no obligation to be loyal. From a utilitarian standpoint, all now have a legitimate claim on the state to protect their well-being, for the public sphere, like others, is to be judged by its consequences for individuals.

In effect, the state's contribution to the well-being of individuals became the standard of its political legitimacy. The state was thus demystified. There was everywhere a secularizing consequence of middle-class utilitarianism. The utilitarian had no obligations to a state that did not protect his interests and, correspondingly, believed that the political loyalty of other social strata would be undermined when their well-being was neglected. It was similarly assumed that political loyalty could be instrumentally generated or deliberately mobilized by aid provided through the state. In short, bourgeois utilitarianism was consistent with the assumptions of the Welfare State to whose development it contributed.

THE UNEMPLOYED SELF

Although subverted and limited by property interests and tempered by a belief in natural rights, "utility" has nonetheless provided a central standard by which middle-class societies evaluate activities and roles. In large reaches of our society and particularly in the industrial sector, it is not the man that is wanted. It is, rather, the function he can perform and the skill with which he can perform it for which he is paid. If a man's skill is not needed, the man is not needed. If a man's function can be performed more economically by a machine, the man is replaced. This has at least two obvious implications. First, opportunities for participation in the industrial sector are contingent upon the usefulness imputed to a man and his activity; so, in order to gain admission to it—and thus to its rewards—a man must submit to an education and to a socialization that early validates and cultivates only selected parts of himself, those that are expected to have subsequent utility. Second, once admitted to participation in the industrial sector, there is a strong tendency to appraise and reward him in terms of his utility as compared to that of other men.

Both processes have, of course, one common consequence: they operate as selective mechanisms, admitting some persons and some talents or faculties of individuals, while at the same time excluding others, thereby roughly dividing men and their talents into two pools, those useful and those not useful to industrial society. The not-useful men become the unemployed and unemployable: the aged, unskilled, unreliable, or intractable. Much the same selective inclusion and exclusion occurs in regard to particular *attributes* of individual persons. The useless qualities of persons are either unrewarded or actively punished should they intrude upon the employment of a useful skill. In other words, the system rewards and fosters those skills deemed useful and suppresses the expression of talents and faculties deemed useless, thereby imprinting itself upon the individual personality and self.

Correspondingly, the individual learns what the system requires: he learns which parts of himself are unwanted and unworthy; he is induced to organize his self and personality to conform with the operating standards of utility, for to the extent he does so he presumably can minimize the friction he feels while participating in such a system. In short, vast parts of any personality must be suppressed or repressed in the course of playing a role in industrial society. All that a man is that is not useful will somehow be excluded or at least not allowed to intrude, and he thereby becomes alienated or estranged from a large sector of his own interests, needs, and capacities. Thus, just as there is the unemployed man, there is also the unemployed *self*. Because of the exclusions and devaluations of self fostered by an industrial system oriented toward utility, many men develop a dim sense of loss, for the excluded self, although muffled, is not voiceless and makes its protest heard. They feel an intimation that something is being wasted, and this something may be nothing less than their lives.

THE PECUNIARY PARADIGM OF UTILITY

In the daily operations of a bourgeois culture utility is commonly measured by the production of wealth and incomes, whether by individuals, enterprises, or nations. This was and largely remains the core meaning, the specifying cultural paradigm, of utility in practical social discourse. As a result, a salient defintion of work and of occupation in our society is that it is "gainful employment" in a pecuniary sense. In such a context, unemployment is the mark of failure, but an unwillingness to work at a remunerative employment is a moral outrage and a mark of degraded character. Correspondingly, sheer wealth or income is a basis of esteem, regardless of how (or whether) it is earned. Utility or imputation of utility thus tends to become an historical ballast that may be dropped; a middle-class culture that initially held that men's rewards ought to be proportioned to their contributions and usefulness eventually yields to one in which the prime consideration is sheer marketability, the pecuniary worth of goods and services quite apart from their imputed utility. In short, the focus comes to be placed on whether they will sell and for how much, and concern centers on improving the effectiveness of marketing rather than the usefulness of what is being marketed.

When the financially gainful employment of time becomes a dominant criterion for human usefulness and social worth, even the most traditionally prized of human activities may come to be viewed as frivolous, empty, or questionable when pursued for its own sake, and often enough it has to be justified in public discourse in terms more "tough-minded," like utility.

Writing poetry or painting pictures may be viewed as an acceptable occupation if it sells; but it is often viewed as dubious, or worse, if it does not. The poverty of the ordinary clergy, however genteel, registers the low market price and marginal place of the values the clergy are supposed to protect. The income of educators in systems of higher learning is correlated with their imputed usefulness in preparing young people for imputedly useful vocations. And in a social world where gainful employment is a measure of human worth, the place of children, young people, and women who earn no incomes is uncertain. In a culture that measures value by gainful employment, of what value are painters and poets, priests and prophets?

In such a culture traditional values come to be regarded as ornamental marginalia: kindness, courage, civility, loyalty, love, generosity, gratitude—all these cease to be viewed as essential to the ordinary routines of industrial work and even of public life. It is not how well a man does his job that counts, nor what kind of job he has, but what he gets from it that makes him count. Values other than utility become, within the work setting and also beyond it to a lesser degree, desirable but dispensable graces. They are the frosting on the cake.

Between a man's legal status on the one side, and his economic utility on the other, there stretches a vast no-man's-land in which his behavior is not deemed to be of public relevance. This, we say, is the realm of privacy and private conscience, in which a man is "free" to be a saint or a brute. Yet what he is there will also, for better or worse, prepare him for his other public roles, just as what he is there will in turn be shaped by them.

To the degree that a man's usefulness becomes a central criterion of public judgment, there is created a protected realm of privacy in which, we often say, his personal characteristics and his *personal* life are "no concern of ours." In other words, a good doctor is a good doctor even if he is Jack the Ripper on his own time. As the occupational world becomes one of specialized experts judged by their usefulness, we increasingly regard the traditional decencies only as private matters. In short, no one wants or assumes responsibility for minding the everyday culture. The man seriously concerned with "private" virtue comes to be regarded as eccentric or neurotic, while, correspondingly, those who pay no attention to the virtues or vices a man manifests privately pride themselves on possessing a suitable "tolerance" of human foibles. Since Rousseau, it has been a matter of common knowledge that those who insist on virtue must be somewhat mad and that, in any event, they lead a lonely life.

In trading virtue for freedom in private life we discover, however, that there is often less of both. There is less virtue because a utility-centered occupational culture, assuring us that it is only "results that matter," inures us to personal viciousness. And we have less freedom too, even in our private lives, because neither the Welfare State nor the private sector of the economy can permit this. The private sector, for example, wants to insure that the wives of its executives are of the right sort and will aid their husbands in their careers. The Welfare State, similarly, wants to be sure that the women for whom it provides "Aid to Dependent Children" will not have further children out of wedlock, whom it will then have to support.

THE WELFARE STATE AND THE DISPOSAL
AND CONTROL OF THE USELESS

A central problem confronting a society organized around utilitarian values is the disposal and control of "useless" men and useless traits. There are various strategies for the disposal and control of useless men. They may, for example, be ecologically separated and isolated in spatially distinct locales where they are not painfully visible to the "useful"! They may be placed, as American Indians were, on reservations; they may come to live in ethnic ghettos, as American Blacks do; if they have the means to do so, they may elect to live in benign environments such as the communities for the aged in Florida; they may be placed in special training or retraining camps, as are certain unskilled and unemployed American youth, frequently Black; or again, they may be placed in prisons or in insane asylums, following routine certification by juridical or medical authorities.

Transition to a Welfare State does not simply mean transition from a standard of individual to collective utility; it also implies a greater involvement of the state in developing and managing the disposal of the "useless." In some part, the very growth of the Welfare State means that the problem is becoming so great and complex that it can no longer be left to the informal control of market or other traditional institutions. Increasingly, the Welfare State's strategy is to transform the sick, the deviant, and the un-skilled into "useless citizens," and to return them to "society" only after periods of hospitalization, treatment, counseling, training, or retraining. It is this emphasis upon the reshaping of persons that differentiates the Welfare State's disposal strategies from those that tended to cope with the useless primarily by custody, exclusion, and insulation from society. The newer strategies differ from the old in that they seek to be self-financing; the aim is to increase the supply of the useful and to diminish that of the useless.

At the center of the Welfare State's failures is the fact that its concern for "welfare" is limited by its commitment to utility: it demands something "useful" in return for what it gives. Another problem of the Welfare State is that it is a treadmill operation; it must continually strive to keep abreast of continuing increases in mechanization and automation, with their inherent tendency to generate at least temporary unemployment of men and continual obsolescence of skills. In the private sector, the useless traits of persons are eliminated, so far as they can be, by creating machines that perform functions once performed by men without, however, being linked to their "useless" traits. In one part, the Welfare State constitutes an effort to use the state to dispose of the use-lessness created by the private sector's own disposal strategies, mechanization and automation.

Within the private sector one of the relatively new disposal strategies is the various programs for "human relations in industry." These constitute an effort to teach management how to utilize or readjust the useless parts of self. The excluded self is now acknowl-edged as impinging on the effective employment of skills; non-pecuniary motives are being seen as affecting productivity. Larger and larger reaches of self and social structure are thus fitted into utilitarian appraisal. Here the system has not changed its values but has simply extended the range of things it seeks to manage from the same utilitarian standpoint. Modern sophisticated manage-ment, for example, seeks to control the "informal" group structures of factory life, which had hitherto provided opportunities for a compensatory expression of the human qualities excluded by tradi-tional utilitarian culture. It also provides psychiatric therapy for executives under tension. Seeing a new significance in these once neglected personality and social structures, management extends the sway of utilitarian standards over them, thereby cutting off the hinterland into which the personality formerly could retreat and from which it once could wage a kind of guerrilla resistance. Individual "privacy" remains, in principle, a community virtue but is increasingly infringed upon by all-seeing organizations.

One of the main disposal strategies of a utilitarian culture, then, is continuously to transform useless things into useful "by-products." Personality components and social structures hitherto regarded as areas of privacy to be ignored or junked, now are viewed as potentially useful. The escape routes thus become ever fewer. With such closure the unemployed self is required either to cease resistance altogether or to come out in open rebellion against the system's utilitarian values.

THE PSYCHEDELIC REVOLT AGAINST UTILITARIANISM

Since the end of World War II we have seen the beginnings of a new international resistance against a society organized around utilitarian values, a resistance, in short, against industrial, not merely capitalist, society. This is essentially a new wave of an old resistance to utilitarian culture, one that had begun almost at once with its emergence in the eighteenth century and that had crystallized in the Romantic movement of the nineteenth century.

The emergence of new, "deviant" social types today—the cool cats, the beats, the swingers, the hippies, the acid-heads, the drop-outs, and the "New Left" itself—is one symptom of a renewed resistance to utilitarian values. The emergence of "Psychedelic Culture," if I may summarize various forms with a single term, differs profoundly from the protest movements and "causes" of the 1930's, however politically radical, for Psychedelic Culture rejects the central values to which *all* variants of industrial society are committed. Not only does it reject the commercial form of industrialization, holding money or money-making and status-striving in disdain, but, much more fundamentally, it also resists achievement-seeking, routine economic roles whether high or low, inhibition of expression, repression of impulse, and all the other personal and social requisites of a society organized around the optimization of utility. Psychedelic Culture rejects the value of conforming usefulness, counterposing to it, as a standard, that each must "do his own thing."

In short, many, particularly among the young, are now orienting themselves increasingly to expressive rather than utilitarian standards, to expressive rather than instrumental politics, to gratification directly achieved with the aid of drugs, sex, or new communitarian social forms rather than through work or achievement-striving via individual competition. To many among them, Psychedelic Culture is just a last fling before they surrender and become the conforming cadres of a utilitarian culture. To some, it is a compensation for their already costly experience of participating in that culture. Yet, to others, it is a full-time commitment sometimes colored by genuine religious overtones. Despite the blatant vulgarities and posturing of some in this resistance movement against utilitarianism, despite their preference for atrocious *art nouveau* styles and their youthful self-certainty, this is, I believe, a very serious movement indeed.

In referring to Psychedelic Culture as a modern version of "Romanticism," I do not intend that characterization in the invidious sense used by such critics of the New Left as Nathan Glazer or Daniel Bell. I believe that such polemical use of the notion of "Romanticism" is not based upon any serious consideration of its intellectual resources or its historical development. What one thinks of Romanticism depends, in part, on one's judgement of utilitarianism. To assert that Psychedelic Culture is a new species of a long-familiar Romanticism is, I think, essentially true; to imply that it is "merely" this is to miss the point of both the earlier Romanticism and its modern forms. Nineteenth-century Romanticism was, from its beginning, a revolt against utilitarian culture. What, after all, was the "Philistine" whom the Romantics held in contempt except a species of utilitarian who saw no use in things that made no money? Recognizing the earlier Romantic antecedents of the contemporary resistance movement should not blind us to the importance of either the old or new version as a reaction against utilitarianism. If nothing else, the long history of Romanticism testifies to the fact that it has not concerned itself with a problem transient or peripheral to the culture.

Recognizing the continuity, however, should not blind us to the differences between the early and the contemporary versions of Romanticism. When Southey remarked that "the principle of our social system . . . is awfully opposed to the spirit of Christianity," he was typical of the many early Romantics who employed Christian values as a standpoint for social criticism. Modern versions of Romanticism do not commonly adopt Christianity as a standard, however strongly religious their impulses may be. In part this is because they often reject the ascetic strain in Christianity; but in greater part it is because, living in the God-Is-Dead epoch, they simply never took Christianity seriously in the first place. Psychedelic Romanticism is, after all, post-Nietzschean and post-Freudian.

Modern Psychedelic Romanticism, unlike the earlier version, has emerged in an economy of affluence, when the industrial economy has reached maturation. In other words, early Romanticism rejected what were then only the promised fruits of industrial society; contemporary Psychedelic Romanticism rejects the actually ripened fruits. Psychedelic Culture therefore represents the rejection of success, or at least of a system that has succeeded by its own standards. If a system cannot hold loyalties even when it has accomplished what it set out to do, it would seem that it has arrived at a deep level of crisis.

The continuing development of Psychedelic Culture with its changing forms of deviance suggests that the Welfare State has not developed strategies to control the middle classes and the relatively well educated. For Psychedelic Culture recruits its members, to a considerable degree, from persons of middle-class origin. The Welfare State, however, still basically conceives its charter as requiring it to cope with the poor, the lower, the working classes.

The periodic recurrence of "call girl," homosexual, and drug scandals suggests that the membrane between the middle class or even "high society" on the one side, and the world of the deviant or *demi-monde* on the other side, is thinning out in many spots. Indeed, this is what makes them public "scandals," instead of merely crimes. With all manner of transitional forms, the middle class is beginning to desert its loyalties to traditional utilitarian culture. This is not altogether new for the elite, and certainly it is not new for the outcasts and poor who live in ethnic casbahs or in the ghettos of the "Threepenny" *lumpenproletariat*. But something new and different is afoot when even the members of respectable civic professions begin to "swing" like and with Bohemian artistic coteries. Insofar as this continues, the rejection of utilitarian culture by the very low can no longer be dismissed as the consequence of failure, that is, as a case of sour grapes.

THE LIMITS OF THE WELFARE STATE

In good time the Welfare State will discover that a very new type of problem confronts it and will once again bestir itself. It is in the nature of the Welfare State to be a counterpuncher, acting only after and in response to the undeniable emergence of a "problem." Yet, insofar as it seeks to mobilize itself against these new problems, it will, I suspect, be even more ineffectual than usual. For one thing, the welfare apparatus that will be used against the middle-class deserters of utilitarian culture will be staffed by their class kindred, who may have already caught or who are vulnerable to the very malaise they will be asked to stamp out. They may, in parts of themselves, be drawn to the subversion of our utilitarian social order. Still, their vested administrative interests will require that they do something. Whatever become their private adaptations, I think it likely that they will seek to publicly define the various forms of resistance to utilitarian culture, especially as manifested by their cultural peers in the middle class, as a "sickness" that requires humane and expert treatment by competent authorities— psychiatrists, social workers, counselors, etcetera.

The problem-solving style of the Welfare State is, I have suggested, a slow, reactive, and *post factum* one. Since its operations are costly, the middle class is loath to submit to taxes except for problems already fully manifest. Rather than taking a lead on the target, therefore, the Welfare State commonly shoots directly at or behind it. But the ineffectuality of the Welfare State derives even more fundamentally from the fact that it must seek solutions within the framework of the master institutions that cause the problem. Accommodate as it must to the private sector, the Welfare State commonly prefers to attack only those problems whose "solutions" yield returns for those involved in producing the solutions, quite apart from the solution's demonstrable effectiveness in relieving the suffering of those experiencing the problem. Nations thus pile up armaments without any relation to the degree that these demonstrably enhance national security. In like manner, the type and level of activity of the Welfare State, and of investment in it often bears little demonstrable connection with the effectiveness of its programs. What frequently determines the adoption of a specific welfare program is not merely the visibility of a critical problem, not only a humane concern for suffering, and not only a prudent political preparation for the next election. What is also of particular importance is that the adopted solution entail a public expenditure that will be disbursed, through the purchase of goods or the payment of salaries, among those who are *not* on welfare. It is this that enables the Welfare State to attract and retain a constituency among middle-class and professional groups.

The Welfare State is thus an *ad hoc* accommodation to group and individual egoism. It is a public sector that attacks problems produced by the nature of the private sector, but must do so in ways that also yield gratifications to those who are *not* suffering from the problems with which the government is attempting to cope. The Welfare State does not oppose but counterbalances the utilitarian assumptions of the middle class; it constitutes an accommodation that allows the private sector to maintain its narrow commitment to utility. The Welfare State becomes the agency through which the "useless" are made useful or are, at least, kept out of the way.

UTILITARIAN CULTURE AND SOCIAL THEORY

A utilitarian culture affects the development of social theory in a variety of complex ways. For one, of course, it exposes theory to the demand that it be formulated in ways and on conceptual levels that facilitate "application" to what are taken to be "practical" questions and obvious social problems. Yet the pressure that a utilitarian culture places on social theory to be "relevant" and to develop technological potency as an applied science, is limited by the rewards that can be given to those who conform to the pressure. In short, while a utilitarian culture always exposes social theory to a demand for practical application, its ability to enforce this demand depends upon the larger society's readiness and willingness to finance such work and to provide careers for those engaged in it. Since such funding did not begin in earnest until the relatively recent maturation of the Welfare State, the fullest manifestations of this pressure toward the applicable, the practicable, and the relevant in social theory and sociology do not appear until well after World War II.

Social theory "for its own sake," or "pure" social theory, is always vulnerable and of challengeable legitimacy in a utilitarian culture. Insofar as "theory" is regarded as the least practicable aspect of social science—that is, as "mere" theory—the social science of a utilitarian culture always tends toward a theoryless empiricism, in which the conceptualization of problems is secondary and energies are instead given over to questions of measurement, research or experimental design, sampling or instrumentation. A conceptual vacuum is thus created, ready to be filled in by the common-sense concerns and practical interests of clients, sponsors, and research funders; in this way sociology is made useful to their interests.

Yet the effects of a utilitarian culture on social theory are even more subtle and complex. Far from limiting social theory to a concern with practical usefulness for limited social problems, utilitarian culture can also dispose theory in the opposite direction, particularly when there are few clients ready to supply extensive funding, toward an abstruse, very general type of Grand Theory.

Essentially, this is rooted in an endemic strain within utilitarian culture, which continually tends to undermine the apprehended reality of the object-world as men have traditionally viewed it and to weaken their image or "social map" of society as they had known it.

A utilitarian culture, like others, shapes man's most deeply held conceptions of what is real. On the deepest level, perhaps, this derives from the kinds of relations and experiences that the culture encourages or constrains men to have with the total object-world, that is to say, with the universe of socially defined "things."

Utilitarianism undermines the world of traditionally defined things, of received, commonsensical, and familiar objects, to which both reality and value had been imputed. Attending as it does to the *consequences* of operating with objects, and especially to their gratification or pleasure, utilitarian culture is constantly withdrawing attention from the object as such and focusing it instead on what one gets from using it. Since this depends on and varies with the use-*context,* the reality as well as the value of objects changes with the relationships in which they are placed. Objects are therefore no longer experienced as having an intrinsic or permanent value or reality. The value of an object varies with the purpose to which it is put, and the nature imputed to it changes with its contextual location. Utilitarianism, then, induces a view of objects as shifting things, lacking in fixity. As attention turns to the use and function of things, it is withdrawn from their stable and structural aspects, from their object-ness. The social world as a world of objects thus tends to sink into subsidiary awareness: "If one switches attention away from the object to the pleasure of the object-relationship, the object is lost sight of. . . ."[4]

Objects then become interpretable primarily as vehicles or terminals of purpose, or as mediators of consequences. Stated in other terms, one effect of a utilitarian culture is that the established cultural mapping of objects, as a socially shared order of reality and value, tends to be attenuated, with the result being that traditional definitions or locations of objects have less power to impose themselves on persons. There is diminished certainty about either their reality or value. On the one hand, this means a greater possibility of individual disorientation and anxiety; on the other hand, it also means a greater freedom to perceive and conceptualize objects in new, unconventional, and non-commonsensical ways. And the two are likely to be connected: the increased disorientation prompts new efforts at conceptual mapping.

Attenuation of traditional mappings of the object-world is congenial to the development of "technical" or "abstruse" social theory, for there are fewer of those firm convictions about "the way things are" that would generate a compelling sense of the *prima facie* inappropriateness of newly offered perspectives. At the same time, as the attenuation of traditional maps frees social theorizing, it may generate compulsive efforts to redefine the social map. That is, now one is not simply free to see the social world in new ways; one is now *impelled* to do so. Under these conditions theory-making is exposed to certain tacit demands: specifically, to provide a map of the world of social objects whose comprehensiveness and order can reduce the anxieties of a disordered personal reality.

Utilitarian culture may thus focus theory-making on *comprehensive mapping* for two reasons. First, because utilitarian culture *prescribes* a concern with situating objects contextually, in terms of their consequences within a network of objects; second, because utilitarianism has the unanticipated consequence of breaking down traditional mappings of the object world. The first creates an expectation and desire for a mapping, which the second makes acutely problematic and necessary. What I am saying, then, is that one implicit task of sociology in the modern world is not simply to study society but to conceptualize and *order* it: that is, to conceptually constitute social objects and to map their relationships with one another. If one looks at what sociologists do, rather than at what they say they are doing, a great deal of it consists of the formulation, exemplification, and presentation of an ordered set of concepts, rather than of laws or empirically verified propositions about the relations between things. In short, much of sociology—from the elementary textbook to the work of Talcott Parsons—is engaged in constituting social worlds, rather than simply in researching them.

Utilitarian culture also has other consequences of considerable importance for social theory. Most particularly, it entails a shift from traditional definitions of the object-world, in which the *moral* dimension (the "goodness-badness" dimension, in Charles Osgood's terms) was comparatively salient, to definitions in which the *power* dimension (their "strong-weak" dimension, again in Osgood's terms) becomes increasingly salient.[5] Utilitarianism's focus on consequences engenders an increased concern with the sheer potency of objects as a way of achieving desired outcomes, independent of the moral dimension. It is thus not simply that utilitarianism fosters a concern with cognitive judgments as distinct from moral evaluations, but that cognitive judgments themselves come to center on judgments of potency. In this view, to know what is, is to know what is powerful; knowledge is power, when knowledge becomes a knowledge *of* power.

With the growing salience of the power dimension of objects, there is a growing sense of a widening split between power and morality, between the real and the ideal. The real now excludes the moral and tends to become reduced to knowing about power, in the same sense that *Realpolitik* implies that a "realistic" politics is one that not only attends exclusively to the power implications of actions but also invidiously counterposes these to the moral implications.

With utilitarianism there is a growing sense that things of power may lack morality and that things of value may lack power. In short, there is a feeling that the world of social objects has become "grotesque," in the specific sense that the "grotesque" essentially involves a *conjunction* of objects (or object attributes) that is felt to be incongruous and ominous. Postulating, as I do, that the equilibrium state in the perception of social objects is one where power and goodness are seen as positively correlated, then the experience of the grotesque as diffusely present in the social world implies a perceptual dissonance to which social theory must in some way accommodate itself and which it will seek to reduce. One can, of course, perceive the social world as having only limited pockets of grotesqueness, but my point here is that a utilitarian culture exerts a general and diffuse strain on the integration of "goodness" and "power." Theorizing that is sensitive to this strain must address itself to the most fundamental "attribute-space" in which social objects are located, that is, to the most general latent structure of the object-world. Rather than focusing on those limited areas in which a dissonance between goodness and power obviously manifests itself, the task of social theory is then to reintegrate and reorganize the most basic coordinates of social space itself.

The effects of a utilitarian culture on the development of social theory, then, are complex; they are by no means limited to exposing social theory to the expectation that it have a practical usefulness. As a result of the attenuation of the object-world and the split between morality and power, a utilitarian culture generates at least two tacit problems for social theory, which, when responded to, are conducive to a distinctive kind of theory, Grand Theory. One is the problem of coping with grotesqueness, or reducing the dissonance between the dimensions of power and goodness in the object-world. The other is the problem of coping with the attenuation of older, traditional maps of the object-world and hence of redefining the objects in the social world and their relationships to one another in a comprehensive manner. Together, these problems constitute two of the tacit parameters that shape and define systematic social theory, Grand Theory.

In effect, although Grand Social Theory may define itself positivistically (or at any rate, may nominally define itself as an essentially scientific activity concerned primarily with furthering "knowledge" about men and human relationships), it internalizes concerns that actually have little need of "research," and for which theory itself is, in some ways, a self-sufficient response. Its social function, in short, is not simply or primarily to provide "facts" about the social world, but to provide an anxiety-reducing reorientation to it, to provide a new, comprehensive mapping which says what things are and where they belong in relation to one another.

Grand Theory differs from "middle range" theory, whose dominant concern is with the empirical verifiability of its implications, not because it rejects the importance of "research" but because a commitment to rigorous and detailed research necessarily and severely restricts the extension or *circumference* of the social world that can be brought into view. Grand Theory is not in conflict with middle range theory but is engaged with a *different* kind of problem; essentially it is a dissonance-reducing, orientational, meaning-constituting, and order-generating task, rather than a knowledge-establishing task.

Middle range theory is an effort to avoid both the proclivity of Positivism to break down into methodological ritualism, as well as the obvious ideological resonance of the more comprehensive map-making impulses of Grand Theory. Middle range theory seeks to map, and proclaims the propriety of mapping, the social world in a limited way—province by province, sector by sector. In so doing, it need not render explicit the larger maps of social reality that it may hold in subsidiary awareness. In some part, middle range theory corresponds to the growth of professional specialization in modern sociology and provides a rationale for its narrowness. In some part, it also corresponds to the closer integration of these specializations into the Welfare State, with its bureaucratically de-limited administrative agencies, each chartered to make only limited reforms in special social sectors. In short, one social function of middle range theory is to facilitate adaptation to bureaucratic organizations with limited social missions. In a different vein, however, Grand Theory seeks the standpoint of total societal reconstruction, of inter-sectorial change; it is oriented to larger social crises that are not or cannot be bureaucratically confined and managed.

NOTES

1. Cesar Graña, *Bohemian Versus Bourgeois* (New York: Basic Books, 1964), p. 107.

2. R. K. Merton, *Social Theory and Social Structure* (Glencoe, Ill.: The Free Press, 1957), p. 157.

3. While there is considerable emphasis upon the utilitarian significance

of knowledge and education in middle-class society, there are also other factors that somewhat attenuate and contravene the utilitarianism of the professional sections of the middle class. The professions have a long and continuous history in which some *non*utilitarian orientations have been protected by professional organizations and transmitted during technical or professional training in schools or universities, which define themselves as guardians of "high" values. Professionals are taught to respect the technical proprieties, on the one hand, and to provide "service" to client *needs*, on the other. The ideology of the civic professions, then, tends to be relatively uncomfortable with money-making, *individualistic* utilitarianism and somewhat more congenial toward a broader, more *social* form of utilitarianism, which may under certain conditions even become anti-utilitarian, calling for "knowledge for its own sake." Some of the significant tensions in modern society derive from this difference between the educated or professional sectors of the middle class and the propertied sectors. One important contemporary expression of this tension arises when education comes to be administered by the educated sectors of the middle class and the children of even the propertied middle class come under their tutelage and thus are exposed to their somewhat different values. Another important modern expression of this tension in the middle class arises with the later development of the Welfare State, which is more congenial to the social utilitarianism of the educated professionals than to the more individualistic utilitarianism of the propertied middle class. The Welfare State, moreover, is also more directly advantageous to the career interests of the educated, professional sector, who become the staff experts and the suppliers or administrators of services provided by the Welfare State. The Welfare State thereby constitutes itself as an alliance between the state apparatus and the educated sectors of the middle class, whose operations are often costly to parts of the propertied sectors and thus more likely to be opposed by them.

4. H. Guntrip, *Personality Structure and Human Interaction* (New York: International Universities Press, 1961), p. 288.

5. Charles E. Osgood, George Suci, and Percy Tannenbaum, *The Measurement of Meaning* (Urbana: University of Illinois Press, 1957).

4

What Happened in Sociology: An Historical Model of Structural Development

I have so far attempted to outline a few characteristics of the utilitarian culture with which middle-class society began; I now want to explore some ways in which these intertwined with the development of sociology itself. In doing so, I also hope to secure leverage for a broader analysis of the *structure* of Western sociology and the dynamics of its development. Thus I shall be concerned here not so much with the substantive content of specific theories as with the historical development of sociology's shared infra-structures, its intellectual and social organization, its differentiation and sponsorship by different nations and social classes, the division of intellectual labor in which sociology has taken a part, and the historical periods or stages in which these structures crystallized or changed.

Much of what I say below shall be in the nature of flat assertions concerning these structures and their development, rather than a probing analysis or an historical documentation. In other words, it is a preliminary effort at constructing a model about what happened to Western sociology. In effect, it is a theory of the development, and an outline for the history, of modern Western sociology.

There have been four major periods in the international development of Western sociology, which are here largely defined in terms of the theoretical syntheses dominant in each:

Period I, *Sociological Positivism*, which began about the first quarter of the nineteenth century in France and to which the key contributors were Henri Saint-Simon and Auguste Comte;

Period II, *Marxism*, which crystallized about the middle of the nineteenth century and expressed an effort to transcend the powerful tradition of German idealism and syncretize it with such traditions as French socialism and English economics;

Period III, *Classical Sociology,* which developed about the turn of the century prior to World War I, and may be conceived as a period of consolidation and accommodation. It strived to accommodate the central developments of the first and second periods by bridging Positivism and Marxism, or to find a third path. It also sought to consolidate earlier developments, often only programmatic in nature, and to embody them in detailed, scholarly researches. It was a "classical" period because most of those scholars now regarded by academic sociologists as "classical" did their work at that time: for example, Max Weber, Emile Durkheim, Vilfredo Pareto;

Period IV, *Parsonsian Structural-Functionalism,* which crystallized during the 1930's in the United States in the evolving theory of Talcott Parsons and was given complex development by the "seed group" of young scholars who early had studied with him at Harvard: for example, Robert K. Merton, Kingsley Davis, Wilbert Moore, Robin Williams, and others.

PERIOD I: SOCIOLOGICAL POSITIVISM

The beginnings of Sociological Positivism were characterized by an ambivalence toward traditional middle-class utilitarianism, being both critical of *and* continuous with it. Following the French Revolution, Henri Saint-Simon—one of the "fathers" of both modern socialism and sociology—formulated his famous parable of sudden death. In this, Saint-Simon invidiously contrasts the useless court with the productive *industriel.* What would happen, he asks, if France one day lost all of its scientists, industrialists, and artisans, and on that same day also lost all the officers of the Crown, its ministers of state, judges, and largest landholders? Of the latter group, Saint-Simon replies, the loss would only be sentimental, grieving the good-hearted French but causing no political evil to the state, for these useless men could easily be replaced. From the loss of the former, however, France would be stricken and would topple from its place as a leading nation. Central to Saint-Simon's judgment on men and society was a powerful distinction between the useless and the useful.

Like Sièyes, Saint-Simon addressed himself to the question, useful for whom? Utility, he said, must be for the nation and, indeed, for humanity as a whole. In his "Letter from an Inhabitant of Geneva" of 1803, Saint-Simon reminds the poor that

you voluntarily concede a degree of domination to men who perform services which you consider useful to you. The mistake which you make, in common with the whole of humanity, is in not distinguishing clearly enough between the immediate and more lasting benefits, between those of local and more general interests, between those which benefit a part of humanity at the expense of the rest, and those which promote the happiness of the whole of humanity. In sort, you have not yet realized that there is but one common interest to the whole of humanity, the process of the sciences.[1]

Among other things, one may notice here the utilitarian and scientific framework within which conceptions of collective welfare, essentially continuous with those later embodied in the Welfare State, are beginning to emerge. That Saint-Simon's anticipation of the Welfare State, and his linking of it to science and sociology, was neither cryptic nor casual may be seen in his remarks of 1825, where he holds that the elite minority need no longer maintain itself by force in an industrial society, and that the problem of integrating the community is now subordinate "to improving the moral and physical welfare of the nation." Public policy, says Saint-Simon, should aim at giving the working class "the strongest interest in maintaining public order . . . [and] the highest political importance," by state expenditures "ensuring work for all fit men," by spreading scientific knowledge among the working class, and by ensuring that the competent—namely, the industrialists—administer the nation's wealth: the public welfare sector is thus to operate within the framework of the private sector.[2] Perhaps the main difference between Saint-Simon's policies and those of the modern Welfare State is that he often places the welfare function in *nongovernmental* hands.

Saint-Simon was also clearly concerned with another question, namely, *what* is useful? Here, as noted above, he especially stressed the utility of science, knowledge, and technology. The central novelty in Saint-Simon's position, then, was not his concern with utility or even his insistence upon social as opposed to individual utility, but was rather his conception of *what* fosters utility, of the things that are useful. It was precisely his emphasis on the utility of science and technology, combined with his relativistic notion of the useful—which allowed that arrangements once useful could cease to be such—that led Saint-Simon's disciples to a critique of private property.

Holding that under modern conditions private property was not conducive to the production of social utility, because private inheritance of property might result in management by incompetents, the Saint-Simonians came to socialism. Far from opposing utility, their "utopian socialism" led to a refined conception of utility as a social standard, and they launched a critique of those institutions that were held to impede utility.

The positivists and utopians, in short, sought to extend and socialize individualistic utilitarianism. While stressing the importance of the economic, they sought to broaden the range of things regarded as economically useful to include, and indeed to center on, the vital significance of technology and science. Perhaps also reflecting the somewhat distinctive tendency of many French intellectuals, then as now, to combine an interest in science with one in politics and art, Saint-Simon seems to have been determined to rescue art from being warped by a narrowly economic valuation; he found a legitimate (because useful) place for artists in the new industrial society by proposing that they become engineers of the soul and an inspiration to collective morale. In so doing, he conceived art as an activity to be judged by its *social* utility. Saint-Simon thus looked beyond the individual person or family to a concern with what was useful for the larger society's coherence or solidarity.

SOCIOLOGY AS A COUNTERBALANCE TO INDIVIDUALISTIC UTILITARIANISM

From its beginnings in nineteenth-century Positivism, sociology was a counterbalance to the requirements of an individualistic utilitarian culture. It emphasized the importance of "social" needs neglected by, and required to resolve the tensions generated by, a society that focused on individual utility. It was a theory to cover what had been left out. The residual had to be added; as some sociologists once said, sociology is an $N+1$ science. In other words, it was a theory of the *complementary* structures needed to make whole the new utilitarian society. While critical of the deficiencies of the new culture, the aim of Positivist Sociology was thus not to overthrow it but rather to *complete* it. What was seen to be wrong with society was the defective structure of the totality.

In its Positivist beginnings, the new social science entailed a "cultural lag" theory. This explained current social tensions as a symptom of the system as a whole, due either to the continued existence of once functional but now archaic institutions, or to the immaturity of the new industrial system that had emerged, but as yet had failed to create appropriate new institutions in other sectors. In short, the new society's flaws were seen as those of an undeveloped adolescence rather than as the decrepitude of old age.

Saint-Simon, Comte, and, later, Durkheim contributed to a socio-logical tradition that stressed the importance of developing shared belief systems, common interests and wants, and stable social groupings. It was expected that they would have a moral authority strong enough to restrict the striving of competitive individualists and provide them with anxiety-reducing group memberships. Tech-nical activities would be controlled by guild-like professional associ-ations that assumed a communal character, and personal life would be regulated by institutionalized arrangements governed by common values. These were to restore what had been "left out," and thus make society whole.

This response intended to counterbalance the operating code of the new utilitarian economy, which, being concerned with the effi-cient use and production of utilities for private gain, stressed un-restricted individual competition, stripped men of group involve-ments that limited their mobility, and transformed them into deployable "resources"—to be used when useful and discarded when not—thus making them adaptable to an ever-changing tech-nology. It was in part because the central emphasis of the sociology of the early nineteenth century focused on what the new utilitarian culture had neglected and on the social problems generated by its assumptions, that it then failed to win stable support from the emerging middle class.

In fine, the newly emerging sociology did not reject the utili-tarian premises of the new middle-class culture, but rather sought to broaden and extend them. It became concerned with *collective* utility in contrast to individual utility, with the needs of *society* for stability and progress, and with what was useful for this. In particular, it stressed the importance of other, "social" utilities, as opposed to an exclusive focus on the production of economic utilities. Sociology was born, then, as the counterbalance to the political economy of the middle class in the first quarter of the nineteenth century.

THE EXTRUSION OF THE ECONOMIC FROM THE SOCIAL

This historical development has had abiding consequences for the place of sociology in the scholarly and academic division of labor. For the sociological focus was and remains centered on a *residual* element in middle-class, utilitarian culture. Sociology made the residual "social" element its sphere.

As it first emerged in Sociological Positivism, and, in particular, in the work of Saint-Simon, it is clear that sociology's historical mission was to *complete* and culminate what it viewed as the still *unfinished* business of the emerging industrial revolution. Saint-Simon thus expressly conceived of sociology as being needed in order to extend the scientific outlook from the physical sciences to the study of man, and thus approach man and society in a manner consistent with the emerging scientific revolution. For Saint-Simon, sociology was required to finish what the other disciplines and physical sciences had still left undone. It was to be a culminating *addition* to the new industrial outlook. It was, in this sense, to be an $N+1$ science.

This $N+1$ conception always has had two somewhat different implications. On the one hand, it involved focusing on intellectual leftovers, on what was *not* studied by other disciplines. On the other hand, it sometimes led sociologists to conceive of their discipline as the "queen" of the social sciences, concerning itself with all that the others do, and more; possessing a distinctive concern with the *totality* of sectors, with their incorporation into a new and higher level of integration, and with the unique laws of this higher whole. This ambitious claim, however, was suitable to sociology only when it was still outside the university before it had to compromise with the claims of other academic disciplines, which regarded such a conception of the sociological mission as, at best, pretentious and, at worst, intellectually imperialistic.

As sociology adapted to the claims of other, more academically entrenched disciplines, it sometimes found the more humble interpretation of itself less provocative. In this *interpretation* of itself, and in its attendent scholarly practice and researches, sociology often came to dwell on those concrete institutional areas and social problems that were not already academically preempted: on the family, ethnic groups, the urban community, on suicide, criminality, divorce. In its scholarly *practice* sociology often became the study of what was left over by other disciplines; it became a residual discipline. But this solution was neither intellectually nor professionally satisfying. On the *theoretical* level, sociology came in time to conceive of and legitimate its place as an *analytic* discipline. It conceived itself as characterized by its distinctive perspectives and concerns, not in terms of the concrete subjects it studied. This meant that, *in principle*, sociology could study *any* aspect of human life, any institution, sector, group, or form of behavior, just as economics could, the difference being the questions and interests it had in them. For some sociologists of a later period, such as Leopold von Wiese or Georg Simmel, this was taken to mean that sociology's domain was in the formal aspects of social relations and processes; for example, in cooperation, succession, competition, integration, conflict, or in dyads, triads, or rates of interaction. The most fundamental of such formal concerns that moved to and remained the center of the attention of academic sociologists—as it had been for Western social theorists since Plato—is the problem of social order: the nature and sources of social integration, coherence, and solidarity.

Sociology thus remains concerned with society as a "*whole*," as some kind of totality, but it now regards itself as responsible only for one *dimension* of this totality. Society has been parceled out analytically, among the various social sciences. From this analytic standpoint, sociology is, indeed, concerned with social systems or society as a "whole," but only insofar as it is a *social* whole.

In theory sociology is now no different from, and certainly no worse than, any other social science, each being characterized by a distinctive analytic interest, its special way of angling into the whole. In practice, however, the specific researches of sociology still frequently focus on concretely different "topics," or on those concrete institutions or problems not traditionally encompassed by other social disciplines. Sociology remains a residual science in its practice, even if autonomous in its self-image as an analytic science focused on the general problem of the integration of groups or societies. There exists in actuality no *general* social science, but only a set of unintegrated and specialized social sciences. (In the academic social sciences there is nothing that corresponds to Medicine.)

This means that Academic Sociology traditionally assumes that social order may be analyzed and understood without making the concerns of economics focal and problematic. It implies that the problem of social order may be solved, practically and intellectually, without clarifying and focusing on the problem of scarcity, with which economics is so centrally concerned. Although aspects of sociological analysis make *tacit* assumptions about scarcity, sociology is an intellectual discipline that takes economics and economic assumptions as givens, and that wishes or expects to solve the problem of social order under any set of economic assumptions or conditions. Sociology focuses upon the noneconomic sources of social order. Academic Sociology polemically denies that economic change is a sufficient or necessary condition for maintaining or increasing social order.

POSITIVIST GRAND THEORY AND THE RESTORATION STALEMATE

In the period of the Positivist synthesis, sociology arose to form a Grand Theory of society, with a distinctive and strong emphasis upon the importance of studying society scientifically: with the same "detached" manner as other sciences study their subject matter, said Comte, neither praising nor blaming it. Positivism emerged in France in the sprawling work of Henri Saint-Simon, following the Revolution of 1789. It was systematized by Comte as a Grand Theory during the Restoration, a time when, following the defeat of Napoleon, the combined military might of the European aristocracy was restoring the French nobility to its control of France.

In brief summary, Restoration social structure, as a matrix for the crystallization of Sociological Positivism, involved the following major factors: (1) a fundamental conflict between the restored nobility and the middle class, involving basic characteristics of the forthcoming society and the essential terms of settlement of the Revolution; (2) despite their mutual opposition, each of the major contending classes was somewhat ambivalent and uncertain of the terms that it would settle for, and the nature of the social map that it would support; that is, there were splits both within the nobility, between moderates and ultras, and within the middle class; (3) nevertheless, a great variety of basic issues were under contention; the fundamental question of which group would control the larger society was critical, because each was supporting a radically different mapping of the total social order; (4) one of the oldest sources of authoritative mapping under the old regime, traditional religion, continued to lose much of its public support and credence, particularly as it gave renewed support to the restored nobility and the Crown; (5) at the same time, science continued to develop and to win public prestige.

It was out of these essential developments that there emerged a set of collective public sentiments which was, on the one hand, detached from *both* major contending social alternatives—old regime traditionalism and middle-class liberalism—and, on the other, expressed a need for a new social map to which men could attach themselves; that is, for a *positive* set of beliefs. It was this new structure of collective sentiment that Sociological Positivism congenially resonated and which, in part, enabled it to find public support.

The program of an important section of the restored elite was not merely a limited political one; divided more in tactics than ultimate purpose, many among the old elite were bent upon transforming the entire social world, and refracting it as far as they could toward their traditional map of the ancient regime. They did not seek piecemeal political reforms, but aimed at a fundamental transformation of the larger social structure. What was at stake in Restoration society, therefore, was not some specific political institution, not some piece of legislation or executive enactment, but rather, the total network of institutions and the total culture that had surfaced during and after the French Revolution.

Important segments among the Royalists believed that their newly restored political power depended for its stability on certain economic and ideological conditions; they believed that their political position could not be fundamentally stabilized without larger changes in the total social structure. Thus, for instance, under Villèle, between 1822 and 1827, laws were passed for the indemnification of the nobility and the preservation of primogeniture, both aiming to restore the nobility's socio-economic position. They also enacted a law of sacrilege, attempted to abolish the Université de France, and proposed various laws bearing on the censorship of the press.

Those among the middle class who wished to defend their newly emerging institutions needed to respond on the same broad institutional level, with more than a political program that might guide them from election to election; they were under pressure to develop a coherent ideology about the social order as a totality. But their own ambivalence toward the Revolution, their fears of renascent Jacobinism and of the urban masses, blurred their vision of what they wanted and blunted their political initiative. Moreover, during the Restoration they were in no mood to share their own newly acknowledged and severely restricted political privileges with unpropertied groups. The people of the middle class thus had few unequivocal conceptions about the nature of the social order they wanted, except that it be constitutional in character, limited in governmental powers, and *laissez faire* in policy. They had, one might say, an image of the shell of a social order, but no firm view of its content; their map of a desirable social order was largely "negative," focusing as it did on the maintenance of individual freedom *from* political control.

This was a period when newly emerging social structures and institutions, far from being taken for granted, were highly precarious; moreover, this precariousness was a visible one, for the contending views were subject to articulate public debate. The most fundamental structures of society were at issue, and the debates concerning them in the legislature were amplified in cafes, in shops, and in homes. In the end, to some extent, each of the powerful contenders nullified the other and undermined the full commitment that might have been given to one or the other's conception of society.

Having once again clearly aligned itself with the nobility, the traditional Church's moral authority was further undermined among the middle class. Thus one of the main forces, which might have presented itself as a nonpartisan alternative and thus resolved the dilemma, had been deeply compromised. Many among both the aristocracy and the middle class became increasingly sensitized to the political uses of religion, and a more instrumental and detached view of religion developed. As George Brandes remarks: "In the seventeenth century man believed in Christianity, in the eighteenth century they renounced and extirpated it," and in the nineteenth century, they looked at it "pathetically, gazing at it from the outside, as one looks at an object in a museum."[3]

Out of this growing detachment there developed, perhaps most acutely among the young, a crisis of belief and a sensed need for new *positive* beliefs. As Madame de Staël remarked: "I do not know exactly what we must believe, but I believe that we must believe! The eighteenth century did nothing but deny. The human spirit lives by its beliefs. Acquire faith through Christianity, or through German philosophy, or merely through enthusiasm, but believe in something."[4] Here, as in other matters, de Staël was a sensitive weathervane, articulating some of the surfacing collective sentiments that Sociological Positivism, then emerging, would express. Positivism would stress the importance of positive beliefs, counterposing them to the negativism of the Enlightenment, as well as advocating a new "religion of humanity."

The period, then, was characterized by a sensed detachment from traditional beliefs and by an expressed need for new ones. Moreover, by 1824, there was a rising new generation, which, by that time, constituted a majority of the European population. They were deeply attached neither to the ideologies of the Revolution nor to those of the counterrevolution, for these had little rooting in their own personal experience. Lacking the loyalties or the bitterness of those who had played a role in the Revolution as adults, the new generation was not moved by the old slogans. They feared neither revolution nor reaction quite as personally as had their parents.

At the same time, the new generation was being exposed to educational institutions increasingly favorable toward the rapid development of science. For example, science was being pursued and taught at the Collège de France, Faculté des Sciences, the Muséum d'Histoire Naturelle, and Ecole Polytechnique. New scientific journals were being established, and science and philosophy were being separated both in France and Germany. There was a growing interaction between science and industry; engineering was emerging as a systematic application of science to industry. The belief was taking hold that there was a single scientific method applicable to all fields of study. The growing prestige of science began, in part, to substitute for the attenuation of traditional religion, and science came to attract those who felt a need for a new and general belief system.

The early nineteenth century had been an emotionally exhaust-

ing quarter-century of revolution and war, and this was com-
pounded by the failure, during the Restoration stalemate, authoritatively to resolve the most basic issues concerning the social order.
The Revolution had deeply undermined the older religious faith,
and the political partisanship of the Church under the Restoration
had done little to restore confidence in its moral authority. At the
same time, however, the Revolution itself was coming to be seen
by many in the middle class from its negative, irrational side, as a
time of anxiety and bloodshed. Many thus experienced detachment
from both of the dominant alternatives. To many, also, the emerging world of peaceful bourgeois routine was bloodless and uninspiring. There was need of a faith that could endow life with a new
meaning, and restore a sense of commitment and involvement.
The new generation, then, had a capacity for detachment, on the
one side, and a readiness for a stimulating new belief system on
the other. Both these sentiments were essentially akin to the standpoint of the Sociological Positivism then developing: the new structure of collective sentiments was congenially resonated by and expressed in the new sociology that extolled scholarly detachment
even as it offered a new religion. The new theory was borne by a
new infrastructure.

Neither the old regime, with its traditional beliefs, nor the anti-
traditional Enlightenment rationalism was sufficient to anchor
personal convictions. Both were out of keeping with the personal
reality that many now experienced. Now, after twenty-five years of
dramatic upheavals, of adrenalizing adventure, of history-making
involvements, the return of peace was, for some, depressing: life
seemed drab and meaningless.

What these individuals sought was a belief system that would
endow the present with drama and color, would invest it with deep
transcendental meaning that would not pale when compared with
earlier enthusiasms and solidarities, and which would enable it to
take on a drama of its own. In short, what was needed was an
ideology that, on the one side, *romanticized* the present, and on the
other, was compatible with the new world-view of science. What
was needed was a view that was both romantic *and* scientific. What
also was needed was an alternative to the traditional map of the
social world, which had been destroyed by the Revolution and,
because of the middle class's disillusionment about revolutionary
terror and its abiding fear of Jacobinism, not been replaced. With
the Thermidorean reaction, the middle class had begun to hedge on
its own vision of the world and the future, and had no clear
position. It was in this social context that Sociological Positivism
developed.

The breakdown of the old regime's old social mappings had

these three aspects: (1) the attenuation of the traditional *image* of the social order, the specific kinds of social identities it had established, the objects it had valued, and their relationships with one another; (2) the failure of the traditional *sources* of authoritative map-making, most especially with the weakening of the Church's social influence; (3) the problem of map-making *methods*. One massive, multifaceted response to the breakdown of the old social mappings was a surge of new, comprehensive map-making efforts on different levels and in different quarters of society. For example, on the state level there was constitution-making, a comprehensive legal effort to order, specify, and give fixity to a social order in minutely legislated detail. From another direction there was "utopian socialism," the socialism of Fourier, Cabet, and the Saint-Simonians, which presented its image of a counter-social order in plans of equally minute detail. Utopian comprehensiveness, we might say, was the emerging Left's map-making counterpart to constitutionalism, while constitutionalism was the map-making utopianism of the liberal middle class. In addition there was Sociological Positivism itself, whose comprehensive map-making took two distinct forms: systematic or Grand Social Theory, as in Comte's work, and the "religion of humanity," with its minutely specified catechisms and holidays and its detailed ritual and symbolism.

Sociological Positivism was related to the breakdown of traditional social mappings in one unique way. This was expressed in its sense of the irrelevance of all the dominant social mappings then available, and in its consequent search for a new *method* of social mapping. Hostile to lawyers and "metaphysicians," it sought for new *elites* that could authoritatively establish the new social maps. For Positivism, the new map-making authorities were to be scientists, technologists, and *industriels*. Its new *way* of making maps for the social world was to be science.

Much the same map-making problem was then being confronted by the German Romantics, but they did not define map-making as a cognitive, rational, or scientific effort; they viewed it as a feat of imagination and spirit. Thus the new map-making elite that the Romantics favored was not scientists but poets and, more generally, artists. But whether scientists or artists, Western Europe was seeking a new elite to fill the vacuum and provide an authoritative source of new social mappings. It would be utterly wrong, therefore, to think of French Positivism and of Romanticism (German or French) as two entirely separate or mutually isolated responses to the map-making crisis of the time. To see this, one need only remember de Staël's enthusiasm for the German Romantics and the French response to her study of them in her book on Germany.[5]

For that matter, we might also recall Saint-Simon's grand offer to marry de Staël, Saint-Simonianism's search for *la femme libre* and its attraction to "free love," or, again, the religion of humanity itself. French Positivism was a *blend* of science and Romanticism, a "scientism," but nevertheless it was a blend in which the scientific element was focal and dominant.

French Sociological Positivism resonated an emerging structure of collective sentiments, in which the world was seen to need new mappings because the moral commitment to the traditional social maps had been weakened while the prestige of science was growing. Positivism was a response to the moral uncertainty and moral exhaustion of the Restoration. It sought to escape from the Restoration stalemate between the nobility and the middle class. Against the clash of right against right, Positivism affirmed the propriety of an *amoral* response to the social world; it stressed the value of knowledge about society and universalized this moral escape by transforming its amoral method for making social maps into a moral rule.

On one of its sides, then, Positivism called for a new, practical, useful, and amoral social science as a tool for making social maps. It would not merely "moralize" about what society should be; it would find out what it was and would be, and, on this basis, would found its new morality. In this methodological posture, Positivism constituted a delaying tactic, implicitly calling for a moratorium on all the map-making that was then going on, a delay that would in effect be indefinite or would presumably extend until Positivism could, through its new methodology, create a new social map. Positivism was conforming to a structure of exhausted sentiments that said, in effect, a plague on both your houses: upon bourgeois and Restorationist, upon feudal traditionalist and middle-class liberal, upon Royalist and Jacobin.

Yet, the Positivists were also infused with utilitarian sentiments that brought them close to a middle-class outlook and led them to expect and to seek middle-class support. This was, in the end, withheld; so, while the Positivists were drawn to the middle class, they were not pulled fully into its orbit, for they resented the middle class's failure to appreciate and support them. Underlying and exacerbating Positivism's detachment, was its disappointment with and resentment of the propertied middle class. To the degree that the middle class withheld active support from them, the Positivists had little choice but to be "above the struggle." Not wishing and not forced to choose among alternatives, what Positivism made sacred, therefore, was not the map itself, but the rules for making it, a methodology. In this distinctive way, Positivism was a social movement that uniquely stressed the possibility of living in the world without a map, with the use only of a method and the sheer information it produced.

This, at any rate, was one distinctive emphasis of Positivism; but there was another, directly contrary, which led it to produce a detailed and "positive" map of the social world. This was Positivism's religion of humanity, for which both Comte and Saint-Simon had designed highly specific blueprints. This utopian aspect of Positivism was the future-oriented counterpart to the backward-looking historical novel of the Romantics; in both, social worlds were being designed and mapped in imaginative detail, and offered as alternatives to the present.

From the beginning, Positivism entailed this deepgoing conflict: the "Positive" meant on the one side, that men should base their map-making upon the *certainties* of science, and, on the other, that they should be not only critical, but also *for* some specific conception of how the world should be. In its first, methodological posture, Positivism counseled patience and warned of premature commitments to social reconstruction. In its second, religion-of-humanity stance, Positivism eschewed "negativism" and forthwith produced a new map of the world. To meet the problem in Restoration society of the loss of the traditional faith, Positivism offered a new religion of humanity.

The study of society, and especially the call for a detached scientific method of studying society, was born of an effort to find an apolitical alternative to political conflicts over the fundamental character of society. As such, Positivism was congenial to those among whom science had prestige, especially educated sectors of the middle class, and who sought a prudent way of producing social change—progress within order, skirting political conflict so as not to risk the mobilization of uncontrollable allies, the radical Jacobin potential, and simultaneously to minimize the reactionary, Restorationist backlash.

The dissonance between these two sides of Positivism began to be reduced by the factional differentiation that emerged among the various disciples of the fountainhead of Positivism, Saint-Simon. Following Saint-Simon's death, two distinguishable groupings soon formed. One of these, centering around Enfantin and Bazard, ultimately syncretized with Hegelianism in Germany—in the work of Marx's teacher, Eduard Gans, among others—and contributed to the development of Marxism. Another faction, centering around Comte, ultimately eventuated in Academic Sociology.

One of the ways in which these two factions differed was in respect to their conception of science itself. Enfantin and Bazard had a rather Romantic appreciation of the actively creative role of hypothesis, intuition, and "genius" in the process of knowing. In brief, they saw science as a "lamp" rather than a "mirror," embodying active forces akin to those that the German Romantics regarded as the source of poetry and art. This positivistic grouping also had a more politically *activistic* component than Comtianism.

When the Comtian faction failed utterly in its efforts to win acceptance for its new map, its religion of humanity, it gave up this effort and became increasingly concerned with the methodology of map-making rather than with the map to be made. Academic Sociology, in its Positivistic heritage, thus emerges from the failure of Comtianism as a practical social movement for cultural reconstruction. Viewed historically, in relation to the Positivist's own aspirations, modern "value free" sociology is the anomic adaptation of Sociological Positivism to political failure, an adaptation that commonly takes a ritualistic form, in which pure knowledge or the methodology of map-making tends to become an end in itself. Continually striving to be "above the conflict," it serves as a refuge for those seeking an apolitical alternative to the dominant images of society that are in conflict. The specifically Positivistic aspect of modern sociology has a political taproot: the failure of middle-class politics to yield a coherent image of the new social order.

DETACHMENT AND OBJECTIVITY

Utilitarian culture, in its confluence with the Restoration crisis, had fostered acute sentiments of detachment. Positivism transformed this detachment into an ideology and morality. Detachment was the characterological foundation of the morality of objectivity, while Positivist objectivity envalued the sentiment of detachment. Objectivity, as a value, prescribed and articulated a detachment that the detached self already felt: ought implied can. The Positivistic demand for objectivity resonated the sense of detachment fostered by a utilitarian culture, in which a sense of the intrinsic value of objects was being undermined by the shifting appraisal of consequences fostered by market conditions. In a market economy, intrinsic object attachments impede buying and selling; here, whether men keep or sell any object depends ultimately on the price offered for it. If they will sell themselves, their time and their services, for a price, there are few things they will balk at selling when the price is right. In such a culture, there is, therefore, less of a strain in the demand that men be "objective."

A concern with the usefulness and marketability of things cripples our ability to love them, and hence to feel loving. There is a negative dialectic between use and love, each one impeding the other. No one sensed this with a surer instinct than the Romantics, who counterposed passionate and personal love to detached and impersonal use; who held, as Goethe had, *Gefühl ist alles;* or who claimed, in Werner Sombart's pointed antithesis: "Either economic interests, in the broadest sense, or love interests, form the central point of all of life's importance. One lives either to work or else to love. Work implies saving, love implies spending."[6] "Objectivity" is the compensation men offer themselves when their capacity to love has been crippled. Thus those who wish to speak in praise of objectivity often know no better way of doing so than to denounce "sentimentality."

On this level, such objectivity is not neutrality, but alienation from self and society; it is an alienation from a society experienced as a hurtful and unlovable thing. Objectivity is the way one comes to terms and makes peace with a world one does not like but will not oppose; it arises when one is detached from the status quo but reluctant to be identified with its critics, detached from the dominant map of social reality as well as from meaningful alternative maps. "Objectivity" transforms the nowhere of exile into a positive and valued social location; it transforms the weakness of the internal "refuge" into the superiority of principled aloofness. Objectivity is the ideology of those who are alienated and politically homeless.

In suggesting that objectivity is the ideology of those who reject both the conventional and the alternative mappings of the social order, I do not, however, mean to suggest that they are equally distant from both; commonly, these "objective" men, even if politically homeless, are middle class and operate within the boundaries of the social status quo. In some part they tolerate it because they fear conflict and want peace and security, and know they would be allowed considerably less of both if they did not tolerate it.

Let me put the matter in another way: sociology emerged in the Restoration conflict, when, as de Staël said, men had lost their traditional beliefs and felt a need to believe in something. It emerged as an objective and detached study of society because traditional values had broken down and there were no firmly delineated alternatives. The soil on which sociology grew was manured by a pervasive anomie. The objectivity of Sociological Positivism arose when men entertained the suspicion that the world in which they lived was passion-spent and had little in it worth living or dying for.

Fundamental to the alienation they experienced was the split in the universe: the cleavage between power and morality. The old patterns of legitimacy were losing or had lost potency, while the emerging locus of power, the new bourgeoisie, had only the thinnest and most dubious legitimacy. One of the most paradoxical characteristics of modern culture is its abiding contempt for the middle class: the very term "bourgeois" has always had an ineradicable edge of derision to it. Sociology and the Positivist demand for objectivity emerged when traditional and middle-class values were, in the first case, unworkable, and, in the second, unheroic or uninspiring.

The Positivist sociologists tried to mend this split between power and morality in various ways. For one, they held that morality could grow out of knowledge of social reality. For a second, they attempted to shore up morality through the religion of humanity. Most important of all, however, and out of an abiding conviction about the corrupting consequences of power, they proposed to separate the "temporal" and "spiritual" orders and constitute them as insulated realms. They did this, in large measure, because they wanted to protect their spiritual order and certain values in it. They wanted to preserve their objectivity and their "dignity"; they did not want to be put to meanly practical uses. While the Positivists proposed to educate and refine the moral sensibility of the new men of power, they intended to do so only from a protected distance. They really did not like these men, if for no other reason than that they were neglected and unappreciated by them. Yet they were ready to use them if they could, and, correspondingly, they were ready to be used—"consulted," in a manner befitting their dignity—and they waited patiently to be discovered. In short, they proposed what was, in effect, a deal: they were to be treated with respect and left in charge of their own spiritual order, and in return they would respect the temporal order as it was, although still attempting to uplift it: they would render unto Caesar. That was the political meaning of Positivism's objectivity.

Even today the value-free, high science sociology that is the heir of Positivism, serves to defocalize the ideological dimensions of decision-making, diverting attention from differences in ultimate values and from the more remote consequences of the social policies to which its research is harnessed. It is congenial, therefore, to an "engineering" or managerial position, in which the client specifies the ends to be pursued while the sociologist provides the means or appraises only their efficacy. Classical Positivism manifested a clear drift in this direction from its inception. Such a conception of the sociological task does not require, and is indeed dissonant with, the more comprehensive, more assertively ideological social mappings of Grand Theory; it seeks, instead, specific knowledge about limited social sectors and requires intensive research for acquiring it. The contradiction between Positivism's scientific ambitions and its map-making impulses remained relatively invisible during its classical period, in part because there was then little support provided by the middle class for intensive social research.

As such funding becomes increasingly available, the emphasis on rigorous methodologies assumes a very special rhetorical function. It serves to provide a framework for resolving limited differences among the managers of organizations and institutions, who have little conflict about basic values or social mappings, by lending the sanction of science to limited policy choices concerning ways and means. At the same time, its cognitive emphasis serves to defocalize the conflict of values that remains involved in political differences, and to focus contention on questions of fact, implying that the value conflict may be resolved apart from politics and without political conflict. Positivism thus continues to serve as a way of avoiding conflicts about mapping. Yet, despite this seemingly neutral, nonpartisan character, Positivism's social impact is not random or neutral in regard to competing social mappings; because of its emphasis on the problem of social order, because of the social origins, education, and character of its own personnel, and because of the dependencies generated by its own funding requirements, it persistently tends to lend support to the *status quo.*

POSITIVISM: BETWEEN RESTORATION AND REVOLUTION

The middle-class society that had, as in France, broken through the old regime, clearly understood that the danger to its further development lay, in important part, in the continued resistance of old institutions and elites. The practical political task confronting the middle class entailed the protection of its newly won positions, against the restoration of the old regime, which it identified with social forces of the historical past. In sort, old elites were still seen as consequential in the present; their continuing power was condemned as illegitimate on the grounds of their present social uselessness, as in Saint-Simon's parable.

The early Sociological Positivists, like many among the emerging middle class, sensed that the past was still alive and dangerous, and they expressed this feeling in a "cultural lag" theory. They conceived of the present as embodying certain tensionful contradictions, which they viewed not as within and inherent to the new bourgeois institutions, but rather as conflicts that existed between them and older, "archaic" institutions lingering on from the past. These contradictions were expected to resolve themselves in the course of social evolution. In this, the archaic past would wither away, and the new society would be *completed* by the rounding-out of its institutional requirements and by developing new institutions appropriate to those middle-class arrangements that had already emerged.

At the same time that the middle class sought to strengthen its new position in society against the older elites, it also found itself confronted with a newly emerging proletariat, the urban masses, who seized upon middle-class revolutionary militancy to advance their own interests. The middle class was thus constrained to inhibit its own revolutionary initiatives, for fear that it would be unable to control the emerging masses. There was, in short, the Thermidorean reaction.

The nineteenth-century middle class was soon in the position of having to pursue its interests by waging a social struggle on two fronts. Change had to be tempered with a prudent concern for social order, political continuity, and stability. The middle class' need to complete its revolution, on the one hand, and its simultaneous need to protect its position and property from urban disorder and proletarian unrest, on the other, help to account for August Comte's twofold slogan, "Order and Progress," and his conception of progress as the unfolding of order. Comte's evolutionary, prophetical sociology held that what was required for completion of the new society was not revolution but, rather, the peaceful application of science and knowledge: Positivism. Comte's sociology reflected the middle class' impulse to fortify its new social position against restoration from above, while avoiding the risks of revolution from below. The new sociology resonated the sentiments of a middle class precariously caught between past and future, between still powerful old elites and emerging new masses.

As suggested earlier, the middle class failed at first to support the new sociology, even though it coincided with their needs and perspectives in some respects. They backed away from it partially because it was critical of their narrowly economic and individualistic version of utilitarianism. Moreover, in focusing attention on sociological structure, sociology tended to diminish the importance attributed to the state. At a time when the middle class was still involved in a struggle for control of the governmental apparatus, Comte had hardly anything to say about the state.

The Positivistic Sociology of the early nineteenth century was not the intellectual creation of the propertied middle class. Its ground-work, rather, was initially laid by the dispossessed aristocracy, including the Counts DeBonald, DeMaistre, and Saint-Simon; their ideas were fused with a concern with "science" attractive to the civic, and especially the engineering, professions then emerging. *Sociology was thus at first the intellectual product of old strata that had lost their social power and of new ones that were still far from fully developed.* The intellectual concerns and cultural traditions of these strata were not identical with the needs of bourgeois property; the noble antecedents as well as the superior education of the men who created the new sociology gave them a sense of their superiority, which troubled the new, often vulgar, men of money. In large measure, the new sociology of Saint-Simon and Comte was the product of a marginal social strata, of those dying or still not fully born. It also won the support of stigmatized groups, like the Jews, and from persons with various individual stigmata, such as pronounced mental illness, marriage to prostitutes, bankruptcy, or bastardy.

These men were commonly viewed with profound discomfort by the propertied middle class. They were disreputables, who had publicly declared themselves for "free love." They were men of dangerous character, who were bundled off to jail and prosecuted. The *arriviste*, the still socially and politically insecure middle class of the early nineteenth century, was not about to ally itself with such men or their sociology. Moreover, the rising middle class did not relish being told, by advocates of the new sociology, that it was science and technology, rather than property, that legitimated authority in the modern world. The middle class had not fought the aristocracy and disestablished the powerful Church, only to be yoked by a seedy little sect. Comte would wait in vain.

It was only as industrialism deepened its hold on society that sociology would come into its own. Only where and when the institutional requirements of commercial industrialism were fully established; only when the middle class was secure from the restoration of old elites; only when it therefore did not look upon the past as a threat and did not believe the future required anything radically different: only then could the middle class relinquish a cultural lag theory that explained away present social tensions as due to old institutions grown archaic. These were among the *necessary* conditions for the acceptance and *institutionalization* of sociology in middle-class society.

Sociology could then relinquish its historical and evolutionary perspectives, curtail its future-orientedness, and live upon the knife-edge of an isolated present. By the classical period, evolutionism began to give way to "comparative" studies and to Functionalism. Functional sociology, with its ahistorical character and its emphasis upon the *ongoing* consequences of existent social arrangements, reflects the loss of historical imagination that corresponds to the mature entrenchment of the middle class, which no longer fears the past and neither imagines nor desires a future radically different from the present. Thus, modern, functional social theory and sociology itself are, at first, largely the product of those societies where middle-class industrialization moved ahead most rapidly: that is, France, England, and, above all, the United States.

PERIOD II: MARXISM

Born of and in capitalism, no less than in a struggle against it, popular, politically powerful, Marxism also placed a central value on social utility, even though it polemicized against Benthamite utilitarianism. From an historical perspective, one function of popular Marxism was to *complete* the utilitarian revolution by overcoming the obstacle that bourgeois property presented to the further extension of standards of utility. It is this which, in part, contains the historically "progressive content" of Marxism. Popular Marxism was not, of course, alone among socialisms to commit itself to a form of popular utilitarianism, as may be gleaned from H. G. Wells' biting criticism of Beatrice Webb, she of the "bony soul."

On the level of publicly affirmed and genuinely believed values, there is no difference in principle between capitalism and socialism with respect to the slogan: from each according to his ability, to each according to his work. The "honest bourgeois" would agree: men should work hard and to the best of their ability; and they should in turn be paid in full what their work is worth.

THE SOCIAL UTILITARIANISM OF MARXISM

Socialist and bourgeois would disagree, however, with respect to the exclusive use of utility as a standard for determining what men receive. Commonly, socialists felt that men's needs, as well as their usefulness, were a legitimate basis for allocating goods and services to them. While insisting that men's wants were corrupted under capitalism, Marx believed that men had certain universal "species needs" as humans, and that, as socialism matured, they would develop more truly human needs. Marx and other socialists believed that men's claims to gratification were ultimately rooted in these needs, and not simply in their usefulness.

On the one hand, Marx, like the Utopian Socialists, acknowledged utility as a standard, and, indeed, sought to overcome impediments to its historical development; he sought to socialize utility. On the other hand, he also sought to balance and temper utility with considerations of human need, even during periods of early industrial development, in the anticipation that utility would be transcended when economic development had vastly increased productivity; and then human needs, no longer corrupted by venal motives, could become more truly human.

Let me be at great pains to insist that Marx's position about utilitarianism was very complex and that it is mistaken to interpret him as an exponent of traditional utilitarianism. Nothing can make this complexity clearer than the polemic Marx mounted against Jeremy Bentham, that "insipid, pedantic, leather-tongued oracle of the commonplace bourgeois intelligence of the nineteenth century."[7] Yet to understand Marx's polemical position on utilitarianism, its strengths and its limitations, it is vital to see his assumptions.

First, Marx insisted that we cannot talk about utility in general, but only about utility for something:

> To know what is useful for a dog, we must study dog nature [and] . . . he who would pass judgment upon all human activities, movements, relations, etc., in accordance with the principle of utility, must first become acquainted with human nature in general, and then with human nature as modified in each specific historical epoch.[8]

Thus Marx insisted that we cannot tell whether anything is useful to man without having a general, universal conception of human nature, as well as an historical conception of it. Second, Marx clearly took exception to the *reductionistic* aspects of utilitarianism, insisting on the autonomy of expressive as well as other motives. This is especially evident in his *German Ideology*, where he condemns efforts to reduce all the various forms of human activity— "speech, love, etcetera"—to a relation with utility in which they are not supposed "to have a meaning peculiar to them." Men sometimes "use" things as means to other ends, in an instrumental manner, but not under all conditions. Third, Marx condemned Bentham's version of utilitarianism because it tacitly premised that what is useful for the English bourgeois is useful to all men. "Whatever seems useful to this queer sort of normal man, is regarded as useful in and of itself."[9] Finally, and central to his analysis of capitalism, is Marx's view of utilitarianism as an *ideology* of the bourgeoisie. Although the bourgeoisie talks about utility, he really means profit, Marx says. The bourgeoisie does not really produce what is useful but what is profitable, what sells. Bourgeois production is commodity production: that is, the production of things that have "exchange-value," not "use-value." Utilitarianism is a false consciousness of the bourgeoisie, a congenial disguise for its venality.

At bottom, then, Marx's critique of utilitarianism centers on its limited bourgeois form; his is an attack upon the pursuit of individual private profit, underneath which is the more classical hostility toward egoism. For Marx, utilitarianism is largely individual egoism, or the modern disguise of it. Marx therefore does not generalize his critique to all forms of utilitarianism but centers it on the bourgeois form. As early as his youthful paper at the Triers Gymnasium, Marx committed himself to a kind of *social* utilitarianism, to the importance of being useful to *humanity*. He remarked there that one must choose a vocation "in which we can contribute most to humanity," and he warned that unless we choose vocations for which we are talented, "we will be useless creatures."

Marx is a "revisionist" utilitarian, a social utilitarian; he wants men to be useful to the collectivity, to society as a whole, to what was emerging in history. In his well-known, and deliberately sloganistic, characterization of *advanced* socialism, where he demands, "from each according to his abilities, to each according to his needs," Marx is, on the one hand, severing the conventional utilitarian correlation between work and reward, but on the other hand, he is also implying that men have a *moral* obligation to be useful to a humane, socialist society. What Marx rejects in Benthamite utilitarianism is precisely its instrumental calculation and expedience; what Marx wishes is a *noncalculating, moral* utilitarianism, where men feel a genuine obligation to be useful to a decent society.

This is a somewhat tensely fine line between Marx's condemnation of individualistic and venal utilitarianism, and his accommodation to a socialized and communal utilitarianism. In some part, this tension was resolved by assigning a different importance to utility in different periods of economic development, holding that it would be ultimately obsolescent under fully developed socialism, where the rule would be, from each according to his abilities, to each according to his need; in earlier, less developed socialism, utility would hold greater sway, and the rule would be, from each according to his abilities, to each according to his work.

The historical outcome was paradoxical. On the one hand, socialists came to view utility as an historically transient and increasingly archaic standard, ultimately destined for the historical rubbish heap; even its current legitimacy was ambiguous and undermined. On the other hand, however, the practical exigencies of successful industrialization and nation-building often led socialists to apply utilitarian standards in daily politics and economic planning, and the transcendence of utility as a social standard tended to assume a millennial character.

Marxism thus tacitly embodied the conflict between utilitarianism and natural rights that had been characteristic of the middle class, even though it was hostile to commercial paradigms of utility and critical of the universal claims of natural rights. Marx himself had envisaged the good society that would ultimately appear as one that severed the correlation between a man's usefulness and what he would get; what a man received would no longer be a reward for his usefulness but his birthright as an individual. This, however, was the Marxist image of the future, not the operating standard of the existing socialist movement. Marxism then was ambivalent about utilitarianism; seeking to transcend it in the future, it accommodated to it in the present; opposed to a venal, individualistic utilitarianism, it still accepted the necessity of a social utilitarianism.

THE BINARY FISSION OF MARXISM AND ACADEMIC SOCIOLOGY

A major structural characteristic of Western Sociology develops after the emergence of Marxism; following this, Western Sociology is divided into two camps, each with its own continuous intellectual tradition and distinctive intellectual paradigms, and each greatly insulated from or mutually contemptuous of the other. After the sprawling genius of Saint-Simon, Western Sociology underwent a kind of "binary fission" into two sociologies, each differentiated from the other both theoretically and institutionally, and each the reverse or mirror image of the other. One was Comte's program for a "pure" sociology, which, in time, became Academic Sociology, the university sociology of the middle class, that achieved its fullest institutional development in the United States. The other was the sociology of Karl Marx, or Marxism, the party sociology of intellectuals oriented toward the proletariat, which achieved its greatest success in Eastern Europe.

Rather than defining itself as a "pure" sociology, as Comte had come to define Positivistic Sociology, Marxism affirmed the "unity of theory and practice." Far from appealing to the middle class, as Comte had, Marxism found its constituency not in classes that were rapidly being integrated into the new middle-class society, but in strata that were still outsiders, marginal to it, lowly, disreputable, relatively powerless, and still very far from enjoying the benefits of the new society. In this last respect, Marxism made the most basic rupture with all previous social theory, which, from Plato to Machiavelli, had addressed itself to and sought the support of

Princes, elites, and socially integrated strata. Marxism took the decisive step when it rejected Saint-Simon's proletarian philanthropy, which provides help from the outside, and opted instead for proletarian initiative and proletarian self-determination.

Marxism was no less one-sided than the "positivistic trash" it deplored, but it did develop precisely those interests that Comte had neglected. Instead of conceiving of society, as Comte had, as tending naturally toward stability and order, it regarded modern society as containing "the seeds of its own destruction." Rather than concerning itself with social stability, Marxism conceived of social reality as process; it sought both to understand and to produce social change. Instead of being in love with order and stability, Marxism—at least in its early, prerevisionist stages—had an amplified sensitivity to the sounds of street-fighting. It did not center attention on small "natural" groups, such as the family, that Comte believed would spontaneously maintain social order; Marxism focused on large social classes whose conflicts disrupted social order, and on planned associations, such as political parties and trade unions, which could rationally modify the social world in accordance with the guidance of a social science. Marxism exalted work, knowledge, and involvement; Comtianism prized morality, knowledge, and scientific detachment. The Comtian formula was: Scientific Method × Hierarchical Metaphysics = Positive Sociology; the Marxian formula was: Scientific Method × Romantic Metaphysics = Scientific Socialism.

Marx accented the economic and industrial focus already present in Saint-Simon, but he conceptualized it as a matter of economics and power rather than of science and technology. Saint-Simon's position on this had developed as early as 1803, when he had expressly argued that "the haves govern the have-nots, [but] not because they own property; they own property and govern because, collectively, they are superior in enlightenment to the have-nots."[10] Marx, of course, came to maintain the very opposite. Marx saw modern society as "capitalist," in contrast to Saint-Simon's conception of it as "industrial." Marx thus centered attention on the variability of property and power arrangements, and their importance for the further development of industrialization. Marx also focused on the conflicts within the new industrial classes rather than on their common interest in opposing the elites of the old regimes, as had Saint-Simon. Where Saint-Simon had stressed their similarities as industrials, Marx split them into proletarians and capitalists.

Comtianism and Academic Sociology became the sociology and ideology of strata and societies that made the first and quickest breakthroughs into industrialization. Marxism became the sociology adopted by underdeveloped or more slowly developing regions, by strata least integrated into industrial societies, by classes who sought but were denied their benefits.

Saint-Simon's doctrines thus underwent a binary fission into two basic theoretical systems that persist until this day. One side of Saint-Simon's work went to his French disciples, Enfantin and Bazard; there it became "Saint-Simonism," which, when fused with the infrastructures of German Romanticism and Hegelianism, contributed to the development of Marxism, in the work of Marx, Engels, Karl Kautsky, Nicolai Bukharin, Leon Trotsky, and V. I. Lenin; and, where it renewed its contact with Hegelianism, it was expressed in the work of Georg Lukács, Antonio Gramsci, and in the contemporary German School of "Critical Sociology" at Frankfurt, including Herbert Marcuse, Theodor Adorno, Max Horkheimer, Leo Lowenthal, Erich Fromm, and Jurgen Habermas. Thus one side of Western Sociology's binary fission produced a protean tradition whose persistent theme has been a criticism of modern society in the name of man's human potentialities and their fulfillment. The other side of this fission at first crystallized as Positivistic Sociology, which provided the roots of conventional Academic Sociology, as it passed from Comte through Emile Durkheim and English anthropology, to become one of the central sources that Talcott Parsons was to draw upon for his own theoretical synthesis. This continuing tradition of Academic Sociology has, as its perduring theme, the need for social order and moral consensus.

POSITIVISM AND SUBSEQUENT FUNCTIONALISM

Modern Functionalism, which emerges later, in the third and fourth periods of sociological synthesis, has part of its heritage in Sociological Positivism. While modern Functionalism renounces certain assumptions important to earlier Positivism, particularly its evolutionism and cultural lag theory, Functionalism has always remained loyal to Positivism's central "programmatic concept"—a concern with the "positive" functions of institutions—and, moreover, to certain of the core *sentiments* adhering to it. The term "positive" is a resonating programmatic concept, like those found at the heart of all major social theories. To grasp the programmatic concept, to see its fundamental domain assumptions and the sentiments that permeate it, is to grasp much of the power, pathos, and appeal of the theory.

To Saint-Simon and to Comte the "positive" had at least two central implications: on the one side, the "positive" referred to the certain, to knowledge certified by science; on the other, it was the opposite of the "negative," that is, of the "critical" and "destructive" ideas of the French Revolution and the *philosophes*. In line with the latter, Positivism was, from its beginnings, bent on displaying the "good" that might reside in institutions and customs; it focused on their constructive, functional, useful side. However, under Saint-Simon's formulations, French Positivism never committed itself to the assumption, "once useful, always useful." Saint-Simon's was not a Panglossian optimism that saw this as the best of all possible worlds, but rather was a vision of the modern social world as incomplete, as suffering from immaturity. It was thus a qualified Functionalism, for it did not fear to criticize what it felt were the residual vestiges of an archaic social past still encumbering progress. It also wanted new social arrangements more in keeping with modern industry, which it was hoped could reunite society. Therefore it adopted a more critical stance than that characteristic of later Functionalism. But in its subsequent academic formulations, particularly by Comte, Positivism aimed primarily at blunting the criticisms that the *philosophes* had directed against almost all the institutions of the ancient regime.

Insofar as the "positive" implied an emphasis upon the importance of scientifically certified knowledge, it was using social science as a rhetoric, which might provide a basis for certainty of belief and might assemble a consensus in society. It preached "an end to ideology" under the formulation of "an end to metaphysics." In other words, Positivism assumed that science could overcome ideological variety and diversity of beliefs. Comte had, in this vein, polemicized against the Protestant conception of unlimited liberty of conscience, holding that this led men each to their own differing conclusions and thus to ideological confusion. This disunifying liberty of conscience was, in Comte's view, to be supplanted by a faith in the authority of science that would reestablish the lost social consensus and thus make society whole again.

Comtian Positivism thus manifested the same fascination with consensus and social cohesion, as well as with the ongoing if hidden usefulness of existing institutions, that later characterized Emile Durkheim and A. R. Radcliffe-Brown. The culmination of this abiding Positivist heritage is reached in Talcott Parsons' Structural-Functionalism, which is quite properly celebrated by E. A. Shils as a "consensual" theory. Championing both order and progress, the Comtians had of necessity sought progress within the framework of middle-class property institutions and of the new industrialism, which they regarded as basically sound even if still unfinished. In this continuity of essentially optimistic sentiments and domain assumptions, on the level of infrastructure, modern Functionalism is the legitimate heir of nineteenth-century Sociological Positivism.

In addition to the deep structural split between Academic and Marxist Sociologies, there has been another, less easily crystallizable cultural cleavage of consequence for sociology. Sometimes this split has been formulated in national terms, as a difference between the French and German intellectual traditions (as, for example, by Raymond Aron); sometimes it has been defined as a split between the German idealistic tradition and the more Positivistic tradition of the other Western nations (as, for example, by Ernst Troeltsch). My own view is that this cleavage is only superficially expressed in national terms, for it entails underlying cultural tensions in all Western industrial nations, which manifest themselves in various cultural sectors—painting, music, theater—as well as in sociology.

Historically, one side of this split appeared in Germany no later than the first quarter of the nineteenth century, with the full emergence of the Romantic movement as a counterstatement to rationalism, materialism, Positivism, and utilitarianism; in short, to the culture of the emerging middle class. Romanticism, however, was not simply a reactionary, right-wing opposition to the middle class and its economic order, but had, as it were, an opening to the left. It had revolutionary potentialities that were, for example, developed in the work of Marx, despite his contempt for earlier Romantics. The revolutionary potential of Romanticism derived, in part, from the fact that although basically a critique of industrialism, it *could* as well be used as a critique of capitalism and its culture. As a critique of industrialism in the period of its emergence, however, Romanticism lent itself to use against the middle class by the embattled older elites, especially the aristocracy, and in *that context* it was often reactionary.

Romanticism was nevertheless capable of being blended with a working-class critique of the middle class. There was, as Henri Le Febvre says, a Romanticism of the left as well as the right. Romanticism tended to be predominantly reactionary in its political effect, when it objected to the early industrial development. Romanticism, however, has had liberative potentialities whenever it has sought to transcend the middle-class limitations of utilitarian culture in *advanced* industrial societies; when it has accepted the irrational or nonrational as a source of vitality, without exalting it; and when it has not been elitist. Freudianism has been one expression of such a Romanticism.

Romanticism has, in various ways, been one of the cultural

syndromes around which there have developed styles of sociology discernibly different from the Positivistic or the methodologically empiricist. "Romantic sociologies" have been different both in substantive theory and in methodology, and have placed themselves in tension with other styles that emulate the physical, high science models. I will argue, in another volume, that Romanticism was *one* of the major cultural influences leading to the development of Marxism. The most important influence of Romanticism on Academic Sociology in Europe, is to be found in the work of Max Weber, while its most important influence on American sociology is through George Herbert Mead and the "Chicago School," on the one side, and Talcott Parsons, on the other.

PERIOD III: CLASSICAL SOCIOLOGY

Classical Sociology emerged during the last quarter of the nineteenth century, a period of consolidating industrialization, large-scale organization, and growing imperialism prior to World War I. Classical Sociology had more diversified national sources than Positivism, including powerful developments in Germany as well as new expressions within the French tradition itself. Nonetheless, each source remained relatively national in character, with little mutual acquaintance and influence among the key contributors. It was also—and this was significant—increasingly institutionalized within the supporting university contexts of the different countries. If the key polemical target of Positivistic Sociology had been the *philosophes* and the French Revolution, the common polemical target of the thinkers of the Classical period was Marxism. Marxism was the crucial intellectual development, and socialism the key political development, that, as antagonists, differentiated the central concerns of the first and third periods in the development of Western Sociology. Classical Sociology was the great achievement of the middle class of Western Europe, in the late nineteenth century, when the individual, competitive entrepreneur was being supplanted by increasingly large-scale and bureaucratized industrial organization, and when in general, the middle class was increasingly threatened by the rise of Marxist socialism.

THE DECLINE OF EVOLUTIONISM AND RISE OF FUNCTIONALISM

Academic Sociology in the Classical period was structurally differentiated, in various ways, from that of the Positivistic period; one of the most important was the atrophying of social evolutionism both in Emile Durkheim's work and in Max Weber's, and its replacement by "comparative" study. This is one reason why Herbert Spencer, with his dominating emphasis on evolutionism, subsequently failed to be regarded as a characteristic thinker of the Classical period. In Germany, especially as epitomized by Max Weber, comparative studies largely focused on Western European societies, or on literate, great civilizations, such as India's. In France, however, comparative studies increasingly incorporated, as in Durkheim's school, materials from nonliterate societies; here they moved toward a juncture with anthropology, and became influential in the development of English anthropology through the work of A. R. Radcliffe-Brown. The decline of evolutionism and the rise of Functionalism were complementary, and shaped the development of sociology and anthropology alike.

The movement away from Positivist evolutionism and toward Functionalism may be examined in detail in Durkheim's work, particularly in comparison with Comte's. Perhaps the crux of the difference was related to the fact that Comte had felt a deep ambivalence toward the past: he was both more linked to it and more afraid of it than Durkheim. Comte had conceived of the new Positivist society as only one stage in an evolutionary process, although he had believed it the highest stage of development that mankind could reach. He knew that in France this highest stage was, in his day, only half-born, and was still floundering between a future not yet fully arrived and a past not yet wholly and safely dead. The basic threat to the new society was, in the early Positivist view, from the archaic remnants of the past still potent in the inevitably incomplete and immature present. In short, there was postulated a theory of "cultural lag."

Durkheim, however, was operating in a decidedly different situation, and it shaped his historical imagination quite differently. Modern industrial society was far more developed in his time than it had been in Comte's; it had reached and gone beyond the takeoff point. The active threat of powerful Restorationist elites was therefore gone, even though "vestigial" institutions remained. The danger, in brief, was no longer seen as located in something essentially of the past, but as more fully rooted in the present.

One of the areas in which this was expressed most clearly was in Durkheim's conception of patterns of inheritance as an "archaic survival." Clearly, however, Durkheim did not regard inheritance in anything like the sense in which Saint-Simon had seen the restored monarchy. It was inconceivable that Durkheim would make the same kind of statement about inheritance that Saint-Simon had made about the monarchy. Yet Durkheim did see inheritance as generating tensions, and as no longer historically necessary, although visibly rooted in the present. The brunt of Durkheim's critique of inheritance saw it as doomed because it has a manifest inappropriateness to other aspects of the society, particularly its contractual ethics, and because it has an injurious effect upon the modern division of labor. In conceiving of inheritance as a "survival," he presented an image of it as a fish out of water, doomed to die a natural death, rather than as something having to be actively and forcefully deposed through revolutionary change. It would be gradually and peacefully closed down, step by step, painlessly put to sleep by a euthanasia administered by guild-like, syndicalist corporations. Removing it required no bloody conflict.

For Durkheim, then, the basic threat to modern society did not come from still powerful remnants of the past, actively hostile and dangerous to the present. He was ready to relinquish this half of the Positivist theory of cultural lag, to forgo that part of it that blamed current ills on the past. To repeat, it was not that he did not see inheritance as causing trouble, but that he did not see it as deeply threatening. Certainly he did not consider it nearly as important as the growth of *anomie,* or the decline of a binding morality that would restrain men. His central concern was not economic poverty, but the poverty of morality.

The important question is how Durkheim viewed this decline of morality. In particular, did he see it in terms of the cultural lag theory, as an expression of an insufficiency natural to a young society, and sooner or later to be overcome *spontaneously,* through its own natural process of maturation? Not entirely. His refusal to take this tack was implicit in his planned effort to surmount the problem *now,* through the deliberate development of syndicalist corporations. This implied that the "poverty of morality" could be overcome in the *present;* it need not wait for the future. In short, while there was nothing in the present that would make this remedy inevitable, there was also nothing in the present that would make it impossible. The outcome depended not upon a future unfolding and maturation, but upon the present and on decisions in it.

Durkheim was thus *beginning* to close down the theory of cultural lag from both ends. It was neither the threat from the past that was most serious, nor the *necessary* incompleteness of the present. Durkheim had no need to curse the past or pray to the future, for things would not be radically different in it. The really serious dangers to society, for Durkheim, were rooted in the inherent insatiability of man, and these would remain the same for all societies and be unchanged in the future. From Durkheim's standpoint, socialism could bring no significant change in this, the essential character of man. Man would be ever the same; there was, in effect, no point in looking forward to the future for a radical change in society. It was the present, therefore, that counted. This had much the same implication as Max Weber's view of modern industrialization as being essentially "bureaucratic" in nature, and his consequent prediction that socialism would be no less bureaucratic than capitalism. There was really no choice, in this respect, between socialism and the present society.

Socialism and Marxism had taken a very future-oriented time perspective, adopting an historical and evolutionary emphasis in which it was stressed that the present society would inevitably be superseded by a radically different one. To this, Durkheim polemically replied that social science was still far too immature to see the future. It was precisely in connection with his polemic against socialism that his opposition to an evolutionary outlook that attempted to predict the future was most explicitly formulated, and his counteraffirmation, that sociology is concerned about what is or was, was most emphatically advanced. While Comte had raised the motto of "Order and Progress," Durkheim, in contrast, felt constrained to place even less emphasis upon "progress" than had Comte; he came to invest his energies almost exclusively in the analysis of "order." In short, Durkheim began to truncate the future orientation of Comtianism in the course of his polemic against the conceived future projected by Marxism and socialism. He thus began the consolidation of sociology as a social science of the synchronic present, which came to culmination in contemporary Functionalism.

At the same time that Durkheim foreshortened the future-oriented perspective of early Positivism, he also began to revise its conception of the past. In his distinction between two forms of society, the organically and mechanically solidary, it was clear that the former referred primarily to modern industrial societies. Indeed, the distinction was, in one way, intended to be a defense of their inherent stability. "Mechanical solidarity," on the other hand, referred to almost *all* earlier societies, or at least to many that had existed at widely different periods. Mechanical solidarity lumped together societies as widely spaced and different as feudalism and tribalism.

The dichotomy between organically and mechanically solidary societies was, in effect, a distinction between "now" and "then." Modern industrial society was being conceptually cut out of its former place in a multiphased series of societies; it was being used as a central point of reference, which gave all that had come before its value and interest. The present was being constituted as an *island* out of time; the past was no longer to be thought to embody its own significant *temporal* gradations and developments, but to be treated primarily as a convenient *contrast* with the present rather than as a preparation for it. Here evolutionism was giving way to "comparative studies."

In some ways, this was similar to the Comtian impulse to see the evolutionary development of society as having come to climactic culmination in Positivist society. Yet, the historical sense of Comtianism, and of classical Positivism in general, had been much stronger; it had, in fact, given birth to new schools of historiography, such as that of Augustin Thierry, Saint-Simon's pupil. If it had viewed the past primarily as preparation for the coming of the Positivist society, it had also insisted upon doing justice to it, by studying the step-by-step, phase-by-phase, temporal process by which Positivism had finally emerged. To Durkheim, however, the past had little value, except when it could, by comparison, help him to understand the present.

Durkheim's move away from evolutionism toward comparative studies had one important intellectual advantage. It became a matter of indifference whether a past society had any known historical linkage with the present, and it thus widened the range of societies that might be considered of interest. This meant that sociology no longer had to confine itself to the European experience or even to great civilizations; it could now include in its comparative data even *tribal* societies. It was in this broadening of his studies to include tribal societies that Durkheim made a most important intellectual advance beyond Comte. This development of interest in tribal societies did not, however, occur in a social vacuum, but was concurrent with the increasing activity of the European powers in Africa and elsewhere, and concurrent with the intensive development of nineteenth-century colonialization. Both of these developments, the European colonialization of other continents and the development of Durkheim's sociology in a nonevolutionary direction capable of incorporating tribal studies, contributed to the critical shift that was to occur in anthropology, particularly English anthropology.

DIFFERENTIATION OF THE GERMAN AND
FRENCH RESPONSES TO UTILITARIANISM

The broadening of the concept of "utility," begun by the Positivists, was carried forward and incorporated into Functionalism by

Durkheim's work, and then diffused into English anthropology. The emerging "functional" theory sought to show how the persistence or change of any social institution or custom had to be understood in terms of its *ongoing* consequences for surrounding institutions and behavior. It had to be explained in terms of its place in and its contributions to the larger society of which it was a part. In other words: "function" was a broad and subtle way of talking about the *usefulness* of *all* (not merely economic) "social" relations, behaviors, and beliefs.

The successful appeal of Functionalism has rested, in part, on its ability to resonate congenially the practical, utilitarian sentiments of men socialized into a dominant middle-class culture, men who feel that things and people must be, and are, legitimated by their ongoing usefulness. Being thus at variance with sentiments of aristocratic insouciance and traditionalism, as well as with socialist critiques of middle-class society as entailing exploitation based on power rather than utility, Sociological Functionalism was congenial to the middle class in its struggle against the new masses and, if need be, against the old elites. The revisionist broadening of utilitarianism occurred mostly in France.

However, Functionalism was seriously alien to cultures, such as the German, having a massive infusion of Romanticism and a mandarin disdain for middle-class culture: Weber rejects Functionalism. German sociology was thus characterized by a radical polemic against utilitarianism, rather than by a broadening and sublimation of it. Culminating around the turn of the century in Max Weber's sociology of religion, it stressed the importance of ideas in general and of religious ethics in particular, as influences upon social development and human conduct. Rather than accounting for social action in terms of its functions or useful consequences, it emphasized that social outcomes were the result of men's efforts to conform with ideas and ideals. As had Romanticism, Weber's emphasis was on the autonomy and importance of the ideas to which men inwardly committed themselves, and on how these shaped history. Weber's position was, in large part, a polemic against the Marxist conception that ideologies were a "superstructural" adaptation to the economic "infrastructure." In contrast, Weber argued that the economic system of Western Europe, capitalism itself, was the unanticipated consequence of conformity with the Protestant Ethic.

Weber's valuation of the utilitarian traditions of middle-class culture was more hostile than was Durkheim's, while Durkheim's was in turn more critical than had been the sociologists' of the Positivist era. Both Weber and Durkheim agreed on the importance of moral values in producing profound, even if unintended, consequences: capitalism for the former, suicide for the latter. Both thus commonly stressed the importance of the *nonrational* in men. Yet there were important ways in which their views of moral values differed. For one, Durkheim stressed the inhibiting and restraining function of moral values; he saw them as limiting men's appetites and thus as preventing anomic insatiability. Weber, however, tended to accent the energizing, motivational significance of moral values; he saw them as stimuli to human striving. For Weber, values express and ignite passions rather than restrain appetites.

Durkheim also stressed the role of moral values, when shared, as a source of social and specifically "mechanical" solidarity; Weber saw men as led into conflict in the defense of their differing values. Durkheim thus regarded moral values as pattern-maintaining, socially equilibrating forces; Weber focused on the power of values to disrupt established boundaries, patterns, and equilibria. For Weber values were significant in lending meaning and purpose to individual life; they have a human significance. But for Durkheim their significance was primarily social: they contribute to the solidarity of society, and to the integration of individuals into society.

Underlying the different treatment of values by Durkheim and Weber was the difference in their critiques of utilitarian culture. Durkheim feared that it would unleash appetites, inflame men with an insatiable lust for material satisfactions and acquisitions. In effect, he saw industrialism as turbulence-generating, anarchy-inducing: in short, as undermining social order. Weber's concern was the very opposite. His essential fear was not of social disorder but of entropy, lifelessness, lack of arousal, lack of passionate involvement. Weber readily acknowledged the efficiency and productivity of modern bureaucratic society, but he feared that it entailed a routinization of life, in which men accommodate themselves to the social machinery and become lifeless, dependent grey cogs. It was not the threat to social order that Weber most feared, but the successful creation of a social order so powerful that it would be autonomous of men; he is, in short, concerned with the problem of human alienation in a utilitarian society. Durkheim, in contrast, regarded this same externality and autonomy of social structures as a normal and healthful condition, needed to constrain men.

Durkheim adopted the position of sublimated, revisionist utilitarianism, insisting on the *usefulness* of the division of labor. He emphasized that it was not only useful economically, as a way of increasing productivity, but also had another, more fundamental function or use, the production of social and specifically "organic" solidarity. Division of labor would do this not so much by enhancing men's individual satisfactions as by making them dependent upon one another and by encouraging in them a chastening sense of dependence on the social whole. It would restrain men. Under "normal" conditions the new utilitarian culture could potentially have a benign effect. But, added Durkheim, the modern organization of the division of labor was not yet normal; what was needed was a new morality that would restrain men's appetites, regulate and interconnect occupational specializations, and make men willingly accept differential roles and rewards. A shared morality that would accomplish this was necessary for the solidarity of modern societies, for only a moral force would be accepted willingly by men. In effect, then, Durkheim's treatment of morality, as well as of the division of labor, focused on its functional importance as necessary and useful for the maintenance of society and social order.

Morality, for Durkheim, is that which contributes to or is useful for social solidarity. Durkheim thus conceived of morality in a way that was congruent with the bourgeois sentiment for the useful. Far from simply being one of the higher refinements of culture, an elegant but useless luxury, morality was held to be essential to social existence. Like those who say that "nothing is more practical than a good theory," Durkheim was saying that nothing is more useful to society than morality. Thus, for all of his polemic against what he correctly regarded as Saint-Simon's utilitarianism, his own critique was itself limited by middle-class utilitarian sentiments of the most popular sort. Such a rationale for morality would have been anathema to Weber, who saw its essential justification in the *meaning* with which it endowed life rather than in its usefulness to society.

CONTINUITIES BETWEEN POSITIVISM AND FUNCTIONALISM

At bottom, Functionalism sought to show that social customs, relationships, and institutions persisted because, and only because, they had some social "function," which is to say, an ongoing usefulness, even if this was unrecognized by those who were involved in them. Functionalists implied that if social arrangements persisted, this could only be because they facilitated exchanges in which all parties involved were benefiting. Usually, however, Functionalists failed to consider what, from the Marxist perspective, is crucial: whether the measure of what is received bears any correspondence to what is given. In short, Functionalism dodged the problem of "exploitation," that is, of giving less than one receives, and instead simply asserted that social arrangements which survive must, in some degree and in some way, be contributing to the welfare of society. It was the job of the Functionalist, sociologist or anthropologist, to exercise his ingenuity to find out how this was being done. The implicit slogan of Functionalism was: Survival implies ongoing usefulness—search it out!

Functionalism thus served to defend existing social arrangements on *nontraditional* grounds, against the criticism that they were based on power or force. From the Functionalist perspective there was a tacit morality in things that justified their existence: the morality of usefulness. Functionalism also sought to show that even if given arrangements were not useful economically, they might still be useful in other, noneconomic ways; in short, they might be *socially* functional. Thus, they attempted to demonstrate that new economic arrangements, such as the intensified division of labor, were not advantageous simply for individual selfish gain, but also had a social usefulness, contributing to the very solidarity of society. Thus, from Positivism to Functionalism, sociology embodied the standard of social utilitarianism: usefulness to society.

This continuity from Positivism to Functionalism will be missed only if one fails to distinguish philosophical utilitarianism from popular, cultural utilitarianism. The latter does not refer only to behavior that is *intended* to be useful, and deliberately and rationally pursues courses of action that optimize desired outcomes; this is only one type of utilitarianism, which might be called "anticipatory" or rational utilitarianism. There is, however, another kind of popular middle-class utilitarianism: a "retroactive" utilitarianism that judged social arrangements in terms of their ongoing consequences, and was quite prepared to believe them legitimate whenever they were useful, without insisting that this utility be planned in advance. This is clearly evidenced by eighteenth-century political economy, which held that individual decisions on the market had advantageous, albeit unintended, consequences for society as a whole: that is, "private vices, public benefits." Popular utilitarianism, then, entailed a concern with judging actions in terms of their useful consequences, but it did not always require that these be anticipated prior to their occurrence.

In both anticipatory and retroactive utilitarianism, the standard of judgment was the useful. It was the sentiment for the useful, not the philosophical theory of utilitarianism, that was central to the bourgeois polemic against the traditionalism of the old regimes. Popular utilitarianism served to draw a line between the parasitical idlers of the old regime and the hard-working middle class, whose new political claims it served to legitimate.

THE PROBLEM OF ANTHROPOLOGY AND SOCIOLOGY IN ENGLAND

The considerations advanced above need to be related to certain peculiarities of English social science: Functionalism has been incorporated primarily in English anthropology rather than sociology; indeed, it is only rather recently that England has developed an academically institutionalized sociology as such. The absence of Functional Sociology, and the weak institutional development of sociology in general, may seem perplexing from a standpoint such as our own, which stresses the link between Functional Sociology and utilitarianism. For, one of the distinctive intellectual developments of the middle class in Britain was precisely its utilitarianism. Why, then, is there a Functional Anthropology in Britain, but not a Functional Sociology? This needs to be explained in a parsimonious manner, consistent with the presence of Functional Sociology elsewhere. That is, the explanation must account for the presence of a Functional Sociology in certain cases, as well as for its absence in others.

Perry Anderson's thoughts on this problem are valuable and relevant here. He suggests that the English middle class, being "traumatized by the French Revolution and fearful of the nascent working-class movement," accommodated itself to the English aristocracy.[11] Instead of wresting hegemony from the aristocracy, the British middle class fused with it to form a "composite" ruling class. British culture therefore remained under aristocratic influence, and middle-class utilitarianism thus never became the dominant *cultural* influence. "The hegemonic ideology of this society was a much more aristocratic combination of 'traditionalism' and 'empiricism,' intensely hierarchical in its emphasis, which accurately registered the history of the dominant agrarian class."[12]

In short, the English aristocracy fostered a culture that was dissonant with a utility-rooted justification for its own preeminent position. The English aristocracy's mandate has never rested primarily on its usefulness to society or to the other classes, or on the social functions it performs. (It took an American sociologist, E. A. Shils, to advance such a view of the English monarchy.) Like other aristocracies, the English did not believe that its social position was justified by hard work and diligent, specialized achievement, but by its gentlemanly cultivation and breeding, the inherited grace that endowed it with a confident sense of its own "natural" superiority. The aristocracy's eminence and prerogatives were held to derive from what history had made it, from what it *was,* and not merely from what it now *did* in society. A sociology that incorporated middle-class sentiments of utility and of legitimacy would subvert rather than sustain such an aristocracy, as was perfectly plain as early as Saint-Simon's parable of the sudden death of the French Court.

A Functional Sociology would be dissonant with the English aristocracy's traditional modes of legitimation. It would also be unattractive to the British middle class, or at least the upper middle class, which merged itself with this aristocracy; which married and bought itself into the aristocracy's style of life and thus accepted family lineage and "connections" as legitimate, and generally placed itself under the *cultural* hegemony of the aristocracy.

This fact bears upon the absence of a Functional Sociology in Great Britain, but it still does not clarify why there has been hardly any academically powerful sociology in Britain. Perry Anderson suggests that this is related to the absence of a powerful Marxist tradition in Britain:

> The political threat which had so largely influenced the birth of sociology [I would say, Classical Sociology] on the continent—the rise of socialism—did not materialize in England . . . the dominant class in Britain was thus never moved to produce a counter-totalizing thought by the danger of revolutionary socialism.[13]

To summarize this in terms of my own formulations above: Functional Sociology is a social theory consistent with the middle class's need for an ideological justification of its own social legitimacy and with its drive to maintain a social identity distinguishable from that of the established aristocracy, at least where such an aristocracy existed. A Functional Sociology, therefore, would not be congenial to a middle class—such as the British—that, fusing with the aristocracy under the latter's cultural hegemony, did not seek a distinctive ideological justification for its legitimacy, since it adopted the aristocracy's, and, far from wanting to maintain an independent social identity of its own, wished to merge with the aristocracy. Correspondingly, the English middle class's domestic influence and legitimacy were not, during the Classical period, threatened from below by a powerful revolutionary socialism or by a systematic Marxism that would stimulate it to formulate a systematic theoretical defense of itself and of its society.

FUNCTIONALISM IN ENGLISH ANTHROPOLOGY

The central role that Functionalism came to play in English anthropology was acceptable under these social conditions because anthropology's focal concern is not with *domestic* English society but with its colonies elsewhere. In this respect, English Functional

Anthropology remains in the tradition set by earlier English evolutionism:

Broadly speaking, it is true of all the evolutionary social theorists that they could recognize the social functions of irrational, absurd, and superstitious practices only provided that they were someone else's, or at least, if present in their own society, that they were merely transitory.[14]

English evolutionary anthropology had largely been an armchair assimilation from secondary sources provided by historians, travelers, and administrators, and it had lacked funds either for field research or for the support of the researcher. As Huxley wrote to A. C. Haddon in the 1880's, "I do not see any way by which a devotee of anthropology is to come at the bread—let alone the butter."[15]

Evolutionary anthropology had been shaped in the period of English dominance, during the consolidation of Empire. It had been created by a society for whom a large part of the world was their domain, their labor supply, and their protected market; it was, in short, made in the world of a confident and ascending middle class, with solid prospects. Functionalism, however, arose following World War I, which is to say, against the backdrop of a violent challenge to English dominion and Empire; it arose when English precedence was no longer taken for granted, when the English could no longer feel confident that their own society represented the culmination of an evolutionary process from which they might look down benignly upon "lower" peoples. Following World War I, the English future was felt as uncertain and was not to be savored in anticipation: doubtful prospects foreshortened future-oriented thinking. In this setting, the prospect was not the inevitable uplifting of backward colonies in their common evolution toward the future; the task was now to hold on to the colonies and to keep them under control. The sanguine expectation of progress gave way to the grim problem of order.

Moreover, if it was now not at all sure that the "absurd" practices of contemporary, domestic English society were transitory imperfections, to be gently erased by inexorable progress, how then could they be happily viewed? Functionalism replied that they really were not absurd at all but actually possessed a *hidden* usefulness and were, at bottom, functional. Functionalism, then, emerged in a Europe where there was a sense of the precariousness of society and a fear that any tampering with the status quo might have dangerously ramifying consequences. Thus, in one of his first papers, Malinowski argued that culture was an integrated whole

comprised of interdependent parts; touch any one of them, he suggested, and there is danger of a general collapse.[16] The emergence
of Functionalism, particularly in anthropology, thus corresponded
to the changing structure of sentiments that was becoming pervasive in Europe.

The two most important anthropologists to move toward a fully
Functional Anthropology were A. R. Radcliffe-Brown and Bronislaw Malinowski. Each of them was deeply influenced by Durkheim's work, although each in a different way. Radcliffe-Brown's
development of Functional Anthropology was very similar to
Durkheim's work, centering as it did on the problem of social order
in primitive societies. There is hardly any institution of primitive
society that Radcliffe-Brown did not view primarily in terms of its
usefulness for social solidarity, be it dancing or subsistence-getting.

For his part, however, Malinowski was engaged in a persistent
polemic against Durkheim, particularly because of Durkheim's
tendency to spiritualize and reify society. Malinowski sought to link
social institutions with species needs, which he saw as foci around
which institutions develop. It was precisely Malinowski's reductionistic tendency to find the roots of social institutions in the common
needs of individuals that was at first more congenial to the English,
because it resonated persisting traditions of English empiricism
and individualism; indeed, it was even consistent with Spencer's
version of evolutionism, which held that "every phenomenon ex-
hibited by an aggregation of men originates in some quality of man
himself."[17]

Individualistic though it was, however, there was also a strain of
Marxist influence in Malinowski's views; stripped of its reductionism, Malinowski's conception of the rooting of social institutions in
universal needs of the individual echoed Marx's concern about
"species" characteristics as foci of social development. There are
other places in which Malinowski's borrowing from Marx, characteristically unacknowledged, seems even plainer. For example,
Malinowski stressed that black magic is an instrument of social
control primarily available to people of power and wealth in primitive societies, and not uniformly accessible to all.

Malinowski insisted that the "oedipal complex" is not universal
and argued that the form it assumed in the Trobriand Islands,
where the child feels hostility against his uncle rather than his
father, was due to the *power* the uncle has over him and to the
constraining authority he exercises. Malinowski also polemicized
against Durkheim's view of the sources of social solidarity, arguing
that even in primitive societies this is due not to the awe in which
the group's "collective conscience" is regarded, but rather to the
practical patterns of reciprocity through which members of the

group *exchange gratifications*. Typically, when Malinowski sought to explain how primitive norms were actually activated and enforced, he noted that this was not an automatic process: the group as a whole did not recoil in collective hostility against those who had offended its moral beliefs, but rather the reaction was mediated by the vested interests of particular individuals who had personally and directly suffered as a result of the offender's behavior.

The difference between Malinowski with his undertow of Marxism and the more orthodox Durkheimian, Radcliffe-Brown, is epitomized in their differing approaches to magic. Malinowski noted that the people he had studied, the Trobrianders, tended to use more magic when they went on hazardous deep-sea fishing expeditions than when they fished the more protected lagoon waters. He concluded that magic functioned to reduce the greater anxieties induced by deep-sea fishing, and was less used in lagoon fishing because the situation there was more controllable. Malinowski held that magic generally served to reduce anxieties that were not technologically controllable, and thereby enabled men to carry out their duties. Radcliffe-Brown, in contrast, focused on magical practices surrounding childbirth and family behavior, and he concluded that magic did not *reduce* anxieties but actually heightened them, and thereby *solemnized* the activities with which they were associated. To Malinowski, then, magic functioned to allow men to go about their business and get their work done; to Radcliffe-Brown, in rather Durkheimian spirit, magic functioned to infuse certain activities with sentiments of solemnity, awe, and humility, ceremonially communicating the high pathos that the society bestowed upon the activity.

Both Malinowski and Radcliffe-Brown agreed, however, on an anti-evolutionary view. A practice, custom, or belief was to be interpreted in terms of its present and ongoing functions in the surrounding society. Nothing, in effect, was any longer to be seen as an "archaic survival," which is to say, nothing was to be understood as a relic that had once been but no longer was useful. The anthropologist was no longer to look to the past in order to understand the present. He was not to reconstruct dubious evolutionary stages in which he could locate and interpret things still presently observable, in order to account for their present condition. In short, they were dealing a death blow to the Positivist's theory of cultural lag.

Malinowski and Radcliffe-Brown are the bridge between Durkheim and modern Sociological Functionalism. Although contemporary Functionalists have sought to purify their discipline of "unnecessary assumptions," which they attribute to these anthropologists, we cannot overestimate their abiding influence. For one,

Anthropological Functionalism powerfully consolidated the anti-evolutionary and *comparativist* orientation that had begun to emerge in Durkheim. Later Sociological Functionalists were deeply influenced by the anthropologists' polemic against evolutionism, especially where it coincided with a similar vector in their own sociological tradition. Modern Sociological Functionalism of the fourth period emerged bereft of focalized historical interests, unconcerned with future-gazing, and embedded in a timeless present.

Having adopted the ahistorical standpoint of an Anthropological Functionalism that often had no choice, since it studied societies without a recorded history, Sociological Functionalism broke entirely with evolutionism, adopting this view even of literate societies for which there was an ample historical record. Influenced by social anthropology's reliance upon methods of first-hand field observation of ongoing social processes, Sociological Functionalists tended increasingly to confine themselves to what could be observed at first-hand. However, they were not able to accomplish what many anthropologists could: to study entire societies seen as a whole. It was possible for anthropologists to do this, despite their use only of first-hand, detailed observation, because the societies they studied were often no larger than several hundred people. But, committed to such methods and to avoiding historical depth, sociologists would find it increasingly difficult to study societies as a whole.

Anthropological Functionalists, furthermore, commonly investigated societies that had not yet developed a modern politics. Thus, in effect, as Durkheim had appeared to cleanse Functionalism of religion, so Anthropological Functionalists appeared to cleanse it of political relevance. Functionalism was not only becoming secularized, it was on the verge of becoming innocuous. Of course, one could not use primitive societies to study modern problems, such as the development of modern socialism, industrialism, or the class struggle. Yet there were other problems of contemporary relevance that anthropologists might have studied, had they been disposed to do so. These other problems they largely chose to ignore, including above all the problems of imperialism and of the conditions underlying native struggles for national independence. That they shied away from these problems was not due to the absence of opportunity. It was rather that this anthropology operated within the context of an imperialism and colonialism that were under increasing pressure.

Distinct from its intellectual intentions, then, the societal, subsidiary task of this anthropology was often to facilitate the administration of tribal people, whose ways were radically different from and troublesomely unfamiliar to English administrators. Functional

Anthropology thus lived something of a double life. If anthropologists played a role for English colonialism, they also often viewed themselves as the paternalistic protectors of indigenous tribal institutions and culture. Often they sought to defend native institutions from the moral indignation and the political expedience of English administrators. In this vein, for example, Malinowski defended black magic among the Trobrianders, viewing it as an indigenous instrument of social control which, as such, should not be attacked by English administrators out of moral zeal.

Anthropological Functionalism based itself on the study of dominated cultures, many of which were still far from national independence and industrialization, a goal which their colonial administrators did not want them to approach. The task of colonial administrators was not to facilitate change but to keep things stable and orderly. They wanted to do this with the smallest investment in state apparatus and the least cost of policing and administration. The colonies, after all, were not meant to be run at a loss. English administrators therefore wanted and welcomed a native social system that was orderly and self-maintaining, and Anthropological Functionalism, which was concerned with these problems, was relevant and congenial.

Yet while administrators and anthropologists commonly wanted these cultures to remain much as they had been, the administrators also wanted natives to pay taxes and to be available for labor. These, of course, were contradictory policies, for inevitably native contact with English values and technology brought change. Early Functional Anthropology usually paid little attention to the relations between the colonial power and the native society, and, when it did, it was commonly viewed as a form of "culture contact," seen from the perspective of its disorganizing impact on the native society. Anthropological Functionalism did not view native societies as being in the process of a lawful evolution, as, for example, the early Sociological Positivists had viewed nineteenth-century France. They did not take it for granted that these cultures were destined to be industrialized or independent. They often counseled tolerance of native institutions and sought to preserve them, sometimes from romantic and sometimes simply from humane motives.

Although Anthropological Functionalism was sometimes critical of English practices toward native institutions, this was marginal criticism, rarely objecting to European domination as such, but only seeking to make this domination better informed and more restrained. Correspondingly, it rarely adopted a critical attitude toward traditional native institutions, but rather more commonly defended them in romantic ways. Its basic posture toward both European and native societies was therefore essentially compatible with the maintenance of European dominance and with the inhibition of the political autonomy and industrialization of colonial areas. And this was compatible with the basic policies of colonialism. While some Functional Anthropologists conceived it as their societal task to educate colonial administrators, none thought it their duty to tutor native revolutionaries.

In approaching English anthropology, it is vital to understand the gentlemanly self-image of its practitioners and of its audience of administrators. As Duncan Macrae remarks, "The subject . . . has prestige. It is associated with colonial administration—traditionally a career for gentlemen . . ."[18] That Malinowski was the scion of a Polish aristocracy never impeded his career or barred his way in English society. Indeed, Malinowski's own views were often informed by assumptions congenial to the aristocracy: he viewed those who wished to outlaw war among native peoples in something of the manner in which the fox-hunting aristocracy views those who wish to put an end to their sport; he had an aristocrat's understanding of the practical value of religion for the maintenance of social order; and he had a Burkean feeling for the wisdom of tradition. "Destroy tradition," he warns, "and you will deprive the collective organism of its protective shell and give it over to the slow inevitable process of dying out."

Aristocratic assumptions were thus combined with a view of society as an organism bound together by the uses or functions that each part contributes to the others. In effect, Malinowski mobilized traditional bourgeois assumptions about utility to defend native society from criticism by this very middle-class *morality,* which he termed the "convention-bound, parochial, middle-class mind." There is, as it were, in Malinowski, a foreground sound and a background sound. Underneath his aristocrat's contempt for the parochialism of middle-class morality was an appreciation of the possible universality of middle-class utilitarianism. And underneath the anthropologist's explicit defense of native institutions was the aristocrat's tacit defense of aristocratic institutions.

Malinowski viewed native institutions from the standpoint of the aristocrat within the anthropologist, with a submerged sense of an affinity between the customs of the aristocracy and those of native societies: dinosaur called to dinosaur. This sensed affinity derived from the fact that both groups' customs were vulnerable to a popular criticism that could condemn each of them as archaic, outmoded, and useless. Thus Malinowski's view of one group's customs resonates his view of the other's; his defense of native customs is *seen* to have implication for the defense of aristocratic customs. Malinowski's emphasis on the functionality of *all* customs —his "universal Functionalism"—was a generalized statement of a narrower impulse, namely, to defend precisely those institutions that seemed devoid of utility to the middle class. It was, above all, a defense of that which the lower middle class regarded as *non-rational,* whether in distant colonies or in England itself. Indeed, Malinowski himself expressly drew the parallel between the "savage customs" of native peoples and "silly" English games, such as cricket, golf, football, and fox-hunting. These were not "wasting time," insisted Malinowski; indeed, an ethnological view would show that "to wipe out sport, or even to undermine its influence, would be a crime." Aristocratic custom, style of life, and leisure, no less than native institutions, now had a common theoretical defense. Behind English Anthropological Functionalism, then, was a hidden impulse to defend the aristocracy against a narrowly conceived bourgeois standard of utility, *in terms of a more broadly conceived standard of social utility.*

To have overtly and systematically defended the aristocracy's position in English society in terms of its ongoing usefulness would have been tactlessly at variance with the self-conceptions of both aristocrats and gentleman-scholars. In short, a Functional *Sociology* would have to join the issue in an overt way, on the level of public discussion. A Functional *Anthropology,* however, need never do this in any pointed and embarrassing way; but it could, and did, establish a tacit line of defense for the aristocracy in terms of the functional methodology it developed, if not in terms of the specific societies to which this methodology was applied.

The domestic implications of this functional ideology were not lost upon the peers who shared its universe of discourse. If English Anthropological Functionalism devoted its focal attention to searching out the hidden functionality of native institutions, there was also, within its subsidiary awareness, a ready sense of the manner in which this same defense might serve gentlemen at home. The utilitarianism on which this defense rested, however, was not the shopkeeper's concern for private gain. It was not a utilitarianism that was desirous, as Sir Henry Maine once put it, of "turning Her Majesty's government into what tradesmen call a 'concern.'" Nonetheless, it remained interested in all that was "useful" for preserving a way of life with arranged privilege. It was a sublimated social utilitarianism blended with a traditionalistic sensibility, concerned to receive and responsibly hand on Empire and to be useful in its governance.

Functionalism, then, was certainly not the ideology of an unreconstructed, highly individualistic, and highly competitive bourgeoisie; the social ideology of this class was "social Darwinism." Instead, Functionalism became the social theory of an upper middle class that did not stress overt individualistic competition because in England its aspirations were to gentility and to an alliance with the aristocracy. And elsewhere the middle class did not stress competition, for it was becoming involved in large-scale industrial organizations with growing requirements for cooperation and integration.

As the middle class becomes constrained to attend to the growing demands of the working class and of other social strata marginal to modern industrialism, it increasingly adopts the standpoint of a *social* rather than individual utilitarianism. It thus moves toward convergence with sociology's own earlier anticipations of social utilitarianism and of the Welfare State. Under these changing social conditions, sociology should receive more sustained support from the middle class, whose own assumptions and sentiments are becoming consistent with it. In short, sociology should come into its own under the Welfare State.

THE EXTRUSION OF RELIGION

One of the important and new characteristics of Academic Sociology in the Classical period was its secularization. In the first, or Positivistic period the characteristic sociologists had treated religion as an area requiring practical pronouncement. Both Saint-Simon and Comte had capped their intellectual careers by proposing and providing detailed plans for new religions of humanity. They regarded their religious plans as legitimate enterprises for students of society such as themselves, and as necessary to give practical implementation to their sociological studies. The "religion of humanity" was the *applied* sociology of Positivism.

By the third or Classical period of sociology, however, the religion of humanity disappeared as a distinct structure in the work of sociologists and was, in effect, replaced by the sociology of religion. The creating of new religions was succeeded by the study of established or historical religions, which were dealt with in terms and standards relevant to the scholarly role as such. Part of what was involved here was not only a change in the subjects now studied, but also a change in the nature of the scholarly role itself. Religion was examined not in the critical manner of the "pre-Marxians," Feuerbach and Strauss, but in the "dispassionate" spirit of the professional scholar.

This does not mean, however, that sociologists of the Classical period viewed religion as just one more social phenomenon, no more important to society than any other. Religion continued to be attributed a very special importance in the affairs of men, but this was now expressed in the formulations and assumptions of scholarly theory and research. The religious concerns of sociology became sublimated and secularized, but they did not disappear. This transition can be clearly seen in the differences between Comte's and Durkheim's treatment of religion.

In the course of his studies of religion, Durkheim developed a conception of the requirements of social order, which premised that society itself was the godhead and that social order depended on the creation and maintenance of a set of moral orientations that were essentially religious in character. In Durkheim, therefore, the religious impulse was no longer expressed, as it had been by Comte, in the formulation of a religion of humanity as a distinct and externalized structure. Durkheim had no religion of humanity as such. He sublimated and depersonalized the manifest religious craving of the Comtian, although he did not eliminate it.

Durkheim thus gave sociology a new, secularized public image. He presented it as a discipline primarily concerned with what is and what has been but not with what ought to be. A "value-free" conception of sociology emerged in Durkheim's work with greater sharpness. In some part this was stimulated by his effort to distinguish sociology from socialism. It was further strengthened by Durkheim's readiness to relinquish in *practice* the earlier, Comtian expectation that sociology could stipulate and legitimate values, even though Durkheim still maintained in *principle* that this would be possible at some future time.

SOCIOLOGY'S INTEGRATION INTO THE UNIVERSITY

This structural change in the sociologist's conception of his discipline and his role during the Classical period was related to sociology's new integration into the growing and renovated university system in Europe. Sociology in the Classical period was no longer the avocation of stigmatized social reformers but the vocation of prestigious academicians. Sociology became a standard full-time career for men who, working in state-sponsored universities, were commonly constrained to accommodate to the claims and sensibilities of theological faculties within the universities as well as to the expectations of state authorities outside of it.

The university itself was, during this period, becoming an agency for the integration of society on a national and secular basis. It contributed to the development of an image of national culture and to a defense of the nation-state as a culture. In this period, then, the growth of technical, intellectual autonomy developed simultaneously with strongly nationalistic identifications by academicians. Academic autonomy comes to be the freedom of each intellectual specialty to hold its own special intellectual standards within (and tacitly limited by) a larger loyalty to the essential institutions of the social order of the nation. Even as they were making claim to intellectual autonomy, the classical sociologists also were expressing strongly nationalistic sentiments, and in 1914 they enthusiastically supported their nations at war. However strong their claims to intellectual autonomy, the classical academic sociologists rarely manifested autonomy from the claims of the nation-state.

By the end of the nineteenth century, the political sphere's autonomy from religion was widely secure in Western Europe, and the states could thus assume a new *modus vivendi* with the established religions. This secularized autonomy of the state from religious institutions was, in some part, carried forward by the state's mobilization of the university as an independent font of culture and ideology: the university had been coopted by the state. The "autonomy" of the university thus, in part, grew out of the state's need for an ally in developing its autonomy from religious establishments. Paradoxically, the autonomy of the university was and is, in large part, an expression of the support given it and hence of its dependence on the state. Once having established its autonomy from religious establishments, the state wished to consolidate the loyalty of its religious constituency and so did not wish to act provocatively toward religious establishments.

As the university became linked with the state and infused with nationalistic sentiments, it began to be penetrated by the socialist movement of student radicals, on the one hand, and by socialists of "the chair," on the other. The new Academic Sociology, then, became constrained to relate to socialism and Marxism within a university structure that was tied to the state. Academic Sociology therefore launched a scholarly critique of socialism and Marxism, to come to grips with them in intellectual terms. Much of the focus of this discussion, evidenced by Durkheim's lectures on socialism, aimed at distinguishing and separating sociology from socialism. In short, sociology was acting to prevent itself from being "confused" with socialism by the public and the state.

There was thus a growing structural differentiation between Academic Sociology and socialism (as well as religion) in the Classical period, and this, as Irving M. Zeitlin's work elaborates,[19] has had enduring consequences for the scholarly efforts of the classical sociologists. This structural differentiation of sociology and socialism was radically different from their manifest fusion by the Saint-Simonians of the Positivist period. Moreover, in the Classical period, the *de facto* split between sociology and Marxism attained a new level of mutual and polemical self-awareness, with intellectual and character-defining consequences for Academic Sociology itself.

The earlier emergence of Marxism had produced a sociological synthesis that was strongly critical of established religions and established states and that had defined both of these as mechanisms for maintaining the existing class system. Academic Sociology, however, accommodated itself to the spiritual claims of established religions and to the expectation of loyalty by the nation-state, by renouncing all claims to itself assert ultimate values, whether religious or political. Sociology became "value free," presumably concerned only with what was rather than with what should be and thereby made itself less suspect both to established religions and to the state. Max Weber's explicit manifesto on behalf of a value-free conception of sociology expressly articulated what Durkheim had clearly but only implicitly moved toward. The emerging conception of Academic Sociology as a value-free discipline, along with a tendency to define sociology as an analytically distinct specialization, combined to encourage a politics of academic ecumenism. This promised, in effect, that sociology would tolerate the claims of other interests in and out of the university, in return for their toleration of sociology's now truncated ambitions. In short, Academic Sociology entrenched itself in the university by accommodating itself to the political and religious status quo.

It was out of this accommodation in the Classical period that the modern structure of Academic Sociology arose with its characteristic focus on the existential (that is, what is or had been) and its avoidance of overt, focalized treatment of the normative (that is, what men should do) along with its correspondingly delimited and specialized structure of emerging professional roles. The Positivists of the first period had divided the social world into two orders, the temporal and the spiritual, and had claimed authority in the latter. The Marxists had unmasked the social role of religion, and then chose to seek power directly, in the political sphere. It was left to sociology in the Classical period to renounce influence in both the spiritual and temporal orders. Its tacit slogan became: give unto both Caesar and the priest the things that are theirs.

Despite sociology's increasing integration into and acceptance by modern society in this period, classical sociologists nonetheless had a growing presentiment that there was something deeply wrong with modern industrial societies. It was a feeling shared by both Durkheim and Weber, from whose standpoints the dangerous pathologies were, respectively, anomie and bureaucratization. In France this pessimism was inhibited and repressed by that nation's traditionally more optimistic and rational culture. In Germany, however, there was a long tradition of pessimism; optimism was widely associated with intellectual superficiality and pessimism with intellectual seriousness: the optimist was rarely judged "deep." Nietzsche's "gay science" was no exception, of course; it allowed optimism only as the grimace of those who could endure the premise of an "eternal recurrence"; it was the desperate "optimism" of the dancer on the grave.

PERIOD IV: PARSONSIAN STRUCTURAL-FUNCTIONALISM

The fourth, the modern period in the intellectual synthesis of sociological thought emerged in the late 1930's in the United States. It gathered momentum in the midst of the greatest international economic crisis that capitalism has known. Sociological Positivism was the Academic Sociology that corresponded to pre-Marxian Utopian Socialism. Classical Sociology was the Academic Sociology that corresponded to and confronted the rise of Marxism, socialism, and their subsequent development of revisionism and reformism. Parsonian Structural-Functionalism corresponds to the period of the communist seizure of state power in Russia and to the subsequent intellectual stasis of Marxism that accompanied the rise of Stalinism. It is rooted in a time when Marxism has achieved state sponsorship and when socialism has come to power in a vast Eurasian land.

STRUCTURAL-FUNCTIONALISM AS A SYNTHESIS OF FRENCH FUNCTIONALISM AND GERMAN ROMANTICISM

Parsons' work began by syncretizing the "spiritual" component of German Romanticism, which focused on the inward orientation of the actor, with the French tradition of Functional theory; however, it was the Romantic component that Parsons first stressed by characterizing his earliest synthesis as "voluntarist." Parsons' theory thus contained two historically and culturally distinct attitudes that coexist in a tensionful relationship. There was French revisionist social utilitarianism, in which social arrangements are explained in terms of their imputed usefulness for or function in the larger group or society, which is seen as a "system" of interacting elements. Also there was the Romantic importance attributed to moral or value elements, where behavior is accounted for by efforts to conform with an internalized moral code and where, it is emphasized, men need pay no heed to consequences but seek to conform to the code for its own sake. Parsons' combination of Functionalism and voluntarism was a reflection, within the idiom of technical social theory, of the continuing conflict in bourgeois culture between utility and morality or "natural rights," and it was an effort to confront and resolve this cultural conflict on the theoretical level.

Parsons added a distinctively American emphasis to the tradition of German Romanticism. This Romanticism had stressed the "inward" significance of ideals that were seen as shaping the private life of the mind within which—in contrast to the public and political spheres—it was felt that true freedom resided. Since Parsons came to German Romanticism largely through Max Weber, who had stressed the *worldly* consequences of certain ideals, he was alerted to the role of ideas as stimulants to outward or public action, striving, and achievement. Parsons went beyond Weber, moving toward a still more Americanized version of Romanticism, by stressing the melioristic potential in the *successful* acting out of one's values. Parsons thus rejected the pessimism that had long tinged German Romanticism and whose gloom had deepened in the post-Bismarckian and post-Schopenhauerian period; he crystallized a more optimistic and more activistic formulation of sociological Romanticism. In short, Parsons Americanized German sociological Romanticism.

Following World War II there was a tendency in American sociology to return to a more *social* utilitarianism, both in Parsons' own work and in Functional theory more generally. Parsons' later work, especially *The Social System* (1951), placed a relatively great stress on the importance of the gratifying outcome of individual conformity with values, and on the contributions of diverse social structures or processes to the integration of social systems. His concern for the usefulness of certain social or cultural arrangements for system equilibrium became focal while his earlier stress on the energizing character of values became subsidiary.

About the same time, Robert K. Merton's version of Functionalism also manifested a tendency to restore social utilitarianism. Merton treated the subjective orientations of persons (the voluntaristic component) in a completely "secularized" manner; viewing them as just one among many analytic considerations and devoid of any special pathos, he explicitly took the functional consequences of various social patterns as his point of departure. This return to a revisionist social utilitarianism in postwar American sociology was then largely completed in George Homans' theory rooted in a mercantile metaphor of "exchange." Homans focused on the individual gratifications "exchange" provided, and he treated moral values as themselves emergents of ongoing exchanges. Here Romanticism received its *coup de grâce* from a Spencerian Positivism allied with Skinnerian Behaviorism and American "tough-mindedness." It is the most unabashedly individualistic utilitarianism in modern sociology. The wave of theorizing that had begun as a form of *anti*-utilitarianism in the United States during the late 1930's thus relapsed into social and even individualistic utilitarianism following World War II.

Still there is no doubt that so far as Parsons' own work is concerned, moral values are always viewed with a special pathos and are always attributed a special importance. He continues to stress moral values, although moving from a more Weberian view that emphasizes their role as energizers of action to a more Durkheimian view that emphasizes their role as sources of social order. Parsons never allows moral values to become just one other variable in the social equation. Paradoxically, however, neither does he ever mount a full-scale and systematic exploration of the nature and functioning of moral values. But this is not peculiar to him.

THE SOCIOLOGY OF MORALS: A STRUCTURAL LACUNA IN SOCIOLOGY

The internal structure of sociology may be usefully characterized in terms of what it does *not* do and in terms of what it excludes. In addition to sociology's systematic neglect of economic factors, there is another generally evident intellectual omission from the internal structure of academic sociological practice: this is the absence of a *sociology of morals or values*. Despite the fact that Academic Sociology, beginning with Sociological Positivism, had hailed the significance of shared moral values, despite the fact that Emile Durkheim had called for and promised to create such a sociology of morals, and despite the fact that a concern with moral values was central to Max Weber's sociology of religion as well as to Talcott Parsons' "voluntaristic" theory, there still remains no concentration of scholarship that might be called a "sociology of moral values" and would correspond in cumulative development to specialized areas, such as the study of social stratification, role analysis, political sociology, let alone to criminology or to family studies.

This omission is paradoxical because the concerns of Academic Sociology, seen as a patterned arrangement of scholarly energies and attention, have traditionally emphasized the importance of moral values both for the solidarity of societies and for the well-being of individuals. Structurally, then, Academic Sociology is characterized both by the importance it attributes to values *and* by its failure to develop—in its characteristic manner which transforms almost everything into a specialization—a distinctive sociology of moral values. This omission is, I believe, due largely to the fact that a full-scale analysis of moral values would tend to undermine their autonomy. Both sides of this paradoxical structure of sociology, however, constitute important problems that can be most fully understood in Talcott Parsons' social theory; I therefore propose to defer further discussion of it until I can address myself to Parsons' work in some detail.

STRUCTURAL-FUNCTIONALISM IN THE CONTEXT
OF THE GREAT DEPRESSION

The anti-utilitarianism of Parsons' prewar theory must be related to its historical context in the Great Depression, while its postwar drift back toward social utilitarianism must be seen in its own, different historical milieu. As I shall later show more fully, Parsons' early *anti*-utilitarian or "voluntaristic" theory was, in part, a response to the social conflicts and demoralization born of the Great Depression. Its stress on the importance of moral ideals was a call to hold fast to those traditional values that called for individual striving in the fact of crisis-induced instigation to change or reject them.

In the 1930's the economic system had broken down. It could no longer produce the massive daily gratifications that helped to hold middle-class society together and foster commitment to its values. If the society was to be held together and its cultural patterns maintained—as Parsons clearly wished—one was constrained to look for *non*economic sources of social integration. In the time-worn manner of the conservative, Parsons looked to individual moral commitment to cement society. Parsons' voluntaristic sociology did not consider the crisis soluble in terms of the New Deal's welfare efforts, so, in effect, it concerned itself with what was necessary to integrate the society *despite* mass deprivation. Parsons expected that morality might cement the society without changes in economic institutions and without redistributions of income and power that might threaten established privileges. In short, Parsons' theory was not congenial—and was, indeed, hostile—to the emerging Welfare State.

Then, of course, came the war. Unlike the period of the Great Depression the state could then act in the name of an all-embracing national unity. It could and did call upon sociologists to use their technical skills on behalf of the collectivity; many sociologists began to be employed by the federal bureaucracy. American sociologists acquired a firsthand and gratifying experience with the power, prestige, and resources of the state apparatus. From that time forward, their relationship with the state was a closer one.

During the war and after it, prosperity returned, at least for the middle class; American society was reknit by affluence and by war-induced solidarity. The working class and its unions became increasingly integrated into the society; the sense of an imminent threat to public order disappeared. Yet many retained a sense of the precariousness of the system that even the new affluence could not completely dissipate; the cleavages of the Great Depression had been repaired but not forgotten. Moreover, New Deal legislation had created new expectations and vested interests among middle-class professionals as well as among the working class, which had acquired a glimpse of what the state might do for them. The Welfare State was, in short, here to stay. Following the war it gradually became involved with problems of racial inequities.

With the return of affluence *and* a growing Welfare State, the maintenance of social order in postwar America no longer needed to rely so exclusively upon moral incentives. Furthermore, in the postwar affluence the more fluid "collective" behavior of the depression receded, and there was less of an intensive street life and on-the-road existence. Social life ebbed back into more clearly defined structures (buildings, offices, and factories) and into more traditional styles of politics: the daily rhythms of social life once again became routine. To see society in terms of firm, clearly defined structures, as Parsons' new theory did, was now not dissonant with the collective experience, the shared personal reality, of daily life. The new structural vision of Parsons' work, like a leaning tower built of concept piled on concept, corresponded to a period of social recoalescence that retained an abiding, though latent sense of the powerful potentialities of disorder. The Great Depression had glaringly revealed the possibilities of social catastrophe. But with success in war and the return of affluence, Parsons' confidence in the society seemed vindicated, and he mobilized himself for the Herculean labor of tidying up the residual social debris. Driven toward an all-inclusive comprehensiveness by an impulse to fill in all the empty spaces, he began to seek a conceptual place for everything in society and to put everything in some conceptualized place; it was search for intellectual order that manifests a certain frenetic character.

The second phase of Parsons' work parallels the accelerated consolidation of the Welfare State. In this period his emphasis is initially placed on society as a *social system* composed of interacting institutions and other components. In the first, prewar period his emphasis had been on the role of values, particularly on the energizing role of values: the voluntaristic dimension. Despite his involvement in Harvard's Paretian circle during the 1930's, Parsons' conception of society *qua* system had then only been sketched. It was in the postwar period, however, that it was first fully elaborated and seen as a self-maintaining, homeostatic system. Later on, and by the 1960's, this "system" focus gradually comes into conflict with emphases that call for political priorities which assign powerful initiatives to the state. Moreover, in his second period Parsons also elaborated the complex variety of specific mechanisms that contribute directly to the internal stability of a society, which goes well beyond the mere affirmation of the importance of shared values as a source of societal stability.

In the prewar period, then, Parsons had focused on moral values as inward stimuli to social action, as energizers of individual effort. In a way, this early period had focused on the importance of maintaining the sheer vitality of the system; it was above all a fight against the entropy of cultural patterns and against the waning of individual loyalty to them; the fundamental support for cultural patterns was seen to reside in the inward moral convictions of individuals.

In the second period, however, the security of the social system was now seen as more dependent upon its *own* special devices, upon the operation of various, autonomous mechanisms of system integration and accommodation, and less on the will, drive, or commitment of persons. Moving from a focus upon individuals, Parsons now was concerned with how the social system *as such* maintains its *own* coherence, fits individuals into its mechanisms and institutions, arranges and socializes them to provide what the system requires. Moral conviction and inwardness of commitment are now seen as system-derived and produced; the focus is no longer on what moral conviction produces but rather on how it is produced by the socializing mechanisms of the system. Thus the reliance on largely moral incentives as the mainspring of social solidarity is reduced in the postwar period, when there is renewed affluence and when, in consequence, other inducements to conformity and social solidarity have been refurbished. An emphasis on voluntaristic individual commitment is supplanted by a reliance on the "socialization" of individuals to produce the choices the system requires.

In the postwar period Parsons saw system-equilibrium as a derivative of system initiatives and processes, as resting essentially on the conformity that all give to the legitimate expectations of each other. This was a vision of societal solidarity that fit in with the Welfare State's practical interest in finding ways to produce loyalty and conformity and with its operating assumption that the stability of society is strengthened by conforming with the "legitimate" expectations of deprived social strata which, in turn, are then expected to have a willing conformity with conventional morality. The operating assumption is that deprived strata will be "grateful" for the aid they are given—rather than assuming, as Durkheim had, that men are inherently insatiable—and that they will therefore conform willingly to the expectations of the giver. In some respects, then, the postwar phase of Parsonsianism was rather consistent with the requirements and assumptions of a Welfare State. As I shall indicate later, however, there were important ways in which Parsonsianism remained a *pre*-Keynesian sociology, still moored in an earlier image of a social order held together by *spontaneous* processes, and thus by no means fully corresponded to the Welfare State's instrumental interest in social order or, for that matter, with its other disposition toward justice and equality.

THE GENERAL CRISIS OF MIDDLE-CLASS SOCIETY AND PARSONSIANISM

The Parsonsian synthesis grew out of the deep crisis in middle-class societies, which had historically been developing well before the Great Depression. This crisis was pervasive, general, and acute; it was economic and political; it was domestic and international. Prior to the Parsonsian synthesis, the crisis had unfolded itself in four major convulsions, each with world-wide ramification:

(1) World War I, which undermined the middle class's confidence in the inevitability of progress, destroyed old nation-states and created new ones throughout Europe, increased American influence in Europe, undermined mass confidence in the old elites, and set the stage for (2) the Soviet Revolution, which for a period, intensified the revolutionary potential in Western and Central Europe, acutely heightened anxieties among the Euro-American middle class, began to polarize international tensions around the United States and the Soviet Union, and, converging with growing nationalism in underdeveloped areas and particularly in Asia, undermined the colonial empires of the victorious Western powers; (3) the Rise of Fascism in Italy and especially of Nazism in Germany, which signaled that the European middle class's anxieties had become a panic that undermined social and political stability throughout the continent; (4) the international economic crisis of the 1930's, which, overlapping with the third wave, created mass unemployment among the working class, acute deprivation to small farmers, sharp status anxieties and economic threats to the middle

class, and finally accelerated the growth of the Welfare State in the United States. With the United States' involvement in the world economic crisis, the international stronghold of the world middle class had been breached.

Parsonsianism does not simply emerge at this specific time, but it emerges also in a specific place, Harvard University. Its emergence there tokened a regional and cultural shift in the center of gravity of Academic Sociology in the United States. Sociology now developed in, and was influenced by, the culture of the Eastern Seaboard rather than that of the American Midwest, in which it had previously developed at Chicago University. Eastern Seaboard culture tends to be somewhat less localistic, parochial, isolationist, and less "down to earth"; it is, correspondingly, more "intellectualistic," more national, and more international in its orientations. In particular, Eastern Seaboard culture has a greater sensitivity to happenings in Europe.

Parsonsianism, in fine, developed in an era when the anxieties of the middle class in different nations came to be shared; these anxieties were focused on a common international danger, the emergence of Communist power in the Soviet Union, as well as on a common international economic crisis, the Great Depression of the 1930's. If the Classical period of sociological synthesis reflected a set of parallel tensions that were viewed by the middle class in terms of national particularities, the Parsonsian era reflected a general, Euro-American crisis of the *inter*national middle class. It reflected the common concerns of relatively advanced or "developed" industrial societies whose elites defined their problem primarily in terms of their common need to maintain "social order."

Social theory could not be relevant to this world crisis if it were formulated solely in terms of (1) social problems in individual institutional sectors, each treated in isolation from the other, or in terms of (2) a monographic historiography that focused scholarship on the special traditions of different nations, their unique types of culture, or their varying levels of industrialization. If social theory was to be revelant to the common problems of such diverse societies, it had to take the problem of social order as central, and it had to be constructed in a relatively abstract manner. The empirical emptiness and abstractness of the Parsonsian analysis of social order reflected an effort to respond to the existence of an international crisis that simultaneously threatened the middle class in capitalist countries on different levels of industrialization and with different political traditions. Despite their many other differences, European societies could then be seen as facing a similar problem, the problem of order, and as having certain crucial likenesses rather than as differentiated national societies: they could more readily be seen, in short, as "cases" in an abstract "social system."

Any sociological synthesis that aimed at being relevant to any one of these societies also had to be applicable to the others. The thrust of sociological synthesis was thus pushed to the highest and most abstract level of generalization. The resultant paradox: the more the theoretical synthesis probed toward the true generality of the existing crisis and was capable of coping with international variety, the more *ir*relevant it seemed to the crisis as it was experienced in any of the nations involved. This was a central paradox of Parsonsianism.

This paradox has lead to a vast misunderstanding of Parsons' work, one which is particularly common in the interpretations of it by liberal sociologists. These critics frequently assert that Parsons' theory lacks concern for problems of contemporary relevance, meaning, I suppose, that it does not directly focus on social problems manifest in the everyday world: for example, poverty, race, war, economic development or underdevelopment. There is a sense in which this criticism is true; but there is a more important sense in which it misses the point. For, the insistence with which Parsons focused on the problem of "social order," most generally conceived, implied that he, rather than his liberal critics, had in fact glimpsed the true extent of the modern crisis; at least he saw it in its full depth, even though defining it from a singularly conservative perspective, as a problem of the maintenance of order.

Parsons' liberal critics reveal their own limitations when they fail to see that there *are* historical eras when the crisis of social order is general and manifest. The depression of the 1930's, which existed when Parsons was writing *The Structure of Social Action,* was such an era. It was a time of mass meetings, marches, demonstrations, shotgun auctions, protests, petitions, welfare demands, militant organizations, street corner meetings, and riots: it was a time of widespread collective unrest. From the conservative standpoint such a period is viewed as an acute threat to social order; from a radical standpoint, however, the time may be seen as one of revolutionary opportunity. The problem of social order, then, is the conservative's way of talking about the conditions when an established elite is unable to rule in traditional ways and when there is a crisis of the master institutions.

However conservative his formulation, Parsons was absolutely correct in insisting that the problem of social order in our time is not merely an academic problem but one of abiding and contemporary relevance. Parsons had seen more deeply into the precariousness of modern society than most of his critics. Unlike some of his critics who, as liberal technologues, view "problems of contemporary relevance" as capable of being resolved if only enough money and expertise are mobilized, Parsons' vision of the contemporary social condition saw that it embodied a more total and general problem that would not be so easily engineered away.

Parsons' shortcoming, therefore, was not that he failed to engage problems of contemporary relevance but that he continued to view them from the standpoint of an American optimism. Because he saw them from this optimistic standpoint, he one-sidedly emphasized the adaptability of the status quo, considering the ways in which it was open to change rather than the manner in which its own characteristics were inducing the disorder and resisting adaptation to it. But for all his optimism, Parsons—unlike his liberal critics—had glimpsed the true depth of the contemporary problem. His abiding optimism, however, led him to believe that the present institutions were viable, that the status quo had not been played out but still had time and resources commensurate to the crisis. Parsons' confidence in the status quo was also buoyed by his sense of the vulnerability of its critics and their alternatives: if things were bad here, they were not manifestly better elsewhere. Parsons' optimism led him to no facile solutions, and he never viewed the agony of his culture, in the manner of liberal technologues, as an occasion to vaunt a brittle technical expertise.

But there is a paradox here that must be faced: How was it that Parsons could remain an optimist, although he had seen so deeply into the contemporary crisis? It is not enough to invoke general American conditions and the prevalence of optimism in American culture. We must also examine the concrete manner in which history and culture intersect with individual biography. In short, we must come closer to the individuated way in which culture becomes embedded in personal reality and influences theory.

The vital statistic here is that Parsons was born in 1902. This means, first, that he did not experience World War I as an adult, being only twelve when it began and only fifteen when the United States entered it. Second, this means that Parsons was a mature man of twenty-seven when the stock market crash of 1929 heralded the coming of the Great Depression. Parsons had, in short, grown to manhood during the booming economic prosperity in the United States of the 1920's. His education had been completed (A.B., Amherst, and Ph.D., Heidelberg) two years before the economic crisis started. By 1929 Parsons had been married and on the faculty of Harvard for two years.

In other words: some of the most fundamental aspects of Parsons' personal reality had been shaped by the economic prosperity of the 1920's, during which time his own personal prospects and position coincided with the general success of the American economy. It was thus not simply that Parsons had witnessed the "success" of the American economy as an outsider, but that as an Instructor at Harvard and as the son of a college president he also participated in it. Much of Parsons' abiding optimism, I would suggest, is rooted in the fact that he viewed the Great Depression from a specific perspective: from the standpoint of a personal reality that had been formed by the experience of success. Parsons encountered the Great Depression as an adult who had already started a career at America's most prominent university. By 1929 Parsons was by no means professionally prominent; yet he was about as successful as a young academician born in Colorado Springs, Colorado, might expect to be.

Seen in the light of the prosperity of the 1920's, the Great Depression seemed to many like a bad dream, frightening but unreal, which in time would go away. With the advent of World War II, it did. For Parsons, then, the Great Depression was an interlude between the prosperity of the 1920's and the later American triumph in World War II and postwar affluence. Linked to the experiences of a powerful and successful middle class, Parsons' optimism was the optimism of those for whom success, of and in the system, was the fundamental personal reality and for whom its failure was an aberration not quite personally real.

INTERNATIONALIZATION OF ACADEMIC SOCIOLOGY

The great thinkers of the Classical period were not only politically but also culturally nationalist in experience and orientation; indeed, even their own social theories were often developed in ignorance of relevant work in other countries. The ignorance Weber and Durkheim had of each other's work is the most notable case in point. Parsons, however, began the assimilation of the hitherto nationally fragmented expressions of European social theory. This entailed a synthesis of Western European social theory within the framework of an American structure of sentiments, assumptions, and personal reality. Parsons did not simply reproduce or transplant European theory into American culture like an emigré; he profoundly destructured, assimilated, and resynthesized it in terms of the different American experience. His synthesis became viable in American academic life while remaining relevant to European culture. It could thus serve as a bridge between European and American intellectual life and as a major step in the internationalization of Academic Sociology.

There is little question but that the crisis of the 1930's intensified American academic interest in European social theory and brought it to the center of intellectual controversy. In particular, the crisis of the 1930's led some American academicians to look to European Academic Sociology as a defense against the Marxism that was recently penetrating American campuses, for Europeans had far longer experience with it. European social theory was thrown into the breach against the crisis-generated interest in Marxism. It was with such ideologically shaped expectations that a group of Harvard scholars, which centered on L. J. Henderson and included Parsons, George Homans, and Crane Brinton, formed a seminar on Vilfredo Pareto, which began to meet in the fall of 1932 and met regularly until 1934.[20] Also attending were R. K. Merton, Henry Murray, and Clyde Kluckhohn.

The political implications of the circle's interest in Pareto were expressed by George Homans, who candidly acknowledged—Mr. Homans never says anything except with forceful candor—that "as a Republican Bostonian who had not rejected his comparatively wealthy family, I felt during the thirties that I was under personal attack, above all from the Marxists. I was ready to believe Pareto because he provided me with a defense."[21] The *nature* of this defense may, in part, be glimpsed in Homans' 1936 article, "The Making of a Communist," where he argued that a "society is an organism and . . . like all organisms, if a threat be made to its mode of existence, a society will produce antibodies which tend to restore it to its original form."[22] Here, then, was their rationale for optimism and conservativism even in the midst of the great crisis.

The location of the Pareto circle in the political spectrum was clearly indicated by Crane Brinton, who remarked that "at Harvard in the thirties there was certainly, led by Henderson, what the Communists or fellow-travellers or even just mild American-style liberals in the University used to call 'the Pareto cult.' " Pareto himself was then called, as Brinton notes, "The Marx of the Bourgeoisie" when he was not, somewhat less grandly, simply termed a fascist. In short, the Pareto circle took a political position far over on the conservative right, placing itself in opposition not simply to Communists but also to "mild American-style liberals." The internationalization of American Academic Sociology thus began on a politically conservative, anti-Marxist basis. The Pareto circle was clearly searching for a theoretical defense against Marxism, and this aspect of their attraction to Pareto was by no means thrust back into the dimmer regions of subsidiary awareness.

Being a member neither of Harvard's Society of Fellows nor of Boston's exclusive Saturday Club—Henderson and Brinton belonged to both, Homans only to the Society—Parsons seems to have been not quite nuclear to the circle, although he was very close to Henderson. His own anti-Marxist position was therefore somewhat different from—less parochial and earlier than—that of the other members of the seminar. Indeed, Parsons had already been familiarized with the European critics of Marxism, particularly Max Weber, during his European studies, which were prior to the depression and to his membership in the Pareto circle. In short, Parsons had his theoretical ammunition in hand before the target came into view on the American scene.

Yet, despite the political and ideological motives that animated American interests in anti-Marxist European theorists, there were important ways in which the Americans' relation to this European tradition remained an external one. While Parsons and others were fully alert to the ideological significance of this European critique, they assimilated it from the standpoint of an American culture in which the socialist tradition and experience were, despite the current upsurge, still little known at first hand. The specific intellectual issues, the changing political conflicts and historical paradigms, on which the European response to socialism rested, were not really a part of the cultural and personal reality of American sociologists. The Marxism they knew was largely known as theory and not as a familiar political expression or embodiment.

Political and intellectual traditions in the United States had not fastened academic attention on the challenge of Marxism as compulsively as it had in Europe. The American theoretical response to the crisis was therefore not impelled to remain locked in a close confrontation with Marxism that would narrowly limit the terms of its rejoinder; and the Americans could use the full variety of the intellectual weapons that had been stored in the European armory. Parsons, therefore, never engaged himself as directly and deeply with Marxism as had the Europeans. He never really came to a conception of its full analytic complexity and, indeed, had committed himself to a view on Marxism before he had any sensitivity to its own internal development. There is little doubt that Parsons has always had a better acquaintance with Marx's critics than with Marx himself. In the 793 pages of his *Structure of Social Action*, Parsons makes not a single reference to the original writings of Marx or Engels, citing only secondary sources. Seeing Marxism primarily as an obsolescent intellectual system rather than as a living culture, as akin more to Hobbes, Locke, or Malthus than to Durkheim, Parsons took his approach to Marxism from the conclusions but not the experience of Weber, Durkheim, Pareto, and Sombart. For these scholars Marxism had been a living culture, and their struggle against it was embedded in their own personal reality. For Parsons, however, Marxism was primarily a cultural record, a thing of books that was never built deeply into his personal reality. Not bound to a tradition of detailed Marxist criticism, the Parsonsian synthesis could be formulated in more abstract terms. Parsons could start with the conclusions of the classical European critique of Marxism and, picking up where these had stopped, could move on to a more general theory rather than pursuing narrow, detailed, historical study in the European manner.

POSITIVISM AND PARSONS: FROM SCIENTISM TO PROFESSIONALISM

At the beginning of this chapter I briefly described the historical conditions surrounding the emergence of sociological Positivism, with a view to understanding certain of the social forces that helped shape it. The restoration context of Positivism may also help to provide some historical perspective on the social conditions that led Talcott Parsons—perhaps more than any other social theorist since Comte—to undertake the formulation of a comprehensive Grand Theory. An understanding of this may be illuminated by noting certain of the important similarities between the periods in which each worked. The most important of these, in my view, is that there was in each period a sharp conflict, a conflict that did not simply involve relatively limited questions about a few issues, but entailed a confrontation between two sharply different and comprehensive mappings of the social order as a whole. In the 1930's one mapping was the traditional free-enterprise image of the middle class in the United States and the other was that offered, first, by Marxism and, second, by the New Deal.

In the America of the 1930's, Marxism was a perspective attractive to only a minority, though it was generally an articulate and energetic minority of intellectuals whose views were clearly visible, within the universities and elsewhere. In this the middle-class map of society was challenged in a most comprehensive manner, and, even though American Marxists were not themselves politically powerful in the United States, they were often associated with a powerful political embodiment of Marxism, the Soviet Union. On a different level, however, the conventional middle-class map was also challenged by the extensive New Deal reforms. While these constituted a far less radical challenge than that presented by Marxism, they were frightening because they were politically powerful, a governmentally sponsored alternative. The extensive changes in welfare arrangements, employment practices, labor relations, and in industrial and banking organization that were proposed or enacted by the New Deal were often far more threatening to parts of the middle class than even the actual economic breakdown itself. In certain middle-class quarters hatred of "that man" Roosevelt sometimes attained paranoiac proportions, even though the point of New Deal reforms was to stabilize the established system in its essentials rather than overturn it. The abruptness of the acceleration toward a Welfare State had made some feel that "society as they knew it" was under radical attack.

Although Marxism and the New Deal represented very different alternatives to traditional social mappings, anxieties about each resonated and amplified anxieties about the other. Anxiety about communism led sectors of the middle class to view the New Deal as more radical than it was, while anxiety about the New Deal led them to view communism as more powerful than it was in the United States. As some viewed it, the New Deal was merely a disguise and opening wedge for international communism. Fused as the two sometimes seemed, traditional middle-class mappings of society thus often seemed to be under attack by an alternative that was both radical and powerful. Thus the real conflict between alternative social maps, which was in fact sharper than it had been in the United States since the Civil War, came to be seen in some quarters as even more acute than it was. The question of the basic character of the social order in its totality often became a matter of extensive public concern and of articulate and visible debate among many intellectuals. The stability and legitimacy of the traditional social order in the United States of the 1930's was no longer taken for granted in anything like the manner that it had previously been.

It is in this respect that there was important structural similarity between Restoration society and American society during the 1930's; in each case the situation was conducive to an effort to provide a comprehensive new mapping of the social order, to clarify its essential elements, to estimate its resources for progress and its prospects for recovery, and to define the sources and conditions of its legitimacy.

Faced with an international and domestic crisis of the most acute sort, for the solution of which their services were not at first sought by public authorities, Parsons and his students began their long march into the inner resources of theory. The crisis of the 1930's gave them few career inducements and little research funding that might have stimulated them to engage themselves with it directly and have diverted them from theory building. There were few opportunities for Parsons and his students to engage in "social engineering" as sociologists, even had they felt this feasible and desirable. As it was, however, Parsons' ideological and theoretical bent—conservative in politics and *laissez faire* in its Paretian implications—did not lead them to believe that such intervention was needed or desirable. Those of more liberal persuasion might and did engage themselves as professionals in governmental service; but, what *could* have been done by academic conservatives who rejected the New Deal, and how *could* they have formulated their work to enhance its practical relevance to the problems of the time?

In some part, then, the Parsonsian withdrawal into technical theory was an expression of the impotence of a conservative outlook during this American crisis. The technical involution of Parsonsian theory was contingent on the lack of external opportunity that might have attracted it to social engineering as well as on its own ideological character and commitments.

But the point here is not the specific ideological character of Parsonsianism, that is, its conservatism; the more important point is that the political impotence of *any* ideological position may become an inducement to compensatory theoretical effort. It is partly, but not simply, that men engaged in active politics usually have little time for extended theorizing. The other fundamental point is that self-involved and technically-engrossed theorizing is an activity that for some intellectuals, whatever their ideology, is *self*-sustaining when the time is out of joint for their political ideologies, be it too late or too early, and when they need to compensate for failure, defeat, or neglect. It is the politically defeated or the historically checkmated who write intensive, technically complex social theory. Such Grand Social Theory is thus, in part, a substitute for politics.

Plato, for example, makes this plain in his seventh Epistle, where he explicitly indicates that he turned to philosophy after his expectations of a political career were disappointed and when neither the oligarchy nor the democracy in Athens satisfied him. Again, the first period of the Positivist sociological synthesis is partly rooted, as I have indicated, in the work of a declassed nobility, the Counts DeBonald, de Maistre, and Saint-Simon, and in the efforts of a nascent technical intelligentsia which was literally disenfranchised. Again, as revealed in the letters he wrote to Saint-Simon in breaking off their relationship, Comte wanted to retreat to a "pure" sociology, feeling that practical men of affairs in his society did not have the wit to understand sociology nor the inclination to honor the sociologist. It is also notable that the most technically involved period of Karl Marx's own productivity largely followed the failure of the Revolution of 1848. And the failure of Max Weber's own political ambitions—culminating in but not limited by his inability to secure nomination for political office—is well known. In all four major periods of sociological development, then, extended and technically-engrossed social theorizing—and perhaps, particularly, systematic, "grand" theorizing—has taken one of its motivations from political frustration and powerlessness.

Sociological Positivism of the early nineteenth century had defined the modern society that was then emerging as "industrial"; they had seen it as the culminating stage in an historical evolution which would be perfected gradually. They believed, on the one hand, that there were archaic social arrangements centering on the elites of the old regime, that needed to be superseded and, on the other, that there were lacunae in the modern arrangements that needed to be filled in. They believed that the new society needed to be integrated or as they repeatedly put it, "organized," and that this required a new moral code appropriate to the emerging industrial, technological, and scientific institutions of the new order. Their central emphasis, however, was on the importance of *science:* partly as an instrument for enhancing productivity and thereby reducing dangerous mass discontent; partly as a method through which men could be persuaded to a consensus in beliefs that could integrate the new society; and partly as a commitment, which, unlike sheer wealth, could lend *legitimacy* to the new industrial institutions and the new men of property who controlled them. Science, for the Positivists, was to be the central source of modern social integration and of the legitimacy of its new elites.

The Parsonsian response to the crisis of the 1930's differed by reason of the different position of the American middle class, the difference in the threats with which it had to contend, and the differences in the bases of its legitimacy and, in particular, in the role of science as a base of legitimation. In the United States of the 1930's science and technology were, of course, deeply entrenched commonplaces of daily life. Yet, while deeply entrenched, they were not altogether unproblematic, for in consequence of the depression they had lost in public credit; in fact, some people then held that the depression itself was attributable to the overproduction caused by a too rapid technological development. Indeed, there was even talk of declaring a moratorium on scientific and technological development. In short, science was being seen as a source of trouble. The American middle class's association with science was therefore by no means sufficient to establish its legitimacy.

Moreover, the abrupt and devastating collapse of the American economy in the 1930's had sharply undermined the legitimacy of the reigning American elite; the gap visible between power and morality in public life was thus dangerously wide. And from Parsons' morality-sensitive perspective, it was precisely this impairment of the middle class's legitimacy that was one of the primary problems. He thus set out in the midst of the Great Depression to mend the rift between power and morality and to find new bases of legitimacy for the American elite.

It is in the conclusions of these efforts that one can see some of the important differences between Parsons and the Positivists. Parsons placed considerably less emphasis on science as a source for elite legitimation and social integration; instead he gave a new emphasis to "professionalism." In his 1938 paper on the professions, he noted that all of the elites of industrial society, businessmen no less than scientists, were now regarded as forming "professions." Indeed, modern society as a whole, he said, was distinguished by the importance of the professions, "which is, in any comparable degree of development, unique in history."[23] Here Parsons had found a way of characterizing modern society without defining it, as Marx had, as "capitalist" and, at the same time, without having to stress its bureaucratic character, as had Weber. It was a "professional society," orderly yet "spiritual"; it was neither bureaucratic nor capitalist.

There seems little question that Parsons' focus on the professions was stimulated by his polemical effort to refute the depression-intensified conception of modern society that had focused on its capitalist character. "If asked what were the most distinctive features [of Western civilization], relatively few social scientists would mention the professions at all. Probably the majority would unhesitatingly refer to the modern economic order, to 'capitalism,' 'free enterprise,' the 'business economy,' or however else it is denominated."[24] For Parsons the focus on the professions was an opportunity to diminish the significance then commonly attributed to the "capitalistic" or "profit-making" aspect of modern society.[25]

The emphasis in Parsons' analysis of the professions is on their similarity to business, on the elements common to both. Hitherto, says Parsons, the common view has had it that the businessman egoistically pursued his own self-interest while the professional altruistically served others. Not so, he says. Business and the professions do not pursue essentially different motives; the difference between them, says Parsons, is "one of the different situations in which the same commonly human motives operate . . . the acquisitiveness of modern business is institutional rather than motivational."[26] Both businessmen and professionals seek "success" and recognition of their success, even though the manner in which success is concretely defined and pursued may differ in each case. Thus professionals are not "altruistic" in the conventional sense, while businessmen are not "egoistic"; both are simply conforming to the standards deemed appropriate in their special areas of activity. Moreover, businessmen and professionals are also alike in their rationality, seeking the most efficient rather than traditional ways of carrying on work; the authority of both is also characterized by their functional specificity, each being an authority only in his own delimited areas; and both are universalistic, governing their decisions by certain general and impersonal rules. Parsons' emphasis, then, is on the characteristics *common* to the professions and business, thus diminishing the significance attributed to the self-interested pursuit of private gain. Parsons thereby envisions businessmen as professionals. To the charge that the professions have become commercialized, he counters by saying it is rather commerce that has become professionalized. Assimilated to the professions, business becomes credited with the moral responsibility traditionally imputed to the professions for collective welfare and thus is legitimated.

Seen as a profession, business comes to be defined as the moral exercise of competence on behalf of the public interest in "productivity." The shift from Positivism to Parsonsianism, then, entails a shift from science to professionalism as the source of elite legitimation; the rational and empirical components of science are not eliminated but are, rather, fused with a moral component, professionalization. There were thus at least two important ways in which Parsons sought to repair the modern split between power and morality and to mend the Positivistic rift between the spiritual and temporal orders; first, by a refocusing that moved the locus of legitimation from science to the professions and, second, as I have earlier emphasized in discussing Parsons' "voluntarism," by a stress on the autonomy and *causal potency* of moral values in determining social outcomes.

At the same time, Parsons also insisted that even the pre-professional captains of industry were not to be understood as having been primarily motivated by expedient or self-interested considerations, for they were always under the heavy influence of essentially moral values, particularly, of the Protestant Ethic or its later, more secularized versions. In short, businessmen were seen as motivated neither as American Populists had viewed them, by greed and venality, nor as the Marxists had, by the structural constraints of the capitalist system; businessmen and business were seen as motivated by moral orientations that were becoming increasingly institutionalized through professionalization. Such a defense of the legitimacy of business, one might add, was more likely to be persuasive to those whose personal reality derived from experience with the older, better-educated, New England business elites, than to those acquainted with the "hog-butchers" of the Midwest.

Another evident difference between Positivism and Parsonsianism is that the former was emphatically evolutionary in outlook, while the latter is nonevolutionary or only marginally evolutionary. That Parsons has lately produced an essay on "evolutionary universals" does no more than suggest that this is of some subsidiary concern to him. But evolutionism was crucial and not peripheral to the Positivists. This difference seems to be related to the fact that, unlike the Positivists, the middle class of Parsons' society was not threatened by an *old* elite which was identified with and drew attention to the past, and thus did not need to look forward to a future in which it would be rid of that incubus. The forces threatening the modern middle class are themselves very future-oriented and look forward to a radically different society. Parsonsian Functionalism, therefore, is grounded in a class experience that has no stimulus to focus upon the past and little desire that its future be radically different. Its impulses are fundamentally conservative: they want more, but more of the *same*. It is thus not seriously evolutionary but, rather, synchronic in its primary emphasis; its concern is with social order, that is, integration. This is particularly reflected in Parsons' later post-World-War-II phase, where he moves from his earlier stress on Weber's interests to those of Durkheim's. Speaking of an article by Kenneth Boulding, Parsons remarks that: "I, for one . . . would endorse what he [Boulding] refers to as a 'strong temptation' to identify sociology with concern about the integrative system."[27]

THE BEGINNING OF A NEW PERIOD: EMERGING TRENDS

MARXISM AND ACADEMIC SOCIOLOGY: SCHISM AND GROWING POLYCENTRISM

Seen from a world perspective, the schism between Academic Sociology and Marxism remains one of the central features of the historical structure of Western Sociology even into the present, the fourth period, which is now ending. Following the Bolshevik Revolution, the subsequent world development of Marxism has been preponderantly influenced by the national sponsorship it received from the Soviet Union. Following the institutionalization of Academic Sociology at the University of Chicago in the 1920's, and most especially after its American center of gravity moved to the Eastern Seaboard, the world development of Academic Sociology has been preponderantly influenced by the United States. The intellectual schism between Marxism and Academic Sociology was not confined to their different sources of support within any country but was paralleled on the level of an international polarity.

The split between Marxism and Academic Sociology has long

induced each to avoid or to excoriate the other in intramural discussions. Yet while there was little open dialogue, there was a limited or subterranean intercourse between them; e.g., Malinowski, Merton, and Bukharin. One might say that in the United States Marxism was part of the suppressed "underculture" of Academic Sociology, particularly for those who matured during the 1930's. Correspondingly, Academic Sociology had a similar position vis-à-vis Marxism in the Soviet Union.

In the latter part of the fourth period, especially following World War II and the demise of Stalinism, the public dialogue between the two traditions grew more open. "Concrete sociology" emerged as an academic discipline in the Soviet Union, while in the United States Marxism increasingly influenced the critique of Parsonsianism—there was the beginning of a more "dialectical" sociology. Both these wings of Western Sociology began to attend the same international conferences of sociologists.

The schism between Marxism and Academic Sociology still remained, however, a major global split during the Parsonsian period. In both the Soviet Union and the United States sociology was used as an instrument of state policy, both with respect to domestic problems and as an instrument for international leverage, influence, and prestige. The Soviet Union had long employed Marxism in this manner; the United States has done this increasingly since the growth of its Welfare State following World War II, and it also has used the social sciences to check the spread of political and intellectual movements friendly toward Marxism and communism. It has sent social scientists to Viet Nam; it has sought to study revolutionary movements in Latin America; it has sponsored the formation of social science organizations in Europe, such as the Italian Social Science Research Council; and it has influenced such international organizations as the OECD.

In consequence of this new American expansionism, the split between Marxism and Academic Sociology has become complicated by the emergence of a somewhat autonomous "Third Force"; that is, by self-conscious effort among some European sociologists to move toward a Pan-European sociology characterized by a rejection of compulsive anti-Marxism and the various American intellectual paradigms. Academic sociologists and Marxists in Europe have manifested an increasing readiness to exchange views: a few random examples are the summer school at Korçula, the *New Left Review*, Lucien Goldmann, Tom Burns.

By the 1960's the polarized structure of Western Sociology had thus become overlaid with, though not superseded by, a polycentricist structure. Polycentrism within Marxism itself was spurred by the drives toward autonomy of East Europeans, by Maoism and

Castroism, as well as by a more scholarly neo-Marxism. Polycentrism was also manifested within Academic Sociology in general and American sociology in particular, on both the institutional and the theoretical levels. On the one side, powerful new centers of study and training sprang up in the United States to challenge the traditional precedence of Chicago and Harvard Universities. On the other, George Homans, Erving Goffman, and Harold Garfinkel formulated theoretical or methodological positions that contrasted sharply and competed with the dominant Parsonsian formulations.

So the new structural characteristic of American Academic Sociology in the late 1960's is the declining centrality of Parsonsianism. We appear to be slowly entering an interregnum, in which the system erected by Parsons—since World War II the dominant theoretical synthesis—is undergoing a quiet eclipse. I shall, in a later chapter, elaborate on why I think this is happening and what it is bringing about. Here, however, I will simply outline the argument briefly and focus primarily on its structural implications.

PARSONSIANISM: IMPENDING ENTROPY

Parsons' system is undergoing a kind of entropy and is taking a declining place in the professional attention of academic sociologists; in consequence, there is no longer a single, organizing, intellectual center for the sociological community. Parsons' system was often a paradigm that gave coherence to the sociological community as much by the controversy it elicited as by the converts it won. Today, however, it is used less as a system than as an encyclopedia: parts of it are used here and there when sociologists remember that it discusses a problem on which they happen to be working; pieces of it are ingested in various areas of specialized work. This is happening, however, not because its opponents crushed it; indeed, in some respects it was never well enough organized to be dealt a crushing blow. It has been not so much exploded as picked apart and now is slowly expiring under the growing apathy of its audience. Parsons' own students grow less distinguishable from those of other schools. In the course of influencing American sociology, Parsons' own system loses its own intellectual distinctiveness and its boundaries become less distinct.

If this leaves a vacuum at the center, we may, however, suspect that it will not long be empty. For, in a way, Academic Sociology is a science of repeatedly new beginnings; which is to say, it has a strange tendency towards amnesia. In my own lifetime I have known three sociologists who have said or publicly announced that

with them, or at least with their students, sociology was at last
going to begin. However much one may deplore this lack of perspective, one can admire the dedication implicit in such an ingenuous view.

To call Academic Sociology a science of new beginnings is to
suggest that it had best be wary of its faddish proclivities. At the
same time, however, it is to call attention to certain of its strengths:
its relative openness to intellectual innovations and its readiness to
deficit-finance them. To call Academic Sociology a science of new
beginnings is to take note of both its sometimes genuine openness
to intellectual novelty and its amnesia about its own heritage.

Among the sources of the impending entropy of Parsons' system,
I shall only and briefly note two factors here: (1) the development
of a distinct culture of the young, and (2) the very rapid growth
of the Welfare State following World War II. A new structure of
sentiments is emerging among important sectors of the younger
generation, in particular among those who are students and thus
very close to the academic establishments within which Academic
Sociology was developed and is taught. This new structure of
sentiments may be summarily characterized as consisting of those
elements expressed in the New Left, on the one hand, and in
Psychedelic Culture, on the other. Both of these are, as I will later
elaborate, deeply dissonant with the sentiments and assumptions
embedded in the Parsonsian synthesis. It is not likely that the
devotees of Psychedelic Culture will find Parsonsianism congenial;
indeed, the mind boggles at the thought of a Parsonsian hippie.
Parsonsianism will be felt to be irrelevant by the young adherents
of the New Left no less than by the exponents of Psychedelic
Culture. But this does not inevitably preclude a "Left Parsonsianism," or a "Neo-Parsonsianism"—in short, a Parsonsianism "stood
upon its feet"—any more than the conventional Hegelianism of
the early nineteenth century precluded a Left Hegelianism or a
Neo-Hegelianism. One cannot preclude the possibility of a radical
(as distinct from a Welfare State) Parsonsianism, even if one
cannot really believe it.

The relationship of Parsonsianism to the Welfare State is a more
complex problem. Modern sociology emerged most fully when the
middle class was free of the threat from the past or where it never
regarded it as a threat. It is apparent that sociology becomes most
fully *institutionalized* under the sponsorship of a powerful middle
class that has freed itself of the hegemony of older elites. Still, if
an industrial society were totally secure, if it had no social problems
that needed to be understood and managed, it would merely appreciate but would not liberally endow a sociology. In almost all of
Western Europe, therefore, the emergence of the Welfare State and

of the problems to which it was a response has been the single most important stimulus for the rapid development of Academic Sociology as a social *institution*. It was the burgeoning of the Welfare State after World War II, with its massive financing and its emphasis on a broader *social* utilitarianism, that provided the most favorable context for the institutionalization of sociology; it is, indeed, slowly accomplishing this even in England.

The modern Welfare State and its accelerated support of Academic Sociology are the responses of a modern middle class which is both entrenched and threatened. No longer living under the shadow of Restorationism, it is a middle class that has great influence on the society and state apparatus. At the same time, this middle class is threatened by the development of international communism and by the collapse of its influence abroad. It is threatened also by growing internal crises at home, by the demands of dissident social strata, like the racially subjugated, the students, the welfare dependents. Modern Academic Sociology and the Welfare State are the interlocking responses of a middle class that does not fear the past but does not look forward to a fundamentally different future. They are responses that seek to reply to current tensions within the framework of the existent master institutions of middle-class society. They are the responses of a middle class wealthy enough to pay the costs of the Welfare State, however reluctantly, and which still believes that its own institutions are fundamentally sound. Being sound, they are not felt to need a radical reformation but only a kind of fine-tuning. Social problems are, then, thought to be soluble by modest inputs of centralized administration, along with expert services, research, and advice, and a modest amount of income redistribution. The problems, in short, are seen in terms of technological paradigms and are thought to be soluble in the manner of engineering tasks.

The needs of the new Welfare State, then, constitute both the growth opportunities and the limiting conditions that shape modern Academic Sociology as an institution; Academic Sociology flourishes in a period when Keynesian economics permit effective intervention with respect to the more traditional economic factors. Sociology is thus the $N + 1$ science of the Welfare State, providing it with an expert, university-based staff which addresses itself to the "other," the noneconomic social problems: racial conflict, deviant behavior, delinquency, crime, the social consequence of poverty. The distinctive focus of contemporary sociology—particularly of Functionalism based on social utilitarianism—is on society as a system of interacting variables, and especially upon the manner in which unanticipated social problems are produced by the complex interaction of these variables, particularly the noneconomic ones.

Sociology as the $N + 1$ science is peculiarly well-suited to the requirements of the Welfare State, which is itself the $N + 1$ State, serving as a kind of "holding corporation" for the diverse social problems that recurrently spin off from the normal operation of the society's master institutions.

While the second phase of Parsonsianism is more fully consonant with a Welfare State, there are, as I suggested earlier, other ways in which it is dissonant with it: most specifically, in its conception of the equilibrating process as largely spontaneous in character and as self-perpetuating. Not starting from a situation in which conformity had broken down, Parsonsian analysis never considered the mechanisms that may be mobilized deliberately, by the state and other institutions, to prime the social process when it has failed. The infrastructure of Parsonsianism remains pre-Keynesian, insofar as it conceives of the relations among institutions, or actors on the tacit model of a spontaneously equilibrated *laissez-faire* economy rather than of a state-managed welfare economy. It still remains deeply committed to the importance of the role of moral values as sources of social solidarity and sees these, in liberal perspective, as elements that should not be instrumentally manipulated by the state. Moreover, the Parsonsian model resonates only one conception of the Welfare State, as a gyroscopic engine of social order, but has little relationship with that conception which views the Welfare State as an agency of justice and equality.

Even the second phase of Parsonsianism, then, does not constitute a social theory that fully corresponds with a mature Welfare State. It has become increasingly refracted toward the requirements of the Welfare State, but it remains only a half-born sociology of the Welfare State; on some of its deeper levels it continues to correspond with the requisites of a "free market" society. Parsonsian theory is thus partly out of phase with a mature Welfare State, and it is considerably out of phase with emerging Psychedelic Culture. It is becoming, at least partially, irrelevant to the administrative needs at the society's management level, while, at the same time, it does not congenially resonate the new structure of sentiments emerging among potential recruits in younger groups. No longer instrumentally or expressively appropriate to the time, it withers as an intellectual paradigm, while theories advanced, say, by Erving Goffman, Harold Garfinkel, or George Homans provide a more recent, significantly different reflection of the period.

NOTES

1. Henri de Saint-Simon, *Social Organization, the Science of Man and Other Writings*, F. Markham, ed. (New York: Harper & Row, 1964), p. 9.
2. *Ibid.*, pp. 26–77.
3. George Brandes, *Main Currents in Nineteenth Century Literature* (New York: Macmillan, 1901), III, 79, 85.
4. Quoted in F. B. Artz, *Reaction and Revolution, 1814–1832* (New York: Harper and Bros., 1934), p. 49.
5. See *Madame de Staël on Politics, Literature and National Character*, Monroe Berger, ed. and trans. (New York: Doubleday, 1964). This includes a translation of her work on Germany and has an excellent introduction.
6. Werner Sombart, *Der Bourgeois* (Munich: 1913), p. 263.
7. Karl Marx, *Capital*, Eden and Cedar Paul, trans. (New York: Dutton, 1930), II, 670.
8. *Ibid.*
9. *Ibid.*
10. Saint-Simon, *Social Organization, the Science of Man and Other Writings*, p. 4.
11. Perry Anderson, *New Left Review* (July–August 1968), p. 12.
12. *Ibid.*, p. 12.
13. *Ibid.*, p. 14–15.
14. J. W. Burrow, *Evolution and Society* (Cambridge: Cambridge University Press, 1966), p. 226.
15. Quoted in *ibid.*, p. 86.
16. B. Malinowski, "Ethnology and Society," *Economica*, II, 208–219.
17. Burrow, *Evolution and Society*, p. 199.
18. Quoted in Anderson, *New Left Review*, p. 48.
19. Irving Zeitlin, *Ideology and the Development of Sociological Theory* (N.J.: Prentice-Hall, 1968).
20. See Barbara S. Heyl, "The Harvard 'Pareto Circle,'" *Journal of the History of Behavioral Sciences*, IV, No. 41 (October 1968), 316–334.
21. Personal letter, quoted in *ibid.*, p. 317.
22. George Homans review of J. Freeman's *An American Testament*, in *Saturday Review of Literature*, XV (October 31, 1936), 6.
23. T. Parsons, *Essays in Sociological Theory Pure and Applied* (Glencoe, Ill.: The Free Press, 1949), p. 185.
24. *Ibid.*, p. 186.
25. *Ibid.*, p. 185.
26. *Ibid.*, p. 187.
27. "My own inclination," Parsons adds, "is to refer above all to Durkheim (*The Division of Labor in Society*, especially) as the fountainhead of the primary fruitful trend." (*et al.*, I, No. 2 [Winter 1967], 6.)

PART II

The World of Talcott Parsons

5

The Early Parsons

We have been looking at the world through the wrong end of the telescope, so that the resultant miniaturization might provide a more comprehensive view both of the forest as a whole and of our own place in it. Having situated ourselves historically, the time has come to turn the telescope the other way around and seek a detailed view of one part of the forest, our part. The preceding outline, protracted as it might seem, was intended only as background for a close examination of the present period in sociology; it was merely a preface. What follows is a critique of the present. The focus will be primarily on contemporary Academic Sociology, indeed, on only a segment of this. In consequence, I shall have all too little to say in what follows about what is fully one-half of Western Sociology, that is, Marxism. When I do discuss it, space will allow me to do so only from a certain limited perspective, namely, its relationship, first, to Academic Sociology in the West and, subsequently, to "concrete sociology" in the Soviet Union. The focus, then, will be on a limited part of the contemporary state of Academic Sociology.

THE IMPORTANCE OF PARSONS

In my view, this means that we must now give concentrated attention to the theoretical work of Talcott Parsons. Some of Parsons' critics will object to the attention he receives here. Disagreeing with his work, they want to ignore it; they would prefer to center attention on those styles of sociology they prefer and believe more intellectually viable or more socially "relevant." But if it is the present we wish to understand, then it is above all with Talcott Parsons that we must be concerned.

Intellectually viable or not and socially "relevant" or not, it is Parsons who, more than any other contemporary social theorist, has influenced and captured the attention of academic sociologists, and not only in the United States but throughout the world. It is Parsons who has provided the focus of theoretical discussion for three decades now, for those opposing him no less than for his adherents.

Parsons' influence has exerted itself not only through his own prolific writings but also through his students, particularly Robert Merton, Kingsley Davis, Robin Williams, Wilbert Moore, as well as more recent students. They have been important because of their intellectual work, as well as their dominant roles as officers of the American Sociological Association and as editors of its journals. Moreover, the work of Parsons and his students is widely known and translated throughout the world of Academic Sociology; it is read in London, Cologne, Bologna, Paris, Moscow, Jerusalem, Tokyo, and Buenos Aires. More than any other modern academic sociologist of any nationality, Parsons is a world figure.

In the United States, where I believe Parsons' influence has reached its apogee, his work retains a considerable audience, and its standpoint still commands considerable respect. Thus, in the 1964 survey that Timothy Sprehe and I conducted among American sociologists, and to which some 3,400 replied, we asked these men to express their views on the following statement: "Functional analysis and theory still retain great value for contemporary sociology." Some eighty percent of the responding sociologists expressed agreement with it in varying degrees of intensity. We must thus center our discussion of the present state of Academic Sociology on Talcott Parsons' theory, if for no other reason than the sheer influence it has had throughout the world.

Yet it is not only the influence that justifies our close attention but also the intrinsic significance of Parsons' theory as theory. For, there is no other work by an academic sociologist today that is as relevant to the entire galaxy of important theoretical issues. To say that Parsons is intellectually relevant is not, of course, to say that he is right. Yet even where he is wrong, as I believe he is in fundamental respects, and even where he neglects certain problems, he constrains us to confront them. If he himself does not directly deal with every important theoretical problem, he brings us to its threshold. There is no other academic theorist today—certainly not Homans and not Goffman—who has half the world-influence or the ramifying theoretical relevance of Talcott Parsons. Though beginning to lose his dominance now, he was and still remains the intellectual anchor of academic sociological theory in the modern world.

Despite Parsons' great significance for technical theory-work, there remains the paradox that his work seems to be detached from the world around it. Of the various social theories Americans have formulated, that of Talcott Parsons appears to be the most unconcerned with the problems of its day. Cast on its high level of abstraction, it does not manifestly center on American society as such or even on industrial society more broadly. Indeed, for long stretches in its presentation it is devoid of almost any kind of data. It employs a terminology that obviously does not coincide with that of everyday usage. If ever a social theory seemed to grow only from purely technical considerations internal to social theory, as if born of an immaculate conception, it is the work of Talcott Parsons.

Yet, as I have shown, this is merely appearance. The reality of the situation, while by no means simple, is quite different. What is usually forgotten, or at least never remarked upon, is that this theory actually emerged in the United States during the Great Depression of the late 1930's. The historical juxtaposition of Parsons' detached, technically engrossed theory and this time of turbulent travail seems so sharply incongruous as to lend almost a *prima facie* plausibility to the assumption that the theory emerged independently of societal pressures. Such an appearance of social irrelevance, however, is totally deceptive. We must not mistake detachment for irrelevance.

UNIVERSITY STRUCTURE AND THEORETICAL DETACHMENT

In the preceding chapter I began to explore this *seeming* disparity between Parsons' self-involved theorizing and the public crisis of the 1930's primarily in terms of the larger societal and international context. In what follows I want to elaborate on this analysis of the social origins of certain characteristics of Parsons' theory. I will begin here by focusing on the *local* institutional setting within which it developed—specifically, the university setting—and then in Chapter 6 return to the macroscopic influences on the theory, as viewed from an historical perspective.

In some part, Parsons' theory must be understood as the product of the social organization characteristic of the intellectual life of this period and, in particular, of the central role of the university in that social organization. The theory was, more specifically, the product of a *relatively* insulated university system, whose own members were not as sensitizingly exposed as were the intellectuals operating independently of it, to the economic crisis of the 1930's. There was, then, a split between those intellectuals who were diffused through urban life and thus relatively vulnerable to the economic hazards and career insecurities of the period, and those academicians who lived a relatively insulated life because their intellectual standards and career interests were rather greatly protected by the *corporate* structure of the university.

Unattached urban intellectuals had nothing like the university traditions and organizational arrangements that protected the continuity of the academic scholars' *technical* interests. They also had nothing like the time-tested, community-enclosed solidarities that guarded the economic and career interests of those in established universities. Academicians, therefore, could continue to lead a comparatively corporate and traditional existence.

Several other specific social conditions that generated distance between American academicians and the crisis of the 1930's also deserve mention. For one, the structure of university financing, particularly in private universities, helped create a feeling of distance from social disruption, for it had the form of independent capital endowments that would continue to provide economic support. This, of course, implies a close tie between the *class* linkages of a university and its capacity to insulate itself from economic crises. This is so for at least two reasons: first, because the size of its independent capital endowment will be related to the extent to which its alumni and students come from, or move into, upper-class strata; second, because its operating costs are more securely provided when derived from tuition fees of students who can easily afford them. In short, the upper-class, private university can better maintain its corporate cohesion during an economic crisis; it will be less disunited by the differential economic security of its academicians on different levels of tenure and seniority.

A second social condition generally conducive to the *relative* insulation of American academicians from economic crises is to be found in certain ecological arrangements. Many American universities are situated in small "university towns" in which the likelihood of continuous and involuted social interaction among academicians—and of corresponding distance from "others"—is heightened, first, by their sheer physical propinquity to one another and, second, by the endemic town-gown tensions that commonly permeate such places. The existence of a common town "foe" often enhances the social solidarity of academicians. In university towns professional *and* personal interaction overlap to reinforce a sense of corporate identity among academicians.

In general, then, one might expect that the corporate and mutual protection of academicians, with a corresponding *relative* tendency toward insulation from economic strains, would be greater in well-endowed than in poorer, private universities. One might also expect some difference in the isolation from societal strains to be manifested by universities in university towns in contrast to those situated directly within great cities, for in the latter there is more intercourse between academicians and other intellectuals, less propinquity among academicians, and, correspondingly, less corporate cohesion among the academicians themselves.

These considerations bear upon the ability of a social science faculty protected by a corporate university structure to define and pursue problems in terms of a relatively autonomous *technical* tradition, rather than in terms more responsive to publicly salient concerns. They do not, however, directly clarify the reason and the manner in which these technically-engrossed concerns will be accepted by the students. Several factors generally relevant to this I shall here briefly mention and later expand upon: the prestige of the faculty and of the university; the career opportunities that the faculty can make available to the students; the extent to which the students themselves *value* such career opportunities and the degree to which they have and/or prefer alternatives to them. In appropriate combination, these three factors may serve as a powerful social control by a social science faculty over its students and thus facilitate its imposition of purely technical interests, despite the students' possible resistance to them and their greater openness to problems of "social relevance."

During the Great Depression, of course, job opportunities of all sorts were scarce. The implications of this for the faculty's control over the students largely depended upon the extent to which the specific faculty could provide jobs for them. The faculty that could not help the students had less control. The more a faculty could do, however, especially in this time of general unemployment, the more valuable the positions and prospects it could make available, the more control it exerted. Furthermore, the more prestigious the faculty and university, the more readily it could help its students start their own careers, and hence the more rather than less success in implanting its technical standards in students during a period of economic crisis. Conversely, in a time of general prosperity, or when the academic labor market is highly favorable to sellers, a social science faculty would have less influence in this respect.

One other element of special importance to Academic Sociology's social isolation, and its corresponding focus on technical concerns during the 1930's, is worth mentioning. This is the fact that this crisis was defined nationally as an *economic* failure and therefore required an economic solution which, in turn, required economists. Sociology, therefore, played hardly any role at all, and sociologists were rarely called upon to contribute to national policy. At that time, few national policy-makers had any clear conception of the kinds of skills that sociologists commanded and of the uses to which they might be put in the ongoing crisis. It was, therefore, not only the corporate and class character of the university, the ecology of university towns, and the state of the academic market that were related to the emergence of Parsons' detached, technically-involved sociology; there was also the fact that there was then no large-scale government market for sociology. There were few who would tempt the "young thing" from a life of virtue. Like the lady who had never been asked, sociologists could remain "pure."

PARSONS AT HARVARD

These generalities, however, need to be applied to the special case of Harvard University, for this was the specific institutional incubator from which Parsons' work emerged. We need briefly to take cognizance of the distinctive institutional character of Harvard, its special history, traditions, and ecological situation. Unlike Chicago or Columbia Universities, which are centered directly in metropolitan complexes and which are therefore more closely linked to the life of their cities, Harvard, of course, is in the university town of Cambridge. It lies at the periphery of Boston, from which it is separated both geographically and symbolically by the Charles River. While Cambridge is adjacent to Boston it is, nonetheless, somewhat psychologically and ecologically enclaved. This enhances Harvard's isolation from metropolitan influence and better enables it to reduce, though not eliminate, stimuli that might otherwise be academically distracting.

Harvard's capacity to maintain control over its own immediate environment is also enhanced by its national eminence and prestige. These enable it to strike a better bargain with local influences and to remain relatively less vulnerable to town pressures than do those less prestigious universities also situated in university towns. During the Great Depression, moreover, academicians—particularly those who were established and had tenure—did not suffer as acutely as did other sectors of the population, whose styles of life were often abruptly devastated. Indeed, tenured faculty were sometimes relatively advantaged. Senior professors with modest savings accounts might, in fact, make a killing on plummeting real estate values, and some were able to buy homes that they could not have previously afforded. The setting of an upper-class university in a university town, then, provided a relatively sheltering environment, to some extent filtering out the crisis in the larger society and permitting a somewhat greater detachment toward it.

In addition, Harvard also has what Robin Williams once aptly termed an "Olympus Complex." It has a rich awareness of its own special traditions and unique history which, in fact, begin before the Congress of the United States. It has a confident sense of its own intellectual excellence, from which it may look down without fluctuating response on every episode in the social upheaval.

There are various ways in which the sheer novelty and the ambitious scope of Parsons' enterprise were deeply dependent upon the aura of Harvard. In accounting for Parsons' novelty, it is important to remember the newness of Harvard's Department of Sociology in the early 1930's. Indeed, the Department itself was founded directly after the crash of 1929; P. A. Sorokin arrived to head it in the summer of 1930, and the Department was officially launched in September of 1931. While intellectual novelty is nominally prized in all scholarly communities, in long-established departments it is often restricted by recruiting practices that prefer men acceptable to the governing professors and is limited by the traditions they have developed. Lacking such limiting traditions and still needing to establish its reputation in the larger intellectual community, a new department may be relatively open to intellectual innovation.

Again, the sheer ambitiousness of any intellectual effort will find congenial support in Harvard's "Olympus Complex" and in the high expectations that it directs towards its faculty. Yet it is not simply that Harvard expects its professors to be outstanding and that, therefore, they strive to be, nor only that it is able to recruit outstanding men with high ambitions. There is something more, of considerable relevance to theorizing, particularly to theorizing which is original in character and ambitious in scope. Theorizing that is novel and ambitious is a risk-taking enterprise that cannot be successfully pursued by those with diminished selves. It requires not only ambition but an appreciable degree of self-confidence to believe that one can produce theory comparable to that created by the great minds that have come before. It requires, in short, a measure of "theoretical conceit." There are many personal sources for such theoretical conceit, but there are institutional and social sources for it as well; to have been selected as a faculty member at a great university is, I believe, one of these. Appointment to its staff is itself easily taken to be validation of unusual individual promise, if not of greatness; the self thus powerfully validated may dare where others only dream. It may be partially for this reason— that is, because Harvard is an institutional incubator of "theoretical conceit"—that so many of the men who have produced important social theory in the present period have done it at Harvard.

Well-endowed, recruiting most of its undergraduates from an elite who had relatively little difficulty in paying the tuition, surrounded and permeated by an aura of money and Family, having regular intercourse with men of power and influence, Harvard is a part of the American Establishment and a training and recruiting ground for its elite. It is a relatively protected milieu, better able than most to maintain the continuity of technical academic traditions, more effectively impose them on local academic interests, more successfully resist the politicalization of graduate students of sociology, and more easily control the press and mute the clamor of current social tensions.

Let me stress, however, that it would be totally erroneous to assume that these young men or their faculty were unaware of or insensitive to the current economic crisis, or that it did not impinge upon their careers in personal ways. There were many among the faculty who closely followed the course of the developing New Deal and the growing world crisis, and who indeed addressed themselves to the problems generated by the politics of social reform— among them C. Zimmerman, J. Ford, N. Timasheff (who gave a comparative course on Fascism, Nazism, and Communism) and E. Hartshorne (who was particularly interested in Nazism). Moreover, some of the students came from poor or modest backgrounds, from urban slums or small Southern farms; and many were aided by government funds supplied by the National Youth Administration and the Works Project Administration, much of which were administered through Zimmerman.

At the same time, however, the central figure was P. A. Sorokin, the Department's first Professor of Sociology, a man of established international reputation even before his arrival at Harvard, and whose reputation doubtless attracted many who came as graduate students. It is certain that Sorokin exerted considerable influence even upon those who found themselves increasingly drawn to the theory being developed by the young Parsons, and that Sorokin did much to center students' attention upon technically complex theory and, indeed, to define it as intellectually pivotal. My central point, then, is not that the Depression failed to penetrate Harvard's Sociology Department but to explain how, despite the manifest attraction of current political and economic problems, a detached and technical, self-engrossed theory was, nonetheless, able to develop momentum.

The very expectations with which some of the graduate students came to Harvard rendered them vulnerable to the detached objectivity that the university sought to inculcate. If some could never expect to be true "Harvard men," since they had done their undergraduate work elsewhere, they could, nonetheless, expect to carry away with them some of the special, advantaged aura of Harvard. A Harvard degree does not merely imply special educational and intellectual opportunities, if it implies that at all, but it certainly means advantaged social and career opportunities. Even some of the poorest young men who then came to study sociology at Harvard were careful to take tennis rackets with them. To those of modest origins the sheer fact of being at Harvard meant that they had already come up in the world. Being at Harvard also implied future social and career opportunities not likely to be totally unimportant even to the most intellectually dedicated among them. Unlike the College of the City of New York (CCNY), for example, Harvard still had rewards and promises that it could use, even without vulgar brandishing, to control and induce restraint among its young men. If there were academic posts to be had, Harvard men had a better chance than most of getting them.

The graduate students who then gathered at Harvard were intelligent and socially-sensitive young men, often of plain if not humble origins. The structure of their sentiments was influenced by the tense disparity between the reality of their personal success and the society's failure. What was happening to them was very different from what was happening to their social world. The society's malaise could not be viewed as a superficial aberration, but it was still a society within which they had excellent prospects. They were thus inclined neither to accept the society as it was nor to rebel against it, they could instead develop a posture of detachment. The ideal aloofness of Parsons' theory made it possible for those who accepted it to look beyond the suffering that the social crisis was creating and to foster a sense of protective remoteness from the society that was engendering it. It insulated them from feeling that they must at once do something to alleviate the suffering or else be allied with the forces that were creating it. They need feel neither responsible for what was happening nor guilty that they did not seek to remedy it: they could, in short, be "objective."

Yet their sense of the new depth of the American crisis made them aware that the conventional diagnoses would no longer suffice. They saw that what was then happening in the United States was not an isolated event but something that was happening to their social world as a whole. They sensed that a new and deeper intellectual approach, with which they themselves associated, would in time be needed. They felt, in sum, a structure of sentiments that was receptive to a new theory in which the society as a whole could be seen at some remove.

Parsons gave his students the hope that something like this was in the offing at Harvard; something that went far deeper than the focus on isolated social problems that had previously prevailed in American sociology; something whose sheer complexity could be felt to be commensurate with the profundity of the crisis they were witnessing; but something which, at the same time, would allow for as well as further their own still buoyant personal aspirations. Parsons' young students could thus respond to the social crisis with the feeling that the most valuable social contribution they could make would be by sticking to their own last and developing a new sociology (and themselves as sociologists) so that, in time, they could provide the scientific help society required. The new theory was not yet ready, while the old ones were manifestly inadequate. Confident in their own growing intellectual skills and hopeful about their own personal prospects, they could wait.

This was also a time, of course, when many young intellectuals throughout the United States were developing an interest in theoretical or ideological systems and, in particular, when some were being drawn to Marxism. Many of Parsons' students found in their teacher's work a theory equally complex, with implications for art, politics, and religion, no less than for economic institutions. Like Marxism, it aimed at understanding society as a total system in terms of the interrelation of its institutions. Parsons' was a world view that promised to compete with Marxism on all analytical levels. For all its technical involution, then, Parsons' theory enabled its young adherents to establish an *ideological* identity of their own, which gave them distance not only from the society-in-crisis but also from its most salient critics. Now they did not need to be either low-brow adherents of the traditional map of the American social order or iconoclastic adherents of the most salient counter-map: they need be neither Philistines nor revolutionaries.

An understanding of the full cultural significance of Parsons' work must see it as in some part an American response to

Marxism. It was an American alternative to Marxism, which through both its intellectual adventuresomeness and its seriousness attracted and held the interest of many young intellectuals who were under pressure to respond to Marxism. It gave them a perspective on the crisis of their society that enabled them to be detached from the society without being opposed to it or allied with its opponents.

In contrast to the system that Parsons was creating at Harvard, Marxism was something that students read about in the library and that was then deadened by Stalinism and not developing. Some of Parsons' students had long since read the key Marxist works and were growing increasingly aware of Marxism's intellectual difficulties from the lectures that N. Timasheff and P. A. Sorokin were at that time giving at Harvard.

Unlike both Marxism and Sorokin's work, however, Parsons' theory then did not present a seemingly completed intellectual system. It required and allowed serious theoretical development. It did not confine ambitious young men to the "dirty work" of dogmatic exegetics or limited research applications. It was, rather, an intellectual system whose manifest incompleteness was experienced as an opportunity-making "openness"; students could buy into it at relatively little cost. It is, in part, precisely because of its "shortcomings" that the ideas of a younger instructor are often more attractive than those of an older and better established professor. For the older man is in a position to make more costly demands on students, and his more polished product seems to leave little work for younger minds. The young man requires allies to protect his emerging theory in its formative period; the older theorist with the finished system has a doctrine to which he seeks conformity: he seeks disciples rather than students. And besides, lacking an impressive bibliography to further their careers, young faculty members are constrained to listen to and seek alliances with students.

Parsons' theory emerged in a period when the previous American tradition of the study of isolated social problems was manifestly incompetent to deal with social strains that obviously ramified through all institutions and social strata, and when the only other established large-scale social theory well known to many intellectuals was a Marxism that was being stultified by Stalinism. It was also a time when many other European theoretical traditions— which had never recovered from the devastations of World War I— seemed to have spent their creative impulse and were floundering. For all his profound immersal in European social theory, the fact that Parsons was an American was not inconsequential for the synthesis he wrought. He could treat French, Italian, and German theorists with little evidence of nationalistic parochialism or of a world-weary pessimism.

Parsons endowed his students with a social theory that had ramifying philosophical roots and promising empirical possibilities. It was a theoretical system which, if not because of its rigor then at least because of its complexity, was something to be reckoned with. It could thus enable its adherents to hold their own in the competitive give-and-take of an academic world that was then still quite suspicious, if not contemptuous, of sociology's intellectual credentials.

Curiously, then, the crystallization of what was to become the new, technical American sociology, and which until World War II resisted immediate social engineering, progressed by capturing conventional loyalties that had been dislodged by a deep social crisis. The full irony of this development lies in the fact that the earlier phase of American sociology, with its more openly practical bent, had been the expression of a more stable society. It had been made by men with greater conviction about their society's inherent soundness and rightness. The emerging Parsonsian phase, with its greater detachment, was made by young men involved in far greater social upheavals and who were much less confident of their society's basic stability.

THE DEBATE ABOUT CAPITALISM

A genetic view of Parsons' work must begin by noting his early and intensive studies of the theories of Werner Sombart and Max Weber, as these had focused on the emergence of modern capitalism. At the very beginning of his work, Parsons manifested the most intense interest in the nature of capitalism, its antecedents, character, and prospects, as well as in theories about capitalism. Parsons' doctoral dissertation at Heidelberg—to which he went after studying under Malinowski at the London School of Economics—was addressed to these problems and, as might be expected, his earliest publications dealt with them. Some time after these, his next publications include a translation of Max Weber's *The Protestant Ethic and the Spirit of Capitalism*.

It deserves notice, even in these brief remarks, that Weber's *Protestant Ethic* was fully compatible with the Durkheimian tendency to transform evolutionism into comparative studies. Weber's central focus was on the origins of modern society. It was an historical analysis in a comparative framework, not an evolutionary analysis. Its concern was with the conditions that had led to the emergence of modern society, and not with a whole *series* of types of societies, in which the modern was seen as but the latest. In the main, Weber emphasized that the spirit of capitalism had been shaped by the Protestant ethic, and he stressed that the hallmark of modern society and its economy is not its venal, profit-pursuing but, rather, its rational mode of production and its rational, essentially bureaucratic mode of social organization. This emphasis made an enduring impression on Parsons' conception of the nature of modern capitalism.

Whatever else may be said about this early work of Parsons, it scarcely can be said to have been of only academic relevance. While the relevance of much of his later work for problems of contemporary significance is not always easily discernible, here, in his earliest work, Parsons was manifestly interested in larger social issues. In the world of the twentieth century, following the successful Bolshevik Revolution in Russia, the defeated revolutions in Germany and Hungary, as well as the downhill flow of revolutionary movements into the Orient, it was quite clear that capitalist societies were being confronted by a vigorous, world-wide opponent that was Marxist in avowal and derivation. This opponent clearly intended to exploit capitalism's vulnerabilities and to hasten its demise, which (it asserted) was in any event "inevitable": it intended to be the historical heir of capitalism.

One common element in the work of both Weber and Sombart had been their polemical yet respectful posture toward the Marxist interpretation of capitalism. In 1928 and 1937 Parsons noted that Marxian theory had formed the focus for the discussion of capitalism in Germany.[1] Indeed, opposition to Marxism was a common quality not only of Sombart and Weber but also of the other social theorists—namely, Pareto and Durkheim—on whom Parsons focused in his 1937 synthesis, *The Structure of Social Action*. A critique of Marxism was not simply a peripheral or incidental by-product of the work of all these men but was, commonly, one of their animating impulses. Sombart, Durkheim, and Pareto had all produced full-scale studies of socialism that were deeply polemical. In Weber's case, his *Protestant Ethic* was directed against the Marxian hypothesis that Protestantism was the result of the emergence of capitalism; more generally, Weber opposed the Marxist conception that values and ideas are "superstructural" elements that depend, in the last analysis, upon prior changes in the economic foundation; Weber, rather, sought to demonstrate that the development of modern European capitalism was itself contingent upon the Protestant ethic.

Parsons distinguished two periods in Weber's theoretical outlook: an earlier phase, prior to his nervous breakdown, which had "a rather definite materialistic bias," and a later phase characterized by "a new anti-Marxian interpretation" of modern capitalism.[2] It is often said, as Parsons does, that Weber was not denying the importance of material factors but merely attempting to correct Marx's *over*emphasis on them.[3] This is specious. It is akin to saying that the enemies of Darwinian evolutionism were not denying that man arose out of lower animal species but were merely correcting Darwin's overemphasis on this! What Weber did was to treat "material" factors simply as one in a set of interacting factors; whereas, despite his emphatic *system* focus, Marx had affirmed the special importance and *ultimate primacy* of material factors. Thus Weber was not merely reducing the "weighting" to be assigned to material factors but was polemicizing against the distinctive *structure* of Marx's explanatory model.

Parsons found himself in a strange situation when beginning to deal with Sombart and Weber. While agreeing with the intent of their anti-Marxist critique, he could not accept their conclusions, since both were deeply critical of capitalism as well. Indeed, Parsons felt that Sombart and Weber were even more deeply pessimistic about industrialism than Marx himself. While Parsons concurred in their anti-Marxism, he was much perturbed by their pessimism and their anticapitalism. In short, one of the important things that stimulated Parsons' own creative effort was *the conflict between his own structure of sentiments and those of Sombart and Weber.*

Both Sombart and Weber had emphasized that capitalism was fostered by certain ideological factors, the capitalist *Geist* or Spirit in Sombart's case and the Protestant ethic in Weber's. Both had stressed that capitalism entailed a distinctive type of morality that transcended individual venality. Sombart, like Weber, had stressed the rational element in the capitalist spirit, particularly in its later phases, although he had also attended to its competitiveness and acquisitiveness. This stress on the rationality of capitalism tended to diminish the Marxist emphasis on the historical uniqueness of socialism; the latter was now viewed simply as a development continuous with capitalism, moving in the same rational direction. Rationality was seen as expressed organizationally in the bureaucratic character of the capitalist enterprise, which was thus, in this respect, viewed as not basically different from the socialist form. Variations in property institutions were, in short, taken to be of secondary significance. In regarding both socialism and capitalism as fundamentally bureaucratic, Weber thus minimized the distinctiveness of socialism; in effect, he argued that if the proletariat had "nothing to lose but their chains" by revolting against capitalism, they also had little to gain. At the same time, however, this also diminished the uniqueness of capitalism, and Parsons objected to this.

Unlike Marx, who had viewed capitalism as developing through a series of economic strains and class conflicts, Sombart saw it in a more Hegelian way, as an unfolding of the capitalist *Geist*. In Sombart's emphasis on the *Geist*, as well as in Weber's emphasis on the role of the Protestant ethic, Parsons was to see a theoretical convergence of considerable significance. This was a convergence that attributed a measure of autonomy to "value elements" or moral values, and which, in his *Structure of Social Action*, Parsons later claimed to be the distinctive focus of social theory in the late nineteenth century. Parsons subsequently developed Sombart's and Weber's critiques of Marx into a systematic discussion of the generalized importance of moral values, thereby confronting Marxism not simply on a specific issue of historical interpretation, but on the broadest possible theoretical level. In short, Parsons' first major work, *The Structure of Social Action*, stems in important part from his earlier interest in these anti-Marxist theories of capitalism. It takes as its point of departure an effort to generalize and extend the anti-Marxist polemics of Sombart and Weber.

As suggested, however, there were important ways in which Parsons in 1928 felt that these anti-Marxist critics had not gone far enough, had accepted too many of Marx's assumptions, and had remained rooted in a theoretical tradition more like than different from Marxism. In particular, Parsons took exception to two aspects of their position: the deterministic metaphysics and the pessimistic structure of sentiment that suffused their work.

In their determinism both Sombart and Weber viewed capitalism as Marx had, says Parsons: That is, as forcing "the individual businessman into the race for profit, not because he is venal by nature, nor because it represents the highest values in life for him, but because his enterprise must earn profit or go under."[4] The fault of capitalist exploitation, thus construed, rests not with the individual capitalist but with the social system that constrains him to exploit or be ruined. Sombart saw capitalism as a powerful mechanism that, during its mature phase, subjugated all to a rationalistic, calculating spirit that was located not even in the entrepreneur himself but rather in the impersonal business organization. Sombart thus saw capitalism, complains Parsons, as a kind of "monster" possessed of its own purposes and going its own way, independently of the will—if not of the activity—of individual human beings. Consequently, says Parsons, Sombart's "view results in fully as rigid a determinism as that of Marx. All the individual can do is to 'express' this spirit in his thoughts and actions. He is powerless to change it."[5] Parsons therefore accuses Sombart of overemphasizing the rigidity of modern society and of succumbing to fatalism and pessimism. Parsons explicitly rejects this pessimism in favor of a gradualistic meliorism: "There seems to be little reason," he says, "to believe that it is not possible on the basis which we now have, to build by a continuous process something more nearly approaching an ideal society."[6]

TOWARD THE PERFECTION OF CAPITALISM

This formulation succinctly exposes both the difference and the continuity between Parsons and Durkheim. Each sought change within the framework of his society's existent master institutions and through a "continuous process." There is, however, a visible difference between the early Parsons' cautious Protestant perfectionism and Durkheim's more Catholic organicism. This may be noted by contrasting Parsons' remarks above with Durkheim's parallel formulation in *The Rules of Sociological Method:* it is, Durkheim says, "no longer a matter of pursuing desperately an objective that retreats as one advances, but of working with steady perseverance to maintain the normal state, of re-establishing it if it is threatened, and of rediscovering its conditions if they have changed."[7] In effect, Parsons' Functionalism is a more optimistic one than Durkheim's. Although Parsons fully shares Durkheim's concern for social order and equilibrium, he in principle, envisions a somewhat more dynamic equilibrium, more susceptible to influence by men's active efforts in pursuit of their moral ideals.

To Parsons, progress is not based on a deterministic evolutionism but is, rather, seen to be animated by men's commitment to the activistic fulfillment of their transcendental values. The contemporary condition of capitalist society, indicates Parsons, does provide a basis for its gradual perfection. It is inherently sound even if presently disrupted: things are not so bad. Indeed, capitalism's sheer technological accomplishments are seen as a source of hope. It is going too far, says Parsons, to deny as Sombart pretty much does, all value to our civilization's conquest of nature. Technological development and industrial society possess value; they do not, as Durkheim claims, dangerously undermine the sources of social stability by exacerbating men's inherently insatiable appetites.

Parsons is as much exercised by Weber's pessimism as by Sombart's. In some ways similar to Sombart, Weber had felt that modern society was being warped by the growth of lifeless bureaucratic routines that increasingly dominated the major institutional areas. In Weber's view, complains Parsons, capitalism presents a dead and mechanized condition of society, in which no room is left for truly creative or charismatic forces "because all human activity is forced to follow the 'system.'" While acknowledging the widespread rationalization of modern life, Parsons challenges Weber's pessimism. Present-day bureaucracy, he says, need not continue to dominate life, and there is the possibility that it may once again be made to serve spiritual ends. Weber's pessimism, says Parsons, derives from his acceptance of the Marxian dualism between material and spiritual forces, but there is no reason to believe that these are the ultimate factors in social development.

Much of Parsons' later theoretical work is shaped by these two powerful impulses clearly manifest in his earliest work: (1) by his effort to *generalize* the anti-Marxist critique, and, (2) at the same time, by his effort to overcome the *determinism*, the pessimism, and, indeed, the anticapitalism of these critics of Marxism.

Stated in other terms, Weber and Sombart—while disagreeing with Marx about the historical conditions that had led to capitalism and, in general, about the role of moral and ideological forces— had, nonetheless, agreed with Marx that the central social problem of modern society was *alienation,* a condition that they opposed, as he did. In this respect the Germans had been of one mind. Since Sombart and Weber, however, rejected socialism, they, unlike Marx, saw no solution. Oddly enough, then, Parsons shares, in full self-consciousness, some of Marx's optimism, the difference being that Parsons believed modern society could be gradually perfected *within* the framework of capitalism: that is, "on the basis which we now have."

In his 1928–1929 articles on capitalism, Parsons was still prepared to believe in a kind of chastened social evolution, "even though it is not so plain as it has been thought, and even though its ethical interpretation in terms of progress is unwarranted," and so long as it was neither "so radically discontinuous nor so radically determined" as that of Sombart.[8] In short, Parsons was ready to accept social evolution if it left a place for moral striving and individual choice. Indeed, he was then even prepared to entertain the thought that capitalism itself might one day be superseded, so long as there was room left for continuity: "in the transition from capitalism to a different social system surely many elements of the present would be built into the new order."[9]

Parsons, then, believed that capitalism as it was, was still not perfected; he had been exposed to the German critique of capitalism and accepted certain aspects of it, particularly its Romantic rejection of "materialism." He maintained that, "it does seem that the apostles of progress and freedom have been somewhat overhasty in their optimism, and it is by no means certain that the conquest of nature alone is sufficient cause to boast the glory of our civilization . . . our tendency to glorify it is evidence of a lack of a proper sense of cultural balance."[10] Here Parsons speaks as a tranquilized Rousseau, prudently acknowledging that the progress of culture and manners may not have kept abreast of the progress of science and technology. He thus looks forward to a gradual evolution that will create a more balanced society in which this cultural lag will be remedied by the blossoming of spiritual culture.

In 1965 Parsons indicates that his patience has been vindicated. He declares the spiritual imbalance to have been redressed and proclaims that "capitalism" is on the verge of being transcended: "democratic government, the welfare state, trade unionism . . . education, science, and even humanistic culture play such important roles that calling [the United States] 'capitalistic' in anything like the classical Marxian sense seems increasingly forced."[11]

Parsons, after all, had studied in the great seats of European culture; he had walked where great thinkers had walked, and he had even glimpsed the Blue Flower. The son of the Congregationalist minister had no vulgarian impulse to surrender to things as they were in the late 1920's. He had wanted to perfect the spiritual aspect of American culture, to make it a fitting capstone of its technological triumph; he had wanted to mend the split between the spiritual and the economic, and he viewed capitalism itself as imbued with a deeply moral element. Indeed, he regarded it as possessing a noteworthy uniqueness, and complained that Weber had lost sight of its organic individuality.[12] Strongly influenced by the Germans in the beginning, accepting their critique of Marxism but not their pessimism about capitalism, Parsons viewed capitalism as in need of a cultural fine-tuning (much as had the early Positivists) but as healthy in its essentials. He saw capitalism from a syncretic standpoint that combined European intellectual perspectives with American sentiments. European theory had, on the one hand, given him some perspective on capitalism, while, on the other—and even before the Great Depression—it had vaccinated him against the most radical of the criticisms of capitalism. When the crisis came he would not be panicked into a shoddy defensive-ness and trivial polemics, but would be able to maintain a steady course in a thoroughgoing defense of his basic vision.

THE DRIFT TOWARD THEORETICAL VOLUNTARISM

Sombart, Weber, Parsons in *The Structure of Social Action,* and the young Marx of the philosophical manuscripts, all agree that a situation in which men are molded by autonomous social forces, and in which their aims and efforts are controlled and overridden, is undesirable. Weber and Sombart tended to see this as unavoidable in modern industrial civilization; Marx saw it as inevitable under capitalism but avoidable under communism; Parsons sees it as avoidable even under capitalism. Indeed, it is a central point of Parsons' "voluntarism" that men's efforts always make a difference in what happens.

Viewing men as goal-seeking creatures whose own efforts can change their lives, Parsons' vision converges with that of Marx, and particularly that of the young Marx of alienation. In *The Structure of Social Action,* however, Parsons is unaware of this partial convergence with Marx. In some part, this is due to Parsons' unfamiliarity with Marx's own writings, and particularly with the earlier, pre-1847 work in which Marx had focused most explicitly on the problem of alienation. Indeed, in 1937 Parsons did not cite a single original Marxian source. Of course, the Marx-Engels Institute had published only the first volume of (what was expected to be) the complete works of Marx and Engels in 1927, and it was only in this and later volumes that the definitive texts of Marx's earlier writings were first made available. Some passages in the *German Ideology* were made available in English by Sidney Hook, but not until 1936; the full manuscript itself was published in English in 1938. Similarly, H. P. Adams' study of Marx's earlier writings appeared in 1940. But Parsons' *The Structure of Social Action* had already been published in 1937. But, despite the subsequent publication of Marxian texts, Parsons never has cited a single one of Marx's own writings, not even in his 1965 paper on Marx.

It is not only, however, because Parsons was unaware of Marx's earlier work that in 1937 he failed to see the convergence between Marx's concept of alienation and his own antideterministic voluntarism. There was another difficulty that impeded Parsons' clear view of this convergence, for, to see the development of Marxism in this way would have complicated, if not contradicted, Parsons' thesis about the development of nineteenth-century social theory. In the *Structure of Social Action* Parsons had held that, in the late nineteenth century, social theory commonly manifested a convergence *toward* a voluntaristic view that saw men's actions as shaped by their own volitions, desires, decisions, choices, and strivings, as a major element in the interacting system of social forces.

Without Procrustean effort, it is quite easy to see the difference between the earlier and later Marx in precisely these terms—but, in the opposite direction. The young Marx had given greater emphasis than the older one to these voluntaristic elements and had, indeed, seen man's species character as entailing such end-directed, goal-shaped strivings. In a class society, however, they resulted in unanticipated consequences at variance with man's true intentions, stressed Marx; indeed, it was this that manifested the alienated condition that Marx sought to abolish. The earlier Marx had thus emphasized a conception of man as making his own history in the pursuit of his goals, while it was the later Marx who had stressed, and decried, the manner in which the capitalist system subjected man to its own blind laws. Under capitalism, man made history, but only in an alienated way; actors were alienated from the consequences of their own actions; they neither knew them as theirs nor controlled them. *Marx's own work, then, manifests a drift not toward but rather away from a voluntaristic social theory.*

Parsons might argue, however, that the development of Marx's work does not essentially fall within the period (the Classical period, as I have called it) with which he was concerned in the *Structure of Social Action.* In other words, he might hold that the voluntaristic drift in social theory was simply a "law" of the third period, while Marx's work largely falls in the second. The question would then arise as to why this should be so; that is, why should the drift manifest itself in the later but not the earlier period?

Here we have to consider Parsons' general explanation of the voluntaristic drift in social theory: He argues that this drift cannot be explained in Hegelian, in Marxian, or in sociology-of-knowledge terms; that is, it was not due to the immanent unfolding of a set of initial theories or to the social conditions of the historical period. Nor, for that matter, he says, was it explainable in empiricist or Positivistic terms, as due only to the accumulation of new facts.[13]

Parsons instead accounts for the voluntaristic drift as due to the *interaction* of the accumulating facts with theory; theory led to the formulation of problems and shaped research interests that generated facts which, in turn, constrained theory toward voluntarism.

But since the theorists that had presumably ended in a common place had begun in different ways, it is difficult to understand how their substantive theories could have contributed to the subsequent, voluntaristic outcome. Parsons is thus unwillingly forced back either to a Hegelian or Marxian account, or to a Positivistic explanation that stresses the importance of the facts. Parsons tries to save his account of the voluntaristic drift by opting for the latter; that is, by giving special importance to the role of facts. In a footnote, Parsons declares that one of the reasons why the voluntaristic drift emerged was its "empirical validity."[14] He acknowledges that "other factors" also conduced to the voluntaristic development without specifying them, but adds, in emphasis, that "had it not been for the fact that its authors observed correctly, and reasoned cogently about their observations, the [voluntaristic] theory . . . would not have developed."[15]

In the end Parsons seems to be holding that the voluntaristic drift in social theory occurred because of the empirical reliability of the observations and the logical correctness of the inferences made from them. In effect, he resolves the conundrum of how *different* theoretical starting points could have had the *same* terminus by minimizing, if not sacrificing, the role of substantive theory. Parsons' explanation of the drift toward voluntaristic social theory, then, largely comes down to a matter of the cumulation of reliable facts subjected to valid reasoning—in short, to a view that stresses the autonomy of social science from social forces, a view surprisingly close to the Positivistic and utilitarian standpoint against which he had polemicized.

It would therefore follow that the reason Marx's work became less, rather than more, voluntaristic over time was that it had *not* been based on reliable facts and/or had *not* subjected them to valid reasoning. Such an inference is, at least, compatible with Parsons' long-standing disposition to emphasize the pre-scientific and ideological, if not religious character of Marxism. Parsons wishes, on the one hand, to underscore the scientific validity of a voluntaristic model of social theory and, on the other, to undermine the contemporary "scientific" standing of Marxism. Since it is the very convergence among theorists that, for Parsons, suggests that "the concepts of the voluntaristic theory of action must be sound theoretical concepts," then the very different line of development of Marx's own work presumably implies that it is unsound.

The difficulties and tendentiousness of Parsons' position become even plainer if the following considerations are added. Even if we confine Marx to the second period, we cannot do so, for Marx*ism*. It continued to develop and change into the third period, the period on which Parsons' voluntaristic thesis is focused. Specifically, it was in the third period that V. I. Lenin emphasized the leadership initiatives of the revolutionary party and mounted his attack against the theory of political sponteneity. In addressing himself to the problem of *What Is to Be Done?*, Lenin gave new importance precisely to the *voluntaristic* component in Marxism. In short, Lenin's political and social theory gave every indication of having moved appreciably toward the very voluntarism that Parsons' attributes to the academic social theorists of the Classical period. Parsons, however, takes no note of this. And if he had, how could he have accounted for it, and remained consistent, except as still another indication of the influence of correct observation and cogent reasoning? One of the important reasons for Parsons' neglecting of both Marx and Lenin, then, seems to have been that in the former instance Parsons would have faced a negative case at variance with his generalization, while in the latter he would have had an embarrassing confirmation of it; it would have required him to endorse the *scientific* character of Lenin's social theory, which would have been at variance with his inclination to expel Marxism from "true," scientific sociology.

There is one other peculiarity in Parsons' development of the thesis of a voluntaristic drift in social theory that should be briefly mentioned. In his 1928–1929 discussion of Sombart's and Weber's treatment of capitalism, Parsons emphasized that their image of capitalism had unduly stressed *non*voluntaristic components: that is, it had manifested a *deterministic* character; had entailed a view of capitalism as being bureaucratic and rigidified; had embodied a unilinear evolutionism; had held that the development of capitalism spelled the destruction of the charismatic elements in social life and the loss of spiritual aims. Parsons accused Weber of saying that the religious values that had originally given capitalism personal meaning had been superseded by an "automatic, mechanistic system" in which material goods had gained an inexorable hold over men's lives.[16] Prior to the Depression, then, Parsons had emphasized *not* the voluntaristic, but the *anti*voluntaristic component of Weber and other third-period theorists of capitalism. It is only after the Depression, in the *Structure of Social Action*, that Parsons sharply recasts his vision of them to emphasize their contribution to the development of a voluntaristic social theory.

The theorists whom Parsons had summoned in evidence of his thesis about voluntaristic development had not changed from 1928 to 1937; it was Parsons who had changed. What happened, in short, was that with the Depression and the growing salience of Marxism in the United States, there was greater pressure to develop and fortify the intellectual alternatives to Marxism, and to expel Marxism from consideration as a sociology much like any other. And, indeed, a similar thing had previously happened to the classical academic theorists themselves, and it had been that very thing which led some of them, too, toward a heightened voluntarism. In brief, one may accept Parsons' thesis about the increased drift toward a voluntaristic social theory among the classical sociologists and attribute it, in some appreciable part, to their own common effort to combat the materialistic determinism of Marxism. But, coming out of the tradition of German idealism, it was the materialistic—and not the deterministic—aspect that they most consistently opposed. Their principal impulse was to resist the devaluation of the "spiritual"; a deterministic *idealism,* a version of the Hegelian *geist,* was actually attractive because it underscored the potency of the spiritual. For its part, Lenin's new voluntarism needs no special, or different, explanation, except that he was looking for a theoretical standpoint that would skirt the deterministic component of Marxism and leave room for revolutionary initiative within the basic Marxist framework. Lenin's voluntarism was, therefore, inserted at the level of a politics, of political organization and strategy, rather than at the level of generalized social theory.

ALIENATION AND VOLUNTARISM

While Parsons is unaware of it, there was a convergence between his voluntarism and that of at least the young Marx, for both agree that man is and should be a goal-oriented, striving creature whose history reflects his own efforts. Parsons' polemic against Marx is, though he is unaware of it, directed primarily against the older Marx, whose work probed the limitations that historically specific social conditions imposed upon men's efforts, both analyzing and *denouncing* the emergence of an autonomous social system that could impose itself on men and override their efforts. But in his quarrel with the pessimism and determinism of Sombart and Weber, and in his one-sided emphasis on the determinism of the older Marx and Engels, Parsons was in unwitting agreement with the young Marx.

Yet this convergence is a limited one. Parsons' voluntarism and Marx's conception of alienation agree only in their view of man as a striving, goal-seeking creature. Both had been shaped in this respect by German Romanticism. Parsons' voluntarism, however, stresses that man's efforts count, not because they are realized successfully but simply because things turn out differently than they would have without them. Parsons does not view as undesirable the difference between man's intentions and the outcomes of his action, but it is precisely this difference that was a central problem to Marx.

Stressing that men themselves should make their social world, Marx decried their being *alienated* from it, not controlling it, not knowing it as a world of their own making. Marx wanted to know the varying and specific historical conditions that led to such alienation, so that it might be overcome; he wanted to reduce the gap between what men intend and the outcomes of their action, between the producer and his product. That men's actions result in outcomes at variance with their intentions was, for Marx, a fundamental social pathology.

Parsons, however, is content simply to suggest that sometimes men achieve what they strive for, sometimes not, and that things are in either event different because of men's strivings. It is this sheer *difference* that is important to Parsons because his voluntarism is primarily an expression of his antideterminism. The values men pursue are not reducible to the social conditions that influence and shape them, *and* do not—as Parsons is at pains to insist—result in conditions that mirror men's intentions. That men's values cannot be reduced to other social conditions implies that they cannot be *predicted from* other social conditions; his point is not, though, that one can predict how outcomes will conform with men's intentions, but only that outcomes would differ, in some unspecified way, if men's intentions differed. Parsons makes no systematic analysis of the diverse forces that shape men's efforts or of what they, in turn, account for.

In effect, then, voluntarism for Parsons serves as a randomizing rather than a structuring mechanism, and is thus expressive of his antideterministic intent.[17] Voluntarism and morality are the equivalent of "free will"; they serve not simply to *qualify* other theoretical models by inserting another variable into the predictive equation, but rather to undermine the entire possibility of any kind of determinism, even that of a probablistic predictability. Moral norms are tacitly the prime starting mechanisms, the unmoved movers.

For Parsons the voluntaristic conception of action refers to a process in which the concrete human plays an active, not merely an adaptive, role; far from being automatic, the realization of ultimate values is a matter of active energy, of will, of effort. Parsons insists on a distinction as well as a connection between "ultimate" moral values, on the one hand, and the specifically *voluntaristic* component, the active, striving efforts of individuals, on the other hand.[18] Whether or not norms are realized, he holds, "depends upon the effort of the individuals acting as well as upon the conditions in which they act." Moreover, Parsons specifically indicates that it is this "active element of the relation of men to norms [which is] the creative or voluntaristic side of it."[19]

Parsons further adds that, while a voluntaristic social theory involves moral norms, it "does not in the least deny an important role to conditional and other non-normative elements, but considers them interdependent with the normative."[20] Voluntarism does not hold that the mere existence and recognition of a moral norm implies automatic conformity with it; and it certainly denies that moral norms are merely manifestations of other forces but themselves lack in causal potency. Both such views, objects Parsons, imply that action is an "automatic process." (This would seem to suggest that here Parsons is polemicizing against the use of mechanical models for social analysis and is, in general, favorably disposed to those more organismic models that stress the importance of emergent forces.) Rejecting both those views of moral norms, Parsons instead holds that moral norms are only one variable in a set of interdependent elements in social action, and that their influence is achieved only by overcoming resistance and obstacles to them.[21]

It is clear that Parsons is attempting to treat the significance of moral norms quite differently than had the Positivists who, from Saint-Simon to Durkheim, had stressed their significance as externals, constraining the individual. In 1937 Parsons instead conceives the significance of moral norms as potent energizers motivating lines of effort and striving, on the one hand, and as bases for selecting and integrating courses of action, on the other. In stressing voluntarism and in placing a concern with moral norms in this context, Parsons is, in effect, expressing the conviction that no more than anything else do moral norms inevitably preclude certain kinds of change. More generally, Parsons is stressing the openness of social action and historical development.[22]

Parsons' voluntarism thus contains a tremendous ambiguity about moral norms. On the one hand, Parsons, like Durkheim, tends to reduce or qualify the importance attributed to them, first, by seeing them as only one in a set of interdependent variables and, second, by stressing that they work their effects only through an intervening variable, the will or effort. On the other hand, however, it is clear that moral elements do have a very special significance for him. They are the only specific mechanism for energizing will that Parsons systematically considers; indeed, he makes a special point of stating that a voluntaristic theory "involves elements of a normative character." *Parsons' voluntarism is an effort to maintain a special place for moral norms, while at the same time rejecting the deterministic framework in which they had hitherto been cast: he is emphasizing the power of morality.*

It is precisely because moral norms serve, in effect, as *anti*-deterministic elements in Parsons' social theory, as determinism-*reducing* elements, that it is intrinsically difficult for Parsons systematically to address himself to the question of where moral norms themselves come from and on what they themselves depend. For, once this is confronted it becomes possible, in principle, to predict the *non*-normative conditions that give rise to norms; voluntarism would tend to break down in the direction of what Parsons calls a "utilitarian" social theory, in which moral forces are treated as manifestations of other real forces. Parsons wants to have his moral norms without paying the Positivist price of a deterministic universe.[23]

To the extent that men attained what they sought, the social world would obviously be predictable and controllable; there would be a measure of determinism in it. Parsons' antideterminism, therefore, leads him to focus on and value the existence of the sheer *difference* between what men seek and what they bring about; this difference is not seen as "bad" and in need of a remedy, but as "good," being, in effect, an evidence of men's freedom. For Parsons it is men's *failure*—their ignorance and their impotence—that marks their freedom, and man's "alienation" is the price of his freedom.

There is thus a tendency in Parsons' theory to stress the presumed need for a sheer *communality* of moral norms, with only the most formal limitation on what these norms might be, other than that they must not be at variance with the requisites of social system survival. His stress, then, is on the *diversity* of possible value commitments that might be made, rather than on the things that limit them. Since it is possible for men to want and pursue widely varying values, and since there is no systematic sociology of morals that might specify the conditions under which different moral beliefs might emerge, Parsons' system tends toward an historical *in*determinism. There is thus a tendency for his voluntarism to come down to the assumption that, with respect to *social change*, many outcomes are possible. But not quite. For there is another element in *The Structure of Social Action* that emphasizes the *un*anticipated consequences of *purposive* social action and, in particular, its difficulties and dangers.[24]

Parsons conceives of man as a creature whose striving influences but does not limit history; he sees this striving as a blind one. Man is seen as bound by nonrational moralities, confined and thwarted by other forces, and repeatedly trapped by the unanticipated consequences of purposive social action. To Parsons, men are free to strive, but are not free to *achieve* what they strive for. Men make a difference, but not the difference they intend. This, indeed, is a picture of Marx's alienated man. But what for Marx is an historical pathology to be overcome is for Parsons the unavoidable and eternal condition of man.

While stressing the importance of the ends and values that men pursue, Parsons never asks *whose* ends and values these are. Are they pursuing their own ends or those imposed upon them by others? He never asks whether men are striving to achieve goals that they themselves have rationally inspected and selected, or whether theirs is the striving of tools, energetically seeking ends that others have programmed them to pursue. And Parsons never asks, under what social conditions can men select their own goals and under what condition will they blindly seek goals set for them by others? Parsons never sees that there is a profound difference between the failure to achieve one's own goals and the failure to achieve goals that others have imposed upon us. He fails to see that the ultimate alienation is not that we fail in what we seek, but that we seek what is not ours. The ultimate alienation is that we live our lives as tools and that we do not live for ourselves.

Parsons' conception of men as "eager tools," willingly pursuing whatever goals have been "internalized" in them, largely derives from the stress he places upon "socialization" as a value-imprinting mechanism; his stress upon socialization implicitly defines men as value-*transmitting* and value-*receiving* creatures rather than as value-*creating* creatures. Here, then, the very agency that is the source of men's humanness, socialization, is also the agency that eternally makes man a tool to pursue the ends of others; man is thus alienated in the very process of becoming human.

Parsons has, in effect, *generalized* alienation, transforming it from an historical condition to the universal fate of men. It is here that he makes his most general reply to Marx. To Parsons, man is alienated not under capitalism alone but in any society; and this very alienation is the condition of his humanity and freedom. Thus, although Parsons begins by objecting to a view of men as automatons, controlled by any social system or by mechanized bureaucracy, he ends by seeing them as necessarily subject to a nonrational morality, bound by goals they do not choose but which are imposed upon them by socialization, and whose pursuit has results that are often at variance with what they seek. Instead of bending his social science to the problem of how men might better control their social world, better realize their own goals, and better reduce the unan-

ticipated consequences of their striving; instead of exploring the
social conditions that make it more rather than less possible for
men to know and achieve their own goals, Parsons simply focuses
on the universal *limits* within which all social action must take
place, on the indeterminism of social action and the sheer contingency of historical development.

In releasing men from the bondage of determinism, Parsons
restricted the possibilities of predictability, control, and successful
achievement. He provides no basis on which men's actions can
achieve their goals or realize their hopes. Voluntarism gives men
the freedom to make things "different" from what they might have
been, but neither the freedom nor the power to get what they want.
In extolling man's creativity, energy, and will, Parsons reassures
men that they and their efforts make a "difference"; but if this does
not mean that they can more fully achieve their purposes, what
difference does this make? Men might as well be bound by history
and evolution. In extolling men's creative initiative without giving
them hope of fulfillment, in extolling their striving despite its slim
success, Parsons, in effect, extols the striving of the blind, who
might indeed do better and be safer if they strived less.

Parsons' voluntarism thus contains a contradiction, particularly
so when he extols men's efforts and strivings but, at the same time,
warns against the unanticipated consequences of purposive social
action. For, the latter is, after all, often an expression of men's
efforts to achieve certain moral values. Taken seriously, such a
warning might be conducive to apathy rather than effort. The
theory of the unanticipated consequence of purposive social action
thus neutralizes the theory of voluntaristic effort. Taken together,
the two in effect seem to say that men can have freedom but not
successful achievement, that they should strive but not hope for
too much. This was clearly an apt lesson in humility for respectable
men caught in the depression. Indeed, much of the clue to this
problem is in the history of the 1930's.

This period was characterized by intensive and concentrated
efforts at purposive social action, whose dominant form—as in the
New Deal—was one that conservatives did not relish. The kind of
purposive social action against which the emphasis on unanticipated social consequences warns is, implicitly, that undertaken on
behalf of only a limited set of moral values, liberal or radical
values. The point of the theory of unanticipated consequences is
not usually aimed, say, at the purposive action of governments at
war. In effect, then, the indeterminism of Parsons is essentially
a *caveat* about liberal or radical change and, indeed, all efforts at
social change that exert a strain on the status quo.

Parsons began by wanting to stress the importance of moral

values and effort against determinism and pessimism. In this, however, he necessarily left the door open to *all* kinds of values and effort, including those that, from a conservative standpoint, are disruptive of the status quo. He was therefore faced with the resultant task of, on the one side, sanctioning morally motivated effort but, on the other, finding a way to discourage certain kinds of moral effort: system-disruptive efforts. Parsons closes the door that his voluntarism had left open by warning of the unanticipated consequences of purposive social action. Parsons' effort to make men free thus operates within the limits of, and indeed conflicts with, his concern about maintaining social order.

In its net impact, Parsons' simultaneous emphasis on voluntarism and on unanticipated consequences is a recommendation that men should strive to realize their values but should not expect too much. It is a theoretical mix that tacitly serves to sustain striving despite the experience of failure: striving should be chastened by awareness of the possibility of failure; it should be a prudent and limited striving, not a zealous and passionate striving. Such a striving will suffice to keep men at their duty, will tone up the existent social system, but will not rock boats.

THE LIBERALIZATION OF FUNCTIONALISM

Seen as a conservative manifesto of antideterminism and antipessimism, Parsons' earliest work should no longer appear so utterly disconnected with the calamitous events in the surrounding society. If one were to regard it as a Shavian piece of "Advice to Intelligent Patriots in the Midst of Social Disaster," it might be thought of as a remonstrance not to despair, but to take heart, to believe that they may yet work their way out of the impasse in which they find themselves, to believe that their own energies and effort do make some difference, and to believe that they should not surrender to false theories that prophesy an end to their way of life. For all its detachment, then, Parsons' early work is very much a response to the crisis of his time.

But it is *not* a response from the standpoint of those whose deprivation was near destitution; it does not, in short, resonate to the suffering of the bankrupt small farmer or the unemployed worker. Indeed, it is only if we expect that a response to social crisis must express sympathy with suffering that we will fail to see Parsons' work as a response. Parsons' response, however, is singularly insensitive to the sheer suffering of the desperately afflicted. Nowhere is the word "poverty" mentioned in *The Structure of Social Action,* although it is written in the midst of a national experience with breadlines, unemployment, and hunger. Instead, Parsons' response is concerned to avoid institutional discontinuities and to maintain traditional loyalties; that is, he is concerned with discouraging radical social change. It is not so much the suffering of individuals as the resultant threat to the established culture, to which Parsons is responding. It is in this way a conservative response to the social crisis.

Yet it also needs to be added that it is a very American form of conservatism, which tempers loyalty to established institutions with individualism. If its response to the vast crisis seems insufficient because it still stresses individual effort rather than collective solutions, and if it neglects the *needs* of individuals, nonetheless it also retains a sensitivity to their potency. Conservative though it was in comparison with the changes upon which the nation was then irretrievably launched, it was, by comparison with Durkheim's social theory, a step toward liberalism. Unlike the latter, it does not obliterate individuals in its concern for social order and solidarity; it does not see them as tools and embodiments of the collective conscience and exoteric social currents; it does not exhort them to be suspicious of industry and of man's greedy insatiable appetites, to bow dependently before society, to like the idea of circumscribed tasks and limited horizons, to curtail ambitions, or to be docile to authority. With the shift from Durkheim's to Parsons' Functionalism, the values embedded in Functional theory have appreciably shifted.

The shift toward this more liberal Functionalism seems, in part, attributable simply to its diffusion from French into American culture, for the latter has always been more individualistically liberal than France with its *étatist* traditions. In other words, the value change in Parsons' Functionalism is to be understood as due to a shift in the *national* culture in which Sociological Functionalism now found itself, rather than to a shift in its *class* sensitivities. Functionalism still resonated an essentially middle-class outlook, but the American and French middle classes differed. From this standpoint Parsons' emerging Functionalism resonates traditional American middle-class conceptions and aspirations, which were intrinsically more individualistic than those traditional to the French.

Parsons' early work, then, may be conceived not as free of any response to the ongoing American social crisis nor as a value-free response independent of class orientations but, rather, as expressing a middle-class conception of, and response to, the crisis. From this standpoint the problem was not sheer suffering or deprivation but rather the danger that these might promote efforts at disruptive social change, radical institutional innovation, and thus might lead to a loss of faith in the traditional middle-class value placed on individual effort.

NOTES

1. Cf. T. Parsons, *The Structure of Social Action* (New York: McGraw-Hill, 1937), p. 495.

2. *Ibid.*, p. 503. Also, see " 'Capitalism' in Recent German Literature: Sombart and Weber—Concluded," *Journal of Political Economy*, XXXVII, No. 1 (February 1929), 40. Here Parsons noted that Weber's Protestant Ethic "was intended to be a refutation of the Marxian thesis."

3. Parsons, *The Structure of Social Action*, p. 511.

4. Parsons, " 'Capitalism' in Recent German Literature: Sombart and Weber—Concluded," p. 35.

5. Parsons, " 'Capitalism' in Recent German Literature," *Journal of Political Economy*, XXXVI (December 1928), 660.

6. *Ibid.*

7. Emile Durkheim, *The Rules of Sociological Method*, ed. E. G. Catlin, (Chicago: University of Chicago Press, 1938), p. 75.

8. Parsons, " 'Capitalism' in Recent German Literature," p. 693.

9. *Ibid.*

10. *Ibid.*, p. 654.

11. T. Parsons, *Sociological Theory and Modern Society* (New York: Free Press, 1967), p. 125.

12. *Ibid.*, pp. 48–49.

13. Parsons, *Structure of Social Action*, p. 725.

14. *Ibid.*

15. *Ibid.*, p. 726.

16. Parsons, " 'Capitalism' in Recent German Literature," p. 43.

17. This may be noted clearly in Parsons' definition of what "ends" are: "An end, then, in the analytical sense must be defined as the difference between the anticipated future state of affairs and that which it could have been predicted would ensue from the initial situation *without the agency of the actor having intervened.*" (*The Structure of Social Action*, p. 49.) The actor, in short, introduces a *non*predictable element. This seems to be the case, even though Parsons is àt pains to emphasize that the striving, volitional component is itself partly structured by moral values, for there is no systematic analysis of the general conditions that shape moral values themselves and lead them to take one form rather than another. Moral values pattern individual action and, when common to actors, are a vital condition of social system stability; but they are not held to produce individual or collective outcomes in accordance with the intentions they foster. They make a difference, but this is unspecified in character.

18. A voluntaristic social theory, such as Parsons espouses in *The Structure of Social Action*, is, he says, one that "involves elements of a normative character" (p. 81). By norms he means "states of affairs which are regarded by individuals as putatively desirable and hence [they] strive to realize them." Here it seems as if Parsons almost equates moral norms and men's active efforts to realize them, although in other places he distinguishes these.

19. *Ibid.*, p. 82.

20. *Ibid.*

21. Thus, "the failure of the actual course of action to correspond exactly with that prescribed by the norm is not proof that the latter is unimportant, but only that it is not alone important" (*ibid.*, p. 251). The existence of this resistance, he adds, as well as the overcoming of it, implies the importance of another element, to wit, "effort." The distinctive element in voluntarism, then, is not moral norms as such; it is, rather, the human *effort* which they may arouse or, for any other reason, activate.

22. What actually happens, he is saying, depends in part on what people strive for and want to happen. What people want, he says, depends vitally but not exclusively on the moral norms that people have; for, in principle, *any* "agencies which stimulate this will" play a very important part in determining historical outcomes. While Parsons, in principle, does recognize that *various* elements can energize will, the fact remains that the only one of these to which he gives express attention is moral norms, thus indicating the special significance he attributes to them.

23. But different levels are distinguishable here. Parsons wants to see moral norms as controlling and restraining *individuals* (structuring and patterning their wants) and also as stabilizing social systems—but not as confining *history*. He wishes, on the other side, to stress that social order and the integration of social action require *common* moral norms, since these are held to pattern and limit the courses taken by individuals; but, on the other side, Parsons also wishes to stress an antideterministic position with respect to *historical change,* and to prevent an evolutionary foreclosure of possible lines of societal development.

24. This can be better seen if we note that Parsons advances his voluntaristic model as an alternative to the "utilitarian" model, against which he polemicizes. In the utilitarian model, as Parsons sees it, men deliberately appraise their social situation and choose courses of conduct by appraising which of them will best realize their goals. His utilitarian model premises that men seek knowledge in order to change, or that in order to change they first need knowledge. His voluntaristic model, however, argues that men's behavior is not basically predicated on a rational survey of their situation or on knowledge of it, but rather on commitments to certain ultimate, non-rational values that the actor takes as given. In effect, then, the tendency of Parsons' voluntarism is to diminish the significance attributed to rationality and knowledge as elements in social action. Parsons' emphasis on nonrational moral values, as opposed to the utilitarian emphasis on knowledge and information, focuses attention on those factors in social action and change that are not amenable to planful control and deliberate use. And even knowledge and science, like other social elements, are seen as having unanticipated consequences. The entire role of social science itself, as a guide to social change, is therefore radically if unwittingly undermined. For what is stressed is that social solidarity or social "health" depends upon the vitality of this nonrational element rather than on rational planning or change.

6

Making the World Whole: Parsons as a Systems Analyst

Undergirding the phantasmagorical conceptual superstructure that Parsons has raised there is an unshakable metaphysical conviction: that the world is one, and must be made safe in its oneness. Its oneness, Parsons believes, is the world's most vital character. Its parts, therefore, take on meaning and significance only in relation to this wholeness. Making conceptual distinctions is not an end in itself for Parsons, but a way of providing ports of access to the whole. In this thrust toward unitariness, Parsons' system has a living connection with the tradition of Sociological Positivism, whose abiding impulse was to "organize" and to integrate the social world, and, further back, with Platonism itself.

I want to begin to explore this aspect of Parsons' metaphysics from a curious standpoint, in terms of what is, as it were, the shell of his work, the "mere" appearance that strikes one almost immediately on picking it up—in short, its literary style. One of the obvious but invariably neglected aspects of any social theory is the fact that it has a form as well as a content. All social theory thus far has had some *literary* form; which is to say, it is written in some style. Since form and content are fused, it may be possible to discern part of what a theory means by examining not only what it says but also how it says this.[1]

It is commonly recognized that the sheer structure of Parsons' work has two obvious and indubitable characteristics. First, it has a powerful conceptualizing drive: it presents and strings together concept after concept; it names concepts, defines concepts, subdivides concepts, exemplifies concepts, categorizes concepts. Second, and I will deal first with this aspect of its literary structure, it is more Delphically obscure, more Germanically opaque, more confused and confusing by far, than that of any other sociologist considered here or, indeed, of any whom I know. Mr. Parsons' style was from its beginning a byword for obscurity among American sociologists. Unfortunately, however, there has been much more snickering about Mr. Parsons' tortured style than there has been serious thought about what it might mean.

NOTES TOWARD A SOCIOLOGY OF THEORETICAL OBSCURITY

The use of such an exceptionally obscure literary style by any writer might token what could be conceived of as the wish for "privatization" of his work or as an impairment of his interest in communication. In brief, Mr. Parsons does not have a strong impulse to be understood by others. In some part, this testifies to Mr. Parsons' conception of his role: he sees his task as a technical and professional one, which admits no responsibilities to a larger audience. Yet the fact is, it is not only a lay audience that finds Parsons' style forbidding, but also other sociologists. This, in turn, would seem to imply that he has not been terribly concerned about communicating effectively even with his peers, or even about being understood by them.

We need to ask how Parsons has been able to get away with this and to inquire into the social conditions that have permitted it to happen. Most generally, it seems to imply a breakdown in the system of social controls that normally shape a scholar's work. In particular, I would like to suggest that Parsons' obscurity may be related to his being protected by Harvard's high social position.

Like any university, Harvard's social position tends to have a "halo effect" on the prestige of its faculty members. Commonly, that is, the higher the national repute of a university, the higher the prestige of those associated with it. Simply by reason of being at Harvard a man gets a substantial measure of "unearned prestige." A university's prestige, of course, affects the bargaining position of its faculty. But "bargaining position" does not refer solely to what a man can command in rank and salary in the national labor market of his profession; it refers also to the treatment of his *work* in its *intellectual* market. The greater the prestige of the university with which a scholar is associated, the greater the readiness to credit his work and to tolerate departures from the profession's conventions, including its literary expectations. Stated otherwise, the higher the prestige imputed to a scholar by his associates nationally, whether because of his own contributions or because of his university affiliation, the greater their readiness to grant him "deviance credits," which, in turn, allow him greater freedom either for creativity or for sheer idiosyncrasy.

This may manifest itself in various ways. For example, when a scholar is confronted with a very prestigious colleague's work, which he finds difficult to understand or to see importance in, he is more likely to blame *himself* than when confronted with similarly obscure work by a less prestigious colleague. Indeed, I can think of at least one important sociologist, a man of outstanding and enduring attainments, who was so traumatized by his difficulty in understanding Parsons' work that he assumed this signified his own impending obsolescence. Faced with the obscure work of prestigious colleagues, scholars are also likely to favor it with the assumption that its manifest muddiness is indicative of a hidden depth. The point is not that obscure work is necessarily fostered by a prestigious university—George Homans' work at Harvard clearly scotches that—but, rather, that such an affiliation can enable a man to escape the neglect that obscurity commonly invites.

A central *social* fact explaining the acceptance and spread of Parsons' work, despite its considerable intellectual fuzziness and obscure style, remains, in my view, that it was developed at and associated with Harvard. For, in addition to the unearned prestige with which this endowed Parsons' publications, being at Harvard also meant that Parsons had access to many first-rate students. Since they were first-rate, and also because they acquired Harvard degrees, these young men soon assumed important positions elsewhere in the academic world, from which vantage points they could, in turn, more readily win additional adherents to his theory. It is my impression that, more than any other contemporary academic social theory, Parsons' has made its way through such a network of adherents who, of course, had a personal stake in winning acceptance for it. The opacity of the master's own words was thus counterbalanced by the devotedness of his students, at least for a certain period, and by the fact that they, unlike Parsons, often could and did write well, and sometimes very well indeed.

Yet it must not be supposed that the obscurity of Parsons' style had only the effect of impeding the understanding and diffusion of his ideas. For, the sheer difficulty in understanding Parsons can be overcome, if at all, only by considerable effort, which constitutes an appreciable personal investment in his work and engenders what is, in effect, a vested interest in it. The scholar's return on his investment may come from discussing Parsons' ideas publicly, either critically or in a favorable spirit; either course probably results in making them better known.

It is also noteworthy that a difficult style may serve to protect intellectual creativity. The task of an intellectual innovator is two-sided. He must *detach* himself from conventional approaches, whether these are conventional to a larger lay public or to a narrower group of specialists like himself; he must, this means, protect himself from the press of conventional approaches, lest his own originality be diluted. An innovator, however, must also find some way of *securing support* for his early still undeveloped, and hence particularly precarious efforts; he must make or win adherents, establishing a new group that will shelter his innovation. Linguistic and stylistic obscurity serves both functions.

Obscurity makes a work relatively costly. It is costly for those bearing conventional views to penetrate its meanings, and they will therefore often ignore it or give it short shrift. This, in turn, relieves the innovator from the pain of adverse criticisms. His work will *at first* often be ignored or only superficially criticized. The innovator can feel, and justifiably, that his critics have not studied it carefully or understood it deeply. He can thus dismiss his critics painlessly and proceed on his own course.

To publish in a very difficult style is almost equivalent to *not* publishing. In reading an extremely obscure work, those first drawn to it are dealing with a not yet truly public object, but with something that is more nearly akin to a "cult object." It is much like reading an unpublished and privately circulated manuscript, which has, in effect, the aura of a "secret teaching." Because of its difficulty the work must be given an "interpretation." Its interpretation and understanding are, in part, dependent upon a personal acquaintance with the author, and knowledge of it often implies a special relation to him.

The early initiates of such a theory may thus feel a lonely but privileged distance from their larger intellectual communities. The very difficulty of interpreting the new doctrine heightens intercommunication among the first adherents, and this, along with its new, membership-symbolizing vocabulary, draws them together into an intellectual community. The new doctrine becomes firmly imprinted in the members as they seek to clarify it for one another and to explain or defend it from outsiders. The result, then, is that the new doctrine is protected by becoming deeply internalized in each adherent and by the developing social solidarity of the first-generation "seed-group." These, in turn, safeguard the intellectual coherence of the new doctrine and reduce its tendency toward entropy.

There are, however, contrary consequences of obscurity, which ultimately do generate entropy-increasing forces. Because the work is obscure, it allows various interpretations that may be appreciably different from one another. This enhances its attractiveness to competitive intellectuals, enabling each to distinguish himself from the other adherents. In time, however, as each continuously develops his own individuated interpretation by cross-breeding with the increasingly differentiated developments of his peers, the coherence of the innovator's original system is attenuated, it blends into the larger intellectual environment, and it becomes increasingly difficult to distinguish from the "background."

There are, of course, various kinds as well as various sources of intellectual obscurity. For example, there is a kind of obscurity that is tradition-protected and, within learned disciplines, is conceived of as a "technical" difficulty. The technically difficult is, in short, obscure only to the uninitiated, and it is a socially sanctioned obscurity, in the view of those initiated. There is also an idiosyncratic obscurity that is not sanctioned by the traditions of any intellectual community but is peculiar to an individual. Much of Parsons' obscurity is of this sort; it is quite distinguishable from the obscurity, says, of Karl Marx's *Capital*, which is obscure only to those uninitiated in the technical idiom of nineteenth-century political economy.

Again, there is a syntactical obscurity as distinct from one of vocabulary. Vocabulary obscurities relate to difficulties in understanding the manner in which objects are defined and their boundaries established, while syntactical obscurities bear upon the manner in which defined objects are related to one another. In Parsons, both obscurities are found frequently. They are so common because so much of Parsons' work entails the presentation of proliferating neologisms and object definitions: this I have previously referred to as his conceptualizing drive. His work is taken up, in large part, with the more or less simultaneous presentation of numerous conceptualized objects while he is trying to establish their relations to one another.

At the core of Parsons' obscurity, then, is the sheer *multiplicity* of objects under examination and the attempted *simultaneity* with which they, and their relations to one another, are presented. By virtue of this "busy-ness," few of them are intellectually inspected long and carefully, and few are illustrated with the kinds of concrete examples that might enhance their intelligibility. Like the juggler who has to keep many balls in the air, he may not touch any one of them more than momentarily.

The sense that one gets in reading Parsons' work is of a kind of headlong rush that does not allow him time to edit what he has written before publishing it. Parsons is telling us quite plainly that, in his understanding of the theoretical enterprise, "neatness" does not count, details that might clarify do not count, and, indeed, no one of the *parts* touched upon at a given moment counts. What, then, does count?

For Parsons what matters above all else is the *whole*, and his ability to sustain contact with his glimpsed apprehension of the whole. He is engaged in a race against the sensed ephemerality of his vision of the whole; his need is to fix and bind it in its wholeness. He must hurry on before it fades. One reason for this is that the structures Parsons "sees" are lacking in *social* reality, in the specific sense that they are not maintained by publicly shared, cultural definitions and traditions; they are, rather, highly private distinctions which, as such, have only a precarious reality. They must be written down quickly, for it is largely through such literary objectification that they may seem real. Intensely preoccupied with the maintenance and inspection of his own precarious vision of the social whole, much of Parsons' theoretical work is an exceptionally privatized effort, little attentive to the anticipated reactions of others and, hence, blind to the obscurity of his own communication.

Parsons' obscurity leads us, I believe, to the central concern of his most basic metaphysics, which clearly devolves from an affirmation of the importance of the whole and its priority to the parts. For, it is his commitment to the whole and his inability to see the parts as having reality except by their involvement in a whole, that lead Parsons to push on and conceptually constitute the total system at once without pausing to work through the clarifying details. There is for Parsons a kind of urgency; he must forthwith constitute the total anatomy of social systems and identify all their components immediately, for without this conceptual constitution of the system as a whole, the parts are uninterpretable:

> The most essential condition of successful dynamic analysis is continual and systematic reference of *every* problem to the state of the system as a whole . . . A process or set of conditions either 'contributes' to the maintenance (or development) of the *system* or it is 'dysfunctional' in that it detracts from the integration and effectiveness of the system.[2]

Each part depends on and contributes to every other, and it is lacking in stable signification apart from what it does for and receives from every other; it thus has no being apart from its involvements and exists therefore only as a "part," which is to say, only in and for something else. Parsons is thus centrally concerned with discerning "the foundational reference of *all* particular conditions and processes to the state of the *total* system as a going concern" (italics mine). It is precisely this organic vision, which implies that parts lack reality without membership in a totality, that induces the multiplicity/simultaneity hastiness that contributes so much to Parsons' obscurity.

THE CONCEPTUAL SYSTEM AS ICON

In general, Parsons' overall style of work seems very similar to Comte's. Indeed, the similarity between the two is not a superficial one, and we might well think of Parsons as a latter-day Comte. For one thing, the taxonomic, formal quality of Parsons' work is strikingly like Comte's compulsive formalism. Comte started, for example, with certain postulates about human nature, beginning with the assumption that it was divided into two parts, intelligence or mind, on the one side, and "heart" or emotion, on the other. Emotions are then dichotomized into sentiments and will. Sentiments are further dichotomized into those that are egoistic and those that are altruistic. The egoistic sentiments are divided into the nutritive, sexual, and material, the military and industrial instincts, and pride and vanity. The altruistic sentiments, for their part, are subdivided into friendship, veneration, and kindness. The "will" is divided into courage, prudence, and steadfastness. Then—going back to the other half of the first dichotomy in human nature—Comte subdivides intelligence or mind into understanding and expression; the former is passive or active; if passive, it is abstract or concrete; if active, it is deductive or inductive. Comte postulates that in the relation between the two basic elements in human nature, intelligence and emotions, the latter governs action; man is basically a nonrational creature; intelligence is noble but weak. There is thus a split in human nature itself, between power and goodness, or between reality and morality.

Parsons' work parallels Comte's both in its taxonomic zeal, crudely utilizing four-fold tables as a logic machine to chop out mountains of conceptual distinctions, and also in its basic assumptions concerning the *nonrationality* of human behavior. It is similar, in short, in both form and content. Man's behavior is shaped not by a utilitarian calculus but by nonrational, ultimate values, according to Parsons. Parsons, however, does not speak of "human nature" but instead moves toward more behavioristic distinctions between types of social action. Insofar as these entail *imputed* states of mind they are not, of course, any more behavioristic or "empirical" than attributes of human nature. The shift, however, does imply an emphasis on the great variety of concrete ends that men may pursue; it implies a drift toward a more relativistic image of man.

Very importantly, it also implies a more *sociologistic* picture of man. While Parsons' voluntarism places great importance on man's effort to realize certain ends, it is paradoxically true that these ends are no longer seen as derived from him; though they reside *in* him, they derive *from* social systems. Man is a hollowed-out, empty being filled with substance only by society. Man thus is seen as an entirely *social* being, and the possibility of conflict between man and society is thereby reduced. Man now has and is nothing of his own that need be counterposed to society.

In his taxonomic fervor—and it is nothing less than that— Parsons postulates that human action is either instrumental or noninstrumental. He is then off and running, and the logic machine goes into high gear. Since the instrumental is for Parsons primarily cognitive in character, it corresponds to Comte's mind or intelligence; the noninstrumental corresponds to Comte's "heart" or emotion. From this point onward, conceptual distinctions fly in all directions and reproduce promiscuously. New distinctions are mated to produce new conceptual offspring, and they, in turn, are bred incestuously either with their parents or with one another to produce still another generation of concepts.

For example, a distinction is made between forms of action in terms of their "motivational" and their "value-orientational" dimensions. The latter refers to culturally transmitted standards or norms by which action is oriented and appraised. The former refers to internalized drives, or urges toward something, and is further subdivided into the cognitive, cathectic, and evaluative forms, which correspond to beliefs, sentiments, and morals. All human action is further categorized in terms of five pattern variables, which are discussed dichotomously. Page after page of concepts and their typological combinations gush forth. Distinctions are made between the cultural, social, psychological, and biological levels—the latter being later added, it seems, for the sake of formal completeness—each of which is seen as a distinctive analytical system. Social systems are analyzed in terms of their role and status organization, their aggregate character as collectivities, their norms and values, their universal functional exigencies and phases, their adjustment to internal stresses or external boundary-exchanges, which are, in turn, combined with the instrumental versus noninstrumental or consummatory dichotomy to produce four system problems: adaptation, goal-attainment, pattern-maintenance, and integration. And so on.

For Parsons, the significant test of these concepts is *not* that they lead to or may be inserted in testable hypotheses or propositions; Parsons seems no more interested in this than the unsophisticated compiler of a dictionary was interested in the sentences in which his inventory of words might be used. The tension-releasing, triumphant moment for Parsons is when he can "show" that one set of his categories or concepts may be applied to *various* social sectors or to *different* levels of social life, thus linking them together. It is when Parsons is able to show the diverse applications of a single set of concepts, thus reducing the dangle of things, that he feels he has demonstrated its worth. Diversity of application of a single category set is his unstated *test* of value. Similarly, Parsons also likes elaborate analogies, for while they do not actually bridge things they resonate a sense of unity.

That different sectors or levels of a universe may be viewed in terms of the same set of distinctions does not, of course, demonstrate that the distinctions yield propositions that are scientifically or practically valuable, or are true or interesting, or lead to the discovery of new facts or the useful reorganization of old ones. One may, of course, distinguish people in countless ways, say, as redheads versus nonredheads, and may find that all human populations are susceptible to categorization in these terms. One may even shout, Eureka! and proclaim that the same is true for horses. But what does this demonstrate about the value of such a distinction? Does it show it to be better than an alternative distinction, which, for example, divides the world into bald and hairy people?

Looked at in its grossest and most manifest terms, Parsons' work is largely a list of combinations of certain kinds of concepts, and, in particular, of those that express *domain assumptions* about man and society. He is concerned, that is, to assert what is presumably true of *all* social action, *all* societies, *all* social systems, etcetera. In a serious sense, then, Parsons is not so much a substantive social theorist as the grand metaphysician of contemporary sociology. If I object to Parsons' metaphysics, however, it is not because I object to metaphysics in general, but only to those that are befuddled.

Yet all this has been said before. Time and again it has been said and shown[3] that Parsons' work is primarily a body of analytic concepts, of categories and typologies of shifting meaning and fuzzy connotation, whose most manifest feature is its obscurity. To let the matter go after having said this, however, is unsatisfactory; it does not tell us how this came to be. In particular, it provides no insight into the *meaning* of Parsons' conceptual effort or into the impulses that drive it. To fully understand Parsons we must see how the many obvious weaknesses in his work are, in a sense, *irrelevant* in the light of what he is attempting in his conceptual fervor. Indeed, we must see how the very structural weaknesses of his work actually express and achieve his intent. In what follows I attempt an understanding not of this or that specific Parsonian concept, but of the *structure* of his intellectual style, which is characterized by his blanketing conceptual drive.

As I have indicated, Parsons believes that no aspect of the social world can be *known* unless it is set within a whole. He does not feel that an empirical understanding of the social world can be seriously furthered unless *all* of its predicates are first laid out in *advance*. Underlying the prolific specification of parts and their relationships is Parsons' impulse to relate all the contents in the whole, leaving nothing without its place. "Exhaustiveness" is the most important criterion that Parsons tacitly employs in viewing his sets of categories.

His concern for exhaustiveness, however, is not simply an expression of his interest in conforming to the logical canons of correct categorization. For, while these canons do, indeed, call for exhaustiveness—that every particular be placeable in one of the concepts in the set of categories—there are, however, other important criteria for correct categorization to which Parsons pays scant attention: for example, the criterion of "mutual exclusiveness," which requires that each individual case be locatable in one and *only one* category in a set. This, however, requires a conceptual clarity and specificity that Parsons little manifests. In addition, Parsons pays little or no attention to the more general standard of parsimony, which prohibits the unjustified proliferation of distinctions and assumptions.

The most important consideration for Parsons, which is closely related to his neglect of the criteria of mutual exclusiveness and of parsimony, is that his concepts and category sets should have no spaces between them into which things might fall and be lost. For Parsons, it is far more important that there be *at least* one concept into which any and every particular might be put, than that there be *only* one concept into which something might be unambiguously placed. For this reason it is not too important to Parsons if his concepts are fuzzy, if they overlap, if they are ambiguous. Indeed, their very ambiguity allows them to be stretched and thus further ensures their exhaustiveness.

For Parsons, then, the making of conceptual distinctions is his way of constituting the *oneness* of the social world. It is his distinctive way of bringing the world *together*. His analysis begins by symbolically constituting a single communality that underlies the entire social world, a single common plastic dimension, social action, which is then differentiated into various others (means, ends, conditions; instrumental and noninstrumental; etcetera) much as a coin is made up of one metal substance of distinguishable elements, some well demarcated, others blurred into one another. Parsons' categories thus function as a symbolic representation and constitution of the social world's *oneness*. This oneness is expressed and communicated by the very *weaknesses* of his work; it is conceptually promoted by the promiscuous combining, blending, bleeding, leaking of his concepts, one into the other, by their fungus-like capacity to grow out in all directions from a single spore and to cover the entire territory in shingled layers.

Parsons' conceptualizations are thus not to be understood merely as scientifically instrumental or as useful for research; indeed, this still remains to be shown. They are, in part, ends in themselves. They really need no research to fulfill their symbolic function. Their very structure represents Parsons' vision of the oneness of the social world. Rather than being exclusively instrumental, they are like icons, whose very form communicates something vital about the world.

The revealing thing about Parsons' individual concepts is that, characteristically, they are not even sensitizing. They do not heighten the reader's awareness of certain parts of his environment; they do not confirm and crystallize his own vague intimations. They are, typically, not insight-inducing conceptualizations, for in the end insight is always an insight into some experience. There is little about the world we experience, whether impressionistically or systematically known, to which Parsons' categories appeal. For they are not intrinsically oriented to any form of empirical sensitivity. Parsons' categories are, more nearly, self-sufficient conceptual extrusions that cover rather than reveal the world. They make the world whole by overlaying its gaps, tensions, conflicts, incompletenesses with a conceptual encrustation. The mountains of categories to which Parsons' labors have given birth are the product of an inward search for the world's oneness and a projection of his vision of that oneness.

PARSONS AS SYSTEM ANALYST

In its holism Parsons' domain assumptions are only superficially similar to the Marxist conception of society as a *system* and to its concern with capitalist *systems*. For, influenced by the Hegelian tradition, Marx had felt that the *divisions* in the world, its negations, internal contradictions, and class conflicts, were its deepest reality. To Marx the cleavages in the world were of its essence. In a way, the world did not become fully real to him until it was divided against itself. It is not the cleavages in the social world that are real to Parsons, however, but its unbroken oneness: the fact that it all grows out of one elemental stuff, social action, into increasingly differentiated structures. At any rate, this is one of the ways in which Parsons constitutes the oneness of the social world. The most important expression of Parsons' vision of the oneness of the social world, however, is his conception of it as a *system*. Parsons thus actually has two different metaphors in terms of which unity is expressed: the social world as organic differentiation from a common substance, and the social world as a single system. The metaphor of organic differentiation is less focal and controlled; the metaphor of system is labeled and deliberately employed. Protoplasmic organic differentiation is the genetics of oneness; system mechanics are the synchronics of oneness. There is a hint of a Rousseaueanism here: social systems are born as living organisms, but everywhere they are becoming machines.

PROBLEMS OF SYSTEM ANALYSIS[4]

From the standpoint of Parsons' system analysis three very general questions emerge. First, as Parsons indicates, "the most general and fundamental property of a system is the interdependence of parts or variables." Questions therefore arise concerning the character of *interdependence*. Second, there is the problem of *system maintenance*. Systems may maintain some measure of stability through processes of "boundary exchange" and through mechanisms which restore their "equilibrium" when this is perturbed. Much of Parsons' system analysis, then, resolves itself into questions either about the nature of system interdependence or about the nature of system-stabilizing forces, boundary-maintaining or equilibrating mechanisms. Clearly, however, system interdependence and equilibrium are analytically independent, for while equilibrium implies interdependence, interdependence does *not* necessarily imply equilibrium. Third, and finally, we will also want to know what Parsons thinks about system change, that is, the ways in which systems may change, either in their internal dynamics or in their structure as a whole.

But even before any of these basic problems can be explored, we must ask how the constituent components of the social system are identified by Parsons. His assumption is, as we have seen, that it is not possible to interpret any single social pattern except by referring it to some larger systemic whole. Parsons assumes that the *whole* system must be conceptually constituted prior to the empirical investigation of any specific part or pattern. In consequence, Parsons is led forthwith to the specification of *all* the parts of the social system, of its entire anatomy, in an effort to identify all of its potentially consequential components. Presumably, this should make it possible systematically to refer any one part to *all* the component structures constituting the system. But since this must take place prior to the empirical study of any one part, all the constituent elements of the whole system can be immediately constituted only by some form of *ex cathedra* postulation.

The problem is that, whether or not a given part of the social anatomy is in fact "there" or whether it is useful even to postulate it, is to an important degree resolvable only by research. The specification of the component elements of a social system is no more attainable by theoretical postulation alone than are the attributes of those "living" systems with which biologists deal. But Parsons makes no systematic use of empirical operations in constituting the elements in his social system, thinking that this must be done *a priori,* in a purely theoretical manner.

Parsons' insistence upon the immediate postulation and constitution of a "social system" as a whole is, he explains, justified on the basis of its superior explanatory power. But its real grounding is in Parsons' metaphysics. So far as I am aware Parsons' recommended procedure has never been *shown* to explain (the variance in) any single problematic social pattern more fully—or in any other sense, better than—some other strategy of explanation.

The main advantage of Parsons' system approach seems to be that it does communicate an *image* of the *oneness* of human groups. Indeed, this is really one of Parsons' most important contributions. More than any other modern social theorist, he has persuasively communicated a sense of the reality of a social *system*, of the boundaried oneness and coherent wholeness of patterns of social interaction. All this, however, is done *entirely*—and this is the paradoxical aspect for those who merely complain about Parsons' literary style—through the sheer force of his conceptualizing rhetoric. For all his ambiguity and obscurity, he has been able to conjure an image of a special something, the *social system*, and to evoke a sense of its reality by what are, in the last analysis, entirely literary means. It is this communicated sense of the *wholeness* of a group, and not any demonstrably great explanatory power, to which Parsons' system analysis owes much of its appeal. It gives sociologists a sense of the tangible substantiality of a special entity that they feel it is their special business to explore, and thereby helps to legitimate their existence as a distinct discipline.

When Parsons stipulates the structure of a "social system," exhibiting the elements out of which he constitutes it, his nuclear conception is of an Ego and an Alter, that is, two or more role players engaged in interaction with one another, conforming to or departing from one another's expectations, having some measure of complementarity in their expectations, so that what Ego regards as his rights are viewed by Alter as his duties, and *vice versa;* this complementarity is, in its turn, dependent upon a common orientation to a set of moral values that they share. It is, in large part, because Parsons centers his conception of social systems on the interaction between Ego and Alter that it has its great appeal, particularly to Americans. The Ego-Alter formulation hints at the *presence* of individuals somewhere in the system by giving them differentiated role locations; the distinctive properties of groups are thus not formulated in a manner that obliterates their connection with individual behavior. Parsons' focus is not, as Durkheim's often was, on the utter autonomy of social phenomena, on the social as a reality *sui generis*, or on the group as an "association" of undifferentiated roles. Thus Parsons establishes the coherence and systemic character of the group as such while still allowing a *place* for persons, if not the persons themselves.

It is clear, however, that, from Parsons' formulation of the social system, elements in men's biological constitution and physiological functioning, as well as features of their physical and ecological environment, are excluded. So too are the historically evolving cultural complexes of material objects, including tools and machines, even though these are man's own unique and distinctive creations, the very products and the mediating elements of his social interaction and communication, and even though they also include those instruments of *transportation* which make possible the very interchanges among social parts that constitute their interdependence. In exiling these "material" elements from the social system, Parsons at best derives a purely formal advantage: that is, the demarcation of a distinct class of systems, which may form the object of a distinct social science discipline. But in doing this he undermines a systematic place for numerous cogent re-searches—perhaps, particularly, the ecological—which, if lacking in formal elegance in this sense, might illuminate the important ways in which social behavior is patterned. Similarly, the actual embodied individual is also exiled from the social system and flits through it phantom-like, only materialized momentarily as he passes through role locations.

To establish the social system in this manner may accomplish the objective of chartering an independent social science. But it seems a Pyrrhic victory, bought at the cost of a scientific ritualism in which logical elegance is substituted for empirical potency. It is vulnerable to Ruskin's sarcasm about constituting a science of gymnastics that postulates men having no skeletons.

SYSTEM INTERDEPENDENCE

The problem of "interdependence" is central to Parsons' concept of a social system, as it is to any. It is notable, however, that Parsons rarely gives the concept of "interdependence" systematic and formal analysis; he tends instead to take it as a given rather than making it problematic in its most general implications. Perhaps the basic reason for this is that for Parsons the concept of system interde-pendence has a *polemical* vector in it. Built into it there is a coun-terstatement against those social theories, such as Marxism, which he interprets as implying that some social factors are *independent,* since they are held to *determine* outcomes in the long run. Thus, for Parsons the initial value of the concept of *interdependence* is that it undermines assumptions concerning the *independence* of certain social factors and, with this, their determinism. Since any change in a system presumably acts on it in numerous ways, an underlying moral of Parsons' system is unpredictability. For Par-sons, a system is a surprise machine.

Interdependence for Parsons is, therefore, antideterministic. In the *Structure of Social Action,* for example, Parsons stresses that system parts are *inter*dependent with one another. And he adds that, "in a system of interdependent variables . . . the value of any one variable is not completely determined unless those of all the others are known." This formulation clearly, albeit only implicitly, reveals the improbability, if not the impossibility, of knowing the value of *any* variable in a social system. For, no one thing can be "completely determined"—in a system—unless everything is; which means, in effect, that nothing is completely determined. It is therefore because the rhetorical function of the concept of system interdependence is, for Parsons, very largely to polemicize against deterministic theories that postulate the independent causal significance of certain social factors, that he has little reason to analyze the concept of a system formally. For him the concept of a system need be clarified only enough to perform its antideterministic function.

Nevertheless, even on a formal level of system analysis, different things may be predicated about systems; it is necessary to choose among competing formal models and to identify those that promise to have a better "fit" to the known, relevant data, for there are significantly different kinds of systems. Mere commitment to the concept of an empirical "system" is empty; it is much as if a mathematical physicist were to commit himself to the use of "geometry" in general, rather than specifying which system of geometry he proposed to use in solving his problems.

The concept of "system" is purely formal and, like those used in mathematics, is devoid of empirical content. When a formal system is applied to a specific subject matter, it is said to be "interpreted." Some formal systems have many interpretations, others have none. The nub of the issue here is the nature of the interpretation to be given, when the formal and empty notion of a system is applied to human affairs. Parsons does, indeed, provide such an interpretation. But it is, at one level of analysis, an *ad hoc* and metaphysically-driven interpretation, because he never sees that, on the formal level, there are different conceptions of systems that might be applied, never explicitly says which one he is applying, what its character is, and why he uses it. This we must, at best, infer from the concrete applications he makes. He tells us what his *social* system is, but not what his social *system* is. In short, he has given only the most primitive analysis to the formal concept of a system, allowing matters to rest very largely with the affirmation that it has the unexamined attributes of interdependence and self-maintenance, or equilibrium.

It makes a good deal of difference, however, whether interdependence and equilibrium are analyzed as dimensions capable of significant variability or, instead, conceptualized as substance-like entities. If this dimensionality is not recognized, there is a compelling tendency to conceive of systems as things that *have* interdependence and *have* equilibrium, and thus to miss that these are the positive values of dimensions. Systems have varying *degrees* of interdependence and of equilibrium, and it is easy to forget that what we have to deal with is not a system but "system-ness." In effect, the Parsonian conception of a system, focusing as it does on only one extreme of the dimension, does not confront the variable states a system might have.

FUNCTIONAL AUTONOMY AND INTERDEPENDENCE

Rather than conceiving of systems in terms of the "interdepend-ence" of their elements, one could just as truly define a system as a group of elements that have low "functional autonomy" with respect to one another. In other words, systems might be conceived of as elements or parts having some interchanges with one another, and each of the parts might thus have varying degrees of depend-ence on or autonomy from the others. Some parts might have all or most of their needs satisfied by such interchanges, while others might have relatively few; the former may be said to have low functional autonomy, and the latter, high functional autonomy. In this sense a system might be defined as a group of elements whose interchanges restrict their functional autonomy.

To conceptualize systems in terms of their interdependence, as Parsons does, tends to focus primarily on the "whole" and on the close connectedness of the parts. It tends to stress the *oneness* of the whole. A conception of systems in terms of "functional autonomy" tends, quite differently, to focus on the *parts* themselves, and it stresses that their connectedness is problematic. A concept of interdependence focuses on the parts only in their implication within a system. It sees them as "real" only in and for a system. A concept of functional autonomy, however, raises the question of the extent of this implication and, more distinctively, focuses on the other, *extra*system involvements of the parts.

In other words, in conceiving of systems as made up of inter-dependent parts, the parts are conceived of only in their system character. In conceiving of systems as made up of more or less functionally autonomous elements, however, the elements are not merely "parts" but are seen to exist in and for "themselves." They are seen to have an existence apart from any given system in which they are involved; their reality does not depend solely upon their involvement in the system under examination. From the standpoint of functional autonomy, then, the analysis of social systems has a different emphasis than does Parsons'. For example, from Parsons' standpoint emphasis is placed on the mechanisms that protect the interdependence and equilibrium of the *system* as a whole; from our standpoint, emphasis would also be placed on the identification and analysis of the mechanisms that protect the *functional autonomy of the parts*. The latter may require the reduction of high degrees of interdependence if they threaten the parts' autonomy, and it may also give rise to a resistance to pressures for equilibrium. In short, parts with some degree of functional autonomy would be expected to resist full integration into or increased dependence upon the larger system or upon other elements in it.

From this standpoint, in fine, two opposing forces are continually at work in all social systems. First, there is the tendency of the parts to protect whatever measure of functional autonomy they already possess or even to extend it further; there is a tendency for each part to maintain its *own* boundaries and to resist fuller and more complete integration into the larger system.

Second, there is the tendency of the system itself, or more accurately, of those parts that are charged or identify with system management, to strive toward fuller integration, reducing the autonomy of the parts and increasing their submission to the requirements of the system as a whole, as they, the system managers, define it. These integrating pressures are exerted by a system part, the managerial element, which, if identifying itself with the entire system, is nonetheless like any other part with its own vested interests in functional autonomy. Integrating forces therefore always contain two opposing elements: those deriving from the intrinsic, but managerially interpreted requirements of the system for a measure of integration, and those deriving from the special interests of the managerial part in the maintenance of some measure of autonomy for *itself*. In short, tendencies toward system integration inherently tend toward "oligarchical" centralization, for they are always interpreted and implemented by some system part which has its own distinct drive toward functional autonomy. Correspondingly, it is precisely these oligarchical tendencies that threaten the autonomy of the other parts of the system, generate opposition to oligarchy, polarize the system around an internal conflict, and, in effect, constitute an "iron law" of *opposition* to oligarchy.

MORAL CODES AS CONDUCTORS OF TENSION

Such as it is, then, the integration of the system is at best an inherently tense and precarious balancing of forces. At any given moment it is the result of the changing balance of power among the parts and of their shifting alliances; it registers the outcome of the various pressures in the negotiated compromises which are achieved. To say this, however, is not to say that moral considerations do not limit autonomy strivings and do not influence the system parts in their effort to preserve or extend their functional autonomy in their negotiations with one another. At the same time, moral considerations and shared values do not fully govern the outcomes. For, on a different level, considerations of morality and considerations of "interest" in functional autonomy are themselves in a tensionful relationship with one another. The conflicts between integration and autonomy are not eliminated, nor for that matter are they merely "controlled" by shared moral norms, for the tensions are, in fact, expressed *through* the moral norms and through their relations to other commitments.

This is so for several reasons. First, due to the very fact that different parts have different degrees of commitment to a given social system, they are differentially committed—some more, some less—to that system's moral code. Second, the moral rules themselves are not given automatic and mechanical conformity simply because they, in some sense, "exist"; the varying degrees of conformity given by different system parts are a function of different parts' bargaining positions; conformity is not so much given as *negotiated*, and this, in turn, will reflect the actors' varying degrees of functional autonomy. Third, there is differential conformity to a single moral rule at different *times*, depending, in part, on whether it restricts or enhances one's functional autonomy; a moral rule is given more support by a part when it furthers than when it restricts or reduces its autonomy. Conformity with or enforcement of the same rule often has different consequences, losses or gains, for the autonomy of different parts. The tension between the parts is reflected *in* the different *interpretations* each seeks to impose on any rule. The rule thus serves as a vehicle *through which* the tension is *expressed;* it becomes a focus around which conflict develops. Fourth, there is usually more than one rule in a moral code that can be claimed to be relevant to a decision and in terms of which it may be legitimated. A central factor influencing one's choice of a specific rule to govern a decision is its expected consequences for the functional autonomy of the part. There is therefore conflict about *which* of several rules applies in any case. Each part tends to opt for the rule that it believes will optimize its functional autonomy. What one conceives to be moral, tends to vary with one's interests.

In any interaction between parts, therefore, the existence of a shared moral code does not *necessarily* reduce friction, for each may define a different rule as governing the interaction and each may interpret the same rule in different ways. Consequently, the fact that the parts all subscribe to a common moral code does not in the least ensure that their relations with one another will be "complementary," and that those things regarded by one part as "rights" will be viewed by the other as "obligations." To the contrary, the underlying impulse of all parts to protect and extend their functional autonomy ensures that the moral code itself often becomes the very language in which their conflicts, competitions, and tensions are expressed. A moral code does not eliminate the tensions inherent in a social system; at the very most it provides a restraint on these inherent tensions; and at the very least it provides a language in which tensions are given public expressions and become the focus around which they are organized. Tensions abide.

THE SOCIAL SYSTEM AND THE SELF[5]

These general considerations, I am well aware, are essentially metaphysical in character, but Parsons is above all a metaphysician. His system metaphysics need to be applied to various levels. For example, when the Parsonsian conception of a system is brought to bear on the relationship between individual persons and the group as a whole, what is emphasized is the individual's plastic potentiality for conformity. Emphasis is placed on the conformity of individuals with the requirements of the social position in which they find themselves or with the needs of the group; thus tensions between the individual and the group are seen not as intrinsic but as fortuitous, not as universal but as situational. Conceiving of the individual as an entirely "social" creature, as an empty, hollowed-out container that depends entirely upon experience in and training by social systems, it denies that there *need* be any conflict. Instead, it draws attention to the power of the socializing process and to the malleability of the individual, which, in principle, might produce so complete a fit as totally to eliminate conflicts between individual and group. A theoretical model that implies this, however, has one fatal flaw: it fails to correspond to the facts known about any social system ever studied.

Indeed, the very malleability of an organism viewed—as in Parsons' model—as susceptible to almost any kind of socialization, by any one social system, is precisely what allows it to be *re*socialized by and in another. Organism-malleability does not ensure the elimination of conflict between the individual and society; quite the contrary, it underwrites a measure of functional autonomy for the person and, with this, an inevitable tension between the group and the individual.

Once socialized, moreover, individuals may remain socialized even though separated from their original system; many persons manifest a capacity to generate an "escape velocity" and flee to refuge elsewhere. Certainly human beings are not invariably characterized by a total dependence upon any one social system. Here it is relevant to note one central difference between the *primary* socialization of young people conducted by families or family-surrogates, which is relatively unspecialized, and the *secondary* and more specialized socialization provided by those groups that train adults. In the course of primary socialization, while the child is prepared to participate in the roles and groups of the larger society, he commonly learns how to participate as a member of various groups. The very nature of primary socialization, then, serves not to provide well-tooled parts for any one specific group, but to ensure a measure of functional autonomy for the *individual* by virtue of preparing him to participate in various different groups: it creates "persons." Primary socialization means that the child's own interests are, in some part, regarded as separate from those of any one particular group; it means that he is being prepared for those diverse involvements that may optimize his unique individual fulfillment. Indeed, the inculcation of motives toward, and skills to facilitate, a measure of functional autonomy is one important function of primary socialization. Characteristically, however, what Parsons emphasizes in such socialization is the transmission of skills and dispositions that make the individual useful to *the system.*

Parsons' description of training for "autonomy" during primary socialization is not only extremely undeveloped and sketchy, but also largely focused on what is required to emancipate the child from his family so that he may then pass on and enter into roles in other groups.[6] For all his polemic against "utilitarianism," the pathos of a utilitarian culture echoes in Parson's Functionalism.

Socialized individuals have some measure of mobility, vertical or horizontal, among the social systems within their society, and they move with varying degrees of ease or stress from one to another. Moreover, they may and do migrate to or sojourn in societies quite different from those in which they were originally socialized. They apparently have considerable, if varying, degrees of functional autonomy relative to all concrete social systems. Consequently, we cannot think of socialized persons as "raw materials" or even as "parts" fashioned by the social systems for their use.

Human beings are as much engaged in using social systems as in being used by them. Men are social system-using and social system-building creatures. They are not merely viewed inadequately when seen one-sidedly as "social products," but are also seriously misunderstood if viewed simply as *social* beings, if by that is meant *sociable* beings, friendly little fellows eagerly waiting to cooperate with others. For, the human self develops and grows with social differences, in part, and consequently often seeks and needs confrontations.

The development of self involves development of the discriminating processes which perceive likenesses and differences. It is not, however, the likenesses but the differences that become crucial in distinguishing the self from others. And furthermore, not all differences between men are equally critical, and none so problematic as those whose consequences threaten or supply gratifications and reduce or avoid deprivations. And it is especially when the differences between men lead them into contention or conflict that these are most likely to be perceived. It is when men differ *with* one another that they are most likely to be aware of their differences *from* one another. It is when Ego demands things which Alter is not inclined to provide that Ego needs to take stock, to clarify his differences with Alter; from this does Ego's perception of his own self grow.

The development of Ego's self depends, in part, not on his involvement in a system of mutual *conformity* with Alter but also on the *breakdown* in their complementarity. The cumulation and organization of his perceived differences *with* others shapes Ego's perception of his differences *from* others, thus forming the boundaries of his self. These differences that Ego has with and from others become introjected and experienced as the critical distinction of himself, as his "individuality." What the self is taken to be and the extent to which Ego is consciously aware of this self is influenced by and realized in his social conflict with others. The self increasingly becomes an object to itself when its impulses are *not* reflexively in keeping with the expectations of the other and as it experiences responses *not* completely in keeping with its own.

The self grows out of social interaction with others, from which its social contents are derived and by which are shaped its shared similarities with, and individual differences from, others. Different aspects of the self are affected by different kinds of social interaction. The self is faced with the task of locating and enhancing itself on both the "goodness" and the "potency" dimensions, and of bringing the two into equilibrium, just as it must for all objects. The self may, for example, experience self-*esteem* when it *conforms* with the expectations of others and with group values; it thus wins approval and experiences itself as "good." But self-esteem is not the same as self-regard, which arises from a sense of the self's *potency*. Unlike self-esteem, self-regard may be experienced when the self *violates* the expectations of others, when the self manifests a capacity to express distance or autonomy from others and their demands, rather than conformity or involvement with them. Self esteem derives from *consensual* validation; self-regard derives from *conflictual* validation, which the self may experience when it manifestly becomes something to be reckoned with, even if not approved by others, and when it thus validates its autonomy. Self-regard may be experienced when the self can realize its goals despite others' resistance and when therefore it may deviate from rather than conform with culturally prevalent standards.

The self experiences itself as "good" when it is approved or loved by others, as in consensual validation, and as potent and autonomous when it stands against others, as in conflictual validation. Consensual validation, however, since it is given for conformity with social values, makes the self like other selves and blurs its identifiability and individuality. Without some tensions with others, without the individuating, boundary-forming sense of difference from others, the line between self and other grows wavery and indistinct. Conflict, therefore, is every bit as important as consensual validation in the development of an individuated, acceptable, and mature identity.

Imagine something like the complete reverse of the experiments conducted by S. A. Asch: rather than subjecting the individual to others who all differ sharply with his judgments, imagine an experiment in which total agreement and consensual validation are given by all others to some individual. He is given everything he wants; he is told that everything he believes is correct; he is shown that everything he says is understood and accepted; never for a moment, then, does anyone in the group differ in any way from him. According to the view that stresses the importance of consensual validation, this man should be fulfilled and happy. According to the view implied in conflictual validation, however, he should at some point manifest stress and distress, for the main-

tenance of self requires some measure of tension with others. Because there can be no stable self without some boundaries and
some differences with others, the self may seek out and sharpen its
differences *with* others so that it may clarify its differences *from*
them. The maintenance of the highly developed self, then, entails
a rift between self and society. Thus the highly developed self,
although emerging in social interaction, is not simply a product of
amiable sociability. It is not totally committed to friendly cooperation with others, but it also requires some measure of conflict
for its very survival: it must at some point fight the system of
which it is a part and those who wish to subject it to that system.

The embodied and socialized individual is both the most empirically obvious human system and the most complex and highly
integrated of all human systems; as a system, he is far more
integrated than any known "social system." In his embodiment,
the biological, psychological, social, and cultural all conjoin. They
are "bound together" in him far more tightly than are the elements
of any other system; embodied, socialized man is not simply a
"part," he is the *nexus* and the bond of all human levels and
systems, the modality in which and through which all their
energies are concentrated and discharged.

The amount of sheer energy located in the embodied individual
is always greater than that available to contain or resist him at the
particular sector of any social system in which he operates; even
when a social system ceases to control him only with "social bonds"
and instead builds prisons, he can find and make his way out.
There is really only one way in which a social system can be
absolutely confident that it controls the man bent on overcoming
its restrictions, and that is to kill him. There is no known social
system whose requirements he cannot evade or which he cannot
shake or destroy. A single assassin with a single gun can, and has,
spread disruption and despair in the most powerful nations on
earth. And a single creative individual, open to the needs of others
and the opportunities of his time, can be a nucleus of spreading
hope and accomplishment. A model of a social system, such as
Parsons', which overstresses the interdependence of system "parts,"
simply cannot come to terms with these and other expressions of
the potency and functional autonomy of individuals.

The system model that Parsons favors conduces to an emphasis
on interdependence-induced oneness and to a lopsided focus on
the ways that individuals are prepared to conform to the expectations of others or to satisfy the needs of their social systems. The
focus is on the mechanisms of social integration that accept individuals into social solidarities or reduce social distance among
them; on the mechanisms of defense that reduce tension among

them; or on the adaptive mechanisms that adjust the system to its environment and that reduce friction with it. All these are vital processes; no analysis of human interaction that ignores them can be adequate. But when they become the overweening focus of social analysis they warp rather than inform it; for they lead the analysis to neglect the equally significant "avoidance" side of the equation, in which socialized individuals, and other social units, commonly and with success seek to resist total inclusion in any social system, for that would involve the loss of their functional autonomy. Parsons' system model tends to assume that the "organization" of a system, that is, the particular arrangement of its parts, provides primarily for avenues of integration among the parts. From the standpoint of a system model responsive to "functional autonomy," however, "organization" serves not only to link, control, and interrelate parts; it serves also to separate them, to maintain distance among them, and to protect their functional autonomy.

Parsons emphasizes that social systems are systems of role behavior and of interaction among *role* players. Here the emphasis is on the ways that personality is integrated into the social system, involved in consistent satisfaction of its needs, and brought into reliable cooperation with others. Roles, in short, are viewed as mechanisms by which persons are integrated into systems. Yet it is of the essence of social roles that they never demand total involvement; even when role obligations are numerous and diffuse the person is never exposed to unlimited obligation. Roles are always construed so as to turn in two directions, toward the maintenance of the system *and* toward the maintenance of a measure of functional autonomy for the participating individuals. To say that a person is an "actor" in a social system, as Parsons does, is to stress that he plays a role in a social system, is subject to some system controls, and has obligations to the group in which his role has a part. At the same time, however, to say that he is a role-playing actor implies, though Parsons too often fails to make it explicit, that the person has only a *limited* involvement in any one social system and, precisely because of this, has a reality and potency apart from *all* social systems.

Although Parsons is at pains to stress the different levels of integration and analysis (the biological, psychological, cultural, and social system levels), in none of these is a conceptual provision made that would focus directly and systematically on a human system, and thus would enable us to take seriously the embodied socialized person who moves in, through, and between social systems, and who uses, creates, and destroys them during the course of his life cycle and career. In Parsons' social world, the human system, the embodied socialized individual, is not recognized outside the other four levels. The human system disappears in Parsons' framework; it escapes through the mesh of his conceptual system. It is as if Parsons' social world consists of a series of partially overlapping circles of light; when the embodied person leaves one circle or social system he disappears, becoming visible again only after he enters and is "plugged into" the next circle. Parsons thus totally inverts the entire world of everyday experience. For, in that everyday world it is the embodied individual that is most continuously in evidence, and not the social systems in which he participates. Paradoxically, then, Parsons transforms the embodied individual from the most to the least visible. It is as if the obvious existence of people is an embarrassment; as his theoretical system develops, especially as it moves from "action schema" to "social system" analysis, the embodied and socialized individual is lost from sight.[7]

ANOMIE AS DE-DIFFERENTIATION

Because Parsons' conceptual system fails to focus on the embodied socialized individual as a distinctive unit, it fails to understand how the continuity of *cultural* (as distinct from social) systems is furthered by and maintained through *people,* and how this continuity may be preserved quite apart from that of specific social systems. When a social system has failed to solve its problems and is destroyed as such, the individuals do not, of course, necessarily disappear with it. The social system often then de-differentiates back into its more elemental components, into smaller primary groups or individuals, which can and frequently do survive. From the standpoint of that specific *social* system this is a period of "disorder" or of anomic crisis. But from the standpoint of both the component individuals *and* the *cultural* system, this is a cutting of bonds that releases them to try something else that might better succeed. Anomic disorder may unbind wasted energies, sever fruitless commitments; it may make possible a ferment of innovation that can rescue the individuals, or the cultural system, from destruction.

When a social system has fruitlessly exhausted its routine solutions for its problems, then anomic randomness may be more useful to individuals and to the culture they bear, than are the treadmill and orderly plying of the old structures. Limited increases in the randomness of social systems—that is, growing anomie—may be useful for the human and the cultural systems. In this view the "anomic" person is not merely an uncontrolled "social cancer" but may be a seed pod of vital culture which, if only through sheer chance, may fall upon fertile ground. The functional autonomy of embodied, socialized individuals, implying as it does the possibility of their survival apart from a specific social system, helps maintain the cultural system. For, the cultural system, the historically accumulated heritage of beliefs and skills, is, at least in some measure, still preserved within embodied individuals even after their dissociation from specific social systems.

The continuity and safety of *cultural* systems as such derive, in some part, from the fact that embodied individuals are always socialized to have a measure of functional autonomy and are invested with far more of the culture than they require for successful operation within the single social system. Indeed, the security of *cultural* systems requires that individuals not be overly specialized vis-à-vis the needs of any particular *social* system. Seen from this perspective the socialized person's functional autonomy serves to enhance the continuity of cultural systems precisely by loosening his dependence upon the fate of his social system. From this standpoint the embodied individual is much more akin to a "seed" or germinal material than to a system "part" or organ, for the latter view sees only his specialized function vis-à-vis a social system. He contains *within himself* the "information" that can reproduce an entire culture, as well as the *energy* that enables him to "imprint" this information upon patterns of behavior and to strand these together into social systems.

In stressing the potency and autonomy of the socialized individual in his relation to the social systems, one must also avoid picturing the individual as passive in relation to the *cultural* systems. For, when cultural patterns fail to gratify the individual in a specific environment, including the social systems, he may and does modify them; that is, the embodied individual can extricate himself from conventional beliefs and traditional skills, no less than from social systems. And he will, as in the occurrence of "organized" deviance, construct new social systems within whose confines he may protect himself from the claims of old cultural patterns and secure support for new ones. If, on the one hand, the individual's extensive enculturation provides him with a measure of functional autonomy in relation to social systems, on the other hand, his capacity to create and maintain social systems provides him with a measure of functional autonomy from specific cultural systems. Each type of system provides him with leverage on the other: *he uses them both.*

WEIGHTING THE SYSTEM ELEMENTS

Throughout these comments I have stressed that "interdependence" is not a constant substance, but a variable dimension. And if there are degrees of *inter*dependence, there must also be degrees of *in*dependence or functional autonomy. Consequently, even within a system of interdependent parts, the various parts can have varying degrees of independence.

Having gone this far, it is now evident that a stress on the "web of interdependence" within a system does not relieve a theorist of the problem of weighting the differential contributions of the different elements to the system outcomes. Different system parts make different contributions to any state of the system; they contribute differentially both to changes in and to the stabilizing of the system, and this needs to be identified systematically and studied empirically. Parsons, however, fails to undertake this, largely because his starting point is a polemic against the view that there are "one or two inherently primary sources of impetus to change in social systems," to which he counterposes an emphasis on the sheer "plurality of possible origins of change."[8] Since his version of system analysis is motivated, in important part, by an effort to undermine "single factor" theories or variants of them, he is largely content to let the matter rest simply with an affirmation of an unspecified "interdependence" of unweighted elements.

System analysis centering on a doctrine of the interdependence of elements had long been a central assumption in the sociological tradition from which Parsons' theory emerges. It was clearly at work as early as Saint-Simon, and it was used by Comte. Not, however, until Radcliffe-Brown and Malinowski was it fully explicated, and Parsons gives it its most methodologically self-conscious treatment. Today, among American Functionalists, the doctrine of interdependence is a domain assumption so widely and uncritically accepted as to be almost an item of professional faith, and more likely to be given ritualistic reaffirmation than rigorous inspection. The doctrine of interdependence appears so intuitively cogent to many social scientists as to be beyond question. It is an almost unquestioned part of their occupational culture.

The formulation of the interdependence doctrine given widest credence is one which asserts that human groups and cutlures are to be seen as composed of mutually influential elements. In this terse but relatively "strong" form the doctrine of interdependence seems persuasive. Yet, in a different but equivalent form this same postulate is manifestly "weak": in social and cultural phenomena, "everything influences everything else." There is no operational, no researchable difference between the strong and weak versions of the doctrine of interdependence. The only difference is in their metaphysical pathos; that is, in the sentiments they resonate congenially. The first version appears cogent, strong, and somehow significant; the second is quite obviously trivial and weak.

The weak form, however, has at least one merit: it makes it evident that a number of important questions are being begged or ignored. Granted that, by one definition, elements in a system are mutually interdependent. Still, one must ask: Are they all interdependent in the same degree, or are some more or less functionally autonomous in relation to the system as a whole or to other elements or subsystems within it? Granted that the elements of a system, by one definition, all influence one another to some degree. One must still ask: Do they all influence one another, or the larger system, to the same extent?

These and related questions cannot be answered simply by qualitative and clinical case studies—indispensable though they are—for their solution demands the use of some kind of mathematics. Such questions imply a quantitative difference in the way the system elements determine any given outcome, and they therefore require quantitative analysis. Until recently, Functionalists were able to beg quantification because it was impossible without the use of mathematical tools which did not exist. A Parsonsian system model that simply made a vague affirmation of the "interdependence" of parts did, however, permit a qualitative analysis. While this engendered, of course, very indeterminate solutions, such empirical operations did resonate the felt sense of the world's oneness, without violating the antideterministic impulse animating the larger theory. The vague doctrine of interdependence permitted Functionalists to conduct and develop their limited empirical explorations of concrete groups and specific societies: it enabled them to do some work.

We may better understand the strengths and weaknesses of the Parsonsian model of system analysis if we understand the model to which it saw itself as responding and, indeed, if we see the larger family of possible models, of which it is only one. The Parsonsian model of system analysis was a polemic against those models that stressed the importance of "one or two inherently primary sources of impetus to change in social systems." We may term the latter model a "single factor model." But the Parsonsian was not the only response to the single factor model, there being another that we will term the "multiple causation model." We can begin with the single factor model that generated two responses, of which the Parsonsian was only one:

The Single Factor Model: In its crudest and "ideal typical" form, this model seemingly asserted, or was taken to assert, that some single factor—for example, economy, race, or climate—accounted for all other cultural and social phenomena at all times and places. Marxism, of course, has frequently been construed precisely as such a single factor model. While this has been debated, I see no profit in pursuing that debate here, since it was often understood by its opponents in this way and it was to this conception of it that they made their response.

What, then, was a single factor model thought to be? In one formulation, such a model could be said to premise a distinction between "dependent" and "independent" variables. The model requires that one examine *many* dependent variables in their relation to *one* independent variable. In other words, it takes as its task to demonstrate the diversity of effects generated by this single independent variable, and to show that changes in any and all of the dependent variables can be traced to a previous change in the preferred independent variable.

Thus simply construed, the single factor model obviously possessed both logical and empirical defects. For example, it failed to make systematic provision for the ways in which the assorted dependent variables mutually affected one another. It also ignored the reciprocal influence of the dependent variables, singly or in concert, on the independent variable. In other words, in practice it entailed focusing on one preferred variable as explanatory of the various others; however, it failed to make explicit that the independent factor accounted for only some, but not all, of the variance in the dependent variables, and thus failed to take as problematic the still unexplained or residual variance in the dependent variables. Essentially, the effort here was to "justify" some general emphasis on the importance of a variable and to demonstrate that it could be ignored only at the analyst's peril. The researcher's interest here was only in the independent variable, and in *legitimating* its place in his theory.

The Multiple Causation Model: This model was one of the two major reactions against the single factor model. In opposition to it, multiple causation counteraffirmed that all social and cultural phenomena were produced by many factors rather than one. Multiple causation focused on the diversity of contributors to the single outcome, and it sought to identify the numerous independent variables influencing the single event. While the single factor model worked with one independent variable and many dependent variables, the multiple causation model typically used *many* independent variables and *one* dependent variable.

In this way, multiple causation lent greater "realism" to theory and research. It congenially resonated the sentiments of the liberal intellectual, who, as liberal, sought to mediate between competing single-factor theories and who, as intellectual, was suspicious of the oversimplification and partiality of any one of the single factor theories. The defects of the multiple causation model were, however, substantial; indeed, they were the mirror image of those manifested by the single factor model. Multiple causation entailed the successive study of the effects of various independent variables, taken one at a time, either with or without the effects of the other independent variables held constant or "partialled out"; in either case, it also neglected the reciprocal influence of the single dependent variable on the independent variables.

Multiple causation commonly violated the canons of parsimony, often tending to the needless proliferation of independent variables. Sometimes, for example, it failed to consider whether the independent variables it added actually provided a better accounting for a greater proportion of the variance of the dependent variable. It also, sometimes, ignored the possibility that the several independent variables were simply outward manifestations of a smaller number of underlying common factors, or of one factor, being but different measures of one and the same thing.

Parsonsian System Analysis: This, like multiple causation, was, as I have suggested, also born, at least, in part, out of a polemic against the single factor model. Parsons' system model rejected the single factor view that, within a given domain, there was some variable that was inherently an independent one; it looked upon all variables as being both dependent *and* independent. In this respect it also broke with multiple causationism, for the latter had also continued to use a distinction between dependent and independent variables, even if it did not regard any specific variable as being inherently one or the other. Parsons' system model conceived of human groups as systems composed of parts that were all interdependent and mutually influential; it viewed each variable as both "cause" and "effect." As I have already indicated, a basic defect of Parsons' system model is that it begs the question of whether all the variables in a system are equally influential in determining the state of the system as a whole or the condition of any of its parts.

The difference between Parsons' system model and the single factor model, if we construe Marxism as an example of the latter, is not so radical as Parsons seems to imply, at least in his polemical formulations that stress their discontinuity. This is so for at least two reasons. First, it is unmistakably clear that Marx *did* think of societies as social systems whose elements mutually influence one another. Marx did, after all, invent the concept of the "capitalist *system.*" In fact, he believed that even the "superstructure" does react back upon the "infrastructure," though he felt that the latter is, in the "long run," controlling. Marx accepted the systemness of human groups as given; his attention was fixed on asserting that certain elements within the system ultimately controlled it. In effect, Marx addressed himself to the question of the *weighting* of the system parts, but he did so under circumstances where the opportunity for a mathematical solution was still far off; he thus did not give his solution a mathematical formulation and did not focus on the *degree* of control or dominance that a factor could have, any more than Parsons focused on the degree of interdependence among variables.

There is a second reason that Marxism and the Parsonsian system model are not as discontinuous as they might seem. While Parsons' system model affirms an amorphous interdependence among system parts, without weighting or formally affirming the dominance of any one part, nonetheless, he—like others in his theoretical tradition, from Comte to Durkheim—has always clearly assigned a very special place to one variable: shared moral beliefs or value elements. Parsons' actual use of the system model is not so radically different from Marx's. The concrete variable to which each assigns special importance is, admittedly, very different, and Marx does it all much more overtly than Parsons; nonetheless, each does, in practice, assign special importance to "one" variable operating within the system of mutually interacting variables. On this level, the differences between the Functionalist and the Marxist traditions are much more, though not entirely, a substantive matter of the specific variable preferred, rather than a matter of the formal *explanatory* model that each uses.

A possible basis for integrating the two traditions can be realized by formulating a fourth model, which I have called a "stratified system model." This model would methodically note that, even within a system of interdependent parts, not all elements are equally interdependent, some having a greater, and others a lesser, degree of autonomy or independence. In designating this a "stratified" system model, the intention is not to emphasize the causal potency of *social* stratification, but rather to focus attention on the differential causal influence of the numerous variables that operate together in a system. The model postulates that the variables comprising a system will be stratified in terms of their differential influence.

The stratified system model shares with both the Parsonsian system model and Marxism an interest in viewing any socio-cultural pattern as an element in a system. Unlike both these other models, however, it seeks, on the one hand, to measure the extent to which this pattern is involved in a given system and, on the other, to measure the extent to which the latter is a system. Unlike the Parsonsian system model, the stratified system model aims to determine the extent to which various components of the system may account for its characteristics, and to weight their varying influences. Unlike the Marxist model, the stratified system model insists on leaving open the possibility that more than one factor may determine the system's characteristics and insists that these others be investigated and their relative influence measured: it does this without assuming that several influencing factors will all be *equally* influential, and without ignoring, as does the Parsonsian model, the question of their differing degrees of influence.

EQUILIBRIUM PROBLEMS

Basic to Parsons' analysis of the social system is his focus on equilibrium and on the conditions from which this derives. For Parsons, what makes Ego and Alter a system is not simply that their behavior is mutually influential or interdependent, but that it contains patterns that tend to be *maintained.* It is not simply that there are regularities, features predictable in their behavior toward one another, for these could be regularities of conflict and change; Parsons focuses on the manner in which these patterns are either protected from change and conflict or, if they undergo it, do so only within a repetitive cycle. In focusing on social system equilibrium, Parsons' concern is with the manner in which patterns of interaction are stabilized and unchanged, or on how, when some changes do occur, still others will result whose effect is to limit the first changes or return the situation to what it had been. He is concerned with the way social systems are endowed with *self*-maintaining elements, with stabilizing characteristics internal to the system. In short, emphasis is on how the system preserves itself; a system has no inherent strains, only situational discrepancies or "disturbing" factors of marginal significance.

More concretely and in Parsons' terms, it is held that a social system is and will remain in equilibrium to the extent that Ego and Alter conform with one another's expectations. The equilibrium of the system is seen as, in effect, largely dependent on the *conforming* behavior of group members. Insofar as Ego does what Alter expects, Alter will be gratified by this and will, in turn, behave so that Ego is gratified, which is to say, in conformity with Ego's expectations; thus, when one behaves in conformity with another's expectations, he elicits a response from the other that leads him to continue doing so without any change.

This model makes a variety of tacit *empirical* assumptions. Most particularly, it assumes that each of a sequence of identical conforming acts will yield either the same or an increasing degree of appreciation, satisfaction, or gratification, and will thereby so reward the conformer as to continue them. This assumption seems to be involved in Parsons' conception of how social system equilibrium is maintained, for, otherwise, it is difficult to understand how he can hold that "the complementarity of role-expectations, once established, is not problematical. . . . No special mechanisms are required for the explanation of the maintenance of complementary interaction-orientation."[9] In other words, once started, this cycle of mutual conformity goes on indefinitely. Now, so far as I am aware, no evidence exists for what this implies, namely, that responses which reward a series of identical conforming actions will either remain the same or increase. On the contrary, both impressionistic observations and theoretical considerations lead one to have the greatest doubt about it.

DECLINING MARGINAL UTILITY OF CONFORMITY[10]

Here, as in the previous discussion of system "interdependence," the subject is best viewed as involving questions of *degree:* Ego's conforming acts always have some consequences for Alter's expectations; expectations are always modified by prior relevant action. But, modified in what manner and to what degree? For my part, I would assume that the longer the unbroken sequence of Ego's conforming actions goes on, the more likely is it that Alter will take Ego's later actions for granted and the less likely is it that they will be given notice.

This, in turn, will elicit tendencies for Ego either to reduce or to increase the extent of his conformity with Alter's expectations. If he reduces them, this may, in turn, lead Alter to reduce his conformity with Ego's expectations still further, and thus generate a vicious cycle of decreasing mutual gratification and conformity, and thereby of growing tension. Conceivably, however, Ego may seek to maintain his former level of gratifications received from Alter by *increasing* his conformity with Alter's expectations, thus seeking to prevent Alter's rewards from declining. This, however, means that Ego's conforming behavior is undergoing an inflationary spiral, later units of conformity being worth less than earlier ones. But, how long can Ego go on increasing his conformity under these conditions? One limit is, of course, set by the sheer extent of Ego's energies, time, and resources. He cannot increase his conformity indefinitely in order to maintain his own former level of gratifications. Moreover, Ego's cost in maintaining such conformity will increase relative to his gains, and thus *alternative* investments of his time and resources will become increasingly attractive and/or rewarding. In short, the probability of the continuance of this line of conduct, or even of the relationship itself, is declining under these conditions.

It is, of course, possible that as Alter's rewards to Ego decline and Ego reduces or halts his conformity with Alter's expectations, Alter will stop taking Ego's conformity for "granted" and will increase the rewards he gives Ego for it. But, in any event, it seems clear that it cannot simply be assumed, as Parsons does, that identical acts of conformity will yield identical increments in group equilibrium. At some point, continued and unchanging conformity exerts strains upon a social system, inducing apathy, or tensions and conflict. Insofar as this leads to Ego's failure to comply with Alter's expectations, or to reduce his conformity with them, this may *recharge* the whole equilibrium process. But this is a far cry from the original conception, which stressed that it was *conformity* with expectations upon which system equilibrium primarily depended.

Parsons' own assumptions therefore lead to the conclusion that system equilibrium requires some *non*conformity with expectations. Moreover, even in Parsons' terms, it appears as if the system does indeed contain its own "seeds of destruction," for, at some point, continued *conformity* produces system *dis*equilibrium. The system disrupts itself. What Parsons fails to see is that considerations of *marginal utility* apply to the gratifications produced by conforming actions. Conformity, in short, has an economic dimension, and its "price" or return is subject to considerations of the *amount* of the supply and demand. Conformity always tends to "glut" the market; it can thereby generate *non*conformity. The stability of a social system may thus be impaired by conformity, while it may be restored or renewed by dissent and nonconformity.

CONSTRAINT AND THE PRICE OF CONFORMITY[11]

Considerations other than the sheer amount or repetition of conforming actions can likewise strengthen the *expectation* of conformity, and thus similarly reduce the return—the "appreciation"
and counterconformity—it elicits. Central among these is the degree to which Alter defines Ego's conforming actions as imposed
upon him: "he was forced to do it." The more that Alter feels this,
the less will he value the actions and reciprocate them; conversely,
the more that Alter defines Ego's conformity as "voluntary," given
"of his own free will," the greater is his tendency to reward it.

There are two types of conditions under which Alter may feel
that Ego's conformity is involuntary or constrained. First, he may
feel Ego's conformity is *situationally* constrained, that he "has no
choice" and conforms out of expedience, in order to get what he
wants or to reduce his own costs. Second, Alter may feel that Ego's
conformity is *morally* constrained, that Ego has no choice but to
conform because nonconformity would be so morally reprehensible.

To understand some of the larger implications of this we must
go back to certain basic elements in Parsons' account of the Ego-
Alter system and to his explanation of its equilibrium. From Parsons' standpoint Ego and Alter will more likely conform with one
another's expectations when they *share* a common moral code, for
this means that each has developed expectations that the other
regards as legitimate and deserving of conformity. Parsons expects
a common moral code to stabilize relationships, and he focuses on
the ways in which it does so. He assumes that the more an expectation is defined as legitimate and is sanctioned by Ego's and Alter's
common moral code, the more likely is it to be given conformity;
thus he sees a moral code as stabilizing and system-equilibrating.
What this ignores, however, is that, while a shared moral code may
increase Ego's disposition to conform with Alter's expectations,
nonetheless, to the extent that Alter defines Ego's conformity as
imposed upon him by this moral code, Alter will tend to reward
such conformity less than he will the similar act of another, which
he defines as having been not morally imposed but as given voluntarily.

In other words, while a shared moral code may increase Ego's
motivation to conform with Alter's expectations, it may, however,
reduce the reward or return that Alter gives Ego for conformity.
And this will be the more pronounced as Ego's conformity is made

more *reliable* by his acceptance of this moral code. A shared moral code thus seems to increase the probability that conformity will be rewarded, but to reduce the *amount* of the reward given.

What Parsons generally fails to communicate is the system of *tensions* that are expressed in and maintained by a moral code. In part, this results from the fact that he makes no general analysis of the conditions under which moral codes develop or of the functions they perform, beyond merely indicating that they serve to harmonize Ego and Alter by establishing a complementarity of social interaction. But, why should any kind of moral code be necessary, except that one party wants something from another whom he sees as *unwilling* to provide it? If he were seen merely as *unable* to provide such compliance, the response would simply involve an effort to *educate* him to do so, by increasing his skills or his knowledge, but would not involve defining the desired performance as *morally* obligatory.

If we postulate—and I will develop this more fully at a later point—that desired performances are defined as morally obligatory when people are seen as able but *unwilling* to perform them, then the very existence of a moral norm premises a tensionful conflict of forces: there is a desire for some action and, counter to this, there is some measure of reluctance to perform it. One need not at all postulate that, say, by their "animal nature" men chafe against moral restrictions. The point is simply that the moral imperative would be unnecessary were there not some contrary impulse. Conformity with a moral norm is thus always a "duty" which is in some degree costly and, for that reason, is contingent. This is precisely why the rewards given by *others* are of special importance in maintaining morally stipulated actions.

Conformity given by Ego is, as I have said, likely to earn only restricted rewards, to the extent that Ego's behavior is defined by Alter as imposed upon him by the moral norms. At the same time, if Alter is also bound by the same moral norm, it obliges him to make an appropriate response and to provide *some* reward for Ego's compliance. Alter too is caught in a tension between opposing impulses. It is not only Ego's conformity with the moral norm, but Alter's response as well, that is highly contingent. The conformity that each gives to the moral norm is precarious, because for each of them it rests on a conflict of internal forces; it is *doubly* precarious, because its maintenance depends on overcoming the conflict of forces *within* each and also on the external rewards that each provides for the *other* by his own precarious conformity. Conformity and system equilibrium are thus far more uncertain, vulnerable, and precarious in the "normal" case than Parsons intimates.

Indeed, a system of social interaction is in part held together *by* this tensionful uncertainty. Ego is, in part, oriented to being mindful of and sensitive to Alter's expectations and behavior because Ego is *far from certain* how he himself should behave and precisely *because* he is far from totally submissive to the moral norms. If Ego were totally under the influence of internalized moral norms he might pay little or no attention to the implications of his own behavior for Alter; he might simply do as the norms required. And if Ego paid no heed to the consequences for Alter but only to his own piety, then the damage would really be done, for no *social* system could long survive with men so moral that they took no heed of one another's needs and responses. In sum, it is not the completely successful but rather the *precarious* internalization of moral norms and the ambivalent conformity to them upon which the survival of social systems depends. Insofar as the system is held together, it is held together not despite but *by* its tensions.

The equilibrium of the system is maintained, *so far as it is,* not simply because Ego's gratifications derive from Alter's responses and vice versa, and not simply because each is thus led to conform with the other's expectations in order to secure gratification of his own. Parsons does see this aspect. What he misses is that it is not merely the mutual *dependence,* but also the sheer *uncertainty* of the gratification that each provides for and receives from the other that also holds the system together; and *this,* in turn, depends partly on the *resistance* that each has to conformity with their shared moral code. What he continually misses is that the equilibrium of the system is, in part at least, dependent upon the *unwillingness* of those in it to conform with the moral code, and thus upon their tendencies toward nonconformity.

SCARCITY AND SUPPLY OF GRATIFICATIONS

As we have seen, Parsons stresses that the stability of social systems derives largely from the *conformity* of role partners to one another's expectations. Presumably, the more people pay their social debts, the more stable the social system. What this ignores is that it is not simply the *payment* of a social debt but the existence of debts still *un*paid, acknowledged "outstanding obligations," that contributes to the stability of the social system. It is obviously inexpedient for creditors to sever relationships with those who still have and acknowledge obligations to them. And it is also inexpedient for debtors to do so, if only because creditors may not again allow them to run up a bill of indebtedness. If this conclusion is correct, then we should not only focus on mechanisms that constrain men to *pay* their debts, as Parsons does, but should as well search out social mechanisms that induce people to remain socially indebted to one another, that *inhibit* their complete repayment, and that conceal or obscure the net balance of reciprocities among them.

Parsons acknowledges, to turn to a related but different consideration, that the stability of a social system requires that there may be some "mutuality of gratification" among the system's members. In other words, he acknowledges that system stability depends, in part, on the exchange of gratifications, those provided by one party being contingent on those provided by the other. This, however, remains a fragmentary insight whose full implications remain unexplored in Parsons' work. Here again it is necessary to raise questions of degree and amount, in this case of the amount of *gratification* that the system supplies its members and of the amount of *mutuality* that exists. Both of these may and do vary.

To take the question of the amount of gratification first: Parsons' Ego and Alter do not seem to live in a world of scarcity; scarcity seems to have no effect on their behavior or on their relationship. Typically, Parsons calculates the stability of a social system in terms of the relationship between men's moral expectations and the conformity given them by others; that is, in terms of the isomorphism between men's performances and their moral code. Parsons assumes men will learn to derive gratification from such conformity and, because their capacity for gratification is extremely malleable, they will learn to accept different amounts and kinds of gratifications. Thus variations in the level of gratification is not problematic, for Parsons. What he is implicitly doing is simply holding constant the level of gratification, because he wishes to stress the other point, namely, the importance of conformity with a shared moral code. Thus the central locus of strain in Parsons' social system is "deviance"—lack of conformity with moral norms —but not *lack* of gratification. In contrast, a full focus on the implications of gratification for social system stability would entail concern with the degree or level of gratification, with deprivation and relative deprivation.

Parsons is undoubtedly correct in indicating that variations in the degree of moral conformity with a system have an effect on its stability. Yet this says no more than that moral conformity makes *some* independent contribution to system stability. It fails, however, to assess the contribution that may be made by sheer gratification, by gratification independent of morality. Parsons tends to reduce gratifications to those derivable from conformity and to emphasize that conformity usually brings gratification. Like Plato, he prefers to believe that the good man is also the happy one. It is easy to understand how a moralist is disposed to claim this, but difficult to understand that anyone describing the world could do so.

Fortunately for them, men can often find gratification in non-moral things, and, often enough, they find gratification in things downright immoral. Parsons' primary emphasis, however, is on the convergence—one might say, the happy coincidence—of morality and gratification: "The normal actor is, to a significant degree, an 'integrated' personality . . . the things he values morally are also the things he 'desires' as sources of hedonic satisfaction or objects of affection."[12] This alleged coincidence of wants and moral values is nothing less than startling in the light of all the cumulative evidence of clinical psychology, let alone everyday observation. In contrast to Parsons, Somerset Maugham seems ruthlessly realistic: Parsons, happy man, knows nothing of "Human Bondage."

In all this, Parsons is once again *making the world whole*. He does so either through a conceptual fantasy that obliterates conflicts and contradictions, or by deprecating their significance while acknowledging their existence in a merely formal and empty way that undermines their reality. Characteristically, Parsons thus adds to the above quotation the routine qualification that, "to be sure, there are, concretely, often serious conflicts in this respect, but they must be regarded mainly as instances of 'deviation' from the integrated type."[13] To be sure.

In emphasizing the coincidence between what men want and what they value, Parsons fails to see sheer gratification as a fully independent standard by which human action is guided and which is not only distinct from but often knowingly at variance with the claims of morality. On the one hand, there is a standard of *gratificational adequacy,* by which we appraise people and things in terms of the enjoyment they provide us and, on the other, there is the standard of *moral propriety*—which is one source, but scarcely exhausts the sources, of gratification—by which we appraise the conformity of things and people with our conceptions of the way they *should* be. There are, therefore, some things we do because we deem them morally obligatory though, nonetheless, ungratifying—for example, visiting a kinsman whom we dislike—and others we do because they are gratifying even though morally improper. Here the list of exemplifying possibilities staggers the imagination.

This distinction is important for many reasons, not the least of which is that men will openly complain of and seek public redress for offenses to their moral standards, while covertly and very persistently seeking remedies for those impairments of gratification that violate no moral standards. In the latter case, the resultant problems simply fester underground, and efforts at remedy, for a while anyway, take the form of guerrilla forays rather than open warfare. But the response to the lack of gratification is just as real and consequential as, even if different in form than, the response to a violation of the moral code.

We would assume, therefore, that two social systems that were alike in all other ways, but differed in respect to the *amount* of gratification each supplied its members—relative to their costs of involvement, on the one hand, and relative to their needs, on the other—would also come to differ in their stability. In short, social systems that supplied their members with *more* gratifications would also be more stable. Again, suppose that with two identical social systems we were to increase the amount of gratifications that one provided its members and decrease that of the other. Is it not very unlikely that the stability of the two systems would remain *un*changed or that they would change in the same direction?

Parsons seems to assume that the scarcity or level of gratifications as such will not effect system stability, so long as Ego and Alter share a common moral code. Presumably, the common code will lead to complementary rights and obligations: Ego will want no more gratifications from Alter than Alter willingly provides. But the gratifications that Alter is willing to provide Ego depend not only on Alter's conception of his duty but also on the costs of his performing it; these costs effect the supply of the gratification Alter provides and, in turn, depend upon the supply available to him. Any party's conformity with his moral obligations is a function of the level, the scarcity or abundance, of his own gratifications, and of the cost of producing them.

RECIPROCITY, COMPLEMENTARITY, AND EXPLOITATION

Once posed quantitatively, it becomes apparent that "mutuality of gratification" is not something that is merely present or absent. It is not an "all or none" matter. Benefits exchanged may, at one extreme, be identical or equal. At the other logical extreme, one party may give the other nothing in return for the benefits he has received. Both of these extremes are probably rare in social relations, and the intermediary case, in which one party gives the other something more or less than he has received, is probably far more common than either limiting case.

It is not simply "mutuality" but, very vitally, the *degree* of mutuality that affects the equilibrium of a social system. While it need not be supposed that an equality of exchanged gratifications is necessary for system equilibrium, it is, nonetheless, clear that as the exchange becomes more and more one-sided, the relations become more precarious. In consequence, an understanding of system disequilibrium requires us to pay particular attention to "exploitative" relations, those in which one party gives more or less than he receives in return.

Although exploitative relations imperil system equilibrium, they cannot, however, be assumed not to occur. Rather, what needs to be explored are the conditions under which they do occur, and how social systems are held together despite their occurrence. In Parsons' work on the doctor-patient relationship, he tacitly acknowledges the importance of exploitation by noting the unique exploitability of the patient, but he tends to see this as a special case; the point, however, should be to recognize medical exploitation as but one case in a larger class of social phenomena of basic significance to theory, rather than giving it only *ad hoc* treatment in a few empirical contexts.

Parsons' failure systematically to analyze exploitative patterns and even to see their general importance is partly related to his failure to explore the *variability* possible in the degree of mutuality of gratification. Another reason for this failure is that much of Parsons' analysis of system equilibrium focuses on the *complementarity* of expectations, though in fact he tends to confuse complementarity and *reciprocity*. Parsons sometimes uses these two terms as if they are synonymous; he centers his own analysis far more firmly on complementarity and neglects systematic analysis of reciprocity, rigorously construed.

Now, complementarity has essentially two meanings: it means, first, that what Ego defines as his right is defined as an obligation by Alter, and, second, that what Alter defines as his duty is viewed by Ego as his right. On the *empirical* level, however, it is possible for one party to conceive himself as having either a right or a duty, though the other does *not* define his own situation in a complementary manner, entailing a complementary duty or right. What should *produce* the complementarity, indicates Parsons, is that both share the same set of moral values. In any empirical case, complementarity means that what is a right of Ego is actually felt by Alter to be his duty.

Reciprocity, however, as distinct from complementarity, implies that *each party* receives something from the other in return for what he has given him. In terms of rights and obligations, this means that reciprocity entails not that one party's rights are the other's obligations, but rather that *each* party has *both* rights *and* obligations, thus increasing the probability that there will be some *exchange* of gratifications. In effect, then, reciprocity of gratifications requires that each role be defined culturally so as to include both rights and obligations.

There are at least two general ways in which complementarity as such can break down. In one, Alter can refuse to acknowledge Ego's rights as being his own duties. In the other, Ego may not regard as his rights that which Alter regards as his own duties. Now it is notable that Parsons gives scant attention to the latter. The reason for ignoring it is obvious: such a breakdown in complementarity is not frequent, nor, should it occur, would it have as disruptive an impact on system equilibrium as the other kind of breakdown; when men are endowed with more rights by others than they themselves wish or claim, their relationship is less likely to be disrupted than when they claim more than the others are willing to acknowledge.

In reality, then, it is not a lack of complementarity as such—as Parsons seems to think—that disrupts social systems, but rather the lack of *one type* of complementarity. It is primarily when men ask for more, not less—and when they give less, not more—than others think their right, that trouble ensues. In noting the significance that shared moral codes have for engendering a system-equilibrating complementarity, Parsons tacitly assumes what Durkheim explicitly postulated, that the main function of moral values is to *restrain* men's wants and claims. Like Aristotle, Parsons tacitly assumes that men are more ready to receive and claim benefits than they are to give them. He is, in short, operating with a domain assumption about human nature, although not explicating it: namely, that men have a tendency toward "egoism," a salient though not exclusive concern with their own gratifications. If this is a valid assumption—and some such assumption appears to be eminently reasonable—then any complementarity of rights and obligations that might be established should be exposed to a patterned and systematic strain, for each party will usually be somewhat more alert and actively concerned to defend or extend his own rights than those of others.

There is nothing in complementarity as such that would seem able to control such egoism. Even if it is assumed that socialization transmits a deeply internalized moral code (with its accompanying conceptions of rights and obligations), there still remains a question as to how this is *sustained* during the person's full participation in the social system. How is complementarity maintained within the context of social interaction? For this we need to look to reciprocity, the process through which *gratifications* are exchanged. For reciprocity, unlike complementarity, actually mobilizes egoistic motivations and channels them into the maintenance of the social system. Egoism can motivate one party to satisfy the expectations of the other, since by doing so he shall induce the latter to reciprocate and satisfy his own. In fine, it is not complementarity by itself, but only when supported by reciprocity, that can yield system stability.

EQUILIBRIUM AND POWER DISPARITIES

Since system stability depends upon the exchange of benefits and is impaired by exploitation, then conditions abetting exploitation must have adverse effects upon this stability. While various conditions are conducive to exploitative exchange, none seem more obvious to me, and less obvious to Parsons, than extensive power differences among the system's members. Where notable disparities in power exist, the stronger is enabled to coerce the weaker, allowing him to extract gratification without providing appropriate returns.

It is characteristic of Parsons' analysis of social system equilibrium that he never clarifies his assumptions concerning the power balance conducive to a stable social system. Power is, in this regard, simply taken as a given. His tacit assumption, therefore, must be that the balance or imbalance of power between Ego and Alter will make no difference for the stability of their relationship, if the other conditions obtain. It would seem, however, that such an assumption is more than dubious—it is either naive or ideologically compulsive. While Parsons assumes that moral values held in common by Ego and Alter are conducive to the stability of their relationship, he never seems to ask about the conditions under which moral values *will* be held in common; he never seems to notice that power differences (among others) are likely to be conducive to differences in moral values and will thus, within his own assumptions, undermine the stability of the relationship in which they exist. Moreover, Parsons ignores the fact that such power differences establish a framework in which one party can, and often does, impose himself on another, with resultant conflict between them, even when they do share moral beliefs. Differential power is thus conducive neither to a consensus in moral beliefs and to an attendant complementarity of expectations, nor to a reciprocity or "mutuality of gratifications." On two counts, then, great power differences will, by Parsons' own assumptions, impair the self-maintaining equilibrium with which he is concerned.

The point here, of course, is not that great power differences necessarily impair system equilibrium because they inevitably lead those with the power advantage to exploit their position selfishly. The point is simply that this potentiality for system-disruption is inherent in the nature of such a power *difference*. Parsons acknowledges that some forms of power may be disruptive, or indeed disintegrative, of social systems, while other forms are integrative. However, the major distinction he makes concerns the *form* of power, whether or not it is "controlled" or "uncontrolled"—the former resulting in integrative, the latter is disintegrative tendencies —rather than the *size of the disparities* in power among system members. Of course whether or not power is controlled, power differences may still vary extensively: one may have "controlled" totalitarian or authoritarian power, or one may have "controlled" democratic power where the power differences are *relatively* small. For Parsons, however, the extent of the power differences among system members is not in itself significant for the stability of their relationship. Presumably, the only way power effects system stability is through variations in the manner with which it is *controlled.*

This seems to mean that differences in power are not consequential for system stability so long as they are morally sanctioned or "legitimate"—and hence constitute not power but "authority"— for it is this that Parsons seems to mean when he speaks of the "control" of power. Yet this misses the problem. For system stability the real issue is whether or not power disparities among system members are consequential for the maintenance of the mutuality of gratification and the complementarity of expectations. To say that "controlled power" is system integrative begs the question: Do great *disparities* in power among system members facilitate or impair the control of power? When Parsons says that power may be controlled or uncontrolled, and that its consequences for system stability vary with this, he means to stress that power is not inherently disruptive (or corruptive). But since, for Parsons, power is *by definition* the capacity to realize the system's collective goals, this simply boils down to the platitude that the capacity to realize the system's goals is not inherently disruptive. Whoever thought it would be?

The problem, of course, is what the consequences are of using power for private or for class rather than system goals; power is simply not power if used in the way Parsons defines it, and the issue disappears through conceptual magic. It is rather as if some-one were to say, "Girls with 'good looks' have special advantages," and Parsons were to respond: "Forget about 'good looks'; let's only talk about 'looks,' and remember, 'looks' are not inherently bad."

Parsons' focus is not primarily on the manner in which the power of one actor may be controlled by the *power* of another, but rather on the restraints that are placed on men's power by a *moral code*. But, if a decisive consideration for system stability is the control of power, this it would seem can be done in various ways, moral restraints being only one of them. It should be obvious, but apparently is not, that, if the aim is to control power, one should prevent its distribution from becoming too one-sided. That Parsons never takes this tack is related to his belief in the functional in-dispensability of social stratification, for this implies that there must be differences in status—in prestige, wealth, possessions, facilities, and sanctions—and, therefore, differences in power. Parsons simply believes that power differences are functionally necessary and indispensable for social systems. Since he generally assumes that social systems do not embody tendencies or processes that are inherently *un*stabilizing, he cannot recognize that great power disparities are inherently unstabilizing.

Parsons' concern, then, is with the moral control of power, which is part of his more general focus on morally sanctioned social patterns, or on patterns seen in their relations to moral beliefs. In other words, Parsons' central concern is with patterns of action and social interaction that are culturally prescribed and institutional-ized. His primary focus is on the *legitimacy* of behavior patterns, on dimension of legitimacy rather than gratification. In effect, Parsons divides the social world in two: behavior patterns that are normatively prescribed, and those that are not. His work thus em-bodies an implicit distinction between an "infrastructure" and a "superstructure"; unlike the explicit Marxist distinction of a for-mally similar sort, Parsons' analysis emphasizes those culturally prescribed moral elements that Marx would locate in the super-structure.

NOTES

1. Compare my discussion of Plato's dialogue form in my *Enter Plato* (New York: Basic Books, 1965), pp. 379 ff.

2. T. Parsons, *Essays in Sociological Theory Pure and Applied*, revised edition (Glencoe, Ill.: The Free Press, 1957), pp. 46–47.

3. See, for example, the excellent article by Max Black, in *The Social*

Theories of Talcott Parsons, M. Black, ed. (Englewood Cliffs, N.J.: Prentice-Hall, 1961), pp. 268–288.

4. This and the next section are more fully developed in my "Reciprocity and Autonomy in Functional Theory," in *Symposium on Sociological Theory*, L. Gross, ed. (White Plains, N.Y.: Row, Peterson, and Co., 1959), pp. 241–270.

5. Parts of this section and the next are developed in A. W. Gouldner and R. A. Peterson, *Notes on Technology and the Moral Order* (Indianapolis: Bobbs-Merrill Co., 1962). See Chapter 3, especially.

6. See T. Parsons, R. F. Bales et al., *Family, Socialization and Interaction Process* (Glencoe, Ill.: The Free Press, 1955).

7. This can be clearly seen when Parsons revises and enlarges his earlier work; for instance, compare his 1940 version of the theory of stratification with that of 1953.

8. Parsons, *The Social System* (Glencoe, Ill.: The Free Press, 1951), p. 494.

9. *Ibid.*, p. 205.

10. I have discussed this in detail in "Organizational Analysis," *Sociology Today*, R. K. Merton et al., eds. (New York: Basic Books, 1959), pp. 423 ff.

11. For a fuller analysis and argument see my "The Norm of Reciprocity: A Preliminary Statement," *American Sociological Review*, XXV (1960), 161–179.

12. Parsons, *Essays in Sociological Theory Pure and Applied*, p. 168.

13. *Ibid.*

The Moralistics of
Talcott Parsons:
Religion, Piety, and the Quest
for Order in Functionalism

For Talcott Parsons the social world is, above all, a moral world, and social reality is a moral reality. It is not what men actually do that is most important to him; these are merely discrepancies, secondary disturbances, erratic departures of some sort. Rather, it is what the group values prescribe they do that constitutes the perspective from which their actual behavior is viewed. There is, thus, a persistent pressure in Parsons' work to ignore social regularities that are not generated by moral codes. This, in turn, means that regularities that derive largely from the competition for or conflict over scarce goods and information, and which are not normatively prescribed or derived (for example, processes of collective behavior such as panics or crowds), tend to be neglected or seen as only marginal.

LATENT IDENTITIES

When Parsons analyzes social systems, therefore, his focus is on the way men's behavior conforms to or deviates from the legitimate expectations of others, and on the way it complies with the requirements of those social statuses or identities that are defined as relevant to the particular social system. This diverts attention from those statuses that people occupy in other social systems and from the other social identities with which they may be endowed. It thus withdraws attention from the way such *latent* identities themselves intrude upon and influence men's behavior toward one another.

For example, there is usually something going on between people by reason of their sexual interests and identities, even when this is not prescribed by the moral values deemed relevant to the particular social system in which they are interacting, or, indeed, by the values of the larger society environing that specific social system. Like most other social system analysts, Parsons takes little note of the fact that Ego and Alter invariably have a gender, except when he is talking about kinship: reproduction, si; sex, no! Yet, one does not have to be a Freud to insist that sex makes a difference in the behavior of the members of a social system; so, too, do identities of an ethnic, racial, or religious character, even though not normatively prescribed by the particular social system. In consequence of his general stress on institutionalized patterns of behavior, Parsons is led to focus his analysis on those manifest social identities of system members that are consensually regarded as legitimate in a situation, and to neglect those latent identities that are not. But latent identities do, of course, systematically shape behavior and social interaction. In particular, they exert a persistent strain on social system stability. They continually dispose people to behave in patterned ways which are at variance with or irrelevant to the normative requirements of their specific social system.

Parsons' neglect of latent identities is merely one expression of his moralistics, that is, of the dominant place that he ascribes to patterns of moral values. In this, however, he is far from idiosyncratic among American sociologists; whether because of Parsons' influence on them, or of their common exposure to larger social forces or to common intellectual paradigms, most American sociologists stress the importance of moral values, particularly as the source of social solidarity. One thing seems certain: the actual evidence for this assumption is considerably less than the overwhelming consensus of American sociologists concerning it would lead one to believe.

That "Functionalists," in particular, place unusual emphasis upon the importance of moral beliefs may be documented, in some part, by the findings of the national survey of American sociologists that Timothy Sprehe and I conducted in 1964. In this survey we sought, among other things, to determine their attitudes toward Functionalism by asking them to respond to this statement: "Functional analysis and theory still retain great value for contemporary sociology." We also asked for a response to the following statement: "The most basic sources of stability in any group are the beliefs and values which its members share." Responses to the first statement were used to determine which sociologists were "favorable" or "unfavorable" to Functionalism, and responses to the second were used as an indicator of the importance that sociologists attributed to shared moral beliefs. The finding was that sociologists "favorable" to Functionalism were more likely than those "unfavorable" to stress the importance of shared moral beliefs; specifically: eighty percent of those favorable to Functionalism, but only sixty-four percent of those unfavorable, agreed with the statement attributing importance to shared moral beliefs.[1]

There would seem to be something of a paradox here: Why should Functional Sociology, which, after all, came to maturity in an advanced industrial civilization, consistently attribute such importance to moral conditions? Why should it emphasize the effect on social order made by morality rather than that made by technologically-produced abundance and gratification?

In this chapter, I shall suggest that the moralistic character of Parsons' theory, which tends to be shared by all those generally congenial to Functional theory, is related to the intellectual tradition from which it derives and, in particular, to certain of its residual dilemmas, as evidenced in Durkheim's early version of Functionalism; that it is related to the fascination with the problem of social order common to Functionalist Sociologists; that it is related, also, to the importance they ascribe to religion, with its distinctive kind of shared moral values, as a source of social solidarity. These considerations largely bear on cognitive consistencies, consistencies of theory and ideology. I shall further locate the moralistics of Functionalism in certain broad social and historical conditions, seeing it as responsive to certain dilemmas found in any kind of social system and, more specifically, as responsive to the forms they take in modern industrial society. I shall begin by examining aspects of the theoretical tradition, the internal subculture, of Functionalism.

THE DURKHEIMIAN DILEMMA

The stress on moral values in Functionalism is associated with its emphasis upon the problem of social order and, in particular, upon certain conceptions of social order and upon certain assumptions concerning its maintenance. The tradition from which Functionalism most directly emerged was epitomized by Durkheim, who assumed that, unless men's wants were morally limited, no technological development, however advanced, could satisfy them and thereby stabilize society. Durkheim, indeed, indicated that technology might increase appetites, and Comte had feared it might generate a dissensus in beliefs, thus further attenuating social order. Technological development, then, was seen *neither* as a sufficient nor as a necessary condition of social stability, in this tradition.

It was, on the other hand, explicitly assumed that shared moral values were a necessary condition for the stability of any society. Indeed, it was tacitly assumed that, given shared moral values in a society, a low level of technology and material scarcity need not be *un*stabilizing. Thus, it made no difference for its stability whether a society had a highly productive technology, or whether it was industrial or pre-industrial. It was the state of the morality, not of the technology, that counted most for social order, from the standpoint of those immersed in this tradition.

Furthermore, shared values were associated with the *spontaneity* with which order was maintained. What was wanted was a spontaneous, self-maintaining social order that, deriving from men's possession of shared values, would facilitate their willing cooperation and their readiness to do their duty. Technology and science, on the other hand, were construed as deliberate rather than spontaneous devices to achieve social order and, thus, as intrinsically unsuitable.

Functionalism differed from Positivism by rejecting the latter's evolutionism and, with this, its slogan of "Order *and* Progress." In separating itself from Positivism, Functionalism relinquished an interest in "progress," which the Positivists had commonly associated with technology, the application of science to industry. The Positivistic theory of cultural lag had intrinsically premised an evolutionary progress spurred by technological advance. The three— evolution, progress, and technology—tended to be associated in Positivism. Functionalism, however, tended to deny the stability-inducing significance attributable to the gratifications that an advanced technology might provide, while it simultaneously brought itself to a narrower concentration on the problem of social order alone. The problem of social order, therefore, had to be solved increasingly in terms of the moral mechanisms on which Comte had placed such reliance.

The initial problem with which we began can be divided into two questions: first, why did Functionalism *continue* to focus on moral values as a source of social order and, second, how did Functionalism come to reject the Positivistic focus on technological progress? The key figure here is Durkheim and the problem he encountered in his critique of Comte. Durkheim's polemic against Comte's argument ·that the division of labor induced dissensus in social beliefs, had brought him to a critique of private property.[2] Durkheim held that it was not the division of labor as such, but only the *forced* division that undermined social solidarity; this division of labor was "pathological" because it was controlled by outmoded institutions, particularly private property. At the same time, however, Durkheim also held that social solidarity was impaired by the lack of a set of moral beliefs adequate to integrate the new specializations—in short, by industrial anomie. He then faced the strategic decision of which of these two impairments of modern social order he would analyze further.

For various reasons, but mainly because it would bring him into an uncomfortable convergence with the socialists, Durkheim backed away from the problem of the forced division of labor and, instead, concentrated on anomie; which is to say, on the *moral* conditions necessary for social order. If Durkheim had followed up his own lead on the forced division of labor, it would have blurred the very difference between Academic Sociology and socialism on which he was then polemically insisting; it would have been difficult to tell the difference between Durkheim and Jaurès. If modern Functionalism had pursued Durkheim's critique of the forced division of labor, it too would have had to move toward *some* form of socialism, and thus reject the master institutions of its society. If Durkheim and modern Functionalism had accepted Comte's critique of the dissensus-producing effects of the division of labor, it would have had to reject *any* form of industrialization. Functionalism did none of these. Its solution was to say, in effect, that the problem of social order could be solved *apart* from questions of economic institutions and technological levels. The problem could, that is, somehow be solved solely in terms of *morality as such*, and thus would not require basic changes in industrialization or in its capitalist structure.

This seems to be part of the historical process by which the Functionalists came to place special reliance on the role of moral values in maintaining social order in industrial societies. Had it followed Durkheim's lead concerning the "forced" division of labor, it would have been led to an analysis of property institutions predicated upon assumptions critical of them. In turning away from this problem and its obvious solution, Functionalism was constrained— given the alternatives it saw—to place an ever greater reliance upon moral values and moral reform as the source of social order. Its focus upon the problem of order and its search for solutions to it, became, in effect, a search for solutions to the problem of order *within* a business-managed industrialism, for solutions that were compatible with this distinctive kind of social order. Functionalism's emphasis upon morality, as the keystone of social order, is characterized by its compatibility with the maintenance of the specific and established form of industrialism in which it found itself, and which permitted it to avoid a critical posture toward its society's hegemonic institutions and classes.

FUNCTIONALISM AND THE PROBLEM OF ORDER

The deepest expression of Functionalism's, as of any social theory's, conservatism is in its fascination with the problem of social *order*. What is it that social theorists are doing when they focus upon social order, either as their central intellectual problem or as their central moral value? What is it that they seek when they seek social order?

To seek order is to seek a reduction of social conflict, and thus it is to seek a moratorium on such social changes as it sought through conflict or which may engender it. To seek order is to seek a predictability of behavior that would, of its nature, be threatened either by social conflict or, for that matter, by individual creativity. To seek social order is to seek order-giving mechanisms that might derandomize behavior. It is to seek "social structures," things that, like rocks jutting into the stream of moving behavior, distribute it in patterned ways or dam it up. This requires that some things be viewed and treated as unchangeable. It expresses an Apollonian vision of a social world composed of firmly boundaried social objects, each demarcated and separated from and setting limits upon the other. The quest for social order expresses an impulse to fix and bind things down from a place outside of, if not above, them. To seek or prefer order is to seek or prefer "structures": the structure of social action, not the *process*.

For all the earnest talk about morality, however, the pursuit of order is only contingently compatible with an emphasis upon moral values; the commitment of those obsessed with order is not to morality as such, but only to *a* moral system that yields order. Both Positivism and Functionalism are really interested only in *certain* kinds of shared moral beliefs, namely, those thought to produce order. Positivism tended to assume that shared moral values that did *not* produce order were, somehow, not "really" moral values.

For instance, when Comte spoke of individual "liberty of conscience," he was clearly referring to a kind of moral value, but,
despite this, he decried it because it led men to differing conclusions and thereby dissolved social consensus. For the classical
Positivist, the truly moral was judged by its consequence, its contribution to consensus; it was as difficult for him as for Durkheim
to resist the conclusion that *anything* that produced consensus,
restraint, and order was intrinsically moral. Order, in short, becomes the fundamental basis in terms of which the moral itself is
conceived.

The overt commitment to social order is a tacit commitment to
resist any change that threatens the order of the status quo, even
when that change is sought in the name of the highest values:
freedom, equality, justice. For this reason it is not uncommon for
social movements and elites that champion social order to betray
even the "superior" morality they claim to embody. A stress on
social order requires those committed to it to harden themselves
against the claims of other high values. Those who seek these other
values are, at bottom, often searching for an improvement in their
own life chances, their own access to scarce goods and dignities.
The demand for the fulfillment of such values commonly expresses
the protest of those who want a better life for themselves and more
of those things upon which this depends. It is thus threatening to
those who are already advantaged, for they fear that it means that
they will have, or be, less.

But since the demand for a reallocation of life chances is made
in the name of high values, to resist it nakedly and only in the
name of maintaining established privilege is to make oneself vulnerable. The advantaged universally tend to resist it, therefore, in
the name of what they claim to be a still higher value: social order.
To pursue and to speak in the name of social order, then, is to
defend, not order and not the status quo "in general," but the
existent order with its specific and differential distribution of life
chances, which endows some with special advantages and others
with special liabilities.

The exponent of order presents the issue as if it were a choice
between "order" and "disorder" (or "anarchy"), and thereby makes
it seem as if a preference for order is the only reasonable choice to
make. Actually, of course, those seeking a redistribution of life
chances are not seeking disorder but a *new* order. And their struggle for a new order is intrinsically no more conducive to disorder
than are the efforts of those who resist the new order in the name
of "order." *Dis*order does not stem from the search for a new order
as such, but is a symptom of the failure of the old order; a rising
"disorder" stems from the breakdown of an old order that is com-

pounded by the compulsive effort to resist the new. It takes two to make disorder. To make social order one's central concern, then, is indeed to be conservative, and not merely in a metaphysical sense; it is to be politically conservative.

A central concern with social order, therefore, underwrites a concern to maintain those established master institutions that allocate life chances. Correspondingly, a concern to maintain social order *through* a reliance upon *morality* requires a distinctive kind of morality, one that maintains the existent patterns of life chances and the institutions through which they are allocated. In this connection it needs to be emphasized that, however much they talk of morality, the champions of social order are not in favor of any and all moral beliefs. For example, and as Comte indicated, they are not in favor of values that individuate behavior or diversify belief. Typically also, they are not in favor of "material" values. Yet to want a car, a clean apartment, a job may be just as expressive of a "moral value" as to want God. Nonetheless, what the champions of order vaunt when they speak of values are not material but "spiritual" values, "transcendental," "nonempirical" values. They prize spiritual values such as temperance, wisdom, knowledge, goodness, cooperation, or a trust and faith in the goodness of God: the quiet values.

While freedom and equality are no less "spiritual" values than goodness and temperance, they are, nonetheless, not those to which the guardians of order refer when they speak of values. For, freedom and equality may be taken to legitimate claims for the redistribution of material goods, and thus threaten property institutions and the existent system of social stratification. This is why an overriding quest for order involves a quest for values that are not merely *different* from liberty and equality, but commonly are *in opposition* to them. The affirmation of morality by the champions of order, then, is not primarily an affirmation of *spiritual* values as such, but only of those values which, eluding the premises of a zero-sum game, are not fixed or scarce, but are available in unlimited supply. "Spiritual" values have historically had this interesting quality: a man may get more of them without taking anything away from others. Spiritual values may thus be achieved without threatening the structure of privilege. The search for order is a tacit search for those specific social mechanisms which allow retention of the existent and basic distribution of life chances, and thus require no change in basic institutions.

Underlying the formal conception of "social order in general" is a tacit, concrete image of a specific order with its fixed distribution of life chances. The quest for order is thus an ideology; it congenially resonates sentiments that favor the preservation of

privilege. And it is a very persuasive one too, for it speaks on behalf of an imputed common interest shared by the privileged and
disadvantaged alike, and it thereby presents itself as nonpartisan.
But it neglects to mention that, while the interest is a common one,
it is not, in the nature of the case, an equal one. Some gain or lose
more than others when order breaks down; that, in some part, is
why it does break down. A social theory that takes as its central
problem the maintenance of social order is thus more ideologically
congenial to those who have more to lose.

One might add, however, that the champions of order may just
as readily oppose changes that would *increase* the deprivation of
the less privileged, and may even seek to ameliorate their lot. In
other words, there seems to be a certain impartiality in their love
of order. In practice, the champions of order often counsel the dominant elites to a policy of restraint: nothing too much. Or in a less
classical idiom: don't make a pig of yourself. But this advice derives from the fear that an elite's efforts to increase its control or
extend its advantage will precipitate counterresistance by the less
advantaged and thus generate open, order-disrupting conflict. What
such counsel of moderation basically seeks is the preservation of
the status quo. It serves, in short, to protect the *given* system of
privileges and liabilities in its essential features. Such counsel,
then, is not impartial to the status quo. It is a policy of *prudence
on its behalf.*

RELIGION AND MORALITY IN FUNCTIONALISM

I have reviewed the manner in which Durkheim's intellectual dilemmas led Functionalism to a great emphasis upon morality. Well
before Durkheim, however, from its birth in Positivism, the new
sociology was conceived of as a "moral science." Indeed, it issued
almost immediately in a sociological religion of humanity. From
the very beginnings of sociology, moral and religious interests were
intimately interwoven. That this conjunction is still present in the
Functionalist tradition that culminates in Parsons' work could not
be made plainer than by Shils, in his encomiums to religion and in
his insistence on its special importance for authority and tradition.[3]
Shils may be right that, for some sociologists, God is dead; but his
very complaint reveals that Functionalists such as himself refuse
to allow Him to be interred quietly.

The unique importance that Parsons attributes to religion in the modern world is expressed in two ways. First, in the *potency* that he ascribes to it in bringing into existence practically all of what he takes to be modern culture and society, including its uniquely *powerful* economy, technology, and science. Second, in the *goodness* that he attributes to it and its products, as substantiated by the increasingly *benign* character of the world it fosters. In short, Parsons here resolves the problem of the grotesqueness of life, the split between morality and power, by affirming that it is increasingly *both* powerful *and* good, and that both aspects have a common root in Christianity. There is no other single institution to which Parsons attributes such potency and goodness: the Church has been the rock and the light of modern civilization.

It was Christianity, Parsons holds, that transmitted ancient culture to the modern world; which, in its medieval synthesis, "produced a great society and culture"[4]; and which, in its Protestant synthesis, was the necessary condition of "the great civilizational achievements of the seventeenth century"—without Protestantism, these are "unthinkable."[5] Parsons reminds us that Weber linked the Protestant Ethic to the development of capitalism not by a "*removal* of ethical restrictions," but rather by a religious mobilization of certain motivations, eventuating in "free enterprise."[6]

"The Christian Church developed for its own internal use," explains Parsons, "a highly rationalized and codified body of norms which underlay the legal structure of the whole subsequent development of Western Society."[7] Moreover, since Christianity "did not claim jurisdiction over secular society," it established the basis for the secularization of society and for its unification in terms of a set of commonly shared values.[8] "Catholic Christianity also made a place for an independent intellectual culture which is unique among all the great religions in their medieval phase."[9] Moving in a similar direction, Protestant cultures were the "spearheads" of the educational revolution of the nineteenth century and the "general cultivation of things intellectual and particularly the sciences."[10]

Not only has Christianity provided the underpinning for the distinctive Western economy, science, intellectual autonomy, legal structure, and secularization, but it has also contributed to the development of individual character, since "the internalization of religious values certainly strengthens character."[11] It is the basis for the dignity of the individual, fostering a "new autonomy for the individual,"[12] which, in turn, has had political consequences: "The most important single root of modern Democracy is Christian individualism."[13] Christianity's respect for the dignity of the individual person, related to its possession of "a certain strain of egalitarianism,"[14] fosters a variety of the humanitarian elements that distinguish modern life: the opposition to discrimination against persons not justified by merit or demerit,[15] opposition to grinding poverty, illness, premature death, and unnecessary suffering; these are all "undesirable from the Christian standpoint."[16] In short, behind the humane Welfare State, Parsons finds Christianity.

In consequence of the benign influence of Christianity, says Parsons, "there can be little doubt that the main outcome has been a shift in social conditions more in accord with the general pattern of Christian ethics than was medieval society."[17] Things, in brief, have never been better, not only in terms of the power, but also in terms of the goodness and morality of modern life. With proper scholarly prudence, Parsons acknowledges that "the millennium definitely has not arrived," but emphasizes that, "in a whole variety of respects modern society is more in accord with Christian values than its forebears have been."[18]

Since Parsons attributes this moral enrichment and humanization of life largely to Christianity, he is faced with the problem of responding to those who declare that there has been a general decline of religion in modern life.[19] Parsons answers that there has *not* been such a decline, and feels called upon to explain why the contrary is so widely believed. He does so, briefly, by holding that moral standards have not deteriorated; rather, modern men are facing more difficult problems, and as a result of television and other mass media, people are now more *aware* of the evil and suffering which has always been in the world.[20] Parsons has looked upon the world and upon the whole history of European civilization and contemporary society; he finds it not only powerful but good, its power and goodness largely deriving from a Christianity that still retains an abiding vitality. Christianity, for Parsons, has been the central source of the order, the unity, and the progress of Western society.

About the only modern developments of significance that Parsons fails to attribute to Christianity are Marxism and socialism. It is hard to see how he overlooks them. Surely any number of talented commentators, engaged in the "dialogue" between Marxism and Christianity, have already related them. Some, like Alasdair MacIntyre,[21] regard Marxism not only as rooted in Christianity but as its only worthy historical successor. And indeed, the case for a Christian rooting of Marxism is a very strong one. Perhaps Parsons is an Edmund Wilson man on this question, seeing Marx as an Old Testament figure. But Parsons' avoidance of this connection is at least more cautious than those he confronts. But it is anomalous in the light of his quest for the universal inclusion of everything under the Christian banner. Undoubtedly it derives from the sheer contradiction it would generate: to deny socialism and Marxism an origin in Christianity is to acknowledge that an enormous part of modern culture owes little to Christianity; to affirm that Marxism is influenced by Christianity is to acknowledge Christianity as a major source of "disorder" and conflict, let alone downright "subversion," in modern society—best, therefore, not to mention it.

To evaluate Parsons' assertions concerning the role of Christianity would take nothing less than a review of Western history for the last two thousand years; but since they are merely assertions it would seem that this could wait upon the presentation of his evidence on their behalf. The assertions are not only undocumented, they are also not terribly persuasive, even impressionistically. Both Stalinist Russia and Nazi Germany were Christian cultures, but neither was impressively concerned with the dignity of the individual, political democracy, intellectual autonomy, or the defense of the individual from arbitrary authority. Correspondingly, Japan is not a Christian culture, yet its development of a modern science, technology, and industrial economy seems in no way impaired by this. Christian churches have, moreover, blessed opposing armies in wars fought among peoples for more than a thousand years, when they have not themselves trumpeted the call for holy crusades and inter-religious massacres; some have sanctioned slavery and opposed child labor legislation, public contraceptive facilities, and legal abortion. Say what Parsons will about the Church's role in furthering science, the history of the warfare between science and religion was not simply the figment of some bigoted historian's imagination: there remains Galileo. My object here, however, is not to refute Mr. Parsons' claims on behalf of Christianity; indeed, the burden of proof is on him. I wish only to make it clear that there is a persistent and systematic one-sidedness in them. They are saturated with a kind of "piety," which, in Robert Nisbet's formulation, "represents a conviction that full understanding of social phenomena is impossible save in terms of a recognition of the unalterable, irreducible role of the religious impulse,"[22] and they verge on Christian apologetics—in the serious scholastic sense, of course.

FUNCTIONALISM AND RELIGION: SOME SURVEY DATA

Parsons' piety, however, is *not* an individual idiosyncrasy; it is, on the contrary, a general disposition of the larger school of modern Functional social theory, of which he is the fountainhead. The best evidence on this matter derives from our national survey of American sociologists, for this clearly shows that the religious orientations of Functionalists differ from the religious orientations of those opposed to Functionalism. Using the question noted above (p. 247), to tap attitudes toward Functionalism, we found that those favorable to it have greater religiosity and stronger religious affiliations.[23]

One question we asked sociologists was whether or not they had ever thought of becoming clergymen, as well as whether or not they were presently members of the clergy. Here we found that, although all groups were *preponderantly* "favorable" toward Functionalism, those who were clergy were only about half as likely to be *un*favorable to it as those who were not clergy. More specifically, about five percent of the clergy were unfavorable, but almost ten percent of those who were not clergy were similarly unfavorable. Leaving aside indeterminate answers, we also found a *slight* tendency for those who were clergymen to be more favorable than were those who had not become clergyman, yet once had thought of doing so; and they, in turn, were also *slightly* more favorable than those who had never thought of becoming clergy. The percentages of the favorable among these three groups were: eighty-seven percent, eighty-six percent, and eighty-one percent.

A similar but more pronounced association was found between sociologists' attitudes toward Functionalism and the frequency with which they attended church. It is instructive to look at the two most extreme groups. Among those *most* favorable to Functionalism only thirty percent *never* went to church, while fifty-five percent of those *least* favorable to Functionalism *never* attended church. Looking at the "most frequent" church attenders, we found among them 27.8 percent of those *most* favorable to Functionalism but only ten percent of those *least* favorable to Functionalism.

If we take frequency of church attendance as an indicator of the degree of religiosity, it seems clear that *those favorable to Functionalism are more likely to be religious than those unfavorable.* This is further confirmed by the response to a question concerning religious affiliation. Table 7–1 plainly suggests that *those without*

*a religious affiliation are more unfavorable to Functionalism than
those having any religious affiliation.*

TABLE 7-1

		RELIGIOUS AFFILIATION				
		CATHOLIC	OTHER	PROTESTANT	JEWISH	NONE
Attitude	(+)	.88	.86	.84	.80	.78
to	(?)	.07	.09	.08	.09	.08
Functionalism	(−)	.05	.05	.08	.11	.14
	N+	320	84	1446	497	1054

This table shows that those *least* favorable to Functionalism are
those who report *no* religious affiliation and whom I would suspect
to be the *least* religious group. Indeed, the percentage of this group
which is unfavorable to Functionalism is more than twice that of
Catholics. Of those reporting some religious affiliation, Catholics
are the most favorable to Functionalism and Jews the least so.

If we wish to grasp why and how Functionalism places such
great stress upon morality, especially upon transcendental and nonempirical values, as Parsons calls them, we must first recognize
that this is compatible with the importance it also ascribes to religion. Concerns with morality and with religion are mutually reinforcing. Certainly, however, the religious side of modern Functionalism is, compared to its expression in Comtianism, much muted.
The modern Functionalist's religious impulse is less Catholic in
tone and more consistent with a soberly rational religion, yet one
which, if it does not pray to Almighty God, still pays its earnest
respects "To Whom It May Concern."

In American Functionalism, the Catholic ritualistic accoutrements of the Positivist religion have been sublimated by its development within a relatively Protestant culture. The religious impulse
is now expressed in a kind of Ethical Culture religion, whose
presence is revealed by and concentrated in the potency and character it ascribes to moral values. What Parsons calls transcendental,
nonempirical values call forth the same sentiments of respect
and the same sense of the sacred as do more traditional attitudes
toward the supernatural. These transcendental values are the invisible ultimates, the final answers to the society's "wherefore?";
they are the that-which-there-is-nothing-higher-than. Under what
social conditions does such a sense of "respect" emerge? How does
such a conception of the sacred arise? Parsons does not so much
wish to explain as to locate it. The sacred is somehow within culture, but how it got there remains mysterious.

The Parsonsian "sacred" thus no longer has an icon, a cult, or a

God. It is an unexplained protoplasmic *sentiment,* a hungry piety that may reach out and endow anything with a touch of divinity. The sense of the sacred is, for Parsons, at the core of the moral system, which is, in turn, at the center of the social universe. The godhead abides, uncelebrated but potent and mysterious, within morality.

For me the interesting problem is not, as it is for Shils, for example, to account for the *lack* of religious sensibility in other sociologists; I am, rather, perplexed at the continued *presence* of a religious impulse in the theoretical tradition of Functionalists. In general, I believe that it is, in one part, due to the tension between men of knowledge and their society; in other words, it is a special case of ambition frustrated. It derives, I would suggest, from the technological weakness of sociology now and from the inability of sociologists to achieve the high place they seek in society through the practical contributions they can make. The religious impulse of sociology, that is, arises and is sustained when sociologists and sociology lack the very power that they attribute to society. It betokens a great gap between the ambitions of sociologists and the means they have to realize them as scientists and technicians; piety, in short, becomes a substitute for power.

The muted religious impulse of sociology, its present piety as well as its earlier full-fledged religious form, is an adjustment to the tension between great expectations and very modest performances; between great opportunities and the inability to seize them; between high hopes and low achievements; between great human needs and sociology's meager capacity to satisfy them with the technology and knowledge it commands. A sociological religion of humanity, or a sociology modeled on religion, seeks to solve the problem of how—here and now, in this very weak condition—the expectations can be fulfilled, the opportunities mastered, the hopes achieved, the needs satisfied, and of how sociology can be made an influence now in the lives of ordinary men. Finding itself still far from able to provide a useful technology, sociology consoles itself and the world with piety.

From the very beginnings of the Positivistic tradition from which Functionalism evolved, sociology has experienced a central dilemma. On one side, Positivism clearly sought to change society and influence the lives of ordinary men. On the other side, Positivism—especially in its Comtian development—manifested a monastic impulse to be detached from man and society; in some part, this was an expression of resentment born of the failure to be heard, to win the support, the recognition, and the influence it believed its due. These two opposing impulses may be discerned in all sociology deriving from the Comtian tradition. The dilemma, then, persists.

There was and still is a persistent tendency to resolve this dilemma by infusing sociology with a religious character. This was done by Comte in his development of a full-fledged sociological religion of humanity. It is done by Parsons, in more muted form, in his development of a social theory that stands witness to the central importance of the sacred in the lives of men, by devoting itself to the celebration of the morality in which the sacred is held to dwell. Faced with a social crisis such as the Depression of the 1930's, the tendency of Functional social theory is to shore up morality. Since it holds that at the heart of morality are sentiments of sacred respect, any crisis of society is seen as the product of a failure of its sense of the sacred, in all the places where, presumably, it dwells: tradition, authority, and religion. Its diagnosis comes down to the unstated conclusion that great evils befall men and society when God dies. Its therapeutic response, therefore, can only be to protect morality, intensify a sense of the sacred, and preserve the godhead. The "consensual sociology" that Shils proclaims involves a consensus between men of worldly authority and priestly sociologists, who between them can reunite the temporal and the moral realms and thus maintain order in society. He understands well and deeply that Parsons has at long last established the theoretical basis for fulfilling the Comtian program.

When sociology infuses itself with a religious character, it does not require a new and potent technology to fulfill or to legitimate its ambitions. In infusing itself with a religious character, sociology can now draw upon those means available to any religion: the protection, revitalization, and transformation of morality, and the fostering of men's submission to it. The essential solution to social problems which this tradition advances is the cultivation of the moral system, to which it now relates itself as guardian and steward. Yet there is a revealing paradox in its "scientific" relation to moral belief. On one side, it extols their potency, but, on the other, it does not profane their sacred character with systematic research. Its attitude toward morality is the attitude of religion and the religious toward the place where the god dwells; it regards it as both potent and untouchable.

There is this fundamental paradox not only in the Functionalist's science of morality, but also in his posture toward practical human problems, concerning which the diagnosis must always be clearer than the remedy. For, while it affirms that the most fundamental root of any social malaise is moral, it cannot grasp and use this in instrumentally manageable solutions, for it conceives morality as sacred, which means that it is not instrumentally manageable. Such a sociology can therefore be made "practical" only in the same way that religion is: by relating men to the sacred. It is made practical by placing at its center a *concern* with what it defines as sacred or, rather, by defining as sacred what it has made central, and by fostering appropriate sentiments and *behavior* toward it.

THE PIETY OF FUNCTIONALISM

If I am correct in believing that there is a religious cast to Functionalism—not merely an "element," but something that pervades its culture—then how are we to judge it? We might begin by noting that our judgment of Functionalism as the embodiment of a religious feeling is not essentially different from that often made of Marxism, although considerably better documented.

When Marxism is judged to be religious, it is often tacitly assumed that this demonstration of a religious aspect discredits the scientific aspect. I believe no such thing. In speaking of Functionalism's religious aspect, I do not for a moment intend thereby to impugn its intellectual merits. These simply must be judged on other, independent grounds. Conversely, it is also often implied, by those who speak of Marxism's religious character, that to demonstrate its lack of conformity with the imputed methods of science must strengthen the supposition that it is religious. It is in this vein that Robert Tucker remarks: "Scientific theories normally arise after their authors have immersed themselves in the empirical data that the theory seeks to explain. But not so with the Marxian science of history according to its founders."[24] This is a merely mythological conception of how scientific theories arise. As is so common, it substitutes the morality of science for the sociology of science, a preconception of how it *should* arise for a study of how it actually does arise. Being no Aristotle in command of all sciences, I shall say only that Tucker's view simply does not conform with what I have seen in the social sciences. And I shall drop the matter by noting that it should be perfectly obvious by now that Talcott Parsons is, in this respect, not one whit better than Marx. Parsons' theory was certainly not based upon an "immersal" in the "empirical data." If, as Tucker holds, Marxism "came into being by means of the transformational criticism of Hegel's philosophy of history," Parsons' theory came into being by means of his criticism of Pareto, Sombart, Weber, and Durkheim.

Even if we were to regard Functionalism and Marxism as both similarly religious, it needs to be added that there are vital differences in the nature of their religions. Indeed, nothing could make this clearer than Mr. Tucker's own study of Marxism as a religious myth. It is one of his central themes that Marxism arose out of a theoretical tradition, from Hegel to Feuerbach, in which there is seen "no absolute difference between the human nature and the divine"; Tucker observes that, in an early article, Engels held that "God is *man*." Yet there was certainly never a contention, at least in Feuerbach and Marx, to the effect that there was no "difference between the human nature and the divine." They never claimed knowledge of a divine nature, but only of human nature, from whose alienated condition, they maintained, there arose a *human conception* of divine nature. Moreover, even if he spoke elliptically, it deserves to be noted that Engels did *not* say, God is *society*. And here is the crucial difference between Marxism and Functionalism.

For, whatever the outcome of the Leninist version of Marxism in Russia, and despite the development of the overgrown, paranoid Stalinist state, the earliest focus of Marx and Engels was on the liberation of *man*, and not of society. The ultimate intention was not merely a withering away of the state which stood above men, but a total transformation of society itself, because it was viewed as subjecting men to a crippling alienation. "It is above all necessary to avoid postulating 'society' once again as an abstraction confronting the individual," said Marx. "The individual *is* the *social* being. The manifestation of his life . . . is therefore a manifestation of social life."[25]

The Marxist focus, then, was on the liberation of "real individual man." In his early manuscripts in particular, Marx speaks of man not only as a social creature but as an intrinsically powerful "species being," whose species *products* are religion, the family, the state, law, science, and economics. The liberation of this species being was intended to be a liberation of the creative and sensuous powers of "real individual man"; that is, of the "five senses" with which embodied man is endowed as a species being. "The transcendence of private property is, therefore, the complete emancipation of all the human senses and attributes." Thus, if Marxism was a religion, it was not a religion of society, as is Functionalism, but a religion of *man*. It was a religion of pride in man and struggle on his behalf, not a religion of piety toward society and quiescent conformity to it. Whatever the scientific demerits of Marxism, it may be placed alongside Functionalism with confidence that it is not *its* moral character that will be found wanting. And since we have here been speaking of Marxism and Functionalism as religions, the question of their moral character is by no means irrelevant.

Although running the risk of seeming to protest too much, I must say once again that, in having noted Functionalism's religious character, I have no sense that I am engaged in an "unmasking." While somewhat surprised at what I found, I am not repelled. I have always thought it odd that men who profess to a respect for religion should act so triumphant when they uncover a religious side to Marxism, and that they should hold this up before us as if it were the conclusive argument. Although I am not "religiously musical"—to borrow Max Weber's term[26]—I do experience this exercise in righteousness as somewhat repellent. I cannot share in this sport of baiting the "false religion," because I have too keen a sense of the close connection that exists between religion, any religion, and human suffering; and I experience contempt for religion as callousness toward suffering. If I disapprove of Functionalism, it is not because it has a religious dimension, but because of the *kind* it has, and most especially because of the *kind* of morality it seems to embody.

Similarly, although I judge the priest by what he serves, I see nothing humorous, contemptible, or degrading in priesthood itself. In writing of Functional Sociologists as men having a priestly side to them, I hope that this communicates what is intended: namely, that they often are men of principle, not pandering opportunists. At any rate, the best of them live for, not off, sociology. If they serve order in society, they are usually acting with authenticity, out of their own deeply felt convictions. If they refrain from social criticism, it is often because of, not cowardice, but a priestly reticence toward public life, and perhaps because they believe that they must deliver unto Caesar the things that are his. Like priests, they feel they must minister to their flocks wherever they are and whatever they do. Yet, like priests, they also have a sense of distance and removal from the society around them, even as they do their duty toward it. And, like priests everywhere, they accept the compromises that they believe must be made to maintain the church. I should note, moreover, that these comments are only about the best among the Functional Sociologists. I am well aware that there are priests *manqués;* that many who enter have no aptitude for the life; and that some join a monastery because they like its wine cellar.

In suggesting that Functional Sociologists have a priestly side and Functional Sociology a religious side, be assured (if you must) that I am not saying that the former wear priestly collars or that the latter has ordained them or is itself conventionally defined as a church. I am, rather, thinking of the moralistic piety with which Functionalists often regard society and indeed science itself.

I have previously indicated what I take to be this pious conception of society. In what follows I want to focus briefly on the conception of *science* congenial to many Functional Sociologists, to show how it is congruent with their conception of society, and, in particular, how it is infused with a sense of sacredness. Just as Functional Sociologists have often conceived of society on the model of a godhead, so too are they disposed to conceive of science on the model of a religion. Functional Sociology, for them, serves as a link between man and the sacred and transcendental power of society, mediated by the activities of a group of priest-like specialists—Functional Sociologists themselves—who have scientific resources, skills, and powers that are sacred.

For Functionalists, science and social science are not merely practical, useful activities; indeed, Functionalists have sometimes gone out of their way to restrain sociology's inherent impulse to be applied; to them science and social science are "high" things of *intrinsic* value. Science is not seen as an everyday, secular activity inherently accessible and akin to the activities of ordinary men. It is, instead, seen as the activity of very special, somber, austere, dedicated, perhaps heroic men; it is to be spoken of deferentially; it is to be treated solemnly; it is to be approached circumspectly; and great care must be taken to conform to its rules and rituals. Indeed, Functionalists often conceive of the contributions of scientists, including sociologists, as a purchase on immortality. With respect to the prescriptions that are deemed appropriate to sociology, the watchwords, as I mentioned earlier, are continuity, cumulation, codification, convergence, the joyless prescriptions of a structuralizing methodology that is the fit counterpart of an Apollonian vision of society. (And one might wonder how it happens that all these watchwords begin with a "c" if there is not just a bit of cabalistic magic in them.) Functionalism, in short, seems to have a distinctive conception of social science and its methodology, as having developed out of and still remaining charged with sacred sentiments that are engaged in a dialectic with a hidden anxiety.

Let me say, however, once and for all, that if I had a choice only between a Functionalist conception of science as "sacred" and a conception of it as a "business," I would have no hesitation in opting for the former. Better pious than crass, better anxious than smug. But I do not believe that these are the only alternatives that sociologists have. Sylvan Tompkins' work on the psychology

of knowledge is valuable here precisely because it begins to formulate alternative views of science and, furthermore, plainly lays
out their links with different domain assumptions about man and
society.[27]

There is, says Tompkins, one conception of science—closely
convergent, I would add, with that held by the Functionalists—
in which stress is placed upon the value of science in separating
truth from falsity, and reality from fantasy. This view of science
emphasizes man's vulnerability to error, the wisdom of the past,
the importance of not making errors, the value of thought in keeping people on the straight and narrow, the necessity of objectivity
and detachment, and the importance of discipline and correction
by facts. Corresponding to this conception of science, suggests
Tompkins, is the conception that man is, at bottom, evil, and that,
therefore, government's first duty is superintendence. In this view
science is something *above* men, controlling and rectifying their
natively untrustworthy impulses and austerely maintaining a safe
distance from those studied.

In contrast to this view of science, Tompkins outlines an alternative which stresses man's activity, his capacity for invention and
progress, and the value of novelty and of intimacy with the things
being studied. Here science does not serve as a suspicious watch-
dog but trusts man's imagination and intuition as contributive to
knowledge. This view of science, says Tompkins, also corresponds
to an image of both man and society; men are felt to be good, and
it is the satisfaction of their individual needs and the promotion
of their welfare that is deemed the most important function of
government.

SOCIAL BASES OF MORAL CONCERN

Thus far, I have related Functionalism's stress upon morality very
largely to elements internal to the theoretical tradition out of
which it emerged or to the special social conditions that theorists,
and academicians more generally, encounter in their larger society.
But if these combine to dispose Functional theorists toward a stress
on morality, it seems doubtful that they alone suffice to sustain it.
I would not want to imply that social theorists foist such views
upon an unwilling society, a society that does not resonate to its
message and has no demand for it. There is, rather, a "fit" between

the needs of the larger society and the moral emphasis of the theory. In other words, living in modern society generates the same deep need for morality in the theorist as it does in others, and an emphasis upon the importance of morality is as much a response to this *personal* experience as it is an "objective" report on the needs of the society.

An understanding of the nature of the experience that generates this personal need for morality in the theorist as in others, may be approached on two levels of analysis: in terms of an analysis of, first, certain existential problems of living in almost any kind of a society and, second, some of the unique problems of living in a modern industrial society. Both approaches will help clarify the role of morality in an industrial society and show why even such a society does not lead men to seek only the distinctive kinds of gratifications that modern technology can increasingly supply.

I shall begin by approaching the problem of the sources of morality on the most general level. The language of morality— hence morality itself, for it is not accessible to study except through its linguistic manifestations—arises in the social world in situations where what men *want,* the gratifications they seek, are precarious and uncertain. The crux of the whole matter is that morality is rooted in the scarcity and contingency of desired objects or performances. The "primeval scene" in which morality first forms has this character: someone *wants* something; but what he wants is something that he cannot procure by his own unaided effort; the satisfaction of his wants is therefore contingent upon what others do, either to aid or hinder him in his pursuits; finally, these others are not altogether ready to provide or do what he wants, or, at any rate, the things desired from them are *felt* to be somewhat contingent. The "primeval" problem, then, is how one man can arrange his relation with another so as to more reliably secure what he wants. We begin, thus, with this deliberately simplified model in which "Ego" wants "O" from "Alter." *Why* he wants "O" is irrelevant here, although it is important to remember that he can want it to a greater or lesser degree.

Having an interest in getting what he wants from Alter, and recognizing that satisfaction cannot be taken for granted, Ego will become interested in his chances for success, and he will develop some ideas about the factors that will affect them. There are at least two aspects of Alter's disposition in which Ego will come to be interested: first, whether Alter is *willing* to do as Ego wants and, second, whether he is *able* to do so. And Ego will make imputations about Alter in *both* terms. Note that, at this point, nothing has been said about whether Ego thinks that Alter *should* do as he, Ego, wants, for we are trying to understand the conditions under which such a morally formulated notion of Alter's duty arises: *that* is what needs to be explained. To further simplify matters, I shall also assume that Ego simply dichotomizes his imputations about Alter's willingness and ability to do as he wants. That is, he assumes that Alter is either willing or unwilling, able or unable, to do so. From this simplified standpoint four possibilities emerge:

First, Alter is seen by Ego as being *neither willing nor able* to do as he wants. Ego then faces the choice of either persisting in what he wants or in some way changing the demand he makes on Ego. In the latter event, Ego will seek "X" from Alter instead of "O." But if Ego persists in wanting "O," and if he believes that Alter is both unwilling and unable to provide it, he is likely to seek another source of supply. The decision is to change either what is sought and/or from whom it is sought. In general, the relative cost of doing each of these and the availability of the alternatives will be among the factors shaping Ego's decision. If Ego can surrender neither his goal nor his wish that Alter himself supply it, he may then simply act in a punitive way toward Alter, substituting an expressive action for an instrumentally suitable one.

Second, and directly opposite to the above situation, is one in which Ego views Alter as *both willing and able* to provide what he wants. In this event there is no problem. Ego can let matters take their course and need not seek to influence Alter's behavior in any way.

There is a third possible situation, in which Alter is seen as *willing but unable* to provide what Ego wants. Here, Ego's reaction will depend upon his view of Alter's inability and the extent to which he regards it as modifiable. If Ego regards Alter's "inability" as unchangeable, his alternatives are essentially those described in the first situation. That is, Ego can change what he wants or can retain his goal but seek it from someone else. If, however, Ego views Alter's inability as changeable, he may seek to render Alter capable of doing what he wants, perhaps by "educating" him in some manner, improving Alter's skills or helping him to improve his resources. Here Ego has no incentive to threaten or punish Alter.

Finally, there is a fourth possible situation, which brings us to the heart of the matter. Ego may view Alter as *able but unwilling* to do as he wants. Here, Ego will attempt to influence Alter in some manner, by exhortation or command, or by supplying incentives or punishments, or by threatening or promising to do so. Whatever the method, the objective here is to modify Alter's *motives*. Here again, however, it needs to be added that this all depends upon Ego's cost. Demographic, ecological, and technological considerations, the number, location, transportability, and availability of other suppliers and supplies will be basic factors shaping the outcome.

It is primarily in this situation, I would suggest, that the language and sentiments of morality—of "ought" and "should"—arise and are most fully developed and used. Morality and moral claims are one basic way in which Ego can get Alter to do as he wants. We view morality as emerging in situations in which there is a scarcity or contingency of desired performances or objects, and when this is defined by Ego as due to Alter's *unwillingness* to provide them, rather than to his lack of skill, competence, or resources and facilities. In sum, morality is more likely to emerge: (a) the more that Ego wants something, and (b) the more that he defines Alter as able but unwilling to provide this thing, and (c) the more costly it is for Ego to remove or replace Alter with someone else.

The problem may be reviewed from another familiar perspective. When Ego judges Alter in terms of his "willingness" and "ability" to do as he wishes, Ego is, in effect, judging Alter's "goodness" and "potency." That is, the judgment of "goodness" is contingent on and connected with a judgment of "willingness." This is not a reversible connection. Ego does not judge Alter as willing because he defines him as good, but rather he judges him as good, in part, because he defines him as willing; and conversely, as bad, because unwilling. "Goodness" or "badness" is a cryptic or disguised judgment that Ego makes of Alter when Ego feels that Alter is willing or unwilling to do as he wants. The "good" object is one that does not frustrate us, does not resist our will, gives us what we want; in short, it is an object that gratifies. But gratification is only nuclear to the "good," not coextensive with it. There is a gap between saying, "He is willing to do as I want,"and saying, "He is good." The problem, in effect, is under what conditions does the primitive feeling, "I *dislike* people who do not do as I wish," come to be translated into, "They are *bad* people."

One such condition, I have suggested, is where Ego holds that Alter is *able* to do as Ego wishes. It is unrealistic and "unreasonable" for Ego to expect something from Alter that he is unable to provide, and Ego can often recognize this. In this sense, "ought implies can." That is, the moral judgment premises a prior judgment of potency. Only potent people, or people to whom a measure of potency is imputed, and who are therefore "responsible for their actions," can be either good or bad. It is only as people gain or accept a measure of autonomy and become loci of potency that they become capable of behaving in a manner subject to moral judgment.

As mentioned above, Ego might get what he wants not only by changing Ego's motives but also by coercing him in some manner. If Ego has power enough to do this, he can "command" Alter's performance. Conversely, Ego might provide positive incentives, benefiting or rewarding Alter for doing as he wishes. The exercise of compulsion or offering of incentive is feasible in this situation because Alter can, if he wants, do as Ego wishes. It is not feasible where Alter is simply unable to do so, or is believed to be unable. There are thus two ways that Ego can proceed: through some "appeal" that aims at modifying Alter's motives, or through some constraint or incentive. Actually, both constraint and incentive will also modify Ego's motives, his willingness or readiness to comply, but this change is *situational,* and when the incentive or the coercion is removed, Alter will probably revert to unwillingness.

Such situation-linked motivation is not a stable, reliable way for Ego to get what he wants from Alter, for it will vary with the vagaries in Ego's situation—with his ill health, bad luck, droughts, or anything else that undermines his ability to coerce or reward Alter. If Alter's compliance is entirely contingent on these situational impulses, the reliability of his future conformity is slight. It may be severely disrupted even by casual impairments of Ego's powers and resources. Ego therefore faces the problem of *persuading* Alter to do as he wishes even when these contingencies occur. Ego must reduce the contingency in Alter's performance that arises from the contingency of his own powers and resources. For indeed, no matter how great Ego's power, it is always possible for Alter to enter into coalitions with others and to mobilize a countervailing power.

Faced with someone who is able but unwilling to do as he wishes, and against whom his own power and his own ability to promise benefits or threaten punishments is always, at some point, limited, Ego must therefore find a way to modify Alter's motives that does not depend upon the benefits or punishments he can provide. This must, then, take the form of some "appeal" that, on the one hand, is not narrowly situational and, on the other, is not related to promised benefits or threatened punishments. This is essentially the character of moral language. It is not situational, for it *always* refers to performance in a *class* of situations and for a category of persons. A moral claim always refers to what should be done in a *type* of situation by a *type* of person. There is no moral claim that is incumbent on only one specific person in only one concrete instance. Behind the specific claim that one friend makes on the other is the assumption that "friends" generally owe this to one another. And, again, moral claims are characteristically not held to be incumbent because of the *consequences* of conformity with or violation of them: that is, anticipated rewards or punishments. They are held to be appropriate "for their own sake."

Morality is a rhetoric Ego uses to mobilize Alter's motives for complying with his wants, without express reference to the manner in which the situation will be changed by improved benefits or by avoided costs. It defocalizes situational consequences. It implies that these are not relevant to the decision to do or not-do what is sought. On the one side, it implies that Alter should do something regardless of whether or not he will gain or lose from it. On the other, when Ego demands conformity with a moral claim, he is intimating that he is not doing so because of any partisan interest or any personal advantage he will derive if Alter complies. The social function of the language of morality, then, is to *induce* actions without the exercise of power or compulsion and apart from the offering of rewards. Making claims in moral terms projects a specific image of persons, as "unselfish." There is, in this sense, always some implication that the moral person is "disinterested." In short, the social function of morality is to stop contention about the distribution of advantages.

Several other functions are also worth noting. One is to resolve *ambivalence* about doing or not-doing something, by throwing support to one side or the other, thus cutting the Gordian knot of sheer indecision; it facilitates the overcoming of internal conflicts. Also, morally sanctioned claims function as "deficit-financing" or credit-creating mechanisms in social relations. Not being situationally narrow, they inhibit Alter from immediately withholding compliance from Ego's demands, even when it is clear that Ego's ability to provide reciprocal rewards may be temporarily impaired. They thus sustain the relation until Ego can resume his benefits to Alter or until it becomes clear that he will never do so.

If morality solves certain problems, it also creates others and generates distinctive kinds of vulnerabilities and costs for social systems. One of these involves the hiatus between the desired and the desirable, between the gratificational nucleus and the moral stipulation. This hiatus derives from the fact that, in pursuing his own wants, Ego is seeking the somewhat reluctant cooperation of others who also have their *own* wants and whose very reluctance to attend to his wants derives, in some part, from the fact that they are much concerned with satisfying their own.

The expression of a want as a *moral* claim intrinsically constitutes a promise of a *mutuality* of gratification. That is, in formulating his claim upon Alter in moral terms, Ego is tacitly promising that he will comply with a similar claim upon himself made by Alter; or that he will support a similar claim made by Alter upon a third party; or that he will support an altogether different claim made by Alter—either upon himself or a third party—which is part of the larger moral code within which Ego's original claim upon Alter is sanctioned. Morality is, in this sense, a tacit promise of mutuality of gratification and for that reason always entails obligations as well as rights for *each* party held to be subject to it.

It is precisely in consequence of this, however, that morality has certain distinctive *vulnerabilities*, for there is always some point at which the fit between morality and gratification is subject to strain. For, every moral code invariably contains tacit promises from which some derive more gratification than others; which are more costly or rewarding for some to comply with than for others; and which, therefore, some are more ready to enforce than others. Every moral code always entails obligations that some are reluctant to perform, although they do admit (in part, *have* to admit) them in order to mobilize support for those other claims in which they happen to be most interested. Every moral code thus involves a "Noble Lie." And some will always be ready to do less than their own moral commitments imply and, at some point, demand. This is not due to a failure of "socialization" or to aberrant disturbances; it is inherent in the nature of a moral code as a system of tacit mutual promises.

Another of the basic problems generated by moral codes derives from the fact that they entail at least some obligations be done "for their own sake alone." At some point, it demands that one do his "duty," even if others have not done theirs in the past and cannot be expected to in the future. It demands that certain things be done for, or to, certain others, regardless of whether they are needy or well-off. In short, it demands that one do the "right thing," without consideration of the consequences. From the standpoint of many moral prescriptions, it is irrelevant how the required action relates to the prior history of interaction among the parties, or even whether it generates consequences hurtful to others.

Moral considerations may therefore lead Ego to withhold assistance from or even to hurt a person who has previously helped Ego. *Moral* considerations may lead him to do things beneficial to those who are already advantaged and not do them for those who are "needy." Conformity with morality may induce a disregard of our past indebtedness to others, our future dependence upon them, and their present needs. Morality may, then, be deeply disruptive of social systems.

A moral "appetite," a hunger after righteousness, may be as insatiable as any other hunger, and as disruptive of social systems as the *anomie* or normlessness that Durkheim deplored. Social systems know no fury like the man of morality aroused. He cares little for the good that others have once done him or for the suffering they now know. There can be more free-flowing sadism in morality at high tide, and hence a greater potential for social system cataclysm, than in even the most expedient behavior. It is not those who have turned their backs on morality who are invariably the most hurtful men. It takes righteous men of great moral indignation to build concentration camps and crematoria.

There is a kind of dialectic between the system of reciprocities and the system of morality. Each has weaknesses that generate a need for the other. It is not simply that power and expedient reciprocities need to be controlled, for so too does morality.

MORALITY AND IMPUTED NONPARTISANSHIP

Although a system of rules may be "morally" sanctioned or legitimated in many different ways—for example, by claiming it to be old, legal, divinely given—all sanctions have one thing in common: they tacitly claim that what they establish does not result in partisan advantage for one group or one sector of the population. Whatever its specific form, the claim to legitimacy is always a tacit claim that there is mutuality of benefits. But how is this mutuality to be known and validated? It is commonly difficult for men to judge, by direct examination, the allocation of benefits yielded by a set of rules, for they may be obscured by the unforeseeable tangle of long-run consequences.

One way in which determination of the mutuality of benefits is, however, commonly made, is by examination of the manner in which the rules arose, or by beliefs about the establishment, derivation, or origins of the rules. The more that rules are believed to have developed in a manner that avoids or dispels suspicion of partisan benefit for certain individuals or groups, the more likely they are to be defined as legitimate. Certain imputed *derivations* of rules are generally more consistent with a belief in their impartiality, and hence their legitimacy, than are others. This means, for example, that rules commonly believed to have been created solely by those benefiting under them are less likely to be viewed as legitimate. Conversely, rules which are conceived of as made by all who were subject to them, or by groups in which all feel themselves to be full members, are more likely to be deemed legitimate.

Similarly, rules that are thought to be a heritage of earlier generations may, to some degree, be above suspicion of special advantage to those who are claimants under them, because they manifestly could not have been made by them. Again, and most important, rules seen as instituted by some agency which is itself believed to be nonpartisan will also be more likely to be judged legitimate than those viewed as deriving from some agency believed to be allied with one of the contending parties. This, of course, is one reason why it is supremely important for the "state" to project and protect a public image of itself as nonpartisan, in relation to the contending claims or interests within the larger society.

One of the most common rhetorics for communicating that the rules governing a group are nonpartisan is to claim that they derive from the gods and are superintended by them. To hold the gods to be the fount of morality is an implicit denial that it derives from, or gives advantage to, the special interests of some limited social group. It is this that vouchsafes the "justice" of a morality held to be divinely ordained. It is not merely that the violation of a morality defined as divinely originated may be viewed as a sacrilege that will provoke an inescapable nemesis—although this too, surely, induces powerful motives for conformity with it. But beyond such considerations, when rules are attributed to gods who stand above human groups and their conflicting interests, this in itself betokens the very impartiality of the rules and thereby endows them with a legitimacy that induces men to give them a willing obedience.

POSITIVISM AND THE MORAL CRISIS OF INDUSTRIALISM

Modern Western industrial society arose after the eighteenth century Enlightenment in Europe, which had severely undermined traditional religious beliefs and conceptions of divinity. Indeed, the very social classes that fostered industrialism were those congenial to the Enlightenment. Industrialism itself, with its utilitarian culture and its affinity for science and rationality, exerted considerable strain on traditional religious beliefs, beyond even any special polemical animus and regardless of whether or not science and traditional religion were judged to be "logically" compatible. The emergence of utilitarian industrialism was accompanied by and induced the sharpest impairment of traditional religious beliefs

—of conceptions of the supernatural and of an afterlife—those which had, hitherto, contributed to the sensed legitimacy of the moral code of Western Europe. The gods began to die, and with their dying the legitimacy of the entire moral system of Western Europe was threatened. And even the most dire expectations of those who foresaw the impending crisis were fulfilled in the rise of figures such as the Marquis de Sade, who concluded that if nothing was absolutely right then absolutely nothing was wrong.

Much of the emphasis on morality in Positivistic Sociology was a response to this emerging moral crisis, an effort to find some other, nonsupernatural, sanctioning of the moral order. In this light Positivism's effort to establish a secular, nonsupernatural religion of man is understandable. Its problem was to find a "secular" religion consistent with the new utilitarianism—that is, one without God and without a conception of an afterlife—that could endow common morality with legitimacy.

At first, Positivists believed that this could be done through science; they assumed that science's imputed certainty and impersonality could underwrite the legitimacy of moral codes with the very nonpartisanship that was required. The impersonal detachment of social science could provide, Comte believed, a morality-legitimating nonpartisanship. Detachment was not simply seen as conducive to better research or to truth for its own sake, or as of value to social scientists alone. Its historically latent function was to underwrite the legitimacy of the social scientist as the giver of a morality that was to come from social science.

This Positivistic effort to legitimate morality through science and a secular religion of man failed. Later developments in social science, from Durkheim to Parsons, record the retreat from Positivistic scientism, while at the same time giving clear expression to the need to find other ways, compatible with a highly rational society, in which Western society's moral code might yet be sustained. Essentially the answer of modern Functionalism comes down to saying that a nonrational morality is *necessary* for the stability of society as a *whole*. Here again, the legitimacy of morality is endorsed by the stress upon its nonpartisan character. There is a paradox in this reply, however, because, in effect, it gives a rational defense of the nonrational. Since it defends morality in terms of its rationally imputed societal *consequences,* these, of course, are always subject to rational dispute and continued reappraisal. Most particularly, the argument is vulnerable to the rejoinder that, while *some* moral code may be necessary for social order, the now existent and specific moral code is not simply conducive to social order in general, but to the stability of a specific society with its differential allocation of advantages and liabilities. In short, the moral code remains vulnerable to the claim that it is the defense of privilege.

The moral crisis, then, has not at all been solved; and, in truth, for many God is no longer dying, but dead. The search for a basis to legitimatize the moral code of Western European culture abides. But it persists under different conditions from those it began under in post-Enlightenment Europe; and for many, if not most, it is no longer a matter of central awareness. The moral crisis has not so much been solved as deferred by the strengthening of the non-moral bases of social order, particularly the growth of the increasingly abundant gratifications that an industrial civilization is able to distribute. Western society was stabilized by enabling many men to gain more gratifications than they had formerly enjoyed—even though continuing to have a great deal less than others around them.

Instead of having to use "spiritual" values as a way of bypassing the social instability induced by a zero-sum game, modern industrial societies used increased productivity. They stopped playing a zero-sum game. There is a very substantial sense, then, in which industrial societies need not be as "spiritual" as previous societies in order to maintain the stability of their systems, for they have, in truth, replaced the spiritual with the "material."

In short, I do not believe that those who speak of a general decline of moral standards in contemporary society, as many have, do so merely because the mass media have made them increasingly aware of evil and suffering in the world, but rather because, in some part, *there is such a decline*. In appreciable degree, this decline is an outcome of the built-in disposition of bourgeois utilitarianism toward anomie. For myself, in contrast to Parsons, there is no dilemma in holding that moral standards are declining, on the one side, and that certain "decencies" of welfare are increasing, on the other. For, rather than viewing such increasing decencies as evidence of an abiding and viable Christian morality, I view them as largely attributable to growing industrialization with its growing productivity and distribution of gratifications.

Moreover, I would add that these growing decencies are not incompatible, but directly correlated, with an increasingly instrumental use of people and with a declining "respect for the dignity of the individual." In some part, this decline is due to the growth of technical and professional specialists, who, quite in character with modern industrialization, consider themselves responsible solely for the application of narrow technical standards to persons, often quite apart from their consequences for improving *welfare:* "the operation was a success, but. . . ." In some part, it is due also to the fact that such specialization, by its very universalism, transforms individuals into "cases." Finally, it derives also from the nonresponsive callousness that power, based on technical expertise, permits professionals in the treatment of "clients." And all this is not one bit mitigated by the benign intentions of those involved. Indeed, if there is any modern organization more callous than the army to the dignity of the person, it is the modern hospital.

A technologically advanced civilization reduces and standardizes the skills required for wanted performances; it simplifies and mechanizes many tasks. It is therefore not as dependent on the rhetoric of morality or the mobilization of moral sentiment to ensure desired performances. Thus, within the technologically advanced sectors of society, individuals are less likely to be required to possess moral qualities and to be treated as moral actors, even as they are ever more "decently" treated. For, men are becoming more interchangeable, more replaceable, and removable at lower costs. Morality has become a "private" matter. Technicians now "process" cases according to impersonal rules and narrow standards. Utilitarian culture has found its hardware embodiment in modern technology and its organizational embodiment in modern bureaucracy; it can now fulfill its promise of treating persons as objects. And all this is happening together with increased health, longevity, literacy, welfare. Everywhere in industrialized societies the "decencies" are growing, and everywhere in them men are being indecently diminished.

In other words, men are less likely to experience themselves as potent and in control of their own destinies as bureaucracy, technocracy, and science become increasingly autonomous and powerful forces by which men feel entrapped. Men's capacity and need to see themselves as moral actors are threatened. Many, therefore, will be disposed either to reassert their potency *per se*, aggressively or violently and without regard to the moral character of such affirmation, or to relinquish the entire assumption that they are moral actors and capable of moral action. The latter, however, implies a radical reconceptualization of our fundamental view of man. I take it that this is, at least in part, Michel Foucalt's basis for noting the recent historical emergence of the concept of "Man" and speaking of the danger that "Man" will begin to die out in the twentieth century as "God" did in the nineteenth century.[28]

MORALITY AND SCARCITY UNDER INDUSTRIALISM

It is, in some part, because men are now increasingly treated as things but still retain the expectation that they will be treated as persons, that there is continued public concern with morality and a sense of endemic moral crisis, even if dulled by the outpourings of new gratifications. But there are other reasons as well and, indeed, some that suggest certain basic contradictions in our culture. One of the most important of these is that the sheer success of modern technology begins, at some point, to devalue its output. Its production of gratifications is not correlated in a one-to-one way with the increases in the gross national product. At some point for all, and more rapidly for the advantaged and privileged, there is a declining marginal utility to the new and additional objects and services. The second television set does not produce as much rapture as the first, the third car not as much bliss as the second. Industrialism is subject to the law of the declining rate of gratification, which, in time, diminishes the value of the very thing it does best. A technologically advanced society, then, can defer the problem of morality, but it cannot abolish it. And this is precisely because men *are* satiable, not insatiable. A rational society that really wanted to optimize its own social solidarity would obviously allocate increases in its output to those who would find them most rewarding, the poor and deprived. But since it is not these relatively weak groups that determine allocations, the powerful groups continue to provide themselves with a wastefully large share of the output.

While there are some social strata in industrial society which are already beginning to experience the consequences of the law of declining gratification, the full impact of this trend is still a long way off. We are now only at the very beginnings of the reaction. For the present, it is scarcity that remains the dominant problem. For, while modern industrial civilizations are far more productive than those in which Positivism first took root, they are still very far indeed from a level of productivity that would enable them to satisfy even the most basic needs of the population of the whole world. And this will become a most pressing requirement as the system of international relations is extended to incorporate new nations, which have a claim to aid either out of humane or political considerations. Even if the existent industrial plants throughout the world were used at full capacity, and if the total output was divided equally among all persons in the world, the results would be far, indeed, from universal security and comfort.

This same outcome would most often be the case if the nation itself were used as the unit of reckoning and the national output divided only among its own citizens, although the average level of gratifications would, of course, be much higher in the industrialized nations. Indeed, this is one reason the nation-state still remains a viable social unit. It provides a mechanism and a rationale for defining privileged access to gratifications, which go, first and most directly, to those who are its own citizens and most involved in their production. It is the viability of the Soviet Union as a nation-state and the pressure to maintain this privilege-defining role, that required and enabled it to resist China's claims that a share of the Soviet Union's productivity should underwrite her own industrialization; this is one of the basic sources of their conflict.

In fine, despite vast increases in industry's capacity to produce gratifications, the world still is living within an economy of excruciating scarcity. This means that the advantaged become powerful centers of vested interest, both between and within nations. These differentials cannot be stably protected by power alone, but require—both to inhibit claims for reallocations and to justify refusing them—a moral code that the parties involved will commonly define as legitimate.

Moreover, it is not only that existent levels of productivity are still far too low; there is the further fact that such productivity as exists is not all invested in producing goods that might further stabilize society by dispersing gratifications. An enormous amount of the gratification-potential of modern industry is drained off for military, the moon-doggle, and other nonproductive purposes. Thus the effective capacity of industrial nations to supply gratifications is presently far smaller than their potential capacity. Even the most industrially advanced nations must supply their own citizens with far fewer gratifications than they might in the absence of continual military involvement and tensions, let alone outright destruction.

And there is something of a vicious cycle here also: the differential ability of nations to provide gratifications to their own members contributes to tensions within and between nations, which, in turn, require military expenditures that still further impair the availability of gratifications. It is, in part, because military expenditures compete with welfare funds that the modern nation's ability to provide stabilizing gratifications is impaired and it must supplement consumer goods with moral restraint. There is the further consideration that the very type of nonproductive activity required here, namely, military service and combat, cannot be motivated by the kinds of gratification that an industrial civilization is intrinsically best at providing. The state's need to maintain men's motivations to fight and to die creates a market for a morality that no amount of consumer goods can by itself supply. Where death is, religion and morality are not far away; let the spectacle be produced under the auspices of The State, and it may then be called "glory."

There is one other fundamental aspect of the functioning of industrial civilizations that is important here. This is the fact that industrial production itself entails great costs for those involved in it. Industrial work requires a great reliability of presence and consistency of performance. Men must appear when and where they are needed and do precisely what is expected, all within a very narrow range of variability, even when their own impulses diverge from these expectations. For many, particularly those doing the unskilled and semi-skilled work, the tasks are arduous, stultifyingly dull, tedious, boring, and degrading. In large measure, the deadliness of much of modern work derives from the manner in which it is organized socially, which, in turn, is a function of both the master institutions that govern industry and the level of technology that it now has at its disposal.

Even where there is extensive unionization, men still have little control over what they produce and how they produce it; what they produce is not "theirs." Why, then, should they invest themselves in it, and how, then, can they derive *intrinsic* gratifications from it? In consequence, the operation of an industrial civilization requires an enormously costly discipline of self-expression and of self by those directly operating it. It requires either habits and values which reinforce this, if men are to work spontaneously, or, in their absence, an extensive bureaucracy and an unflagging totalitarian superintendence. This problem is particularly acute at the early stages of an effort at industrialization, when older work patterns are being rejected, when industrial discipline is new, and when the still low level of industrial productivity is as yet insufficient to compensate for the costs involved. In some measure, Stalinism was a response to this problem.

Yet even in advanced industrial societies the problem remains endemic. If the discipline required is more familiar, for many it still remains unspeakably tedious and costly. As a result, part of the very abundance of advanced industrial societies is used up in compensating people for the new burdens that it has itself generated. Much of the new gratification produced by industrialism must therefore go to sheer self-maintenance; that is, some part of the gratification produced serves to keep people producing it *despite* the costs. Although individual improvement is often experienced and many people are better off than they formerly were, this betterment does not serve to strengthen men's loyalty and indebtedness to the system as much as it might otherwise, for much of what they receive is experienced as a compensation for costs they have already incurred. They often see themselves as getting little more than they have earned, as having already paid for what they get. Thus they often experience themselves as being "even" with the system and may have no stabilizing sense of gratitude or of "outstanding obligations" to it.

For these several reasons, then, modern industrial civilizations have urgent need of viable moral systems, despite their increasing capacity to produce gratifications. Modern morality has grown out of and remains rooted in scarcity. It is this that lends a measure of realism to social theories that stress the significance of morality; it is this that generates structures of feeling which such social theories resonate meaningfully. At the same time, however, it is this also, that makes it exceedingly plain that when social theories fail to see and to say that what men need is an end to wars, an end to inequalities, an end to scarcity, and an end to dehumanized work, this makes them an ideology for accommodating to the present, rather than one that might transcend it.

The strength of such social theories is precisely that they enable some men to feel that they conscientiously *can*, and realistically *must*, accommodate themselves to the here and now. The vulnerability of such theories is that they of necessity counsel right-living, temperance and restraint, gradualness, patient acceptance of deprivation and of the accumulated hurt of living to those vastly less advantaged. Clearly the trouble with Functionalism is that it is committed to the present society, with all its dilemmas, contradictions, tensions, and, indeed, with all its immorality. The trouble with Functionalism is, in a way, that it is not really committed to social order in general, but only to preserving *its* own social order. It is committed to making things work despite wars, inequities, scarcity, and degrading work, rather than to finding a way out.

That there are some problems, human finiteness and death, from which there is no way out, is no excuse. This is not a social system problem, but a human problem, and is, indeed, not even within the special province to which such a social theory limits itself. Whether human beings will ever resign themselves to the fact that they are mortal is, to my mind, doubtful, but it is irrelevant to the issue at hand. That men are mortal is no excuse for accommodating to, but a good reason for opposing, societies that make the little time that we do live so terribly much less than it might be.

SOME DILEMMAS AND PROSPECTS

I shall briefly review some of the major assumptions I have made here and outline a few of their implications. The level of gratifications supplied by a society and the level of moral conviction or conformity within its culture—the latter may be included within but far from exhausts the former—are both prime sources of social solidarity, the willing mutual accommodation among men and groups. In some measure, each is an alternative to the other as a source of social solidarity; this means that, to some degree, each is in competition and conflict with the other. The relative importance of moral and nonmoral gratifications for the solidarity of society thus varies under different conditions. In particular, since technology is one of the major sources of nonmoral gratification, the relative contribution of moral and nonmoral gratifications to social solidarity will depend greatly on the level of technology in a society and on the changes in this level. Given a relatively primitive technology, then, social solidarity (so far as it exists at all) must rest more heavily on morality.

Correspondingly, however, as technology develops, it commonly undermines traditional moralities. Thus a great development in technology may mean a corresponding impairment of the moral sources of social solidarity, and, as a result, the "net" growth in the stability of the technologically advancing society will by no means have a one-to-one correlation with the growth of its technology. As technology develops, and to the degree that it produces a corresponding attenuation of the traditional moral code, a greater proportion of the solidarity of a society will depend upon the gratifications supplied by its technology. In time, however, the latter is subject to declining marginal utility—there are both short-range cycles and long-range trends by which the gratifications persons derive from technology are felt to decline. As this happens, the moral bases of social solidarity and the "moral problem" tend to become more salient.

But different parts of the moral code become salient to different groups; since they receive different benefits from the technology, the "moral problem" tends to be experienced differently by each. Specifically, those whose relationship to the technology advantages them are more disposed to view questions of moral *meaningfulness* as important. Conversely, those less advantaged with respect to the technology tend to place greater emphasis on improving their access to the gratifications it can provide, and to raise questions concerning the morality of allocation. In some measure, the disadvantaged seek to defend their claims in moral terms, and the advantaged, in turn, seek to protect their established positions in similarly moral terms. Both therefore are inclined to stress the importance of morality, but with different ends in view; each tends to stress the moral components that sanction their own claims. The disadvantaged stress the importance of justice, of equality, and of such freedom as is needed to pursue their claims to improved gratifications. The advantaged, for their part, tend to stress the importance of order. Thus the endemic strain upon a moral code that is exerted by the numerous changes attendant upon a developing technology are further and acutely complicated by differential interpretations given to the moral code by contesting groups.

With the Industrial Revolution at the end of the eighteenth century, a fundamentally new situation was created in the relative contribution that moral and nonmoral gratifications made to social solidarity. The new technology immensely increased the importance of nonmoral gratification. At the same time, however, continuing and accelerating technological change has meant that the relatively short-cycle changes that had hitherto been made to readjust to small technological changes were no longer possible: they were not made, in some part, because they could not be, shooting as they would have to at a continually changing target; and, they were not made, in some part, because they need not be, since the technology kept on providing more solidarity-producing gratifications. There has, in consequence, been a growing hiatus between the moral and technological sources of social solidarity in advanced industrial nations. As Durkheim saw—but for different reasons—the solidarity of industrial societies rests increasingly on nonmoral gratifications: the role of the "collective conscience" has diminished.

Since the moral code of these nations is gravely attenuated and continuously subjected to conflicting interpretations by those differently advantaged, contention concerning the allocation of gratifications cannot be resolved by direct mutual negotiation. The integration of these societies depends increasingly upon the control and mediation of conflicts from the state level. While the state can and does periodically deplore the decline of "moral fiber," it can mediate these conflicts with instrumental effectiveness only in two ways: either through some development of its repressive apparatus, moving in the direction of a "police-state," and/or through the manipulation of the technological fruits by income reallocations, the Welfare State. In either case, the state apparatus is greatly enlarged.

Moreover, all modern police-states also serve or promise to re-distribute such gratifications, as Fascism and Nazism did. Corre-spondingly, all Welfare States tend, with their welfare activities, to coordinate new policing functions and to bolster more traditional sources of "law and order." It is all a question of proportions, but these are vitally important, for they define, on the one hand, the degree of "freedom" that the parties will have, to pursue redistribu-tions congenial to themselves and, on the other, the extent to which allocative problems will be solved by the acquisition of booty through aggression and war.

From this standpoint it seems possible that the Soviet Union, with the continuing improvements in its technology, will, in time, move increasingly away from a repressive system of state control and toward a Western type of Welfare State. At the same time, however, there will be a corresponding decline in the influence of the moral-ideological bases of the Soviet Union's solidarity, with a resultant growth of anxieties, particularly to those most advantaged and socialized by its system; as a result, its transition to a Welfare State will be neither frictionless nor swift.

While the American Welfare State is based upon the most pro-ductive economy in the world, it is and will continue to be a deeply ambivalent structure. For, in one part, it is oriented to a concern to maintain social order and, in another, to a concern to do justice and remedy inequality. The order-oriented component has real po-tentiality for transition to a "police-state." The equality- and justice-oriented component must, in order to finance and supervise the welfare process, concern itself with efficiency and accommodate itself to the demands for fiscal economy from the order-oriented component and from the private sector more generally. Although much less drastically than a police-state, the Welfare State, then, must continually intrude into privacy and the other traditional lib-erties of both those who pay for and those who receive its bounty. And this, in turn, will further sharpen certain of the strains in the moral code.

The integration of American society in the foreseeable future promises to rest increasingly upon the development of a technology that could, on the one hand, facilitate effective administrative control by the state apparatus and, on the other, increase the gross national product and thus permit increased individual gratifications without changing the *proportions* allocated to different groups. The two main internal contingencies in this development are: first, the enormously disruptive impact that a serious economic depression would have on a society thus maintained; second, the increasing pressure for some total redefinition of the traditional moral code, a pressure which may take the form of a new, mass social movement for "cultural revitalization." This last is already in evidence with the emergence of the new psychedelic and communitarian counter-cultures.

NOTES

1. The following survey figures are *not* reported in Sprehe's doctoral dissertation, cited previously; they were obtained from my own analysis of the raw data.

2. For a fuller discussion, see my Introduction to E. Durkheim, *Socialism and Saint-Simon* (New York: Collier Books, 1962).

3. See E. Shils, "The Calling of Sociology," in *Theories of Society*, T. Parsons, K. D. Naegle, and J. R. Pitts, eds. (New York: Free Press, 1961), II, 1405–1448.

4. T. Parsons, *Sociological Theory and Modern Society* (New York: Free Press, 1967), p. 398.

5. *Ibid.*, p. 409.

6. *Ibid.*, p. 406.

7. *Ibid.*, p. 398.

8. *Ibid.*, p. 393.

9. *Ibid.*, p. 399.

10. *Ibid.*, p. 409.

11. *Ibid.*, p. 417.

12. *Ibid.*, p. 394.

13. *Ibid.*, p. 406.

14. *Ibid.*, p. 409.

15. *Ibid.*

16. *Ibid.*

17. *Ibid.*, p. 408.

18. *Ibid.*, p. 417.

19. *Ibid.*, p. 398.

20. *Ibid.*, p. 419.

21. Alasdair MacIntyre, *Marxism and Christianity* (New York: Schocken Books, 1968).

22. Robert Nisbet, *The Sociological Tradition* (New York: Basic Books, 1966), p. 261.

23. The following statistics are *not* reported in Sprehe's doctoral dissertation, cited previously; they were obtained from my own analysis of the raw data.

24. R. Tucker, *Philosophy and Myth in Karl Marx* (Cambridge: Cambridge University Press, 1961), p. 171.

25. *Marx's Concept of Man*, E. Fromm, ed. and T. Bottomore, trans. (New York: Ungar, 1961), pp. 130–131.

26. And to use it with about as much truth as it had in his case.

27. S. Tompkins, "Psychology of Being Right—and Left," *Trans-action*, III, No. 1 (November–December 1965), pp. 23–27.

28. See M. Foucault, *Les Mots et Les Choses* (Paris: Gallimard, 1966), pp. 396–398.

CHAPTER

8

Parsons on Power and Wealth

In his 1937 *The Structure of Social Action,* Parsons treated the role of "force" in social life as a marginal and residual problem, allowing it four pages (p. 288 ff.) in a volume of nearly eight hundred pages. While this would be a patent absurdity today, several wars and more than 200,000,000 deaths later, in 1937 it was characteristic of most American sociologists. Until quite recently, most of them had practically nothing to say about war or internal violence except under the nonpolitical rubric of crime and "deviance."

Parsons' treatment of force in 1937 emerges in his discussion of Pareto's emphasis on the role of force and fraud in social life, which, says Parsons, leads people of liberal "antecedents" to criticize Pareto's work for having a Machiavellian cast. "To avoid misunderstanding," Parsons points out that there was, for Pareto, an association between force and idealism: "the man of strong faith turns readily to force." In short, the use of force sometimes testifies to the existence of a powerful *moral* impulse and thus to the viability of what is, for Parsons, the single most important source of social integration. Force, therefore, cannot be *all* bad.

Far more realistic than many academic sociologists of this period, Parsons then shrewdly observes that "the role and significance of both [force and fraud] has undoubtedly been seriously minimized by the 'liberal' theories of progress and linear evolution." While they are a symptom of the breakdown of moral restrictions on ways of getting things done, and are for Parsons to that extent unwelcome, still force, unlike fraud, "frequently attends the 'creative' process by which a new value system becomes estab-

lished in a society through the succession to power of a new elite."
Parsons thus sees force as being "midwife" to the new value system
that may reintegrate society, and not as inherently egoistical as
fraud tends to be.[1] Moreover, force is used by the state "as a means
of enforcing commonly accepted rules." Constrained to choose,
Parsons—unlike Goffman—aligns himself with the "lions" rather
than the "foxes."

In 1940 Parsons formulated his "Analytic Approach to the
Theory of Social Stratification,"[2] in which stratification is conceived
of as the "differential ranking of the human individuals who com-
pose a given social system" for which a moral sanction is claimed.[3]
Among the six "bases of differential valuation" that Parsons men-
tions here, the sixth and last, acknowledged by him as a "residual
category," is power. In 1953 Parsons published an extensive revision of this paper, which outlines his new thinking about the problem and then applies it to the American system of stratification.[4]

The paper begins by stressing certain general points. For example, that "social stratification is a generalized aspect of the
structure of all social systems" and is thus universal. Second, that
"it is a condition of the stability of social systems that there should
be an integration of the value-standards of the component units to
constitute a 'common value system,'" and that "stratification *in its
valuational aspect* . . . is the ranking of units in a social system in
accordance with the standards of the common value system."[5] In
other words, while acknowledging that stratification as evaluation
is stratification seen from only one limited perspective, specifically,
in relation to the shared moral code, Parsons, nonetheless, chooses
to emphasize this one aspect of it. Here, power is regarded as the
"actual state of affairs," in contrast to the normatively defined ideal
ranking in value terms.[6] Power, Parsons then explicates, "is the
realistic capacity of a system-unit to . . . attain goals, prevent un-
desired interference, command respect, control possessions, etcetera," that is, in Parsons' terms, to actualize interests.

The ideological character of Parsons' theory of stratification
becomes increasingly manifest in this 1953 paper. In 1940, when
still within the shadow of the Great Depression, Parsons had con-
ceded that "in a business economy the immediate end of business
policy must, in the nature of the case, be to improve the financial
status of the enterprise . . . the earnings of the business have become the principal criterion of its success.[7] But if in 1940 Parsons
had acknowledged that the aim of business was profit, by 1953 his
emphasis came to be placed upon "productivity;" he then holds that
American society gives first place, in its value emphases, to the
contribution that units make "to the production of valued facilities . . . whatever these may be. . . . This puts the primary emphasis

on productive activity in the economy."[8] Profit thus disappears as the "principal criterion" of enterprise success, vanishing into the conceptual recesses of various "valued facilities."

The image of the American system of stratification that emerges in the 1953 paper is as follows. It is, above all, a system dedicated to the improvement of productivity. It is also "individualistic" (in the sense of a "pluralism of goals"), in that its concern is with "the production of valued facilities for unit-goals, whatever, within the permissible limits, these may be."[9] This sounds suspiciously like a backhanded way of asserting the cultural dominance of the very utilitarianism that Parsons had, in *The Structure of Social Action*, been at pains to criticize. While there is no one overriding goal to which the system as a whole is committed, Parsons adds that there is a *primary* system goal, namely, "the maximization of the production of valued possessions and cultural accomplishments." This formulation raises science and technology into a prominence equal to that of possessions, like property and wealth, as objectives of the society. Parsons, however, does acknowledge that interest in science and technology is a consequence of their contribution to productivity and thus that this interest "is derivative rather than primary."[10] In short, science is commonly seen in our culture from an instrumental and "applied" perspective.

American society is also regarded as placing an unusually strong stress on "equality of opportunity" and thus on the conditions requisite for it, namely, health and education. This, in turn, is seen to entail a measure of government involvement, so that health and education should not depend entirely on an ability to pay for them. Here, Parsons emphasizes that increased governmental action is now a "necessity" that derives most strongly from "the present position of high responsibility of the United States in the world."[11] It is not at all clear from Parsons' statement, however, who has placed this global responsibility upon the United States, or, indeed, whether increased American involvement abroad is at all a moral "responsibility" rather than an imperial ambition. In any event, Parsons has here become an exponent of American Destiny.

Parsons also maintains that, in the occupational system, "status is a function of the individual's productive 'contribution' to the functions of the organizations concerned."[12] Status therefore depends on capacities and achievements on behalf of the organization. "Of course," acknowledges Parsons, "there are innumerable ways in which it fails to work out," for differences in power based on differential command of possessions increase discrepancies between contribution and status. These discrepancies, he reassures us, are, however, "secondary from the point of view of the broad characterization of our stratification system."[13]

"Our system of stratification," holds Parsons, "revolves mainly about the integration between kinship and the occupational system,"[14] family income and status being derivative of occupational earning and position. (Equal emphasis is not, however, given to the reality of the converse, where occupational earning and position are derivatives of family income and status.) There is no fixed, unambiguous class system in the United States, says Parsons, hardly any development of an hereditary upper class, no clear-cut hierarchy of prestige, considerable mobility between groups, and much tolerance for diverse avenues to success.[15] As a result of the American tax system as well as of the separation between management and ownership, there is no American elite whose position is family-transmitted. The American elite is open and shifting.

Lines between classes are blurred at all levels of the hierarchy. As a result of automation, "it looks very much as though the traditional 'bottom' of the occupational pyramid was in [the] course of almost disappearing."[16] The enormous increase in the productivity of the American economy is a "big positive opportunity-producing factor,"[17] and, in effect, now serves as a substitute for the closed frontier. The main source of upward social mobility is not access to possessions but to college. For those in metropolitan areas, who can live at home while attending college, "the economic difficulties of going to college are not the principal barriers even for those from relatively low-income families . . . the available evidence suggests that it is less important than is generally supposed." In accounting for the failure of some to achieve upward mobility through education, Parsons therefore stresses that "an unexpectedly heavy emphasis falls on the factor of *motivation* to mobility . . . as distinguished from objective economic opportunity for mobility."[18] In short, upward mobility now presumably depends largely on education, and education on ambition, or "git up and git."

In sum, in 1953 Parsons looked upon his American system and found it good. While acknowledging certain "discrepancies" between achievement and reward, he holds these to be of "secondary" importance; while observing the discriminated position of the Black population, he has confidence that it will, in good time, be remedied through the inexorable working of universalistic values with their stress upon equality of opportunity; while noting that science and education are subordinated to utilitarian purposes and to enhancing productivity, he finds this no cause for indignation. While not perfect, it is perfectly clear that, from Parsons' standpoint, ours is the best of all possible social worlds.

Although many important problems in Parsons' analysis remain, and I shall return to some of them later, here I simply want to comment on a curious anomaly in Parsons' moral posture, in his "moralistics." Parsons' fundamental vision requires systematic and repeated affirmation of the importance of looking at the social world in relation to its moral code. And Parsons does this ceaselessly. Yet the differences that he observes between reality and morality never disturb and certainly never outrage him; they are, for him, always temporary discrepancies, secondary aberrations, marginal deviations of no consequences in the larger scheme of things. Parsons is a rare creature: the contented moralist. And for all his talk about the "voluntaristic" component, Parsons' own behavior clearly reveals that moral values do not always lead to energetic striving on their behalf, but may, on the contrary, induce a smug satisfaction with things as they are. His moralistics consistently takes the form of piety, of apology for rather than criticism of the status quo. Parsons persistently sees the partly filled glass of water as half-*full* rather than half-*empty*.

Essentially Parsons accomplishes this by absorbing reality into morality, focusing only on those aspects of reality that coincide with morality, as, for example, when, in his revised theory of social stratification, he tells us blandly that he shall be concerned primarily with its "valuational aspect." Part of the reason for this is that Parsons' metaphysics stresses the coextensivity of morality and reality. He really doubts the fundamental reality of the nonmoral. There is thus a surprisingly strong Platonic component in Parsons; both focus on order, morality, hierarchy, and, as we shall see, in the last resort, on "force." These metaphysics emerge with even greater clarity, if that is possible, in Parsons' subsequent analysis of power.

THE PROBLEMATICS OF POWER

In 1961 and 1962 Parsons turned, for the first time, to a fully systematic discussion of both force and power, apparently prompted by a conference called to discuss guerrilla and counterinsurgency warfare. It then seemed as if American "responsibilities" abroad were about to lead Parsons to a new interest in power and thereby remove its residual character in his theory. As we shall see, however, nothing of the sort happened.

These new analyses of power centered on a detailed and, indeed, an elaborate discussion of "the polity as a societal subsystem theoretically parallel to the economy,"[19] in which: (1) imputed characteristics of the economy are, presumably, used as a basis to develop a theory of power, and (2) power is treated as analogous in the polity to money in the economy, and where (3) power is therefore viewed as a generalized medium of interchange in the polity, that is, "as a circulating medium," and therefore (4) the focus is not on *who* has how much power relative to others or on the *consequences* of such power differences, but where (5) power, like money, is seen as an "input" that can be combined with other elements to produce certain kinds of "outputs" useful to the system as a whole.

From Parsons' standpoint power is now to be viewed as a "generalized capacity to secure the performance of binding obligations by units in a system of collective organization, when the obligations are legitimized with reference to their bearing on collective goals and where, in the case of recalcitrance, there is a presumption of enforcement by negative situational sanctions."[20] His requirement that, for power to be power it must be "generalized," stems, as far as I can see, simply from the analogy with money; in any event, and like his other inferences from the analogy, it produces no theoretical consequences of any significance or originality. The focus on legitimacy is, for its part, typical of Parsons' abiding emphasis on the integrative importance of morality, and is not derived from the analogy with the economy or with money.

Parsons stresses that "securing compliance with a wish . . . simply by threat of superior force, is not an exercise of power." Parsons' systematic discussion of power, then, is not really concerned with all forms of power but, at most, with only one kind, namely, the "institutionalized power system" which secures conformity to *obligations* deemed *legitimate* by reason of their imputed contribution to collective goals. In short, Parsons is concerned primarily with *morally* sanctioned power, and not at all with power as it has been commonly understood by most political scientists and sociologists.

Indeed, Parsons himself acknowledges, "most political theorists would draw the line differently,"[21] because *they* regard threats of superior force as exercises of power. Parsons might have added, in candor, that he now not only disagrees with other theorists but also with his own earlier position on the character of power. For, in his 1940 paper Parsons had expressly stated that "a person possesses power only insofar as his "ability to influence others and his ability to achieve or secure possessions are *not institutionally sanctioned.*"[22] In 1962 Parsons has, in effect, chosen to talk about something else, something different from what most social theorists regard as power. He has chosen, we might say, to confine himself to a discussion of "establishment power," power used in, by, and for established social systems and established elites.

Parsons might hold that his idiosyncratic conception of power should be appraised in terms of the theoretical consequences that it yields. In my judgment, his entire analysis of power, with its central and repeated analogy with money, yields consequences of absolutely no intellectual significance. Thus, for example, Parsons concludes, on the basis of this analogy, that "force" bears the same relation to power as gold bullion bears to money, that force is a reserve on which the system can fall back in case other measures fail. In short, it is the ultimate deterrent, the instrument of last resort in a "showdown." It would hardly seem that his elaborate discussion and analogy are justified by this banality or by the others that it yields. For example, he tells us that "the danger of war is endemic in uninstitutionalized relations between territorially organized collectivities."[23] In other words, there is always a danger of war between sovereign states. In a similarly enlightening vein, Parsons remarks that it is not the possession of weaponry or the threat to use it that is the "principal 'cause' of war." Never have theoretical mountains labored harder to produce tinier and grayer mice.

The utter speciousness and uselessness of Parsons' analogy with money is evidenced by the fact that his conception of force as an instrument of "last resort" was formulated as early as 1941 and in total independence of that analogy: though "force is not the only or even in any general way the most important or effective means of controlling others, under certain circumstances it is the last resort."[24] The really significant questions about force, namely, who has routine access to it and on behalf of which interests, remains unexamined in both the early and later versions of Parsons' theory.

To return, nevertheless, to the theory itself, we recall that intrinsic to Parsons' conception of power is legitimacy: "the threat of coercive measures, or of compulsion, without legitimation or justification, should not properly be called the use of power at all, but is the limiting case where power . . . merges into an intrinsic instrumentality of securing compliance with wishes, rather than obligations."[25] Here, Parsons' response to the split between power and morality is, primarily, to deny or minimize its significance and reality; shoving it over into a corner of his attention, he gives it only an occasional glance.

For Parsons, the normal case is one in which the use of coercion is justified, thus providing a vivid demonstration of how it is possible to be both empirically correct and intellectually absurd. Parsons is empirically correct, in that even the most brutal exercises of coercion are commonly *held* to be justified by those committing them. The Nazi invasion of Europe and slaughter of the Jews was, indeed, justified, by the *Nazis*. His position is intellectually absurd, however, because he does not specify *who* must regard coercion as justified, before it can be defined as "true" Parsons-1962-type power. Since practically everyone regards his own use of coercion as justified, pure coercion and compulsion will be rare indeed: all will be "power." While Parsons sees that power entails the means of acquiring legitimacy, he fails to see that this does not simply imply access to "sanctifying" agencies, much less the making of claims to obedience on grounds that others regard as independently valid and would normally acknowledge. He fails to see the literal sense in which coercion, violence, force, and all forms of might *make* right. He fails to see that might creates its own legitimation and is not merely willingly "exchanged" for it.

Those who obey because they are afraid do not like to think themselves unmanly or cowardly; in an effort to maintain a decent regard for themselves, the fearful frequently find ingenious ways in which they can define almost any demand made upon them as legitimate. Correspondingly, those demanding obedience often dislike viewing themselves as engaged in an unmanly brutalization of the weak; to maintain a decent regard for themselves, they use all the resources at their command to convince others that they are justified in their brutality. Legitimacy, in short, may be born of a tacit alliance and trade-off between the criminal and his victim: the victim conceals his *impotence* by acknowledging the legitimacy of the claims made upon him, while the criminal conceals his brutality by forcing his victim to acknowledge the legitimacy of his claims. Thus are power and morality brought into equilibrium. This is not to deny a potentially significant autonomy to moral considerations; it is simply to insist on the fully reciprocal nature of their relations to power. Like any other behavior, the judgment that something is legitimate can be coerced and rewarded situationally.

Power will often, but not always, be defined as legitimate by those exposed to its most brutal forms, because a perceived malintegration between power and morality generates anxiety and, in turn, a dissonance-reducing drive. The chasm of meaninglessness must be closed. Precisely because power may be so brutal, men will strive to believe that it is not morally irrelevant. Yet simply to define power as legitimate, as Parsons does, is an exercise in conceptual license as futile as it is sterile. Parsons' extension of the sovereign domain of morality is an inverse form of Machiavellianism. It is one more indication of the fact that the theorist lives in the same constraining world as those he theorizes about, and has their common need to reduce the dissonance between power and morality.

In the formulations above, it may seem as if I am talking only about the manner in which *extreme* threat—the "last resort" of force—generates a readiness to obedience that is rationalized in other, more moral terms. It is not only, however, when power is brutal and not only when it is poised to express itself as force, that its presence is sensed in social relationships and generates motives for *willing* obedience. Power also exists quietly, as it were, and is fully real even at the lower ranges of intensity. It makes its presence felt continuously, underneath and alongside of "legitimacy" and all moral motives for obedience. In some of his formulations, Parsons, like many other sociologists, seems on occasion to regard power and "authority," or morally legitimated power, in two ways: either as two different *stages* in development, in which, for instance, power is viewed as the degenerate or the immature form of authority; or as two alternative ways in which one person or group can structure the behavior of others. In both cases they are viewed as mutually exclusive, as if, when one exists, the other does not.

This image is misleading. It exists largely because power and authority are being looked at from the standpoint of superordinates, those on top. If it had been looked at from the standpoint of *subordinates* in the social world, power and authority would more likely be viewed as dual structures, both *simultaneously* present, in subtle and continual interaction. Power, in short, exists not simply when authority breaks down or before authority has had a chance to mature. It exists as a factor in the lives of subordinates, shaping their behavior and beliefs, at every moment of their relations with those above them. Attitudes toward their superiors are continually influenced by the *awareness*—sometimes focal and sometimes only subsidiary—that superiors can give or withhold at will things that men greatly want, quite apart from their own agreement or consent, and that crucial gratifications depend upon allocations and decisions by their superiors. It is the sheer ability of the powerful to do this, quite apart from their *right* to do so, that is an independent, ever-present element in the servile attitudes that subordinates often develop toward their superiors. Legitimacy and "authority" never eliminate power; they merely defocalize it, make it latent. How could "authority" eliminate power when authority is not merely some unanchored "legitimacy," but the legitimacy of *power*?

The extreme displays of power, or the "last resorts" of force, even when directed toward others, and, indeed, toward others whom one may believe "deserve" it, serve as symbolic reminders that power is continuously present in the lives of all. The occasional lynching of a Black, the occasional firing of an employee, the occasional parental flare of temper toward the child, the occasional punch in the nose, all—however occasional, and even though aimed at someone else—remind men that there are limits. The exercise of the "last resort" is the symbol of a *continuing presence;* the mild, routine exercises of power are chastening reminders of the availability of nonroutine last resorts.

Utopian as his analysis frequently is, there are moments when Parsons' discussions of power and force threaten to be realistic. For example, he sees that even institutionalized power has its limits and vulnerabilities. He thus remarks that the obligations of power, like the obligations of a banker, are always larger than it can fulfill at any one moment. If the demands made on power, he says, are too rapid, it can become "insolvent." Yet this is a warning not only that power can be broken, but also that it can be terrible. "At the end of the road," warns Parsons, "lies the resort to force in the interest of what particular groups conceive to be their rights."[26] This comes down to saying that, pressed too fast and too hard, the system will bloody those who insist on demanding their rights. Presumably, therefore, claimants must seek justice slowly and gradualistically, lest they provoke the powerful to the wrathful use of "extreme" measures.

It is notable that it is only here, with respect to the extreme resort to force, but not with regard to the routine exercise of power, that Parsons speaks of "what particular groups conceive to be their rights." For, if the routine, institutionalized exercise of power were seen in this relativistic manner, it would imply that power inherently entails a tendentious self-interest. And this would be fundamentally incompatible with Parsons' ideologically compulsive conception of power as that which disinterestedly serves not partisan but *collective* goals.

In maintaining that men who demand that "power" fulfill its legitimate obligations "too rapidly" can undermine a power system, Parsons tacitly assumes that "power" *normally* fails to discharge certain of its obligations, or leaves them unmet. Surely this implies that power is normally in arrears in meeting its moral obligations. This, in turn, implies that, far from being mutually adjusted, there is usually some tension between power and morality. This implication fails to be made explicit, however, because it contradicts Parsons' basic emphasis on the coextensivity of power and morality.

Once the moral defaults of power are made focal, then the next question inevitably becomes: *Whose* legitimate claims are being met and whose are being ignored? Will it be assumed that the moral defaults of power are *random,* relative to all actors in a social system, or are these defaults in some way patterned and skewed? Parsons absolutely must maintain that they are random and not patterned. He must, that is, maintain that the chances that power will slight the legitimate claims or rights of actors depends in no way upon their position in the social system, or upon their power itself. Should he admit that the moral defaults of power are related to the very power that people have, then his fundamental conception of power as disinterestedly serving non-partisan *collective* interests collapses utterly. At this point, therefore, Parsons' fall into realism must and does stop.

What Parsons must ignore is how the possession of power itself enables some to *default* on their moral obligations; how the lack of power constrains others to accept less than they might legitimately claim; and how this very default of morality is itself established as *customary* on the basis of the power distribution. In short, what Parsons must ignore is what I will call "normalized repression."

Every social system entails some degree of failure to conform with the full requirements of its moral code. There is always some latitude in what is taken to be acceptable conformity with the requirements of any moral value; but this will vary considerably, depending upon whether the persons judging it are those giving or those receiving such compliance with the moral code and upon their power relation to one another. One reason for this universal disparity between moral principle and customary practice is that, often, those who profess a given value do not, and never did, believe in it, at least in anything like the generalized manner in which it came to be formulated publicly. Men often experience neither guilt nor embarrassment at doing less than a value requires, because they were never committed to all that it prescribed. Values are continually susceptible to attenuation in practice, because people frequently are induced to promise performances that they do not want, and perhaps never intended, to keep. This disparity between values and "wants" leads to a gap between principle and practice, which, in time, attains a kind of equilibrium in custom and usage. The young are socialized to *expect* its occurrence. To demand full compliance, they are told, is impractical, unrealistic, and naive.

Yet not all are able to default with equal impunity on their moral obligations. Some pay more costs, others less. Some hang for stealing the goose from off the commons; others steal the commons from under the goose without penalty. While a set of moral values may be shared in common, men are not equally interested in all moral values, and the power to enforce moral claims is never equally distributed. The level at which moral default comes to be stabilized is, in large part, determined by the relative *power* of the groups involved. The more powerful are, in consequence, both ready and able to *institutionalize* compliance with the moral code at levels congenial to themselves and more costly to those with less power. Power is, among other things, just this ability to enforce one's moral claims. The powerful can thus *conventionalize* their moral defaults. As their moral failure becomes customary and expected, this itself becomes another justification for giving the subordinate group less than it might theoretically claim under the group's common values. It becomes, in short, "normalized repression."

If morality seems coextensive with power, it is not only because power influences the *levels* at which conformity to moral values becomes conventionalized, but also because power can actually shape the definition of *what* is moral (and, indeed, of what is "real"). For, in any given case, what is moral is often uncertain, frequently disputed, and invariably resolved in a situation where some have more power than others. Those with more power therefore exert more influence in determining which moral rule applies and what a rule means in any given case. That is, they define what is moral. Morality fits power, therefore, because the powerful have the Procrustean ability to mold morality. While not creating the moral code out of whole cloth, they can cut and tailor it to suit themselves.

MAKING AMERICAN SOCIETY WHOLE: THE IMPORTANCE OF BEING RICH

In a society with democratic values, where the principle is "one man, one vote," and where it is held that a man's reward should depend on his contribution, the position of the "rich" is an anomalous one. Since it is at variance with the values publicly affirmed, their exceptional power and privilege must be muted. A public charade is therefore often played, in which people act as if there were no one here except "middle-class" people, and being rich is treated as if it had no special consequences. Being "rich," then, often comes to be a latent identity.

The importance of being rich largely disappears in Parsons' mythos of the franchise. He tells us that, in the "largest and most highly differentiated systems . . . the most 'advanced' national societies, the power element has been systematically equalized through the device of the franchise"; and he adds that "the same basic principle of one member, one vote, is institutionalized in a vast number of voluntary associations." Moreover, "equality of power through the franchise is so great empirically that the question of how it is grounded in the structure of social systems is a crucial one."[27] It is characteristic of Parsons' moralistics that he finds this grounding in a value principle, universalism, which involves treating people of the same merits or demerits in the same manner. It is equally characteristic that he makes no mention of the many bitter struggles that took place, from Chartism onwards, to extend the franchise to the working class, to women, to the Blacks, and of how these were won only against the bitter resistance of the propertied and prejudiced. Somehow the universalistic value principles of the rich have frequently and mysteriously not led them voluntarily to honor the principle of one man, one vote.

Again, Parsons rather typically makes no mention of the fact that, though this principle is "institutionalized in a vast number of voluntary associations," this has not prevented practically all of them from being ruled by oligarchies. Parsons' essay on power might well have begun by asking, "Who now reads Robert Michels?" It is only the empirical importance of the *principle* of equality, not, in Parsons' view, its continuous and routine *violation* in common practice that is worth mentioning. That men in the "advanced" countries are born enfranchised but everywhere live under oligarchies neither perturbs nor puzzles Parsons deeply.

It is noteworthy that in the mid-1940's and in the 1950's there was much discussion among sociologists interested in organizational analysis and political sociology—for example, Philip Selznick, S. M. Lipset, and myself—of the problem of oligarchy, that is, the rule of the few. Much of the controversy centered on Michels' "iron law" formulation, which sees oligarchy as an inevitable, though perhaps, "unanticipated" consequence of internal organizational imperatives. The issue was, in part, one of pessimism versus optimism concerning the possibility of successful social change in democratic directions and with democratic means. The Michelsians, of course, were pessimistic, and others of us opposed them largely because they seemed to preclude democratic change. Michelsian pessimism concerning oligarchy was then congenial to socialists disillusioned with the Soviet Union and, more generally, hostile to those who they felt encouraged "utopian" and unrealistic expectations of social change. Disagreement tended to focus on the causes of oligarchy. It pitted those who stressed the origins of oligarchy in characteristics common to all organizations, and who were therefore rather pessimistic, against those of us who saw oligarchy as more susceptible to some kind of control and remedy, partially because we tended to stress its historical origins. We never disagreed, however, about the data, or, at least, we commonly accepted the fact that most organizations were, indeed, oligarchical.

In the 1960's, however, interest in oligarchy waned among sociologists; there is now little pessimism and, in fact, little concern shown about it either as a political or as a theoretical problem. Nor, for that matter, has anyone indicated a belief that the facts have changed and that organizations are now growing democratic. What has happened, rather, is that the fact of oligarchy has simply ceased to be a value-resonating problem for most sociologists. There has been an intellectual *accommodation* to the existence of oligarchy, which largely takes the form of neglect.

The earlier period of pessimism about oligarchy had entailed a critique and a generalized suspicion of power; it had stressed the selfish and partisan uses of power by office-holders, whatever their ideology. The Michelsian theory of oligarchy had then congenially resonated the sentiments of young socialists, who were starting careers as sociologists but were still distant from sociology's centers of power and, at the same time, were also critical of the Soviet alternative. The generalized suspicion of power, which the Michelsian theory validated, was congenial to those involved in career-building efforts that would have been diverted or permanently impaired by involvement in any reform "movements." (Indeed, I still recall receiving a letter in the mid-1940's from a leading American criminologist, discouraging me from applying for a post in his Department because he had me marked down as a "social reformer.") If the earlier concern with the problem of oligarchy derived, in part, from its congeniality to a rising professional cohort, its neglect today is part of the ideology of a now well-established cohort. The current conception of power as a resource for fulfilling collective or public goals, rather than the selfish ambitions of office-holders, reflects the sociologist's access to and ease with established power centers, all of which has been greatly accelerated by the largesse of the Welfare State. But so far as I am aware, the facts remain unchanged and unchallenged: practically all organizations are oligarchical.

Were the prevalence of oligarchy in the modern association seriously acknowledged, the problem would, of course, have to be carried to the level of the polity as a whole. Here, anyone with an ounce of empirical curiosity could not help but wonder how it could be possible for the man with a million dollars to be content to have no more of a vote than the man living on public welfare, particularly since the latter could vote to tax his fortune. The Parsonsian answer, I suppose, would be that, being imbued with universalistic value principles, the rich properly accept the "very strictly binding" consequences of equality under the franchise. The "rich" therefore receive no special mention—indeed, hardly any mention at all—in Parsons' elaborate and spacious discussion of power. They merely do not appear. Parsons' political sociology keeps them invisible. The rich are a very "latent identity" indeed, as embarrassing to Parsons' esoteric sociological theory as they are to the commonplace political ideology that it embodies. Like Ernest Hemingway, Parsons believes that the rich are like everyone else, in relation to the power system of advanced nations: they have been "systematically equalized."

For my part, I am confident that it was not Hemingway but F. Scott Fitzgerald who was right on this matter: the rich *are* different. They are not just like everyone else. They are certainly not about to limit their political power to that which the principle, one man, one vote, allows them, nor need they do so. What the "extension" of the franchise has meant is that the rich continue to exert power, far beyond their votes and numbers, largely through *non*parliamentary or *non*congressional means, just as they always have.

The rich exercise power, including political power, though not by voting and not by getting elected to office. They do it in these ways: primarily through their control of great foundations, with their policy-shaping studies and conferences and their support for universities; through a variety of interlocking national associations, councils, and committees that act as legislative lobbies and as influences upon public opinion; through their membership among the trustees of great universities; through their influence on important newspapers, magazines, and television networks, by virtue of their advertising in them or their outright ownership of them, which, as Morris Janowitz once observed, sets "the limits within which public debate on controversial issues takes place"; through their extensive and disproportionate membership in the executive branch of the government, their financial contributions to political parties, their incumbency in major diplomatic posts; and through their control of the most important legal, public relations, and advertising firms. Granted that these observations are in no way as original as Parsons' observation that force is an instrument of last resort. Nonetheless, they still bring us close to the most important problems in the analysis of a business society's class system, and help us to see certain fundamental difficulties in Parsons' treatment of it.

In his 1940 paper on stratification, Parsons insists that wealth is only secondarily a *criterion* of status—that is, one is given approval or prestige not primarily *because* one has wealth but, rather, because wealth has "primary significance . . . as a symbol of achievement." That is, Parsons holds that a capitalist society stresses the value of achievement and therefore gives wealth in recognition of and, indeed, in *proportion* to achievement. Here one might have paused briefly to wonder why it was, and what it meant, that a society with such a strong pecuniary concern should be so reluctant to award approval or prestige simply for wealth alone. Why does it not openly honor the rich in the same fulsome way that ancient Greece awarded prestige for sheer physical prowess in war? While Parsons understates the extent to which sheer wealth has, in fact, always been a basis on which prestige has been awarded, he is, I believe, correct in noting that there is a certain embarrassment in doing so. The "rich" are, in part, a latent identity. The use of wealth as a criterion of status is not as open and easy as might be expected in a business society such as our own.

Essentially this has to do with the fact that wealth itself, and particularly differential wealth, has always been in *need* of justification and legitimation, even in a middle-class and pecuniary society. Commonly, even people in a middle-class society have been interested in knowing what gives the wealthy a *right* to their wealth. Traditionally, the middle-class answer has argued that it is based on their talent and individual achievements. In this vein, Parsons remarks that wealth "owes its place as a criterion of status mainly to its being an effect of business achievement."[28] At any rate, this has been the fundamental middle-class ideology.

Yet Parsons also acknowledges a certain "complicating" factor, to wit, "inheritance of property." In consequence of this, he must admit that wealth "gains a certain independence so that the possessor of wealth comes to claim a status and have it recognized, regardless of whether or not he has the corresponding approved achievement to his credit."[29] But if wealth, as Parsons says, owes its importance as a criterion of status to its association with achievement, why should a claim to status, on the basis of inherited wealth alone, be acknowledged?

In his effort to explain this paradox, Parsons has to abandon his most fundamental assumptions, which, being Functionalist, would ordinarily lead him to search out the ongoing contributions that a practice makes to a social system. Here, instead, he invokes a *pre*-Functionalist explanation to account for the practice of honoring the unaccomplished wealthy, characterizing it as a vestigial "tradition." Thus Parsons holds that "in our society . . . there is a tradition of respect for birth and inherited wealth which has never quite been extinguished." But, *why* does this tradition *persist*? In particular, *how* can it persist if it is in flagrant violation of the society's dominant values, which, being "universalistic" and achievement-oriented, call for all rewards to be apportioned to specific achievements?

The answer, of course, is that respect for inherited wealth and the granting of status based upon it, is not an anomaly in capitalist societies but is, rather, consistent with and supportive of its institutionalized pattern of property and inheritance. The inheritance of wealth is intrinsic to the system of private property characteristic of capitalism. On the principle that it is better to be wealthy and secure than very wealthy and insecure, the rich have compromised with progressive taxation and with universalistic and achievement values. They bend and compromise, but they do not compromise themselves out of existence. To have any degree of stability and legitimacy, a capitalist system must win some measure of acceptance for its own distinctive principle, namely, that some have a *right* to something for nothing, to approval and prestige because of their sheer wealth alone. The system must mobilize every resource at its command to prevent the violation and to guarantee the acceptance of this principle.

But this principle contradicts universalism and achievement. How this is possible, and why this is possible, are secondary issues. The first and most important thing is to see that the contradiction *exists*. And it is this—and the basic implication it entails—that Parsons is most desperately laboring to avoid. He is trying to avoid acknowledging that middle-class property is *il*legitimate from the standpoint of important middle-class values; for, this might imply that middle-class society has built into it a fundamental contradiction between its property system and its cultural values that inherently unstabilizes its social system and undermines its moral code. Stressing, as he does, the importance of morality for the stability of a society, Parsons is caught in the contradiction of maintaining that contemporary society is fundamentally sound, even though its property system is at variance with its own moral code.

Parsons argues tautologically that possessions or "facilities" are optimally allocated when given to those who can use them most effectively within and for the values relevant to the system in question. He then transforms this into the statement that differences in facilities (possessions) *follow* upon and correspond to differences in the contributions people *do* make to the functioning of the system, so that "the rank order of control of facilities should tend to correspond to the rank order of the evaluation of unit-function in the system."[30] In short, possessions and prestige should and do correspond, because both are given to those scarce individuals competent to use them on behalf of the social system as a whole. "Any lack of such correspondence," Parsons reassures us, is merely a "disturbing factor in the situation."[31]

This trivial "disturbing factor" turns out, on inspection, however, to be nothing less than private property and inheritance. But Parsons simply cannot acknowledge this in anything like its full importance, for he expressly holds "that it is a condition of the stable state of a [social] system that the reward system should tend to follow the same rank order as the direct evaluation of units in terms of their qualities and performances."[32] In other words, Parsons holds that the stability of a social system depends upon "the principle . . . of reward in proportion to 'desert.' "[33] (Which, of course, was exactly Plato's point: That is, the stability of a society depends upon doing "justice," in the sense of giving a man his due.) But since, as Parsons also acknowledges, "control of possessions is inevitably correlated with high status,"[34] those with possessions continue to get their rewards regardless of whether or not they earn them, and all the more so as the possessions themselves are inherited rather than earned. The modern development of a separation between ownership and management in the corporation sharpens the problem of the legitimacy of the rich. Moreover, with the development of trust companies, which invest inheritances (and help avoid inheritance taxes), it is now possible for the rich to remain so, and, indeed, to grow richer, without managing either production or investment enterprises. The rewards of the rich then continue, without their having to lift a finger or twitch a brain cell and without any correspondence to their contribution or "deserts." By Parsons' own assumptions, therefore, a business society fails to meet the requirements of a stable social system as he himself has outlined them.

As will later be noted, Parsons is ready to acknowledge that our *family* system, in which children share and inherit parental advantages without earning them, violates universalism. He acknowledges that the "preservation of a functioning family system even of our type is incompatible with complete 'equality of opportunity.' " But this acknowledgment too is ideologically distorted, for the present family system is incompatible with anything remotely approaching equality, let alone "complete" equality and opportunity. The reference to "complete" equality simply serves to make the existent disparity between the two seem inevitable and thus to make the demand to reduce it seem impractically idealistic. Yet while Parsons acknowledges the incompatibility between the family and the moral code, he is unable to acknowledge the same contradiction between private property and the moral code. The point, of course, is that Parsons is not engaged in a polemic against Plato, who was the first to see the full implications of the contradiction between the family system and private property, but against Marx; acknowledgment of the contradiction between property and the moral code would undermine Parsons' position here.

The fundamental dilemma that Parsons faces is that *capitalism does not comply with the requirements of a stable social system* as he himself has formulated them: for, how is it possible to maintain a willing mutual conformity to the common moral code on which social equilibrium rests, according to Parsons, when the code itself is violated by the property system and when some are enormously wealthy and powerful by reason of property that they have often inherited and never earned? When some are so much more rich and powerful than others, is there not a continual possibility that they may, with relative impunity, ignore rather than be sensitive to, and depart from rather than comply with, the expectations of others? Is there not a continual temptation for the rich and powerful to minimize compliance with their obligations and to maximize compliance with their rights, thus exerting a continuous strain on the "complementarity" of the social system and increasing its exploitative patterns? Is there not a continual inclination for them to rationalize, to equate the "needs" of the collectivity with the vested interests inherent in their own advantaged position? And quite apart from their immediate interests, is there not a continual tendency for the rich and the powerful to make decisions not in terms of the needs of the collectivity or the requirements of its moral code, but to protect their own capacity to influence *subsequent* decisions?

TOWARD A SOCIOLOGY OF PROPERTY

It would be a mistake to believe that the differential and special power of the rich derives only from the size of the resources they have at their command, from what they can buy with or exchange for these resources, or even from their prestige—be it earned or unearned—in society. The power of the rich is most deeply rooted in the nature of property itself, in the structure of property as an institution, and in its relationship to social systems. To understand the most crucial aspects of systems of social stratification it is necessary to explore the nature of property institutions in society.

It is one of the most disturbing, though characteristic, aspects of Parsons' social theory that it has undertaken only the most superficial probing into the nature of property. Still, Parsons is, in this respect, somewhat better than other Functionalists.[35] Thus when Neil Smelser undertakes a brief but systematic analysis of the *Sociology of Economic Life*,[36] meant as a serious and scholarly work, he finds no occasion to present any sustained discussion of the nature of property itself. And when Smelser and Parsons collaborate in their *Economy and Society*,[37] or when Parsons considers the issue by himself, the problem of property is presented in only the most cursory manner. This is particularly noteworthy because Parsons has always presented himself as a systematic and comprehensive theorist, concerned to consider all important variables, and not limited by narrow, conventional definitions of what are appropriately "sociological" subjects for investigation. In what follows, my attention will be primarily directed to one form of property only, the private or individually owned, and specifically to its implications for "social systems" as these are conceived of by Parsons.

Insofar as Parsons, like other Functionalists, confronts the analysis of property, he tends to stress its *similarity* to social role behavior and to discover in it the kinds of "rights" that inhere in any "social role." For example,

> Property is a bundle of *rights* of possession, including above all that of alienation . . . in a highly differentiated institutional system, property *rights* are focused on the valuation of utility, *i.e.*, the economic significance of the objects . . . the most important object of property comes to be monetary assets, and specific objects are valued as assets, that is, in terms of potentials of marketability. Today . . . *rights* to money assets, the ways in which these can be legitimately acquired and disposed of, the ways in which the interests of other parties must be protected, have come to constitute the core of the institution of property.[38]

In short, there has been a "monetization of property." It would seem that essentially what Parsons is talking of here is "bourgeois" property.

To repeat: what Parsons has done, for the most part, is to interpret property and possessions in terms of role theory; thus, in *Economy and Society* he and Smelser remark that property is "the institutionalization of rights in objects of possession or nonsocial objects,"[39] which are used as production facilities or rewards to the factors of production. Yet the relationship of the "possessor" to the thing possessed differs from role relationships. In other words, the relationship between possessor and possessed is not a relationship of Ego to Alter, or of two role players, because an Alter is a role player, not a thing. This is recognized in the following insightful observation: "Put another way, the differences between

possession and occupation lie in the fact that things are not expected to interact in the same way as persons."[40]

Where, then, are the mutuality and complementarity characteristic of stable, social, Ego-Alter relationships? This is answered
with a homely example. "The expression 'my hat' refers not only
to the fact that I 'have' and am at liberty to wear a particular hat
at will, but also to the fact that others are, under most circumstances, restrained from taking possession of or using my hat
without my permission."[41] In other words, Ego as "possessor" has
certain rights of use, control, and alienation over his hat (he can
sell it, give it to charity, or bequeath it to his nephew, Rameau);
to this right there corresponds a "restraint" upon Alter, which
means he cannot "steal" it or otherwise use it without permission
of its owner.

Presumably, then, possession is a "role" relationship, like any
other, in that it entails certain rights for those playing the role of
possessor vis-à-vis certain (unstipulated) others, who, in turn,
have corresponding, supposedly complementary obligations to the
possessor. The question, however, is whether this is, indeed, a
role relationship or a system of social interaction fundamentally
like any other, and whether a possessor is, in fact, a "role" whose
"rights" to use, control, or alienate the object he possesses are
rights like others found in *role* relationships, and, if so, with *whom*
does a possessor have a role relationship?

We may notice immediately that it is not said that "others" are
obligated not to take possession of Mr. Parsons' hat without his
permission. What is said, rather, is that others are "restrained"
from doing so. Is this a slip of the tongue? I think not. The point
is that there is a very special consequence should others walk off
with Mr. Parsons' hat; and there is a very special identity assigned
to them. They are reported to the police, tried in court, and put in
jail if convicted; they are called "thieves," and their behavior is
called "stealing."

In most social relations, however, this does not happen when
people fail to meet their obligations. One man may alienate the
affection and love of another's wife, but neither the wife nor the
seducer is clapped into jail. A man may undermine the authority
of another, violate his obligations as a friend, lie, and cheat, and
misrepresent, all to his own advantage and all in flagrant violation
of the other's role "rights." For the most part, all that the injured
party can do is call upon his friends to rally round, ask that
onlookers observe the violation of the elementary decencies, and
seek the unorganized protection of his immediate community. (In
other words, the victim is in serious trouble.) In the normal course
of role relationships, one man can destroy the life work of another

and, in the process, violate the most sacred role obligations, yet he may at most be subject only to frowns, criticism, or loss of reputation. But heaven help him should he deliberately walk off with the other man's hat. The police apparatus would be mobilized, weapons inspected, warrants issued, jail keys turned.

Ownership, then, seems to have some very remarkable attributes, which are not at all common to other social roles. In particular, it has an ease of access to legal enforceability. The inviolability of property rights is more closely monitored and protected by the legal and state apparatus, in the normal course of events, than any other "right" except that of protection from bodily harm. The use of the state's force to protect property is not at all an instrument of "last resort," but a *routine* method of enforcement. Normally, one does not bargain, negotiate, remonstrate, or appeal to a thief; one calls the police. This, implies something about the priorities that the state assigns to the protection of property rights; but, more than that, it implies something about the nature of the state itself.

There is another peculiarity of property and property rights that distinguishes "owners" from role players. Those playing social roles are usually doing so in some relationship with another, *focalized* role player. If one is an employee, husband, father, friend, one is always an employee *of* some employer, husband *of* a wife, father *of* a child, etcetera. Alter, the reciprocal role player, is always fully evident as a member of the relationship in which Ego plays some role and in which each rewards the other for conforming to his rights. The characteristic thing about owners, however, is that their culturally *focalized* relationship is not with another private person or another role player, but rather with some *thing* or object; one is owner of a house, a business, a patent. This is not to say that property does not "implicate" an owner in some social relationship with other private persons, for it does. But this relationship is *only* implicit; such a relationship is normally only within an owner's subsidiary attention, particularly insofar as his *obligations* are concerned, unless the "others" violate what he takes to be his rights. The basic effect of defining an object as someone's "property" is to *exclude* all others except the state; it establishes, by *prima facie* definition, that others have no rights in this object except insofar as the proprietor expressly permits them such rights.

Stated in other terms: the private "others" to whom one is related as an "owner" constitute only a *negative* and *residual* social identity. Vis-à-vis an owner who has not expressly undertaken obligations, all private persons are interchangeable "others." There is no point in distinguishing them from one another, for they all stand in the same relation to the owner. All alike are commonly excluded from the use and enjoyment of "his" property. This, indeed, is the central consequence of establishing objects as private property. Others thereby have no obligations of any positive sort to the owner; they are not obliged to help him but only to avoid intrusion on his rights. Correspondingly, an owner has no positive obligations to help others, but only to avoid such uses of his property as would intrude upon their rights.

The property relationship, then, is fundamentally one of mutual avoidance and forbearance. Others, consequently, take on a clear, focal, and differentiated identity vis-à-vis an owner only when they *violate* his rights (though not when they respect and conform with them) or when he employs his rights to make special promises to certain others. It is primarily in the latter case that an owner and others have positive rights and obligations to one another. But such undertakings are not incumbent on an owner. And unless such undertakings are specifically entered into, "others" do not normally receive "rewards" for conforming to an owner's rights, but only punishments for violating them. In their most costly form, these punishments are usually administered not by the owner himself, but by a third party: the police, the courts, or, more generally, the state.

Since there is no "social relationship" between an owner and other private parties in the same sense that one exists between two *role* players engaged in social interaction, an "owner" is not in a social role in the conventional sociological sense. It is precisely because of this that an owner is culturally defined as being in a role relationship not to other *persons* but to the *object* he owns. This is how "possession" is normally viewed, or culturally focused in our society; and, we may say, the "culture" knows whereof it speaks. The most binding and continuous social relationship that an owner as owner enters into is with those upon whom he relies to protect his property rights—the agencies of the state—not with merely private parties, whether they violate those rights or honor them.

Indeed, with our strong cultural emphasis, which tends to define property as a "sacred" and hence absolutely inalienable right, even the state—as the Declaration of the Rights of Man expressly indicated—cannot appropriate a man's property without due process and reimbursement. This means that the general presumption is that possession is absolute, which is to say, noncontingent on any performance by the owner; it does not require that he perform certain obligations to others as the *condition* for the maintenance of his property. Before he has entered into some contract, no party other than the state has a claim upon an owner. And he has no obligation to enter any contract.

An owner's rights are therefore noncontingent in relation to all others except the state; they are valid and enforceable quite apart from any fulfillment of obligations to others and quite apart from whether others *believe* they have obligations to the owner. In sum, ownership does not in itself implicate an owner in any social relationship with any private parties that necessarily entails reciprocal and complementary rights and obligations. To say that private property exists in a society is to say that some considerable part of the valuables in that society has been preempted by individuals who have the legal right to exclude all others from their use, whatever their "need" may be. The net effect of ownership is to exclude all other private parties from the use, control, or alienation of certain objects, and to limit the claims that any role player may make upon any other, regardless of the roles they have. Ownership thus establishes the presumption that certain objects and the rights to them are excluded from all social relationships, unless they have been expressly included or are required by the state.

"Social space," then, may be conceived of as divided into two types: one type consists of parcels or areas preempted by "ownership," the other of "free space" that has not been thus enclosed. It is in the free social space that "social systems," as they are conceived by Parsons, are established. A "social system" is therefore a *residual* organization of social relationships, in that it may deal with only those things that are "left over" after property rights have been established. Such social systems as come to exist may develop only in the free social spaces, the interstices that have not been previously preempted by property rights. Property is an encumbrance on social relations. It is a prior claim, or a claim treated as prior, to those involved in the role relations that constitute "social systems." Property constitutes the "givens" or the limiting conditions for the construction and development of social systems in the Parsonian sense; to property, it is assumed, all else must and will adapt. Property is thus the infrastructure of social systems.

If "social systems" are social relationships entailing mutual obligations and rights—a complementarity and reciprocity of obligations and rights—then ownership does *not* constitute a social system. Property is closely linked to the legal structure and the state apparatus precisely because it does *not* necessarily implicate the owner in a self-maintaining, spontaneous social system with other private parties. Ownership as such does not obligate the owner to other private parties: it does not obligate him to *reward* those who respect his rights, and it inherently allows him certain rights quite apart from what he does or provides for others. He may thus secure conformity with his own rights in certain objects without giving reciprocal conformity to the expectations of others. The social relations established between owners and other private parties thus cannot be stabilized by reason of their willing mutual conformity.

Moreover, property rights differ from other kinds of role rights in that they may be assigned, bequeathed, given, or sold to others. An owner may assign his property rights to others unilaterally, without the *moral* approval and permission of any other except the state. If the state regards such a transfer as legal, no one else need define it as morally justified in order for it to proceed. Hence, *property inherently entails power over others*, the ability to achieve certain aims despite their resistance.

The rights of owners, therefore, do not and cannot rely for their protection upon the moral approval of other private parties, for it is intrinsic to property rights that they are valid despite the absence of such legitimacy. In consequence, they must and do find their protection elsewhere, through their ability to invoke the aid of third parties, specifically those in the state apparatus. This means that the protection of property rests on access to and use of force, *not* as a matter of last resort, but personally, directly, and routinely. Even without involving the police or the state, one may personally and immediately exercise "reasonable" force in the protection of his property. The *presumption* is that the storeowner may shoot to protect his cash register, and the householder to protect his personal belongings. Since property as such does not require or allow reciprocal and complementary expectations, or mutual rights and obligations among private parties, it exists apart from a social system whole stability relies upon men's willing mutual conformity. Indeed, property is essentially a mode of protecting advantage without involvement in a self-maintaining social system, as Parsons has conceived this.

In stressing that ownership as such does not implicate owners in self-maintaining social systems, my point, of course, is *not* that ownership does not constitute a social relationship of any sort; it constitutes a very distinctive kind of social relationship, one which does *not necessarily* entail reciprocal and complementary rights and obligations that might constitute a stable, self-maintaining social system. It is precisely for this reason that private ownership is, paradoxically, a social relationship in which owners have more power than nonowners and, indeed, power *over* nonowners, but in which this power is inherently precarious, always vulnerable to the threat of other private persons and vulnerable to the state itself. This extreme vulnerability of private property is, in large part, an intrinsic consequence of its being defensible *apart* from self-maintaining social systems involving other private persons. It is therefore a locus of endemic conflict in societies. Parsons explicitly agrees on this point, even if he fails to see its full importance: "There is obviously a distributive aspect of wealth and it is in a sense true that the wealth of one person or group by definition cannot also be possessed by another. . . . Thus the distribution of wealth is, in the nature of the case, a focus of conflict of interest in a society."[42]

But again, it is not that private property cannot and does not shape social systems or become a focus for their establishment. It can and does do both, and this is part of what I imply in referring to it as an infrastructure of social systems. Since private property entails a monopolization of certain rights in objects, with a corresponding exclusion of others, possession *allows* the proprietor to give others contingent "easements" on the use and enjoyment of his property, either by contract or informally. To possess, therefore, is to have rights in valuable objects that may be used to initiate or enter into social systems. The proprietor controls objects that may gratify others and which he may therefore use to secure desired performances from them. Property may thus be used to obligate others to the owner, thereby establishing a social system. Thus property need not only exclude others; it can also be used to establish social solidarities. In particular, it allows the owner initiative in establishing social systems centering on and advantageous to himself, especially as his rights are anchored in and protected by the state apparatus *outside* that social system.

The use of objects in common is one of the ways in which the very boundaries of social systems are established and determinable. This implies that owners may determine or shape the boundaries of social systems; for, to the degree that an owner determines who may use or enjoy certain objects, he is free to determine who are and are not members of the particular social system, as well as their function and status in it, for both function and status are importantly definable in terms of access to and use of objects. Indeed, in some part, what defines a group is its common access to and use of a concrete set of objects. The solidarity of a family, for example, is importantly influenced by the fact that its members have special access to the use and enjoyment of many objects, a common obligation to protect them from outsiders, and a special expectation of inheritance.

Insofar as men can enter into and establish stable social systems only by fulfilling certain obligations which provide others with gratification, it may be noted that there are two ways in which this can be done. One is by undertaking certain *personal* performances for others, using skill and time; the other is by using *property*, which is to say, allowing others to have certain uses or control of one's objects. In the former instance, where personal service or performance is used to discharge or to create obligations, this is subject to limitations of time. The capacity to do as others desire through the performance of a personal service is limited to the twenty-four hours in a day. Capacity to do as others desire by allowing them access to one's property is not, however, limited by time, but only by the size of these property holdings. The ability to meet or to create obligations through the employment of property is, therefore, practically unlimited. One's ability to establish and to participate in social systems, the power that they have and the power that one has in them, are thus a function of one's property. Clearly, "ownership" entails an enormous capacity to generate social systems and a relatively great mobility in relationship to concrete social systems; in effect, "markets" allow owners routinely to enter into or depart from specific social systems, insofar as holdings in them may be bought and sold.

On the one hand, then, property gives its owner leverage on social systems and, on the other, it allows him to elude the claims normal to most social systems, extricating him from the usual liabilities of membership. I have stressed that the latter potentially generates a certain vulnerability, for it thereby also excludes him from the protections that the mutual exchange of gratifications usually establishes. Intrinsically, private ownership is a game that one man plays against all others; in it, what one man owns another may not own. It therefore does not enclose him in protective solidarities, except to the extent that he forgoes his right to exclude others or he allows others easements on his property. But the point, of course, is that private property does not *obligate* an owner to do this, except for those in his family, and even this is not necessarily a legally enforceable obligation. To hold property is to hold it against all others and to be on guard against them.

The ultimate paradox is this: men seek property because they do not want to (and, indeed, have found themselves unable to) rely entirely on other men. To seek property is to seek security and the enjoyment of advantage, despite the faithlessness, disloyalty, envy, and turpitude of men, which are amply evidenced in all social systems. Men seek property as a hedge against the deficiencies of social systems, most particularly because the disadvantaged will not reliably protect the advantages of others, for not uncommonly they want them for themselves. Yet in seeking to protect advantage by constituting it as property and establishing it apart from social system involvements and obligations and apart from the good will and trust of others, they create new vulnerabilities for this very advantage. Property owners therefore have to look elsewhere for the protection of their property than to ordinary social systems composed of persons like themselves.

They look to the state. It is with the state that the owner's rela-

tionship is likely to be mutually reinforcing and relatively stable—
rather than with other private persons—and it is by the state that
his property rights will be most rigorously enforced. The state
provides ready and willing protection for property, and, in return,
owners provide the state with the resources and moral support
needed to maintain its activities on behalf of "law and order."
Although there is usually some disagreement over the price paid
for the state's protective services—in short, taxes—the state and
property owners commonly develop mutual understanding and
appreciation. For in the end the greed of the state is less costly to
property owners than would be the need of the disadvantaged. Relatively willing and able to support the state, and defined therefore as
responsible, loyal, and reliable, property owners can commonly
rely on the state's reciprocal responsiveness to their interests.

This is by no means identical with the classical Marxian formula
characterizing the state as the "executive committee of the ruling
class," for it premises an appreciable, if unspecified, degree of
autonomy of the state from the rich and property-owning, and a
corresponding degree of need and dependence by the latter in their
relation to the state. At the same time, however, neither is this
formulation identical with the traditional *liberal* conception of the
state as a nonpartisan force, independent and equally impartial to
the claims of all, for my formulation premises that commonly the
state will be particularly close and especially responsive to the
claims and interests of property owners.

TALCOTT PARSONS ON C. WRIGHT MILLS

In this connection it is worth noting some of Parsons' criticisms of
C. Wright Mills's *The Power Elite* and, more generally, his views
on the role of the business class in the power system of American
society. Parsons acknowledged, in his critique of Mills, that, "given
the nature of an industrial society, a relatively well-defined elite or
leadership group should be expected to develop in the business
world."[43] This, however, he holds is due not to the cumulative
advantages derived from property ownership, but largely to
certain unspecified functional imperatives of the social system.
It is Parsons' tendency generally to deemphasize the importance
of property and wealth as a source of power in society and even
within the economy itself. (He thus maintains that the business

elite itself "is no longer an elite of property owners, but [of] professional executives or managers."[44]

Parsons adds, moreover, that the elite in the economy is not
identical with that in the society as a whole. One reason for this,
according to Parsons, is because eliteness is not exclusively manifested in the *power* or influence of persons or groups. There are,
Parsons says, groups and persons that are functionally indispensable to modern society—his example: families and women—but
which are not powerful as such. Mills's argument, however, in no
way premises that power derives from the functional importance
of persons or groups, but, if anything, stresses that powerholders
can control those who are functionally important. And while Mills
does not hold that only the rich have power, he does stress the
importance of the "corporate rich" in the total "power elite," which
for him also includes the top military and top professional politicians. That the rich have more power than they can, or wish to,
manage personally, and therefore hire others to do so, simply
means that they do not exhaust the membership of the corporate
rich and not, as Parsons seems here to imply, that they have been
replaced by professionals. The fact remains, moreover, that professional managers own more corporate stock than any other occupational group, and they are very important property owners; they are
not only economically but also socially intermingled with the rich
in style of life, schooling, and organizational membership.[45]

Mills had argued that governmental regulatory agencies did not
effectively control business. Parsons replied that this must be
wrong, because if "effective controls had not been imposed, I find
it impossible to understand the bitter and continuing opposition on
the part of business to the measures which have been taken."[46] He
concludes, therefore, that "there has been a genuine growth of
autonomous governmental power . . . and that one major aspect of
this has been the relatively effective control of the business system."[47] Actually, of course, two of the three main centers of Mills's
"power elite" are the top military and the professional politicians,
which would imply that Mills acknowledged a substantial measure
of government autonomy.

One must also add here that, if business opposition to government control is evidence of their effectiveness, as Parsons holds,
then the subsequent acceptance of government regulation suggests
that it did not prove to be very effective for very long or that
businessmen changed their minds concerning its implications.
Indeed, Parsons does make it quite clear that the Republican Party
—"the party of the bigger sector of business"[48]—now vies with the
Democratic Party "in promoting the extension of social security
benefits . . . [and] on the whole, business groups have accepted the

new situation and cooperated to make it work."[49] Yet, why should businessmen now accept governmental influence, regulation, and spending if they have not found it to their net advantage? And in another part, it seems reasonable to view this initial resistance and later acceptance as consistent with businessmen's membership in a larger elite, in which some sectors play a leadership role and, for a while, act against the wishes and even the policies of others, some of whom in time see they were mistaken in believing that such leadership initiatives were against their interests. In point of fact, businessmen have never been equally and universally opposed to all controls over all business activity; they have often accepted regulation of their own making, through cartels and price-fixing arrangements, as well as many governmental forms of regulation. Moreover, the resistance of some is not evidence of the resistance of all sectors of business, for they do, indeed, have some important interests at variance with one another. For example, there are some business interests that are advantaged by military policy and expenditure, while others lose if they result in a decline in welfare expenditures.

It should also be noted, in this connection, that here Parsons rather abruptly dismisses his own ordinary emphasis on the *systemic* character and mutual *interdependence* of different sectors of society. One would have thought that, rather than emphasizing the *autonomy* of government in analyzing its relationship with business, Parsons' system model would have led him to stress their mutual dependence. Parsons' emphasis here on the autonomy of government seems attributable not to his theoretical commitments but to his overriding ideological predilections.

At one point he opts not only for the autonomy of government but also for the societal dominance of politics: "In a complex society the primary locus of power lies in the political system."[50] At the same time, however, Parsons also recognizes that business leaders have traditionally been the leaders of the larger American community, at least until quite recently. The key turning point, he seems to suggest, was the Great Depression of the 1930's. (According to his line of reasoning, one must also conclude that prior to the stock market crash the United States was not a "complex" society.)

Parsons' analysis of power in America is an unstable mixture: of the realism of the conservative, who knows—from the inside, as it were—the importance of business as the "natural" leader of the community; combined with an ideological embarrassment at the implications this has for traditional democratic ideology; and spiced, as Parsons commonly prefers, with a dash of "up-to-date" theoretical developments, which is, in this case, the pluralism of some political scientists. Emphasis on government autonomy is thus combined with a hard-headed realism about the importance of business leadership. Parsons thus has no doubts that "a relatively well-defined elite . . . should be expected to develop in the business world," nor any doubt that the hitherto conventional role of this business elite was to lead the larger community. There has been, he says, a " 'natural' tendency for a relatively unique business leadership of the larger community."[51] At the same time, however, he sees this leadership as no longer unequivocal, and the question arises as to how he views the present and forthcoming role of business in the larger community.

One part of an answer is implied by Parsons' observation that there has been a growing autonomy of the government sector. While part of this may result from an effort to cope with the effects of increasing industrialization, another source, which Parsons is at pains to emphasize, is "the enormous enhancement of American responsibility in the world [which] has taken place in a relatively short time."[52] This, in large part, is seen as a response to the revolutionary threat that the Soviet Union has posed for "our own national values and interests . . . [and] only American action was able to prevent Soviet domination of the whole continent of Europe."[53]

This rise of American "responsibility" in the world has, of necessity, entailed a greater role for government and a corresponding intrusion of new governmental elites on the traditional position of leadership that business has held in the American community: "the business group has had to give way at many points."[54] Parsons also seems to attribute some special importance to the Depression of the 1930's as a crucial factor in the undermining of the role of business leadership in the larger community. He points out that this major crisis was solved not by them but by government leaders.[55] While Parsons does not expressly maintain that this began a process which undermined the *legitimacy* of the business elite as leaders of the community, for that would be a devastating critique from Parsons' standpoint, he does characterize the role of business in the 1930's as a "major failure."[56]

At any rate, there seems to be no question but that, in Parsons' view, the business elite can no longer lead the American community in the future as they have in the past. At least, not in the same manner or in the same degree. The national elite of American society is thus, in his view, undergoing some still uncompleted transition, involving a relative decline in the prominence of business and a need for other, more political and governmental elements to assume increasing importance: "the tendency will be toward a strengthening of the element of professional governmental officials who are essentially independent of short-run 'politics' . . . the military officer is a special case of this type."[57] But this is still a new tendency, and, at present (1960), "a clearly defined nonbusiness component of the elite has not yet crystallized . . ." Thus, "the striking feature of the American elite [is] . . . its fluid and relatively unstructured character."[58]

This last statement, however, should at most be interpreted to mean that the American national elite is not a closely knit, politically concerted, "capitalistically" dominated group, and, in particular, an hereditarily transmitted position. For Parsons, the important consideration is the *legitimacy* of the elite, resting particularly on its achievement; while he insists on this, he never doubts for a moment that there is and must be an elite within business and within the community at large. If anything, Parsons' point—as we shall see—is that there is a need for further development of the elite, and, in particular, for a strengthening of its nonbusiness elements: Parsons is an unembarrassed elitist.

Parsons' analysis of power is essentially one that is compatible with and reflects the development of the Welfare State: "it is necessary for the older balance between a free economy and the power of government to be considerably shifted in favor of the latter. We must have a stronger government than we have traditionally been accustomed to, and we must come to trust it more fully."[59] It is notable that Parsons does *not* say that, with this increased power of the centralized government, there must also be a corresponding strengthening of the power of the electorate and of representative institutions, or even of the protection of popular rights against infringement by this increasingly powerful government. Parsons looks to a strengthening of the essentially "republican" and elitist features of rulership in the United States, rather than of the democratic. He calls for citizens to have a greater sense of their duties rather than their rights. And he wants governors who will have greater sense of moral responsibility, technical competence, and public service, rather than responsiveness to their constituencies. He wants a leavening of established business leadership with professional, competent groups, all drawn from social strata privileged enough to prepare them for devotion to and development of a tradition of full-time "public service." What the country needs, in short, is increased governance by Harvard-type men.

"The changed situation in which we are placed demands a far-reaching change in the structure of our society," says Parsons portentously.[60] When his proposals are viewed in detail, however, it becomes apparent that the change to which he refers is not at all so "far-reaching"; indeed, it fundamentally entails acceptance of and accommodation to the traditional power of business as well as a movement in the direction of a more diversified power elite, which in any event, has been occurring. The new situation, says Parsons, demands, above all, three things:

The first is . . . to encourage the ordinary man to accept greater responsibility. The second is the development of the necessary implementing machinery. Third is national political leadership, not only in the sense of individual candidates for office or appointment, but in the sense of a social strata where a traditional political responsibility is ingrained.[61]

The most important of these requirements, holds Parsons, is the third, which seeks an elite stratum for which political responsibility is traditional and which can provide a recruiting ground for those who actually wield power. In my view, it is certain that such a stratum must become hereditary.

What will be the role of the business elite in the enlarged national political elite, as Parsons sees it? His answer is blunt and clear:

Under American conditions, a politically leading stratum must be made up of a combination of business and nonbusiness elements . . . political leadership without prominent business participation is doomed to ineffectiveness and to the perpetuation of dangerous internal conflict. It is not possible to lead the American people *against* the leaders of the business world . . . yet the business world cannot monopolize or dominate political leadership and responsibility.[62]

In effect, Parsons conceives of the business elite as having a veto power within American society. For, to say and emphasize that American society cannot be led "against" the business leaders clearly implies that, while no longer able to take initiatives as formerly, they can still stop what they do not want. It is notable that Parsons never makes any comparably flat statement about the veto power of any other single segment of American society, regardless of their functional importance. He never says that it is *impossible* to lead American society against the wishes of the purely political elite, the military, the civil service, the church, the university, or even mothers. Surely this implies that business leaders still are and must remain the single most important force in the American political elite, despite the increased autonomy of government and the primacy of the political center in complex societies.

On a purely theoretical level, one cannot help but wonder how such a conclusion derives from Parsons' repeated insistence on the *plurality* of the sources of social change and the mutual *inter-*

dependence of various institutions, as stressed in his own *system* model of society. For all of Parsons' repeated insistence on the manner in which his empirical conclusions are guided and informed by his theoretical position, here, and not for the first time, the theory seems to imply one thing while the empirical conclusions to which he comes are quite another. This is certainly not the first time that such a disparity has occurred in the work of a systematic theorist; and, in a way, it is to Parsons' credit that he recognizes that logical consistency must be subordinated to empirical considerations. Apparently there are some things one learns, by reason of what one has seen and where one has been, that will not be subordinated even to one's own theory.

Other substantive implications of the position Parsons takes here are also worth noting. For one, if it is the case that American political leadership is doomed to ineffectuality without the active participation of business—and I would agree that, in our society, this is "telling it as it is"—it is clear that the business group can demand an extremely high price for its participation. A second important implication warrants elaboration. While Parsons stresses that the American community cannot be led without and cannot be led against the business leadership, he also implies that it cannot be led *by* them. Certainly it cannot now be led by them as *once* they led it. This would seem to portend two other social trends. (1) If there is a business elite with a *continuing* veto power in American political life, as Parsons indicates, but which can no longer lead the larger community as businessmen, then, certainly, it will seek *other roles* and social arrangements in which it can express and wield influence. And it continues to hold the power to win access to these new positions. (2) If it is true that new, nonbusiness segments must play an increasing role in the national elite, it is certain, given Parsons' own assumptions concerning the continued business veto power, that the former must accommodate themselves to the business leadership and, in effect, negotiate an alliance with them.

From both sides, then, this implies a growing national "power elite," with an interlocking membership and mutual understandings, within whose broadened membership the business elite will and does continue to play the single most important role. In effect, Parsons comes surprisingly close to agreement with some of the most fundamental conclusions which C. Wright Mills had arrived at. The crucial difference between them on this involves primarily not the empirical imputations about what is happening to the structure of power in the United States, but rather the *legitimacy* of this development and of the new power elite itself.

In short, there seems to be much more agreement between Parsons and Mills about the facts than their conflicting evaluations might imply.

It is notable that there is, in all of Parsons' discussion of power, not a distinct word about the role of the *propertied middle* class in America. In a way, this may be another expression of Parsons' realism, for this middle class seems increasingly to have lost its will to power as well as its hold on power as it becomes the increasingly suburbanized, deployable tool of corporate bureaucracy. Meanwhile, the effective arena of political decision moves to the higher, national levels.

In Parsons' conception, the propertied sectors of the middle class have disappeared in the new power elite. They have been ground between the more traditional business elite with its abiding veto power, and the newly emerging elites in the civil service, the military, the professions more generally, and the universities which are their training grounds. The fundamental Parsonsian map of the new social elite sees it as composed of two parts, business and "nonbusiness" (as Parsons sometimes calls it) or, in other words, the professions. His fundamental map of society is bicameral, divided between the temporal lords and the spiritual mandarins. The words are the new words of Parsons; but the thought is the abiding thought of Comte.

Clearly, there are deep and enduring structures in the development of Academic Sociology that link nineteenth-century Positivism to twentieth-century Functionalism. The academic sociologist still speaks from the standpoint and represents the claims of the educated nonpropertied sectors of the middle class, who now find the Welfare State a uniquely suitable fulfillment of their vested professional interests, their elite ambitions, and their liberalism—which is to say, their social utilitarianism.

ACHIEVEMENT, ASCRIPTION, AND THE FAMILY

Parsons, as we have seen earlier, argues that equality of opportunity is never fully possible, because differential advantages accrue to children in different families and vary with the social rank of the family. Leaving aside consideration of whether "complete" equality of opportunity is ever attainable, Parsons is certainly correct in observing that children born to different families

have different advantages. What he systematically fails to see, however, is that "advantages" may be of fundamentally different sorts.
Some, like attitudes, motivations, social skills, cultural competencies, and aspirations, are, while family-linked, basically different
from *property*. The inheritance of property is the inheritance of
advantage of a special kind: it is the inheritance of *rights*—of
legally protected rights in valuable objects. Given the existence of
inheritable property, men are endowed at birth not with the same
but with very unequal positions.

The property endowments that children derive from their families reflect institutional commitments of the larger society that are
fundamentally at variance with the culture's avowal to reward its
members on the basis of their demonstrated merit and their capacity to produce desired performances. Possessions, however, advantage the child for reasons that have nothing whatsoever to do
with what he himself has accomplished or can do and, in that sense,
provide "unearned income." Other family-transmitted endowments
may also advantage children, but they do so mainly with respect
to opportunities for "earned income." It is differential access to
*un*earned income that is most at variance with the standards of
universalism and, especially, achievement.

While it is true that the elimination of private property and its
inheritance would by no means eliminate all inequalities—and,
indeed, was never expected to do so by any socialist thinker—it
would reduce differentials in opportunities for unearned income.
It seems clear that Parsons' ideal society is one in which rewards
are allocated universalistically on the basis of individual achievement. Parsons does recognize that his own ideal society is dissonant with family-transmitted advantages, but he fails to see that
these are not all of one piece; the *reduction* of opportunities for
unearned income is by no means utopian or impossible, for the system of inheritance and existent property institutions might be
changed without necessarily destroying the stability of the family.

One can assume that families wish to advantage their children
and will do so differentially under any inheritance and property
system, without assuming that they can do so only under existent
institutions of inheritance or property. Yet this is largely what
Parsons tends to believe. Moreover, even though such change would
by no means eliminate all opportunities for unearned incomes or
eliminate all power differentials, it would reduce them substantially.

This would, in turn, have two consequences. First, it would
bring the actual societal allocation of rewards into greater conformity with the universalistic and achievement standards of the
society itself, and thus would reduce the disparity that exists be-

tween current practices and moral ideals; to that extent it would contribute to the long-range stability of the society. Second, it would reduce, though not eliminate, power differentials, with a similar stabilizing consequence. Such a change would, therefore, contribute to both the stability and the self-maintaining character of the larger social system. Such change seems compatible with views expressed by the early Parsons, to the effect that it is possible to build on the basis that we now have a more perfect society. The question, of course, is what shall we regard as the unchangeable basis: private property with inheritance, or universalistic and achievement standards. (It is paradoxical that, although Parsons' model of stable, self-maintaining social systems is a generalization from certain characteristics of a capitalist, free-market economy, a fuller realization of this self-maintaining, stable social system does not seem possible in such a society.)

One basic way in which these implications are theoretically obscured in Parsons' own work is through his distinction between "ascribed" and "achieved" status, or, as he later came to call it, the "quality" versus "performance" pattern variable. By ascription or quality standards, rewards are allocated to persons on the basis of the culturally standardized identities assigned to them. That is, if persons are defined as having, or being of, a certain sex or race, they will, because of this assigned identity, have more or less opportunities and rewards. Where achievement or performance standards are employed, however, persons will have varying opportunities and rewards allocated to them not on the basis of their imputed cultural identities, but on the basis of the imputed degree of correspondence between what they *do* and a certain norm or standard.

The difficulty with using the achievement-ascription distinction is that rewards that are allocated on the basis of achievement often depend upon *prior* differential opportunities, which might not have depended upon *achievement*. Achievement standards and rewards based on them may conceal and *legitimate* an *earlier* allocation of rewards and opportunities based upon ascription. This is the case with differential family-transmitted advantages, and it is deeply involved in ethnic discrimination, such as that to which Blacks in the United States are subjected.

The whole achievement-ascription distinction obscures the actual mechanisms that make for differential rewards. The distinction makes it seem as if they are only of two kinds: ascriptive mechanisms, which provide rewards based on cultural identities and which largely use natural or biological attributes as their foci (sex, age, race, ethnicity); or achievement mechanisms which provide rewards on the basis of individual merit. What is glossed over is that achievement standards, in fact, often function to conceal and to *legitimate* the prior operation of *non*achievement standards. In short, what is presented as an honest competition has actually been "fixed." What is missed is the dynamic relationship between the two sets of standards, which must be systematically seen as applying to different points in the life cycle. Achievement standards thus become another manner in which an advantaged elite can legitimate and perpetuate itself societally, without threatening those of its advantages that are not legitimate by these same standards.

The achievement-ascription distinction also makes it seem that rewards are allocated *either* in terms of how well the individual does *or* else in terms of his imputed cultural identities, both of which are culturally *valued* attributes. What this distinction ignores is that individuals may receive differential advantage simply because of what they *have*, their possessions, resources, facilities, rather than because of their cultural identities of their individual efforts. The child who inherits property is not advantaged either because of what he has done or because of his imputed cultural identity; his property advantages him simply because he can use it to buy and control things that he desires. Moreover, he can also buy further opportunities for unearned income, which, with modern institutions of investment, may take little or no individual judgment or merit. That he may sometimes lack individual judgment and invest unwisely, ultimately losing his advantage and wasting a social resource, is simply another expression of his differential opportunity, signaling the inherent social dysfunctionality of unearned income.

ANOMIE AND PROPERTY INSTITUTIONS

Parsons' achievement-ascription distinction comes down to saying that, in the public sphere, we have a choice between rewarding men on the basis of their merit or on the basis of some culturally valued status or identity. As we have seen, this ignores the fact that their merit often depends on and derives from their ascribed status. Furthermore, it also ignores the fact that what men are given as rewards in either way constitutes only a part of their access to *life chances*, their access to "the good things of life." Such access is only partly a "reward" for the manifestation of valued qualities; it derives also from the *possession* of scarce goods, however these have come into their control. Access to life chances is, therefore, structured by the institutions governing the accumulation, use, and transmission of property. What men can do or can get depends not only on what they are thought to do or be; it also depends upon what they *own*. Access to life chances is thus systematically allocated in ways that often have nothing to do with their recipient's culturally valued qualities, even if distributed in accordance with institutionally sanctioned allocating systems.

The institutionalized allocating systems are, in this respect, not integrated with the value system. He who has wealth and the power it brings may enjoy more gratifications than those who manifest or conform to the society's values, even though he himself does not. There are few pleasures that a man must forgo, and there need be none denied his children, if only he is wealthy enough. There are few powers and honors that are perpetually immune to the blandishments of the wealthy. The tone-deaf may have the best seats at the concert, the color-blind the best paintings, the undiscriminating the best foods, the impotent the most exciting women, the politically inept the highest offices. Given an institutional system that endows men with great possessions quite apart from their valued qualities or achievements, all this and more is possible.

Here, then, is a basic *source* of the failure of moral values that Parsons ignores, despite his stress upon morality and his belief that the stability of social systems rests upon it. For values will be conformed with to the extent that men are given gratifications for doing so. But under these conditions only a part of the gratificational resources of a society may be utilized to foster conformity with its moral values. Institutions which transmit possessions and wealth through the testamentary or hereditary succession of private individuals thus demoralize men and conduce to anomie; because of them a significant supply of the reinforcing gratifications is withdrawn from support of the society's value system, and it is thus weakened. This is rather different from saying, as Robert Merton does, that anomie results from the malintegration between means and ends, or arises when individuals lack institutional means to realize the cultural goals they have been taught to want. For here, men who attempt to live by the value system are demoralized not simply by their *own* lack of means and their own *failures*, but also by witnessing that *others* may *succeed* even though they lack valued qualities. Indeed, the demoralization is often similarly experienced by those advantaged by these conditions, for they have seen from birth that gratification is possible to them without conformity to the society's values.

Robert Merton's analysis of anomie starts with the assumption that there *is* a malintegration between means and ends.[63] His structural analysis of the social conditions from which it derives in the United States focuses on the nature of the class system, which he characterizes as an "open class system." By reason of its *openness,* presumably all are taught to seek the same cultural goals; by reason of its being a *class* system, some have less means to realize their aspirations, and thus anomie is said to arise for them. But those at the top of the class system, *because* they inherit, do not have to *achieve* their gratifications. Indeed, they can neither succeed nor fail, because they inherit. And there really is no evidence that they are less anomic than those who fail; it is only that they lend support to a status quo that provides them with their superior life chances.

It is one thing to assume and quite another to *account* for the generalized possibility of a malintegration between means and ends. This potentiality derives, in large part, from the inherent nature of certain of the "institutional means," and specifically, from the institutionalized transmission of private property. Given this institution, there *must* be some malintegration between institutionalized means and cultural goals. For, this institution guarantees that some men will be more and others less gratified, even though the former may manifest less and the latter more valued qualities. It is crucial that we understand that it is this—property and inheritance—which explains how it happens that some *have* less "means" while others *have* more.

The allocation of the means to succeed and, with this, of position in the class system is, in appreciable part, a function of the institution of private property and its hereditary or testamentary transmission. Thus the distribution of anomic responses is a function of this institution. But, to repeat, it does not follow that those on the top of the class system are less anomic, if by this is meant that they have more of a genuine belief in and devotion to the culture's moral values. Indeed, there is reason to predict that their genuine commitment to these moral values is undermined by the very institution from which they derive their advantages. For this institution makes it possible to sever the connection between gratifications and conformity with cultural values. From this standpoint, then, any institution—whether private property or another—that allocates life chances in a manner that does not depend upon the recipient's manifestation of valued qualities thereby undermines the value system of its society and spreads anomie. In short, the spoiler of the society's morality is, in the Veblenian sense, "vested interest," the right to something for nothing. And this is precisely the nature of the hereditary transmission of property: it is the *right* to give valuables to someone who has not earned them, and the corresponding *right* to receive them and use them as if they were earned.

DIFFERENTIATION OF THE PRESTIGE
HIERARCHY AND MORAL CODE

The relationship between property and the moral code is a particularly important aspect of the relationship between the larger system of stratification and the society's value system. My previous point has been largely to stress that the existence of individual property constitutes a preemption of certain advantages or gratifications. It is consequential for conformity to the moral code, first, because it involves an entailment upon and hence a net reduction of the supply of gratifications that might be mobilized in support of moral conformity and, second, because it attenuates the relationship experienced between moral conformity and gratification.

It is of fundamental importance to know *why* it is that men conform with any moral code and under what conditions they will continue or cease to do so. It is not enough simply to assert that they *do*, and that courses of action differ as a result. This is merely to assert that values make some difference in social outcomes and that they are autonomous factors in producing social change or social stability. This, we might say, is simply a form of *Vulgar* Idealism. The Vulgar Idealist is, however, sometimes a good observer, for he correctly notes that men often experience themselves as conforming with certain values without regard to the consequences, the rewards or costs, because of the intrinsic worth imputed to them. Where the Vulgar Idealist goes wrong is in his failure to see that this in itself is something that requires explanation and that varies with certain conditions. If, in effect, the Vulgar Idealist is one who imputes importance to values but fails to explain why, the Vulgar Marxist, we might say, generally depreciates the importance and autonomy of values. The Vulgar Marxist tends to stress the correspondence between values and interests, and hence assumes there is no value autonomy that needs to be explained.

My own position is that there is ample evidence for a *measure* of autonomy in moral codes and in morally oriented behavior, in the sense that men can and do act at variance with certain of their "material," or economic and class, interests. At the same time, however, it does not at all follow from this that these are the only interests that may bind men to moral courses; that moral behavior is *absolutely* autonomous; that it is an unmoved mover; that once committed to a moral course of action men never swerve, but continue to pursue it indefinitely; and that we should not seek to account for the conditions under which men continue to pursue a set of values or withdraw from such efforts in order to seek or pursue different values. In short, neither Vulgar Marxism nor Vulgar Idealism suffices.

My most basic assumption is that the extent to which men conform with a given value or set of values is a function of the rewards or gratifications associated with such conformity. (In other words, I do *not* assume that morally conforming action must always yield gratification, or that it is always *intrinsically* satisfying.) Thus I generally assume that men's commitment to a moral code will tend to continue as long as the gratifications associated with it continue, though, as indicated earlier in my discussion of declining marginal utility, I do *not* expect that there will be a one-to-one correspondence between increments of conformity and increments of gratification. Moreover, and as another basic assumption, I assume that the gratifications experienced in pursuing a given moral norm or code bind the actor to it to a degree which is also affected (in general, diminished) by the costs, the difficulties, the exertions he must put forth in pursuing it, as well as by the gratifying alternatives that the exertions of the pursuit necessitate he forego. In short, I assume that men will drift (not leap) to where the gratification is.

To some extent, however, *what* they experience as gratifying is a function of what they believe to be desirable or moral; in turn, what they believe to be desirable or moral is a function of the gratifications produced in pursuing this. There is thus, to *some* degree, a benign, mutually supportive interaction between gratification and moral conformity. It is, in part, this that gives moral norms the deceptive appearance of autonomy. But there would never be any *non*moral behavior or any changes in a moral code, if the only gratifications men could experience were from *conformity* with *it*, if the amount of gratification men received from conformity with a moral norm never changed, if the costs of conformity never changed, and if new possibilities of gratification alternative to established morality were never made possible. In actuality, however, *none* of these conditions obtain. Most crucially, men can and commonly do experience gratifications from immoral and nonmoral behavior, the costs of moral conformity to a particular moral norm are continually changing, and the alternatives men have vary in their attractiveness, partly as a function of the other changes; this last, in turn, causes changes in the costs and gratifications of continued conformity to *established* moral norms.

I have said that the extent to which men will conform with a set of values is a function of the gratifications that are associated with such conformity. There are four main types of rewards that can yield gratifications. Two of these, power and wealth, are "extrinsic" to moral conformity as such; that is, they may be attained quite apart from moral conformity, either as a result of chance opportunities to acquire them or as a result of institutionalized arrangements such as allocations made through inheritance. Moreover, power itself is inherently the opportunity to achieve one's aims despite the resistance, which may be expressed as moral disapproval, of others. In short, power enables men to get what they want even when what they want and the way they seek to get it is at variance with conventional morality. This is not to say, however, that power and wealth are not more securely held to the extent that others believe their possessors to have come by them and to exercise them in conformity with moral norms; it *is* to say that power and wealth are and may secure gratifications not necessarily contingent on the moral approval of others.

At the opposite end of the continuum are the "intrinsic" gratification-yielding rewards; these are essentially a form of *self*-approval, a feeling of rectitude or of good conscience that one experiences simply by reason of conformity with the moral code. This is an aspect of the seeming autonomy of morality. But since, as mentioned previously, moral conformity always entails the cost of overcoming one's internal ambivalences, it cannot be expected to continue indefinitely (even if it does continue for an appreciable period) by reason of self-approval alone and without other auxiliary gratifications. Somewhere between the "extrinsic" and "intrinsic" gratifications, with which moral conformity may be rewarded, is the approval—the prestige, respect, or affection—given by others to those who conform with a moral code.

There are inherent difficulties in using wealth and power as rewards for conformity to a moral code: first, because, while not fixed and inelastic in quantity, they are nonetheless scarce, so that people who have them are loath to part with them; and, second, because those who possess them can, in the nature of the case, effectively resist their redistribution to others. In contrast, however, both self-approval and approval by others for moral behavior can be awarded without *directly* threatening existent distributions of power or wealth. The use of approval or prestige as a reward for moral conformity does not require that property institutions be

changed or that existent allocations of power and wealth be reformed in a manner costly to those already advantaged by it.

The line of "least resistance," then, is to promote moral conformity by mobilizing gratifications that derive from the approval
of others or from self-approval. This means that men must be
taught to express or give approval to those conforming with a
moral code and that they must be taught to place value upon the
sheer approval of others, thus enabling them to derive gratifications from it; and/or that they must be trained ("socialized") to
have a "good conscience" when they do conform to a moral code,
or a bad one when they do not; and, finally, that such approval,
from self or other, be given in some positive relationship to the
moral conformity shown.

Essentially, then, the stability of a moral code within a society
having a significant measure of class stratification will depend on
the society's ability to mobilize *approval* or prestige for conformity
with its prescriptions. This means that approval must be given for
things other than wealth or power themselves, and yet things defined as being of great importance. Without this, the poor and the
powerless would have only the slimmest chance to achieve the
gratifications necessary to sustain their conformity with the moral
code, for there would be few important values that they might
share with the advantaged. It is thus essential to the requirements
for both a stable class and power system and for a stable moral
code, that the prestige hierarchy achieve a measure of differentiation from the wealth and power hierarchies, so that a man be
capable of achieving high prestige even though poor or powerless.

It is in this context that we can perhaps better understand why
the moral codes of Europe have traditionally, insistently, and, indeed, polemically differentiated "spiritual" from "materialistic"
values: the latter are associated with power and wealth and the
worldly comforts, while spiritual values are not only set apart from
but *above* these, and held to be achievable by *all*, and sometimes
even more readily when the worldly comforts are *lacking*. In such
a value system, with its basic distinction between material and
spiritual values, there is a built-in disposition to "give unto Caesar,"
which produces a readiness to accept the given distributions of
power and wealth. The really important values, it is implied, are
not these, but rather the "goods of the soul," which are not scarce
and may be achieved without requiring others to have less of them.

To the extent that a moral code stresses spiritual values and
defines them as superior to materialistic values, it therefore reduces
the pressure on established wealth and power hierarchies. It diminishes motivation to reform or change by enabling the poor and
powerless to achieve gratifications through approval or a sense of

rectitude. It thus commits them to value elements they may share with the more fortunate, and thereby contributes to the maintenance of the given social system. With the development of a moral code stressing spiritual values rewarded by approval of self or others, the "moral identities" that men have—that is, whether they are "good," "bad," respectable, honest, etcetera—become both culturally salient and distinct from class identities. Such a moral code can create distinctions that obscure and compensate for those worldly distinctions established by the wealth and power systems. With such a moral code, it is no longer only men's "worldly" conditions that count, but their moral status as well. A man may be satisfied by feeling he is "poor but *respectable*."

I have suggested, then, that the "goods of the soul" can be obtained without impairing vested interests or shaking the class system and thus, in effect, provide a spiritual reform that serves as an alternative to earthly revolution. Yet this is not altogether successful as a protection to the class and power system, for, to the extent that the moral code and the prestige hierarchy become differentiated from it, they inevitably generate certain strains upon the class and power system. The dilemma is this: the class and power system require, for their stability, a differentiated moral system and a rewarding prestige hierarchy; but the more "autonomous" they become, the greater becomes the likelihood of strain between the two systems. In other words, one major source of the endemic tension between the "ideal" and the "actual" in social systems is that a distinct class and power system *must* create a moral system whose values oppose it.[64]

Insofar as men may acquire prestige in a community apart from their possession of either wealth or power, and, in particular, to the extent that prestige is scrupulously allocated in universalistic ways—that is, in proportion to conformity with the group's values —those who are high and mighty within the power and class system may come to have *less prestige* than those lower in it. The high and mighty may, indeed, be judged to be neither the best nor the most competent men, and thus is set in motion an endemic drain on their legitimacy. This is all the more likely to happen to the extent that wealth and power are transmitted by hereditary succession. Moreover, to the extent that there develop groups with relatively high prestige but of no particular advantage in the society's power and wealth hierarchies, these groups may use their prestige to mobilize support for modifications in the wealth-power hierarchies, either on their own behalf or on that of the collectivity, as they view it.

One of the most fundamental and abiding problems of such societies is to develop a variety of accommodations to control, mitigate, or conceal this tension between the differentiated moral code and prestige hierarchy, on the one hand, and the power and wealth hierarchies, on the other. For one, the culture may emphasize that the rewards of the conforming moral individual will be secured in an afterlife. Again, there may be a development of secondary adjustments that provide opportunities for upward social mobility in the wealth and power hierarchies for those judged to manifest appropriate virtues or competencies. A different, but most pervasive accommodation is "normalized repression," which, in effect, simply makes it traditional or customary for men to be given less than they might claim under the moral code, and *justifies* it simply in terms of "realism" or "practicality."

THE NATURE OF FUNCTIONALIST CONSERVATISM: A SUMMARY AND OVERVIEW

That the ideological character of Functionalism is conservative in nature, should, by this point, be perfectly clear; yet what this "conservatism" *means* still requires some overall, summary clarification. I might begin by suggesting that Functionalism's conservatism is more a quiet than a militant one, whose character has had to accommodate to Functionalism's self-image as an objective, politically neutral discipline. Ever since Durkheim, Functionalism's concern with social "order" has served to project an image of itself as being committed only to the common needs of *all* elements of modern society, and as, presumably, nonpartisan. At the same time, however, this same concern with order has commonly made Functionalism uneasy about demands for a basic reallocation of social advantages, thus allowing it to work within and for the particular form of industrialism under which it first came into existence: until recently this has been essentially capitalist in character.

Yet this is not equivalent to saying that Functionalism is inherently and necessarily *capitalistic* in its ideological commitments, for, as I shall more elaborately maintain later, I also believe Functionalism to be congenial to *socialist* forms of industralization, *at a certain level in their development.* In holding that Functionalism is not *inherently* procapitalist or prosocialist, however, I am not saying that it is neither conservative nor radical. I am, in fact, maintaining that its very adaptability to both capitalism and socialism (at certain levels in their development) is precisely what

makes it essentially *conservative* in character. In this regard Functionalism is at one with the Positivism that Comte earnestly promised would "consolidate all power in the hands of those who possess
this power—whoever they may be." The conservatism of Functionalism is akin to that of the Catholic Church, which is by no means
linked to capitalism any more than it was to feudalism and which
has, indeed, found ways of adapting to socialist societies.

Although Functionalism is adaptable to all *established* industrial
systems, it is not equally responsive to *new* orders that are only
coming into being, for these may be the foes of those already
established. What makes a theory conservative (or radical) is its
posture toward the institutions of its own surrounding society. A
theory is conservative to the extent that it: treats these institutions
as given and unchangeable in essentials; proposes remedies for
them so that they may work better, rather than devising alternatives to them; foresees no future that can be essentially better than
the present, the conditions that already exist; and, explicitly or
implicitly, counsels acceptance of or resignation to what exists,
rather than struggling against it.

Functionalists, then, constitute the sociological conservation
corps of industrial society. They are conscientious "guardians"
devoted to the maintenance of the social machinery of whatever
industrial society they are called upon to service. They pray to the
gods of the city—whoever they may be, and wherever they may
be. When Functionalists are, at length, unavoidably drawn into the
problems of developing industrial societies in "underdeveloped
areas," they characteristically tend to conceive of the task as a
problem in "modernization" or "industrialization." They focus on
those elements that any and all forms of industrial society share,
thus once again backing away from the hard question of choosing
among sharply divergent forms and, in effect, accepting the
property and class system in existence.

The historical mission of Functionalism is not to help bring
industrialization about; it is to bulwark it, once it has come, it is
to provide aid to industrial society, after it has been established
and calls for help. One is reminded of the legend about Comte,
sitting in his office, every day, patiently, waiting for the sympathetic
man of business who never came to call. He was, as Marx said of
Saint-Simon, ahead of his time. For Comte's heirs, however, the
waiting is now at an end. Established industrial societies have a
need for social scientists, who can help maintain and operate them
smoothly; who can be trusted conscientiously to conserve the
established machinery and keep it running; who may be called
upon to speed up or slow down the motor, "customize" a body job,
and even, occasionally, to recommend nonstandard replacements

for a part; but who, nonetheless, are restricted to maintenance and operation activities, and are not expected to design new machinery or the totally new plants that could produce them.

Functionalism's essential posture, it is apparent, is not necessarily anti-socialist or even procapitalist. But it is nonetheless conservative. It can and it will work to conserve either form of industrialism, once it is established. Although it does not quite see how to go forward, or toward what, Functionalism is not "reactionary" in its intent: it does not believe in going back. Functionalists are not Pollyannas who see no fault in the status quo. But neither do they see possibilities of a future significantly different from the present.

It is this conservative character, this disposition to support whatever powers are established, that makes it understandable that Functionalism could depart from its traditional neglect of the state, and even move toward an alliance with the Welfare State, at least after it had been developed in society and widely accepted even by elements that were politically conservative. At that point the *social* utilitarianism long embedded in Functionalism and Academic Sociology more generally, was freed to be mobilized in support of state initiatives and controls. At that point Functionalists were able to define themselves as moderate "liberals" and align themselves with others of that political persuasion.

FUNCTIONALISM AS VALUE UNFREE

The ideological resonance of Functionalism is most visible when cast in the form of large-scale, grand theorizing, such as Talcott Parsons'. It should not be assumed, however, that "middle range" theories are devoid of such ideological implications. Indeed, it is a latent function of the middle range style of theorizing—in which each small intellectual garment is peeled off one at a time, in a kind of ideological strip tease—to conceal the nature and, indeed, the very existence of its underlying, larger view of the good society and the good man; thus the theorist reinforces his image of himself as a "value-free" scientist.

Modern Functionalism often projects an image of itself as politically and ideologically neutral. It sees itself as above politics and partisanship and, to that extent, as "value-free." While acknowledging that ideological commitments may be found in the work of some individual Functionalists, it avers that these are idiosyncratic expressions, random individual biases that are not intrinsic to Functional theory "as such." Though this concedes that some individual Functionalists do manifest ideological biases, this defense of Functionalism avoids examining their source, and thus it can provide no basis for understanding how other Functionalists can or do avoid them. It simply implies that, in some unexplained manner, some Functionalists may overcome the bias-inducing forces to which others capitulate. Containing neither an argument nor a proof of its contentions, it is simply an affirmation of its own position and a denial of the other.

Robert Merton's essay on manifest and latent functions argues that Functionalism is neither intrinsically conservative nor intrinsically radical.[65] The structure of his argument is worth attention. First, he attempts to defend this assertion by showing that Functionalism has been attacked as being both conservative and radical. Then he is at pains to show that there are certain convergences between Marxism and Functionalism, for he is taking special care to defend Functionalism against the accusation of conservatism. This would seem to suggest that he is less perturbed by the accusation of "radicalism." One of Merton's central premises is that, if Functionalism can be shown to converge with Marxism, then a *prima facie* case has been made that Functionalism must be free of a conservative bias. But this, of course, assumes that Marxism is, in all respects, a radical ideology. His entire approach requires that the focus be turned on the ways in which conservative and radical ideologies *differ,* and, in consequence, it neglects the manner in which both are, in some ways and at some times, *alike.* Insofar as Functionalism embodies ideological components that conservatism and radicalism share, then to say that Functionalism has been accused of having both ideological tendencies is not, of course, the same as saying that Functionalism is value-free. Indeed, it was Merton's central concern not to do this but to show that the values with which Functionalism is imbued are not necessarily conservative. However, merely to show that Functionalism has been *accused* of both ideological tendencies is not to show that both accusations are *equally well-founded;* nor should the sheer existence of each accusation be deemed sufficient to discredit the other.

It seems clear that both Western capitalism and socialism do, at least, converge on certain industrial values; they also converge in other ways. During certain periods of their development, both alike have extolled a value system based on self-sacrifice and self-control. Both have invoked a gratification-deferring and self-denying ethic of restraint. It is, therefore, not only in their industrialism that they have sometimes been alike, and not only, as Emile Durkheim said, in their commitment to economic or "material" values. And, although it does so with considerable ambivalence, Marxism shares a measure of social utilitarianism with Functionalism: both agree that men must be useful for the larger collectivity. Both also share certain "spiritual" or ascetically tinged values and commonly call for the postponement of individual gratifications, at least during certain periods of their development, in the name of something higher and better.

Simply because certain brands of conservatism and radicalism are profoundly different in *some* respects does not mean that there are *no* other values which they share. Mr. Merton was led down this path, I suspect, not primarily because he wanted to demonstrate that Functionalism was ideologically neutral. He did so, I would conjecture, because he sought to make peace between Marxism and Functionalism precisely by emphasizing their affinities, and thus make it easier for Marxist students to become Functionalist professors.

The ideological dimension in Functionalism—its value-unfree element—becomes most evident when its affinities with certain elements common to both Marxism and conservatism are seen. That these convergences may, today, be seen more readily is attributable to a number of social processes that have advanced markedly since 1949 when Mr. Merton first wrote his defense of the ideological character of Functionalism. For one, the crisis of Marxism has grown continuously since then; in particular, it has involved the mounting sense, even among Marxists, that the Marxism they knew was often lacking in radicalism. In large measure, the turning back to the "young" Marx of "alienation" is an effort to rescue a viable *radical* element in Marxism. The search for the young Marx suggests that Marxism, in some of its dominant historical embodiments, is no longer felt to be radical, and thus no longer sufficiently different from forms of contemporary conservatism.

In saying that Functionalism's ideology is conservative, I mean to suggest, primarily, that its fundamental posture toward its surrounding society entails an acceptance of its master institutions, but not that it is *necessarily* procapitalist and antisocialist. Committed as it is to the value of order, it can do no other than accept the kind of order in which it finds itself. This commitment to order has two sides, which, taken together, spell out what I believe to be the core of Functionalism's conservatism. On the one side, it is disposed to place itself and its technical skills at the service of the status quo, and to help maintain it in all the practical ways that a sociology can. It is ready and willing, even if not able to do so. On the other side, it is not disposed to a public criticism of the master institutions of the larger society. Functionalism's conservatism is expressed, then, in both its reluctance to engage in social dissent or criticism and its simultaneous willingness to help solve social problems within the context of the status quo.

Functionalism's attitude toward social criticism is very much at the heart of its conservatism. It cannot be supposed, however, that its conservatism implies that it is devoid of all critical impulse; for it no more feels that all is right with its world than does the ordinary, sociologically unsophisticated conservative. Functionalists have their own reasons for feeling a *genuine* ambivalence toward their society, however little the critical side of this ambivalence may be given overt expression. These have several sources. Functionalism's vested interests, its practical interests as an academic discipline, require that there be work for it to do, in order to win its mandate and sponsorship from some sector of the society. This certainly would not be forthcoming if sociology were to respond to societal needs with bland reassurances that things as they are, are really for the best. It thus has to be able to acknowledge and share the self-criticisms of society's managers. But there is much more to it than that. Still another source of Functionalism's ambivalence derives from its central concern with the problem of societal order. To men who respect order, the status quo, indeed any status quo, is surely not the best that can be imagined. Moreover, their conception of themselves as "value-free" scientists, while not accurate, does reflect an underlying structure of *sentiment* that entails a certain remoteness from the rhythms of contemporary society, a feeling that they are marching to a somewhat different music. To some degree, it expresses a remoteness common to all withdrawn scholars. In addition, it also derives from the feeling of some Functionalists that they are the guardians of certain precarious values (and particularly, order), toward which they have a special duty.

Although Functionalists have added a concept of the "dysfunctional" to their inventory of concepts, it is difficult to avoid the impression that this was done in part for the sake of formal completeness. It was a belated finger in the dike, rather than part of the dike itself. It was not, in short, an expression of the infrastructure of sentiments animating Functional theory. Nor do I consider it amiss to take note of the fact—a social fact that means something and has, somehow, to be explained—that Functionalists do call their theory "Functionalism; they do not call it "*Dys*functionalism." Can it be assumed that this is a mere happenstance, and that they might just as easily call it "Dysfunctionalism"?

Some years ago Marion Levy maintained that American Functionalists had mistakenly defined the concept of "Function." What they usually call "Function," Levy said, referring as it does only to *successful* adaptation, should properly have been called *Eu*function, which would be a logical counterpart to the notion of *un*successful adaptation entailed by the concept Dysfunction.[66] The term "Function," said Levy, was mistakenly equated with the term "Eufunction." But, how did this "mistake" happen, and what does it mean? Typical of the manner in which sociologists exempt their own behavior from serious analysis, Levy approached this question as he would never approach a similar problem in studying the language behavior of ordinary laymen. He simply treated it as an error in logic. I, however, regard this as a revealing symptom of the underlying metaphysics or background assumptions of Functionalism, and one which accurately expresses the conservative commitments it embodies.

NOTES

1. Parsons seems to assume that fraud is, by definition, the pursuit of "selfish" goals. This is an unfortunate exercise of conceptual license, which limits observations of the empirically various ways by which social systems may be integrated. The "noble lie" is a fraud presumably perpetuated on behalf of the collective welfare; and "tact" may be thought of as an altruistic form of fraud on a "small group" level.

2. T. Parsons, *Essays in Sociological Theory Pure and Applied* (Glencoe, Ill.: The Free Press, 1949), pp. 166–184.

3. *Ibid.*, pp. 166–167.

4. *Class, Status and Power*, R. Bendix and S. M. Lipset, eds. (Glencoe, Ill.: The Free Press, 1953), pp. 92–128.

5. *Ibid.*, p. 93.

6. *Ibid.*, p. 95.

7. Parsons, *Essays in Sociological Theory Pure and Applied*, pp. 178–179.

8. Bendix and Lipset, *Class, Status and Power*, p. 112.

9. *Ibid.*

10. *Ibid.*, p. 113.

11. *Ibid.*, p. 114.

12. *Ibid.*, p. 116.

13. *Ibid.*

14. *Ibid.*, p. 120.

15. *Ibid.*, p. 122.

16. *Ibid.*, p. 125.

17. *Ibid.*, p. 126.

18. *Ibid.*, p. 127.

19. T. Parsons, *Sociological Theory and Modern Society* (New York: Free Press, 1967), p. 297.

20. *Ibid.*, p. 308.

21. *Ibid.*

22. Parsons, *Essays in Sociological Theory Pure and Applied*, p. 172. (Italics mine.)

23. Parsons, *Sociological Theory and Modern Society*, p. 316.

24. Parsons, *Essays in Sociological Theory Pure and Applied*, p. 50.

25. Parsons, *Sociological Theory and Modern Society*, p. 331.

26. *Ibid.*, p. 288.

27. *Ibid.*, p. 324.

28. Parsons, *Essays in Sociological Theory Pure and Applied*, p. 179.

29. *Ibid.*

30. Bendix and Lipset, *Class, Status and Power*, p. 104.

31. *Ibid.*

32. Parsons, *Essays in Sociological Theory Pure and Applied*, p. 105.

33. *Ibid.*

34. *Ibid.*, p. 109.

35. An honorable exception is Wilbert E. Moore, *Industrial Relations and the Social Order*, revised edition (New York: Macmillan, 1951). See especially pp. 51–58, 598–604.

36. Neil Smelser, *The Sociology of Economic Life* (Englewood Cliffs, N.J.: Prentice-Hall, 1963).

37. Neil Smelser and Talcott Parsons, *Economy and Society* (Glencoe, Ill.: The Free Press, 1957).

38. Parsons, *Sociological Theory and Modern Society*, pp. 319–320. (Author's italics.)

39. Parsons and Smelser, *Economy and Society*, p. 123.

40. *Ibid.*, p. 113.

41. *Ibid.*, p. 113.

42. T. Parsons, *Structure and Process in Modern Societies* (Glencoe, Ill.: The Free Press, 1960), p. 220.

43. *Ibid.*, p. 211.

44. *Ibid.*, p. 212.

45. See, for example, *The Business Establishment*, E. F. Cheit, ed. (New York: Wiley and Sons, 1964); and G. W. Domhoff and H. B. Ballard, *C. W. Mills and the Power Elite* (Boston: Beacon Press, 1968), especially p. 270.

46. Parsons, *Structure and Process in Modern Societies*, p. 213–214.

47. *Ibid.*, p. 214.

48. *Ibid.*

49. *Ibid.*, p. 231.

50. *Ibid.*, p. 212.

51. *Ibid.*, p. 232.

52. *Ibid.*, p. 206.

53. *Ibid.*, pp. 209, 227.

54. *Ibid.*, p. 232.

55. *Ibid.*, p. 234.

56. *Ibid.*

57. *Ibid.*, p. 217.

58. *Ibid.*, p. 233.

59. *Ibid.*, p. 241.

60. *Ibid.*, p. 246.

61. *Ibid.*

62. *Ibid.*, pp. 246–247.

63. See, R. K. Merton, *Social Theory and Social Structure* (Glencoe, Ill.: The Free Press, 1957), pp. 131–194.

64. Cf. Wilbert Moore's emphasis on the "lack of close correspondence between the 'ideal' and the 'actual,'" as a "universal feature of human societies," and which simply takes it as a given, a kind of tragic universal, that "ideal values are not generally achieved." Wilbert E. Moore, *Social Change* (Englewood Cliffs, N.J.: Prentice-Hall, 1963), pp. 18–19.

65. See R. K. Merton, *Social Theory and Social Structure*, pp. 37 ff.

66. See M. J. Levy, Jr., *The Structure of Society* (Princeton: Princeton University Press, 1952), pp. 76 ff.

PART III

The Coming Crisis of
Western Sociology

9

The Coming Crisis of Western Sociology, I: The Shift toward the Welfare State

Functional theory, and Academic Sociology more generally, are now in the early stages of a continuing crisis. What follows in this volume is an effort to clarify the symptoms and sources of this crisis and to elucidate some of its possible outcomes. I shall also maintain, although I can develop this only in a cursory manner here, that much the same thing seems to be imminent for Marxism. It, too, is in or approaching crisis. Since I regard Academic Sociology and Marxism as the two major, structurally different aspects of Western Sociology, I therefore regard Western Sociology as a whole as facing a "coming crisis." It is with this problem that I reach the summit of my concerns in the present volume.

The central implication of a crisis is *not*, of course, that the "patient will die." Rather, the implication is that a system in crisis may, relatively soon, become something quite different than it has been. A system undergoing crisis will change in significant ways from its present condition. While some of these changes may be only temporary and may soon restore the system to its previous condition, this is not the distinctive implication of a system crisis. A crisis, rather, points to the possibility of change that may be more permanent, producing a basic metamorphosis in the total character. When a system undergoes crisis, it is possible that it will soon no longer be the thing it was; it may change radically or may even fail to survive, in some sense.

Systems, of course, are always and continually changing, but this does not necessarily mean that they are in crisis. A crisis implies that taxing changes are proceeding at a relatively rapid rate; that they entail relatively sharp conflict, great tensions, and heightened costs for the system undergoing them; and, finally, it also implies the possibility that the system may soon find itself in a significantly different state than it had recently been. Essentially, this is my contention about Functional theory, Academic Sociology, and Western Sociology most broadly.

THE WELFARE STATE AND FUNCTIONALISM

We may start with the observation (discussed in the last chapter) that, in his later writings, Parsons has become increasingly outspoken in his support of governmental regulation of the economy and of some version of the Welfare State in general. This is a key transition in his standpoint. It is a key transition, however, not only in Parsons' own standpoint but also in the larger tradition of theory from which it derives.

Throughout its development, from its heritage in Positivism, its development in English anthropology, and its formulation by Durkheim during the Classical period, Functional theory, much as it was sometimes concerned about the state, attributed relatively little importance to it or to its initiative and responsibility for the management of the social problems produced by a market economy. The focus of early Positivistic Sociology was largely on "spontaneous" social arrangements that grew "naturally." It polemically counterposed such spontaneous patterns to those that were planned and deliberately instituted, as, for example, the constitution-making drive of the classical, continental bourgeoisie. Positivism, then, did not greatly concern itself with the contribution that "politics" or the state might make to social stability. It saw stability as deriving largely from the new technology, science, the division of labor, or the development of a new morality appropriate to the emerging industrial society. The Positivists, in short, tended to minimize, if not deprecate, the role of the state, even when (as did Saint-Simon) they stressed the importance of remedying the conditions of the emerging working class.

Functional Anthropologists, for their part, found themselves studying native societies dominated by foreign states, and their usual neglect of the specifically imperialist relation between the native society and the colonial power necessarily meant a neglect of the state apparatus that was in effective control of native societies. Moreover, these societies commonly did not have a native state apparatus or a native politics in anything like the sense that European societies possessed them. Again, Durkheim, in his time, regarded modern industrial societies as needing not a stronger state apparatus but a new social structure to mediate between individuals and the state. There is no doubt that Durkheim believed the state incompetent to manage what he regarded as the decisive problem of modern Europe, its "poverty of morality," *anomie*. The syndicalist-type "corporations," with which Durkheim proposed to revitalize morality, were carefully to maintain their independence of the state. He also conceived of them as the new basis of political organization and as the fundamental political entity, minimizing the importance of the territorial bases of social organization and thus of the state.[1] In a similar vein, early Parsonsian theory, warning of the unpredictabilities of "purposive social action," expressed suspicion of the Welfare State then crystallizing in New Deal reforms. Early Functionalism and the tradition from which it emerged, then, did little to focus attention upon the role of the state; the Parsonsian accommodation to the Welfare State after World War II was, indeed, a significant shift.

Functional Sociology corresponds to the standpoint of a society, or of those groups within it, that does not conceive of its social problems as rooted in its basic property institutions, but which must regulate the disruptive impact of its market institutions and adjust its allocative arrangements, lest these result in threats to the property institutions. Insofar as Functional Sociology conceives itself as a science of purely "social" relationships, which premises that social order can be maintained regardless of the level and distribution of economic gratifications, and thus treats economic arrangements as "givens," it is somewhat remote from the income-reallocating strategies of the Welfare State. Yet its social utilitarianism may induce Functionalism to accept various kinds of social rearrangements, including the Welfare State, that promise to control or remedy the socially disruptive impact of individualistic market competition.

Sociological Functionalism's emphasis on the role of moral values and on the significance of morality more generally, often leads it to locate contemporary social problems in the breakdown of the moral system; for example, as due to defects in the systems of socialization and as due to their failure to train people to behave in conformity with the moral norms. To that extent, also, Functionalism's accommodation to the instrumental and technological emphases of the Welfare State must be tensionful, requiring considerable internal readjustment in its own traditional theoretical emphases. Moral conceptions of social problems may lead to new programs of education or training or even to an emphasis on the importance of more effective police systems and punishment. But this moral vision of social problems, however, does not readily lend itself to the instrumental management of adult populations in industrial societies. It is, rather, technological conceptions of and solutions to social problems that tend to proliferate with and are demanded for the development of the Welfare State. The Welfare State becomes infused with technological approaches to social problems and becomes increasingly staffed by liberal technologues. It becomes the centralized planning board and funding agent for numerous *ad hoc* technological solutions to modern social problems; these, in turn, are congenial to the working assumptions of bureaucratic elites and the technostructure in the *private* sector as well. On one of its sides, then, Functionalism, as a social theory with an embedded vein of social utilitarianism, can and is *ready* to adapt to the Welfare State; on another of its sides, however, as a theory with a focus on morality, it may be expected to have difficulty in adapting to the technological and instrumental emphasis of the Welfare State.

PRESSURE OF THE WELFARE STATE

It is basically only after World War II that Functionalism, in the United States, began to give explicit support to the Welfare State as a way to satisfy the need for action to regulate the economy and to protect the society against the "international Communist threat." This entailed a fundamental change in the Functionalist conception of government and the state. This ninety-degree turn was also made possible by another element long embedded in Functionalism. At a deep level in its own infrastructure, Functionalism, like Positivism, has had an abiding conservative disposition to respect and accommodate to "the powers that be," and thus to accommodate to the state power, whatever its ideological and social character.

The growth of the Welfare State has meant the emergence of a new power in society with an ever growing number of personnel and an increasing variety of social functions. What has most directly linked this new state apparatus to the sociological establishment and brought sociologists into closer ties with it is its vastly increased level of funding, some significant part of which is available to the social sciences and directly provides new career-supporting resources. Functionalism's acceptance of the Welfare State, then, derives not only from the general reality but from the immediate power of the Welfare State itself and, most particularly, from its articulated and real support for sociology and the social sciences. The social sciences increasingly become a well-financed technological basis for the Welfare State's effort to solve the problems of its industrial society.

Above all, what one sees is a vast growth in the demand for *applied* social science: the *policy*-oriented use of social science by governments, both for welfare and warfare purposes, and by industry, though cn a considerably smaller scale, for purposes of industrial management. The rate of institutional growth of the social sciences in the past decade has, in consequence, approached revolutionary proportions. This development hinges on the increased level of government investment in the social sciences; the sheer magnitude of these is itself worth documenting.

For example, in 1962 the U.S. federal government spent $118,-000,000 in support of social science research. In 1963, $139,000,-000 was spent. In 1964, $200,000,000 was spent. In the space of three years, then, *federal* expenditures alone increased by about seventy percent—and this, starting from a comparatively high absolute level. It is not, however, only in large countries like the United States that one sees this change. Even in small countries, such as Sweden or Belgium, government expenditures have increased greatly; in Belgium, for example, from 2.9 million dollars in 1961 to 4.8 million dollars in 1964.[2] For our purposes here, it suffices to emphasize the gross features of the new situation: namely, that there has occurred a world-wide and unprecedented growth in social science funding, based largely on vast new resources supplied by government.

This growth is of significance for sociological theory generally, and for Functional theory in particular, because governments expect that the social sciences will help solve ramifying practical problems. In particular, it is expected that the social sciences will help administrators to design and operate national policies, welfare apparatus, urban settlements, and even industrial establishments.

In these new circumstances Functional theory is under great pressure to change, quickly and radically. The applied social theory now being sought to aid policy makers and administrators cannot be one that merely shows how social arrangements that already exist are—manifestly or latently—for the best. What the state apparatus now needs is a social theory that is focally, and not peripherally, concerned with how conditions can be *made better*, how domestic problems can be reduced, how American power abroad can be protected or extended. This raises problems for Functionalism, however, not because it is unwilling, but because certain of its central assumptions and traditional commitments impede its application for such practical purposes.

Functionalism, at first, responded to this pressure, in some part, by reemphasizing the concept of *dys*functions. A. R. Radcliffe-Brown had early formulated a concept of "dysfunction," but this concept, it is notable, was given life in American sociology only during World War II, in the context of a unified national effort that mobilized many sociologists to help in solving the problems of the national administrative systems; that situation required a theory that could *systematically* help overcome social tensions, conflicts, and problems. Yet this conceptual shift toward concern with "dysfunctions" proved insufficient.

The demand on social science, today, to help in practical problem-solving has generated pressures hostile to the assumption, so fundamental to Functionalism, about the "cunning" of society. Functionalists of diverse tendencies commonly assume that, when problems arise in a group, there spontaneously emerge *natural* "defense" or adaptive mechanisms that serve to restore order and equilibrium. In the tradition of Comte, who decried deliberate intervention in social systems, Functionalists usually have expected that the order-maintaining mechanisms in society would work best when they worked "spontaneously"—one of Comte's favorite eulogisms—that is, without rational planning and without deliberate intervention. It was in this spirit that Functionalists cautioned against the unanticipated consequences of purposive social action in the midst of the Great Depression. But, at that time, sociology was scarcely mobilized for national purposes. Today, however, it is being heavily supported, and *not* to show how things work spontaneously or naturally; it is being supported to show how organizational management, through *deliberate planning and governmental intervention,* can make things work better. As Herman Kahn, who should know about these matters, has observed: "It simply isn't worth, say, $150,000 of anybody's money to find out that they are doing everything right."[3] In response to this new pressure for deliberate and rational policy-making, which Functional theory has such difficulty with, there is now a rapid growth of new theories, such as decision theory, cybernetics, and operations research, that seek to do precisely this.

With the growing demand for theories that can guide applied social science and facilitate decision-making, some of the most basic assumptions of Functionalism are being placed under pressure. For example, one of Functionalism's basic methodological precepts is that there are no "causes." Functionalism thinks of systems as mutually interacting variables rather than in terms of causes and effects. Functionalism's elementary domain assumption has always come down to this: everything influences everything else. But Functionalism has had no theory about the weighting to be assigned to different variables in the system. It has had no theory about which variables are more, and which are less important in determining the state of the system as a whole.

Administrators want to be able to appraise the differential costs and effects of intervening in different ways, at different points, and with different kinds of leverage. They therefore need to know which variables are more powerful. This is one reason why there is today a growing interest in those American sociological statisticians, such as Herbert Blalock, who are returning once again to the problem of making *causal* inferences. Administrators cannot be content with a theory such as Functionalism, which placidly reassures them that "everything influences everything else." To say this is to say that one of the major domain assumptions of Functionalism, the concept of functional interdependence, does not suffice for purpose of application. It is likely, in consequence, that this basic assumption of Functional theory will be ignored increasingly. One begins to detect a certain musty odor coming from Functional theory.

Functionalism has long tended polemically to oppose any theoretical model that stressed the primary importance of any one or several forces or factors in producing social change. The development of the Welfare State however, implies that there is a growing readiness to cope with social problems by assigning special importance to a special factor, the role of governance and the state. It is especially notable, therefore, that Neil Smelser, one of Parsons' former students and collaborators, when he seeks to formulate a new "general theory of social change," assigns a new and special importance to government:

If any variable were to be singled out as determining the long-term direction of change (that is, type of outcome), this would be the status of the social system's government-and-control apparatus. As we have seen, the initial impetus disposes the social system to some kind of change, but this disposition is very indeterminate. The direction of change depends at every stage and in large part on the activities of the government-and-control apparatus–its planning, its ability to mobilize people and resources in periods of strain, and its ability to guide and control institutional innovations.[4]

Smelser's formulation indicates that Functionalism is under and is responding to pressure to transform itself into a sociological version of Keynesianism.

This new pressure, however, is a source of strain on the theoretical model that Parsons and other Functionalists had developed earlier. In particular, it is a strain on Parsons' previous commitment to a "voluntaristic schema" that identified moral values internalized in individual persons as the key source of energy inputs into the social process, and which he later "circuited" into self-maintaining "social systems." In contrast to this, to accept the Welfare State is to see the state or polity as the master source of power and initiative in society and as the essential societal stabilizing factor. To be concerned with the Welfare State is also to premise the existence of inherent social "imbalances" of a sort that needs to be corrected, changed, rather than to assume there is, fundamentally, a *self*-maintaining social system, as Parsons does in his essential conception of the "social system."

For these reasons, among others, there is an appreciable strain between Parsons' earlier system focus and his later commitments to the Welfare State. As the last chapter indicated, and as our reference to Smelser reiterates, Parsons and other Functionalists are now prone to abandon older system assumptions and, instead, to look upon the society as requiring some central management stemming from the polity and government. Parsons' earlier theoretical views were grounded in a personal reality, domain assumptions, and structure of sentiments derived from experience and socialization in a successful *pre*-Welfare State. The voluntaristic schema extolled individual striving, and the social system model extolled spontaneously regulated patterns of cooperation; both are idealized requisites of a "free enterprise system." Both, in short, are implicit generalizations from an image of a free market and a *"laissez-faire"* economy that Parsons projected onto the society at large. In effect, then, there was a tacit ideological apologetics in Parsons' early theory—in the implication that, if all social systems would only operate like self-regulating enterprises in a market economy, they would operate better—which is dissonant with an acceptance of the Welfare State.

Despite his reference to the importance of a mutuality of gratifications, and despite even his later talk about "productivity," Parsons' fundamental concern had hitherto been primarily with the morality, responsibility, and legitimacy of the system managers, and not with the technical efficacy of the system or its success in producing and distributing goods and services. Insofar as Parsons' analysis bore on the efficacy of a system, it saw this as derivative largely of two factors: first, the moral commitments and restraint of the actors involved and, second, the spontaneity and self-regulating character of their relationship. This focus, however, remains appreciably distant from the instrumental strategies of the Welfare

State, which places its great emphasis on achieving goals through fiscal and monetary management and income reallocations through taxation.

The growth of the Welfare State and its increasing support of the social sciences, therefore, exerts serious pressure on the social sciences in a variety of ways. This new support largely derives from increased governmental commitment to intervene deliberately in society, whether one's own or others, and whether directly through the activities of the national government or indirectly through such agencies as UNESCO or OECO. Governmental commitment to deliberate intervention on the *international* level coincides with the breakdown of the older forms of colonialism and imperialism, with the competition between the United States and the Soviet Union to control the form that industrialization will take in the "Third World," as well as with the resultant bargaining power that certain developing nations have, to constrain the major powers to assist in their industrialization.

Governments also seek to intervene deliberately in their own societies, as a consequence of: the pressure exerted by relatively deprived social strata or regions, by the "lower" class, whether Black or working or unemployed; a concern to even out and control the oscillations of their economy and to maintain continuing economic growth; and, finally, prevailing conceptions of justice and equity. In response to these massive changes on a world scale, there is a growing level of governmental management of society; largely by channeling new funds into the social sciences, this has caused important changes in the latter's own local and national institutions, which mediate—conveying, defining, and sometimes amplifying—the new government pressures and opportunities. Thus, directly and indirectly, from remote and from local influences, there develop mounting pressures to change the theories and styles with which sociology today operates.

In addition to those already mentioned, these pressures have certain other common tendencies. For one thing, they are aimed at acquiring technological resources to facilitate planned and deliberate *change* in certain social conditions; in short, they entail governmental commitment to certain social "reforms." Second, this commitment itself must also be *justified*. There are continuing pockets of resistance to governmental intervention, partly in consequence of the higher levels of taxation required to finance it and partly because certain vested interests oppose some of the changes sought. The state, therefore, does not only require a social science that can facilitate planned intervention to resolve certain social problems; it also requires social science to serve as a *rhetoric*, to persuade resistant or undecided segments of the society that such problems do, indeed, exist and are of dangerous proportions. Once committed to such intervention, the state acquires a vested interest of its own in "advertising" the social problems for whose solution it seeks financing. In other words, the state requires social re-searches that can *expose* those social problems with which the state is ready to deal.

Prior to the state's assumption of increased control over them, these various problems had been handled by other social groups or agencies in the society, usually on a local, regional, or municipal basis. So, as the centralized government on the national level becomes involved in and seeks a mandate for the management of these same social problems, it enters inevitably into competition with the groups that had been traditionally responsible for their management; it infringes upon and threatens their vested adminis-trative interests in the control of these problems. There is, then, a resultant competition between new and old forms, and between higher and lower levels of problem management.

This creates a situation in which the new and higher levels have an interest not only in exposing the existence of a social problem, but also in unmasking the inadequacy of the older arrangements for dealing with it and in undermining the local elites formerly in charge of these arrangements, and whom the higher levels now wish to displace or to bring under their own control. There is, consequently, a tendency of the new and higher governmental levels to foster what are, in effect *"evaluation"* researches, studies that analyze the effectiveness and, most especially, expose the *in*effectiveness of the elites and of the traditional procedures on the lower, local levels. The upper apparatus of the Welfare State, then, needs social research that will "unmask" their competitors; it needs a kind of limitedly "critical" research.[5]

These interlocking needs of the Welfare State, however, are deeply at variance with certain of the technical commitments of Functional theory, as well as with certain aspects of its underlying structure of sentiments. For example, the state's need now is for instrumentally manageable techniques of solution, but Function-alism has traditionally focused on the importance of moral ele-ments that are not instrumentally manageable, short of totalitarian superintendence. Moreover, as we have seen, Functionalism has a persistently optimistic view of contemporary society, seeing it as almost the best of possible worlds, and tends to deemphasize the pathologies and problems of modern society; but the Welfare State needs to bring some of these into focus, if only to mobilize support for its programs. Functionalism tends to have a "positive" and appreciative perspective, but the Welfare State requires, at very least, a limited sort of *critical* sociology. These, then, are some of the important ways in which Functional social theory comes into conflict with the requirements of the Welfare State, and in which the Welfare State contributes to the crisis that is developing for it. This crisis intensifies to the degree that the Welfare State provides sociology with improved support.

It is, in appreciable part, as a consequence of such support that there has been, since the mid-1950's, an intensification of work that takes as its point of departure the analysis of "social problems," and which does not conceive of them as secondary aberrations, but unbegrudgingly assigns reality to them. Rather than see such social problems simply as disruptions in order and stability, much of the research on racial discrimination for example, sees it within a framework concerned with the general inhibition or violation of freedom and equality; this of course, it tacitly or overtly opposes. The support for such social problem–oriented studies does not, however, derive only from the material resources or funding of the Welfare State, but also from the great civil rights struggles and the closely connected "war on poverty" movement of the 1960's. Indeed, in less than one decade a distinct specialization, "the sociology of poverty," has taken on a new lease on life. It has drawn to itself a cluster of new recruits whose basic concern is to remedy the problem and change the society. Although these impulses for change are limited, they are, nonetheless, distinctly different in emphasis from the order-oriented assumptions characteristic of Functionalism. It is partly around this substantive issue that the long-severed connections between sociology and economics have begun to be mended, and that sociologists have begun to read more economics than ever before. While most of these social problem studies are fundamentally expressive of a sociological Keynesianism, operating within the limits of the Welfare State, and while it is thus not the spirit of C. Wright Mills that is abroad in them, it is also clear that neither is it the spirit of Functionalism and Talcott Parsons that manifests itself here.

CHANGE THEORY

The growth of the Welfare State entails, above all, a commitment to certain social changes and, therefore, requires a fundamentally different approach toward social change from that traditional to Functional theory. The major locus of strain within Functional theory, as a consequence, centers persistently on its analysis of social change.

The Parsonsian treatment of social change manifests anew the evident inconsistencies and the strains to which Functionalism has been exposed almost from its beginnings. There are signs, however, that the tension is becoming increasingly acute for Functionalists. Most specifically, I shall suggest in the following that: (1) it is in its treatment of social change that Parsonsianism will most likely abandon some of its most fundamental domain assumptions and that, most especially, it will manifest a *tendency* to shift abruptly over to radically different domain assumptions, particularly those of Marxism; and (2) that the pressure for this shift is mounting, to the point where certain Functionalists are now, explicitly and openly, attempting to solve problems in the analysis of social change by deliberately borrowing from Marxism. In short, the analysis of social change is increasingly leading Functionalism toward a convergence with Marxism.

Rather than focus on change, Parsons' analysis of social systems long tended to emphasize that they are governed by self-maintaining processes and to highlight the *order*-maintaining mechanisms inherent in them. Along with this he had a pronounced and one-sided tendency to conceive of conformity—with the expectations of others and with the requirements of moral codes—as conducive to the stability of social systems. The Parsonsian "social system" is a social world with its own ramifying network of defenses against tension, disorder, and conflict: pierce one, and another springs up, ready to cushion shock. This system's stability may be contingent, but it is never precarious. What is stressed is its almost endless capacity to absorb and nullify shock; what is painstakingly displayed is an intricate and interlocking network of mechanisms that binds the system's energy into itself, that swiftly and efficiently distributes it to stress-points, and that never dissipates any of it.

The Parsonsian social system is one whose equilibrium, once established, is conceived to be perpetual; whose essential reality is believed to be its inner coherence, rather than the conflicts, tensions, and disorders that are usually considered secondary disturbances or aberrations and that are never seen to derive from the necessary and inevitable requirements of social life; whose "actors" are, like fresh blotters, ready and willing to absorb the ink of an imprinting socialization, and who therefore need never be constrained, for they always act willingly, out of an inward motivation. It is a social world where scarcity seems not to matter or intrude, though, if acknowledged, it is always capable of being nicely managed by moral codes; it is a world where men use power benignly on behalf of the common interest and collective goals, and where power differences rarely tempt the stronger to take more than morality dictates. The Parsonsian social system is, in brief, a perpetual-motion machine.

In suggesting, as I have above, that Parsons does not conceive of social conflicts and tensions as deriving from the *necessary* requirements of social life, I am talking about what Parsons implicitly takes to be "real" in social systems: that is, about his most basic, if rarely stated, domain assumptions concerning social systems. The tendency of Parsons' thought is to assume that it is possible *not* to have these conflicts. Their existence is an entirely contingent one, depending on how the stability-ensuring mechanisms work at any moment. Conflicts and disorder are viewed not as part of the necessary order of things; they are more nearly akin to the fortuitous illnesses of the body than to the aging body's certain infirmity and inevitable death. Parsons operates with the assumption that there is nothing necessarily in a social system that will bring it to an end, seriously disrupt it, continuously subject it to strain, or even radically change its structure from time to time. In other words (and we shall probe this further in the next chapter), Parsons has conceived of a social system that is immortal. It is, in large part, because Parsons has been animated by a desire to endow his "social system" with immortality that it is difficult for him to understand the ways in which social systems must necessarily and lawfully change, and it is why he is led, in *The Social System*,[6] to a bleak pessimism about the very possibilities of understanding this.

ASPECTS OF PARSONS' CHANGE ANALYSIS

If, as Parsons assumes, a stable system of interaction, once established, tends to "remain unchanged," then logically he also tends to assume that changes in a social system arise from external pressures that have somehow overwhelmed or penetrated the system's defenses, or from pressures that are random—in their origin if not in their permeation—relative to the system's essential characteristics. The essential characteristics of the system will not engender critical structural changes *of* the system, but only cyclical or rhythmical changes *in* it. It seems no wonder, then, that in *The Social System* Parsons says:

a general theory of the processes of change of social systems is not possible in the present state of knowledge. . . . We do not have a complete theory of the processes of change in social systems. . . . When such a theory is available the millennium of social science will have arrived. *This will not come in our time and most probably never.*[7]

What must be noted here is the extreme pessimism, indeed the despair, that Parsons manifests about a "complete" theory of the change of social systems. In order to make such despair seem justifiable, Parsons changes the issue in the above quotation, talking first of a "general" and then of a "complete" theory. Surely a general theory is not necessarily a complete theory, unless by some idiosyncratic definition of these terms. Surely a complete theory of anything is rarely possible. And surely it is strange that Parsons— Parsons of all people!—here holds that such a theory must wait upon the prior development of *knowledge*. Why is it that a lack of knowledge should bar development of a theory of the change in social systems, but a similar lack of knowledge provides no impediment to Parsons' theory of social system equilibrium and order? Why is Parsons so bleak and hopeless about a theory of change, but not about a theory of order? Why is it that Parsons, suddenly and out of the blue, here adopts a Positivistic assumption to the effect that theories must wait on prior knowledge, when he never does so anywhere else?

The inconsistency of Parsons' argument here contrasts oddly with the depth of his pessimism. One is inevitably reminded of Socrates doggedly trying to prove the immortality of the soul; all one is sure of is the compulsiveness with which the point is being made, and one suspects that logic is being placed in the service of a prior impulse. The very thought of tackling the problem of system change seems to induce a kind of shrill distress, much as it might in a modern theologian called upon to discuss the nature of the devil.

THE DRIFT TOWARD MARXISM

In *The Social System* Parsons does, nevertheless, present some partial canons for analyzing social change. Interestingly enough, these center on the concept of "vested interests," around which resistance to change is held to be organized. Parsons holds that, so far as an effort to make "change" impinges on institutionalized patterns, "change is never just 'alteration of pattern' but alteration by the overcoming of resistance."[8] But it is not at all clear why "vested interests" should only give rise to *resistance* to change, and why they do not also promote tendencies for change as well. Nor does Parsons systematically note that different parts of a social system do not have an equal "vested interest" in its maintenance; some have different degrees of functional autonomy, some have more and some less of a vested interest in maintaining the system. Moreover, is not Parsons' statement that change takes place by overcoming resistance an acknowledgment, albeit only a tacit acknowledgment, that change takes place through *conflict*? If men have a vested interest in resisting change in order to *maintain* their gratifications, will they not tend equally to labor for change which will *expand* their gratifications? And once this is postulated, has there not then been postulated a cause, tending toward conflict, *inherent* in social systems?

More generally, once Parsons takes the plunge and does confront issues of social change, either *in* or *of* social systems, he seems constrained to mobilize a totally new set of domain assumptions concerning the character of social reality. His efforts to analyze social change seem to lead him suddenly to enlist domain assumptions not only extrinsic to those he uses in analyzing order, but contradictory to them—and which he expresses in the Veblenian notion of a "vested interest" and in the concept of a "resistance to change." One specific origin of the latter assumption is probably in Freudian theory. What should also be mentioned is that this specific assumption is common to Marxism as well. Parsons fails to note that this assumption, which happily seems, at first, to be consistent with and to account for the stabilizing tendency of systems, is actually consistent as well with an inherent tendency toward *conflict;* for, if there were no resistance to change, there would not, in Parsons' own view, be conflict. The very same tendency that, in one circumstance, stabilizes systems leads, in other circumstances, to their instability. The system is hoist by its own petard.

But Parsons does not see this side of it. He tends, instead, to mobilize different assumptions to account for stability and for change, or, at least, to think of them as if they were different. It is almost as if two sets of books were being kept, each operating under different assumptions: one for the analysis of change, and another for the analysis of social equilibrium. This was present even in Parsons' earlier analysis of "The Problem of Controlled Institutional Change," where he attempted to develop a strategy for coping with conquered Germany after World War II.

In this analysis, Parsons stresses that: "The conception of a completely integrated social system is a limiting case. Every at all complex society contains very important elements of internal conflict and tension." But why only complex societies? why not all social systems, even the simplest of them? Moreover, even though there is a certain "realism" in acknowledging the existence of such conflicts, this does not necessarily change Parsons' assumption concerning their character, for they are still not necessary and intrinsic to the society. He does not say that every society "generates" but that they "contain" conflicts, or "elements" of conflict. Parsons also notes, in this same article, that though one of the sides in a social conflict may impede change, the other side may be enlisted as an ally of change or the change efforts. In short, the change process is, again, almost explicitly seen to entail a struggle and conflict of some sort.

Parsons further comments that the most vulnerable point of the Junkers is their economic base; their position in society, he says, sounding like a Marxian journalist, can be attacked as a case of exclusive class privilege.[9] Again, the conservatism of the German civil service is also explained in class terms, being held to depend on the "class basis of recruitment of the higher personnel."[10] Even Parsons, when he comes to the analysis of *change,* begins not merely to acknowledge but, in fact, to stress the importance of class structures, of vested interests, and of conflicts, and to stress them in ways that are not intrinsically derivable from his theory of order. At this juncture the theory manifests a modest but perceptible drift in a Marxist direction.

As still another case in point, we might note his position concerning the role of ideas, regarded from the standpoint of social change. While his primary emphasis in the earlier *Structure of Social Action* was on the interdependence of belief systems with other variables, he now shifts to an emphasis on their "dependent" character, even if continuing to insist formally on their interdependence with other forces.

It is one of the important results of modern psychological and social science that, except in certain particular areas, ideas and sentiments, both on the individual and mass levels, are dependent manifestations of deeper-lying structures—character structure and institutional structure . . . than independent determinants of behavior.[11]

This conception of the matter seems clearly convergent with the position toward which Durkheim had been moving, in his analysis of the place of moral beliefs in society; both imply a distinction between superstructure and infrastructure that is similar to that made by the Marxist.

There is, then, something schismed in Parsons' social theory.

There is an unexpected hint of dualism in his view of the world. On the one side, there is Parsons' model of an immortal and unchanging social system, his version of the changeless Platonic Idea or Form. On the other side, there is his assumption that the natural world of men is, in its appearance, changing and falling away from the Eternal Model: "Every at all complex society contains very important elements of internal conflict."[12] It is as if in his theory of equilibrium Parsons speaks as a Comtian, but, when he addresses himself to a theory of change, he is suddenly transported and mysteriously finds himself speaking with Marx's voice. No wonder, then, that he shuddered at the prospect of turning from the analysis of equilibrium to that of social change. This Marxist tendency is not at all a new one; it was manifested in his *The Social System* as well as earlier, and it continues to be found even in his more recent analyses of social change and evolution.

DIFFERENTIATION: THE FORCES VERSUS THE RELATIONS OF PRODUCTION

In his paper on "Some Consideration on the Theory of Social Change," Parsons focuses on social change as entailing a process of differentiation.[13] By this he apparently means that social change, in part, occurs through the development of new and distinct arrangements and structures for performing certain functions. With the emergence of newly differentiated structures certain of the moral norms governing each unit change, as do the relationships among them. "Differentiation" not only means a change in the activities of some previously established unit; it also means a *loss* of certain activities, of the right to perform them, of the rewards and gratifications provided for performing them, and of the power to perform them. This emphasis on "differentiation" is reminiscent of Spencerian evolutionism, and Parsons' rediscovery of it is, indeed, coincident with his turn toward evolutionism (which I shall discuss shortly). If, as Parsons asked in 1937, "Who now reads Herbert Spencer?," the answer in the 1960's must be, Parsons himself.

Differentiation means the creation of a new unit, which assumes the functions and powers of an older one; so the growth of the new unit entails some loss and a threat of possible annihilation to the old one. Because the new unit must impair the older's vested interests, it will be resisted, with resultant social conflict. Much of this is not particularly new and is either already explicit or implicit in *The Social System*. A somewhat new element becomes manifest, however, when one asks, what conditions give rise to differentiation and upon what does its successful completion depend?

Parsons' reply assumes that the process begins with some kind of an "input deficit" with respect to goal-attainment, which, even when successfully arrested, is tensionful. In other words, some function is being performed; there is an expectation of some service that one system is committed to supply, though it, for some reason, is not performing satisfactorily. The recipient system is therefore exerting pressure upon the supplying system; the quantities, qualities, timing, or rates of exchange are thus made problematic. The recipient system exerts pressure for more, better, faster, or cheaper service than the supplying system, with its established arrangement, has been providing. The recipient system seeks to change the supplying system in some manner that satisfies it.

It is important to note that this "imbalance" is simply taken as "given" by Parsons. Since Parsons postulates that a social system will remain in equilibrium so long as each party to it conforms with the other's expectations, the only way in which he can get the system *out* of equilibrium is by sheer postulation. So he starts here with the assumption that it is already out of equilibrium; one of the parties is simply *assumed* not to be conforming with the expectations of the other. Differentiation, then, as a form of social change, is primarily a way in which the system adapts to and copes with a prior but unexplained impairment of equilibrium. There is, therefore, still nothing in the system itself that should necessarily throw it out of equilibrium or lead one party to frustrate the expectations of others. Disturbance is taken to be largely fortuitous, relative to the system itself.

For my part, however, I have repeatedly suggested that this is not the case; for example, there is an inherent tendency toward the declining marginal utility of gratifications; an inherent ambivalence in complying with even the morally sanctioned expectations of others; a greater readiness to demand conformity with one's own rights than with another's; a selective support for moral norms that are advantageous and a relative neglect of those that are not; there are inherent consequences of power differences, enabling the stronger to enforce his own moral expectations and resist the weaker's demands for such conformity, with resultant "normalized repression"; and there is a general inclination of those disadvantaged to give less support to an existent arrangement for the allocation of gratifications and to the moral code that sanctions this. For Parsons, however, there is still nothing *in* a social system that need inherently disturb its equilibrium.

For Parsons, moreover, successful differentiation is always a process that remains subject to the social systems' dominant values, which are "the highest-order component of its structure."[14] While the ways in which the values are applied may be changed and while the social units to which they are applied may also be changed, Parsons emphasizes that his "whole discussion has been based on the assumption that the underlying value-pattern of the system does not change as a part of the process of differentiation."[15] In other words, he is dealing with only a limited type of differentiation, *institutionalized* differentiation. He is dealing with a process of differentiation that is compatible with a system's primary value commitments and that remains *under control.*

But under what conditions do proposed differentiations remain under control? Suppose that established units resist their loss of old functions and, moreover, have sufficient *power* to make their resistance effective? The capacity to impose a shift of function from an old to a new unit is presupposed by Parsons, which implies that the shift is one within the power of those wishing to make it. In short, institutionalized differentiations, of the sort to which Parsons addresses himself, premise the maintenance of existent power arrangements, and are thus implicitly limited to those found acceptable by the powerful elites advantaged by them.

The course of a differentiation process will not develop equally from every person's experience of "input deficits." Under most conditions the "input deficits" of some will count for more than those of others. The "input deficits" of some persons and groups may long frustrate them and may fester without producing differentiation, while others' "input deficits" will lead to prompt and routine efforts at differentiation. Blacks in the United States, for example, have long experienced an "input deficit" with respect to the education their children receive; this has long been frustrating to them and long known of by others, but to this time there is no remedy for this in sight. Moreover, such "differentiation" as did develop— in short, discriminatory and segregated schooling—was developed and is maintained in order to remedy the "input deficits" not of Blacks but of Whites. Furthermore, *this* discriminatory pattern of educational differentiation was always at variance with the egalitarian value system to which American society nominally subscribes, but it will not be changed without violating the discriminatory value system to which, in fact, many American Whites do subscribe.

Underlying Parsons' analysis of social differentiation is an assumption that there is some constant function that must be performed, some unchanging need *of the system as a whole* that must continue to be satisfied. Increased differentiation is a way in which this same system need is transferred from one to another unit, where it is then better satisfied. The need that may produce social differentiation, however, may not be that of the system as a whole, but only of some part of the system. The crucial problem in transferring system needs from an old to a new unit is surmounting the resistance and vested interests of those advantaged by the established way of meeting it. And this largely depends, first, on the latter's power to resist, and, second, on their readiness and willingness to resist, which, in turn, is a function of whether their access to gratifications is either lost or imperiled, or improved and advantaged, by the impending transfer. For, the point of transferring a function may not be an improvement in the performance of the single system need or even of the system as a *whole;* in other words, transfer of a function may serve or aim not to improve the functioning of the group but to improve the advantages of only some within it.

Differentiation, as Parsons views it then, is largely a way in which social systems change in an "orderly" manner, without changing the fundamental allocation of advantages, and thus change, in short, in a manner acceptable or not threatening to existent power-centers. Still, what is interesting about this analysis is the extent to which it requires Parsons to accent his usual assumptions differently, and the way in which this veers him closer to a Marxist model. For example, Parsons' analysis of differentiation indicates that it begins in some conflict, entails threat, and engenders resistance. If the social system does not inherently entail conflict, *change* of system does. The supplying system is viewed as being under pressure to employ either new devices, or new arrangements for the use of old devices, to improve its performance. One way to improve its challenged performance is to assign it to another unit as a *specialized* function: to differentiate the established system. Let us examine how this works. The system under such pressure is presumably receptive to new devices that would improve its performance; it either tries to create them or it searches for those that have already been created elsewhere. If it succeeds in inventing or borrowing a new device, it must then arrange for its use within its own established system. To maximize the effectiveness with which the new device may be used, the system tends to create new kinds of organizational units, to which it assigns responsibility for the functions that the new device performs. But since the *functions* to be performed are not new, for only the manner in which they are performed is being altered, they must have been previously performed by already existent units within the social system. Therefore the "residual" unit has now lost a function to the new unit; its vested interests are impaired, and its continued access to its former facilities is thrown into question.

This model of change suggests certain parallels and begins to converge with the Marxist conception, which holds that societal change is brought about by a conflict between the *forces* and the *relations* of production. In Marxism, it is conceived that new forces of production (or functional "outputs") are first developed or acquired *within the existent relationships of production* (for example, the existent level of differentiation), but, at some point, become incompatible with these and burst them asunder. What Parsons has done, then, may be conceived of as generalizing the Marxist change model from society to all social systems.

What seems to happen is that, as Parsons shifts from analyzing the sources of system equilibrium to analyzing the sources of system change, there is a noticeable but unacknowledged shift from Comtian to Marxian domain assumptions, a shift toward a new metaphysics, which presently remains unresolved. This leaves the Parsonsian system operating dualistically. I would not, however, wish to overstate the extent of Parsons' shift in a Marxian direction. It is clear that Parsons by no means drops all of his former assumptions, even when he comes to analyze change; manifestly different ones are accented, and new ones make their appearance at that point, but it is also certain they do not have unchallenged control of the analysis, and they are assimilated into the older infrastructure of his theory.

For example, Parsons' analysis of differentiation transforms the Marxist mechanism of *revolution*—the conflict between the forces and relations of production—into a mechanism of *evolution.* The tension between the old residual unit and the newly differentiated one is viewed as remaining under central control. There is a "gray flannel" competition rather than a violent conflict between the units. Considered as a "myth of origins," the Parsonsian theory of social differentiation could be seen in the image of asexual reproduction: of a thing dividing itself but still remaining one thing; of a formless protoplasm gradually dividing itself but remaining integrated.

THE PARSONS-MARX CONVERGENCE
IN EVOLUTIONISM

It is precisely with respect to issues of social change that Parsonsian theory is most unstable, and thus is constrained to converge with models most at variance with its dominant commitments. This was once again indicated by Parsons' sudden turn toward evolutionism in the mid-1960's. That this was less a matter of the immanent internal development of Parsons' previous commitments, and more a matter of adapting to pressures in the intellectual surround—as well as to the pressures that produced these—is suggested by the opening remarks in his article on "Evolutionary Universals in Society." "Slowly and somewhat inarticulately," says Parsons, "emphasis in both sociological and anthropological quarters is shifting from a studied disinterest in problems of social and cultural evolution . . . to an evolutionary framework."[16] In short, Parsons noticed a gap between intellectual developments surrounding his own theoretical system, and he moved toward evolutionism to reduce the tension by "assimilating" it into his own system.

The focus of Parsons' effort here is his concept of "evolutionary universals," which he defines as "structural innovations" that "endow their possessors with a very substantial increase in generalized adaptive capacity, so substantial that species lacking them are relatively disadvantaged in the major areas in which natural selection operates, not so much for survival as for the opportunity to initiate further major developments."[17] An evolutionary universal is an innovation so "important to further evolution that, rather than emerging only once, it is likely to be 'hit upon' by various systems operating under different conditions."[18] This view of evolutionary universals as first *arising* under unspecified, "different" conditions suggests, as is, in fact, borne out by his entire analysis, that Parsons has no explanation of how they *originate*, of the conditions under which they do or do not occur. The origin of evolutionary universals is, in effect, seen as random mutation; their significance derives from their fortuitous creation of an increase in generalized adaptive capacity, which enables the innovation to survive, whatever the causes that first led it to emerge.

Although it is only implicit, there is a tacit "two-stage" sequence in Parsons' evolutionary model. Most specifically, there is a beginning or starting stage that is essentially that of primitive or tribal society. This is characterized by the dominance and pervasiveness of kinship institutions; as Parsons notes, social status is here largely ascribed to "criteria of biological relatedness."[19] This phase is largely an unanalyzed residual category, and only the starting point for subsequent development or evolution; it is that which must be broken out of for the second, equally amorphous, stage to begin. This second stage is everything that comes afterward—after the "seamless web of kinship" has been disrupted—and it is here that "evolutionary universals" develop. In short, all of "history," in effect, constitutes one and the same stage, after and relative to the breakdown of tribalism.

This breakdown occurs, in part, as a consequence of the appearance and operation of certain evolutionary universals. Two evolutionary universals, says Parsons, are most closely related to "the process of 'breaking out' of what may be called the 'primitive' stage of societal evolution."[20] These are, first, a system of explicit cultural legitimation of differentiated societal functions (particularly, political functions) apart from kinship and, second, "the development of a well-marked system of social stratification." More than that, Parsons also assigns priorities between these two starting mechanisms. "I am inclined to think," he adds, "that stratification comes first and is a condition of legitimation of political function."[21]

Once again, this is surprisingly reminiscent of Marxism, and particularly of Marx's and Engels's discussion of social evolution in the Communist Manifesto. Here, Marx began by holding that "the history of all hitherto existing society is the history of class struggles," to which Engels—in the English edition of 1888—appended a footnote, holding that this referred to "all *written* history." Engels then pointed out that in 1847, when the Communist Manifesto had been written, the "pre-history of society . . ." was all but unknown, but that, after that time, Haxtausen, Maurer, and Morgan had published their work analyzing the importance of communal land ownership as the foundation for the development of the Teutonic tribes, and of the nature of the *gens* and its relation to the tribe. "With the dissolution of these primaeval communities, society begins to be differentiated into separate and finally antagonistic classes."[22]

Engels, then, made a basic distinction between the stage of (1) prehistory or primeval societies and (2) all subsequent written history, that is akin to Parsons' distinction between the primitive and post-primitive stages. Engels, in effect, also operated with a kind of "two-stage" theory, holding that the stages of evolution to which Marx gave detailed analysis were, in effect, sub-stages located in the second, "historical" stage. Parsons, again like Engels, also assigns special importance to the role of social stratification in disrupting tribal societies, although his conception of social stratification differs substantially from that of Marx and Engels.

In addition to an explicit system of cultural legitimation and a well-marked system of social stratification, Parsons also focuses on four other "evolutionary universals": a markets and money system, bureaucracy, a universalistic legal system, and democratic associations. One of the most surprising lacunae in Parsons' analysis of evolutionary universals is the scant mention that he makes here of science and of technology. It is strange that these are not given emphatic mention as "evolutionary universals," for it seems obvious that they, no less than those mentioned, also produce a "very substantial increase in generalized adaptive capacity." Science and technology are mentioned in conjunction with the evolutionary universals only incidentally, in two brief sentences just a paragraph before the end of the entire article. Here it is acknowledged that they are as important for modern society as the last four evolutionary universals mentioned above, although they themselves are not stated to be "evolutionary universals." Why is this so?

An answer to this question, I believe, must proceed on two levels, one having to do with Parsons' technical analysis of evolution and the analytic distinctions that it involves, and a second having to do with the *ideological* character of Parsons' discussion, which itself is not independent of the first level but provides an infrastructure for it. As to the technical level: prior to his specification and direct analysis of the six evolutionary universals, Parsons makes an anterior distinction, differentiating what he calls the "pre-requisites for socio-cultural development"[23] from the "evolutionary universals." It is in these "pre-requisites" that Parsons locates *technology*, along with three others: language, kinship, and religion. Considerable (and characteristic) emphasis is given to the significance of religion. Cultural patterns, he holds, are "properly conceived in their most fundamental aspect as 'religious' ... I am inclined to treat the entire orientational aspect of culture itself, in the simplest least evolved forms, as directly synonymous with *religion*."[24] These four "pre-requisites," then, religion, communication through language, kinship organization, and technology, says Parsons, constitute the "very minimum that may be said to mark a society as truly human." Indeed, "no known human society has existed without *all* four in relatively definite relations to each other."[25]

Thus one formal reason that Parsons cannot allow technology to be an "evolutionary universal" is that he has previously defined it as a "pre-requisite." Presumably it cannot be both. Yet to deny that it can be both is arbitrary and contradictory; Parsons' own definition of an evolutionary universal, after all, simply holds that it is an innovation that produces a very substantial increase in generalized adaptive capacity, and technology is precisely the most generalized producer of "adaptive capacity." This is one of the main reasons that it can be diffused, with *relative* ease, among societies otherwise quite different. In short, technology has a relatively high degree of functional autonomy both between and within social systems.[26] The higher the level of technology, the more there is of a generalized adaptive capacity, at least of the same sort that results from any of the innovations that Parsons characterizes as evolutionary universals. Technology is a producer of generalized adaptive capacity in society in at least two important ways. First, it is a source of *non*-zero-sum gratifications; men "playing a game against nature" may use technology to increase the total assets available for distribution among themselves, thus making it easier for each to obtain increased gratifications without reducing the gratifications of the others. They thereby reduce the pressure to reorganize the system of stratification, and, to that extent, heighten system loyalties and stability. Second, technology is a major source of power, enabling systems that have higher technologies to compete more effectively against and impose themselves on those with lower technologies.

In his general concept of "pre-requisites," Parsons once again partially "converged" with Marx and Engels; and, although limited, it is a noteworthy convergence. In *The German Ideology*—and particularly in their critique of Feurbach—Marx and Engels stress the importance of certain "aspects" of social activity, or of certain "moments." These, they insist, are not different *stages* of evolution but "have existed simultaneously since the dawn of history . . . and still assert themselves in history today."[27] The first of these moments, they assert, is that men must be in a position to live in order to be able to make history; having a certain physical constitution, men need food and shelter, so their first historical act is the production of the means to satisfy these needs: they produce tools or means of production. Second, the satisfaction of one need creates new needs, presumably those devolving around production and technology.

> The third circumstance which, from the very first, enters into historical development is that men . . . begin to make other men, to propagate their kind: the relation between man and wife, parents and children, the FAMILY. The family which to begin with is the only social relationship, becomes later . . . a subordinate one.[28]

In connection with their discussion of these universal "moments," Marx and Engels also stress the importance and antiquity of language and religion: "Language is as old as consciousness, language is practical consciousness, as it exists for other men."[29] Central to this consciousness is a consciousness of nature, which, at first, appears as an all-powerful alien force: ". . . a purely animal consciousness of nature" (natural religion). We see here immediately: this natural religion or animal behaviour towards nature is determined by the form of society and *vice versa.*" At this point, then, several things are quite clear: first, that what Marx and Engels speak of as "moments" of social activity that always assert themselves in history, is the same kind of analytical category as the "pre-requisites" for social development of which Parsons speaks; and, second, we may also note that there is a considerable similarity in the specific things included in their parallel categories.

Despite this notable similarity, however, there are a number of important differences in their treatment of these pre-requisites or moments, of which I shall here only mention one. This, of course, centers on the special importance attributed by Marx and Engels to the forces of production, including (but not confined to) technology. While acknowledging the fundamental importance of the family, while stressing the significance of language and communication, while noting the interaction between society and religion, nonetheless, Marx and Engels assign a kind of priority to productive forces, distinguishing them from the other "pre-requisites" or "moments." Parsons does not do this, although, given his own assumptions, there are reasons for doing exactly that. After all, Parsons does assign special importance to those innovations that increase a society's generalized adaptive capacity, which is precisely what the growth of productive forces and technology do; moreover, these grow relatively autonomously, cumulatively, and at increasingly rapid, if uneven, rates. But, rather than acknowledge that technology has important differences in this respect from language, kinship, and religion, Parsons submerges it among these other "pre-requisites" in a way that obscures its special character as an unusually important source of generalized adaptiveness.

That he does this undoubtedly derives, in some part, from his abiding polemical commitments against Marxism,[30] and against any other theoretical model that assigns special importance to one or a few factors. But there is, I suspect, another, more narrowly ideological problem that Parsons faces in the present case and which disposes him to play down the significance of technology. This can be seen by reviewing the specific factors that Parsons defines as evolutionary universals, and most particularly, those that he regards as fundamental to the structure of modern societies. These, he holds, are "bureaucratic organization . . . money and market systems, generalized universalistic legal systems, and the democratic association with elective leadership."[31] What this implies is that the "free enterprise system" of American society is a uniquely powerful embodiment of all the important evolutionary universals that, according to Parsons, have ever been invented. That is, it implies that the United States of America represents the apex of evolutionary development, that it is the most advanced of modern nations.

While Parsons does not state this explicitly, he does directly argue one central implication of such a viewpoint; namely, that the United States' chief world competitor, the Soviet bloc of nations, lacking certain of these evolutionary universals, is inherently unstable and can be no match for the United States. Speaking of the market complex, Parsons holds that "those that restrict it too drastically are likely to suffer from severe adaptive disadvantages in the long run."[32] And "in the long run"—as the Marxist formulation also puts it—adds Parsons, "communist totalitarian organization will probably not match 'democracy' in political and integrative capacity . . . it will prove to be unstable."[33] In effect, then, Parsons uses his concept of "evolutionary universals" to demonstrate the superiority of the American system over the Russian. Now, if Parsons explicitly included technology, science, and general productive forces among his evolutionary universals, this ideologically resonant conclusion could by no means be as readily drawn as it is; that political inference would certainly be dubious, indeed, if special importance were assigned to technology. For, at the very least, the Russian buildup of "generalized adaptive capacity" through technology has been tremendous in the last fifty years, and the *rate* at which it has grown considerably outdistances that of America in that same period.

Behind the conceptual shuffling of evolutionary universals and "pre-requisites," then, there is an effort to deal out an ideologically strong "hand" for the United States and its social system; but, to do this, technology was a card that had to be assigned a low value. This can, I suppose, be appreciated by those with a taste for theoretical games. Still, one cannot but be half-amused (and half-amazed) that in a discussion of evolution, with its fundamental concern for what is surviving and what is not, anyone could have missed the *fact* that, in just fifty years, the Marxist-socialist nations have come to control half the world.

What Parsons' theory of evolutionary universals does is to give the West a consolation prize: a theoretical "victory" in place of a socio-political, real one. Now, at last, Parsons has turned the tables on Marx's "death prophecy" for capitalist societies; Parsons can hold that it is their social system, not ours, that will be buried by history. Marx's death prophecy has not only been "refuted," but a kind of retribution has been exacted.

SMELSER AND MOORE: THE FUNCTIONALIST CONVERGENCE WITH MARXISM

The analysis of social change leads Parsons repeatedly in the direction of Marxist assumptions and models, even as he continues to conduct a polemic against them. This tendency is less ambivalently and much more openly expressed today among other Functionalists. Increasingly, Functionalists are now moving toward a convergence with Marxism and are often doing so with unconflicted self-awareness. Not only is Marx referred to more and more often in the recent work of Functionalists, but they are also becoming openly appreciative of his work, although scarcely uncritical. Thus Wilbert E. Moore remarks:

> Some Marxian analysis was by no means as mechanical and mindless as it has been depicted at times, for Marx took fairly full account of the purposive character of social action—and not solely in his theory of revolutionary change. The Marxist position . . . did emphasize interplay of systemic elements and the dynamic consequences. Marx's intellectual heirs were never quite caught up in the extremes of static "functionalism" that came to represent a dominant theme in anthropological and sociological theory.[34]

Thus Moore makes it explicit that the deepest tensions in Functional theory derive from its analysis of social change, and it is in connection with this that his attitude toward Marxism becomes more appreciative.[35]

In his "Toward a General Theory of Social Change," Neil Smelser clearly indicates that Moore's recent work entails a move toward a convergence with Marxism:

> Like a Marxist, [Moore] views conflict and tension as normal and ubiquitous; but unlike a Marxist, he sees this as stemming from a variety of sources. . . . Like a classical functionalist, he sees social adjustment as responsive to disruptive influences; but unlike a classical functionalist, he does not assume that the adjustments necessarily reduce the tension—indeed, changes may generate even greater conflict and tension.[36]

In a similar vein, Smelser's own analysis in this same essay spends considerable time attempting to codify the Marxist theory of change and deliberately to unite it with his own reinterpretation of Functionalism, while, at the same time, differentiating his own views from those of "classical" Functionalism. That the convergence between Marxism and Functionalism in Smelser's work is not only a central but also a *self-conscious* effort is evident throughout his last essay, most particularly in his concluding remarks: "Hopefully this strategy may work toward overcoming the explanatory shortcomings of the classical functionalist and classical Marxist approaches."[37] There are, then, in both Moore and Smelser indications of the potential development of a kind of "left Parsonsianism."

To sum up, thus far: I have held that Functionalism—the most influential theoretical standpoint in contemporary Academic Sociology as a whole—is undergoing a deepening crisis. Much of this crisis is precipitated by the sharp emergence of the Welfare State. For, while there are structures deep in Functionalism that dispose it to ally itself with the Welfare State, there are also important ways in which it has considerable difficulty in adapting to the change-promoting requirements of the Welfare State. In its "classical" or "static" form, Functionalism cannot provide the Welfare State with the kinds of intellectual resources that are required. In one way, then, the crisis of Functionalism is a crisis *internal* to it. In its Parsonsian form, Functionalism is ready to ally itself with the Welfare State, but, at the same time, however, it lacks the intellectual tools *and* the deep-lying impulse to deal with the problems of social change so central to the Welfare State. In another way the crisis entails a tension *between* the Welfare State and many important aspects of the subculture and intellectual tradition of Functionalism. Futhermore, the enormous growth of the Welfare State has directly funneled vast new funding into sociology and the other social sciences. Functional Sociology has, thus, not only been exposed to tension-producing constraints, but also to new *opportunities* that have been no less tension-producing. Finally, I have also suggested that the central locus of this tension in Functional theory is in its ways of dealing, or not dealing, with social change. Functionalism's drift toward a convergence with Marxism is an effort to cope with the tensions it feels in this intellectual area, as well as an indication of the mounting crisis it is undergoing.

That this growing crisis of Functionalism is vitally related to the growth of the Welfare State means that it is related to social developments of the utmost power and continuing significance. It thus means that Academic Sociology as a whole will itself be subjected to powerful forces that may change it profoundly. There will be changes produced within Functional Sociology that will ramify outward into Academic Sociology and to which other intellectual standpoints also will have to adjust. To the extent that Functionalism loses its hold on the intellectual terrain, this will provide competing standpoints with important new growth opportunities, and this in turn, will intensify the crisis for Functionalism. Again, by reason of the direct support that the Welfare State gives to the "social problem" sociologies compatible with state interests (yet still competitive with the interests of Functionalism), it will weaken the latter's position and exacerbate the tensions present in Academic Sociology more generally. In the chapters that follow, some of these complications will be given closer examination. An attempt will be made to elaborate a larger variety of the indications and of the sources of the crisis in Functional social theory and Academic Sociology today.

It is noteworthy, particularly from the standpoint of a general interest in how social theory itself changes, that none of the changes discussed have derived from the accumulating empirical basis of sociology. There is really no evidence that the changes that Functionalism has already manifested and promises to further undergo—for example, its drift toward Marxism—have anything whatsoever to do with the researches and the findings these have produced, either within or outside of the framework of Functional theory, since Parsons' *The Structure of Social Action* was published in 1937. If we may regard our analysis here as an intensive case study of how one social theory changes, there is no evidence that it changes in the way that the conventional "methodological model" suggests it does, namely, out of its interaction with or as a response to new *data*. It is not the data that are changing Functionalism in any significant respect; and, indeed, the very problems that Functionalism is attending to now are themselves not new. What has happened is that old data and old problems have, largely for reasons exogenous both to the theory and research of sociology, come to be assigned new value, significance, and reality. In short, the *relationship* between the technostructure and the infrastructure of sociology has changed and has become increasingly tension-laden largely because of changes in the latter. This, primarily, is why major theoretical changes are now occurring and impending.

NOTES

1. For fuller discussion, see my Introduction to E. Durkheim, *Socialism*, A. W. Gouldner, ed. (New York: Collier Books, 1962), pp. 7–31.
2. On this and other comparative data, see *The Social Sciences and the Policies of Governments* (Paris: Organization for Economic Development, 1966).
3. *The New York Times Magazine*, December 1, 1968, p. 106.
4. N. J. Smelser, *Essays in Sociological Explanation* (Englewood Cliffs, N.J.: Prentice-Hall, 1968), p. 278.
5. For a detailed application of these considerations to the tradition of "deviant" behavior study, largely led by Howard S. Becker, see A. W. Gouldner, "The Sociologist as Partisan: Sociology and the Welfare State," *American Sociologist* (May 1968).
6. T. Parsons, *The Social System* (Glencoe, Ill.: The Free Press, 1951).
7. *Ibid.*, p. 534. (Italics mine.)
8. *Ibid.*, p. 491.
9. T. Parsons, *Essays in Sociological Theory* (Glencoe, Ill.: The Free Press, 1949), p. 325.
10. *Ibid.*, p. 326.
11. *Ibid.*, p. 336.
12. Parsons, *The Social System*, p. 317.
13. *Rural Sociology*, XXVI, No. 3 (September 1961), 219–239. Reprinted in *Social Change*, A. Etzioni and E. Etzioni, ed. (New York: Basic Books, 1964).
14. *Ibid.*
15. *Ibid.*
16. T. Parsons, "Evolutionary Universals in Society," *American Sociological Review*, XXIX, No. 3 (June 1964), 339.
17. *Ibid.*, p. 356.
18. *Ibid.*, p. 339.
19. *Ibid.*, p. 342.
20. *Ibid.*
21. *Ibid.*
22. *Handbook of Marxism*, E. Burns, ed. (New York: International Publishers, 1935), pp. 22–23.
23. Parsons, "Evolutionary Universals in Society," p. 356.
24. *Ibid.*, p. 341.
25. *Ibid.*, p. 342.
26. For data and discussion bearing directly on this issue, see especially (but not exclusively) Chapter four of A. W. Gouldner and Richard A. Peterson, *Technology and the Moral Order* (Indianapolis: Bobbs-Merrill, 1962). I take it that this stress on the *relative* autonomy of technology is consistent with and, at least, implicit in Marx's emphasis on the importance of, at some point, the conflict between the forces and relations of production. This relative autonomy of technology is one of the reasons that it is possible for it to conflict with the relations of production.
27. Karl Marx and Friedrich Engels, *The German Ideology* (New York: International Publishers, 1947), pp. 17–18.
28. *Ibid.*, pp. 16–17.
29. *Ibid.*, p. 19.
30. The abiding character of this polemic and, in particular, its special relevance to the analysis of societal evolution, from Parsons' standpoint, may be noted in the closing comments in his monograph, *Societies, Evolutionary and Comparative Perspectives* (Englewood Cliffs, N.J.: Prentice-Hall, 1966), p. 115. He remarks, "Once the problem of casual imputation is formulated analytically, the old chicken and egg problems about the priorities of ideal and material factors simply lose significance. I hope that the present

treatment of the problems of societal evolution, though brief, will help lay to rest this ghost of our nineteenth-century intellectual past."

31. Parsons, "Evolutionary Universals in Society," p. 356.

32. Ibid., p. 350.

33. Ibid., p. 356.

34. Wilbert E. Moore, Order and Change (New York: John Wiley and Sons, 1967), p. 7.

35. See also the following appreciative remarks by Moore: Marx's analysis was . . . in effect far more sociological than that of his predecessors . . . Marxian and Weberian interpretations remain significant and controversial . . ." (ibid., p. 35). "Marx correctly observed . . ." (ibid., p. 46). "His position is a useful basis for discussion. . ." (ibid., p. 123). "Certain points in the Marxian tradition have had a continuing viability . . ." (ibid., p. 298).

36. Smelser, Essays in Sociological Explanation, p. 279.

37. Ibid., p. 280.

10

The Coming Crisis of Western Sociology, II: The Entropy of Functionalism and the Rise of New Theories

The impending crisis of Academic Sociology is, in some part, born of its success in the larger world, as the impending crisis of Functionalism is born of its success within Academic Sociology. Our national survey of American sociologists in 1964 revealed that an overwhelming majority of them, indeed, some eighty percent, were favorably disposed toward Functional theory. In that sense, Kingsley Davis's Presidential Address to the American Sociological Association in 1959 was quite right in saying that Functionalism and Academic Sociology had become one.[1] If I understand Mr. Davis's argument properly, he seems to hold that there is now nothing validly distinctive about Functional analysis, and that whatever validity there was to Functional analysis is now common to all sociological analysis. Where the two still differ, he suggests, it is to the discredit of Functional analysis, being expressive of the latter's merely philosophical assumptions, which lack scientific validity.

Looked upon not in terms of the validity of its arguments, but rather as a symptom of the state of Functionalism as a school of thought, Davis's thesis implies that the boundaries between Functionalism and other schools have become difficult to discern. It is quite clear that Davis's article was not announcing a marriage betweeen Functionalism and other sociologies; it was, rather, a notification that a wake was to be held for Functionalism as a distinctive school. Davis's comments are significant, then, not merely because they directly argue that Functionalism has lost its distinctiveness, but also because, as a polemic against his former

Functionalist colleagues, they are in themselves a symptom of much the same boundary-dissolving drift in Functionalism. Essentially, Davis's article is an expression of his defection from Functionalism. This is no small event, considering that Davis was one of the earliest and best known adherents of Functionalism. Davis's arguments express the cleavages, challenges, and crisis that await Functionalism in its hour of triumph.

In contrast to Smelser's and Moore's critique of Functionalism from the "left," Davis's renunciation of Functionalism—or, as he quite correctly calls it, the "Functionalist movement"—expresses what one might call a critique of Functionalism from the "right." It is a critique that belabors Functionalism for its lack of "detachment" (again, quite correctly), which he sees from the methodological perspective of a more Postivist standpoint. The importance of Davis's critique for us, however, is that it is one of many indications of the growing variability and individuation, manifested even by the pre-World War II generation of Parsons' students. That Davis could emphasize the indistinguishability of Functionalism and sociology is, in part, due to the spreading influence of Functionalism, but also to the fact that through its growing internal variability it does, indeed, become more difficult for it to maintain its intellectual coherence and the clarity of its own theoretical boundaries. In short, it is, in some ways, growing difficult to see—at least with casual inspection—a difference between Functionalist and other sociologists, not because there do not remain modal differences between them, but because Functionalists manifest an ever larger variability around their central tendencies. In some part, this is an expression of the *entropy* of Functionalism and is another indication of its impending crisis.

ENTROPY AND THE SEED GROUP

The entropy of Functionalism derives, in one part, from its very success and influence. As is true of other standpoints, it was easier for Functionalism to maintain the clarity of its own distinctive commitments while it was a minority view, in opposition; but having come into respectable eminence, its new position exposes it to pressures that dilute its distinctiveness.

If nothing else, the success of Functionalism has meant an increase in the sheer number of its productive adherents. This quantitative increase by itself should be expected to engender greater variability in its theoretical posture. Such variability, moreover, is all the more likely to develop since its adherents, new and old, are individualistic intellectuals who are impelled to win their place by competitively distinguishing themselves from one another and by expressing their intellectual differences publicly.

There are, however, other sources from which the growing entropy of Functionalism derives. These are related to the fact that Parsonsian Functionalism was diffused by a "seed group" that, from its very beginnings, manifested tendencies toward individual variability. Several characteristics of this seed group are worth mentioning here. First, they have been a prolific *training* cadre. This is easily overlooked, in focusing on their work as researchers, writers, and publishers. Within a surprisingly small time since the late 1930's, they themselves have trained not one but several generations, who, in turn, have trained succeeding generations. Variability in the work of Functionalists has thus been heightened not only by the competitive individualism of the original seed group, but also by that of the younger generations, and by the tensions between them and their elders, and by the intra- and cross-generational borrowing and diffusion of their individual innovations.

A second characteristic of the original seed group, conducive to the growing entropy of Functionalism, is that it achieved national academic prominence at what, compared with European possibilities, was a relatively early age. They attained prominence while still young and intellectually productive. They are presently very much alive and active, writing and publishing, and are exposed to the growing variability in the work of their own generation's peer group, as well as that of their students'. Their own work thus grows more individuated in character, interests, and style; and, because of their eminence, this validates the individuation of the younger, lesser-known men, and contributes to the boundary-attenuating variability of the Functionalist school as a whole.[2]

Because the Functionalist seed group was relatively young when it achieved national professional prominence, it was subjected to still other variability-engendering pressures. For one thing, they early achieved almost all the rewards that the sociological establishment could give them. Many of them have already been President of the American Sociological Association, even though they are still in their prime. This seed group has been so early and so thoroughly honored in this way that one would be hard pressed to find others in it upon whom to bestow this prize. As a result of their youthful success, there is very little more with which their own professional community can meaningfully reward them, even supposing they still retained an appetite for further honors.

This, in turn, suggests that their professional community has a dwindling set of social controls that it can exert upon them to limit their individuality. Correspondingly, it also means that these still productive men may tend to look elsewhere for their rewards— beyond the confines of their own professional community—to different professions, to new problem areas, and to new reference groups within public life. Here indeed, there are still "new worlds to conquer." But this, in turn, can only further augment the variability of their intellectual production.

As a final source of the increasing variability of the Parsonsian seed group, brief mention might be made that, vigorous though they are in so many ways, they are still older than they once were. They are now thus surely looking at their work in the light of a different structure of sentiments and a different "personal reality" or experience than they had in their youth. Their new work is subject to new conditions of the most intimate and personal character. It is shaped by the long backward look as well as by the shorter prospect before them. While looking backward to their youth, they are also looking forward to their historical future. Some will use the time they have to more deeply imprint, sharpen, fix the public image they leave behind them; some will mellow and grow more tolerant of intellectual differences, seeking to enjoy the present without rancorous polemic; some will drift still further away from the public life of their professional community and will bend all their efforts, in Hemingwayesque morality, "to get their work done." All this is bound to have still further individuating results that will heighten the variability of their forthcoming work, and reduce the coherence of Functionalism and the clarity of its boundaries. These, then, are among the endogenous sources of the impending crisis of Functionalism as a distinct intellectual sub-culture.

THE DISAFFECTION OF THE YOUNG

Another source of the crisis in the offing for Functionalism is suggested by an examination of the differences in the *ages* of those sociologists who are most favorably, and least favorably, disposed toward it. As previously mentioned, the national survey of American sociologists conducted by Timothy Sprehe and myself asked them to express their agreement or disagreement with the statement: "Functional analysis and theory still retain great value for contemporary sociology." We found that, for the group as a whole, the replies were overwhelmingly favorable. Yet it is notable that not all age groups were equally favorable or unfavorable. The percentage of those expressing *un*favorable views of Functionalism increases gradually as the respondents become younger. Five percent of the group over fifty are unfavorable to Functionalism; nine percent of those between 40–49 are unfavorable; eleven percent of those between 30–39; and fourteen percent of those from 20–29. There is no doubt that these differences are small and that those unfavorable are clearly in the minority in any age group. Nonetheless, the trend is very consistent and significant. It is clear that the youngest respondents tend to be more hostile toward Functionalism and, indeed, more than twice as much so as the oldest.

If there is any sharp dividing line among them, it seems to lie between those over and those under fifty years of age. The group over fifty seems to be the most favorable (and the least unfavorable) and, thereafter, as one goes down the age line, the percentage of favorable responses declines and the percentage of unfavorable ones increases. The "breaking point" seems to be between those who were professionally trained before or during World War II and those who were trained after it. Moreover, there is some indication, from examination of the more indeterminate or "neutral" responses, that these manifest a small but steady decline, from the older to the younger groups. In short, the middle ground seems to be disappearing, and there are signs of some polarization. The growth of unfavorable responses derives both from the decline of neutral or uncertain attitudes toward Functionalism, and the decline in the proportion of those favorably oriented toward Functionalism. But still the most relevant finding here is that the young are defecting from Functionalism or are more likely to be repelled by it. Small though the differences are at this point, this trend is so distinct that there is considerable reason to expect that it will continue, and that Functionalism will have increasing difficulty in winning the young to its standpoint. And surely, when a theoretical viewpoint manifests a declining ability to attract the young, there are solid grounds for asserting that crisis is impending for it.

Since 1964, when our survey of American sociologists was begun, and 1966, when I first reported on it at the national meetings of the American Sociological Association in Miami, there have been a number of other indications of a growing disaffection among the young, toward Functionalism in particular, but also toward Academic Sociology in the United States more generally. The sharpest public expression of this was, as I have previously noted, at the Boston meetings of the American Sociological Association in 1968. It took a variety of forms, among them the formation of the "radical caucus," organized largely around young militants fresh from their demonstrations at Columbia and other universities. Disaffection was indicated in its reply to the Secretary of the Department of Health, Education, and Welfare, in its "walk-out," and in its resolutions at the business sessions of the Association. The activities of the radical caucus were further intensified and extended at the San Francisco meeting of the ASA in 1969, and clearly evidences that the dissatisfaction of the young is now moving from individual expressions of dissent to organized forms of resistance against what are taken to be the dominant views in sociology.

The declining attractiveness of Functionalism to the younger sociologist was certainly earlier evidenced in the augmented publication of polemical criticism against the Functionalist model during the 1950's and 1960's. These criticisms seem to have been most particularly voiced by scholars still under fifty, by men such as Ralf Dahrendorf, Peter Blau, David Lockwood, Dennis Wrong, myself, and others. In some part, moreover, there is considerable reason to believe that the criticisms of Functionalism made by C. Wright Mills also struck a particularly responsive chord among the young.

Among other signs of the impending crisis of Functionalism is the emergence of radically different and comprehensive theoretical models, whose formal stipulations, and underlying assumptions and sentiments, differ importantly from the Parsonsian model in particular, and from Functionalism in general. Among the most important of these new theoretical models is the social psychology of Erving Goffman, surely the most brilliant of his group.

OTHER SYMPTOMS OF THE CRISIS: GOFFMAN'S DRAMATURGY AND OTHER NEW THEORIES

Goffman's is a social "dramaturgy" in which appearances and not underlying essences are exalted. It is a dramaturgy in which all appearances and all social claims are endowed with a kind of equal reality, however disreputable, lowly, and deviant their origin may be. In short, unlike Functionalism, it has no metaphysics of hierarchy. In Goffman's theory the conventional cultural hierarchies are shattered: for example, professional psychiatrists are manipulated by hospital inmates; doubt is cast upon the difference between the cynical and the sincere; the behavior of children becomes a model for understanding adults; the behavior of criminals becomes a standpoint for understanding respectable people; the theater's stage becomes a model for understanding life. Here there is no higher and no lower.

Goffman's avoidance or rejection of conventionalized hierarchicalizations has, however, important ambiguities to it. On the one side, it has an implication of being *against* the existent hierarchies and hence against those advantaged by it; it is, to this extent, infused with a rebel vision critical of modern society. On the other side, however, Goffman's rejection of hierarchy often expresses itself as an *avoidance* of social stratification and of the importance of power differences, even for concerns that are central to him; thus, it entails an accommodation to existent power arrangements. Given this ambiguity, response to Goffman's theories is often made selectively, the viewer focusing on that side of the ambiguity congenial to him, and thus some among the rebellious young may see it as having a "radical" potential.

Goffman's is a sociology of "co-presence," of what happens when people are in one another's presence. It is a social theory that dwells upon the episodic and sees life only as it is lived in a narrow interpersonal circumference, ahistorical and noninstitutional, an existence beyond history and society, and one which comes alive only in the fluid, transient "encounter." Unlike Parsons, who sees society as a resilient, solid rubber ball that remains serviceable despite the chunks torn from it, Goffman's image of social life is not of firm, well-bounded social structures, but rather of a loosely stranded, criss-crossing, swaying catwalk along which men dart precariously. In this view, people are acrobatic actors and gamesmen who have, somehow, become disengaged from social structures and are growing detached even from culturally standardized roles. They are seen less as products *of* the system, than as individuals "working the system" for the enhancement of self. Although disengaged or partly alienated from the system, they are not, however, rebels against it.

In Goffman's social world, it is not the moral code (or "respect") but "tact" (or prudent sociability) that cements. Such social order as exists for Goffman depends upon the small kindnesses that men bestow upon one another; social systems are fragile little floating islands whose coasts have daily to be shored up and renewed. In

Goffman's view of the world (to borrow George Homan's phrase),
men are coming back into the picture—tricky, harassed little
devils, but still men—and the sturdy social structures drift away
into the background. There is communicated a sense of the precariousness of the world and, at the same time, of zest in managing oneself in it.

Rather than conceiving of activities as a set of interlocking functions, Goffman's dramaturgical model advances a view in which
social life is systematically regarded as an elaborate form of drama
and in which—as in the theater—men are all striving to project
a convincing image of self to others. Here men are not viewed as
trying to do something but as trying to *be* something. (The "third
estate" is still trying to be "something"; now, however, it is taking
short cuts.) If life is a "countinghouse" for the Republican Bostonian of "comparatively wealthy family," for whom the essential
relation is one of exchange, for Goffman it is a *theater* where all
are engaged in a perpetual play and all are actors. (Actually, however, Goffmn's dramaturgy is based upon a limited type of theater;
it takes its departure from what might be termed the "neo-classical"
drama, which is quite different from, say, the "guerrilla" theater or
the "living" theater, both of which commonly portray strong passions and are openly infused with moral purpose.)

Goffman thus declares a moratorium on the conventional distinction between make-believe and reality, or between the cynical
and the sincere. In this all-the-world's-a-stage world, what is taken
to be real is not the work that men do or the social functions they
perform. Rather, human conduct is seen as essentially concerned
with fostering and maintaining a specific conception of self before
others. The outcome of this effort, moreover, is not seen as depending on what men "really" do in the world, on their social functions,
or on their worth, but on their ability skillfully to mobilize convincing props, settings, fronts, or manner. A man's value in this
world, then, depends upon his appearances and not, as it had to the
classical bourgeois, on his talents, abilities, or achievements.

While Goffman's theory may be viewed as a kind of "micro-
functionalism," concerned to identify the mechanisms that sustain
social interaction, he fails to ask the central questions that a functionalist would pose, concerning the presentations of self that are
made. He does not explain, for example, why some selves rather
than others are selected and projected by persons, and why others
accept or reject the proffered self. That is, seeing this largely as a
matter of maintaining a consistent image of self, he does not ask
whether some selves are more *gratifying* in their consequences, to
self and other, and whether this shapes their selection and acceptance. Nor does he systematically clarify the manner in which

power and wealth provide resources that affect the capacity to project a self successfully.

At the same time, however, Goffman's dramaturgy is plainly not an expression of aristocratic insouciance or of disdain for bourgeois industriousness. Aristocrats believe in what they are and its worth; Goffman's actors are busy contrivers of the illusion of self. What has happened, then, is not that we have left the world of the bourgeois, but that we have entered deep into the changed world of the *new* bourgeois. The dramaturgical model reflects the new world, in which a stratum of the middle class no longer believes that hard work is useful or that success depends upon diligent application. In this new world there is a keen sense of the irrationality of the relationship between individual achievement and the magnitude of reward, between actual contribution and social reputation. It is the world of the high-priced Hollywood star and of the market for stocks, whose prices bear little relation to their earnings.

Dramaturgy marks the transition from an older economy centered on production to a new one centered on mass marketing and promotion, including the marketing of the self. It betrays the change from a society whose heroes, as Leo Lowenthal[3] has put it, were Heroes of Production, to one where they are now Heroes of Consumption. In this new "tertiary economy" with its proliferating services, men are indeed increasingly producing "performances" rather than things. Moreover, both the performances and products they produce are often only marginally differentiated; they can be individuated from one another only by their looks. In this new economy, then, sheer appearance is especially important.

When men have no *real* choices, not only in the economic but also in the *political* marketplace, appearances come to count most heavily. Thus many Americans were drawn to President John F. Kennedy because, as they held, he had "style." In an economy and politics without significantly different alternatives, varieties of style sustain the illusion of choice. Style becomes the strategy of interpersonal legitimation for those who are disengaged from work and for whom morality itself has become a prudent convenience. A dramaturgical view of social life resonates the sentiments and assumptions of the new middle class: of the "swinger" in the service-producing sector of the economy, of the status-conscious white-collar worker, professional, bureaucratic functionary, and of the educated middle class, rather than of the propertied groups.

Goffman's is a social theory appealing to men who live in or must deal with large-scale bureaucracies that have a juggernaut momentum of their own and are little amenable to the influence of individuals. Thus Goffman does not deal with how men seek to change the *structure* of these organizations or of other social systems, but, rather, with how they may adapt to and within them. It is a theory of the "secondary adjustments" that men may make to the overpowering social structures that they feel must be taken as given. His theory of "total institutions" clearly communicates his sense of the crushing impact of organizations on persons whose individuality is viewed as protected largely by wiliness. In modern and large-scale organizations, individuals become more readily interchangeable, and their sense of worth and potency becomes impaired. Having little impact on the organization as a whole, they focus on the management of impressions, seeking to be noticed and differentiated from others, and attempting thereby to establish their individual worth and potency. In a large-scale organization, men are closely dependent upon the responses of others, and they know that they are. Those who are more dependent, and more sensitive to their dependence, will be more concerned to manage the impression of self they communicate. The management of impressions is a strategy of survival more likely to be emphasized by persons whose assumptions remain individualistic and competitive, but who are now dependent upon large-scale organizations. Goffman is, in effect, depicting and defending the wily strategies by which such persons protect themselves and seek to maintain a sense of their own reality and potency under these conditions.

This newer middle class is *not* a social stratum that, cushioned by independent means and appreciably "independent" of others, can say: let the public be damned. The new bourgeois world of "impression management" is inhabited by anxious other-directed men with sweaty palms, who live in constant fear of exposure by others and of inadvertent self-betrayal. The management of impressions becomes problematic only under certain conditions: when men have to *work* at seeming to be what others expect them to be. But why should men have to work at this, unless they are no longer spontaneously disposed to do or be this? In short, the moral code shaping social relationships has become less fully internalized in them; while remaining a fact of social reality, it tends to become a set of instrumentally manageable "rules of the game" rather than deeply felt moral obligations.

Social relationships thus become an interaction of espionage agents, each seeking to convince the other that he really is what he claims to be, and each seeking to penetrate the other's "cover." Under these conditions, "there is no interaction in which the participants do not take an appreciable chance of being slightly embarrassed or a slight chance of being deeply humiliated. Life may not be much of a gamble, but interaction is."[4] For all of its claim to reality, then, the new dramaturgical world of appearances is a thin crust on which men must tread lightly lest it cave in and reveal—what?

Goffman's dramaturgy is an obituary for the old bourgeois virtues and a celebration of the new ones. This is its most fundamental difference with Parsons' theory, which remains rooted in the classical bourgeois virtues—in its belief in the importance both of utility and of a genuinely held morality. Goffman's sociology believes in neither, at least not in anything like their former sense. For Goffman, what counts is not whether men *are* moral but whether they *seem* moral to others; it is not morality as a deeply internalized feeling of duty or obligation that holds things together, in Goffman's view, but rather as conventional rules required to sustain interaction and treated much as men do the rules of a game.

In their capacity as performers, individuals will be concerned with maintaining the impression that they are living up to the many standards by which they and their products are judged. . . . But, *qua* performers, individuals are concerned not with the moral issue of realizing these standards, but with the amoral issue of engineering a convincing impression that these standards are being realized. Our activity, then, is largely concerned with moral matters, but as performers we do not have a moral concern in these moral matters. As performers we are merchants of morality.[5]

Moreover, it is not the utility of men or their activities—and, indeed, not even the *appearance* of utility—that is held to matter. What counts is whether the appearance is *acceptable* to or desired by others (in short, whether one can sell it), and not whether the appearance bears any relation to an underlying usefulness. We might say that Functionalism was based upon a conception of men and their activities as "use-values," while dramaturgy is based upon a conception of them solely as "exchange values." (I remember one occasion after a long negotiating session with a publisher for whom Goffman and I are both editors. I turned to Goffman and said with some disgust, "These fellows are treating us like commodities." Goffman's reply was, "That's all right, Al, so long as they treat us as *expensive* commodities.") Dramaturgy reaches into and expresses the nature of the self as pure commodity, utterly devoid of any necessary use-value: it is the sociology of soul-selling.

Goffman's dramaturgy is therefore anti-utilitarian only in the sense of being opposed to a now historically declining form of utilitarianism. While alienated from this old form, which held that men could and should be useful in what they did, it relishes a new marketing utilitarianism; it believes in the usefulness of sheer appearances: the presentation and management of the self. Classical utilitarianism always insisted on the need to maintain a relationship between a man's utility and his reward, between his individual ability and his social mobility. Dramaturgy, however, is a social theory in which this connection is totally severed. Bewitched with consequences, classical utilitarianism always maintained that it was "results that count," and it thus always had a built-in disposition to an amoral calculus of pure efficiency—in short, to anomic normlessness. Yet the *inherent* drift of classical utilitarianism to anomie was partly inhibited by its theory of "natural rights" and by its counterbalancing morality. Its venality was therefore disguised by unctuousness and hypocrisy. The marketing utilitarianism on which dramaturgy is based lacks such moral scruples. While it, too, believes that "it is results that count," it interprets this to mean that "anything goes." Moving increasingly from an inner- to an other-directed social world, dramaturgy capitalizes on the natural culmination of utilitarianism in *anomie*. In other words: dramaturgy is not the antidote to utilitarianism but the symptom of its pathology. Disdaining the inhibitions of the older, somewhat "square" utilitarian culture, the dramaturgist is determined to outwit it at its own game. He is, at bottom, moved by an impulse to get something for nothing, and therefore insinuates that there is nothing to get and nothing to give: all is appearances.

Dramaturgy thus premises a disenchantment with the older utilitarian culture. It uses the new utilitarian culture as a standpoint for an implicit critique of the old, and in this, enables men to disengage themselves and maintain emotional or role distance from it. Bennett Berger deftly lays this matter open in characterizing Goffman's as a "demonic detachment." It is demonic—or Goffmaniac, if you will—in that, while it denies a distinction between appearances and reality, by insisting on taking appearances seriously, it must also devalue, as just one more "appearance," those things that men have conventionally prized. Thus loyalty, sincerity, gratitude, love, and friendship are seen as forms of maudlin sentimentality. Goffman's is a demonic detachment, for the way of life that it celebrates is a form of "camp"; even those who relish its precious cleverness remain visitors to it. Goffman lays bare the elaborate strategies by which men ingeniously contrive to persuade others to buy a certain definition of the situation and to accept it at face value. It is thus deeply ambivalent toward the status quo. It is a clever unmasking of the clever and, at the same time, a how-to-do-it manual of the modern utilitarianism of the new middle class. It is an invitation to the *enjoyment* of appearances. Goffman is to the sociology of fraud what Fanon is to the sociology of force and violence.

To view the world as "drama" is to resonate the sentiments that we normally direct at theatrical drama. Although the dramaturgical model assures us that acting is very serious work, nonetheless, to commend a view of life as a kind of play is still, for most of us, an invitation to view it as an arena of limited and tentative commitment. After the play or game is over, normality returns. "Normality" is an arena characterized by cumulating commitments, where our previous efforts either fail or pay off, either limit or extend our future opportunities. But a single drama does not encumber the next; each opening night is a new beginning. Dramaturgy, then, is a solution to the problem of how to charge life with renewable excitement even when there is no real hope for a better future; it is a way of getting "kicks" out of the present.

Insofar as this model embodies an ideology, rather than being only a limited research heuristic (and the ideology is usually disguised in the method), it must inevitably activate and trade on the pathos with which we ordinarily regard dramas. Which is to say, it refines our capacity to make commitments tentatively and thereby to maintain our distance from things. It enables us, in short, to keep our "cool." The dramaturgical model allows us to bear our defeats and losses, because it implies that they are not "for real," or at least allows us to define them as such after their occurrence. In this respect the dramaturgical model itself is—to use one of Goffman's early formulations—a way of "cooling the mark out," of accommodating losers to failure. However, it may also undermine the satisfaction of winning or of desirable outcomes, because, by the same token, the dramaturgical model implies that our victories too are not for real. Thus winning and losing both become of lesser moment. It is only the game that counts.

Dramaturgical models are most convincing when adapted to only partial social sectors or limited periods of time. When life is looked upon as a drama, the focus must be given over to necessarily restricted situations and personnel. The story can be told only under the spotlight and while the curtain is raised; each drama is an entity independent of the others.

In effect, then, the dramaturgical model invites us to live situationally; it invites us to carve a slice out of time, history, and society, rather than to attempt to organize and make manageable the larger whole. In this respect it is vastly different both from the more traditional religious standpoints of Western society and, for that matter, from the more classical evolutionary social philosophies and the theories of total society that emerged in Western Europe during the first half of the nineteenth century. Rather than offering a world view, the new model offers us "a *piece* of the action."

And yet it does this in a world that is becoming increasingly interdependent. This would seem to imply that the drama to which it invites us is a game to be played within the interstices of social life and within the framework of the dominant institutions. A dramaturgical model is an accommodation congenial only to those who are willing to accept the basic allocations of existent master institutions, for it is an invitation to a "side game." It is for those who have already made out in the big game, or for those who have given up playing it. It has appeal to those members of the middle class who generally mask their alienation out of a concern to maintain a respectable appearance, and to those "dropouts" in the Psychedelic Culture who feel no need to conceal their alienation; both groups are alike in that they are not moved to protest against and actively oppose the system that has alienated them.

Goffman's dramaturgy is a revealing symptom of the latest phase in the long-term tension between the middle class's orientation to morality and its concern with utility. In its earliest development, the middle class had denied the existence of such a tension, or, if it perceived one, often vigorously came to the defense of morality.

That the modern middle class had to travel a long way to reach Goffman's world of vaunted appearances could not be made plainer than by contrasting it with Rousseau's altogether different standard. The comparison is relevant because, like Goffman, Rousseau, too, was obsessed with the world of appearances; but for Rousseau appearance was the mask of insincerity, the barrier that isolated men from one another, the glittering exterior that alienated him from himself.[6] Appearances, in short, were not vaunted but damned. As Rousseau declaimed in 1750 in his Dijon essay,

What a happiness it would be to live amongst us, if our exterior appearance were always the true representation of our hearts; if our decency were virtue, if our maxims were the rules of our actions. . . . Dress will set forth the man of fortune, and elegance the man of taste; but the wholesome robust man is known by others . . . all ornaments are strangers to virtue . . . the honest man is a champion who wrestles stark naked; he disdains all those vile accoutrements which prove only incumbrances. . . . In these our days the art of pleasing is by subtile researches, and finery of taste, reduced to certain principles; insomuch that a vile deceitful uniformity runs thro' our whole system of manners. . . . Politeness constantly requires, civility commands; we always follow customs, never our particular inclinations: no one nowadays dares to appear what he really is. . . . Shall we then never rightly know the man we converse with? . . . Friendships are insincere, esteem is not real, and confidence is ill-founded; suspicions, jealousies, fears, coolnesses, reserve, hatred, and treasons, are hid under the uniform of a perfidious politeness.

This passionate demand for artless "sincerity," and this moral outrage at the constraint that custom imposes on the baring of the heart, is rooted in the assumption that man is at bottom good and he therefore need not fear self-exposure or the possibility that he would be less than he should be if he trusted his own impulses. It is rooted in the assumption that man need *not* betray himself: "I have only to consult myself concerning what I ought to do; all that I feel to be right, is right; whatever I feel to be wrong, is wrong . . . conscience never deceives us."

The transition from Rousseau's to Goffman's social world was a long passage: from men capable of moral indignation to "merchants of morality"; from men of self-absorbed Calvinist conscience to gamesmen adroitly making their moves, not in accord with inward consultation, but in shrewd anticipation of the other's countermove; from the outsider—to whom everything came so painfully hard—to those who feel there is no outside and no inside, but only different situations that yield to different strategies; from the criticism of "insincerity" to the acceptance that all is insincerity; from the desperate plea for the baring of the heart to the cool sneer at sentimentality.

Eighteenth-century "sentimentality" was the self-expressionism of those who wanted to be and to be known as moral, who understood morality as the capacity to feel, who feared that utilitarianism was drying up something human and was isolating men. *Contempt* for sentimentality, however, is a fear that feeling and love expose one, that they bind us to others in ways that limit the means we can employ, that they lock us into relationships and impede our movement from game to game. Sentimentality is the effort—by those who fear isolation—to overcome it, to find some human connection, and to express a human solidarity. Contempt for sentimentality is the hardening of the self to *endure* isolation in order that one's market options should not be preempted. Sentimentality was the counterfeit of feeling and of love; fear of sentimentality is the counterfeit of objectivity.

For Rousseau, the conflict between utility and morality was as fully evident as was its solution: "how often have we not been told by the monitor within, that to pursue our own interest at the expense of others would be to do wrong!" But he insisted that the conflict could be solved and that the way to do so was to yield to the promptings of the conscience: "Reason deceives us but too often . . . but conscience never deceives us. Whoever puts himself under the conduct of this guide, pursues the direct path of nature, and need not fear to be misled." Conscience, it was supposed, was essentially harmonious.

In the Classical period of the sociological synthesis, however, not only was the tension between morality and utility acknowledged by Max Weber, but he held that their relationship entailed a dilemma that was *not* soluble in any generalized manner. Weber argued that there was an inexpungeable tension between two kinds of ethics: an "ethic of absolute ends," on the one side, in which men opted for certain courses solely because they believed in their moral propriety, and an "ethic of responsibility," on the other, in which courses of action were selected by weighing, in more utilitarian fashion, their possible consequences. Weber was leaving a place for utilitarianism, but only a very special version of social utilitarianism in which courses of action were selected in terms of their expected contribution to the *nation-state*. In short, like many other academics of the Classical period, Weber was a nationalist.

Weber believed in the validity of both a *social* utilitarianism *and* an ethic of transcendental or absolute morality; nevertheless, he acknowledged that each was somewhat inimical to the other and that the single-minded pursuit of either one undermined the other. He saw no way of resolving this dilemma in general, but only on the level of individual choices made by inner-directed persons aware of the peculiarities of each specific case. The individual was expected to shoulder resolutely the difficulties in balancing the two kinds of considerations.

From one standpoint, we might say that Weber was less hypocritically pious about morality and more "realistic," having "hardened" himself against Rousseauian "sentimentality." Like Rousseau, he believed that men should consult their consciences in choosing their paths; unlike Rousseau, however, he stressed that the pursuit of one value might undermine realization of another. Men need, therefore, to steel themselves to violate some of their own values if they are to achieve others: men must be "hard" in order to endure. There was, in short, no promise of an essential harmony in the world, but, rather, of an intrinsic disharmony: the world was seen as demonic. For Goffman's "merchants of morality," however, this dilemma simply does not exist; all conflicts may be remedied by the manipulation of appearances.

Goffman's dramaturgy is one more effort to resolve the tension between utility and morality; it responds to this dilemma not by doggedly holding on to both of its horns, but by releasing both. Goffman, simply and deftly, sidesteps the issue, substituting the standpoint of a sociological aesthetics for both morality and utility. Despite this, however, his solution premises the continued existence of individualistic and social utilitarianism as well as of the social strata on which they rest. Dramaturgy is, as it were, an interior decoration that provides a new look to these older furnishings.

The sociology of Erving Goffman is, in my view, a complexly

articulated theoretical expression that resonates the new experience of the educated middle class. This new experience has generated new conceptions of what is "real" in the social world, along with a new structure of sentiments and domain assumptions that are dissonant with the kind of utilitarianism once traditional to the middle class. Most particularly, the middle class now lives in a world in which conventional conceptions of utility and morality are less and less viable; in which rewards often seem to bear little relation to men's (or things') usefulness or morality; in which men can get ahead without the conventional talents or skills necessary in the old production-centered middle-class economy. In short, the new middle class has become sensitized to the irrationalities of the modern system of rewards. These irrationalities have at least three distinct forms. First is an heightened *market* irrationality, in which "stars" and other highly advertised and speculative commodities reap enormous gains, soaring to great heights one day and sometimes collapsing the next. A second and increasingly pervasive form of reward irrationality, which might be termed *bureaucratic* irrationality, draws totally arbitrary lines between those who "pass" and "fail"—and thus between those who are admitted or promoted and those who are not—often doing so on the basis of the most minuscule distinctions in performance. (Contemporary student revolts are, in some part, exacerbated by this form of bureaucratic irrationality.)

These rather modern forms of reward irrationality exist along with the most classical, bourgeois form; namely, the provision of special rewards and opportunities on the basis of property rights alongside of but without any regard for the allocative standards either of the market or the bureaucracy. There is thus a growing confluence of new and old irrationalities in the reward system now, which together seriously attenuate its public legitimacy as well as the authority of those who "succeed" and come to the top through its operations.

Where the irrationality of the reward system grows pronounced, where the relationship between what a man does and what he gets develops considerable slippage, it may be expected that a continued commitment to conventional middle-class modes of winning rewards—to morality and/or utility—will wane, and that new ideologies accounting for or accommodating to this slippage will grow stronger. There will be a stress on good luck, on the importance of power and personal connections, on ritualistically "playing the system," and (as in Goffman's case) on the significance of sheer appearances.

Goffman's sociology corresponds to the new exigencies of a middle class whose faith in both utility and morality has been gravely undermined. In this new period, traditional moralities and religions continue to lose their hold on men's faith. Once sacred symbols, such as the flag, are mingled defiantly with the sensual and become, as in some recent art forms, a draping for the "great American nude." "Pop art" declares an end to the distinction between fine art and advertising, in much the same manner that dramaturgy obliterates the distinction between "real life" and the theater. The "Mafia" become businessmen; the police are sometimes difficult to distinguish from the rioters except by their uniforms; heterosexuality and homosexuality come to be viewed by some as akin to the difference between righthandedness and lefthandedness; the television program becomes the definition of reality. The antihero becomes the hero. Once established hierarchies of value and worth are shaken, and the sacred and profane are now mingled in grotesque juxtapositions. The new middle class seeks to cope with the attenuation of its conventional standards of utility and morality by retreating from both and by seeking to fix its perspective in aesthetic standards, in the appearances of things.

ETHNOMETHODOLOGY: SOCIOLOGY AS A HAPPENING

Among other emerging theoretical standpoints based upon infrastructures fundamentally at variance with the Parsonsian is that advanced in Harold Garfinkel's Ethnomethodology.[7] Like Parsons, Garfinkel is deeply interested in the requisites of social order. Unlike Parsons, however, he assigns no special importance either to the role of a mutuality of gratifications or to that of shared moral values. Instead, and in a more Durkheimian manner, Garfinkel is concerned with the cultural level and, in particular, with a kind of *secularized* "collective conscience." Influenced by Alfred Schuetz's phenomenology, his attention is focused largely on the structure of the shared and *tacit*—that is, ordinarily unutterable—rules and knowledge that make stable social interaction possible. For Garfinkel, then, the social world is held together not by a morality tinged with the sacred, but by a dense collective structure of tacit understandings (what men know and know others know) concerning the most mundane and "trivial" matters, understandings to which no special importance, let alone sacred significance, is normally attributed if, indeed, they are noticed at all.[8]

Like Goffman, Garfinkel focuses on everyday life and on routine activities, rather than on critical events or dramatic public incidents. He regards all people as being "practical theorists," collaboratively creating meanings and understandings of one another's activities. His methodology has a strongly monistic vector, there being no radical difference between sociologists and other men. At the same time, however, Garfinkel criticizes all normal sociology for failing to understand this properly. In other words, while he sees the continuity between professional and practical theorists, he also wants professional social theorists to behave in a more self-conscious manner than practical theorists, by becoming aware of their own involvement in the common sense world. Seeing social reality as created and sustained in the mundane activities of ordinary men, Garfinkel seeks to understand social situations from the "inside" as it were, as it appears to the men who live it; he seeks to communicate *their* sense of things, with an almost Nietzschean hostility to conceptualization and abstraction, and particularly by avoiding the conceptualizations conventional to normal sociology. Thus he erects few or none of the conceptual towers that both Parsons and Goffman like to build.

Even though he stresses the significance of time as intrinsic to meaning, Garfinkel's, like Goffman's, social world is a world outside of time. He is ahistorical and does not limit his generalizations to a given era or a specific culture. While deeply concerned with how definitions of social reality become established, he is not interested in why one definition of social reality becomes prevalent in one time, or place, or group, and another elsewhere. The process by which social reality becomes defined and established is not viewed by Garfinkel as entailing a process of struggle among competing groups' definitions of reality; and the outcome, the common sense conception of the world, is not seen as having been shaped by institutionally protected power differences. There is a way in which Garfinkel's concern with the anchoring character of shared meanings expresses a sense of a world not in conflict so much as in dissolution, of a diffuse multiformity of values rather than a clearly structured conflict of political and ideological groups. He seems to be responding to a social world in which sex, drugs, religion, family, school, all are uncertain, and in which the threat is more of an entropic winding-down rather than of taut conflict.

In an old conceptual distinction, Garfinkel is the ethnographer of the folkways rather than of the mores. Quite unlike Parsons, Garfinkel apparently does not believe that social stability requires that the rules or values be deeply internalized within persons or their character structure. In fact, the tacit implication of his ingenious and upsetting "experiments" is that men (most particularly college students) may rather easily be made to act at variance with them.[9] In this, Garfinkel seems to operate with much the same assumption that Goffman does: that is, both seem to premise a social world resting on tacit understandings that, however important as a foundation for all else, are still fragile and rather readily eluded. The cultural foundation, in short, is precarious, and its security apparently rests, in some part, on its sheer invisibility or taken-for-grantedness. Once made visible, however, it rather readily loses its hold. Unlike Parsons, Garfinkel communicates no sense of the unshakable stability of social foundations.

The concrete differences in the specific character of these varying tacit rules is not examined by Garfinkel. His attention, rather, is largely focused, first, on demonstrating their sheer existence, and, second, on demonstrating their role in providing a secure background for social interaction. As a result, there is a strong tendency for each rule thus exposed to appear somewhat arbitrary, for each is assigned no distinct function or differential importance and is, in effect, interchangeable with a variety of others, all making some contribution to a stabilizing framework for interaction. To perform this stabilizing function, some other rule might conceivably do just as well. His emphasis, then, leads to a conception of these rules as conventions, and thus to a view of society as dependent on the merely conventional—that is, on what are, in effect, rules of the game. Garfinkel normally exposes these rules through game-like "demonstrations" of what happens when some men, without informing others of their intent, deliberately proceed to violate these tacit understandings. And all parts of society, including science (with its rigorous method), are seen to depend on these common sense, arbitrary rules and procedures.

Unlike Goffman, Garfinkel takes no sensuous delight in the world of appearances. Rather, he conceives of the truly important part in the social world as practically invisible, as so familiar that it is a world taken-for-granted and unnoticed. The task Garfinkel sets himself is to destroy this taken-for-grantedness and to strip the cultural foundation of its cloak of invisibility. He is not engaged in locating the familiar commonplaces within the framework of some theory thereby to endow it with deeper meaning and enrich experience with it, which is one of the most deeply Romantic of Goffman's tactics. Garfinkel aims, primarily, at baring and unmasking the invisible commonplace by violating it in some manner until it betrays its presence.

It would be a mistake, however, to conclude that Garfinkel is engaged only in an archaeological excavation of hidden cultural foundations, for his excavations proceed largely through the demolition of small-scale worlds. If Goffman's work may be conceived of as an attack upon certain forms of lower-middle-class smugness, or morality, Garfinkel's is an attack upon the common sense of *reality*. Thus students are instructed to engage friends or acquaintances in ordinary conversation and, without indicating that anything special is afoot, to pretend ignorance of everyday expressions: "What do you mean, she had a 'flat tire'?" "What do you mean, 'how is she feeling'?" Undergraduates are assigned the task of spending time with their families, all the while acting as if they were boarders in their own homes. Again, students are instructed to engage someone in conversation and, while doing so, to assume that the other person is trying to trick or mislead them; or they are instructed to talk with people while bringing their noses almost to the touching point.

At first blush, these demonstrations seem to have a prankish collegiate quality, but this view of them as "harmless fun" wears thin as one reads the reactions of the "victims," as Garfinkel sometimes correctly calls them[10]: "She became nervous and jittery, her face and hand movements . . . uncontrolled."[11] "Quarreling, bickering, and hostile motivations become discomfitingly visible."[12] There was "irritation and exasperated anger,"[13] "nasty developments frequently occurred."[14] "I actually came to feel somewhat hated and by the time I left the table I was quite angry."[15] "Attempted avoidance, bewilderment, acute embarrassment, furtiveness, and above all uncertainties of these as well as uncertainties of fear, hope, and anger were characteristic."

These, then, are the pained responses normal to persons whose conceptions of social reality have been violated, and, indeed, quite deliberately assaulted. It must be understood, however, that painful though they are, these responses are not unanticipated but expected by Garfinkel. As he says in one connection, the responses "*should be* those of bewilderment, uncertainty, internal conflict, psycho-sexual isolation, acute, and nameless anxiety along with various symptoms of acute depersonalization."[16]

The cry of pain, then, is Garfinkel's triumphal moment; it is dramatic confirmation of the existence of certain tacit rules governing social interaction and of their importance to the persons involved. That he feels free to inflict these costs on others, on his students, their families, friends, or passersby—and to encourage others to do so—is not, I would suggest, evidence of a dispassionate and detached attitude toward the social world, but of a readiness to use it in cruel ways. Here, objectivity and sadism become delicately intertwined. The demonstration is the message, and the message seems to be that anomic normlessness is no longer merely something that the sociologist studies in the social world, but is now something that *he inflicts upon it* and is the basis of his method of investigation.

There is nothing that is quite so reminiscent of Garfinkel's demonstrational methodology as the "happening," which, however, usually lacks the unblinking hurtfulness of Garfinkel's techniques, and may also have a larger social purpose. In the "happening," something like this occurs: shortly before noon, say, in Amsterdam, a group of youths gathers in one of the busier squares and, just as luncheon traffic begins to mount, they release into the streets one hundred chickens. These, of course, distract and amaze the drivers; accidents may happen; traffic halts; crowds gather, further tying up traffic; routines come to a stop as everyone gathers around to watch and laugh as the police attempt to catch the chickens. Garfinkel might say that the community has now learned the importance of one hitherto unnoticed rule at the basis of everyday life: chickens must not be dropped in the streets in the midst of the lunch hour rush.

Behind both the "happening" and the ethnomethodological demonstration there is a common impulse: to bring routines to a halt, to make the world and time stop. Both rest on a similar perception of the conventional character of the underlying rules, on a view of them as lacking in intrinsic value, as arbitrary albeit essential to the conduct of routine. And both are forms of hostility to the "way things are," although the ethnomethodologist's is a veiled hostility, aimed at less dangerous targets. Both communicate at least one lesson: the vulnerability of the everyday world to disruption by violation of tacitly held assumptions. Underneath the ethnomethodological demonstration, then, there is a kind of anarchical impulse, a genteel anarchism, at least when compared with the "happening." It is an anarchism that will, to some extent, appeal to youth and others alienated from the status quo, and that may also congenially resonate the sentiments of some on the New Left. It is a way in which the alienated young may, with relative safety, defy the established order and experience their own potency. The ethnomethodological "demonstration" is, in effect, a kind of microconfrontation with and nonviolent resistance to the status quo. It is a substitute and symbolic rebellion against a larger structure which the youth cannot, and often does not wish to, change. It substitutes the available rebellion for the inaccessible revolution.

In any event, it seems quite evident that, while nominally centered on the *analysis* of social order, Garfinkel's ethnomethodology is infused with a structure of sentiments directly at variance with the Parsonsian. The very frequency with which its often dense and elephantine formulations are attractive to the young is indicative of its congeniality to the new structure of sentiments held by some of them, as well as of their readiness to seize upon almost anything that promises an alternative to Parsonsianism. If Goffman's social theory was a "cool" or "hip" sociology congenial to the politically passive 1950's, Garfinkel's is a sociology more congenial to the activistic 1960's, and particularly to the more politically rebellious campuses of the present period.

HOMANS: THE TOUGH-MINDED WORLD OF EXCHANGE

Still another set of theoretical models significantly different from the Parsonsian is that which has been developed by George Homans and Peter Blau in their theories of social exchange. One characteristic that sets them well apart from the Functionalist model is the insistence with which they spell out their economic assumptions and place them at the center of analysis. Men are seen as exchanging gratifications. Indeed, all forms of behavior come to be viewed as having certain market characteristics, as susceptible to variations in supply and demand, as subject to considerations of marginal utility. The effort is to get beneath morality, to discover an abiding substructure upon which morality itself depends and on which institutional survival rests. The aim is to probe underneath culturally structured social roles for the more elemental units of behavior. In Homans' work, as in Goffman's, there is a backing away from established institutions and culturally given roles; men appear not only as members of a specific society "but as members of a species." And also like Goffman, Homans now has an increasing and new awareness of the *precariousness* of things.

Unlike the Functionalist, Homans places no special reliance upon legitimacy and social norms to account for an institution's stability. Rather, Homans sees these as themselves dependent upon the gratifications that must come in forms men can enjoy not simply because they have been taught to do so, "but because they are men." Men as *homo sapiens*, embodied men, have come back into the picture, and Homans tells social scientists to stop talking as if society "were the big thing." The secret of society, he says, "is that it was made by men."

For all his behavioristic psychology, then, Homans is at one with Goffman and Garfinkel in assigning an active role to men as builders and users of social structures and social orders, and not simply as their receivers and transmitters. They are thus quite different from the more mechanistic, later Parsons, though sympathetic to the "voluntarism" that Parsons has long since abandoned. Despite the differences in their theoretical antecedents—for Homans it was B. F. Skinner, for Goffman, G. H. Mead and Kenneth Burke—and despite their very different conceptions of science and scientific method, they have these important convergences.

The difference between Goffman's and Homans' most basic metaphors—theater and exchange—reflects, in some part, their sensitivity to different layers in modern middle-class life. Goffman is open to the new middle class, while Homans is open to the assumptions and sentiments of its older, more solidly established, propertied segments. Homans unabashedly insists on the importance of what men get from and give to one another, on their mutual usefulness, as the central source of social solidarity. Goffman, however, says that it is illusions that count and, in the tradition of Barnum and other great "merchandisers," he holds that one does not sell the frankfurter but the sizzle. Homans rejects Parsonsian Functionalism, at least in part, from the standpoint of a no-nonsense tough-mindedness that wishes to accept the reality of social life without the illusions of morality. Goffman also is tough-minded, but he denies that there is any hard core of underlying reality; he denies that either moral values or usefulness are what hold society together, but sees this, instead, as resting on the mutual acceptance of illusion.

What I have said above of Goffman's, Garfinkel's, and certainly Homans' work is, of course, sketchy and incomplete in the extreme. My aim has not been to present a systematic discussion of their theoretical views, but only to describe them sufficiently to indicate the manner in which their domain assumptions and sentiments are notably different from those embedded in the dominant Functionalist model and thus to suggest how deep is the challenge they now pose for it.

THEORY AND ITS INFRASTRUCTURE

To some degree, the elaboration of a social theory has a life of its own; technical concerns provide it with a measure of autonomy. At the same time, however, theory is embedded in and shaped by a variety of other potent forces; the sentiments, the domain assumptions, the conceptions of reality accented by personal experience, all these constitute its individual and social grounding. This grounding or infrastructure links the theory, on the one side, to the individual theorist and, on the other, to his larger society. For, this infrastructure is "in" the theorist, but, at the same time, it derives from his experience in society where it is shared by some others.

Social theory, then, changes in at least two ways and for two reasons. First, it changes through "internal," technical development and elaboration, in conformity with such distinctive rules of relevance and decision-making as it may have. Second, social theory may also change as a consequence of changes in the infrastructure in which it is anchored: that is, as a consequence of changes in the social and cultural structure as these are mediated by the changing sentiments, domain assumptions, and personal reality of the theorist and those around him. Any effort to deal with the *extra*-technical sources of theoretical change, if it fails to locate the theorist in society, can only produce a "psychology" of knowledge, overstating the importance of the unique characteristic of the theorist as a person; correspondingly, any such effort that does not relate the theory to the person of the theorist can produce only an unconvincing "sociologism" that fails to explain *how* the society comes to affect social theory; in the end, it can discover only a "Hamlet without Hamlet." Our concern with the infrastructure of sentiments, assumptions, and personal reality is an effort to avoid this Scylla and Charybdis: to find a way of coming close to the human system, the theorist who does theoretical work, and, at the same time, to provide systematic connections with the other systems, the society and culture to which his work is related and by which it is influenced.

Social theory then lives on two levels, its technical or formal level, and its infrastructure. And it changes for reasons that involve the relationship of the two levels in subtle and complex interplay. Much of the stability and continuity of any social theory, or its instability and change, derive from the way these two levels interact. In a general way, we can suggest that tensions always arise within theories—or, more exactly, in the course of men's efforts to work with and relate to them—when there develops some kind of disparity, disjunction, malintegration, or "contradiction" between these two levels.

For example, the technical elaborations of a social theory may so outrun and overwhelm its original anchorages in some infrastructure that the theory may come to be seen by some as "trivial" or "formalistic." In other words, the technical development of a social theory may lead it to lose contact or to conflict with the personal reality, domain assumptions, or sentiments of some, who then react by feeling that the theory is not "telling it like it is"; they may find that the theory is "absurdly" unconvincing, or that it inhibits certain feelings they already have, or that it activates certain sentiments that are unpleasant. When a theory resting on one infrastructure, one specific set of sentiments, domain assumptions, and personal reality—is encountered by those whose *own* infrastructure is quite different, the theory is experienced as manifestly unconvincing. This may also occur when men's infrastructures are changing, when people with new sentiments, assumptions, or personal reality are emerging and are encountering social theories that embody older infrastructures.

The theory that we "see," whether "housed" in lectures, articles, books, or conversations, is always a product of technical concerns and infrastructures in mutual interaction. The more that a theorist defines his work as "complete" or "finished," the more he presents it in a public rather than private performance, and the more that he communicates it to technically specialized audiences, then the more will he tend to present it as if it were an "autonomous" performance made in sole and exclusive conformity with the special rules of theorizing, and the more will he omit and conceal indications of its linkages to the extratechnical infrastructure. The theory will, in short, be "dressed up" and made presentable; the infrastructure's implication in the theory will be secreted—suppressed or repressed—and hidden from the theorist's audience and, indeed, often from the theorist himself.

In any event, a major source of change in social theory, and particularly of shifts in the fundamental paradigms of a theoretical community, is when the technical directives of social theory have become dissonant with the dispositions arising from the infrastructure. Such a dissonance eventuates in apathy toward or criticism of the existent theory; it generates pressure to change. If the dissonance between these two levels is sharp enough, the resultant pressure can be thought of as precipitating a theoretical crisis. It is, in large measure, because I believe that this is what is presently happening, and, most particularly, that changes in the social and cultural structure have produced among the younger generation new infrastructures which are dissonant with Functional theory, that I foresee a crisis intensifying and deepening in the near future. The most important indication of the new, theoretically consequential infrastructure of the younger generation is, I believe, the emergence of the New Left.

NEW LEFT AND NEW INFRASTRUCTURE

The "New Left" or the "New Radicalism" is a world-wide phenomenon. It is a social movement of loose and sprawling boundaries encompassing a very heterogeneous variety of political dispositions whose coherence rests, at this point, primarily on the new infrastructures—rather than on political programs or articulated ideologies—of the younger generation. In the United States it is closely linked to the rising civil rights movement for "Black Liberation" and has roots both in the agricultural communities of the South and in the ghettoes of the city, North and South. Among Blacks, in particular, this struggle is oriented to "stomach questions" as well as to related issues of civil liberties. This movement has developed with a rapidity that has confounded and antiquated those trained in the older theoretical and political traditions. Within the space of hardly a decade it has moved from the call for "Freedom Now" to the demand for "Black Power."

The civil rights struggle has been a training ground, inspiration, and stimulus to the New Left, composed of articulate, increasingly radicalized college students, and, perhaps, particularly those who have been herded together in the mammoth, bureaucratized public universities. The "stomach questions" are not central for them, although they do lend support to the struggle of the welfare poor and Blacks against such deprivation. Crucial to the *consolidation* of the new student radicalism in the United States is the increasing opposition to the war in Vietnam.

Far from being "materialists," these students are often deliberately "utopian" and activistically idealistic. The value emphases of the new student radicals center on equality and freedom, but they do not stop there. They also include disgust at affluence without dignity; desire for beauty as well as democracy; belief in creativity rather than consensus; wish for community and communal values, and vehement rejection of depersonalized bureaucracy; desire to build a "counter society" with "parallel institutions" and not simply to be integrated into and be accepted by the dominant institutions; hostility to what is conceived of as the dehumanization and alienation of a cash-nexus society; preference for individuated, intensely felt, and self-generated interpersonal style, including fuller sexual expression and experimentation. They want what they think of as warm human relations and a kind of "inventive sensuality," rather than the rational discipline of either the independent professions or the bureaucratic establishments.

Radical as it is, the New Left does not engage in hero-worship of Marx. It often critically distinguishes the younger Marx of "alienation," whom it prefers to the older anti-utopian Marx, and it frequently rejects the *Realpolitik* of historical Marxism. Far from uniformly relying on the working class for support, the student radicals sometimes fear that it can be bought off—as some of them also believe the Black ghettoes will be—by the affluent Welfare State. If they want a working-class alliance, they also seek allies among the members of the different cultural ghettoes, among whom they include: college students; the alienated rich, whom they are often prepared to treat instrumentally; the inhabitants of the welfare and Black ghettoes, even though some may doubt their long-range commitment to basic social change; and members of different types of deviant groups. New Left youth are often hopeful about the role of artists, believing them to be a group whose work embodies a sharp critique of conventional values as well as manifesting a new vision of alternative values. Implicit in their interest in the artist, and in aesthetics more generally, is their conviction that what is now required by American society is a great deal more than an economic or material change: rather, it is a change in the total culture.

This radicalism seems to be a genuinely new social movement, in the United States as elsewhere, having jettisoned some of the most basic ground rules of the older liberal-left politics; it promises to be of abiding significance. Aside from the fact that it is, on one of its sides, firmly rooted in the massive needs of the Black population, and thus in problems that are not momentary, we must also remember that its university-based contingent is of growing importance. This is so, if for no other reason than that there are now more than 7,000,000 college students in the United States. There are more college students than farmers.

The New Left, the growing radicalization of the student in the United States, promises to be of particular importance for the future of Functionalism and Academic Sociology. This is because the group's domain assumptions, its structure of sentiments, and its personal reality are deeply at variance with those embedded in Functional theory. The New Left in the United States speaks, in a deliberately utopian voice, of Freedom Now, while Functionalism has never centered its interest on freedom or on equality, but has rather, invested itself in *order* and social equilibrium. The New Left is willing to support all manner of effort to achieve its values, and, even where it advocates "nonviolence," it is clear that social change is more important to it than is social order. It is not obsessed with order and is quite ready to risk disorder if it feels this to be justified by the high values to which it is committed. Indeed, going to jail on behalf of a good cause has become a mark of pride and prestige among the youth of the New Left.

Far from advocating moral consensus, which is so crucial in Functionalism, sections of the New Left want "parallel institutions" or a total "counter society"; their appetite is for the sharpest criticism rather than for consensus and continuity. Indeed, their movement has broadened from a limited opposition against conventional domestic politics to a resistance against official foreign policy and, in particular, its imperialistic expressions. Thus, far from being imbued with the mystique of authority and the metaphysics of hierarchy, many of them are utopian democrats and dissensualist rebels against constituted authority. Their ingrained anti-authoritarianism is also manifested in their preference for leadership and organizational forms that minimize the role of formal authority: they will brook no talk about the "functional indispensability of stratification." And far from supposing, as Functionalists often do, that the great cementing sentiment in society is "respect," what they often seek in human relations is "warmth," spontaneity, and sensuality in its broadest sense. Unlike Functionalists who stress that social system stability depends upon conformity with self-restraining and self-denying moral values, the new radicals speak in the name of gratification, and against all poverty, material and emotional. For these and other reasons, it is clear that there is the sharpest difference between the domain assumptions and sentiments underlying Functionalism and those of the New Left.

While this New Left is still far too young to have produced its own social theory, it is plain that its new structure of sentiments and domain assumptions are already leading it to exert the sharpest pressure upon Functionalist professors and Functional theory. Its admiration for the young Marx is only incidentally an index of commitment to a specific brand of theory. Interest in the *young* Marx is, most fundamentally, a way of expressing the desire to be radical; it constitutes a search for a symbol and a theory that may correspond with the new structure of sentiments. The shift to the young Marx is thus expressive of the emergence of a new structure of sentiments among the young; a structure of sentiments deeply incompatible with that found in Functionalism and one which will, I am convinced, in time produce the audience for and the creators of significantly new social theories, even as it is already undermining the appeal of Functionalism.

The New Left is at the very center of the changing academic atmosphere. In this changing college atmosphere with its manifestly changing structure of sentiments, the old rhetorical strategies of Functionalism lose their appeal and persuasiveness. The young new radical is not persuaded that Functionalism is not conservative by a rhetoric that seeks to show the convergences of Functional theory with Marxism. For many of the new radicals, unlike the student generation of the late 1940's and 1950's, to whom Robert Merton first made that appeal, have little sentimental attachment to Marxism; indeed, some not only regard it as devoid of radical sensibilities but as downright "square."

It is not simply, however, that the old distinctions between the political right and left are increasingly experienced as irrelevant, and it is not simply that orthodox Marxism itself is sometimes alien to the new structure of sentiments that has arisen among the new radicals. It is that, to some young radicals Marxism and Functionalism may, indeed, seem more alike than different—just as Merton claimed—but it is precisely because they see them as similar and as offering little to choose between, that they will reject Functionalism no less than vulgar Marxism, and thus compound the crisis of Functionalism.

SOCIAL THEORY AND THE UNIVERSITY

The importance of these young people of the New Left and their various sympathizers is not only in their numbers but in their social *location*. What makes them of special significance for Functional theory, in particular, and social theory, in general, is that they are often college students. The appreciable extent to which students exert *intellectual* pressure upon teachers is something that academic establishments have for long managed to keep a "dark secret." The decisive consideration, here, is that because so many in the New Left are students, they are directly involved in the very academic establishments in which social theory today is made and taught, daily reproduced and informally tested. Students are an integral part of the very social system that transmits and produces social theory. It is inevitable, therefore, that they will exert considerable pressure on any social theory, whether established or newly developing, in American universities today. Any systematic social theory about social theory must, at some point, explore the manner in which the "academic" context and the student-teacher, or disciple-master, relationships in it affect the course of theory-work and influence theory-products.

Since the Classical or third period in the development of Academic Sociology, the production of social theory has been almost entirely the monopoly of academicians working in university milieux; consequently, almost any major change in the organization of the university or its personnel is a potential source of change in social theory. Paradoxically, however, even though most social theorists today are academicians, they have given little systematic analysis to the role of the university in shaping social theory. The tacit assumption seems to be that the university shapes social theory—insofar as it does so at all—primarily by housing theorists, by allowing them to get on with their individual efforts, and by providing them with a vague collegial stimulation and with research facilities that enable them to "test" theory, once it is formulated. Above all, theory-making is commonly regarded as a totally *faculty*-centered activity, one that can be understood entirely apart from the faculty's relationships with the students.

It is tacitly assumed that changes in a faculty's relationship with students or changes in the orientations and interests of students themselves may be safely ignored in accounting for the career of a theory. The student is largely seen as the passive recipient (or audience) for a theoretical product or performance, but his reaction to specific social theories is, presumably, not consequential for their content, focus, character, or development. The assumption seems to be that whether or not a student finds a theory interesting or boring, relevant or irrelevant, will have no consequences in his behavior toward those who present it to him; or that such responses do not affect the faculty member toward whom they are directed; or that, if they do affect him, it is only in his capacity as an educator but not as a working *theorist*.

Even when theory is located in the context of faculty-student relationships, this is usually seen as a one-way influence. The faculty is seen as "transmitting" or "teaching" the theory to the student, but no reciprocal influence by the student is expected to be of consequence for the theory. Yet from the standpoint of the most elementary precepts of sociological analysis, which do, indeed, insist on the importance of a measure of mutuality and reciprocity as intrinsic to the nature of any social relationship, such a one-way image of faculty "transmission" to passive, recipient students must be regarded as marvelously wrong-headed—particularly when held by sociologists. One must insist, rather, that sociologists are like other men; their work performances and products are shaped in essentially the same manner as are other men's, and social relationships in which they are involved are essentially like those that others experience. In short, there are serious theoretical grounds for holding that *even* the work of social theorists may be influenced, and *even* by their students. It is, very largely, because of this that I have stressed the importance of the emerging changes among students, and, in particular, their growing radicalization, in appraising the prospects of development in social theory.

THEORY, INFRASTRUCTURE, AND NEW GENERATIONS

To sum up briefly thus far: every social theory rests on some infrastructure of tacit domain assumptions, on some set of sentiments, and on some set of experiences, which define what people take to be real: that is, their personal reality. Every social theory has certain implications and consequences for the infrastructure, which is, on the one side, embedded in the theorist and his audiences and, on the other, affected by the larger cultural and social surround. This infrastructure of domain assumptions, sentiments, and the sense of what is real mediates between social theories and other parts of the social world. Every social theory resonates congenially or discomforts some sentiments more than others, but certainly not all equally. Every social theory has implications about what is real in the world, and thus has implications about what is both desirable and possible in the social world. Every social theory "fits" certain infrastructures and is dissonant with others.

Tension-generating dissonances that affect social theories may thus arise in two fundamental ways. For one, the theories may be elaborated and developed in formal or technical ways, and this may make them lose contact or come into tension with their once supportive infrastructure. For another, the infrastructure itself may change radically in consequence of changes in the larger society, with the possible result—even without any new disconfirming evidence at all—that the established theory begins to seem irrelevant, absurd, disinteresting, or manifestly false, to those within whom the new infrastructure has most fully and sharply developed.

The emergence of such a theoretically-consequential new infrastructure is most important when it is strong enough to sustain and express itself despite the disapproval and resistance of those bearing the traditional infrastructures. New infrastructures that affect theoretical development tend to be collectively expressed, therefore, in the experiences and lives of numbers of people, rather than in only a few isolated individuals; in particular, they are often borne by a cohort of age peers, a new generation. A new generation is, at times, raised in a new and yet common way, under new but common conditions, and confronting new problems in common. While new and old generations may then confront the "same" political or social issue, for example, a war, a revolution, a depression, this is not the same *experience* or "reality" for them; for the old generation, of course, interprets it in the light of their own longer and previous experiences. It is, in consequence, a *different* experience for them than it is for the younger generation, and all the more so as the younger also assumes the older generation to have been responsible for its management or mismangement.

Moreover, by reason of their shared experiences, members of the younger generation develop solidarities that support and validate the new infrastructure and that provide informal contexts in which it may be given open and easy expression, even before they have developed a new "language" that can articulate their new assumptions, sentiments, and experiences. A new generation, then, can often provide group support for emergent infrastructures that make established social theories seem obsolescent. It can often mount an active attack upon established theories, providing leverage that facilitates mass disengagement from old theories and, at the same time, by providing mutual encouragement for the development of new theoretical alternatives. This is, in large measure, the significance of the current development of the New Left, whose members clearly manifest a new infrastructure and who also have clearly developed a protective sense of generational solidarity.

SOCIOLOGY AND THE NEW LEFT

The New Left, to repeat, is no one, single ideological or political outlook. It is a very loose network of different, vaguely defined reactions to a social situation in which there has been a continual deterioration of conventional conceptions for both morality and utility, attended by a growing sense of institutional hypocrisy. The New Left characteristically denounces both the moral hypocrisy of the older generation and, as well, the "irrelevance" of its own education. Some sections of the New Left are presently pursuing a search for a new sociology appropriate to the new social reality they experience, largely by attempting to refocus Marxism in the young Marx of alienation, the most *anti*-utilitarian phase of Marx's work. Whatever form it finally assumes, it seems likely that the sociology of the New Left will be influenced by the new character of the utilitarian culture in which it now finds itself. Utilitarianism will remain one base for the transition to a new radical sociology, while morality will be the other. Just as classical Marxism was complexly influenced by the older utilitarianism, it seems almost certain that a new radical sociology will, *mutatis mutandis*, be influenced by the new utilitarianism.

Despite Marx's biting theoretical critique of Benthamite utilitarianism, Marxism also embodied an underlying structure of sentiments partly congenial to the culture of utilitarianism. On the level of their structures of sentiments, the traditional bourgeoisie and traditional Marxist may therefore feel closer to one another than to the new radical. Indeed, there is a middle-aged counterpart to the "trust no one over thirty" generational solidarity of the New Left, which sees all other political ideologies as united in opposition to the New Left. Thus in a hostile review of Daniel and Gabriel Cohn-Bendit's *Obsolete Communism: The Left-Wing Alternative*, one reviewer remarks that it "will appeal only to the profoundly disoriented and totally alienated. . . . For the rest of us, conservative, liberal, socialist, and even communist, it can serve only as a warning."[17]

Marxism never really doubted the importance of being useful, although it insisted that this be a usefulness for humanity. Its fundamental objection to capitalist society was to the dominating significance of exchange-value, not to use-value. It objected to the transformation of men's labor into a commodity, but it continued to emphasize the value and importance of work. Marx's critique of utilitarianism was arrested by his simultaneous critique of the bourgeois morality of natural rights, as well as by his polemic against utopian socialism for having mistakenly relied upon morality as a lever for social change. The latter polemic, which viewed morality as superstructural, came to overshadow the critique of utilitarianism and finally to edge it into a subsidiary place, particularly as historical Marxism came to define itself as a "scientific socialism."

In some part, Marx's critiques of morality and utility were polemics against sham and hypocrisy, against a society that claimed to produce useful things and against men who claimed to be respectable, but both of whom would produce anything— useful or not—to turn a profit. Marx looked to history as a substitute for morality and utility. For men would do what they were constrained to do by their social position in a given society at a certain stage in the development of its contradictions. Historical necessity was thus regarded as resolving the contradiction between morality and reality. Marxism saw men as agents of history and sometimes came to believe that they might be used to further it.

The modern radical, however, is faced with a different situation. He has encountered not only the venal hypocrisy of the bourgeoisie, but also the *Realpolitik* of its enemy, historical Marxism. As part of the post-Stalinist generation, the young radical clearly recognizes that no one has clean hands. He lives in an historical period in which the viable alternative to the market, namely, the bureaucratic organization, is seen to possess its own distinctive irrationalities; thus it is not only (as it was to an earlier generation of radicals) the sheer venality of the system, not the doing of terrible things to acquire money and property, which disgusts him. He also sees that men will do awful things for the collective welfare no less than for individual gain: for God, country, history, and socialism. And now, moreover, living in an increasingly automated society, the young radical observes that it is not merely labor but self as well that is bought and sold. One of the distinctive responses that he therefore makes is his great insistence on the importance of an ethic of absolute ends; his rejection of the present is formulated in terms of moral outrage and disgust.

It is thus not at all the sheer difficulty of "getting ahead" that underpins the new radicalism. Nor is it the lack of means adequate to the achievement of individual success. This was a source of much of the radicalism of the depressed 1930's, but it is not central to the experience of the affluent 1960's. Much of the new radicalism today is a response to the *meaninglessness of success* rather than to the lack of it. Success is often experienced as meaningless because many who have been visibly successful are judged not to deserve it, by virtue either of their moral qualities or of their talents and utility to society. Success is not viewed as proving anything about the worthiness, and hence the legitimacy, of the successful.

The process through which success is achieved is viewed increasingly as a "game," and, indeed, this is one of the social sources of the increasing popularity of game models in the social sciences. For, in such games winning is understood to be partly a matter of luck and partly a matter of a limited cleverness in adapting to those "rules of the game" whose only justification is that they allow one to get on with it; lacking any intrinsic or higher legitimacy, the rules are not deeply internalized. In "games" certain means of playing are "ruled out," but not because they are felt to be either immoral or ineffective.[18] Neither sheer utility nor morality governs the rules by which ends are pursued in games. A "good" game is not necessarily one in which the player wins, or wins anything of value. As Goffman indicates, the point of a game is absorption in its ongoing *process*.

As the modern radical views it, the trouble with the social order is not that it fails to pay off, but that it pays off in a worthless currency. Modern radicalism of the New Left variety expresses the experience of those who are already included in the system but who want "out," rather than of those who, marginal or excluded, want "in." Modern radicalism, therefore, is based upon a personal reality and a corresponding structure of sentiments in which moral rather than stomach issues are the central concern. Modern student radicalism is the radicalism of affluence: it is the radicalism of those whose hopes have been destroyed rather than of those whose bodies have been stunted or whose ambitions have been thwarted. (In the United States this has become a major source of divergence between the New Left and the movement for Black Liberation.) For the middle-class student radical, the affluence and temperate moderation of the system are not experienced as compensations for what is felt to be the system's most inexcusable failure—its aimlessness.

The modern radical is faced with an utilitarian culture that exists on various interlocking and contradictory levels. He may feel opposed to all of them, but he has also been exposed to all of them, and, indeed, he is sometimes critical of one level only from the standpoint of the other levels he has partially assimilated. Its three distinguishable levels are: individualistic, social, and marketing utilitarianism. Each emerged during different periods in the history of the middle class, but all three continue to exist into the present, superimposed on one another like overlapping shingles. Individualistic utilitarianism was largely the product of the early, family-centered entrepreneur, and was predominantly economic and individualistic in its focus. Social utilitarianism took hold among the middle class during the period of the growth of large-scale, bureaucratic, industrial organization and was consolidated during the emergence of the Welfare State. Marketing utilitarianism, the most modern form, arises among the new middle class in a tertiary economy where the relation between utility and reward is increasingly irrational and has an arbitrary, game-like character.

In some part, the New Left both adopts and rejects all three utilitarian standpoints. Some young radicals regard social utilitarianism from the standpoint of the older, and more individualistic, utilitarianism and see it, for example, as producing a deplorable dependence of deprived strata on the Welfare State. Nevertheless, they may also believe it deeply wrong to allow such deprivation to go unremedied and feel that society has a collective responsibility to help. One distinctive element in the standpoint of the modern radical, however, is his new distrust of the bureaucratic expressions of social utilitarianism and, correspondingly, the renewed vigor of his individualism. Indeed, the politics of some in the New Left may be closer in its audacity to the "public be damned" individualism of the Robber Barons than to the unctuous social utilitarianism of old line social workers.

Many among the New Left also view marketing utilitarianism with deep contempt; they counterpose to its other-directed concern for appearances an insistence that each man "do his own thing," regardless of what others think or of how it looks. At the same time, however, there do seem to be some tendencies in the New Left that bring it close to the dramaturgical perspectives of a marketing utilitarianism concerned with sheer appearance. It occasionally seems that some regard the "revolt" against the establishment as a "happening" that is gratifying in and of itself, and quite apart from its demonstrable effectiveness in transforming the status quo. Yet the New Left also welcomes such revolts because it believes they unmask and strip the status quo of its protective appearances and reveal its hidden, deeper reality.

Many among the New Left of today have little sympathy left for an "ethic of responsibility"; in short, they reject a prudent concern for consequences. Not a few among the New Left have a similar disdain for keeping up "appearances." The New Left is tired of computing consequences and is tired of people who, it feels, have long done this without any substantial return for the moral costs they have paid. Its dominant drift will, I suspect, be toward an anti-utilitarian sociology; hence its already obvious attraction to the "critical sociology" of the Frankfurt School. Yet there are those in its own ranks who are quick to indicate that planless rebellion converges at some point with dramaturgy, and that the revolution as theatrical "happening" is not enough. In short, there are those who will look to tomorrow in a more utilitarian vein; they want to know what was won by today's sacrifices.

In the end, I suspect, the future sociology of the New Left will seek both an economically sensitive neo-Marxism, which has an "opening" toward the practicality of utilitarianism, and a morally sensitive or critical sociology, open to a critique of the system from some external standpoint. To the extent that both dimensions can be brought together in some mixture that enables them to keep their contradictions in suspension, then such a new radical sociology may be able to avoid some of the pitfalls of a Marxism that embodies both moral and utilitarian sentiments, without fully

acknowledging either, as well as of an Academic Sociology that
rejects both political and moral responsibilities, while continuing
to produce political and moral consequences.

RÉSUMÉ

The coming crisis of Western Sociology, then, and particularly its
expression in Academic Sociology, is manifested: (1) by the drift
of the dominant Functionalist and Parsonsian models toward a
convergence with Marxism, which is to say, toward what was
previously one of its main polemical targets; (2) by the emerging
alienation of young sociologists from Functionalism; (3) by the
tendency of such individual expressions of alienation to develop
collective and organized forms; (4) by the growing technical
criticism of Functional theory; (5) by the transition from such
negative criticism to the development of positive and alternative
theories, embodying importantly different sentiments and assumptions, such as Goffman's, Garfinkel's, and Homans'; and (6) by the
development of a middle-range "social problems" research and
theory that are often oriented to values of "freedom" and "equality"
rather than of "order," as Functionalism tends to be.

Three forces contributing to this crisis have been considered:
(1) the appearance of new infrastructures, dissonant with established Functional theory, among the middle-class youth who have
a strategic closeness to the university milieux in which social theory
is made and transmitted; (2) developments internal to the Functionalist school itself, which have entailed a growing variability
and inviduation in its work—an entropy—and thus have obscured
the clarity and firmness of its theoretical boundaries and muddied
its distinctness as a special school; (3) the development of the
Welfare State, which has rapidly and greatly increased the resources available to sociology. Functionalists have been disposed
to accommodate to the Welfare State; but, at the same time, this
has been done only by generating tensions for assumptions that
have traditionally been central to the Functionalist model.

NOTES

1. K. Davis, "The Myths of Functional Analysis in Sociology and Anthropology," *American Sociological Review*, XXIV (1959), 757–773.

2. The growing variability in the interests and work styles of this seed group cannot be underestimated. Robert Merton's publication of *On the Shoulders of Giants* is only one noteworthy example; it is important not only as an indication of his own personal interests and unique style, but also as a particularly dramatic symptom of the growing individuation of styles in his peer group as a whole. In short, it has a sociological as well as a personal significance. This unusual book is noteworthy because of Mr. Merton's national eminence as an "elder statesman" of Functionalism and thus because of its variability-legitimating significance.

3. L. Lowenthal, "Biographies in Popular Magazines," *Radio Research 1942–1943*, P. E. Lazarsfeld and F. Stanton, eds. (New York: Duell, Sloan & Pearce, 1944).

4. Erving Goffman, *The Presentation of Self in Everyday Life* (Edinburgh: University of Edinburgh, 1956), p. 156.

5. *Ibid.*, p. 162.

6. For a discussion of the implication of Rousseau's work for the theory of alienation, see Iring Fetscher, *Rousseau's Politische Philosophie* (Neuwied: Hermann Luchterhand, 1960).

7. Harold Garfinkel, *Studies in Ethnomethodology* (Englewood Cliffs, N.J.: Prentice-Hall, 1967). Garfinkel is at pains to express his indebtedness to Parsons: for example, "The terms, 'collectivity' and 'collectivity membership' are intended in strict accord with Talcott Parsons' usage in the *Social System* . . . and in the general introduction to *Theories of Society*." (P. 57. Cf. also p. 76, Footnote 1.)

8. In consequence of his interest in this, Garfinkel explains that "the *et cetera* clause, its properties, and the consequences of its use have been prevailing topics of study and discussion among the members of the Conferences on Ethnomethodology that have been in progress at the University of California, Los Angeles, and the University of Colorado since February 1962, with aid of a grant from the U.S. Air Force Office of Scientific Research . . . extended studies will be found in unpublished papers by Bittner, Garfinkel, MacAndrews, Rose, and Sacks; in transcribed talks given by Bittner, Garfinkel, and Sacks . . . and in Conference transcriptions." (*Ibid.*, p. 73.)

9. Thus, in probing the no-bargaining, one-price rule, Garfinkel indicates that "because of its 'internalized' character the student-customers should have been fearful and shamed by the prospective assignment (that is, to bargain over "one-price" goods), and shamed by having done it," but, by and large, he claims this was not the outcome. Many students, says Garfinkel, simply learned that you can, indeed, bargain. (*Ibid.*, p. 69.)

10. *Ibid.*, p. 44.

11. *Ibid.*, p. 43.

12. *Ibid.*, p. 46.

13. *Ibid.*, p. 48.

14. *Ibid.*, p. 49.

15. *Ibid.*, p. 52.

16. *Ibid.*, p. 55. (Italics mine.)

17. *Times Literary Supplement* (London), November 28, 1968, p. 1328.

18. Cf. B. Suits, "Life, Perhaps, Is a Game," *Ethics*, 1967.

From Plato to Parsons:
The Infrastructure of
Conservative Social Theory

To understand the social character of Functionalism, and to appraise its adaptability in the face of crisis, it is important to see that the infrastructure on which it rests is not peculiar to a business society such as our own, or even to modern industrial societies more generally. It is clear, for example, that if we wanted to understand the social role of the Catholic Church, it would be important to remember that it does not exist only in capitalist societies, that it has existed in a variety of previous, very different economies, and that, as institutions go, it is a rather old one. There is an important sense in which much the same may be said about Functionalism.

Most particularly, the infrastructure on which Functionalism rests is a very ancient one, and its existence can, in some important respects, be traced back through European history to the pre-Christian era. The infrastructure of Functionalism cannot be understood solely as the product of a capitalist culture or of a middle-class or industrial society. This infrastructure does not become a type of modern sociology until fused with a scientific technostructure which is relatively new, yet this should not obscure the fact that the infrastructure itself is something much older and deeper. The infrastructure of Functionalism is consequential for the latter's ability to cope with the crisis it faces and to adapt to new situations within our own society or, for that matter, in societies that differ importantly from ours. For this reason, I shall attempt to document the antiquity of this infrastructure by comparing it, on a number of points, with that which may be found in one of the oldest systematic accounts of the human condition in the Western tradition, namely, Platonic theory.

My motive in doing this is not to demonstrate that Alfred North Whitehead was right in holding that all subsequent philosophy has been in the nature of a series of footnotes on Plato. And it is certainly not to demonstrate that the Greeks said it all, first! My point is, rather, that both Platonic and Functionalist theory have been rooted in an infrastructure, a set of domain assumptions and sentiments, that has been significantly consistent and that each, Platonic Philosophy and Functionalist Sociology, is, in part, to be understood as the expression of this common infrastructure that has been culturally transmitted and socially reproduced for some two thousand years. In short, my argument directs attention to the possible importance of a common, underlying, enduring pattern for understanding the social character and for appraising the future of Functionalism.

This comparison may seem an odd one, perhaps particularly to those sociologists who believe that theirs is a "young," immature, or adolescent discipline. It implies that the claim about the "youth" of Functional Sociology is a dubious one, if this is meant to refer to the most basic assumptions and sentiments with which it examines man and society. This, in turn, implies that those who speak of the youth of sociology have centered their conception of and hopes for sociology—far more narrowly than their complaints about "dust-bowl" empiricism might lead one to suspect—on the development of techniques and methods of research. The similarities to be shown between the infrastructures of Functionalism and Platonism will also imply that the development of Functionalism's *substantive* sociological theory has been operating within far more rigid limits than one might be led to think by the detailed technical elaborations given this theory during the last twenty-five years. A comparison between Platonism and Functionalism will imply, then, that such theoretical developments as have been made by the latter have often been variations on (and within) certain limited and ancient themes. The image of Academic Sociology that emerges is, in its dominant form, of a marriage between an octogenarian dowager and a young stud, between an ancient infrastructure and modern science. Fascinated by the new sciences, bent on assimilating and emulating them, Academic Sociology has scarcely noticed that its energies have often been leashed by the venerable lady ensconced in the new household.

THE PARTIALLY GOOD WORLD

We might begin by remembering that Plato[1] insists that God is good, which means that he has created everything "for the best." In the *Laws*, he maintains that men would do well to remember that each thing, down to the smallest, was created to perform a certain role in the world, and that each has its place in the cosmic organism. Plato begins with a kind of "teleological" Functionalism —assuming, that is, that the fit and goodness of things are not accidental but are brought about by mind. In the social world, as in the cosmos more generally, Plato feels that each thing has a special niche for which it has been intended in the larger world organism and, indeed, that each man has, and should adhere to, the special and single role in which he can best serve the society as a whole.

Plato, however, soon comes to believe that, while each thing was initially *created* for the best, it did not long remain that way. (From Plato's viewpoint, the Athens that killed his teacher and comrade, Socrates, was certainly far from the *best* city.) Plato, therefore, retreated from teleological Functionalism to his Theory of Ideas or Eternal Forms. In the latter theory, he says that things are the way they are not because this is "for the best," but insofar as they partake of their Ideal Form, a kind of hyper-spatially located Eternal Idea. Yet since Plato holds that God has used these Ideal Forms to impose an initial patterning on things, then, insofar as things do conform to an Ideal Form, they still have some, but a corrupted, good in them. The theory of Ideal Forms thus entails a kind of chastened Functionalism.

Although not teleological, Functional Sociology also began with an assumption that things in the social world are "functional" or, more plainly, for the best. The "trick of the game" was to find out how. How this was so, the way in which this happened, was the puzzle that the sociologist had to solve. Functionalists were enjoined to explain the persistence of seemingly senseless social patterns by diligently searching out the "hidden" ways in which they were functional or useful. As the English anthropologist, Audrey Richards, has understated it, this sometimes led to certain Procrustean explanations. Yet just as Platonism came to recognize that some things in the world were clearly not for the best, so did Functionalists come to recognize that social patterns should not be examined solely from the standpoint of their "functions" but also from the standpoint of their "*dys*functions;" they might, in effect, have a "corrupted" side to them.

And just as Platonism postulated that there are certain universal and Eternal Ideas, so did Functionalists postulate that social systems have certain "needs," "functional requisites," or "system problems." These, like Plato's Ideas, were also universal and eternal; and it is believed that, if men fail to satisfy or conform with their requirements, this produces difficulties and problems for social systems. Both theories, then, had an ahistorical approach to human disorders, and both centered their attention on ills that were not peculiar to any one time, place, or social system.

AMBIVALENCE TOWARD SOCIETY

Partly for this reason both Functionalism and Platonism also contain an ambivalence toward the status quo; both provide a basis for social criticism, but only a limited criticism, a criticism from within. The sources of such a limitation are built into some of the central domain assumptions of each theory.

In operating with a theory of Eternal Ideas or Forms, Platonism, for example, was provided with a basis for criticizing existent social institutions. It never had to say that "whatever is, is right." Since it assumed that the world of men participated in the Eternal Forms only imperfectly, Platonism could be assured that whatever is, is partly *corrupt*. Platonism *could* therefore take a critical and negative view of the world around it. But the theory of Eternal Forms also postulates that, if the social world is corrupt, this is because it is an inadequate copy of some Eternal Idea. Now, if every existent institution, say slavery, has somewhere a perfect and harmonious model of it—an Eternal Idea—then slavery must in some form be indispensable. The theory of Ideas, then, encourages a criticism of the very institutions for which, at the same time, it provides an apology. It was thus only the historically transient expressions of slavery that were criticized by Plato, but never the institution of slavery itself. The theory of Ideas implies that slavery was *sound* in its fundamental essence, even if corrupt in its historical form. While Platonism presented itself as an impartial and nonpartisan theory of social order, it was, however, a theory that postulated the permanence of *some* form of slavery. While Platonism presented itself as a theory of social order in general, valid for all time and all societies, it was, in fact, a social theory of a very limited kind of social order.

A similar contradiction permeates Functional theory, for a similar reason. Corresponding to the Platonist's Eternal Forms, Functionalists postulate that there are certain universal requisites or needs of social systems. On the one hand, the concept of Functional Requisites provides a potential standard for social criticism; societies that fail on these requirements are deemed flawed, and are seen as lacking in ways that will require remedy. On the other hand, because these Requisites are viewed as universal, as always required for the stability of all societies, they can also be used to provide an apologia for the status quo and to restrict change. In postulating a set of Universal Requisites of society, Functionalism postulates that, even if a society might be reformed in some ways, there are other profound ways in which it cannot be reformed and which men must accept. While Functional theory thus has both critical and apologetic tendencies, these mutually inhibit one another, and Functionalists are, at most, disposed only to a *limited* criticism of society. When it becomes involved in the world, then, Functionalism may be assimilated into an "administrative" sociology that can be used by organizations as a tool to change the social world, but only within very restricted limits.

Both Functionalism and Platonism are thus similar, but not identical, in their critical postures. Both theories provide similar ports of entry for ideological commitments. One port of entry is found at the point where the theorist must formulate particular *specifications* of an Eternal Form or of a Universal Requisite. For example, Plato does not believe that "dirt" or "hair" have Eternal Forms, but he believes that slavery does. Why one and not the other? There is also room for ideology when a decision is made about the level of abstraction in terms of which the postulated Requisite or Form will be formulated. For example, instead of postulating that "slavery" has an Eternal Form or is a Universal Requisite of societies, one could just as logically postulate some "system of production," of which slavery might be one possible, but not a necessary, Form. In choosing the level of abstraction for formulating a Universal Requisite or Form, the theorist has ample opportunity to express and protect his own ideological commitments.

There is another and more general way in which these elements, in both Platonism and Functionalism, embody ideological commitments. Both place their central value on social stability and order, on permanence rather than on change and growth. This is clearly inherent in the Platonic Theory of Forms, for these are conceived of as eternal and unchanging. Correspondingly, the

Functionalist notion of Functional Requisites specifies Eternal Requisites of social stability, not Requisites of change. To know the conditions necessary for stability—which is what is focal to and specified by the Functional Requisites—is not to know the conditions necessary and sufficient for any kind of a social *change.* Both theories thus focus on the need and strategies for social order and not on the need and strategies for social change.

The concept of Functional Requisites is objectionable, not because it provides a general reminder that all social worlds operate within *some* limits, but because it states that all social worlds operate within the *same* limits. A warning that all men must have some limits would be salutary. An insistence that all men have the same limits is merely arbitrary. When a social theorist in the 1960's claims, in effect, that he knows the ways in which all societies, from here to eternity, from Planet Earth to Planet Venus, must be limited, he is affirming a metaphysics of society. This is not objectionable as such, but is objectionable to the extent that those accepting it fail to see it as a metaphysics and, most especially, when they lack awareness of the way values are built into it. Having masked one's own values in a set of assumptions about the way the social world *is,* a theorist may then proceed without having to specify what his values are or even having to admit that they exist. Now, the theorist need only say: this is the way the world is; how convenient that it corresponds to the way I think it *should* be. This is what Macaulay did, for example, when he proclaimed that "universal suffrage is incompatible with the very existence of civilization." When social theorists affirm the existence of certain eternal limits in the social universe, they are creating real limits, but only on their own intellectual creativity.

IS EVIL REAL?

Plato was much perplexed about whether every specific particular had an Ideal Form or Idea to which it somehow, if only partially, corresponded. Does dirt, mud, or hair have an Ideal Form which it approximates, he had asked of the young Socrates. From Plato's viewpoint the answer to this embarrassing question must be and was, no. This implies that, for Plato, "dirt"—more generally, "evil" —is unreal; lacking an ideal form it lacks true being. From Plato's standpoint evil is not a positive or real thing, but rather the *absence* of the good; it is a negative and residual category. In other terms, the domains of the real and of value are seen as coextensive and isomorphic.

To the Sociological Functionalist also, social evil—the *dys*functional—is similarly negative and lacking in true being. It is the *failure* to satisfy a social need, to conform with a system requirement, to solve a system problem. *Dysfunctions* entail failure to comply with a tacitly premised need. They are, in that sense, "negative" things that happen when the "right" thing is *lacking*, because of the *breakdown* of a mechanism of social control, through the *deficient* training of the young or others, or because of the *absence* of regulative values. To the Functionalist, socially nonvalued things are not simply empirically different from the functional; that is, it is not simply that they have different consequences or are made evident by different signs but, rather, that they are also less real. Nothing could make this clearer than Parsons' inclination to think of all departures from his normatively centered models as aberrations, minor flaws, or secondary contradictions.

THE WORLD AS GOOD AND EVIL

If both Platonism and Functionalism agree that evil is not real, they tend also to split good and evil apart, and each assigns good to one realm and evil to another. In neither theory is it possible for both good and evil to be intrinsic parts of one and the same realm. Reality is not contradictory. The theories differ, however, in one crucial respect, which concerns the realm to which the world of ordinary men and everyday appearances is assigned.

Platonism held that such good as the world manifested was not its own; the good came from outside, from God acting through the Eternal Forms. If left to its own devices, the world would be expected to drift back toward chaos and disorder. Platonism, therefore, vacillated between responding to the world either with a recoiling absolute no, or with a dogged partial no; but there was little question of a partial yes, and still less of an absolute yes. It was not the world and man, but God and the Forms that were good. Platonism's first impulse was therefore to say yes to a good that was not conceived as being of this world and, correspondingly, to say no to a world that it conceived of as corrupted.

Functionalism's answer to the half-full/half-empty glass of water problem was different, because it located the good *in* the world, or at least in a part of it. Functionalism saw good as being intrinsic to the *social* world, and evil as not being so. If left to its own devices, the Parsonsian social system would not drift entropically into disorder, but would have a perpetual equilibrium; it is immortal. It is this aspect of the structure of sentiment that Functionalism embodies—its "optimism"—that sometimes conveys a strange air of unreality to those whose feelings and assumptions differ and that makes it seem not only conservative but naive. Yet it is also the related side of Functionalism, its feeling that evil in society is *not real*, that makes it compatible with a liberal sensibility. Feeling that society is intrinsically good, it looks around itself tolerantly and views social problems as surmountable imperfections. Functionalism is thus disposed to see the glass as half-full rather than half-empty, and to give a partial yes to the world. This is its optimism.

Functionalism did not remove the split between good and evil, however, but only rearranged it. Indeed, it built the old split into the world. It defined *society* as good-and-real, but it cast a shadow on the goodness and the reality of *man*. Society thus conceived is the hidden godhead; it is the sociological equivalent of Plato's God-and-Eternal-Forms. The Functionalist split between the semi-real-man-who-lacks-true-humanness-apart-from-society and real-society-from-whom-all-humanness-flows reproduces *within* the world a split akin to that which Plato created between the world and God-and-the-Eternal-Forms. Functionalism assigns to man the very ephemeral properties that Plato had assigned to matter. Functionalist man is good-and-real only insofar as he is filled with and shaped by a power above him, but he is otherwise intrinsically chaotic, filled with lawlessness, or else is simply empty.

NO SOCIETY, NO HUMANNESS

In both views, then, men are viewed as lacking reality, or true humanness, apart from their involvement in or dependence upon either God or Society. Men are thus a kind of raw material. It is no idle academic exercise but a small-scale morality play that is being enacted when the sociology textbook brandishes before the student the dreadful example of the "feral child"—or the maltreated and isolated child—who, abandoned of contact with the nourishing mother society, grows up witless. The catechism is: no society, no humanness. Yet dogs and cats can be surfeited with human attention but never learn to do more than bark or purr. What the Functionalist does not say is that society is no more than a *necessary* condition for humanness and is certainly not a sufficient condition of it. Witness the ants. What the Sociological Functionalist largely leaves out, very much as the Platonist deplores it, is a simple thing, the human body, a human race, with a distinctive kind of anatomy, physiology, and biology. "Oh, that!" says the Functionalist, which is not far from saying "Damn that!" as the Platonist did.

It is probably no more mistaken to say that societies are the raw material of *homo sapiens* than to regard *homo sapiens* as the raw material of societies. Humanness is surely the result only of an interaction between the biological species *homo sapiens* and society. And if one is to be told that societies have enabled the species to better satisfy their biological needs and to survive the rigors of nature, we might reply that sometimes it is only through the joys that a body permits that human beings have been able to survive the rigors of society.

The impulse of both Platonism and Functionalism to view men as the raw materials of society is related to the organismic metaphor in terms of which both view society. Such a metaphor secretes an unctuous pathos in whose cozy blur society becomes not only a reality independent of man but something that is and should be *over* him, or into which he smoothly fits or should be made to fit. The organismic metaphor is plain enough in Plato. Its counterpart in Functional theory is the concept of a social *system*, which is an abstraction from and formalization of earlier organismic models still quite evident, for example, in Durkheim's and Parsons' work. The Functionalist model is explicitly a system model, but underlying that is the tacit background assumption and image of an organism whose parts are not merely interconnected but must work together and be subordinated to the interests of the whole. Both Functionalism and Platonism, then, are infused with a metaphysical passion for "oneness." As I have shown in Chapter 6, it is one of the central thrusts underlying Parsons' conception of the role of "Grand Theory" to exhibit the wholeness of the social world and, indeed, through his "general theory of action," to find one theoretical language that can unify the diverse social sciences.

THE METAPHYSICS OF HIERARCHY

Underneath the organismic image's rhetoric of interdependence there is the spiny substance of hierarchy. It is a function of an organismic image to make a centralized administration of the division of labor, in which some command and some obey, seem intuitively appealing, by making this social arrangement appear to be part of an eternal and immutable order. Both Platonism and Sociological Functionalism focus on the social mechanisms by which men are molded and shaped, by which norms are imposed upon them, and by which they are made to *want* what a particular social system happens to require. In benignly labeling these as mechanisms of "social control" or as forms of education or "socialization," it is clear that Functionalism regards them not simply as requisites but as "goods," for they might no less accurately be termed mechanisms of "domination." And since both Functionalism and Platonism conceive of values as imprintable or transmissibles, both theories tend to divide mankind into two groups, into masses and elites, into those who are to be educated and those who are to educate them. Both theories thus operate with and require a hierarchical metaphysics. In Plato we need not look far for this, for he tells us so. The entire cosmos is a hierarchy to Plato, and hierarchy, he believes, must prevail in all its parts.

One finds a similar metaphysics of hierarchy in Functionalism. This is plainly revealed in E. A. Shils' encomiums to "Authority." Again, it is instructive to recall those occasional shots-in-the-library exchanged between Melvin Tumin and such (one-time) spokesmen of Functionalism as Wilbert Moore and Kingsley Davis. Moore and Davis argued that some form of social stratification was inherent in society. What makes their position metaphysical is that they did not simply affirm the functionality of a specific form of stratification in some time and place, but rather insisted that some social stratification is universally necessary. When someone asserts that something about society is going to be true forever and ever, he is likely to be expressing a domain assumption or a metaphysical conviction that existed prior to his specific argument on its behalf; the felt cogency of the specific argument probably derives as much from the way it resonates the domain assumption as from its internal logic. One ought further to be aware of the ideological resonance of this specific metaphysics, namely, that if the social world is for all time divided into rulers and ruled, then equality is a dream;

some must and should dominate others; only "evil"—social disorder, tension, or conflict—can come from efforts to remove the domination of man by man or to make fundamental changes in the character of authority.

AN ORDERLY WORLD

A central similarity of Platonism and Sociological Functionalism is their common disposition to take as their key intellectual problem, and their central moral value, a concern with social *order*. Rather than focusing, as they conceivably might and as other social theories have, on freedom, equality, or happiness, both Platonism and Functionalism place their intellectual and moral center of gravity elsewhere. A key concern of Functionalists, no less than Plato, is that social systems should be orderly—not free, not equal, not happy—and both largely believe that this depends on men's conformity with their society's shared values. Indeed, both theories account for social order in very similar ways; both focus on and give special stress to the role of shared moral values as central sources of social order. Plato, for example, says that men do not quarrel over things that can be weighed or counted, but over different ideas of Justice and the Good, of what is dear or valuable. For Plato the intellectual task was to discover what men *should* believe or value. Functionalism is the descriptive counterpart of Platonic moralism. For much of Functionalism the crucial intellectual task is to show how values (especially shared values, conceived of in certain ways I shall soon discuss) contribute to social order. This has been the stress of the entire theoretical tradition from which Functionalism evolved, through Durkheim and, earlier, through Auguste Comte.

As a result of the special place that they assign to shared values as a source of social order, both Platonism and Functional Sociology (from Durkheim to Parsons) also place a special emphasis on early education and socialization, and thereby on the processes through which values are internalized in persons. The Platonic stress on the socialization of children was every bit as emphatic as that of the Functionalists. Plato not only emphasized the importance of formal tuition but went on to stress the significance even of children's games and play behavior for the stability of the entire society, and he manifested a great concern for what is now called "youth culture." Unlike Jean Piaget, for example, who is sensitive to the ways in which children may, in part, generate their own values, both Functionalism and Platonism conceive of values in their character as transmissibles rather than as emergents. Both Platonism and Functionalism thus see values as "imprintables"— that is, as patterns that are initially *outside* of the persons to whom they are to be transmitted—and both are much concerned with the way values may be put *inside* persons.

To the Functionalist this "outside" is, of course, the parent or the teacher; in a larger sense it is the "culture," or in Emile Durkheim's language, the "collective conscience." To Plato, the outside source is, cosmically, the Idea or Form that God imprints upon matter; in fact, he conceives of this Form as coexistent with and outside of God himself. Since both the Functionalist and the Platonist see values as coming from outside of and, indeed, from *above* the things on which they will be imprinted, neither, therefore, ever fully confronts the question of how values themselves emerge, develop, and change. Values are conceived of not so much as man-*made* but as man-*transmitted* and man-*received* things.

Since both conceive of externally derived values as the source of individual control, both theories entail an image of men as inherently lacking built-in self-regulators, and as needing control from something outside of and above themselves if social order is to be maintained. In neither theory, therefore, is "man the measure of all things." To the Platonist the measure is "God," and to the Functionalist it is "society." These are the imprinters of value.

THE LEGITIMATE AND THE AUTHENTIC

Functionalists do not seem particularly aware of the way in which the concepts of "values" and "legitimacy" have assumed for them a kind of heightened pathos and almost sacred potency, much as the "goods of the soul" had for Plato. From a different standpoint, one that focuses not on the socially legitimate and the value-sanctioned but on the "authentic," it would be not right or moral behavior that would be invested with a special reliance but, instead, behavior that expresses personal conviction and is deeply felt. "Authenticity" is indicated by a congruence between what men want—as distinct from what they *should* want—and what they do. It is indicated by a congruence between choice and personal conviction. "Legitimacy," however, is indicated by the congruence between what men want or do, on the one hand, and moral values, on the other.

To those concerned with the problem of values and legitimacy, the implicitly held conception is of the "true self" as the value-embedded self, the self formed around certain socially sanctioned values and certain socially legitimated identities. To those, however, concerned with authenticity, the "true self" is one moved by any strong desire or strangely claimed identity, including those that are body-linked and regardless of whether they are lowly or disreputable from the viewpoint of "respectable" claims. In making this distinction, my intention is to indicate that there is more than one conception of self for which a social theory can opt, and that the Functionalist has tacitly opted for an "Apollonian" rather than a "Dionysian" self, although he seems scarcely aware that he has these and other alternatives, let alone that he has chosen among them.

The difference between Functionalism's concern for legitimacy and a concern for authenticity reflects the difference between the former's devotion to the claims of society and the latter's somewhat greater concern with the claims of individuals. It is, in part, a difference in the basepoints for judgment. Functionalism focuses on the need of men to *conform* with their social roles and social values as these have been received, and not on the need to change them. It is the requirements of these roles and values and of the society that they constitute that are problematic for Sociological Functionalism, and not the needs of individuals, which are taken as given.

A stress on authenticity implies that a concern with the claims of society is necessary but not enough either for the fulfillment of individuals or even for the effective operation of society. In the modern world, conformity and success are somehow increasingly experienced as disappointing, even by those who pursue and achieve them. The "lonely crowd" is not composed of the outcasts and failures alone; it is the failure of successful conformity to produce gratification that is at the bottom of the modern plea for authenticity.

The search for authenticity implies that some kinds of conformity are self-deceiving, self-destructive, and life-wasting. One of the central reasons for this is that there are very different motives that may lead men to conform. It is obvious, for example, that men may conform because they truly believe the claims made upon them are right and proper. But it is also obvious that they may conform simply out of expediency, to cut their losses or to build their winnings, without any conviction concerning the propriety of their behavior. It is one thing to believe in the propriety of a claim because it itself is experienced as intrinsically right, but another to accept the claim because one wants to be approved or loved by others, or because one is afraid. It is one thing to believe in the propriety of a claim that, when given conformity, is experienced as gratifying, and another to so believe despite one's own disappointment when conformity is given. It is one thing to believe in the propriety of a claim because it is intrinsically satisfying to conform with it; it is quite another to *believe* in its propriety because one has a need to feel safely at home among others.

The central consideration, however, is that our very commitment to a system of moral values invariably creates an interest in seeming to be, and seeming to do, what the values require. Our most idealistic commitments therefore induce us to deceive ourselves and to lie to others. It is not only egoistic self-interest but morality as well that is a root of "bad faith." It is thus not only when men conform without belief, but when their very belief leads them to continuing self-deception, that men may manifest inauthenticity.

If the advocate of authenticity says that it is not enough to conform, he also recognizes that some men may, nonetheless, conform authentically; legitimacy and authenticity are not necessarily at odds. Individuals can truly want what they should want. Nor, in this view, is deviance an invariable guarantee of authenticity, for deviance from the values of one group may be motivated by a conformity with the values of another that may be no less mindless, even if this other is a small and unpopular group. There remains, in short, the question of the authenticity of deviance no less than of conformity.

DEVIANCE AND ANOMIE

Still another similarity between Platonism and Functionalism is to be found in their *explanation* of deviant behavior, which both often approach in fundamentally the same manner. Having the advantage of some two thousand years, Functionalists have, of course, developed the theory importantly, but the basic structure of the explanation of deviance frequently remains the same in both Platonism and Functionalism. To both, deviant behavior often involves a "falling away" from something, a departure from or

lack of something, particularly of certain kinds of moral norms—
that is, in Durkheim's revealing term, a *"poverty* of morality."

Central to the Functionalist's explanation of deviance has always
been the concept of anomie, which, of course, comes from the
Greek concept of *anomos,* meaning without law, lacking in restraint, devoid of temperance, form, or pattern. It is to be *without*
morality. This approach to deviant behavior is fundamentally different, in its most basic model, from, say, the Freudian or the
Marxian, in which tensions are not necessarily seen as due to the
lack of something, but may, indeed, derive from conformity *with*
certain moral values or may be due to a conflict between opposing
forces, all of which are simultaneously present.

One of the merits of Robert Merton's theory of anomie is that,
tacitly basing itself on certain Marxian domain assumptions—
especially those concerning the "internal contradictions" of a
system—it pointed to the manner in which a commitment to
certain culturally transmitted values may, when unrealizable, induce anomie. But here too the pathological terminus, anomie itself,
entails an ultimate renunciation of or disbelief in the socially
shared values. Yet it is not only the unrealizability of such values
that may sometimes warp a man, but all the things that he *can*
and *must* do to realize them successfully; there is the sickness of
the successful. And correspondingly, one might add (but usually
does not) that when a man pursues goals he has been taught to
prize, and then finds them unrealizable, it is quite sensible for him
to renounce these goals; there is, then, a rationality in deviance.

The central civic pathology with which Plato concerned himself
was "injustice," and he saw this as entailing a lack of restraint
such as arises when men fail to mind their own business, when
they violate the Socratic rule, "One Man, One Task," and when
they do not limit themselves to performing their own role obligations. To the contemporary Functionalist, "system disequilibrium"
is similarly held to arise when men fail to perform their role
obligations; when they do not confine themselves to those things
which their culture sanctions and therefore violate the expectations
of those who do.

Neither Platonism nor Functionalism seems to recognize that
when men limit themselves to what their culturally standardized
roles presently sanction, they may be prevented from acting in
ways that might remedy problems that have arisen only after the
earlier crystallization of social roles. They do not recognize that, at
some point, the world simply cannot be kept livable, unless some
men are courageous enough to *shirk* the duty that respectable or
powerful men around them define as theirs. (What, after all,
entitled Socrates—the son of a midwife and a stonecutter—to

become the philosophical gadfly of Athens? Certainly it was not anyone else's conception of his role that required this of him. It was only his own interpretation of the Oracle of Delphi; it was, in short, his own charisma.) Undoubtedly a man gets into trouble and runs risks when he behaves this way, as Socrates' life plainly testifies. But the original question was not, What is a safe way for men to live? It was, Do men and societies always benefit when men mind their own business and limit themselves to the prerogatives and duties of their incumbent roles? Neither Platonism nor Functionalism seems to understand that there are times when men must be intemperate and risk living *without limits,* for both theories are spellbound by a sculptural Apollonian ideal of man as firmly bounded and contained, as temperate and restrained.

It is thus characteristic of Functionalist analysis of deviance that it centers around the *acceptance* and the *nonacceptance* of culturally prescribed means and ends. But there is, at least, a third choice that men have: to fight. Men's "nonacceptance" of social values is not the same as active struggle against those values with which they disagree or on behalf of those in which they believe. Conforming "ritualistically" without belief is not the same as submitting under bitter *protest.* Struggle, conflict, protest seem to find no firm and distinctive place in the Functionalist inventory of men's responses to society, where they remain blurred and ghostly concepts. These are clearly not forms of conformity. And it is not enough to describe them as *non*conformity, for that results in the drug addict and the civil rights protester, those who organize criminal syndicates and those who organize the poor to wage their own war on poverty, those who march for peace and those who engage in delinquent "rumbles," being somehow all placed under the same conceptual umbrella. In focusing on their common character as "deviants," Functionalism sees no significant differences in the nature of their active resistance to society. Only a marginal reality is assigned to those who *oppose* social establishments actively and who struggle to change its rules and membership requirements.

Implicit in this Functionalist perspective is an image of the *good* man, the man who fits into the Functionalist image of the good society. He does his duty in the role in which he finds himself; he may even do it "creatively," yet somehow he manages to remain agreeable. No belligerent troublemaker, he is, rather, a man who usually conforms with a will to the expectations of others. He supports authority in its efforts to bring deviants under control and is docile even when he himself is admonished. He drinks the hemlock when the jailer brings it.

In Functionalism's implicit image of the *good* man, there has been a fatal confusion between the sociable and the social. When the Functionalist says that men's humanness derives from their social experience, this tends to slide softly into the implication that a man's humanness derives from cooperative sociability. Yet what makes a man human is not only the limits that others set upon him and to which he is sensitive, but also that he resents and resists these limits when they chafe. If men cannot become human apart from society, neither can they become persons except in the course of some conflict with it. A man develops his human self as much by his resistance to the requirements of his social roles, as much by struggling against them and other persons, as by conformity and cooperation. He is every bit as human when he bares his teeth as when he bares his heart. While human beings are no more devil than they are angel, they are, after all, an evolved animal species that was long and hard in the coming.

A man who never knew conflict would not be an individual person but some kind of an appendage. Yet both Functionalism and Platonism have been much and deeply discomfited by human individuality, because each senses this as entailing a variation dangerous to consensus among men and inimical to order in society. From wives or property in common, to setting the city distant from the sea, there is scarcely a social remedy that Plato ever proposed that does not aim at a de-individuating consensus. Functionalism has cautioned against that variability in men which is at the core of individuality, not so much in open challenge to it but in affirmation of what it takes to be higher values, social order and the need of society for consensus. When Talcott Parsons comes to the heart of his conception of how equilibrium may be maintained in the relations among men, he sees it as derived from the willingness of each to do as the other expects, which ultimately requires both to share the same value system.

THE COSTS OF CONFORMITY

Neither Platonism nor Functionalism sees the full danger in the *restriction* of gratification, for each is primarily concerned that men live in conformity with morality; and each tends to assume, rather than show, that such conformity produces gratifications. Neither Platonist nor Functionalist recognizes that conformity is a social product whose supply may glut the market and bring a small price. Plato attempts to reassure men that a life of virtue will make them happy, although he somewhat vitiates this reassurance by remarking that he might say this even if it were untrue. Functionalists, for their part, seek to close the gap between practiced conformity and experienced gratification by focusing on the extent to which gratifications are learned, by stressing human plasticity and men's capacity to derive gratification from almost anything. In effect, Functionalists deal with the observable gap between conformity and gratification by holding that it is, in principle, possible to socialize men to want no more than others are trained to provide them willingly, and to provide willingly no less than others are trained to want. That no human society known has ever succeeded in living up to this principle is treated as owing to failures merely idiosyncratic to each society, not as intrinsic to the human condition.

Far from seeing the costs of conformity and the rewards of nonconformity, Functionalists and Platonists focus on the rewards of conformity and the costs of deviance. One would never guess from reading Functionalist texts on socialization that training children can be a continual room-to-room battle, invariably exhausting to parents and frequently repellent to the children. (In this respect, Plato was immensely more realistic.) Instead of stressing that men's quest for gratification has a healthful side, both stress its dangers. Rather than seeing the dangers in the restriction of men's quests for gratification, they stress the necessity of such restriction. Both have theories of deviance which are less disturbed by the failure of gratification than by the failure of restraint. They assume that the quest for individual gratification must at some point fail, but that the demand for individual restraint need not; yet this last assumption is as utopian as the first is prudent. In this, once again, the Functionalist reveals that he tacitly takes society and not man as the measure; he is usually more concerned to protect society from the failure of individual restraint than to protect the individual from society's failure to gratify him.

Both theories commonly stress that social stability requires the internalization of moral values that restrict and control the pursuit of gratification. Both theories commonly neglect analysis of the ways in which social stability may be enhanced by increasing men's gratifications, either by developing technologies that increase abundance, by reorganizing the mechanisms that allocate differential incomes, or by freeing men from an unthinking bondage to an earlier training that makes adult gratification needlessly difficult. Platonism and Functionalism thus differ deeply from both Freudianism and Marxism; The basic *goal* of these latter—as distinct from their *means*—is to free men from outmoded social and character structures and, through this, to enable them to enjoy greater fulfillment and development. Platonism and Functionalism, in contrast, aim at inducing men to live a value-disciplined existence, and both endorse a conception of values as that which shapes and disciplines the appetites, and produces *un*freedom.

INSATIABLE MAN

Pinning their hopes for stability on a moral restriction of men's wants rather than on efforts to increase their satisfactions, neither Platonism nor Functionalism takes serious account of the vast productive powers of science and technology. Underlying this is the assumption that men are inherently insatiable. This assumption serves, in effect, as a justification for ignoring the great variations in economies and their enormous differences in scarcity and abundance. Assume that men are insatiable, then all economies must, relative to these insatiable wants, be essentially alike; all are economies of scarcity. The assumption that men are insatiable is a domain or metaphysical assumption. It is usually notable that this assumption is in the nature of a complaint, but it is, of course, a complaint about others, not about the self. It is the time-worn complaint of the well-fed against the hungry, of the oligarch against the *demos,* of the entrenched elitist against the reformist egalitarian, of the enlightened philosopher against the ignorant "common man." Those complaining of the insatiability of others tacitly imply their own freedom from the malaise, and they thus belie the very universality that they attribute to human insatiability.

It may be that insatiability will, in time, prove a temporary and historically limited problem. Indeed, it may in the end be a problem of much less danger to society than the situation that breeds *ennui* and boredom and thus loosens men's hold on life. "Need and struggle are what excite and inspire us," said William James, "our hour of triumph is what brings the void." Insatiable men at least want something and, therefore, will remain involved in their groups and cultures, if only to attack them. Thus, while insatiability has, from Plato to Parsons, commonly been assumed to be purely pathological, it may, nonetheless, have a benign side; it may stave off the "void" and serve to keep successful men contributing to group life.

Impulse-negating values, appetite-restricting values, values conceived as restraints, are especially needed in an economy of scarcity. For here, men will be dangerously tempted to get what they want—and indeed, may only be able to do so—by taking it away from somebody else. The historical development of so-called "spiritual" values occurs in economies of scarcity, where they serve and are needed as a restraint on men who may be prompted to improve their lot by injuring others. The "goods of the soul," as Socrates calls spiritual values, are distinguished by the fact that they can*not* be won from or lost to others, and they cannot be depleted. Spiritual values are thus like the magical pitcher of milk; they can never be emptied and always have sustenance enough for everyone. The problem of material scarcity is solved by creating a substitute, spiritual abundance. But spiritual values that are used to keep deprived men quiet come in time to be viewed as a form of social fraud, and they serve as a mechanism of domination by those who do have material abundance over those who do not. In both Platonism and Functionalism, morality is tacitly invited to serve as a substitute for productivity.

Sociological Functionalism, like Platonism, has a strong vein of underground asceticism in it. It entails a tacit dualism of body and mind, in which mind or "self" is the higher and better part. It is a social theory that hardly acknowledges that men have bodies. Scarcely ever, in its many studies of factories, offices, hospitals, and political parties, does it take note of the fact that organization members have a gender. Hardly ever does it consider sex except as a force in reproduction, to fulfill the "Universal Requisite of society." Nor does it intimate that "socializing" the resultant children is a struggle that requires, among other things, abundant physical energy or sheer good health. Talcott Parsons, for example, formulates his conception of the "social system" in such a way as to exclude from it the elements of man's biological constitution, physiological functioning, physical and ecological surround, his tools, machines, and other material artifacts—even though the last three are all directly made by men themselves—and banishes them to the *environment* of social systems. This is a kind of academic exorcism of man's baser animal nature, a form of theoretical purification. It is an effort to use social theory to do what ascetic religions and philosophies have sought to do for centuries. Modern Sociological Functionalism focuses on "social systems" that are seen primarily as systems of symbolic interaction, not between embodied men but between disembodied "role players"; between psychic "selves" who communicate-from-a-distance but who seem never to touch, to hold, to feed, to strike, to caress.

Functionalism, then, is a sociology of asceticism; it is a sociology of angels-without-wings. It is a sociological version of the Platonic dualism between the body and the soul.

PESSIMISM: DEATH AND THE HUMAN CONDITION

Can there be any significant similarity, however, between Functionalism with its optimism and Platonism with its thick vein of pessimism? Can there be any similarity between Parsons, who tends to see ours as the best possible of worlds, ever growing better, and Plato, who believed that in the end all fails, and who said: "Human affairs are hardly worth considering in earnest and yet we must be in earnest about them—a sad necessity constrains us." Here we must return for a closer, more probing and patient look at Parsonsian "optimism."

Clarification of this problem will require us to see that there are different things to which pessimism or optimism can be attached, and that optimism can exist at one but not necessarily another level. Parsons differs from Plato, because his focal concern is with the *social* condition, while Plato's is with the *human* condition. Parsons is optimistic about the social but not the human condition. Indeed, Parsons and Plato are both pessimistic about the human condition, and their pessimism at this level is, in both cases, linked to the same problem: human death. But since Parsons does not normally focus on this human level, his pessimism about it remains subsidiary and is rarely exposed. For Plato, by contrast, the human and social condition are not separated sharply and his focal attention is given over to the encompassing human condition; hence his pessimism is more visible. The manifest optimism that Parsons has about the social condition is, I shall suggest below, not only coexistent with a subsidiary pessimism about the human condition but also is to be understood as an effort to *combat* pessimism on various levels.

To most Greeks of Plato's time, death was regarded as "the bitterest of evils," and concern with death was a central component of Greek pessimism. Plato attempts to combat this pessimism by seeking a rational basis on which men can believe in such immortality as they may have, immortality of the soul. While there are important ways in which Plato succumbs to pessimism and surrenders to death, his search for a rational proof of the immortality of the soul expresses a fantasy-wish to live forever; it is a denial of death. Again, his conception of the Eternal Forms as the truest existence is a resistance to the natural corruption that overtakes the things of this world; it is a fight against death. Death was a focal anxiety to Plato and to the Greeks of his time; but to Parsons, as to most other Americans—perhaps, in part, because we live so much longer than the Greeks did—death is normally only a matter of hidden, subsidiary attention, although still deeply laden with anxiety. Nevertheless, defocalized though this anxiety may be, one of Parsons' most flatly pessimistic statements, that "tragedy is of the essence of the human condition," appears in conjunction with a discussion of death and religion.

Parsons' statement on death is worth quoting here, for its style is both characteristically tortured and revealing. He tells us that "the fact that though we all know we have to die almost no man knows when he will die is one of the cardinal facts of the human situation."[2] In this ambiguous statement, it is not the fact that men must die—and not even that all *know* this—that is "cardinal" but, rather, that few know *when*. In effect, it is not the fact of inevitable death that is accented in this formulation—indeed, it is blurred—but rather the anxiety and uncertainty about its timing. Parsons thus quickly slides over the fact of inevitable death as such; he only implies it. But even if he obscures the matter, it is clear that, for Parsons, the source of the tragic is somewhere in the vicinity of death; it is death-linked.

Parsons' sentiments are thus split concerning different levels of human existence. He is, indeed, optimistic, glowingly optimistic, as we have seen repeatedly, about *social* systems and especially about American society. His pessimism is tied to another level: it is man, individual, embodied man, that he is pessimistic about. His pessimism, in contrast to Plato's, does not encompass man's refractoriness, limitations, or irrationality, for all these are somehow manageable by "socialization." His pessimism centers more narrowly on man's *mortality*, the "tragic essence" of the human condition. Over and against man's animal mortality, Parsons designs a "social system" that, with its battery of defenses and equilibrating devices, need never run down. What Parsons has done is to assign to the self-maintaining social system an immortality transcending and compensatory for man's perishability. It is thus that Parsons' social system extrudes all embodied mortal beings and, indeed, almost any kind of perishable "matter," and the system is instead constructed of "role players" or roles and statuses that transcend and outlive men. Much of Parsons' theoretical effort, then, is, I suspect, an effort to combat death. But it does entail a denial not only of the death of individuals, but also of the death of society and, particularly, American society.

Remember that Parsons, in his articles of 1928 and 1929, began by conducting an intellectual war on two fronts: against Marxism, on the one hand, and its critics, Sombart and Weber, on the other. And he opposes them all for much the same reasons, because they are antagonists of capitalist society, and because they are all—Sombart and Weber, as well—deeply pessimistic about it. Central to Marxism, of course, was its "death prophecy" concerning capitalism; Marxism said that capitalism contained "the seeds of its own destruction" and vowed that it would bury capitalism. At the very source of Parsons' whole intellectual effort, then, was an effort to combat this death prophecy; to seek or formulate a social system so general in character that it need never die; to endow it richly with a perpetual, self-maintaining character; to remove or iron out all hint of internal disruption and decay; and, finally, to cap it all (as he does in his article "Evolutionary Universals") with a "proof" that it is *not* our system but *theirs* that will die. In effect, Parsons' proof of the self-equilibrating, self-maintaining character of the "social system" is akin to Plato's "proof" of the immortality of the soul. The immortality of man, however, is no longer vouchsafed by the immortality of his soul but now, in Parsons, by the immortality of his social system.

I have repeatedly insisted that it is of basic importance in understanding Parsons to remember that his theoretical system emerges in the midst of the mounting crisis of Western societies, makes its first serious appearance during the Great Depression, and develops in a world in which, as Parsons conceives it, the United States is confronted by the dangerous revolutionary power of the communist system.[3] Parsons' optimism, his very optimism concerning social systems, is of a special sort. It is an optimism in the face of pessimism, an optimism that rejects and is against pessimism. Optimism need not be of that sort. It can simply be born of the prospects, excitement, and enjoyment of life; it can express a sense of the juices that run through one. Not so, Parsons' optimism. His is a determined optimism, a polemical optimism, an antipessimistic optimism; his optimism is more like an atheist's vigorous denial of God than an agnostic's unpolemical uncertainty. It is precisely because it has this overreactive component that it is ridden with a kind of compulsiveness that is so one-sided, so little able to acknowledge any serious difficulty in our society or to see any of its problems in their full profundity.

THE VIABILITY OF THE FUNCTIONALIST
INFRACTRUCTURE

I have suggested that both Platonism and Functionalism are built upon similar infrastructures, and both are plainly infused with certain common sentiments, domain assumptions, values, images of what man and society *should* be, and assumptions concerning what they *are*. Their values center on an ethic of restraint and the negation of the private self; upon a concern that men do their duty but without a corresponding concern for their gratification or for their rights. Both are impregnated with some version of an ethic of restraint, temperance, and decorousness. In both, expressive discipline and impulse control are central values. They are based upon a metaphysics of order and hierarchy, with the result that they set small store on human love—which they see as a socially disruptive force—but rather affirm the more temperate affection involved in friendship. Both premise that the cementing social sentiments are neither love, nor a sense of human fraternity or common human destiny, but rather are esteem, prestige, and, above all, respect. They are also suspicious of change and manifest a greater concern for the claims of conformity and consensus—regarded as the more important and valuable attributes of society—than for the claims of liberty and equality.

There is, then, a common infrastructure of domain assumptions, of sentiments, and of conceptions of the real that are shared by both Functionalism and Platonism. The point of this observation is not to deny that Functionalism is "new" or to claim that the central features of Functionalism had long ago been "anticipated" by classical Platonism. If only in its scientific commitment, in its insistence on the importance of *empirical* components of knowing, and in its focus on what "is" rather than on what "should be," Functionalism is, indeed, by no means reducible to or identical with Platonism. It is true that Functionalism has made many of the value concerns that were central to Platonism equally central to its own models of the social world; but it has placed these *within* the framework of a concern with the empirical or existential that are primary to it, at least in principle.

Our implication, therefore, is not that Functionalism in any sense constitutes a "reworking" of Platonism in the framework of an empirically oriented sociology. It is certainly not that Platonism was a philosophical tradition which had first been known to and assimilated in technical detail by Functionalists and then applied to a new set of problems or data, in the manner, say, that Hegelianism had been by Marx. Both Platonism and Functionalism, rather, simply rest on an infrastructure that has important common components. The point is not that Platonism shaped Functionalism, but that both have been influenced by underlying, historically perduring forces. In comparing Functionalism with Platonism, my central concern has been to exhibit the communality of certain important aspects of their infrastructure and, thereby, the antiquity of the infrastructure which underlies Functionalism.

The antiquity of this infrastructure suggests its potency and its continuing potentiality as a theory-shaping force. I do not, however, believe that this infrastructure is unchangeable or eternal. Indeed, it may be that the great growth of modern industrialization, which is a very recent development in the long-time perspective that we are dealing with here, may well have established conditions that have already started to undermine this infrastructure and may do so increasingly, particularly as technological developments begin to bring about a radical change in the fundamental problem of scarcity and provide new mechanisms of social control. Yet even though this infrastructure may be in the process of becoming antiquated, and even though there may be a sense in which "its days are numbered," still I do not believe its day is already *over*. Nor will it be in the immediate and foreseeable future. It seems more probable that this infrastructure will continue to be reproduced, at least for some appreciable time, among privileged and elite sectors of the population. It seems likely to continue, as it has in the past, to serve as a theory-shaping influence and, thus, as a force contributing to the persistence of social theories essentially continuous with those that emerged in Positivism and later evolved into modern Functionalism.

This does not mean that the Functional model will survive the present crisis unchanged; nor does it mean that its present crisis is not a grave one. The very sharpness of the present crisis and its repercussions on Academic Sociology as a whole are, in part, a consequence of the abiding resources that Functionalism can draw upon, to resist the challenge of new theories that rest upon new or different infrastructures and to resist other pressures toward theoretical change. My central conclusion, therefore, is that Functionalism will not collapse in any radical manner, and that it will not manifest anything like the rather abrupt discontinuity, say, that "evolutionism" did during the third or Classical period in the development of sociological theory.

I would also conclude, from the potency of the Functionalist infrastructure, that the movement of theorists with *prior* Functionalist commitments toward a Marxist model will be a *limited* one. This movement toward convergence with Marxism will generate increasing strains for those who had initially made Functionalist commitments, because it is dissonant with the infrastructure they are likely to embody. I would guess, then, that the movement *by older Functionalists* toward a convergence with Marxism, while it will go further than that manifested earlier by Durkheim and others, will essentially entail an effort to assimilate Marxism *into* a Functionalist technostructure and infrastructure. The convergence effort then—when it is made by Functionalists—will not be made from some neutral ground that is *equally* open to the claims and impulses of *both* theoretical models. (Much the same is likely to be true in similar efforts made by Marxists toward convergence with Functionalism.) This, however, does not mean that sociological models unambivalently or fully committed to Marxism will not become increasingly important in Academic Sociology. It suggests, rather, than one ought to expect these to be developed by younger people and by those who have not been committed to Functionalism previously, and who embody infrastructures different from those characteristic of Functionalism.

THE POTENTIAL OF A RADICAL SOCIOLOGY

In emphasizing the power of the infrastructure on which Functionalism rests, I do not mean to suggest the unchangeability of the conservative character either of Functionalism or Academic Sociology. My point, rather, has been to indicate why I think an important part of academic social theory will remain essentially continuous with Functionalism and why, further, the changes in Functionalism that one can expect are probably limited. My view is that an infrastructure conducive to a functional theory will persist for the foreseeable future. At the same time, however, I expect it to have a less commanding influence on Academic Sociology as a whole, leaving increasing room for the development of social theories of a less conservative character and, indeed, I expect that a part of sociology will become increasingly radicalized. There will, in short, be a growth of a "radical sociology" which, while never the dominant perspective of Academic sociologists, will grow in influence, particularly among the younger, rising generation.

There are three basic factors on which the future of this radical potential in Academic Sociology will depend: (1) the changing political *praxis* and, in particular, the growing efforts of some sociologists, again, particularly the young, to actively change the community and the university in more humane and democratic directions; (2) the increasing interaction between Academic Sociology and Marxism, particularly the more Hegelian versions of Marxism; and (3) the inherent contradictions of Academic Sociology itself which generate certain instabilities and open it to a measure of change.

The growing political activism of sociologists, especially younger ones, is partly evidenced by the increasing development of the "radical caucus" in the American Sociological Association; by the disproportionately large number of sociology students involved in university reform movements; and by the prominence of sociologists among those faculty members against whom career reprisals have been made by the administrations of various universities. In addition to its value to the community and the university, the radical political activity of such sociologists is significant because of its self-transforming consequences for the persons involved. It can activate a new structure of sentiments and generate a new experience with the world that can change the pretheoretical impulses from which new, articulate sociologies emerge. The "radicalization" that such political activism generates develops new infrastructures conducive to new and better sociologies, and certainly to sociologies different from Functionalism.

Again, there is no question that throughout Academic Sociology in the United States there is clear evidence that it is involved in a growing dialogue of increasing intensity with various versions of Marxism. Those who want to change the character of Academic Sociology and accelerate the development of a radical sociology will promote such a dialogue even where they themselves are far from satisfied with the intellectual or political adequacy of classical Marxism. The theoretical effect of such increased interaction between Academic Sociology and Marxism will not and cannot be one-sided. It will not simply be Academic Sociology that is transformed in the process but also Marxism itself. Such radical potential as Academic Sociology possesses, then, will not be brought about in isolation from Marxism but will be furthered as interaction with it grows. Both Marxism and Academic Sociology need one another for their mutual continued development. To the degree that such interaction grows, the basic structural cleavage in world social theory between Academic Sociology and Marxism, a cleavage that has persisted since the nineteenth century, will move to a new historical level and, partly through the *struggle* between these viewpoints, it may be that a new theoretical synthesis (not simply a compromise) is being developed.

Finally, the potentialities of a radical sociology will also be influenced by the existence of certain contradictions inherent in Academic Sociology, to which I have referred at various points earlier in this volume. It is, therefore, useful to review briefly certain of these contradictions.

One of the central contradictions of modern sociology, especially in the United States, derives from its role as market researcher for the Welfare State. This role exposes sociologists to two contradictory, even if not equally powerful, experiences: on one side, it limits the sociologist to the reformist solutions of the Welfare State; but, on the other, it exposes him to the failures of this state and of the society with whose problems it seeks to cope. Such Academic Sociologists have a vested interest in the very failures of this society —in a real sense their careers depend upon it; but at the same time their very work makes them intimately familiar with the human suffering engendered by these failures. Even if it is the special business of such sociologists to help clean up the vomit of modern society, they are also sometimes revolted by what they see. Thus the sociologists' funding tie to the Welfare State does not produce an unambivalent loyalty to it or to the social system it seeks to maintain. To be "bought" and to be "paid for" are two different things—and that is a contradiction of the Welfare State not peculiar to its relations with sociologists.

A similar contradiction is involved in the call for "objectivity" so central to the methodological canons of Academic Sociology. For while a belief in objectivity fosters the sociologists' accommodation to the way things are, it also fosters and expresses a certain amount of distance from the society's dominant values. The sociologist's claim to objectivity is not simply a disguise for his devotion or capitulation to the status quo, nor is it an expression of a true neutrality toward it. For some sociologists the claim to objectivity serves as a facade for their own alienation from and resentment toward a society whose elites, even today, basically treat them as the Romans treated their Greek slaves: as skilled servants, useful but lower beings.

The call for "objectivity" serves as a "sacred" justification to withhold the reflexive loyalty that society demands, while at the same time providing a protective covering for the critical impulses of the timid. Under the protection of his claim to objectivity, the sociologist sometimes engages in a bitchy and carping, tacit and partial unmasking of society's failures. Challenged, the sociologist can always scamper back behind the parapet of his "objectivity," claiming that it is not really he who has pronounced a judgment on society, but that it is the impersonal facts that have spoken. In its present, historically developed form, as a claim of the contemporary professional social sciences, "objectivity" is largely the ambivalent ideology of those whose resentment is shackled by their timidity and privilege. Behind objectivity there is a measure of alienation.

One of the most basic contradictions of Academic Sociology resides in the domain assumptions intrinsic to the sociological perspective. This is the contradiction betweeen sociology's *focal* assumption that society makes man, and its *tacit* assumption that man makes society. The former assumption is focal, in some measure, because it is in the interest of Academic Sociology to emphasize the manner in which society, groups, social relations, social positions, and culture shape and infuse men. While this assumption, that society and culture shape men, served at one point to liberate men from biological or supernatural conceptions of their destiny, it becomes an increasingly repressive metaphysics in a more fully secularized and bureaucratized society such as our own, particularly when it encourages a view of social forces as an independent social reality, apart and autonomous from men's actions. If this assumption began by encouraging a liberation of men from their position as the puppets of God and biology, it came to entail a vision of them as the passive raw materials of society and culture, inviting them to bow the knee in gratitude toward a "society" upon which, they are told, nothing less than their very humanness depends.

There is an important truth in this vision of society as an autonomous force. It reflects the despair of secularized men who, told that it was they who made the world, nonetheless found that this world was out of their control and was not really theirs. But the trouble is that the sociologist's conception of society and social forces as autonomous tacitly takes this alienated condition as *normal* and inevitable, rather than as a pathological condition to be fought and surmounted, an effort that finds support in the view that it is men who do indeed make society.

These central domain assumptions of sociology and their structure—that is, the present dominance of the belief that social forces shape men, and the subordination of the assumption that men make society—not only reflect the larger alienation of industrial societies since the French Revolution, but they are also rooted in and confirmed by the special experience of academicians, particularly their political impotence in the university and their docility toward its authorities.

For tenured faculty, the university is a realm of congenial and leisured servitude. It is a realm in which the academician is esteemed for his learning but castrated as a political being. Indeed, it is this trade-off, in which the academician has the right to be a tiger in the classroom but the need to be a pussycat in the Dean's office, that contributes so much to the irrational posturings and theatrics of the classroom. Like other academics, the Academic Sociologist learns from the routine experience of his dependency within the university that he can strike terror only in the hearts of the very young—and now they want to strip him of even that privilege—but that he himself is the gelded servant of the very system in which he is, presumably, the vaunted star. He has thus learned with an intuitive conviction that "society shapes men" because he lives it every day; it is his autobiography objectified.

It is precisely here that the *praxis* of the radical sociologist has its greatest intellectual potentiality for, through it, he learns and teaches a different set of assumptions: that men can resist success-fully; that they are not simply the raw materials of social systems; that they can be the shakers and makers of worlds that are and worlds that might be. It is such *praxis* that can help transcend the contradictions of sociology and release its liberative side. No "sociologist" has ever written a single sentence; no sociologist has ever done a single research or had a single idea; it is the entire man who makes sociology. Those who are whole men, or struggle against their incompleteness, will make a very different sociology than will those who passively accept the crippling that their worlds have inflicted upon them.

In its political and ideological character, then, Academic Sociology is an ambivalent structure which has both liberative and repressive sides. Although its conservative-repressive dimension dominates it, Academic Sociology is not unequivocally such. To miss this is to miss the opportunity and the task. To miss this is also to increase the danger of fostering a primitivistic regression to an orthodox (if not vulgar) Marxism, and to encourage a mindless know-nothingism content to delude itself into believing that Academic Sociology has accomplished absolutely nothing at all in the last thirty years, thereby inhibiting its use as one important stimulus for a continuing development of Marxism itself.

To repeat, there are powerful contradictions within sociology which provide leverage for the transformation of sociology itself. These suggest that radicals are not justified in viewing sociology in the way that Rome looked upon Carthage. Just as Marx extricated the liberative potentialities of a Hegelianism which was previously dominated by its conservative aspect and delivered from it a left or neo-Hegelianism, so, too, is it possible to transcend contemporary Academic Sociology and to deliver from it a radical or neo-sociology.

Because of these contradictions, Academic Sociology, even with its profoundly conservative structure, still retains politically liberative potentialities that can be useful in transforming the community. While there is no doubt that Academic Sociology has neglected the importance of power, property, conflict, force, and fraud, it has (not despite, but because of this) focused attention on some of the new sources and sites of social change in the modern social world.

For example, to be provocatively invidious about it, it was not Marxism but Talcott Parsons and other Functionalists who noticed early the importance of the emerging "youth culture" and at least lifted it out as an object for attention. It was the Academic Sociologists, not the Marxists in the United States, who helped many to get their first concrete picture of how Blacks and other subjugated groups live, and who contributed to such practical political developments as the Supreme Court's desegregation decision of 1954. It is the ethnography of conventional Academic Sociologists which has also given us the best picture of the emerging psychedelic and drug cultures.

Again, it was Max Weber and other Academic Sociologists who forced us to confront the problem of bureaucracy in the modern world in all of its profundity and pervasiveness. Unlike many Marxists, the Academic Sociologists refused to confine their view of bureaucracy to the state levels alone; they did not view it as a social epiphenomenon that would automatically be overcome with the achievement of socialism, as Karl Kautsky did; and, unlike certain Soviet scholars, they did not view bureaucracy as some kind of social "vestige" possessed of an unexplained viability in the contemporary world.

It is precisely because so much of Academic Sociology is polemically and compulsively anti-Marxist and anti-socialist that it was led to explore parts of the social world ignored by the Marxists and to focus on, and often exaggerate, every new social development that meant bad news for Marxism. Indeed, Academic Sociology has often provided a systematic awareness of those very social processes which, because they were lacking in the awareness of Marxists, have contributed to the latter's failures. That Academic Sociology has commonly been animated by politically inspired motives does not necessarily vitiate the fact that it has often explored hitherto unknown social worlds, and that what it has found is often usable in transforming the modern world.

The task, then, is not simply to denounce Academic Sociology, but also to understand that it contains viable elements and liberative potentialities. The problem is to crack these out of the conservative ideological structure in which they are embedded, to rework them thoroughly, and to assimilate them in a social theory which is not limited and confined to the assumptions of our present society. The problem is not only to denounce Academic Sociology but also to transcend and sublate it.

A NOTE ON THE FUTURE OF SOCIOLOGY

It should be clear then, that I have not meant to suggest that the crisis in Academic Sociology will be resolved by a return to the *status quo ante*, or that there will be no major changes in its larger structure. Far from it. First, as I have suggested, I see a continuing movement of Functionalism (of what is even now beginning to be called "classical" or "static" Functionalism by certain Functionalists themselves) toward a convergence with Marxism; but what I have said above means, in effect, that this drift will stop a good deal short of a full blending with, let alone a surrender to, Marxism. It will be an assimilation accommodative to the infrastructure of Functionalism discussed here. My conjecture is that the equilibrium point in this development, that is, the point at which it will stop moving toward Marxism, will be a kind of "Keynesian" Functionalism, which gives special weight to the role of the government and the political process, and which will be pervaded by a more instrumental mood.

At the same time, however, I also expect, as I have indicated, that there will be increased development of a more distinctly Marxist and radical sociology that will have an autonomous base in the emerging generation of younger sociologists, even though they will not be the only ones contributing to it. The hard social core of this development, then, will not consist of defecting Functionalists but of those who were never committed to Functionalism in the first place, who were largely trained in the period after Functionalism came under mounting theoretical attack, and who were congenial to and experienced the emergence of the New Left.

In effect, the movement toward more Keynesian and Marxian views signals a transformation of the total structure of academic sociological perspectives; it will not simply be an addition to an essentially unchanged structure. It means that the range or spread of the ideological perspective of Academic Sociology will be greatly extended. In particular, it means that there will be something that has hardly ever before existed, particularly in American Academic

Sociology, namely, a "left" that will openly accept Marx and Marxist works as theoretical paradigms. There will emerge, both by reason of the Keynesian drift in Functionalism and by reason of the development of a separate Marxian Sociology, a general shift to the left in the community of Academic Sociologists. That the New Marxists and the New Leftists will not view even the Keynesian Functionalists with much greater regard than they have the "classical" Functionalists—in short, that they will continue to view them as conservative—should not obscure the fact that the intellectual structure of Academic Sociology itself will have, nonetheless, undergone a major reorganization.

So far as theoretical and intellectual perspectives are concerned, certain other developments may be expected. Among these, one may expect a continued interest in Goffman's dramaturgical standpoint, and other perspectives allied with it, such as Howard Becker's work on deviance, which constitute a new stage in the development of the "Chicago School." Along with Garfinkel's ethnomethodology, these promise to resonate the sentiments and assumptions of some young people oriented to the new Psychedelic Culture, and perhaps even of some of the New Left. It should be expected that these standpoints will continue to win support from sections of the younger generation.

While George Homans' standpoint is imbued with a much less romantic perspective than Goffman's and is disposed toward a rather different, a more "high science" methodology than those deriving from the Chicago tradition, there are, nonetheless, certain points of affinity among all of them. For one, they share a common focus upon "small groups" research. More important, however, they are all commonly nonhistorical in their perspectives; the world with which they attempt to deal is a world outside history. Partly for this reason, they are rather sharply differentiated from the emerging Marxian sociology which is, of course, traditionally historical in perspective. Nonetheless, I suspect that, faced with a choice between neo-Marxists and neo-Functionalists, some in this new group, particularly those with a Chicago heritage, may find the Marxists closer to their own alienated dispositions and share with them an amorphous sympathy with underdogs and victims.

With respect to its theoretical and intellectual dispositions, then, as well as with regard to its ideological ramifications, the structure of Academic Sociology promises to become much more polycentric than it has been. It will, also, become more ideologically resonant than it has been. But one may conjecture that there will increasingly emerge a tensionful polarization between this development and the growth of an instrumental orientation. This growing instrumentalism, accelerated by the increasing role of the state, finds its expression in "theoryless" theories, a kind of methodological empiricism in which there is a neglect of *substantive* concepts and assumptions concerning specifically human behavior and social relations, and a corresponding emphasis upon seemingly neutral methods, mathematical models, investigational techniques, and research technologies of all kinds. Among the most notable instances of this are operations research, cybernetics, general systems theory, and even operant conditioning. Indeed, Parsons himself has already manifested certain inclinations toward a kind of general systems theory.

Such a conceptually uncommitted and empty methodological empiricism is particularly well adapted to service the research needs of the Welfare State. This is so, in part, for precisely the reason that Comte anticipated, namely, that their "hard" methodologies function as a rhetoric of persuasion. They communicate an image of a "scientific" neutrality and thereby presumably provide a basis for political consensus concerning government programs. Furthermore, their conceptual emptiness allows their researches to be formulated in terms that focus directly on those problems and variables of administrative interest to government sponsors. They thus avoid any conflict between the applied interests of their government sponsors and the technical interests of a theoretically guided tradition. In effect, the methodological empiricists are increasingly becoming the market researchers of the Welfare State.

These theoretical changes and developments in Academic Sociology will be occurring in a society in which a Welfare State has been institutionalized and exerts great pressure on the social sciences, especially through funding and other resources. The Welfare State will continue to influence the Functionalists, and it will strongly support methodological empiricism. It will also influence studies carried on in the Chicago tradition, exerting pressure on it to focus its alienated component on the unmasking of the low level administrators in charge of "caretaking" operations in local communities, and thus facilitate their subjection to control from the administrative center at the national level.[4] Nor is there the slightest reason to suppose that the Marxists themselves will be exempt from the blandishments and pressures of the Welfare State. It is likely that many will, in the end, become "Marxists of the chair." Some who began by denouncing "consensus" theories in favor of "conflict" theories will "transcend" this Hegelian thesis-antithesis with a new dialectical "synthesis" calling for "cooperation." One should not be surprised to find erstwhile "conflict" theorists, such as Irving Louis Horowitz, capitulating completely to Parsonsianism and solemnly announcing, "Indeed the drive of a social system is toward structure and ultimately toward the maintenance of order."[5]

And there will also be increasingly fine distinctions made by Marxists and other sociologists, about which government agencies it is permissible to ask money from, some feeling that the Department of Defense is tainted but that the State Department's money is clean. In short, all schools of sociology will face the common problem of eluding the confining perspectives of the Welfare State, though some will do so more than will others.

NOTES

1. I have outlined my views on the nature and origins of Plato's social theory at some length in A. W. Gouldner, *Enter Plato* (New York: Basic Books, 1965), particularly in Part II. Here, of course, I can only sketch them briefly. I indicated in *Enter Plato* that this study was undertaken not out of antiquarian interest but precisely to help diagnose the *present* condition of social theory.

2. T. Parsons, "Religious Perspectives of College Teaching in Sociology and Social Psychology," in A. W. and H. P. Gouldner et al., *Modern Sociology* (New York: Harcourt, Brace & World, 1963), p. 488.

3. One might add that Plato's thought also is environed by a similar threat, but one which has already culminated: by the climactic experience of Athens' defeat by Sparta, by the destruction of the Athenian empire, by the later defeat of Sparta herself, and with this, the destruction of the Hellenic citadel of traditionalism, which could then no longer provide either a living embodiment of the aristocratic oligarch's aspirations or a safe political refuge.

4. For a fuller discussion, see my "Sociologist as Partisan: Sociology and the Welfare State," *The American Sociologist* (August 1968).

5. I. L. Horowitz, "Radicalism and Contemporary American Society," p. 569, S. E. Deutsch and J. Howard, *Where It's At, Radical Perspectives in Sociology* (New York: Harper & Row, 1970).

Notes on the Crisis of Marxism and the Emergence of Academic Sociology in the Soviet Union

Though Functionalism in the United States is involved in a crisis, its world career is far from at an end. Indeed, the career of Functionalism, and of Academic Sociology more broadly, is now just beginning in Eastern Europe and in the Soviet Union. Both are becoming increasingly attractive to intellectuals in the Soviet Bloc of nations. Even as the American reaction to the work of Talcott Parsons seems to be increasingly critical or apathetic, there is a growing interest in it among European scholars, both Marxist and non-Marxist alike.

I have suggested earlier, in Chapter 4, that world sociology underwent a binary fission; one "half" of it became Academic Sociology, in which the Functionalist tradition finally became the dominant theoretical synthesis, while the other "half" of world sociology became Marxist. Until after World War II each tradition was greatly isolated from, not to say contemptuous of, the other. This changed radically, however, after World War II and especially after the "thaw" in the Cold War, when there was renewed interaction between the two traditions.

It would be overstating it, however, were I to suggest that, prior to that time, both traditions developed in total isolation and without any mutual influence. Indeed, much of the history of Academic Sociology during the Classical or third period is unintelligible except as a response to and a polemic against Marxism. Had there been no Marx, the emphases and character of the work of Max Weber, Emile Durkheim, and Vilfredo Pareto would have been vastly different. Moreover, Marxism and Functionalism did exert mutual influence and pressure upon one another well before World War II. If, as seems to be the case, Marxism influenced Functionalism more than vice versa, it was largely so because Functionalism was still continuing to develop long after World War I, while the intellectual development of Marxism was blighted as Stalinism strengthened its hold on the Soviet Union.

One most interesting, early indication of the influence of conventional Academic Sociology on Soviet Marxism may be found in the work of Nicolai Bukharin, who was fully familiar with most of the great sociologists of the Classical period. It appears that Bukharin was working his way toward a formally developed and generalized social "system" model of analysis.[1] An important expression of Marxist influence on work of a specifically Functionalist character, although characteristically unacknowledged, may be found in the theory of the Polish anthropologist Bronislaw Malinowski. The Marxist influence—particularly of some on its highest level domain assumptions—on the theory of Robert K. Merton is also notable and significant.[2] In general, however, Marxist influence seems decidedly stronger in anthropology than in sociology. This may be due to the far greater interest that anthropologists traditionally have in the "material" conditions of life, in artifactual, biological, and even evolutionary concerns, as well as to anthropology's being a far more "romantic" discipline than sociology, resonating more congenially to the more romantic domain assumptions of Marxism. (While I cannot develop it here, it should at least be clear at this point that I do not in the least regard the "romantic" as intrinsically "conservative" or "reactionary" and do not use the terms in a dyslogistic way.)

The influence of Marxism on Functionalism was, until recently, rather difficult to see or document, for it was usually unfootnoted and unacknowledged. It was, nonetheless, often a part of Functionalism's viable culture and, as such, more visible to those who actually participated in it on that level than to those who had to rely on the record deposited in publications. Marxism's influence on Functionalism is part of the still unwritten history of the Functional Sociology that developed in a middle-class society where Marxism was politically anathema, where the taint of Marxism could cripple academic careers, where Marxism was often dismissed out of hand as an outdated theory or as a mere ideology or, as a "religion" by those same people who otherwise professed to a respect for religion. In such circumstances, some Functionalists found the use of Marxism so inexpedient and dangerous that they repressed their own awareness of their own actual reliance upon it, so that they would not feel anxious about using it, and, at least, simply screened out its open manifestations so they would not be subject to reprisals. If this conception of the matter seems discrepant with the self-image that academic scholars in the West have of their own intellectual autonomy and moral courage, those who lived through (and still allow themselves to remember) the impact of the McCarthy repression will know that it is not overdrawn: if generals and senators were intimidated, so too were professors. Thus some Functionalists borrowed from Marxism, but discreetly or somnambulistically.

Still, this borrowing was only a part of the deviant "underculture" of Functionalism and not its dominant public posture. The dominant situation was one of relatively great mutual isolation, of polemical criticism, and of often unalloyed ignorance between the Functionalist and Marxist traditions. (The relationship between diehard Sociological Positivism and Marxism was even more strained.) The Functionalists missed the point that Marxism filled a void to which they themselves had, by their own one-sidedness, contributed. Focusing on the manner in which societies maintain themselves spontaneously, Functionalists were not prepared for the development of the Welfare State and for the day when they would be called upon to provide tangible aid to facilitate state control of domestic and international problems. The Marxists, for their part, could not imagine that they too would one day have need of a social science that specialized in the study of social order and consensus. Escalating Lenin's rhetoric about the "lapdogs of imperialism," certain Soviet Marxists saw no humor in berating graying academicians in small midwestern colleges as the "sharks of imperialism."

If I have not misread the signs, there is a basic shift impending on both sides of this great historical division. As I have said, some Functionalists have in recent times manifested a clear and open drift toward Marxism. Correspondingly, many Marxists, in the Soviet Bloc as elsewhere, manifest a growing attraction to Academic Sociology, including Functionalism and even Parsons himself. The Functionalist heirs of the Positivist tradition and the adherents of Marxism are moving now, each toward the other, cautiously and tentatively, to be sure, but moving, nonetheless. Each side is now less concerned than before with merely polemicizing against the other and is more deeply involved in attempting to learn about the other's position in its full complexity.[3]

As a result, world sociology is now closer than ever before to transcending the schism with which it has lived for more than a century. To say that this potentiality is now greater than ever is, however, very far from saying that it is something that will happen tomorrow. Moreover, while all men of good will cherish a vision of human unity and desire the decline of all factors that contribute to mutual antipathy between the two greatest powers of the modern world, still it must not automatically be supposed that, even were this theoretical rapprochement to be consummated, it would un- equivocally be "good" for human welfare. The meaning and con- sequences of such a rapprochement would depend on the basis on which it comes to rest, on the uses to which it is put, and on the needs and values it serves. I shall return to this question at a later point.

The movement of Soviet Marxists toward an increased apprecia- tion of Academic Sociology is certainly consistent with the funda- mental assumption of Marx and Engels that their own theory, and working-class culture more generally, must and should assimilate the best in bourgeois thought. But the modern interest in Academic Sociology by Soviet Marxists cannot, of course, be explained as a *result* of this assumption, precisely because it is a relatively new turn. Moreover, I do not believe that this turn to Academic Sociol- ogy is attributable to a belief that a theoretical retooling of Marxism is necessary to manage its intellectual difficulty in dealing with the new social structures and problems—the rise of the "new" middle class, or the separation of management and ownership, for instance —that have appeared since the emergence of Marxism, or because these are regarded as disconfirming the expectations and predic- tions of Marx. The difficulties of the Marxian thesis concerning the "increasing misery" of the proletariat, or of the thesis about the polarization between capital and labor—these and many other problems were long familiar to Marxists. This "disconfirming" evi- dence, then, cannot account for the modern interest of Soviet Marxists in Academic Sociology, any more than the recent shift in Parsonsianism toward Marxism may be explained as a result of its own empirical difficulties or its failure to be supported by the facts. This shift is an expression, rather, of a crisis in Marxism which parallels that in Functionalism and, in large part, derives from the conflicts and problems of Soviet society itself.

Among the various contemporary expressions of this crisis in world Marxism is the growing variety of neo-Marxisms. This is, in part, indicated by increased interest among independent Marxists living in the West in the earlier contributions of Georg Lukàcs and Antonio Gramsci; and by the strongly Hegelian work of the Frank- furt School, including Herbert Marcuse, which is accepted by cer- tain Marxists as a contribution to the development of Marxism itself; and by the anti-Hegelian work of communists such as the French philosopher Louis Althusser,[4] who are strongly attracted to the "structuralism" of Claude Lévi-Strauss and who, like other Marxists working in France (for instance, Nicos Poulantzas[5]) are fully abreast of developments in Academic Sociology, including the work of Parsons; and the *differences* between Althusser and certain other French Marxist philosophers, such as the more humanistic Roger Garaudy.[6] Along similar lines, expressing the growing differentiation in Marxism, is the pronounced emphasis by certain Poles and Yugoslavians on the humanistic dimension in Marx.[7] Very closely related to such interests is the continued emphasis on the importance of the young Marx, which is as pronounced among younger men throughout Western Europe as it is in the United States. This commonly entails a focus upon alienation, which comes to be viewed increasingly not only as a phenomenon of capitalism but as a more pervasive pathology, and one which may be found, as Adam Schaff,[8] the Polish communist philosopher, has argued, even within socialist society. This growing variability in Marxism, then, is expressed not only by nonaffiliated Marxists but also by those affiliated with various communist parties, sometimes on high leadership levels, and by those within the Soviet Bloc of nations as well as outside it. The implications of this growing variety of interpretations of Marxism have been well expressed by Norman Birnbaum, who has remarked:

> The question is, how much further can Marxism be opened without itself undergoing a radical transformation. . . . It may be, however, that those sociologists most aware of their debt to the Marxist tradition will have to transform and transcend it; if so, the crisis in Marxist sociology may mark the beginning of the end of Marxism.[9]

One important factor underlying this growing differentiation in interpretations of Marxism is the diversity of the national experiences and interests of Marxists in various cultures. Where, as in China, Cuba, and Yugoslavia, they came to power largely by their own revolutionary efforts, with little or no Soviet aid, this is commonly taken as a basis for theorizing that is independent of and divergent from the Soviet model. Also underlying the crisis of Marxism was the blunting of its own "critical" impulse after it became the official theory and ideology of the Soviet State and of the mass communist parties of Western Europe. While Marxism remains a basis for a critique of the bourgeois world, its capacity to serve as a basis for a critique of communist state apparatuses, societies, and movements was impaired, particularly as it came under the control of the party apparatus, who often used it more to legitimate policies than to arrive at them. With the communist seizure of state power in Eastern Europe and the growing entrenchment of communist parties in Western Europe, Marxism found itself in a totally different position than when it had first been seeking to establish a political foothold.

Seeking to protect its own society from the uncertain outcomes of international tensions, the Soviet State has inhibited socialist movements elsewhere from risking revolutionary lunges to power that might, it fears, provoke international conflagrations into which it could be drawn; and it has come to rely upon its own military power rather than on support from revolutionary groups elsewhere. The Soviet State now does not believe that war with the West is inevitable. This impulse toward an accommodation between the Soviet Union and the West, no less than the Soviet Union's internal need for the stabilization of its own society, has been conducive to an academization of Marxism that dulls its critical and revolutionary edge. Similarly, as the mass communist parties of Italy and France become firmly established in their own societies, they also become increasingly committed to a search for power through parliamentary means; they seek to ally themselves with, placate, or neutralize other forces in their society to further this objective. Thus one finds a continuing and growing dialogue between Western Marxists and theologians, and a correspondingly greater readiness of Marxists to be less critical of religion and to see it as something more complex than "the opium of the people." Viewed from the standpoint of some young revolutionaries in Western Europe, Marxism—particularly in its Soviet manifestation —often seems an increasingly conservative force, either dampening their own revolutionary élan, or, in Cohn-Bendit's term, simply an "obsolete" thing. At the same time, however, Soviet Marxism-Leninism still does not provide Soviet leaders, managers, and administrators with the concrete kind of instrumental technology that they increasingly seek to further their governance and to help them in equilibrating their society. In short, both the conservative and revolutionary wings of the communist movement today are often seriously dissatisfied with the present state of Marxism-Leninism.

THE CRISIS OF SOVIET MARXISM:
THE LINGUISTICS CONTROVERSY

The emerging crisis of Soviet Marxism was clearly evident well before the 20th Congress of the Soviet Communist Party and, indeed, was quite visible even during Stalinism. One of the most interesting expressions of this was, I believe, initiated by Stalin himself, in 1950, in the guise of a discussion of certain technical problems of linguistics.[10] This took the form of a critique of the views that a Soviet linguist, N. Y. Marr, by then dead, had earlier advanced about the nature of language.

Marr had been confronted with the problem of where to locate language in the Marxian framework: Was it a part of the economic-production "foundation" or a part of the ideological and social "superstructure"? Since there was little in Marx that would allow language to be characterized as part of the economic foundation, Marr quite naturally opted for the superstructure, in any case a residual concept of sprawling looseness. Stalin, however, firmly denied this, arguing that, if language were part of the super-structure, then, like other such elements, it should have changed with the shifts in the Russian economic foundation from feudalism to capitalism to socialism. Yet, it is apparent, he says, that "the Russian language has remained essentially what it was before the October Revolution." Well, he was asked, is language part of the economic foundation? No, it is not, according to Stalin. In despera-tion he was then asked, Is language an intermediary phenomenon, located midway between the economic base and the social super-structure? No, says Stalin, it is not. Stalin's position, in effect, added a third general category to the traditional Marxist distinction between infrastructure and superstructure, and this was accepted by Soviet scholars. This third category includes social phenomenon, such as language—which in an interesting convergence with Par-sons is a "prerequisite" of social development—as well as mathe-matics, symbolic logic, and the facts (as opposed to the interpreta-tions) of science. These, it seems, are now regarded as independent of the economic infrastructure and do not vary with changes in it.[11]

It is clear that this issue was not half so important in its specific implications for language as in its general consequences for classi-cal Marxism as a theoretical system. Classical Marxism had dichotomized the world of social phenomena, holding that every-thing in it was either part of the economic infrastructure or of the social superstructure. What Stalin was, in effect, doing was ac-knowledging that this conceptual dichotomy so central to Marxism was unworkable. The position he took had inevitably to create pres-sure for a more general and drastic overhauling of Marxism, and not merely of its peripheral elements but of its very fundamentals.

Some of the reasons for this theoretical shift can be gleaned from Stalin's discussion of the "class" character of language. Like an orthodox Marxist, Marr had held that language was influenced by the system of social classes within the society in which it existed. Language, however, answered Stalin, is not a class phenomenon but is essentially a "national" thing. Here, as elsewhere, let me stress that I am not concerned with whether Stalin was empirically correct in what he said about language. What I am interested in are the implications of his position for Marxism as a general theory. Here, again, these seem clear. In this case, they involve a turn from the traditional Marxist emphasis on the significance of class phenomena to a greater emphasis on the autonomy of language and its *national* character, which had previously taken a secondary place in classical Marxist theory.

Marr had also believed that language, like other social phenomena, changed and sometimes changed with sudden rapidity. As a Marxist, Marr had held that social phenomena, language included, could develop with sudden revolutionary leaps and bounds. "Marxism," however, replied Stalin, "does not recognize sudden explosions in the development of languages, the sudden death of an existing language and the sudden creation of a new language." Here, once more, Stalin went out of his way to declare that established Marxist domain assumptions, in this case those concerning the potentially sudden character of great changes, are inapplicable.

It seems clear from this that classical Marxism, essentially a change-oriented, revolutionary, and crisis-sensitive sociology, was not merely becoming intellectually troublesome to the Soviet *rulers*, but that, in certain ways, Stalin was beginning to regard it as *politically* dangerous. Stalin makes this evident when he adds that the Marxist theory of sudden change is no longer *generally* applicable to Soviet society.

It should be said in general for the benefit of comrades who have an infatuation for such explosions that the law of transition from an old quality to a new by means of an explosion is inapplicable not only to the history of languages: It is not always applicable to some other social phenomena of a basal or superstructural character. It is compulsory for a society divided into hostile classes. But it is not compulsory for a society which has no hostile classes.

By which, of course, he meant the Soviet Union.

Well before the 20th Congress of the Soviet Union's Communist Party, then, the "Marr Controversy" had already made it plain that the critical, change-oriented, and revolutionary character of Marxism was discomfiting to some Soviet political leaders; that sectors of the Soviet leadership were disposed to pay greater attention to societally *integrating* forces such as language, or to "natural" foci of social organization such as nationality and ethnicity, and thereby to place greater emphasis upon gradual rather than sudden change. In particular, the Marr Controversy indicated that the dichotomous, hierarchical view of social reality, so intrinsic to Marxism, was under pressure. The Marr Controversy thus indicated, on the one side, that the most essential characteristics of Marxism itself were beginning to be experienced as dissonant with the new needs of the Soviet State; on the other side, it also revealed some of the specific assumptions around which a different and more congenial social theory, very much akin to Functionalism, would be likely to develop. The need for a sociology oriented to the problem of *integrating* society was thus already manifest in Soviet society well before the thaw inspired by the 20th Congress of its Communist Party, though it became fully manifest only after that Congress.

FUNCTIONALISM GOES EAST

A systematic analysis of the diverse symptoms and sources of the emerging crisis of Marxism, in and out of the Soviet Bloc, is a task well beyond the scope of the present study. It is a problem every bit as complex and demanding as an analysis of the parallel crisis of Academic Sociology. In the foregoing I have sought tentatively to explore and to sketch only a very few of the dimensions of the problem.[12] In what follows, I shall confine myself to one aspect of the crisis of Soviet Marxism, namely, the emergence of Academic Sociology in the Soviet Union itself, and I shall limit myself to observations and conclusions about this that are based primarily, though not exclusively, on my own personal observations in Eastern Europe and my discussions with sociologists and other scholars there.

Marxism was, at least in one major part, a theory of how to change the world. It was the mirror image of the Comtianism from which Functionalism developed, and it never centered its attention on the problem of stabilizing society. Yet as East European nations today begin to achieve heightened industrialization, they too seem to manifest a need for a theory that focuses on the spontaneous mechanisms conducive to social stability and order. Indeed, it appears that this is one reason for the emergence of "Liebermanism" in the Soviet Union. Liebermanism is a theory of the *spontaneous* or market-like mechanisms useful for maintaining economic growth and stability. Liebermanism focuses on the "natural" and spontaneous mechanisms of economic order; some version of Functionalism is needed to provide sociological underpinning for its economics.

For what it is worth, I might mention that I presented this thesis —concerning the growing attractiveness of Functionalism to Eastern European sociologists—at a conference held by some of them, at which it was a subject of discussions conducted in my absence. The following comments were written by an Eastern European sociologist concerning this discussion:

The idea that Functionalism has begun a victorious march to the East was considered as a valid one. Some papers prepared for the convention . . . as well as some comments made there in discussion may be taken as new evidence in this sense. A paper written by a [nationality designation] sociologist was done in the best or the worst Parsonsian terms, far more closer to Davis and Moore than to Tumin's views. Of course, there was and there is a disagreement whether this turn to Functionalism is something to be welcomed in every respect.

The significance of Parsons' equilibrium analysis for the Soviet Bloc is that it is concerned, in the Comtian tradition, with the manner in which social systems *spontaneously* maintain *themselves* and that it focuses on the internal conditions that contribute to such spontaneous societal self-maintenance. The crux of Parsons' importance here is in how he formulates the equilibrium problem; he wants to know how it is *self*-governing, self-adjusting, self-correcting, self-maintaining. His analysis is valuable not because it tells us what actually happens, but because he focuses on how social systems might be *made* more self-maintaining.

There is no question, in my mind, that many of the details and many of the fundamental assumptions that Parsons advances in attempting to solve the equilibrium problem are wrong. There is also no question that Parsons has, nonetheless, developed an analysis of this problem that goes well beyond that of his predecessors. He has gone far in setting out elements that need to be considered and in establishing firmer ground for continuing work on it. Anyone concerned with this matter must and can use Parsons as a point of departure and as a grindstone on which to sharpen his own thought.

Parsons' abiding focus on this problem is, at once, both the least useful and the most promising of his contributions, for there are some social systems in the world today that are primarily girded for change, while others aim at stabilization. The underdeveloped "third" world is not now fundamentally concerned with the social problem of how to develop a self-maintaining equilibrium in its social system. Its problem, rather, seems to be much better conceived of as how to change, if not disrupt, its old social system, and how to mobilize "starting mechanisms" to generate a new rate and direction of development, so that it may enter the industrial "take-off." While even here there are important questions as to how self-maintaining mechanisms can be built into this development, so that a benign cycle of continual development may occur, nonetheless, for many of these countries the central issue is how to break out of their old social system and start a new one. To this extent, Parsons' focus on self-equilibrating social systems is, from their standpoint, useless. It provides little guidance for the "take-off" problem, and for the revolutionary transformations that will precede it.

At the same time, however, there are other major regions of the world (most particularly, the Soviet Bloc in Eastern Europe) where, within the last half century, old social systems have been replaced and new ones developed. Here, the starting problem has been solved and the industrial take-off achieved. With this achievement, however, the ground is prepared for a shift to a more conservative interest in maintaining what has been achieved and, with this, to a growing interest in the kinds of self-regulating systems which Parsons—as the culminating figure in the Comtian tradition—has done most to develop. Parsonsianism and Functionalism are congenial to those who, like some in the Soviet Bloc, are more concerned with the problem of *stabilizing* their society. Moreover, Parsonsian equilibrium analysis is probably most compatible with the more *liberal* initiatives of these cultures; self-regulation in the Soviet context means the relaxation of the massive centralized controls which they had established. The irony is that Parsonsianism may now have greater practical use in the very society which it was developed in opposition to. No Hegelian could have asked for more.

As the nations of the Soviet Bloc seek mechanisms to protect themselves against a recrudescence of Stalinism, their intellectuals increasingly stress the role of morality; they discuss "Marxism and Ethics" and place great emphasis on the importance of the very self-restraining moral norms that Functionalism has always stressed. In my discussions with sociologists in Eastern Europe during 1965 and 1966, the importance of ethics and moral values was repeatedly emphasized. In my discussions with Soviet sociologists, they also dwelt on the importance of strengthening what they called "self-control" among Soviet citizens. There are, I was told,

difficulties in getting people to exert self-control. For example, we have had legal studies of the Soviets. Our legal scholars tell us that we do not need to be given new rights; the problem is to get people to use the rights they were given twenty to thirty years ago. The same is true in other spheres of life, in factories and elsewhere. A habit of waiting for directives from the top has emerged in the past, from past situations, and it is hard to change this habit, but we are trying. We are trying to extend democracy in our country and, with this, a greater respect for the individual person.

Soviet sociologists, like those in Poland, generally emphasized the importance of developing what they termed the "spiritual life" of their countries. It is not merely the analytic uses, then, but the very nature of Functionalism's built-in morality that makes it attractive to Eastern Europeans. As the Soviet Bloc strives toward heightened industrialization, as it explores political and economic decentralization, as it seeks to consolidate and to enjoy what it has accomplished, and most important, as it encounters the "impatience" of its own younger generation, about whose restiveness it is deeply concerned, it may very well turn increasingly toward Functional theory, precisely because it is a conservative theory, a theory of social order and restraint.

Relative to the political conditions prevailing in these countries, however, Functionalism is *not* a conservative but a *liberal* theory of social order, for, at least prior to its turn toward the Welfare State, it has usually emphasized the importance of the spontaneous and self-maintaining mechanisms of social control rather than of state regulation and control. It might be added, however, that Functionalism is a liberal position not only relative to *political* conditions in the Soviet Bloc, but also when compared with the ideological implications of certain of even the newer social science orientations there. In the discussions about "Liebermanism" in the Soviet Union, it seems clear that certain groupings within the social science community have, in fact, opposed its liberalizing potentialities, arguing that decentralized, spontaneous market mechanisms may not be necessary to solve the problems of Soviet planning. Specifically, some apparently hold that the problems of centralized planning, even on the macroscopic national level, may be managed successfully in the Soviet Union by developing new computer facilities. It is thus quite clear that even the supposedly neutral technologies of science, such as computerization, may have an ideological disposition; specialists in them are sometimes moved by vested interest in their own technology to support politically centralized controls and oppose decentralization. (Something quite similar may also be expected from "program budgeting" in American governmental administration; as Aaron Wildavsky remarks, "As presently conceived, program budgeting contains an extreme centralizing bias.")[13]

ACADEMIC SOCIOLOGY IN THE SOVIET BLOC

The social theory of the Soviet Union and of the Soviet Bloc, then, no less than that of the United States, is moving toward significant change. While I cannot explore the Soviet side of this development in any detail, I shall allow myself a few generalizations derived from my observations and discussions in three Eastern European countries—Poland, Yugoslavia, and the Soviet Union itself—during 1965 and 1966.

1. It seems indisputable that there is a growing and increasingly *autonomous* body of distinctly sociological theory and research within these countries. This is not a revival or reactivation of Marxism. Institutionally and intellectually it is, and is intended to be, distinct from conventional Marxism as such. It is not a "neo-Marxism." It is intended to be something new; it is an "Academic Sociology." In some places it is, in fact, expressly characterized as an assimilation of "Western" sociology. In the Soviet Union it is taking its deepest root in Moscow, Leningrad, and Novosibirsk, and is judged there by standards that are quite distinguishable from those of traditional Marxism-Leninism. It is creating new research institutes. It is publishing an increasing number of translations of American theoretical works, including the strongly functionalist *Sociology Today;* and while it is often focused on, it is not confined to, merely technical volumes on research methods. Young people especially, I was told, are widely and greatly interested in the emerging sociology.

2. While the development of sociology in the Soviet Bloc is, of course, very uneven, it is also producing interesting theoretical work, as evidenced, for example, by the *Polish Sociological Bulletin,* which, notably, is published in English. In particular, perhaps, their grasp of stratification theory is increasingly sophisticated. Soviet work on organizational analysis also manifests a rapid growth in sophistication. Some of the applied communications research both at Talinn and Novosibirsk seems to be of a high order, as is the demographic work at Novosibirsk. More generally, the Novosibirsk group seems to be producing very creditable mathematical social science.

It is my impression that some Soviet sociologists are in no hurry to make systematic contributions to social theory—on any level of complexity—because they fear that this will have a disunifying effect upon the emerging Soviet sociology. In brief, they seem to fear that theory-making may accentuate the differences among Soviet sociologists, and that such intellectual divisiveness would be particularly injurious at the present stage of the institutional development of Soviet sociology. The development of Soviet sociological theory would also be more likely to increase the strain between Soviet sociology and Soviet Marxism. Many Soviet sociologists, then, are building their new institutions with a great deal of self-consciousness, though it does not, of course, imply that all are. This suggests that they will give fuller rein to those forms of work—such as "concrete" or quantitative researches or methodological developments—that are apt to win easier acceptance and to generate more consensus among themselves. In short, quantitative and methodological interests are more compatible with the present, still early stage of the institutionalization of Soviet sociology, since they constitute solidarity-enhancing foci.

3. As the foregoing implies, there was in 1966 an increasing openness in Eastern European nations to the work of American sociologists. Their interest in reading more American sociology, and in having access to work by American sociologists, whether translated or in English, was repeatedly evidenced. Their complaint was not that political authorities prevented these books from entering, but that shortages of library funds were inhibiting them. Some young people specifically volunteered a desire to read the recent mathematical work of James Coleman and Harrison White. Their elders wanted more opportunities for face-to-face contact with American sociologists and were, at that time, clearly vying with one another to be able to attend the conference of the International Sociological Association to be held at Evian in 1966. They look forward to more foreign exchange programs between their scholars and our own.

4. They make quite realistic judgments about the technical worth of their work thus far and evidence a determined ambition to improve it. Soviet sociologists feel that their as yet unpublished work is decidedly superior to that which has recently been published in Russia and also to much that has been translated into English recently.

5. Corresponding to their sober appraisals of Soviet sociology, they also seem to have a growing realism in their judgments about Soviet institutions and social stratification, which augurs well for the quality of future research. Thus, for example, one Soviet specialist in social stratification had this to say:

Our conceptions of social stratification have changed greatly. . . . We once thought—or Stalin said—we only had two strata or classes, intelligentsia and workers-farmers. Now we know better. There are many, and many new ones, In the 1930's we thought that the differences between strata would soon disappear, but we see that they haven't. And they won't disappear for . . . certainly another fifteen years. The differences between them are more than matters of income. They are also differences in education, culture, prestige. It will take more than increased education to eliminate them. It will also need technological development and automation. Today it is often difficult to get people to take or stay at dull jobs. Well, we will get rid of the dull jobs with technological change. But the interesting jobs of today will be viewed as dull when technology develops. Social mobility today is also not what we had thought; the sons of workers are also more likely to be workers themselves.

6. Soviet sociology has given considerable stress to what it characterizes as "concrete" research. "Concrete" is the resonating programmatic concept around which much of the new development of Soviet sociology is formed and without an understanding of which it cannot be properly assessed. Suffice it to say here that the term "concrete" does not seem simply to recommend empirical research on practical problems. The concept of a concrete sociology does not simply give positive affirmation to a new program of empirical work, but also implies a tacit critical judgment of older forms of theoretical analysis. It seems to embody a growing readiness to reject theoretical work that is not empirically founded and, indeed, to reject all self-sealing and self-validating approaches to social theory. It also appears to express reservations about more speculative, future-oriented work and to entail a greater focus upon contemporary conditions. The concept of concrete sociology, then, is both the sloganistic spearhead of a new program of research and a terse, implicit critique of an older style of speculative theorizing.

7. Accompanying this is a more flexible and, indeed, a more rigorously scientific attitude among Eastern European sociologists toward Marxism and Historical Materialism itself. I should mention that I deliberately went out of my way to learn what Soviet sociologists thought about the relationship between the new concrete sociology and traditional Marxism-Leninism. I made a point of asking what they thought would happen if research results appeared to invalidate Marxism. The answers were various; some intelligent, some courageous, some ingenuous, and some not. Yet the central tendency seems to come down to this: there is a growing conception of Marxism as a guide to research, which is to say, as a researchable model, rather than as a self-evident, self-sufficient metaphysics. Indeed, Marxism itself was on several occasions

expressly and, I think, significantly characterized as a "model."
Here I have in mind informal comments by various Soviet sociologists, such as those that follow:

Many of our philosophers write books on Historical Materialism. We
believe there need not be only one approach or one way of presenting
Historical Materialism and that it is good that different men should
write about Historical Materialism. . . . First, it must be remembered
that Historical Materialism is a theory and that life is more complex
and larger than any theory. All theory has limitations. Second, if life
differs from the theory it may be not because the theory is wrong, but
because conditions have prevented the theory from being fulfilled. So
one has to change the conditions. . . . Marxism is not the Bible. It does
not stay still for all time. . . . A theory is a theory. Concrete sociology
may add something new. Old truths may be improved. Concrete research
is a deepening of theory. It checks up on how theory conforms to reality.

All this does not imply, however, that Soviet sociologists regard
the results of concrete research as defining the essence of Soviet
"reality." What Soviet sociologists conceive of as "real" is still
greatly shaped by their larger social theories and domain assumptions—in short, by Marxism. In this, however, they do not appear
to be radically different from those Western sociologists, committed
to Functional theory, whose conceptions of social reality are also
influenced by the metaphysical commitments of their own social
theory. The decisive consideration is the extent to which these
metaphysical commitments are viewed as susceptible to empirical
disconfirmation, the extent to which they are conceived of either
as a "model" of reality or as indisputably real apart from their
researchable implications. In these respects, Soviet sociologists
appear to be converging with their Western counterparts.

8. The growth of a distinct sociological specialization in Eastern
Europe is not to be understood as the reassertion of "antisocialist"
or "antiparty" views by the older intelligentsia of the universities.
First, the real vitality of Eastern European sociology is often among
the younger men. Second, and more important, the new sociology
is often led today by men who enjoy positions of trust within the
communist parties of their countries and who are unquestionably
loyal to them. Indeed, so far as I could judge, some of the best
sociology—some of the most theoretically sophisticated and empirically rigorous sociology, even by American standards—is being
produced by Communist Party members.

It would be absurd to assume that the emergence of Soviet
sociology and its larger meanings have somehow escaped the notice
of the leaders of the Communist Party. It is far more realistic to
assume that these developments are taking place with the *tentative*
sponsorship of highly placed party leaders, in the course of which

the political leaders themselves are taking liens on new, as yet undeveloped, policy options, unlocking if not yet opening new doors, and enlarging their arena for political maneuver.

It should be added that this is a door that could be locked once more. The future of Eastern European sociology is most directly —but not entirely—contingent upon the continuance of liberalizing trends within the Soviet Union, particularly those that have manifested themselves—albeit with powerful counter-movements —since the 20th Congress of the Soviet Communist Party; it is contingent, also, upon the maintenance of certain levels of national autonomy and political freedom in the countries of the Soviet Bloc.

SOCIAL SOURCES OF ACADEMIC SOCIOLOGY IN THE SOVIET UNION

What were some of the societal factors contributing to this recent growth or revival of an Academic Sociology in the Soviet Union? This is worth exploring, because, in pursuing it, we can learn something more about the conditions that are, in general, conducive to an Academic Sociology anywhere, including the United States. Furthermore, since an answer to this question must entail some concern with the nature of the societal mandate within which Soviet sociology operates, it may help us to formulate a more realistic conjecture of the course of its future development.

Starting with the fact obvious to most observers of recent Soviet events, it is clear that the 20th Congress of the Soviet Communist Party in 1956 was the first move in the events that led to the emergence of Soviet sociology, and of Yugoslavian and Polish sociology as well. The attack upon Stalinism launched what came to be called the "thaw." The thaw remains precarious, and Eastern European intellectuals are often as mindful of this as we; but despite the profoundly illiberal implications of the Soviet invasion of Czechoslovakia in 1968 and the icy blasts that this brought, the Soviets are still far, indeed, from returning to the rigidity of the Stalin era. Muddied and slowed, the thaw remains, if one compares the present situation with the Stalinist baseline.

The thaw had, at least, two consequences. First, it relaxed political controls over cultural life and, in general, permitted the different cultural sectors and the various technical intelligentsia in charge of them a larger area of autonomy. It established a greater measure of security for cultural and intellectual innovation. There is no question that the reemergence of an Academic Sociology throughout Eastern Europe is associated with this move toward liberalizing Soviet life. Second, the official exposure of Stalinism also engendered a period of widespread disillusionment with and increasing skepticism about official accounts of life in the Soviet Union and elsewhere. The attack on Stalinism meant that Soviet authority was being discredited *authoritatively*. There arose a "crisis of confidence" concerning official communications and media, and this brought increased public interest in those descriptions of life that were untainted by association with official sources.

It was not simply, however, that the Soviet "man in the street" wanted to know what was really going on in the world and could now more freely express this interest; it was also that Soviet managers had a similar need, and that the new Soviet political leaders had to satisfy this need in order to restabilize their leadership. They had to overcome the attenuated relationship between leadership and masses that had developed during the Stalin era, and, to do this, they needed to know what the people were thinking. It was in this period that public opinion polls also emerged in the Soviet Union, reflecting the new Soviet leadership's inability to operate within the previously official myth of a unanimity of opinion and, at the same time, symbolizing and evidencing their greater readiness to be responsive to some of the varied preferences and wants of the Soviet public.[14] The new Soviet interest in sociology, then, derives partly from an interest in a more believable and realistic picture of the world. Soviet sociology serves as a kind of academic "journalism" in whose reports one can have relative confidence; and Soviet leaders and managers are themselves not just a little interested in having such reports.

Since it was an act of political liberalization that clearly expanded the framework in which Soviet sociology could emerge, it would be very surprising if the vested interests of Soviet sociologists and those of their public did not, in some part, serve to shape their conceptions of their societal mission. Soviet sociologists do not, to put it mildly, see it as their job to restore Stalinism. How then do they see their role and the role of sociology?

THE MANDATE OF SOVIET SOCIOLOGY:
SOCIETAL INTEGRATION

In attempting to talk about this with me, Soviet sociologists frequently spoke of "disproportions" and "imbalances" in their society, and of the need to correct them. It is this, far more than their involvement in industrial sociology and social psychology, that provides the best clue to Soviet sociologists' deepest conception of their societal mandate. It was in the language of "disproportions" and "imbalances" that they sought to communicate what they were up to, and, in the end, this comes down to the problem of *integrating* the society:

As our country becomes developed and more complex the balance of relationships needs to be understood. Sociology is the instrument which *connects* economy with social life, economy with spiritual life. It helps to *integrate* different sectors of society–not that our society is unintegrated–but to help realign proportions and mechanisms of *inter*relationships. There are the *connections* in social life to be understood and explained [author's italics].

Quite independently, so far as I could see, some Yugoslavian sociologists also conceived of their tasks in the same manner. In short, the rhetoric in terms of which Soviet sociology's societal mission is legitimated is almost identical with that which Saint-Simon had used to legitimate his new science of society. It is the rhetoric of integration and "organization."

As an example of the kind of problem that Soviet sociologists characterize as involving "imbalance" of "proportions," they referred to the work of their demographers, who had pointed to an impending demographic "burst," when large numbers of their young people would be graduating from school and would have to be fitted into jobs. The young were repeatedly characterized as having unrealistically high job expectations, which suggests that they were being overeducated relative to the available labor market. As one Soviet colleague said, "not all young people can be cosmonauts." Soviet sociologists are, in general, much interested in the problems that arise in "fitting" young people into the society that has been constructed.

The problem of "proportions," then, is a problem of fine-tuning, of fitting square pegs into round holes, perhaps reshaping them a bit so they will fit: or, of making outputs roughly equal to the available markets. This essentially technological conception of sociology's mission in society entails the tacit assumption that one takes as *given* the jobs that have to be done, the basic social roles for which people have to be prepared, and the basic institutions in which these have to operate. For this reason there has been a growing interest in the sociology of industry, particularly for the leverage this may provide in finding *extra*-wage motives and *non*pecuniary incentives. (As one Soviet colleague explained, "Men work for different reasons, out of a sense of responsibility or merely for the wages. Wages are so highly emphasized and other values are still underdeveloped.") But the Soviet sociology of industry is concerned with only a special case of the larger task, the task, as one man put it, of "adjusting expectations to reality." Nothing could make it clearer than this statement does that Soviet sociology, like Western Functionalism, takes certain parts of its social world as given and views its mission as making these work together more smoothly. The problem is one of getting men to fit into and accept social institutions that are treated largely as givens. To conceive of integration as a problem of "proportions" is to conceive of it in terms of a model which views the system as having "requisites" and "parts" that remain essentially stable, though their links with one another may be strengthened or modified.

The new Soviet sociology—like the Western tradition of sociology from Comte to Parsons—is committed to its own established economic institutions and to the basic rudiments of its system of stratification. It defines its task, essentially, as making these run effectively and making the rest of society fit smoothly into the boundaries which these establish. The most basic assumption of Soviet sociologists, like that of most American Functionalists, is that the major problems of their economy have, indeed, been solved, and, in particular, that they can now take their economy as given, and proceed from that point:

> Our first need was to establish the objective conditions of a good group life–the foundation. We have done that. Now we face the problem of developing social relations, the spiritual life, culture. . . . We used to and had to think mostly about economic things, but now we can think about social and spiritual things.

The emergence of a "Western-type" Academic Sociology in the Soviet Union, then, is premised on the development of the Soviet economy and its industrial basis. If the liberalization of Soviet politics provided the opportunity for Soviet sociology to emerge, it was the maturation of Soviet industrialization—and the growth of technical and administrative strata whose careers depend on their technical effectiveness—that often provided the motives to take advantage of that opportunity. Soviet industrialization is the essential premise of Soviet sociology. The problems of integrating and managing the Soviet form of industrialization define the main problems to which Soviet sociology will dedicate itself.

A MODEL OF THE STRUCTURAL SOURCES OF THE INSTITUTIONALIZATION OF ACADEMIC SOCIOLOGY

Seen from the standpoint of an interest in the sociological analysis of sociology itself, the development of an Academic Sociology in the Soviet Union may be taken as one case in a larger set of cases; namely, those evidencing the successful institutionalization of Academic Sociology. The Soviet case thus enlarges the "sample" of such cases and, along with those others, both the successes and failures provides a basis for further refining our views concerning the social conditions under which an Academic Sociology becomes institutionalized. Recognizing that the Soviet case has important historical and national differences from others, we may employ it, nonetheless, to propose a provisional model that outlines the social conditions under which an Academic Sociology generally becomes institutionalized. The development of an Academic Sociology in the Soviet Union makes it evident that this is not necessarily linked to a specifically capitalist form of industrialization, and suggests that it is likely to occur in *any* type of industrial society at a certain stage in its development.

An Academic Sociology becomes institutionalized:

1. Where industrialization has, at least, reached the "take-off" point and become self-sustaining.

2. Where, in consequence, social theorists and others can more readily define and conceptualize their society's problems as non-economic or purely "social," which is to say, as distinct from economic problems.

3. Where, in consequence of its productivity, the new technology can provide mass gratifications and thus win the loyalty of large groups.

4. Where, in consequence, the threat of "restorationism" has been defeated. Thus the master institutions and the national elites, by which industrialization is developed and controlled are now widely accepted by members of the society. The remaining issues under contention are not viewed as matters having to do with the

strategy of industrialization and of the social classes that will control it, but are regarded essentially as a question of tactics. (Thus what is now being experimented with in the Soviet Union is decentralized management, and while this is important, it certainly does not entail any thought of a return to private ownership and to the inheritance of factories.) Under these conditions, the residual political contests are not defined as entailing differences about the most basic interests and issues, concerning which men feel so strongly that they will not accept political defeat without resorting to force and civil war.

5. Where, in consequence of all this, forms of political liberalization may be permitted and extended, for the differences among contending factions are now less critical, and ruling political factions may accept the loss of office peacefully, because they do not believe that their successors will change the society in ways that violate their most fundamental values and commitments.

6. As industrialization proceeds there is a growth in the numbers of the technical and administrative elites, and in the specialization and professionalization of a management whose authority rests upon an imputed competence based on technical skills, reliable information, and scientific methods. Their careers come increasingly to depend upon their demonstrable effectiveness, or the "results" they produce, and other considerations become more extraneous, particularly as the "restoration" or counterrevolutionary threat is defeated or subsides. The technical-administrative elites increasingly desire and press toward larger areas of discretion for themselves and have a vested interest in increasing "sector autonomy."

7. Partly as a result of this, greater autonomy will be developed and permitted among different sectors of the society. For now each sector of the society is under less pressure to testify to its basic political loyalties and can be allowed greater freedom to operate in terms of its own specialized standards and different technical criteria—in other words, more "autonomously."

8. Where, in consequence, the problem of the coordination of different social sectors grows, but comes to be seen in a distinctive way; that is, as a task for public authority, but one that is not primarily political but technical in character. In other words, difficulties of coordination—"imbalances"—are not defined as due to disloyalty, or resistance and deep-going hostility, toward the society's master institutions and national elites. Public problems are less likely to be defined as expressing a deliberate intent to overthrow or subvert the master institutions.

9. The institutionalization of Academic Sociology, then, is essentially a part or a special case of the more general development

of sector autonomy. It is both a symbolic and an instrumental response to the growing problem of integrating social sectors that are becoming, all the while, increasingly autonomous and differentiated. It is "instrumental" in that it contributes, in practical and "applied" ways, to the efficient integration of different social sectors and levels. It is "symbolic" in that it concerns itself with formulating a "mapping" of the society that locates different social parts, symbolically connecting and representing them as part of a larger social whole.

Whether symbolically or instrumentally significant, an Academic Sociology becomes institutionalized when the integration, the sector coordination, of an industrial society is defined as the responsibility of public authorities, and as a technical task rather than as a problem in policing and political mobilization. The public authority is seen ultimately as contributing to the mutual self-coordination and "self-control" of various sectors, and not as a substitute for them.

This, in turn, is compatible with a view of the various sectors as basically loyal and functionally differentiated, rather than as "subversive" and hierarchically stratified. There is therefore less inclination for the public authority to superintend closely each sector in its relations with others. Such an inclination corresponds to a conception of a society as a "system," in which emphasis is placed on the interdependence of its parts because of their specialized functions, and where this mutual dependence—and not only external imperative control—is expected to foster social integration. It is under these conditions that social integration comes to be defined as a "balance" problem, as the mutual accommodation of parts to one another, rather than as the imposition of the central control of one part over all the others. Integration is then seen as deriving from an internal and "spontaneous" balance rather than as entailing an external control.

The Soviet and the American systems have moved toward this common conception from opposite directions. The Soviet system has been moving toward it from a highly controlled and centralized state apparatus, and its movement entails a relaxation of public authority. The American system has been moving toward it from a state relatively *laissez faire* in character, and its movement entails an increase in public authority. While both, therefore, are attracted to a conception of a society as self-maintaining and self-coordinating, what is problematic in the American system is to legitimate the increase in public authority, while what is problematic in the Soviet case is to legitimate the decrease in it. What is important, therefore, for American theorists operating within the tradition of Functionalism is to find a way of incorporating

the growing state initiative and political control into their traditional theoretical focus on system analysis. What is important for
Soviet theorists, however, is to find or develop a social theory that
stresses a non-hierarchicalized view of system interdependence,
while minimizing conflict with the Soviet commitment to Marxism
and its essentially hierarchical domain assumptions.

Paradoxically, then, an academic conception of sociology seems
to arise where, for all its talk about the importance of moral values,
men seem to have at least tacitly acknowledged the priority of the
economic process and to have committed their loyalty to a specific
form of industrialization. It is then that a sociology can be permitted to hold that it is objective, value-free, and above the political
struggle; the society is no longer engaged in a critical struggle
about what are felt to be its most basic values, and its elites are
correspondingly confident that they can rely on the support of its
social scientists, at least on the most basic issues. In other words,
a sociology with a nonpartisan self-image can become institutionalized when the elites of a society are confident that its social
scientists are, in fact, *not* neutral.

I would not, however, wish to suggest that Soviet sociologists
no longer have any need to put forth evidences of their "loyalty"
to Soviet ideology. It seems to me that there still is such a need,
as evidenced, for example, by the continuing and ritualistic use of
quotations from the classical Marxist literature, and by the many
articles and books that Soviet sociologists still write which are
compulsively critical of American sociology. Nonetheless, this need
to provide public evidence of one's loyalty seems to be declining,
and there is a correspondingly greater emphasis on operating with
the special and relevant standards distinctive to sociology itself.
While I heard no claim among Soviet sociologists that theirs was
a "value-free" sociology, they did vigorously remark upon the
importance of maintaining "objectivity" in the social sciences. In
a similar vein, they also complained about some Soviet historians
who had rewritten history to laud the contributions of certain
political leaders; such work, they said, only made people lose confidence in historical writings in general and undermined their
public credibility.

As conditions generally conducive to an "objective" style of
Academic Sociology emerge in Eastern Europe, the most general
framework is being established for a more favorable reception of
and dialogue with Functionalism. This cannot fully develop, however, without fundamental changes in Soviet conceptions of their
own future and, in particular, in their attitudes toward the coming
of a full-fledged communism. Correspondingly, the growth of Soviet
interest in Functionalism *will* imply that these future-oriented atti-

tudes[15] have already begun a massive recession. To say that Functionalism is growing and will grow in appeal in Eastern Europe, is to say that the millenarian expectations of Soviet Marxism will decline; it is to say that Soviet society is slowing its forward lunge toward a radically different or "communist" future; it is to say that its desire for a "communist" future radically different from and superior to the "socialist" present, is diminishing in vitality. It is to imply that Soviet men are coming to live in a present that they hope to improve substantially, but which they do not expect to undergo basic structural changes.

Correspondingly, a key index to be watched in the work of Soviet sociologists, and one which will signify that their transition to a Functionalist model is fully underway, is whether they continue to use or to reject a "cultural lag" theory to explain the deficiencies of their own society. Characteristically, Soviet social scientists of earlier generations explained the deficiencies of Soviet society in terms of a theory of cultural lag. That is, they explained flaws as due to the remnants of a bourgeois society that had still not withered away. For this reason, I thought it particularly significant that—whatever they say publicly—hardly any of the Soviet sociologists with whom I spoke privately employed such an explanatory gambit. To speak, as I have earlier, of the growing "realism" of Soviet sociologists is another way of saying the same thing.

In seems likely that any decline in the future-oriented perspective of Soviet sociologists will more likely be evidenced first and most fully in the more microscopic, quantitative studies of specific organizations and establishments than in the more macroscopic studies of their society's basic institutions, its stratificational system, its science and technology, or its kinship and community structures. It is likely that much the same distinction could be made for American sociology as well, for it too is, in part, constrained by the very nature of the research methods it uses in the more microscopic studies. One might also expect that the shift to less future-oriented researches will take place along generational lines, the younger being less future-oriented, while the older generation will still give greater emphasis to more macroscopic, future-oriented work.

It does seem probable, however—and it should be expected—that Soviet sociologists will, in general, remain more future-oriented than are American sociologists. However, it is possible that *some* part of this is not peculiar to Soviet society or Marxism, but may be a common characteristic of Europe and European sociology more generally. Before making a judgment about the extent of the future-orientedness of Soviet sociology, one must be careful to distinguish between it and a more general *historical* orientation. In my opinion a decisive question is the extent to which Soviet scholars manifest a belief that future Soviet society will be both radically different from and clearly superior to *present* Soviet society and, if so, on what this difference and superiority is felt to be based. There seems little question that Soviet social scientists presently believe that the future Soviet society will be a better one. They believe, however, that this improvement will come from the development of science and technology, and not from changes in the other master institutions. In short, while glowing hopes are still held for the future, these rest upon factors already found in the present, which, apparently, is now being seen as more continuous with the future than it once was. At the same time, however, there are also indications that technological developments are increasingly being seen not only as producing progress, but, to some extent, as producing problems as well. The growing interest among Soviet and Eastern European sociologists in moral beliefs, ethics,[16] and individual character and values would seem to signify a decline in the reliance they place on science and technology or in their belief that the future development of these alone can solve their society's problems. In other words, the sheer shift in intellectual interests that this new emphasis on morality manifests probably indicates something of a decline in future-orientedness.

When the social conditions outlined above are more fully established, the sociologies of West and East will manifest a growing convergence and a common interest in the maintenance of domestic order, in working out the "residual" frictions in their societies, in balancing and fine-tuning the relations among their different sectors. Commonly committed to the maintenance and development of their own forms of industrialization, and taking these ends as given, sociology both East and West will stress the importance of objectivity. In its larger societal implications, this means that they will adopt a technological view of the management of society, appraising the operation of its various sectors primarily with a view to increasing their *efficiency*, reducing the costs and frictions of their operation within the context of the master institutions governing the industrialization, and accommodating other social arrangements to them. It is then that a sociology concerned with the metaphysics of "system" and "function," a Functionalism, can develop.

THE COMING READJUSTMENT IN WORLD
SOCIOLOGY

The development of an Academic Sociology in the Soviet Union implies that Marxism today, no less than Functionalism in the United States, is confronting new problems and difficulties of major proportions. The sheer development of Academic Sociology in Eastern Europe is a symptom not only that these new problems have emerged, but also that they have already been at least partly recognized by leading members of the Communist Party, who sense the need for new intellectual tools. Surely they know, and expect, that a developed "concrete" or Academic Sociology will have to interact with "Historical Materialism" or Marxism-Leninism; and, in point of fact, no scholar with whom I spoke in Eastern Europe expected that such an interaction would produce only one-sided effects. There is every likelihood that the continued growth of an Academic Sociology in Eastern Europe means that Marxism itself will develop and change substantially.

A major intellectual development in world sociology is impending, and it will be accelerated to the extent that Marxism and Academic Sociology move into increasing contact and mutual dialogue. The most basic historical hiatus in world sociology, which divides the heirs of Comte and of Marx, seems to be beginning a readjustment, a readjustment expressed in their relationship with one another and in their own internal organization. This mutual interaction and readjustment does not necessarily mean that they will both end in the same place or converge on a single model, but it seems likely that, in some respects, they will come closer together than ever before. How rapidly this will occur remains an even more difficult question, and it would be easy to confuse the visibility of the process with its speed. It needs to be remembered, for example, the the Soviet Sociological Association was founded only in 1958 and that the first cross-republic meeting of Soviet sociologists occurred only in 1966. We are, then, probably dealing with a process that will take another generation at least to achieve a new equilibrium.

I have suggested earlier in this chapter that any social change that contributes to peaceful cooperation between the United States and the Soviet Union has a claim upon the favor of all men of good will; nonetheless, a larger judgment on the growing convergence between their social sciences must also seriously consider the *basis* on which this convergence may come about. There is, after all, always the possibility of a Metternichian unity. The terms of an agreement, or *what* the parties agree on, is an important problem deserving of special consideration. If, for example, the sociology of the United States and the Soviet Union should commonly evolve toward methodologically empiricist standpoints, such as cybernetics, systems analysis, or operations research—a development by no means impossible—it will presage a culture dominated by spiritless technicians, useful and usable creatures, where any form of sociological humanism has been blighted. Far better Functionalism, even "static" Functionalism; far better Marxism, even "vulgar" Marxism.

The nature of the readjustment that is and will be taking place between Marxism and Functionalism will depend, in important part, upon the manner in which each develops internally, as well as on the kinds of influence each exerts upon the other. This, in turn, means that it will partly depend upon the manner in which "concrete" or Academic Sociology in the Soviet Union itself develops and, most especially, on the way in which it resolves some of its most important internal tensions. The central conflict in Soviet Academic Sociology is between those, on the one hand, who conceive of and support it primarily as an instrumental tool, because of its usefulness as a technological aid in administration and management, and those, on the other hand, for whom Academic Sociology is ideologically rooted in their own liberal impulses and who want to see it developed because they believe it will contribute to a more humanistic culture. This is a tension by no means peculiar to Academic Sociology in the Soviet Union, for it is found throughout Europe, East and West, and in the United States as well.

While Academic Sociology today manifests a variety of internal tensions, I do not believe that its most basic one exists between those who are methodological empiricists and those who favor theory-oriented research, or between research and theory, or even between proponents of "applied" and "pure" research. Robert Merton and Henry Riecken have rightly suggested that there has been a strong tendency for the empirical research of the new Soviet sociology to involve a kind of "practical realism," with little interest in pursuing the theoretical implications of what has been observed.[17] I do not believe, however, that those Soviet sociologists who object to such "practical realism" see the alternative merely as a "pure" sociology with a strong theoretical commitment. They have a broader vision of the new sociology, being sensitive to its ideological and value implications; above all, they often see it as part of a larger liberalization of Soviet life. If such men may be said to be drawn to some version of a "critical" sociology, the practical realists are, in their turn, essentially supporting an "administrative" sociology. That is, the latter are not simply engaged in a form of research but are agents of *social control*, while the former are not simply interested in building a pure sociology but a more humane society.

The meaning of a rapprochement between Soviet and American sociology, or between Academic Sociology and Marxism, will depend greatly on the extent to which each is committed to an administrative or managerial sociology. An administrative sociology is essentially an instrument for making the status quo work better. If it supports new programs and new policies, it does so within a framework whose aim is to protect and strengthen the existent master institutions of its society, rather than examine them as a source of the society's problems. An administrative sociology views the world from the standpoint of the values and needs of the administrative elites in the society and is shaped by the initiatives, perspectives, and limits of such elites. An administrative sociology fosters an understanding tolerance of the status quo. While acknowledging that it has problems, it regards these as surmountable within the framework of the master institutions and without making basic changes. And the solutions it seeks, appraises, and evaluates are limited to those compatible with the fundamental lineaments of the status quo and its master institutions. The central social function of an administrative sociology is to find less costly and more effective ways of satisfying the distinctive requirements of the institutional status quo.

An administrative sociology commonly tends to have a mechanical and technocratic view of the alternative solutions for the problems of the status quo. It commonly fails to see that policies are accepted not because they are the most useful to society as a whole, but because their proponents are the most powerful, and the alternative they support most useful to *them*. In short, an administrative sociology misses the nature of the competition and struggle between alternative solutions. It fails to see the *political* character of the process by which one alternative wins out over its competitors, and it systematically neglects the power dimension in its explanatory analyses. Administrative sociology thinks bureaucratically rather than politically. It is, in effect, simply searching for less costly and more effective ways of meeting the basic requirements of the status quo, outside of the political process.

INSTITUTES AND UNIVERSITY CONTEXTS
FOR SOCIOLOGY

The relation between such an administrative sociology and a "critical" sociology, the balance of power between them, is a function of several influences. One is the immediate institutional milieu in which a sociology develops and operates on a daily basis. Broadly speaking, there are two distinct sociology-shaping local milieux, the "university" and the "institute." This structural differentiation is not peculiar to Soviet or Eastern European sociology, and may be found throughout all of Western Europe and in the United States.

In the United States, sociological and social science institutes are likely to be somewhat "entrepreneurial" organizations, actively initiating research projects; they serve as middlemen or brokers between, on the one hand, a variety of clients with interests in various forms of applied sociology and, on the other, the university faculty with the skills and interest in performing such services. Eastern European institutes, while by no means devoid of entrepreneurial inclination, are somewhat more closely affiliated with the state apparatus and more fully dependent upon the funding it provides. The Eastern European institutes thus tend to be more closely controlled by the Communist Party than are the sociological faculties primarily located in universities. Indeed, there is often a visible difference in the intellectual perspectives of sociologists operating in these two contexts, accompanied by patterns of differential association, not to speak of incipient tensions between them. There seems little question that, everywhere in the world, the institute context provides a more favorable milieu than the university for the development of an *administrative* sociology. If the institute is the institutional incubator of an administrative sociology, however, it is not its ultimate source of power and support. In the first and last analysis, this power derives from the political initiatives and massive funding provided by the state, and it is on the support of the state that the prospects of an administrative sociology—in and out of the Soviet Union—most depend.

Despite the fact that, for this reason, an administrative sociology in Eastern Europe will commonly be less liberal in its political undertones, it is an exasperating contradiction that the dominant elites within American sociology are most often likely to favor the very kind of Soviet sociology that is typical of the institutes. Specifically, they are more likely to favor the more hardware-using, high science–oriented, methodologically empiricist work congenial to the needs of an institute-based administrative sociology. Para-doxically, then, the international influence exerted by the official spokesmen of American sociology is often likely to support the more communist-controlled and less liberal wing of Soviet sociology.

NOTES

1. N. Bukharin, *Historical Materialism: A System of Sociology* (New York: International Publishers, 1925).

2. I have in mind especially Merton's analysis of anomie, in which he argues that, as a result of a specific type of class system, members of the lower class are socialized to desire the same goals as the middle class, but, being lower class, lack the same opportunity to realize these goals and may, therefore, become anomic. Here, in effect, Merton uses Marx to pry open Durkheim. See Merton's "Anomie and Social Structure" in his *Social Theory and Social Structure* (Glencoe, Ill.: The Free Press, 1957).

3. See, for example, Peter L. Berger, ed., *Marxism and Sociology* (New York: Appleton-Century-Crofts, 1969).

4. Louis Althusser, *Pour Marx* (Paris: Maspero, 1968); Louis Althusser, Jacques Rancière, and Pierre Manchery, *Lire Le Capital,* Volume I (Paris: Maspero, 1968); Louis Althusser, Etienne Balibar, and Roger Establet, *Lire Le Capital,* Volume II (Paris: Maspero, 1968).

5. Nicos Poulantzas, *Pouvoir Politique et Classes Sociales de l'Etat Capi-taliste* (Paris: Maspero, 1968).

6. For example, Roger Garaudy, *Peut-on être communiste aujourd'hui?* (Paris: Bernard Grasset, 1968).

7. See, for example, the collection in E. Fromm, ed., *Socialist Humanism* (Garden City, N.Y.: Anchor Books, 1966), as well as the Yugoslavian peri-odical *Praxis.*

8. Adam Schaff, *Marksism a jednospka Pudzka* (Warsaw, 1965).

9. Norman Birnbaum, "The Crisis in Marxist Sociology," *Social Research,* XXXV, No. 2 (Summer 1968), 350–380.

10. A collection of articles bearing on this discussion is to be found in John V. Murra et al., ed. and trans., *The Soviet Linguistic Controversy* (New York: King's Crown Press, 1951).

11. Recent discussions by Soviet scholars of this infrastructure-superstruc-ture problem are to be found in the writings of V. P. Tugarinov (*Voprosy filosofi,* 1958); M. Kammari (*Kommunist,* 1956); A. E. Furman (*Filosofskie Nauki,* 1965, and *Voprosy filosofi,* 1965).

12. Important contributions to the discussion of this problem have already been made by scholars such as Herbert Marcuse and Norman Birnbaum. See H. Marcuse, *Soviet Marxism: A Critical Analysis* (New York: Columbia Uni-versity Press, 1958).

13. A. Wildavsky, "The Political Economy of Efficiency: Cost-Benefit Anal-sis, Systems Analysis, and Program Budgeting," *Public Administration Re-view,* XXVI, No. 4 (December 1966), 305.

14. See Paul Hollander, "The Dilemmas of Soviet Sociology," in Alex Simirenko, *Soviet Sociology* (Chicago: Quadrangle Books, 1966).

15. For a discussion of the importance of these see George Fischer, *Sci-ence and Ideology in Soviet Society* (New York: Atherton Press, 1967).

16. Among the prominent expressions of such concerns, that found in the work of L. Kolakowski is one of the most important.

17. See R. Merton and H. Riecken, "Notes on Sociology in the USSR," *Current Problems in Social-Behavioral Research,* Symposia Studies No. 10 (Washington, D.C.: National Institute of Social and Behavioral Science, No-vember 1962).

PART IV

Epilogue: The Theorist Pulls Himself Together, Partially

13

Living as a Sociologist:
Toward a Reflexive Sociology

I have come to the end of my work here, and I am aware that ending may be resisted for the wrong reasons. Yet there remains the uneasy feeling that something more needs saying, even in this limited effort. I sense that something has been omitted or glossed and that if I fail to clarify it the preceding work will be not only incomplete but dishonest. To be explicit, I believe that, having spent much time baring the assumptions in the work of others, I should now do the same with my own work here. Presumably, I should now be able to dissect myself; ideally, and without defensiveness or self-flagellation, I should be able to outline my own major assumptions in some modestly coherent manner, if not evaluate them. But I also believe that such an effort is doomed to failure. For no man can be his own critic, and, in pretending that he can, he promises to deliver far more than he really wants. Still, some self-knowledge is possible, and if I make the effort to disclose my operating assumptions, while warning of the distortion and incompleteness to which this effort is inevitably subject, I may render it easier for my critics to perform their own task.

SOCIAL THEORY AND PERSONAL REALITY
IN "THE COMING CRISIS
OF WESTERN SOCIOLOGY"

With this, we come to certain difficult, not to say delicate, questions. For it ought now to be perfectly plain (at least to some) that there is a deep convergence between what Gouldner has, in this volume, claimed to see in the world of sociology and what the earlier Gouldner had been doing all along in that same world. There is a congruence between what Gouldner has here said is happening in modern sociology—most especially, his thesis about the growing convergence between Functionalism and Marxism—and what he himself has been trying to do for more than twenty years now. Is it not "suspicious" that the one very thing Gouldner has spent his life doing as a sociologist should also turn out to be, as he declares, the same thing that is happening, objectively, out there in the world of sociology at large? Is it not possible, therefore, that Gouldner's report of what he has seen in the world of sociology is "merely" a projection of his own ambitions, a fantasy-fulfillment of his own wishes, a justification of his own values, and, indeed, of his own existence? I readily admit this is quite possible. Yet, without stopping here, we must also go on and ask: Suppose this to be true—what does it mean?

Does it mean that what Gouldner has said about the world of sociology and the trends in it has necessarily been distorted or falsified by his own experience with it, his activity in it? I believe not. For, surely men may be led to truth no less than to falsehood by their socially shaped personal experiences in the world. Indeed, there is no other way in which they can approach truth. Surely truth, no less than error, must be born of social experience. Whether or not any work presents us with reality or illusion cannot be determined by knowing the life that the thinker has led. In the end, this can be appraised only by looking at the work alone and not at the life; the work can be judged only in terms of standards appropriate to it, and by seeing how well it bears up under criticism.

But if neither the truth nor the falsity of this, or of any other, work can be judged by understanding its rooting in the lives and times of those who produced it, why bother to locate a work in this manner? The answer, of course, is that we do not want only to appraise the truth-value of any work, but we also wish to *understand* it. That is, we seek to understand why it has taken one direction rather than another, pursued one problem and ignored others, accented certain parts of social life but neglected others, and been formulated in this but not in other ways. Throughout this study, one of Gouldner's efforts, my efforts, has been to *understand* social theories and theorists, which is to say, to understand the work and the men who crystallize the "collective conscience" of the sociological community and provide it with self-awareness. The task here is essentially the same as that undertaken in *Enter Plato*. The present study, like *Enter Plato*, is a case study of social theorists; its *ultimate* objective is to contribute to a more general theory about social theorists, which may illuminate the manner in which theory-products and theory-performances are generated and received.

My own conception as to how social theory is actually made is very different in its central vision from that conventionally emphasized by those methodologists who stress the interaction of theory and research. Most generally, I believe that it is impossible to understand how social theory is actually made, or how it makes its way in the world, in terms of an assumption that one-sidedly stresses the role of rational and cognitive forces and that tends to prejudge what is essentially an empirical question, subordinating it to a methodological morality.

Starting with the very primitive assumption that theory is made by the praxis of men in all their wholeness and is shaped by the lives they lead, and pursuing this into concrete empirical contexts, one is led to a very different conception of what generates social theory and of what it is that many theorists are trying to do. Having pursued this conception, one is better able to see just how complex a communication social theory really is. It is a complexity that cannot even be glimpsed, let alone grasped, if we fail to see the ways in which theorists are entrenched in their theories.

Most of the theory-work and many of the major shifts in social theory examined here simply were not occasioned by the theorists' needs to assimilate the reliable facts painstakingly yielded by rigorously designed social research. Nor, very often, did theorists seem much interested in preparing the groundwork for future research. Indeed, questions of fact—that is, concern with what the facts are—seem to enter surprisingly little into much social theory; at any rate, they seem to have far less importance for theory-making than the methodologists and logicians of science suggest. Perhaps one reason for this is that most such methodologies and logics have been shaped largely by what may well be the very different experience of the physical sciences and that they may not, for this reason, well apply to or describe the behavior of *social* theorists.

It often seems that the making of social theory can get under-way, and be sustained, only when questions of fact are deferred or ignored. In other words, social theorists frequently take certain "facts" as given. They do so because these "facts" have often been yielded by their personal experience rather than research; rooted in this personal reality, they believe in them utterly. The theorist becomes involved in, sees, and experiences such things as the French Revolution, the rise of socialism, the Great Depression of 1929, or a new world of advertising and salesmanship. These "facts" are not problematic to him in their factuality; the reliability of what he sees is not, so far as he is concerned, in question. The important issue is not the determination of the facts, but rather the ordering of them. Social theorizing, then, is often a search for the meaning of the personally real, that which is already assumed to be known through personal experience. Basing itself on the imputed reality of the ordinarily experienced, much of theory-work begins with an effort to make sense of one's experience. Much of it is initiated by an effort to resolve unresolved experience; here, the problem is not to validate what has been observed or to produce new observations, but rather to locate and to interpret the meaning of what one has lived.

Commonly, the social theorist is trying to reduce the tension between a social event or process that he takes to be real and some value which this has violated. Much of theory-work is initiated by a dissonance between an imputed reality and certain values, or by the indeterminate value of an imputed reality. Theory-making, then, is often an effort to cope with threat; it is an effort to cope with a threat to something in which the theorist himself is deeply and personally implicated and which he holds dear.

SOCIAL WORLDS, PERMITTED AND UNPERMITTED

We might suggest that, to a theorist, there are two kinds of social worlds: permitted (or "normal") worlds, and unpermitted (or "abnormal") ones. The theorist often begins after he sees (or perceives the possibility of) an unpermitted world. Some part of his theory-work constitutes an effort to transform an unpermitted into a permitted world and thus normalize his universe: he must eliminate or reduce the threat of the unpermitted, or strengthen and fortify the permitted. Theorists thus tacitly seek to effect a discovery; namely, the conditions under which unpermitted worlds can be transformed into permitted ones or under which permitted worlds can be prevented from becoming unpermitted.

Generally speaking, we might suggest that two of the most important ways in which the theorist does this are, first, by communicating the importance, necessity, or potency, as well as the goodness and value, of what he takes to be a normal world; and, second, by denying, deprecating, or ignoring the potency or value of what he takes to be an unpermitted world. For example, in Parsons' analysis of "evolutionary universals," with its more than implicit counterposing of the United States and the Soviet Union, each of these is (for Parsons) a paradigm, respectively, of a permitted and of an unpermitted world. Much of Parsons' theory here and throughout the larger body of his work is animated by an impulse to bolster both the potency and moral worth of the permitted world and to deny these to the unpermitted; to endow the first with immortality, and to eliminate the second.

We may postulate, as Charles Osgood does, that the entire world of social objects has certain fundamental coordinates, certain latitudes and longitudes, and that men locate all social objects in a multidimensional attribute-space in terms, most crucially, of good-bad and potency-weakness dimensions. This implies that the impulse to assign meaning to social objects will, at a minimum, entail judgments concerning both their goodness and their potency. It also implies that, insofar as social theorizing is engaged in mapping meanings, it too is engaged in assigning objects to places along the goodness and potency dimensions. If we assume, as we must, that social theorists are fundamentally like other men, then we must also assume that, whatever their professions of being "value-free," they too assign meanings to social objects not only in terms of their potency, but also in terms of their goodness.

In a scientific, "value-free" social theory, it is not that the theorist fails to situate his social objects along a good-bad dimension, but only that this assignment, having been conventionally defined as irrelevant to his task, is now defocalized and done covertly rather than being openly accomplished. Yet, if given subsidiary attention only, it continues to function actively, nonetheless. In short, the pressure to situate social objects in terms of their moral value abides and shapes the work of social theorists, whatever their professed conception of their technical role.

Value judgments may, for example, come to be secreted in judgments of potency of power: social objects to which potency is assigned are tacitly held to be *good* things. (Thus, for example, while Parsons' major focus on shared moral values is one that stresses their sheer potency—by emphasizing the sheer difference that they produce in the social world—and while he rarely makes an explicit judgment about the sheer *goodness* of such values, there can be no doubt that Parsons believes that they are not only potent but also good.) This tendency, however, is only one special case of a larger set of cases, namely, a general tendency to define *permitted* social worlds as, among other things, those in which power and goodness are positively correlated. Such a correlation is a general condition of all permitted social worlds. Correspondingly, *un*permitted worlds are those where (1) good objects are seen to be weak, or (2) bad objects are seen to be strong.

It is my suggestion that a significant part of social theorizing is a symbolic effort to overcome social worlds that have become unpermitted and to readjust the flawed relationship betweeen goodness and potency, restoring them to their "normal" equilibrium condition, and/or to defend permitted worlds from a threatened disequilibrium between goodness and potency. With the Depression of 1929, for example, the middle and upper classes were increasingly seen as incompetent and callous powers in society; that is, they were seen as potent but immoral, and their authority was undermined even though their power remained. When Parsons strives to show that these classes are becoming increasingly "professionalized," what he is stressing is that they behave with a moral sense of collective responsibility. He is, thereby, acting theoretically to re-equilibrate power and goodness.

It is as extremely painful and threatening for a man to believe that what is powerful in society is not good, as it would be for a religious believer to feel that his God was evil. The tensions of such unpermitted worlds, however, need not be reduced only by tacitly assigning "goodness" to the powerful, but may also take place in other ways. One of the most common of these is to demean or to forbid the making of any judgment in terms of the goodness dimension, while accentuating the importance of making judgments in terms of potency. Machiavellianism—a *Machtpolitik* or a *Realpolitik*—exemplifies this tendency within the political realm; a value-free conception of social science does much the same in the realm of sociology.

If we recall that modern sociology was crystallized in the Positivistic period, it is plain that the "fathers" of Academic Sociology had no doubt about the ultimate potency of the industrial society that they then saw emerging, but had many doubts about its goodness or morality. They thus, at once, declared that there was a need for a new morality and religion. More than that, they offered science in general and social science in particular as a way of discovering a new morality and of legitimating the new middle class and its institutions. Despite their growing power, the new middle class had appreciable difficulty in getting other social strata, indeed almost all other social strata—whether the old aristocracy, the new working class, or the intellectuals—to view them as fully rightful incumbents of social power. The middle class has continued to live with this abiding tension between its established potency and its challenged goodness.

Theorists may accommodate to such unpermitted worlds by intimating the goodness of the powerful; this is essentially what the Functionalist does by showing that those social objects that survive have an ongoing "usefulness," for, in our world, to be useful is to be good. Again, theorists may accommodate to unpermitted worlds by stressing the potency of the good, as Parsons does in emphasizing the empirical importance of shared moral norms. Accommodation may also be sought be declaring certain kinds of judgments—specifically, value judgments—to be out of bounds or beyond one's competence, as value-free sociologists do. A value-free conception of the social sciences is one way in which Academic Sociologists may accommodate to living in an unpermitted world; for, within such a value-free conception, sociologists are allowed to say that it is not their task to restore the equilibrium between power and goodness, thus permitting them to accommodate to a power that they themselves may deem of dubious morality.

This last strategy is essentially a way to avoid the tension by denying one's responsibility for coping with it. Avoidance, however, may employ a rather different strategy. One may simply omit reference to, or deprecate the empirical importance or statistical frequency of, unpermitted worlds or unpermitted states of the world. Thus, the significance or prevalence of sheer power, force, coercion, conspiracy, or violence in the world has long been ignored or deprecated by liberal sociologists, who, to this day, have scarcely ever confronted the problem of war, either empirically or theoretically. Parsons tells us that he is, at last, going to confront the problem of power, but, as we saw, he is able to do so only by tacitly redefining power as authority; in short, he can confront power only by anointing it with rightful legitimacy. It may seem as if he has talked of power, but he has not. Indeed, in this respect, neither Goffman, Garfinkel, nor Homans seems very different. All commonly avoid intellectual confrontation with the reality of sheer power. To most Academic Sociologists power without legitimacy is an embarrassing, dissonance-generating aberration. A world in which power exists without legitimacy will not, they usually stress, long survive. In effect, this is not so much a report on what they have found, but a form of *reassurance*. Academic Sociologists manifest the common impulse to bring power and goodness into some equilibrium. In a social world in which men doubt that the powerful are the good, avoidance of the reality of power is a dissonance-reducing strategy as fundamental as the avoidance of value-judgments, with the result that, in the end, the sociology thus warped loses as much in its empirical realism as it does in moral sensitivity.

The foregoing remarks, focusing on the response to a dissonance between power and goodness as a theory-shaping force, have been intended only to exemplify the very different perspective on theory-making that arises when one starts with the assumption that theory is made by a man in all his wholeness, and then pursues this assumption seriously. It is, to repeat, intended only as an example of the productivity of such a standpoint; it was not intended to assign any exceptional significance to the power/goodness dissonance in comparison with other forces, or to enumerate the variety of theory-shaping forces mentioned in the course of my work here; and it was certainly not intended to present a systematic social theory about the extra-scientific forces at work in social theory. The presentation of that theory will have to wait for a later work; what we have in the present volume is but a case study in preparation for the ultimate undertaking.

My concern with a theory of social theories is only one part of a more encompassing outlook; in particular, it is a part of a larger commitment to a "sociology of sociology." For while social theory is vital to the development of sociology as a whole, it is just one element in its intellectual apparatus; this intellectual apparatus is, moreover, only a part of sociology seen as a social and cultural system. To secure an intelligible perspective on the present volume, therefore, I must attempt to outline the larger whole of which it is but a segment and to exhibit briefly the conception that I have of a more general "sociology of sociology." Since I do not believe that there is one and only one sociology of sociology, I shall signal my distinctive conception of it by giving it a distinctive name; I shall call it "Reflexive Sociology." The following account of Reflexive Sociology will, in effect, be the framework within which I shall strive to indicate the domain assumptions underpinning the present study.

TOWARD A REFLEXIVE SOCIOLOGY

Sociologists are no more ready than other men to cast a cold eye on their own doings. No more than others are they ready, willing, or able to tell us what they are really doing and to distinguish this firmly from what they *should* be doing. Professional courtesy stifles intellectual curiosity; guild interests frown upon the washing of dirty linen in public; the teeth of piety bite the tongue of truth. Yet, first and foremost, a Reflexive Sociology is concerned with what sociologists want to do and with what, in fact, they actually do in the world.

The intellectual development of sociology during the last two decades or so, especially the growth of the sociologies of occupations and of science, is, when fused with the larger perspectives of the older sociology of knowledge, one promising basis for the development of a Reflexive Sociology. We have already seen some of the first stirrings of a Reflexive Sociology, in one form or another. Indeed, I believe we have already also seen the emergence of defensive reactions that, in effect, seek to contain the impact of a Reflexive Sociology by defining it as just one other technical specialty within sociology.

What sociologists now most require from a Reflexive Sociology, however, is not just one more specialization, not just another topic for panel meetings at professional conventions,[1] and not just another burbling little stream of technical reports about the sociological profession's origins, educational characteristics, patterns of productivity, political preferences, communication networks, nor even about its fads, foibles, and phonies. For there are ways and ways of conducting and reporting such studies. There are ways that do not touch and quicken us but may, instead, deaden us to the disorders we bear; by allowing us to talk about them with a ventriloquist's voice, they only create an illusion of self-confrontation that serves to disguise a new form of self-celebration. The historical mission of a Reflexive Sociology as I conceive it, however, would be to *transform* the sociologist, to penetrate deeply into his daily life and work, enriching them with new sensitivities, and to raise the sociologist's self-awareness to a new historical level.

To the extent that it succeeds in this, and in order to succeed in it, a Reflexive Sociology is and would need to be a radical sociology. Radical, because it would recognize that knowledge of the world cannot be advanced apart from the sociologist's knowledge of himself and his position in the social world, or apart from his efforts to change these. Radical, because it seeks to transform as well as to know the alien world outside the sociologist as well the alien world inside of him. Radical, because it would accept the fact that the roots of sociology pass through the sociologist as a total man, and that the question he must confront, therefore, is not merely how to *work* but how to *live*.

The historical mission of a Reflexive Sociology is to transcend sociology as it now exists. In deepening our understanding of our own sociological selves and of our position in the world, we can, I believe, simultaneously help to produce a new breed of sociologists who can also better understand other men and their social worlds. A Reflexive Sociology means that we sociologists must—at the very least—acquire the ingrained *habit* of viewing our own beliefs as we now view those held by others.

It will be difficult for many sociologists to accept that we presently know little or nothing about ourselves or other sociologists or, in point of fact, that we know little about how one piece of social research, or one sociologist, comes to be esteemed while another is disparaged or ignored. The temptation is great to conceal our ignorance of this process behind a glib affirmation of the proprieties and to pretend that there is no one here but us scientists. In other words, one of the basic reasons we deceive ourselves and lie to others is because we are moral men. Sociologists, like other men, confuse the moral answer with the empirical and, indeed, often prefer it to the empirical. Much of our noble talk about the importance of "truth for its own sake" is often a tacit way of saying that we want the truth about *others*, at whatever cost it may be to *them*. A Reflexive Sociology, however, implies that sociologists must surrender the assumption, as wrongheaded as it is human, that others believe out of need while we believe—only or primarily— because of the dictates of logic and evidence.

A systematic and dogged insistence upon seeing ourselves as we see others would, I have suggested, transform not only our view of ourselves but also our view of others. We would increasingly recognize the depth of our kinship with those whom we study. They would no longer be viewable as alien others or as mere objects for our superior technique and insight; they could, instead, be seen as brother sociologists, each attempting with his varying degree of skill, energy, and talent to understand social reality. In this respect, all men are basically akin to those whom we usually acknowledge as professional "colleagues," who are no less diversified in their talents and competence. With the development of a Reflexive Sociology that avoids becoming molded into just another technical specialty, such rigor as sociology attains may be blended with a touch of mercy, and such skills as sociologists possess may come to yield not only information but perhaps even a modest measure of wisdom.

The development of a Reflexive Sociology, in sum, requires that sociologists cease acting as if they thought of subjects and objects, sociologists who study and "laymen" who are studied, as two distinct breeds of men. There is only one breed of man. But so long as we are without a Reflexive Sociology, we will act upon the tacit dualistic premise that there are two, regardless of how monistic our professions of methodological faith.

I conceive of Reflexive Sociology as requiring an empirical dimension which might foster a large variety of researches about sociology and sociologists, their occupational roles, their career "hangups," their establishments, power systems, subcultures, and their place in the larger social world. Indeed, my emphasis on the empirical character of a Reflexive Sociology and my insistence that the methodological morality of social science not be confused with the description of its social system and cultures, may seem to express a Positivistic bias. Yet while I believe that a Reflexive Sociology must have an empirical dimension, I do not conceive of this as providing a factual basis that determines the character of its guiding theory. Which is to say that I do not conceive of the theory of a Reflexive Sociology merely as an induction from researches or from "facts." And more important, I do not conceive of these researches or their factual output as being "value-free," for I would hope that their originating motives and terminating consequences would embody and advance certain specific *values*. A Reflexive Sociology would be a moral sociology.

Perhaps this can be adumbrated by clarifying my conception of the ultimate objective or goal of a Reflexive Sociology, in regard to both its theory and its researches. The nominal objective of any scientific enterprise is to extend knowledge of some part of the world. The difficulty with this conception, however, resides in the ambiguity of its core notion, namely, "knowledge." This ambiguity is of long standing, especially in the social sciences, where it has been particularly acute. Although expressible in different ways, this ambiguity will be formulated here as meaning that knowledge may be, and has been, conceived of as either "information" or "awareness."

Since the nineteenth century, when a distinction was formulated between the natural sciences, on the one hand, and the cultural or human sciences, on the other, this implicit ambiguity in the meaning of "knowledge" was imported into the social sciences and has remained at the core of certain of its fundamental controversies. Those believing that the social sciences were a "natural" science, like physics or biology, took an essentially Positivistic view, holding that they should be pursued with the same methods and objectives as the physical sciences. They largely conceived of knowledge as "information," as empirically confirmed assertions about "reality," whose scientific value derived from their implications for rational theory and whose larger social value derived from technologies based upon them. In short, science thus construed aimed at producing information, either for its own sake or to enhance power over the surrounding world: to know in order to control.

So long as this was a conception of the physical (as distinct from the social) sciences, it was an ideology (1) behind which all "humanity" might unite in a common effort to subdue a "nature" that was implicitly regarded as external to man, and (2) with which to promote technologies that could transform the universe into the usable resource of mankind as a whole. Such a conception of science was based upon an assumption of the essential unity and the common interests of mankind as a species. It was also a tacitly parochial conception of the relationship of the human species to others; it postulated humanity's lordship over the rest of the universe and its right to use the entire universe for its own benefit, a right tempered only by the species' expedient concern for its own long-range welfare. If such a view of science was an expression of the unthinking ethnocentrism of an expanding animal species, it was also an historical summit of this species' idealism; limitations were ignored in the flush of an optimistic sense that the newly realized universalism of science constituted an advance over narrower and more ancient parochialisms—and so it was.

The humanistic parochialism of science, with its premised unity of mankind, created problems, however, when the effort was made to apply science to the study of mankind itself. It did so partly because national or class differences then became acutely visible, but also, and perhaps more important, because men now expected to use social science to "control" men themselves, as they were already using physical science to control "nature." Such a view of social science premised that a man might be known, used, and controlled like any other thing: it "thingafied" man. The use of the physical sciences as a model fostered just such a conception of the social sciences, all the more so as they were developing in the context of an increasingly utilitarian culture.

This view of the social sciences was fostered by French Positivism. In opposition to it, largely under German auspices and the Romantic Movement with its full-scale critique of utilitarian culture, there emerged a different conception of social science. This required a different method, for example, *verstehen*, clinical intuition, or historical empathy—an inward closeness to the object studied rather than an antiseptic distance from it, an inward communion with it rather than an external manipulation of it. This conception of social science held that its ultimate goal was not neutral "information" about social reality, but rather such knowledge as was relevant to men's own changing interests, hopes, and values and as would enhance men's awareness of their *place* in the social world rather than simply facilitating their *control* over it.

In this conception of social science both the inquiring subject and the studied object are seen not only as mutually interrelated but also as mutually constituted. The entire world of social objects is seen as constituted by men, by the shared meanings bestowed and confirmed by men themselves, rather than as substances eternally fixed and existent apart from them. The social world, therefore, is to be known not simply by "discovery" of some external fact, not only by looking outward, but also by opening oneself inward. Awareness of the *self* is seen as an indispensable avenue to awareness of the social world. For there is no knowledge of the world that is not a knowledge of our own experience with it and our relation to it.

In a knowing conceived as awareness, the concern is not with "discovering" the truth about a social world regarded as external to the knower, but with seeing truth as growing out of the knower's encounter with the world and his effort to order his experience with it. The knower's knowing of himself—of who, what, and where he is—on the one hand, and of others and their social worlds, on the other, are two sides of a single process.

Insofar as social reality is seen as contingent in part on the effort, the character, and the position of the knower, the search for knowledge about social worlds is also contingent upon the knower's *self-awareness*. To know others he cannot simply study *them*, but must also listen to and confront *himself*. Knowing as awareness involves not a simple impersonal effort of segmented "role players," but a personalized effort by whole, embodied men. The character and quality of such knowing is molded not only by a man's technical skills or even by his intelligence alone, but also by all that he is and wants, by his courage no less than his talent, by his passion no less than his objectivity. It depends on all that a man does and lives. In the last analysis, if a man wants to change what he knows he must change how he lives; he must change his *praxis* in the world.

Knowing as the pursuit of information, however, conceives of the resultant knowledge as depersonalized; as a product that can be found in a card file, a book, a library, a colleague, or some other "storage bank." Such knowledge does not have to be recallable by a specific knower and, indeed, does not have to be in the mind of any person; all that need be known about it is its "location." Knowledge as information, then, is the attribute of a *culture* rather than of a person; its meaning, pursuit, and consequence are all depersonalized. Knowledge as awareness, however, is quite another matter, for it has no existence apart from the persons that pursue and express it. Awareness is an attribute of persons, even though it is influenced by the location of these persons in specific cultures or in parts of a social structure. A culture may assist or hinder in attaining awareness, but a culture as such cannot be aware.

Awareness entails a relationship between persons and information; yet information, while necessary to, is not sufficient for awareness. Awareness turns on the *attitude* of persons toward information and is related to their ability to hold onto and to use information. The crux of the matter is that information is rarely neutral in its implication for men's purposes, hopes, or values. Information, therefore, tends to be experienced—even if not expressly defined—as either "friendly" or "hostile," as consonant or dissonant with a man's purposes. It is the relation of information to a man's purposes, not what it is "in itself," that makes information hostile or friendly. News of the stability of a government is hostile information to a revolutionary but friendly to a conservative. An openness to and a capacity to use hostile information is awareness. Awareness is an openness to bad news, and is born of a capacity to overcome resistance to its acceptance or use. This is inevitably linked, at some vital point, with an ability to know and to control the self in the face of threat. The pursuit of awareness, then, even in the world of modern technology, remains rooted in the most ancient of virtues. The quality of a social scientist's work remains dependent upon the quality of his manhood.

Whether "hostile information" refers directly to some state of the larger world itself, or, rather, to the deficiencies of an established, perhaps technical, system of *information* about the world, an openness to it always requires a measure of self-knowledge and courage. The self of a scholar may be as deeply and personally invested in his work on information systems as is a revolutionary's on a political system. Both have conceptions of their work that may, at some point, be maintained only through the blunting of their awareness. A politician's capacity to accept and use hostile information about his own political efforts and situation is often referred to as his "realism." A scholar's ability to accept and use hostile information about his own view of social reality, and his efforts to know it, is part of what is usually called his "objectivity."

As a program for a Reflexive Sociology, then, this implies that: (1) The conduct of researches is only a necessary but not a sufficient condition for the maturation of the sociological enterprise. What is needed is a new *praxis* that transforms the person of the sociologist. (2) The ultimate goal of a Reflexive Sociology is the deepening of the sociologist's own awareness, of who and what he is, in a specific society at any given time, and of how both his social role and his personal praxis affect his work as a sociologist. (3) Its work seeks to deepen the sociologist's self-awareness as well as his ability to produce valid-reliable bits of information about the

social world of others. (4) Therefore, a Reflexive Sociology requires not only valid-reliable bits of information about the world of sociology, and not only a methodology or a set of technical skills for procuring this. It also requires a persistent commitment to the *value* of that awareness which expresses itself through all stages of work, as well as auxiliary skills or arrangements that will enable the sociologist's self to be open to hostile information.

Conventional Positivism premises that the self is treacherous and that, so long as it remains in contact with the information system, its primary effect is to bias or distort it. It is assumed, therefore, that the way to defend the information system is to insulate it from the scholar's self by generating distance and by stressing impersonal detachment from the objects studied. From the standpoint of a Reflexive Sociology, however, the assumption that the self can be sealed off from information systems is mythological. The assumption that the self affects the information system solely in a distorting manner is one-sided: it fails to see that the self may also be a source both of valid insight that enriches study and of motivation that energizes it. A Reflexive Sociology looks, therefore, to the deepening of the self's capacity to recognize that it views certain information as hostile, to recognize the various dodges that it uses to deny, ignore, or camouflage information that is hostile to it, and to the strengthening of its capacity to accept and to use hostile information. In short, what Reflexive Sociology seeks is not an insulation but a *transformation* of the sociologist's self, and hence of his praxis in the world.

A Reflexive Sociology, then, is not characterized by *what* it studies. It is distinguished neither by the persons and the problems studied nor even by the techniques and instruments used in studying them. It is characterized, rather, by the *relationship* it establishes between being a sociologist and being a person, between the role and the man performing it. A Reflexive Sociology embodies a critique of the conventional conception of segregated scholarly roles and has a vision of an alternative. It aims at transforming the sociologist's relation to his work.

Since the 1920's when American sociology began to be institutionalized within universities, it has held firmly to one operating methodological assumption, despite the other changes it has undergone. This assumption can be called "Methodological Dualism." Methodological Dualism focuses on the *differences* between the social scientist and those whom he observes; it tends to ignore their similarities by taking them as given or by confining them to the sociologist's subsidiary attention. Methodological Dualism calls for the separation of subject and object, and it views their mutual contact with concern and fear. It enjoins the sociologist to be detached from the world he studies. It warns him of the dangers of "over rapport." It sees his involvement with his "subjects" primarily from the standpoint of its contaminating effect upon the information system.

Methodological Dualism is based upon a fear; but this is a fear not so much of those being studied as of the sociologist's *own self*. Methodological Dualism is, at bottom, concerned to constitute a strategy for coping with the feared vulnerability of the scholar's self. It strives to free him from disgust, pity, anger, from egoism or moral outrage, from his passions and his interests, on the supposition that it is a bloodless and disembodied mind that works best. It also seeks to insulate the scholar from the values and interests of his other roles and commitments, on the dubious assumption that these can never be anything but blinders. It assumes that feeling is the blood enemy of intelligence, and that there can be an unfeeling, unsentimental knower. Methodological Dualism is, in fine, based on the tacit assumption that the goal of sociology is knowledge conceived as information. Correspondingly, it serves as a powerful inhibitor of the sociologist's awareness, for it paradoxically presupposes that the sociologist may rightfully be changed as a *person* by everything *except the very intellectual work* which is at the center of his existence. In effect, Methodological Dualism prohibits the sociologist from changing in response to the social worlds that he studies and knows best; it requires him to finish his research with the same self, the same biases and commitments, as those with which he began it.

Methodological Dualism is based on the myth that social worlds are merely "mirrored" in the sociologist's work, rather than seeing them as conceptually constituted by the sociologist's cognitive commitments and all his other interests. The Methodological Dualist commonly conceives his goal to be the study of social worlds in their "natural" or uncontaminated state. In effect, he says, like the photographer, "Don't mind me; just be natural, carry on as if I were not here." What this ignores, however, is that the reaction of the group under study to the sociologist is just as real and revealing of its "true" character as its reaction to any other stimulus, and, furthermore, that the sociologist's own reaction to the group is a form of behavior as relevant and significant for social science as is anyone else's. There is not as great a difference between the sociologist and those he studies as the sociologist seems to think, even with respect to an intellectual interest in knowing social worlds. Those being studied are also avid students of human relations; they too have their social theories and conduct their investigations.

Believing that he should not influence or change the group he

studies—except in those limited ways that he plans during experimentation—the sociologist would also like to believe that he does not. He prefers to believe that he is what he *should* be, according to his methodological morality. He thus commonly fails to attend to the ramifying range of influences that he actually exerts upon social worlds and, to that extent, he obscures what, in point of fact, he does and is. The notion that research can be "contaminated" premises that there is research that is not contaminated. From the standpoint of a Reflexive Sociology, however, all research is "contaminated," for all are conducted from the standpoint of limited perspectives and all entail relationships that may influence both parties to it.

Methodological Dualism entails a fantasy of the sociologist's God-like invisibility and of his Olympian power to influence—or not influence—those around him, as he pleases. In contrast, the Methodological Monism of a Reflexive Sociology believes that sociologists are really only mortal; that they inevitably change others and are changed by them, in planned and unanticipated ways, during their efforts to know them; and that knowing and changing are distinguishable but not separable processes. The aim of the Reflexive Sociologist, then, is not to remove his influence on others but to know it, which requires that he must become aware of himself as both knower and as agent of change. He cannot know others unless he also knows his intentions toward and his effects upon them; he cannot know others without knowing himself, his place in the world, and the forces—in society and in himself—to which he is subjected.

Methodological Dualism stresses the "contamination" possible in the research process itself; it sees the main danger to "objectivity" in the interaction between those studying and those studied. In effect, this is the narrow perspective of an interpersonal social psychology that ignores the biasing effects of the *larger* society and the powerful influences it exerts upon the sociologist's work through the intervening mechanism of his career and other interests. What Methodological Dualism ignores is that the sociologist does not only enter into consequential relations with those whom he studies, but that these relations themselves operate within the orbit of the relations that the sociologist has with those who, directly or indirectly, finance his researches and control his occupational life and the establishments within which he works. In ignoring these larger influences, Methodological Dualism in effect boggles at a gnat but swallows a camel. Its claim to "objectivity" is, in effect, commonly made in such a way as to give least offense to those who most subvert it.

A Reflexive Sociology, for its part, recognizes that there is an inevitable tendency for any social system to curtail the sociologist's autonomy in at least two ways: to transform him either into an ideologue of the status quo and an apologist for its policies, or into a technician acting instrumentally on behalf of its interests. A Reflexive Sociology recognizes that the status quo often exerts such influences by the differential rewards—essentially, research funding, academic prestige, and income-earning opportunities—that it selectively provides for scholarly activities acceptable and useful to it. The most fundamental control device of any *stable* social system is not its use of crude force, or even of other, nonviolent forms of punishment, but its continuing distribution of mundane rewards. It is not simply power that an hegemonic elite seeks and uses, but an authority that is rooted in the readiness of others to credit its good intentions, to cease contention when it has rendered its decision, to accept its conception of social reality, and to reject alternatives at variance with the status quo.

The most effective strategy possessed by any stable social system and its hegemonic elites to induce such conformity is to make it worthwhile. What elites prefer is not craven expedience, but pious opportunism. Conformity with the basic principle of establishment politics—that is, accepting the image of social reality held by the hegemonic elite or at least one compatible with it—is, however, nothing less than a betrayal of the most fundamental objectives of any sociology. The price paid is the dulling of the sociologist's awareness; it is a surrender in the struggle to know those social worlds that are and those that might be.

Reflexive Sociology, then, rests upon an awareness of a fundamental paradox: namely, that *those who supply the greatest resources for the institutional development of sociology are precisely those who most distort its quest for knowledge.* And a Reflexive Sociology is aware that this is not the peculiarity of any one type of established social system, but is common to them all. While a Reflexive Sociology assumes that any sociology develops only under certain social conditions which it is deeply committed to know, it also recognizes that elites and institutions seek something in return for the support they provide sociology. It recognizes that the development of sociology depends on a societal support that permits growth in certain directions but simultaneously limits it in other ways and thus warps its character. In short, every social system is bent upon crippling the very sociology to which it gives birth. A claim to "objectivity" made by a sociology that does not acknowledge this contradiction, and which lacks a concrete understanding of the manner in which its own hegemonic institutions and elites are a fundamental danger to it, is a tacit testimonial to the successful hegemony of that system over that sociology. It evidences a

failure to achieve that very objectivity to which it so proudly pledges allegiance.

A Reflexive Sociology can grasp this hostile information: *all the powers-that-be are inimical to the highest ideals of sociology.* At the same time, it further recognizes that most often these are not external dangers, for they produce their most powerful effect when allied with the dispositions and career interests internal to sociologists themselves. A Reflexive Sociology is fully aware that sociology is most deeply distorted because and when the sociologist himself is a willing party to this. A Reflexive Sociology therefore prefers the seeming naivete of "soul-searching" to the genuine vulgarity of "soul-selling."

Insofar as a Reflexive Sociology focuses on the problem of dealing with hostile information, it confronts the problem of a "value-free" sociology from two directions. On the one hand, it denies the possibility and, indeed, questions the worth of a value-free sociology. On the other hand, it also sees the dangers, no less than the gains, of a value-committed sociology; for men may and do reject information discrepant with the things they value. It recognizes that men's highest values, no less than their basest impulses, may make liars of them. Nonetheless, a Reflexive Sociology accepts the dangers of a value commitment, for it prefers the risk of ending in distortion to beginning in it, as does a dogmatic and arid value-free sociology.

Again, insofar as a Reflexive Sociology centers on the problem of hostile information, it has a distinctive awareness of the ideological implications and political resonance of sociological work. It recognizes that under different conditions an ideology may have different effects upon awareness; it may be liberating or repressive, may increase or inhibit awareness. Moreover, the specific problems or aspects of the social world that an ideology can make us aware of also change over time. A Reflexive Sociology must, therefore, have an *historical* sensitivity that alerts it to the possibility that yesterday's ideologies may no longer enlighten but may now blind us. For since hostile information entails a *relation* between an information system and the purposes of men, *what* is hostile will change with the changing purposes that men pursue and with the changing problems that their pursuit encounters under new conditions. What was formerly hostile information may cease to be so; and what was hitherto friendly may become hostile. Thus, for a part of the middle class—the new "swinging" middle class—as the "sexual revolution" has progressed, Freudianism has ceased to be the liberating force it once was. Furthermore, insofar as Freudianism becomes part of a larger movement that interprets social and political dissent as symptomatic of mental illness, it increasingly becomes an instrument of social control and begins to play a sociologically repressive role.

Similarly, the "good news" and the liberating effects of the scientific revolution may now also need to be seen as an historically limited liberation. What is now required is to confront that hostile information which suggests that the scientific revolution has, under present social conditions, opened the prospect of global self-destruction and, more generally, that science has become an instrument through which almost all contemporary industrial social systems maintain themselves. What made Nazi Germany blind was, among other things, its irrational racial ideology; but what made it uniquely dangerous and destructive was its effective mobilization of modern science and technology on behalf of this. This was an extreme case; but it is far from the only instance in which modern societies use science as an instrument of domination, in much the same way that rulers of the "ancient regimes" of the eighteenth and nineteenth centuries once used institutional religion. Despite this, however, the conventional Western view of science is still largely that of the Enlightenment, seeing it as a source of cultural liberation and human welfare that is marred only occasionally, marginally, accidentally.

SOCIOLOGY AND THE LIBERAL TECHNOLOGUES

In a similar vein, the liberal ideologies shared by most American sociologists were, prior to World War II, a source of enlightening awareness. Today, however, in the context of a burgeoning Welfare-Warfare State, these liberal ideologies serve instead to increase the centralized control of an ever-growing Federal Administrative Class and of the master institutions on behalf of which it operates. Liberal sociologists have thus become the technical cadres of national governance. Here, in the post-World War II period, there has been a marriage of the sociologist's liberalism and his career interests. Its eager offspring is the liberal technologue who produces information and theories that serve to bind the poor and the working classes both to the state apparatus and to the political machinery of the Democratic Party, while, at the same time, helping the national bureaucracy to unmask the inept, archaic *local* bureaucrats and to subject them to control from the national center.

Under the banner of sympathy for the underdog, the liberal

technologues of sociology have become the market researchers of the Welfare State, and the agents of a new managerial sociology. While sometimes moved by a humane concern for the deprived and the deviant, the liberal technologues of sociology are creating, in effect, a new "ombudsman sociology" whose very criticism of middle-level welfare authorities and establishments serves as a kind of lightning rod for social discontent, strengthening the centralized control of the highest authorities, and providing new instruments of social control for the master institutions. The liberal technologues in sociology present and experience themselves as men of good will who work with and for the Welfare State only because they want to relieve the distress of others within the limits of the "practicable." They say nothing about the extent to which their accommodation to this state derives from the personal bounty it provides them.

If it is often said, and truly, that most American sociologists today regard themselves as "liberals," it also has to be added that the character of liberalism has changed. No longer is it the conscientious faith of an embattled minority fighting a callous establishment. Liberalism today is itself an establishment. It is a central part of the governing political apparatus. It has a powerful press whose pages distort the truth just as systematically as does the conservative one. The liberal establishment of the Welfare State has its heroes whose virtue may not be slighted with impunity, and it has its myths whose distortions may not be challenged without reprisal. Like any establishment, the liberal establishment rewards the lies that sustain it and punishes the truths that embarrass it.

As a part of the liberal establishment, liberal sociologists are expected to defend the cause. In short, there are times when they are expected to lie. In return, they are allowed to share in the career-battening support of the social service and the research funding supplied by the Welfare State. It has become the essential role of the sociologist-as-liberal-technologue to foster the optimistic image of American society as a system whose major problems are deemed altogether soluble within existent master institutions, if only enough technical skills and financial resources are appropriated. It has, in other words, become the function of the "sunshine sociologist" to assure American society that the cloudy glass of water is really safe rather than dangerous to drink.

American sociology is manned increasingly by men of liberal ideology who are allied with, consultants to, and celebrants and dependents of, the Welfare State. At the same time, however, many of them have a genuine distaste for American policy *abroad*. One way in which some accommodate to this anomalous condition is by splitting their image of the American State apparatus. They tend to conceive of it as composed of two separate parts: a benign and humane Welfare State, on the one side, and a malign, imperialistic Warfare State, on the other hand. In short, they assume that the Welfare State is not organically linked with the Warfare State, in one Welfare-Warfare State. They are, therefore, prone to regard the Warfare State and its reactionary foreign policies as if these were isolated anachronisms, having no significant connection with the domestic reform policies of the Welfare State.

Because they do this, these sociologists are unable to come to any serious understanding of the interrelation of domestic and foreign policy, of the manner in which both are interdependent, and of how both relate to the crisis in the society's master institutions. Yet the sociological unity of the Warfare and Welfare State, the integration of foreign and domestic policies, is thoroughly visible on the political level, where both policy strands come together in the machinery of the Democratic Party. For the Democratic Party has been, *par excellence*, the unifying agent forging both the welfare and the warfare sides into a single coin. It has been the party of active imperialistic adventures abroad, on the one side, and of welfare legislation, on the other. The alliance of the liberal technologue with the Welfare State through the Democratic Party, therefore, cannot help but be an alliance with the Warfare State.

In this specific historical context, it is the liberal establishment and its political ideology that is most responsible for blunting the awareness of American sociologists. The ideological distortion of American sociology does not derive, in any appreciable measure, from conventionally conservative or reactionary—to say nothing of radical—commitments. The development of American sociology, the deepening of its awareness, therefore, is now primarily contingent upon dissociation from the Bismarckian policies that pass for liberalism today. The historical mission of a Reflexive Sociology is to foster a critical awareness of the character of contemporary liberalism, of its hold upon the university and upon American sociology, as well as of the dialectic between Welfare and Warfare policies, and of the liberal sociologist's role as market researcher on the behalf of both. Reflexive Sociology premises that the character of any sociology is affected by its political praxis and that further development of sociology now requires its liberation from the political praxis of liberalism.

REFLEXIVE SOCIOLOGY AND RADICAL SOCIOLOGY

It is, in some part, because I have serious reservations about the historically limited, elite-distorted character of traditional humanism that I have stressed that a Reflexive Sociology requires a radical character. To say that a Reflexive Sociology is radical does not mean, however, that it is only a nay-saying or a "critical sociology"; it should be just as much concerned with the positive formulation of new societies, of utopias, in which men might live better, as it is concerned with a criticism of the present. To say that it is a sociology critical of the present does not mean that it merely entails elitist criticism of mass culture or the evils of television, or even of the foreign or domestic policies of government. It wants to know how these are shaped by the given power matrix and by the institutionally entrenched elites and classes.

Moreover, a radical sociology is not simply a criticism of the world "out there." The acid test of a radical sociology is not its posture (or its posturing) about matters remote from the sociologist's personal life. The quality of its radicalism is as much revealed by its daily response to the commonplace vices of the everyday surround, as it is by its readiness to pass resolutions that denounce imperialism and to sign petitions that seek to remedy mass deprivation.

The man who can voice support for "Black Power" or who can denounce American imperialism in Latin America or Vietnam, but who also plays the sycophant to the most petty authorities in his university, is no radical; the man who mouths phrases about the need for revolutions abroad, but who is a coiled spring ready to punish the rebels among his own graduate students, is no radical; the academician who with mighty oaths denounces the President of the United States, but subserviently fawns upon his Department Chairman, is no radical; the man who denounces opportunistic power politics, but practices it daily among his university colleagues, is no radical. Such men are playing one of the oldest games in personal politics; they are seeking to maintain a creditable image of themselves, while accommodating to the most vulgar careerism. Such men are seeking neither to change nor to know the world; their aim is to grab a piece of it for themselves.

pends on its ability to resist *all* merely authoritative definitions

The integrity of a radical, and hence a Reflexive Sociology depends of reality, and it is most authentically expressed in resisting the irrationalities of these authorities met daily in eye-to-eye encounter. A Reflexive Sociology insists that, while sociologists desperately require talent, intelligence, and technical skill, they also need a courage and valor that may be manifested every day in the most personal and commonplace decisions. Something of what this means in a university context is suggested by Karl Loewenstein's personal appreciation of Max Weber:

> He could not hold his peace. In all the eight years that I knew him, he was forever involved in scholarly and political feuds which he waged with implacable intensity. . . . He had an innate and inflexible sense of justice that made him take the side of anyone whom he thought was being unjustly dealt with.[2]

The core of a Reflexive Sociology, then, is the attitude it fosters toward those parts of the social world *closest* to the sociologist—his own university, his own profession and its associations, his professional role, and importantly, his students, and himself—rather than toward only the remote parts of his social surround. A Reflexive Sociology is distinguished by its refusal to segregate the intimate or personal from the public and collective, or the everyday life from the occasional "political" act. It rejects the old-style closed-office politics no less than the old-style public politics. A Reflexive Sociology is not a bundle of technical skills; it is a conception of how to live and a total praxis.

REFLEXIVE SOCIOLOGY AS A WORK ETHIC

As a *work ethic,* a Reflexive Sociology affirms the creative potential of the individual scholar, which it opposes to the conformity demanded by established institutions, by professional organizations, by university gentility, and by culturally routinized roles. It opposes the inherent tendency of any professional role to become standardized and to be ridden with the smugly self-satisfied. A Reflexive Sociology repudiates the tendency of professionals to prefer the sure thing, with its modest and steady rewards, to the high-variance bet. It prefers men with a capacity for intellectual risk-taking and with the courage to compromise their careers on behalf of an idea. In truth, a Reflexive Sociology is concerned more with the creativity than the reliability of an intellectual performance: it shuns the domestication of the intellectual life.

A Reflexive Sociology, as a work ethic, speaks against all pedestrian and indifferent performances. It detests the impulse to transform all intellectual tasks into impersonal routines, the impulse which, after all, is at the center of sturdy, "sober" professionalism. It insistently demands from a thinker all the freshness and seriousness of response of which he is capable. A Reflexive Sociology knows how very little it takes to be a respected member of an established profession; it knows that pyramids of respect are often erected on a semblance of sobriety and conformity rather than intellectual quality and achievement. And always and everywhere, it warns the individual scholar that there is a crucial difference between himself and his profession; that his profession has a kind of immortality, while he himself is only mortal. He must speak his own piece here and now, mobilize all the resources of creativity that he has, and use all of himself, whether or not it fits neatly into the standardized requirements of his professional role.

When men fall spellbound before the demands of cultural prescriptions, when they fail to heed their own inner impulses, fail to know their own special bents or aptitudes, fail to grasp that there are *many* valuable ways they can live and contribute as scholars, it is then that their lives must be tragic. Men may escape tragedy, when they recognize that they need not allow themselves to be assimilated to their cultural masks; when they insist on the difference between themselves and their roles; when they insist that it is they who are the measure and who do the measuring: one man with, or one man against, other men, and not one man against the standards of culture and the requirements of roles.

To do this, men must accept their own unique talents, varying ambitions, and experience of the world, as authentic. If they find these are distant from the requirements of their culture and role, they should, at least, face up to if not accept the difference. They must consider the possibility that their personal experiences, impulses, and special talents have as much right to be heard as the cultural norms, while all the while granting the possibility that they may simply be in the wrong business. When *ordinary* men can do this, they need no longer be inescapably burdened by a sense of their own failure and inadequacy. When *great* men can do this, they need no longer project an inflated image of themselves as gods. When ordinary and great men can do this, they will both recognize the value of their human contribution as sufficient to justify their lives.

Men surmount tragedy when they use themselves up fully, when they use what they have and what they are, whatever they are and wherever they find themselves, even if this requires them to ignore cultural prescription or to behave in innovating ways undefined by their roles. The tragic sense does not derive from the feeling that

men must always be less than history and culture demand; it derives, rather, from the sense that they have been less than they
could have been, that they have needlessly betrayed themselves,
needlessly forgone fulfillments that would have injured no one. The
sociological enterprise, like others, becomes edged with a tragic
sense when men suspect that they have wasted their lives. In confining work to the requirements of a demanding and unfulfillable
paradigm, sociologists are not using themselves up in their work
and are, indeed, sacrificing, leaving unexpressed, certain parts of
themselves—their playful impulses, their unverified hunches, their
speculative imagination.

When sociologists commit themselves compulsively to a life-
wasting high science model, they are making a metaphysical wager.
They are wagering that the sacrifice is "best for science." Whether
this is really so, they cannot confirm; but they often need no
further confirmation than the pain this self-confinement inflicts
upon them. My point, of course, is not that a sociologist can live
without making such a metaphysical wager, but rather that various
wagers are possible. He may bet that the paradigm or model of
science presently prescribed is more right and trustworthy than his
own "errant" impulses. In short, he may bet *against* himself. He
may, however, bet *on* himself. That is, he may trust his own
individuating impulses, personal experiences, unique aptitudes,
and all the fainter powers of apprehension (as Gilbert Murray
called them) with which these endow him. To say that the sociologist need not make only one kind of bet, however, is not to say
that the number of bets he can make is unlimited. If the basic
problem is how to link himself as a person with the requirements
of his role as a sociologist, there would seem to be, for sociologists
as for others, a limited number of solutions.

The culturally standardized role of the sociologist, like any other
social role, can be thought of as a "bridge"—both facilitating and
limiting, enabling men to "overcome" certain obstacles at the price
of limiting what "other side" they may achieve. Social roles, furthermore, are always unfinished, invariably incomplete bridges; they
reach out only part way across the void. It is their incompleteness
that is the eternal problem, and thus even those who respect the
bridge can never entirely rely upon it to get them safely across.

There are a limited number of attitudes one can adopt toward
this situation. For example, a man can say: So be it; if this is the
way of bridges, then we must learn to live with them, imperfect
though they be. He may, thereafter, parade back and forth along
the completed section of the bridge, sometimes dangling his feet
over the unfinished edge, looking down. Another man, however,
may say: We must be grateful for whatever we have and, repaying

those who built it, we must continue working, each adding his own modest plank to the unfinished end; occasionally resting at the edge, he may dangle his feet over it. In both cases, however, one is bound to have something of a tragic sense, a sad whimsical wish that things were not like that.

But there is still another possibility. A man might feel that one thing is certain: while the building of this bridge will never be completed, his life will surely have its end. A man might therefore risk a running leap from the unfinished edge to the shore that he thinks he sees ahead. Perhaps he has seen right and has estimated his own powers correctly. In which event, applause. Perhaps he has badly miscalculated, on both counts. In which event, a certain dampness sets in. Maybe he can swim back to safety, even if somewhat less than applauded. In any event, he has found out how far he can see and how well he can jump. Even if he is never heard from again, perhaps those who are still dawdling at the edge will learn something useful.

HISTORY AND BIOGRAPHY: A SLIPPAGE

A Reflexive Sociology is an historically sensitive sociology, as it must be; for, to deepen the awareness of sociologists, it must, in part, offer them an awareness of themselves, of their own historically evolving character, and of their place in an historically evolving society. It sees all men as profoundly shaped by their shared past, by their evolving cultures and social systems. Yet it does not see men either as the helpless agents of some inexorable social force to which they must bow, or as the omnipotent overlords of an historical process that they can neatly engineer. A Reflexive Sociology believes that there is an inevitable "slippage" between man and society.

A large part of this slippage between man and society, as well as between man and history, derives from man's character as a biological creature and as an evolving animal species. Man's unique character is embedded in a species nature that endows him with the tissue, organ, and chemical potentiality for both reason and passion; each of these is rooted in his animal nature. Each of these sides of man is both limited and strengthened by the other. Without the chemistry of passion man would be a computer; without the symbolic powers of reason he would be a "naked ape." Man's capacity for creativity, sociability, and solidarity, on the one hand, as well as for mutual destructiveness and aggression, on the other, are both as much embedded in his animal passions as they are uniquely shaped by his reason and symbol-making powers. No animal with man's enormous powers of reason can be wholly vicious or mindless of the needs of others; and no animal with man's highly charged, ever-ready potential for sexual arousal can be wholly reasonable or compliant. Those who want man totally amiable and controllable had best geld him. We must not confuse man's need for sociality with a single-minded impulse toward amiable sociability.

If the historically evolved needs of society set limits within which men must seek their survival and development, men's own individual and species needs also set limits with which any society must, in its way, come to terms. Men do not only seek to satisfy wants that they have learned in society or that their "culture has taught them." They strive also to fulfill their own individual and species potentialities, and they seek fulfillment no less than tension-reduction. In this view, then, society is made by and for the human species, as much as man is made by and for society. The species uses the given society so long as it satisfies human needs and increases man's ability to fulfill himself. The human species and its various societies are not wedded until death do them part. In time, they come to confront one another as antagonists; then, as often before, the species puts aside the society it has created and moves on.

From the viewpoint of much of the sociology dominant in the United States today, it is not man but society that is the measure. This conception of sociology and of society once had value, because it stressed the extent to which men are shaped by an environment of other men, are dependent upon one another, suffer from or take pleasure in one another; because it stressed that men are not simply the slaves of natural, biological, or geographical forces. This view of man and society was, once, a benign antidote, at least when devoid of medieval nostalgia, to the individualistic and competitive bourgeois culture crystallizing in the nineteenth century. Today, however, the context is a growingly bureaucratized, centralized, and committee-shackled Welfare-Warfare State. So, this sociology's inherent subordination of the individual to the group serves, not so much as a reminder to men of their debt to one another, but as a rationale for conformity to the status quo, for obedience to established authority, and for a restraint that makes haste slowly; it becomes a warning about limits rather than an invitation to pursue opportunities.

If a Reflexive Sociology rejects the imperialistic ideology of men who seek to dominate a universe that they tacitly view as "theirs," at the same time this sociology also recognizes that there are some provinces within that universe that properly are or should be men's, and that these are the provinces of culture and society. Thus a Reflexive Sociology has, as a central part of its historical mission, the task of helping men in their struggle to take possession of what *is* theirs—society and culture—and of aiding them to know who they are and what they may want.

From the standpoint of a Reflexive Sociology, men live in society, but not there alone; they live in history, but not there alone. Individual men do live out the cycle of their existence, pursue their careers, and establish their families within encompassing civilizations, cultures, and societies. The concerns and interests of men do, in large part, derive from and coincide with these larger entities; but they do so, however, only in part and never *in toto*. However deep men's identification with and dependence upon a larger cause or group, and however successful the cause or however benign the group, there are always points in the lives of men when they must go their own ways, when it becomes painfully evident that their cause and their group do not constitute the totality of their personal existence.

Central to this disparity between biography and history is the fact that men die. There is an ongoing and irreducible tension between the passion with which we can surrender ourselves to our social commitments and the fact that death can, at any moment, remove us totally and eternally from these same involvements. At moments, the inconceivable permanence of death becomes conceivable, and our single-minded social involvements may suddenly appear as radically ephemeral as a child's game. There are the quiet moments when we glimpse that, to lie for money, to do violence for power, to inflict hurt for love, are as insane as killing an opponent just to beat him at chess. Yet if we flee or withdraw from passionate commitment, if we refuse to take it seriously, we surrender our destinies to the control of those who do. We must be involved, then, because a "sad necessity" constrains us; but we may be involved *gladly*, to the extent that we struggle against an inhumane existence and that, in this struggle, we achieve a sense of our own powers and worth, and aid others to do the same. The very ephemerality of things makes it more, not less imperative to wage a struggle to fulfill the limited existence that men have.

A Reflexive Sociology, however, insists on the reality of these different levels on which men live—on the reality of the difference between society or collective history, and individual biography—and it recognizes that men are compelled, openly or tacitly, to confront this difference and to assign some meaning to it. Conventional Academic Sociology is based upon a metaphysic that blunts awareness of this. A Reflexive Sociology, though, insists upon the reality of these different levels and of the tensions among them. It sees that history, culture, and society never exhaust biography, that everywhere men live with the "loose ends" of an existence that they are constantly striving to pull together.

In some measure this effort at integration was once the task of religion. Western religions sought, among other things, to bridge the different levels of existence by affirming their common origin in and governance by a Supreme Being. As the traditional religions broke down in the eighteenth and nineteenth centuries, science came increasingly albeit surreptitiously to serve as an integrating philosophy of life. Instead of seeing man, society, and species as part of a God-created whole, science sought to integrate existence by tacitly premising the unity and the hegemony of the human species. Instead of placing God at the ideological center of gravity, it placed man and society. From this standpoint the rest of the universe was an empire that stood waiting to be claimed, conquered, and exploited for man's advantage. Presumably, it was there to be known, and it was to be known in order that it might be used. Science, in fine, sought to unify human experience by sanctioning and empowering the imperialism of the human species, and by dangling before men the promise of undreamed riches born of its new power. It may be that, underlying the world of science-fiction, or, for that matter, the recent scientific efforts to scan the universe for signals of intelligence elsewhere, mankind has begun to have a vague sense of the grim deficiencies of human ethnocentrism: the suspicion that *homo sapiens* is not alone in the universe is a suspicion that the universe may not be ours. It is part of the absurdity of our time that the world of science fiction may sometimes be based upon a more humane ethic—if not a sounder perception of "reality"—than the world of social science.

REFLEXIVE SOCIOLOGY LOOKS AT ITSELF

This conception of a Reflexive Sociology outlines those domain assumptions that I know I hold and which have inevitably informed my discussion of social theory. Yet it is only one such statement, and is similar to others that are now emerging among other social scientists. It is, I believe, one of the varied signs of an impending transformation in the social sciences. All of these, however, manifest a common concern with deepening the social scientist's self-awareness and his praxis, which often takes the form of an effort to construct a sociology of sociology. Why does such an effort emerge today? What are the conditions under which there now emerges an expressed need for a reconstruction of sociology—for both a critique and a reconstruction of conventional Academic Sociology are implicit in the movement toward a sociology of sociology. Can a sociology of sociology, or a Reflexive Sociology as one version of this, account for itself?

While, at this juncture, I can do no more than venture a guess about this, I suspect that these new trends in sociology imply a growing detachment from the sociology once conventional in the United States. What is it that fosters such a detachment? It derives partly, I suspect, from the growing detachment of sociologists and others from the *larger* society in which they work and live, *and,* at the same time, from their mounting awareness of the ways in which their sociology is becoming inextricably integrated into this very society. That is, alienation from the larger society would not, of itself, have disposed sociologists to a critique of their own discipline and its establishments, did they not feel that the latter were entangled with the larger society. But as their discipline and its establishments become increasingly supported by and openly involved with the Welfare State; as sociologists wing their way back and forth between their universities and the centers of power; as they are heard ever more frequently in the councils of power; and as their most immediate work environments—the universities themselves—become drawn into the coalescing military-industrial-welfare complex, it becomes unblinkingly evident that sociology has become dangerously dependent upon the very world it has pledged to study objectively.

This dependence is dissonant with the ideal of objectivity. It becomes ever more difficult for the sociologist to conceal from himself that he is not performing as he had pledged, that he is not who he claimed he was, and that he is becoming more closely bound to the system from which he had promised to maintain his distance. A crisis is emerging in sociology today, not merely because of larger changes in society, but because these changes are transforming the sociologist's *home* territory, his own university base. "Corruption" is now not something that one can pretend is going on only "out there" in the base world surrounding the university, or something that one reads about only in the newspapers; it has become all too evident in the eye-to-eye encounter of daily life in the college corridor. A man may begin to move away from others of his own kind when he no longer takes pride in his likeness to them.

The older or classical "sociology of knowledge" arose, we might say, in response to a very special experience and the special personal reality it generated: the experience of the intellectual distortions subtly produced by *class*-rooted differences in political ideology. The older sociology of knowledge was rooted in the awareness that intellectuals or academic men could be shaped, could be informed or deformed, by these other, these "alien" involvements of the scholar. A Reflexive Sociology or a sociology of sociology, however, is based on a somewhat different kind of experience; one that warns that it is not only forces external to the intellectual life, but also those *internal* to its own social organization and embedded in its distinctive subculture, that are leading it to betray its own commitments. It is based upon an awareness that the academician and university are not simply put upon by the larger world, but are themselves active and willing agents in the dehumanizing of this larger world. The unpermitted world has all too plainly penetrated the once seemingly protected enclave and the enclave itself has come increasingly to be seen as an unpermitted world.

This crisis cannot be resolved by retreating to traditional conceptions of a "pure" sociology. This is so, if for no other reason than that the world outside the university will not leave it alone, and because, for good reasons and for bad, the world inside the university does not want to be left alone. Sociology today has "succeeded," at least in its worldly ambitions, only too well; in "arriving" it discovers that its new success threatens it with an ancient failure. The new, self-critical conceptions of sociology and the growing detachment from "normal" Academic Sociology are part of a search for escape from the pressures and temptations of the world that surrounds and penetrates the university; but, at the same time, they also press toward a new self-image and an historical mission that would enable sociology to act humanely in the larger world. They seek to retain their new found potency without surrendering their older values. Of the many who hear the call to this new mission for sociology only those will be "chosen" who understand that there is no way of making a new sociology without undertaking a new praxis.

NOTES

1. Maurice R. Stein has made me particularly aware of this danger.
2. Karl Loewenstein, *Max Weber's Political Ideas in the Perspective of our Time*, R. and C. Winston, trans. (Amherst: University of Massachusetts Press, 1966), p. 100.

Index